lonely planet

Jordan

Jenny Walker, Paul Clammer

PLAN YOUR TRIP

ON THE ROAD

ZOONAR RF/GETTY IMAGES ©
FLOATING IN THE DEAD SEA P111

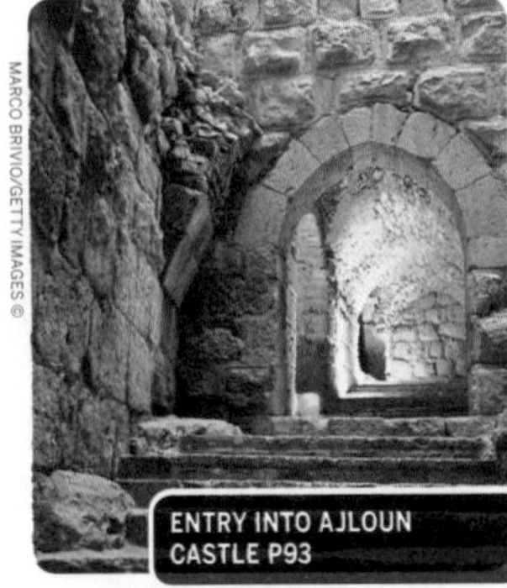
MARCO BRIVIO/GETTY IMAGES ©
ENTRY INTO AJLOUN CASTLE P93

ALEXEY PEVNEV/SHUTTERSTOCK ©
WADI RUM P209

Contents

CHAMELEONSEYE/SHUTTERSTOCK ©

ARABIC COFFEE JUG AND SWEETS P288

SPECIAL FEATURES

Welcome to Jordan

A safe haven in a region of conflict, Jordan has delighted visitors for centuries with its World Heritage Sites, friendly towns and inspiring desert landscapes.

Ancient Hospitality

Jordan has a tradition of welcoming visitors: camel caravans plied the legendary King's Highway transporting frankincense in exchange for spices while Nabataean tradesmen, Roman legionnaires, Muslim armies and zealous Crusaders all passed through the land, leaving behind impressive monuments. These monuments, including Roman amphitheatres, Crusader castles and Christian mosaics, have fascinated subsequent travellers in search of antiquity and the origins of faith. The tradition of hospitality to visitors remains to this day.

Desert Landscapes

Take a ride through Wadi Rum at sunset, and it's easy to see why TE Lawrence (Lawrence of Arabia) was so drawn to this land of weathered sandstone and reddened dunes. But Jordan's desert landscapes are not confined to the southeast: they encompass a salt sea at the lowest point on earth, canyons flowing with seasonal water, oases of palm trees and explosions of springtime flowers scattered across arid hills. Minimal planning and only a modest budget is required for an adventure.

Petra: A World Wonder

Petra, the ancient Nabataean city locked in the heart of Jordan's sandstone escarpments, is the jewel in the crown of the country's many antiquities. Ever since explorer Jean Louis Burckhardt brought news of the pink-hued necropolis back to Europe in the 19th century, the walk through the Siq to the Treasury (Petra's defining monument) has impressed even the most travel weary of visitors. With sites flung over a vast rocky landscape and a mood that changes with the shifting light of dawn and dusk, this is a highlight that rewards a longer visit.

Safe Haven

It takes tolerance to host endless waves of incomers, and Jordan has displayed that virtue amply, absorbing thousands of refugees from the Palestinian Territories, Iraq and most recently Syria. Despite contending with this and with large numbers of tourists who are often insensitive to conservative Jordanian values, rural life in particular has managed to keep continuity with the traditions of the past. While Jordan faces the challenges of modernisation and growing urbanisation, it remains one of the safest countries in which to gain an impression of the quintessential Middle East.

Why I Love Jordan

By Jenny Walker, Writer

From the first *'ahlan wa sahlan'* said in welcome, I knew that Jordan was to become a lifelong friend. After going in search of TE Lawrence as a student, I have returned many times to the low-slung tents of the Bedouin, sipped tea with rug-makers and walked in the wake of shepherds. Beautiful though it is, and blessed with a disproportionate number of wonders, Jordan inspires this loyalty primarily because of its spirit of generous optimism – opening its arms to strangers and sharing its meagre wealth with neighbours in need.

For more about our writers, see p344

Above: Sharif Al Hussein Bin Ali Mosque (p199), Aqaba

Jordan

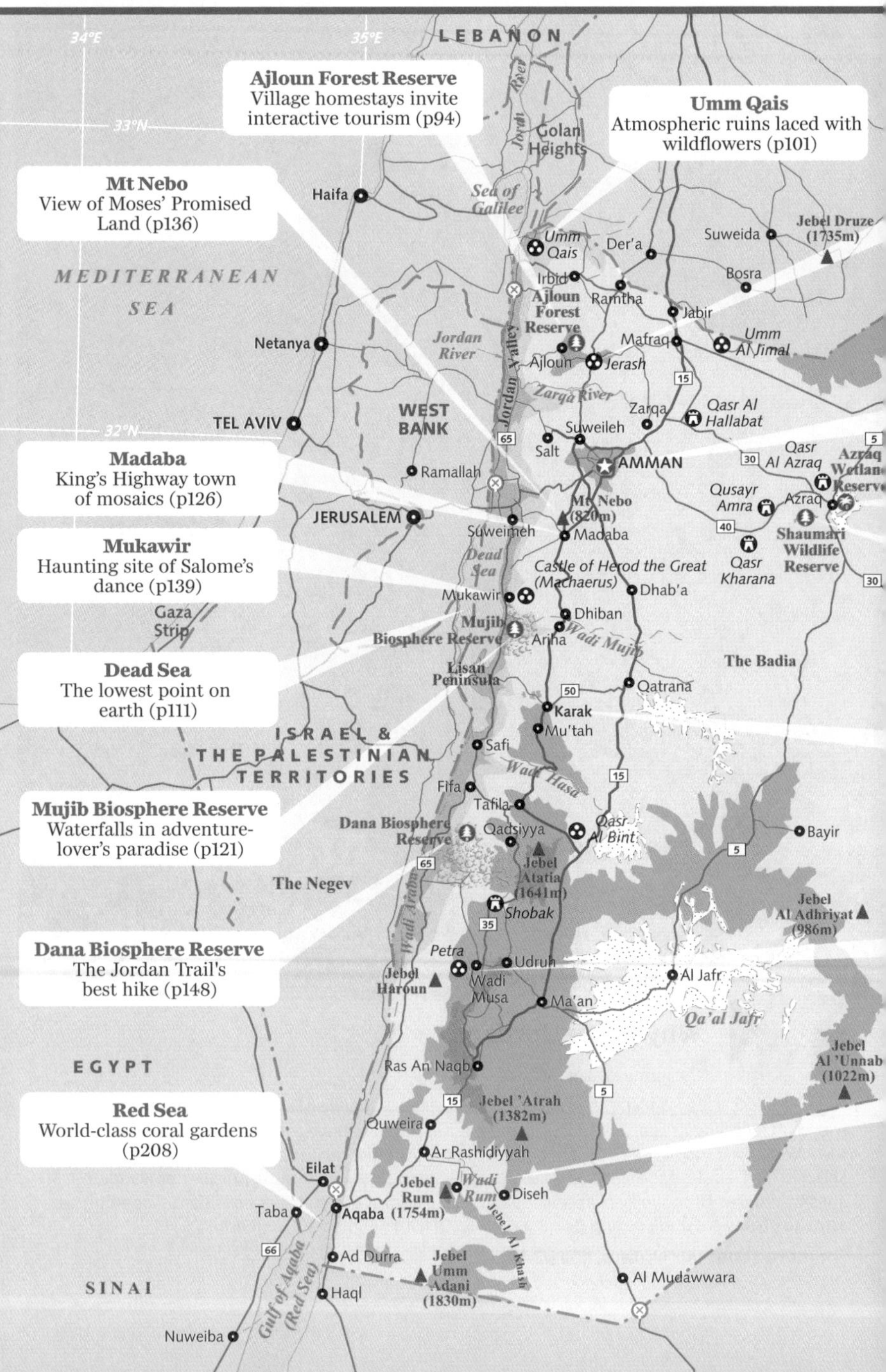

LEBANON
Ajloun Forest Reserve
Village homestays invite interactive tourism (p94)
Umm Qais
Atmospheric ruins laced with wildflowers (p101)
Mt Nebo
View of Moses' Promised Land (p136)
Madaba
King's Highway town of mosaics (p126)
Mukawir
Haunting site of Salome's dance (p139)
Dead Sea
The lowest point on earth (p111)
Mujib Biosphere Reserve
Waterfalls in adventure-lover's paradise (p121)
Dana Biosphere Reserve
The Jordan Trail's best hike (p148)
Red Sea
World-class coral gardens (p208)
MEDITERRANEAN SEA
Haifa
Netanya
TEL AVIV
WEST BANK
Ramallah
JERUSALEM
Gaza Strip
ISRAEL & THE PALESTINIAN TERRITORIES
The Negev
EGYPT
SINAI
Eilat
Taba
Nuweiba
Gulf of Aqaba (Red Sea)
Golan Heights
Sea of Galilee
Jordan River
Jordan Valley
Zarqa River
Umm Qais
Irbid
Der'a
Ramtha
Jabir
Mafraq
Suweida
Bosra
Jebel Druze (1735m)
Umm Al Jimal
Ajloun
Jerash
Zarqa
Qasr Al Hallabat
Suweileh
Salt
AMMAN
Qasr Al Azraq
Azraq Wetland Reserve
Qusayr Amra
Azraq
Shaumari Wildlife Reserve
Qasr Kharana
Mt Nebo (820m)
Suweimeh
Madaba
Castle of Herod the Great (Machaerus)
Dhab'a
Mukawir
Dhiban
Ariha
Wadi Mujib
Lisan Peninsula
Qatrana
The Badia
Karak
Mu'tah
Safi
Wadi Hasa
Fifa
Tafila
Qasr Al Bint
Qadsiyya
Bayir
Jebel Atatia (1641m)
Shobak
Jebel Al Adhriyat (986m)
Wadi Araba
Petra
Udruh
Al Jafr
Jebel Haroun
Wadi Musa
Ma'an
Qa'al Jafr
Ras An Naqb
Jebel Al 'Unnab (1022m)
Jebel 'Atrah (1382m)
Quweira
Ar Rashidiyyah
Jebel Rum (1754m)
Wadi Rum
Diseh
Jebel Al Khash
Aqaba
Ad Durra
Jebel Umm Adani (1830m)
Haql
Al Mudawwara
34°E
35°E
33°N
32°N

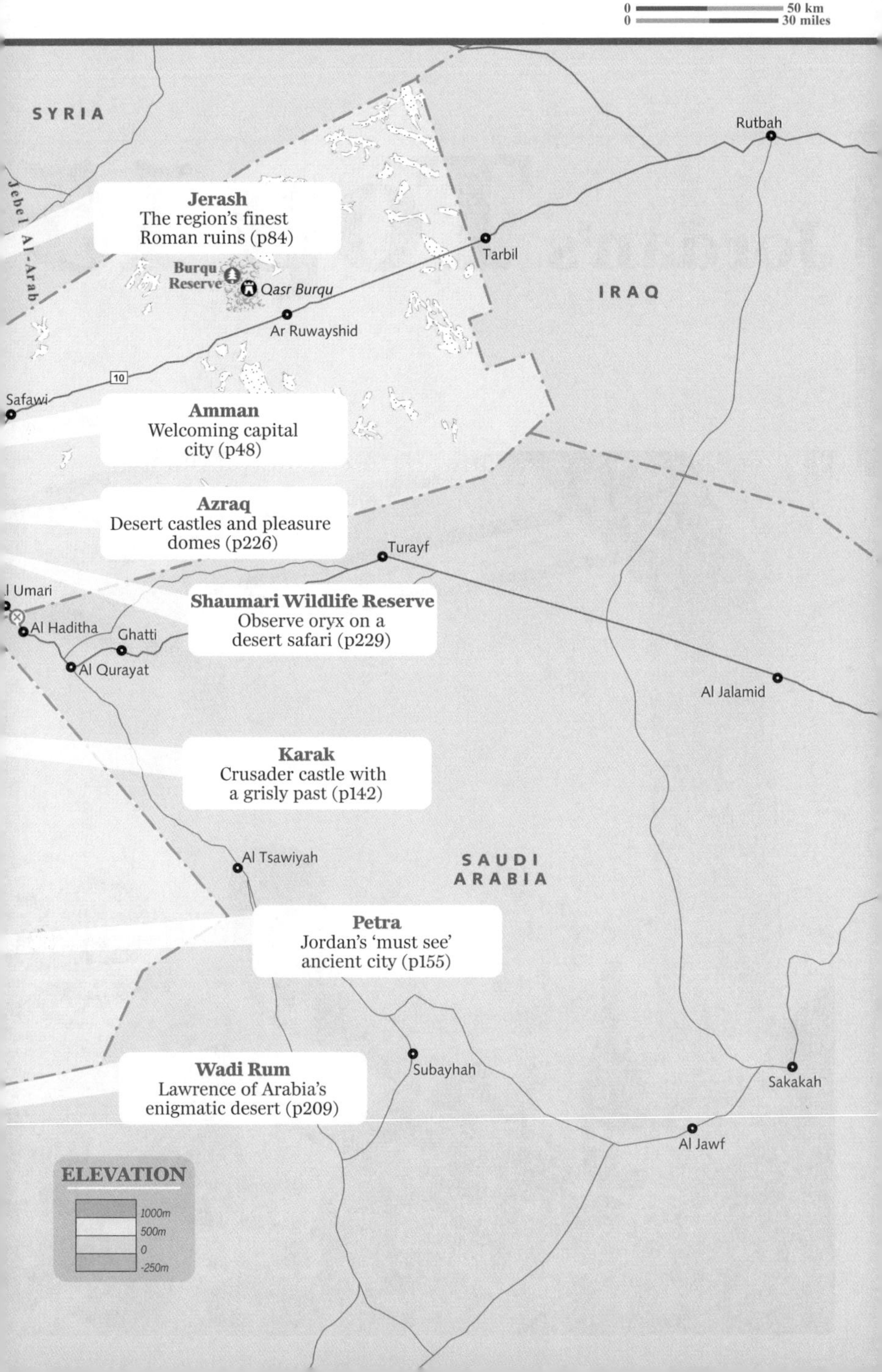

0 — 50 km
0 — 30 miles

SYRIA

Jebel Al-Arab

Jerash
The region's finest Roman ruins (p84)

Rutbah

Tarbil

Burqu Reserve

Qasr Burqu

IRAQ

Ar Ruwayshid

10

Safawi

Amman
Welcoming capital city (p48)

Azraq
Desert castles and pleasure domes (p226)

Turayf

l Umari

Shaumari Wildlife Reserve
Observe oryx on a desert safari (p229)

Al Haditha

Ghatti

Al Qurayat

Al Jalamid

Karak
Crusader castle with a grisly past (p142)

Al Tsawiyah

SAUDI ARABIA

Petra
Jordan's 'must see' ancient city (p155)

Subayhah

Sakakah

Wadi Rum
Lawrence of Arabia's enigmatic desert (p209)

Al Jawf

ELEVATION

1000m
500m
0
-250m

Jordan's Top 15

1

Amman

1 In a country strewn with the ruins of former civilisations, it can be difficult to remember that Jordan isn't just a relic of the past, it's very much a forward-thinking nation with a vibrant contemporary culture. There's no better place to feel the pulse of modern Jordan than in Amman with its international restaurants, trendsetting nightlife and fashionable shopping districts. For those who can't let history sleep, however, the capital boasts its own treasures, including fine Roman ruins and the excellent Jordan Museum (p51).

Below left: View of Amman from Cantaloupe (p70)

Biblical History

2 For many people Jordan is more than just a traveller's destination: it's a place of Christian pilgrimage. Sites resonating with spiritual significance abound in a country delineated by the Jordan Valley. This is where John is believed to have baptised Jesus at Bethany-Beyond-the-Jordan (p115), and where, according to the Bible, the towns of Sodom and Gomorrah attracted the wrath of God. It is at Mt Nebo, however, with its view of the Promised Land, that one most senses that for many people this is 'hallowed, holy ground'.

Below right: Fresco of Jesus Christ, Bethany-Beyond-the-Jordan

SUNNY FITZGERALD/LONELY PLANET ©

BILL PERRY/SHUTTERSTOCK ©

Community Tourism

3 For many years, the northwestern part of Jordan has been at the forefront of community-based tourism with creative initiatives arising out of the Royal Society for the Conservation of Nature's commitment to working with local villages. At Ajloun Forest Reserve (p94; pictured below top), promotion of cottage industries ensures local people benefit from tourism in their backyard. Opportunities for sustainable tourism include following the Al Ayoun Trail, a community-run trail with village homestays. In Umm Qais, classes are offered in foraging, cooking, beekeeping and basket weaving.

Diving the Red Sea

4 It's no secret that the Red Sea (p207) is home to some of the most beautiful underwater seascapes in the world. Jordan's Red Sea shoreline along the Gulf of Aqaba is admittedly short, but this comparatively unexploited stretch of water encompasses pristine reefs, crumbling wrecks and kaleidoscopic coral gardens. Snorkelling and diving among damsel fish, turtles and seahorses is a memorable experience easily arranged through dive centres in and around the lively seaside city of Aqaba (p195). Access is both from the beach and by short boat-ride. Bottom left: Lionfish

Crusader Castles

5 As a frontier in the battle for the soul between Muslim and Christian forces, the Levant is dotted with castles. In Jordan, there are well-preserved examples at Ajloun and Shobak, but Karak Castle (p143; pictured opposite top), commanding the semi-arid hills above the King's Highway, is the most atmospheric. You don't need to be military-minded to be impressed by the enormous ramparts, but imagination helps to hear the dying howls of those pitched from the parapet by sadistic Renauld de Châtillon.

3

OMARDAJANI/SHUTTERSTOCK ©

4

RICH CAREY/SHUTTERSTOCK ©

TOM MACKIE/LONELY PLANET ©

Wadi Rum

6 It wasn't just the dramatic vistas of Wadi Rum (p209), with its burnished sandstone cliffs and vivid-coloured dunes, that impressed Lawrence of Arabia as he paced on camelback through the land of the Bedouin. He was also impressed by the stoicism of the people who endured the hardships of desert life. Today, it's possible to get a glimpse of that traditional way of life (albeit with a few more creature comforts) by staying in one of the Bedouin camps scattered across this desert wilderness.

Below: A Bedouin guide leading camels, Wadi Rum

ANTON_IVANOV/SHUTTERSTOCK ©

6

JAN WILLEM VAN HOFWEGEN/SHUTTERSTOCK ©

King's Highway

7 It may not be a literal path of kings, but the King's Highway follows some big footsteps. These include those of the Nabataeans, whose fabled city of Petra lies at the south end of the highway; the Romans, whose military outpost at Umm Ar Rasas is a Unesco World Heritage Site, and the Crusaders who built Karak and Shobak Castles. Smaller footsteps belonged to Salome in her 'Dance of the Seven Veils' at the desolate hilltop of Mukawir (p139; pictured top left). Only a four-hour direct drive today, the highway is better appreciated over two days.

Petra

8 Ever since the Swiss explorer Jean Louis Burckhardt rediscovered this site in 1812, the ancient Nabataean city of Petra (p155) has been drawing the crowds – and with good reason. This is without doubt Jordan's most treasured attraction and when the sun sets over the honeycombed landscape of tombs, carved facades, pillars and sandstone cliffs, its magic is irresistible. At least two days is needed to do the site justice and visit the main monuments at the optimum times of day. Top right: Treasury (p160)

Madaba's Mosaics

9 For centuries, Madaba (p126), at the head of the ancient King's Highway, has been a crossroads for camel caravans transporting goods, legions of armies pushing the borders of various empires, and Christian pilgrims driven by faith in search of the Promised Land. To this day the town, with its churches, mosques, museums, markets and craft workshops, retains the marks of those cultural exchanges. Perhaps the best evidence of this rich past is Madaba's collection of mosaics, a heritage continued through the town's unique mosaic school. Opposite top: Modern replica of the Madaba Map (p127)

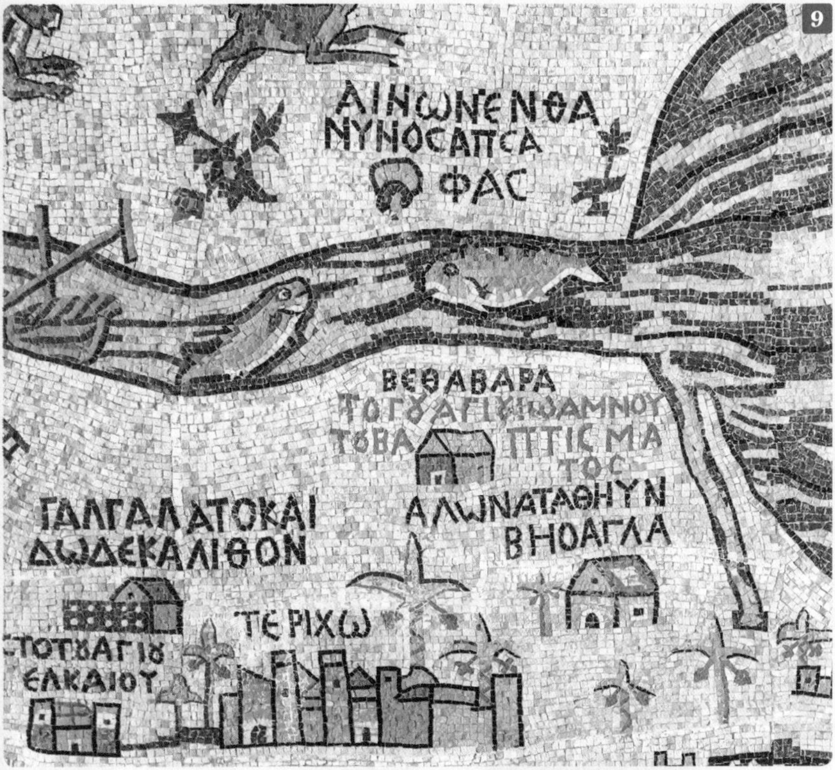

Roman Ruins

10 Jordan punches well above its weight in world-class monuments, with some of the finest Roman ruins outside Rome. In addition to the Citadel and the well-preserved Roman Theatre in Amman, the black basalt ruins of Umm Qais and the Colonnaded Street in Petra signal the Roman presence at either ends of the country. The true highlight, however, is Jerash (p84) with its extensive amphitheatres and colonnades. From the site's well-preserved hippodrome, it's easy to imagine chariots tearing around the track in this ancient outpost of Rome. Right: Roman columns, Temple of Artemis (p85)

The Dead Sea

11 Floating in the Dead Sea (p111) is one of the country's great natural experiences. Floating is the right word for it: with an eye-stingingly high salt content it is virtually impossible to swim in the viscous waters of a sea that is 415m below 'sea level', and equally impossible to sink. The experience is usually accompanied by a mud bath, a bake in the sun and a luxurious, health-giving spa treatment at one of the modern pleasure palaces lined up along the Dead Sea's shores.

Exploring Desert Castles

12 The plains of eastern Jordan are home to the 'desert castles', a collection of early Umayyad pleasure palaces, bathhouses and hunting lodges that appear strikingly incongruous in the barren surroundings. Brooding Qasr Kharana (p235; pictured bottom) tops the list, but other highlights include Qusayr Amra's saucy frescoes and TE Lawrence's winter redoubt at Azraq. The off-road Eastern Badia Trail, recently developed by Wild Jordan, links Azraq Lodge with a new community-based tourism project at Burqu in this region of surprises.

11

12

13

14

MARK DAFFEY/GETTY IMAGES ©

15

BORYA GALPERIN/SHUTTERSTOCK ©

Wadi Mujib

13 Fresh water is in short supply in Jordan, and it has already become an issue of intense political importance in dialogue with neighbouring states. Various projects, such as the 'Red to Dead' Sea Canal and a pipeline from Wadi Rum's aquifers to Amman, are being explored with ever-greater urgency. That's one reason why the natural springs of the Mujib Biosphere Reserve (p121) are a highlight. The other reason is that the water flows through a spectacular wadi into a series of deep pools – paradise for the adventure-seeking traveller.

Shaumari Wildlife Reserve

14 Comprising large areas of *hammada* (black flint), Shaumari Wildlife Reserve (p229) sits on the edge of the great wilderness that stretches into unending distance. The first of Jordan's nature reserves, established as part of a mission to reintroduce the oryx, it has recently undergone a decade of redevelopment. Highlights of a visit include an oryx safari and the opportunity to see rare breeds, such as goitered gazelles and Persian onagers, in their desert enclosures. With Azraq Wetland Reserve nearby, a visit to Shaumari helps prove that the desert is not deserted.

Top right: Ostriches in Shaumari Wildlife Reserve

The Jordan Trail

15 In a region not commonly associated with hiking, Jordan has a surprising number of good walking paths. Trails thread through the northern forest reserves, above wadi waterfalls in Mujib, and along livestock trails in Petra and Wadi Rum. Now it's possible to string many of these destinations together on the 650km, 36-day (42 days with rest stops) Jordan Trail (p37). Named by *National Geographic* as one of the best hikes in the world, the trail includes trekking through four biospheres in the Dana Biosphere Reserve.

Need to Know

For more information, see Survival Guide (p299)

Currency
Jordanian dinar (JD)

Languages
Arabic, English

Visas
Visas, required by all visitors, are available (JD40 for most nationalities) at the international airports and most of Jordan's land borders. Buying a Jordan Pass (www.jordanpass.jo) online before entering gives free access to many sites in Jordan, including Petra, and waives the visa fee.

Money
ATMs are available throughout the country and credit cards are widely used.

Mobile Phones
There is expansive coverage in Jordan for mobile phone networks. Local SIM cards can be used for international calls and can be topped up with readily available prepaid cards. 4G is increasingly available.

Time
Jordan Time (GMT/UTC plus two hours)

When to Go

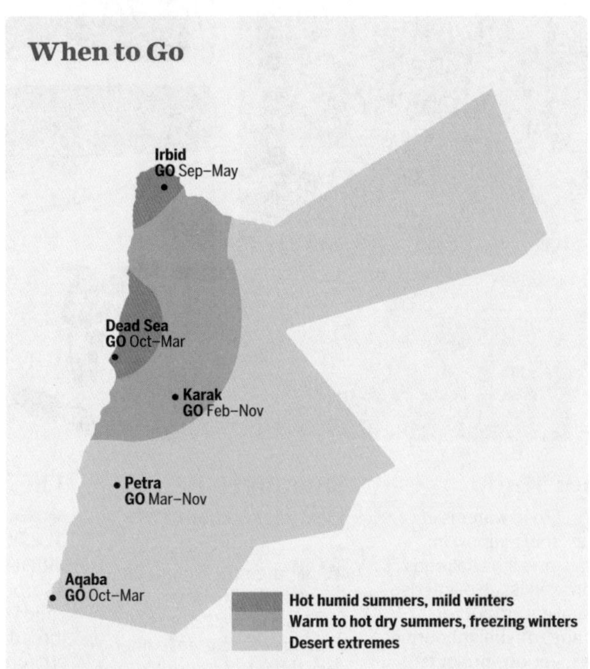

High Season
(Mar–May)

➡ Perfect weather throughout Jordan with warm days and cool nights.

➡ Northern Jordan is blanketed in wildflowers in April.

➡ Reserve rooms in main tourist areas and expect higher rates.

Shoulder
(Sep–Feb)

➡ The best time to visit the Red Sea; prices in and around Aqaba rise accordingly.

➡ Bitter nights in the desert with rain or snow curtail many activities, such as camping.

Low Season
(Jun–Aug)

➡ The desert in the middle of the summer is extreme. Temperatures throughout Jordan can be stifling.

➡ Prices are at their best but many places close in the low season.

Useful Websites

Jordan Tourism Board (www.visitjordan.com) Excellent official website.

Lonely Planet (www.lonelyplanet.com/jordan) Destination information, hotel bookings, traveller forum and more.

RSCN (www.rscn.org.jo) Online booking for accommodation and eco-adventures in nature reserves.

Bible Places (www.bibleplaces.com) Biblical sights in Jordan.

Important Numbers

Jordan's country code	☎962
International access code	☎00
Ambulance, fire, police	☎911

Exchange Rates

Australia	A$1	JD0.56
Canada	C$1	JD0.57
Egypt	E£10	JD0.40
Europe	€1	JD0.84
Israel & Palestinian Territories	1NIS	JD0.20
Japan	¥100	JD0.64
New Zealand	NZ$1	JD0.51
UK	£1	JD0.92
US	US$1	JD0.71

For current exchange rates see www.xe.com.

Daily Costs

Budget: Less than JD40

- Shared room in budget guesthouse: JD10–40
- Street fare and local markets: under JD5
- Public transport: JD5

Midrange: JD40–120

- Double room in midrange hotel: JD40–90
- Eating in local restaurants: JD5–10
- Car hire: JD50
- Entry costs/unguided activities: JD10

Top End: More than JD120

- Double room in five-star hotel: from JD90
- Buffet lunch/dinner: from JD15
- 4WD car hire: JD120
- Guided activities: JD50

Opening Hours

Opening times vary widely across the country. Many sights, government departments and banks close earlier in winter and during Ramadan. The following opening hours are therefore a rough guide only. The official weekend in Jordan is Friday and Saturday, so expect curtailed hours on these days.

Banks 8am–3pm Sunday to Thursday

Restaurants noon–midnight daily

Cafes 9am–midnight daily

Bars and Clubs 9pm–1am daily

Shops 9am–8pm Saturday to Thursday; some close 2pm–4pm

Souqs 9am–8pm daily

Arriving in Jordan

Queen Alia International Airport (south of Amman) The Airport Express Bus (JD3) runs to Amman every 30 minutes (from 6.30am to 5pm); the night bus runs hourly (5pm to midnight). Taxis cost JD20 to downtown Amman (around 45 minutes). Car hire is available in the arrivals hall.

Ferry Terminal (south of Aqaba) A taxi costs JD8 and takes 20 minutes from the ferry terminal and border to the centre of town.

Wadi Araba (Yitzhak Rabin) Border A taxi from the border costs JD11 and takes 15 minutes to central Aqaba (JD50, two hours to Petra).

Getting Around

Public transport is limited to intercity buses and buses that serve the needs of local communities, making it hard for travellers to reach key destinations without time and patience.

Car Hiring a car is recommended, especially for visiting the Dead Sea, Eastern Desert and King's Highway. Driving is on the right.

Private Minibus Some hotels in Amman, Madaba, Petra and Aqaba organise minibus shuttle services and/or tours to key tourist destinations, including Eastern Desert sights.

Taxi Many locals get around by shared taxi. Negotiating a half- or whole-day rate with a taxi driver is a useful alternative to car hire.

For much more on **getting around**, see p314

If You Like...

Roman Ruins

Pillars, pediments and pavements from ancient Rome are liberally strewn across Jordan, making the country one of the best in the world to see evidence of this once mighty empire.

Jerash Centurions once clashed swords in the hippodrome in the extensive ruins of Jerash. (p85)

Umm Qais (Gadara) With a view of the Golan Heights, these atmospheric ruins still command a strategic location. (p101)

Pella Little visited, these ruins represent one of the 10 cities of the ancient Decapolis. (p105)

Citadel Perched above the modern capital, these ruins afford a vantage point of Amman's ancient amphitheatre. (p51)

Colonnaded Street, Petra The Roman presence at Petra is found in the detail – in a hero's tomb or fallen pillar. (p164)

Views of the Promised Land

On the east bank of the Jordan River, latter-day pilgrims can follow in the footsteps of former prophets. More than 100 sites in Jordan are mentioned in the Bible.

Bethany-Beyond-the-Jordan The most important biblical site in Jordan, this is the suggested location of Jesus's baptism. (p115)

Mt Nebo Moses supposedly finally saw the view of the Promised Land from here before dying. (p136)

Madaba Famed for the earliest map of the Holy Land, Madaba is notable for its Christian population. (p126)

Castle of Herod the Great Only a pillar remains atop the hill where Salome is said to have danced in Mukawir. (p139)

Lot's Cave She looked back, and for that Lot's wife allegedly turned into salt. (p123)

Jebel Haroun Revered equally by Muslims and Christians, this sacred site is thought to be Mt Hor of the Old Testament. (p172)

Moses' Spring Moses allegedly struck the rock either near Mt Nebo or in Wadi Musa near Petra. (p138)

Crusader Castles

You don't need to be a kid to love a good castle, and Jordan has plenty. Once guarding ancient trade routes or repelling religious adversaries, their crumbling battlements are a highlight of Jordan.

Karak Castle The king of castles, the Crusader stronghold of Karak commands sweeping views of the valley below. (p143)

Shobak Castle Built by Crusaders in the 12th century, this is the most picture-perfect of Jordan's castles. (p153)

Ajloun Castle Commanding the high ground, this castle was part of Saladin's defensive fortifications against the Crusaders. (p93)

Qasr Al Azraq The winter home of TE Lawrence and Sharif Hussein bin Ali in 1917, Azraq Castle protected an important oasis. (p230)

Castle of Herod the Great This is the haunting site of Salome's seductive dance in Mukawir. (p139)

Qasr Kharana One of the collectively misnamed Eastern 'castles', this quirky Umayyad building invites exploration of the surrounding desolation. (p235)

Springs & Bathhouses

Jordan boasts dozens of thermal springs where the water averages 40°C and is rich in health-giving minerals. For those who like their bath with bubbles, the Dead Sea spas offer paradise.

Top: Starry sky above Wadi Rum (p209)

Bottom: *Mensaf* (a Bedouin dish of lamb on a bed of rice)

Hammamat Ma'in Steam vents pepper the hillside at this spring near Madaba; it's suitable for single women. (p121)

Hammamat Burbita West of the King's Highway near Tafila, these springs have pools and basic facilities. (p147)

Al Pasha Turkish Bath Steam rooms, Jacuzzi and obligatory scrubbing are available at this Amman favourite. (p66)

Petra Turkish Bath With separate baths for women, this is the place to unwind after hiking in Petra. (p183)

Dead Sea Spas Offering the ultimate in healthy bathing and luxurious pampering. (p113)

Flora & Fauna

The desert may look dead, but it is home to the greatest survivors – both animal and vegetable. The desert comes alive in spring, from early April to late May.

Wildflowers In profusion across Jordan in mid-April, the best floral displays are around the northern hills near Gadara. (p101)

Strawberry Oaks Ajloun Forest Reserve protects this rare woodland of red-barked trees. (p94)

Birdwatching Azraq Wetland Reserve hosts migrants and residents in the heart of the desert. (p229)

Black Iris Jordan's national flower blooms with deep purple petals at Dana Biosphere Reserve – if they escape the resident ibex! (p148)

Oryx Showcased at Shaumari Wildlife Reserve, these elegant antelope are back from the brink of extinction. (p229)

Fish The Red Sea is renowned the world over for underwater diversity – as seen from Neptune Submarine Vision. (p199)

Royal Botanic Garden Home to many of Jordan's native species, this botanic garden is located 25km north of Amman. (p85)

Crafts with a Conscience

The revival of cottage industries is helping to sustain traditional ways of life in Jordan. Madaba offers souvenirs that leave as much as the buyer takes away.

Hand-loomed Rugs Goat-hair rugs are bringing life-changing opportunities to the women of Bani Hamida Weaving Centre. (p140)

Palestinian Embroidery The Haret Jdoudna Complex in Madaba provides an outlet for the once-dying art of cross-stitch. (p134)

Mosaics Associated with mosaic-making for centuries, Madaba's Lawrence Arts & Crafts makes portable tree of life designs. (p134)

Painted Ostrich Eggs Ostriches once roamed the region; the art of egg painting has been preserved at Azraq Lodge. (p232)

Environmentally Friendly Products Wild Jordan Center in Amman sells a range of ecocrafts from Jordan's nature reserves. (p75)

Lawrence of Arabia

Jordan is 'El Lawrence' country, the land the eccentric, camel-riding, dagger-wielding Englishman made his own during the Arab Revolt of 1917–19.

Wadi Rum Lawrence's ghost haunts Wadi Rum, which he termed 'Rumm the Magnificent', passing cliffs named 'Seven Pillars of Wisdom' in his honour. (p209)

Hejaz Railway The goods train rattles by on the mended tracks of the Hejaz Railway once dynamited by Lawrence. (p59)

Dana The 'chess-board houses' of Dana, within today's Dana Biosphere Reserve, overlook Wadi Araba, 'fresh and green, thousands of feet below'. (p147)

Azraq Castle Lawrence was proud to ride between Aqaba and Qasr Al Azraq in three days; the journey now takes one. (p230)

The West Lawrence left Azraq riding into the sunset while flocks of cranes flew in company overhead – just as they do from Azraq Wetland Reserve today. (p229)

Bedouin Experiences

For centuries the Bedouin have inspired admiration for their adaptation to the harshness of desert life. Nowadays many make their living sharing that life with visitors – an experience not to be missed.

Camping under Goat Hair With stars, tea and storytelling, Bedouin camps such as Rum Stars at Wadi Rum offer a night to remember. (p218)

Camel Trek More driven than ridden nowadays, camels are still available for hire at Rum Horses and within Petra. (p216)

Sampling Mensaf In Petra you can try *mensaf*, the Bedouin lamb, rice and pine nut speciality served, for example, at Oriental Restaurant. (p187)

Ammarin Bedouin Camp The museum in this camp outside Petra features the lives of the local Bedouin tribe. (p192)

Bedouin Staples Camel's milk, dates and goat's cheese are staples of Bedouin food; learn how they are prepared at Feynan Ecolodge. (p151)

Walks on the Wild Side

Exciting hikes across sand dunes, through forests and via the lush gorges of seasonally dry riverbeds (wadis) are possible mid-March to mid-October. See Di Taylor & Tony Howard's *Jordan: Walks* and their *Walks, Treks, Climbs & Caves in Al Ayoun* for details.

Jordan Trail Tracing the length of the country, this new trail (representing around 40 days and 650km of hiking) is Jordan's defining trek. (p37)

Siq Trail This rewarding scramble (2km, three hours) leads through Wadi Mujib in knee-high water. (p121)

Wadi Dana Trail A classic Dana hike (16km, six hours), this steep trail descends through Bedouin grazing grounds. (p152)

Prophet's Trail Winding through Ajloun's orchards, this hike (8.5km, four hours) leads to Prophet Elijah's alleged birthplace. (p96)

Makharas Canyon Hike This plod through soft sands (8km, 2½ hours) opens up the best of Wadi Rum. (p216)

Wadi Muthlim Enter Petra the Indiana Jones way (5km, 1½ hours) through this unnervingly narrow slot canyon. (p167)

Month by Month

TOP EVENTS

Jerash Festival, July

Hiking Season, March–April

Peak Wildflower Blooms, April

Dead Sea Ultra Marathon, April

Petra Desert Marathon, August

January

If you thought the desert was hot by default, think again! The desert is bitter cold until March. But while most of Jordan shivers under chilly skies, those in the know head for Aqaba.

Red Sea Snorkelling & Diving

Aqaba, with its warm winter sunshine, hosts the annual holiday exodus of urbanites from the hills. The winter months, from December to March, are perfect for an underwater adventure, with clear skies and crystal-clear waters.

April

April is the most popular month to visit Jordan, and with good reason. The weather is balmy and the semi-arid hills of northern Jordan burst into magnificent, knee-high bloom.

Dead Sea Ultra Marathon

Not just for a few crazed locals, the Dead Sea Ultra Marathon attracts athletes and amateurs – all heading below zero. The 50km race begins in Amman at 900m above sea level and ends 400m below the international tideline. (p113)

Jordan Rally

The annual Jordan Rally (www.jordanrally.com) attracts cheering crowds to the Dead Sea shore. The world's leading rally drivers participate in this 1008km route.

ABDALLAH DARABSEH/SHUTTERSTOCK ©

Waterfront in Aqaba (p195)

Nature Walking

Spring, from late March to mid-May, is the best time to visit Jordan's nature reserves. The elusive black iris (Jordan's national flower) blooms and nature lovers can hike through narrow wadis without fear of flash floods.

May

Still peak tourist season, the country heats up in May leaving low-lying areas toasting. It's also peak season for flowering oleander, making the wadis pretty in pink.

Hiking & Camel Trekking

It may be heating up in Petra and Wadi Rum, but the desert is a quintessential experience in the heat. With sizzling days and breezy nights, you quickly slip into the rhythm of Bedouin life, rising early and napping after lunch.

Independence Day

On 25 May, Jordanians celebrate national day with bunting and flags and military parades in the capital. It's a good excuse for a chat, water pipe and mint tea with friends, and visitors are always made welcome.

Ramadan

During the 30 days of Ramadan, Muslims must refrain from eating, drinking and smoking between dawn and dusk. While there are some restrictions for visitors, Ramadan (mostly in May until 2021) also brings special delicacies unavailable at other times.

Top: Man dressed as a Roman soldier, Jerash Festival of Culture & Arts (p91)

Bottom: Black iris (Jordan's national flower)

June

Until 2021, the months of May and June are associated with high points in the Islamic year, the exact dates of which are based on the lunar calendar.

Eid Al Fitr

Marking the end of Ramadan, Eid Al Fitr is a time of festivity for Muslims. Disruptions to opening hours, and heavily booked transport and hotels are likely; on the upside, an invitation to join the party is an opportunity not to be missed.

July

The midsummer month of July brings hazy skies and suffocating heat and few choose this time of year for a visit. Thankfully, it is cheered up by open-air cultural events.

Jerash Festival of Culture & Arts

Hosted within world-class ruins, Jordan's best-loved cultural event brings ancient Jerash to life with plays, poetry recitals, opera and concerts. Held annually since 1981, the festival usually spans three weeks of the summer months. (p91)

Traditional Concerts & Plays

In July and August traditional concerts and plays are held at the Odeon and Roman Theatre in Amman, as well as in Salt and Fuheis.

ISLAMIC HOLIDAYS

Ramadan, the month of fasting, and the two main Islamic holidays in the year, Eid Al Fitr and Eid Al Adha (marked by feasting and family festivities), are observed throughout Jordan. The dates are governed by the lunar calendar and therefore advance by roughly 10 days each year.

August

Just when you think it can't get any hotter, August arrives with high temperatures radiating off the parched earth. Little wonder visitors are few.

Eid Al Adha

Marking the end of Hajj, the annual pilgrimage to Mecca, this Islamic holiday falls in July or August until 2021. Shops close as owners join their families on these important days of celebration.

Petra Desert Marathon

When the heat is at its most extreme, marathon runners take to the near vertical ascents around Petra in a bewildering act of self-punishment (www.albatros-adventure.com/petra-desert-marathon).

October

Residents of Jordan sigh with relief in September as temperatures show signs of cooling and markets abound with figs, corn and fresh olive oil.

Jordan Running Adventure Race

Covered in a single stage usually between Petra and Wadi Rum, this 160km ultra trail (www.tendao-run.com/jrar_english) has become an established part of Jordan's sporting calendar. A shorter route attracts less masochistic participants.

November

Blustering with wind and heavy rains, November signals flash flood season as water chases through sun-dried wadis towards Wadi Araba. Not the best month for hiking, but good for sightseeing.

Floating in the Dead Sea

With fewer tourists than in spring, you may be bobbing alone in the Dead Sea in November. Early harvests of mangos and bananas from the Jordan Valley give extra enticement!

Itineraries

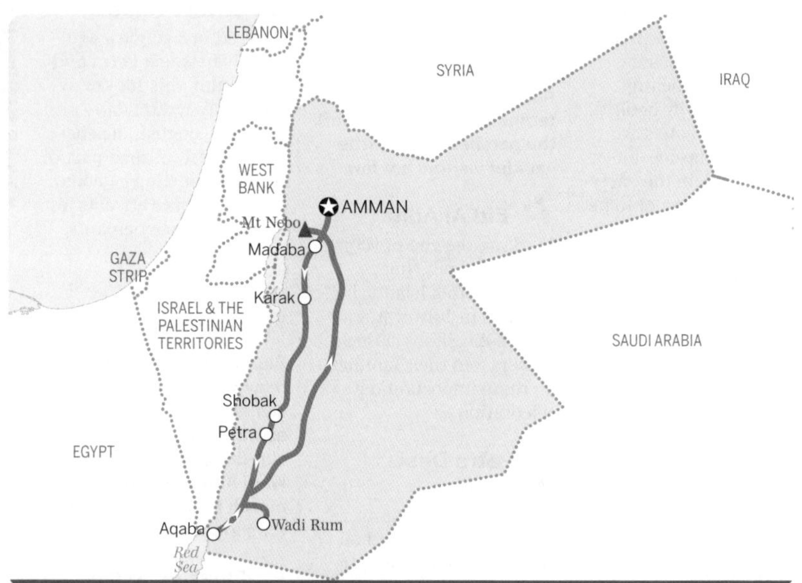

In the Footsteps of Kings: Amman to Aqaba Return

Thanks to its relatively compact size, Jordan rewards even the shortest of getaways, especially if you're prepared to hire a car. This route takes in most of Jordan's key sites in a journey along the King's Highway, the ancient backbone of the country.

On day one, experience modern Jordan in the souqs of **Amman**. On day two, piece together a biblical history in the mosaic town of **Madaba** and, like Moses, survey the Promised Land from neighbouring **Mt Nebo**.

Spend day three following the caravans of history along the King's Highway, crossing mighty Wadi Mujib. Visit the Crusader castles in **Karak** and **Shobak** and listen for ghostly hooves against cobbles.

Rise early on day four to experience the Siq at **Petra** and climb to a High Place for lunch. On day five, attempt the back trail to Petra and watch the sunset at Petra's iconic Monastery. Proceed to the seaside town of **Aqaba**, two hours away. On day six, wash off the desert dust in the spectacular Red Sea before returning to Amman (four hours via the Desert Highway) on day seven; with an early start, a desert lunch is possible at **Wadi Rum** en route.

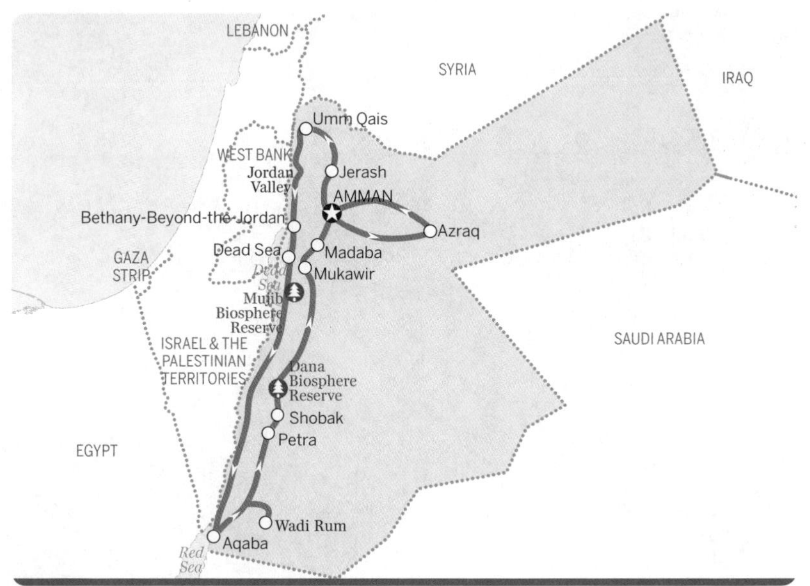

The Best of Jordan

With around 21 days, you can unravel a path through Jordan's most famous sites, travelling in the footsteps of Roman legionnaires, Crusader craftsmen, Islamic warriors and Bedouin nomads. This route takes you on a comprehensive tour of all Jordan's main highlights and throws in a few wild cards too.

Begin with two days in **Amman** and a third day at the spectacular Roman ruins of **Jerash**. For a springtime flower show, camp overnight at the oak woodlands of Ajloun Forest Reserve or spend day four wading knee-high among daisies at the ruins of **Umm Qais**. On day five descend to the subtropical Jordan Valley, pausing at the point where Jesus was allegedly baptised in **Bethany-Beyond-the-Jordan**.

Follow Jordan River towards a night of luxury at the **Dead Sea**, followed by an early morning float on day six at the world's lowest point. Survey the West Bank from a higher vantage at the Dead Sea Panoramic Complex en route for **Mujib Biosphere Reserve**. Splash, swim and struggle through 'Petra with water' on the unguided Siq Trail. Dry out along the Dead Sea Highway to Lot's Cave and swap stories about the adventure over a vegetarian supper at candlelit Feynan Ecolodge.

Begin week two chilling in **Aqaba** for two days, sparing time for a dive or snorkel in the fabled Red Sea. With batteries recharged, tackle a hike in **Wadi Rum** on day 10 and stay overnight in a Bedouin camp. Spend the next three nights in Wadi Musa, joining Petra by Night for a magical introduction to the world wonder of **Petra**.

Head north from Petra via the ancient King's Highway on day 14, sparing time to pause at the imposing castle of **Shobak**. Break the journey at **Dana Biosphere Reserve** and relax on day 15, taking village walks or longer guided hikes.

Spend day 16 making the most of the King's Highway to Madaba, pausing at Karak and Herod's Castle in **Mukawir**. Allow day 17 for souvenir shopping in **Madaba**, the closest town to Queen Alia Airport, or at craft shops in Mt Nebo. From days 18 to 20, cross the desolate Eastern Badia, overnighting at Burqu's ecolodge and Azraq Lodge, touring the desert castles, birdwatching at **Azraq's wetland reserve** and going on oryx safari at nearby Shaumari Wildlife Reserve.

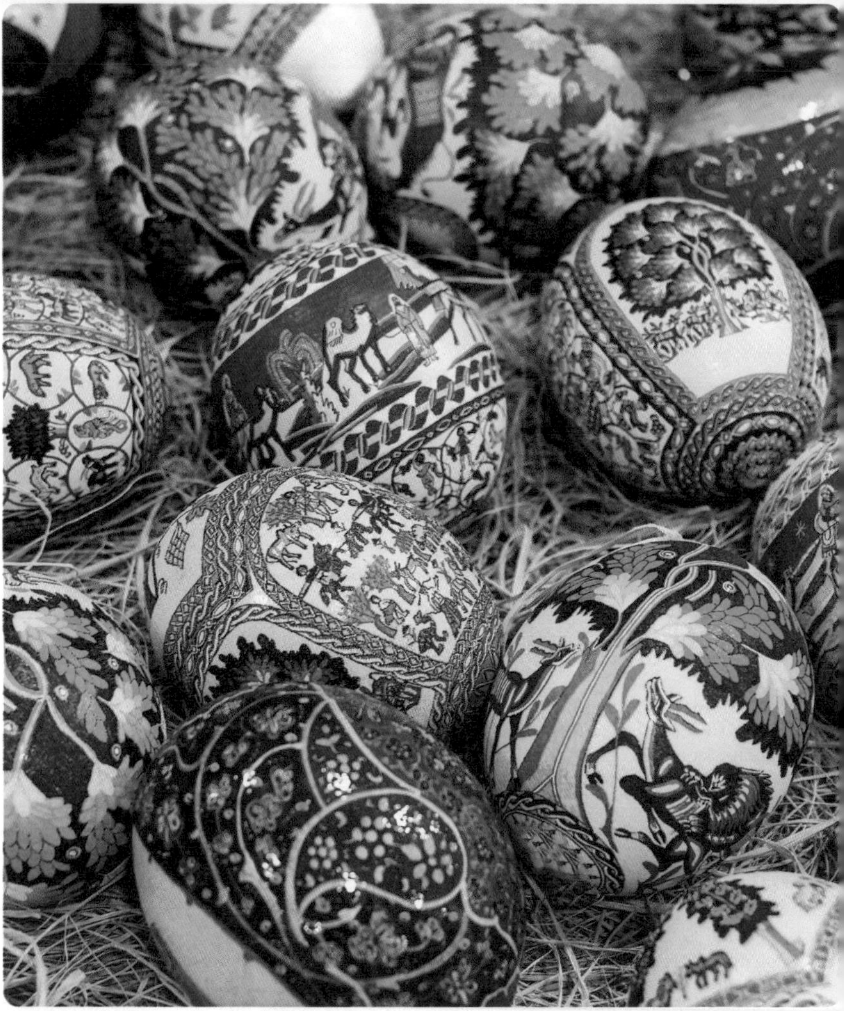

RICHARD YOSHIDA/SHUTTERSTOCK ©

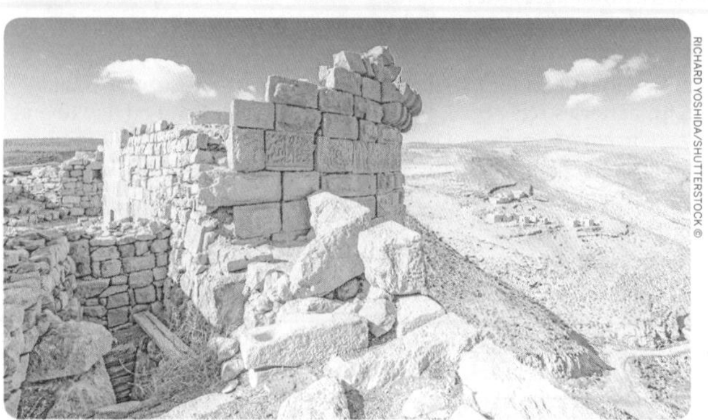

Top: Painted ostrich eggs (p282), Amman

Bottom: Ruins of Shobak Castle (p153)

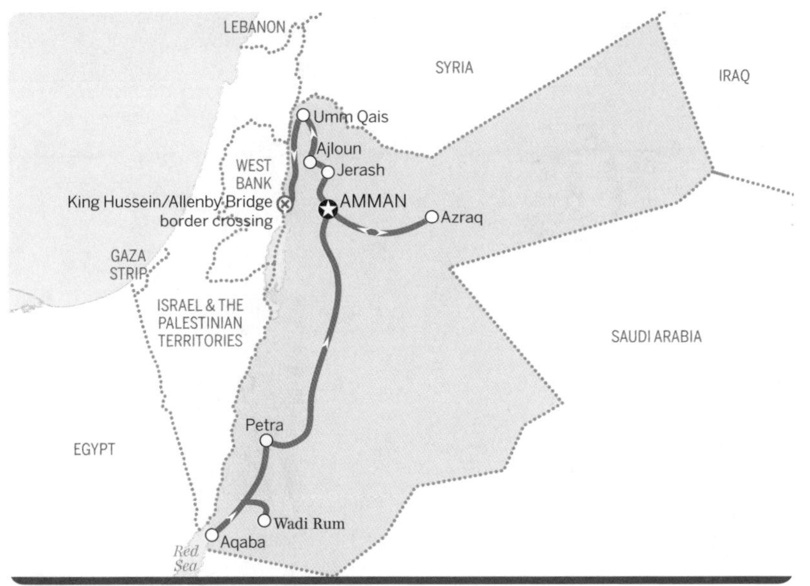

Middle East Heartland: Border to Border

Jordan is plumb in the middle of a richly historic region, making it essential to a Middle East adventure. This 14-day route by public transport assumes entry by ferry from Egypt and exit by bus to Israel and the Palestinian Territories. Check the latest travel advisories before making this trip as the security situation in South Sinai (Egypt) is changeable.

Spend the first two days relaxing in **Aqaba**: Jordan has a distinct character, immediately felt in the souqs and open-air restaurants of this seaside town. Spare time for a swim – Jordan's access to the Red Sea may be diminutive, but the coral gardens are pristine and relatively unvisited. On day three take the morning bus and go in search of 'El Lawrence' in magnificent **Wadi Rum**. Hop astride a camel and head into the sand dunes for a camping experience with the Bedouin.

On day four rise at dawn with the locals, ready to catch the minibus to **Petra**. With two days in the 'Pink City', you can hike to the High Places, learn to cook Jordanian food at Petra Kitchen, watch the sunset from the Monastery and enjoy an evening in the famous Cave Bar.

On day six head north to **Amman** on frequent Desert Highway buses via Ma'an. Sample the city nightlife, including an evening's stroll downtown through Amman's Roman ruins. Hike from the Citadel on day seven and reward the effort with the capital's best-loved Arabic street food at Hashem Restaurant.

Take an overnight trip on days eight and nine to **Azraq** and the desert castles. Azraq Fort was Lawrence's winter hideout. Nearby Azraq Wetland Reserve is a reminder of the fragility of life in the black Badia (stone desert). Given the context, the shrunken waters of the oasis seem miraculous.

Head for the Roman ruins of **Jerash** on day 10. After visiting the extensive site the following morning, spend two nights in **Ajloun**. With its crumbling castle, nature reserve, Al Ayoun Trail and village homestays, Ajloun offers a rare chance to engage with rural life in the Middle East. Travel up to peaceful **Umm Qais** on day 13 for a spot of basket weaving before heading along the Jordan Valley to the border with Israel and the Palestinian Territories on day 14.

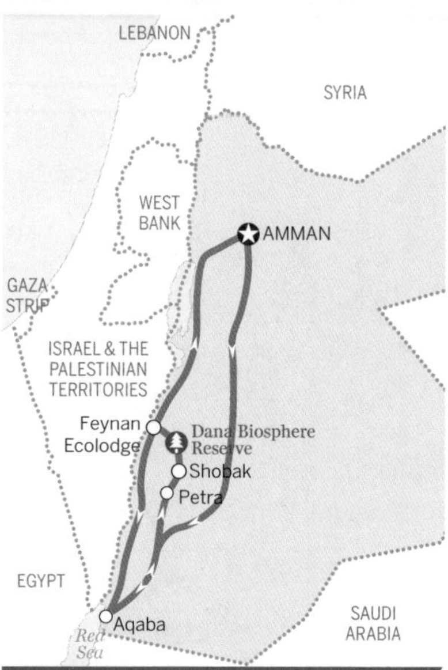

4 DAYS Gems in Northern Jordan

With a long weekend, most visitors head straight for Petra on an overnighter from Amman. For a more rewarding use of time, leave the 'Pink City' for a longer visit and focus instead on Jordan's gems in the north. This trip bypasses the capital.

Hire a car or take a taxi from the airport in **Amman** and head to the Roman ruins of **Jerash**. On day two, amble down to the Jordan Valley via **Ajloun** and the Islamic Ajloun Castle. Pause at the point where John allegedly baptised Jesus at **Bethany-Beyond-the-Jordan** and book in for some extreme R&R at the lowest place on earth at the **Dead Sea**. On day three, tear yourself away from the fluffy towels of the region's best spas (which come complete with a bob in the Dead Sea and therapeutic mud pack) and drive via the Dead Sea Panoramic Complex to nearby **Mukawir**, where Salome reputedly danced for John's head on a platter. Skirt the plateau ridge to the friendly mosaic town of **Madaba** and on day four visit **Mt Nebo** or the dolmens of Wadi Jadid. From Madaba, allow an hour to return to the airport in Amman.

6 DAYS Petra Plus

Travellers often ask: 'Is it worth making the effort to get to Petra with only limited time?' The answer is yes! While you can cover Petra in an exhausting day trip from the capital, this route takes you on a more rewarding route through the south if you're prepared to use taxis.

From **Amman**, take the bus along the Desert Highway to **Aqaba**. With plenty of accommodation, a lively ambience and excellent seafood, it'll be hard to leave town on day three. Take the early bus to Wadi Musa, the town closest to the Nabataean treasures of **Petra**. Amble through the Siq at midday, missing the morning tour groups. Watch the sunset turn the Royal Tombs pink, and return to the lively traveller scene along the town's Tourism St.

Follow the ghosts of Crusaders along the King's Highway to **Shobak** on day four and stay overnight at **Dana Biosphere Reserve**. Hike down to **Feynan Ecolodge** on day five, prearranging transport along the Dead Sea Highway back to Aqaba (or north to Amman) on day six.

Plan Your Trip

Red Sea Diving & Snorkelling

Crystal-clear water, coral gardens and multicolour fish: these features have drawn expert divers to the Red Sea for years. But in Jordan you don't have to be certified to have fun – even the casual swimmer can easily and affordably don goggles and enjoy the spectacle.

Planning Your Dive or Snorkel

The Red Sea has a legendary reputation among underwater enthusiasts. Conglomerations of coral rise from the seabed, shallow reefs teem with brightly coloured fish, sheer drop-offs disappear into unplumbed depths and an eerie, ethereal blue pervades the cut-glass water.

While it is no secret that the Red Sea is one of the world's finest marine destinations, it's less known that Jordan has 27km of precious access to this underwater wonderland alongside the Gulf of Aqaba. This is good news for those divers and snorkellers who seek pristine reefs. It is also good news for those who favour an altogether low-key experience; indeed, the whole diving scene here is delightfully relaxed and unpretentious. Even if you have no intention of diving and snorkelling, you may just find yourself lured into the water regardless by the friendly staff at the travellers' camps along the shore.

For a more structured experience in luxury surroundings, the Tala Bay complex offers a full range of underwater activities without the need to shuttle to and from Aqaba.

Best Water Activities

Best Dive

Cedar Pride The coral-encrusted hulk of this sunken ship is Jordan's most famous dive site.

Best Snorkel

Japanese Garden Shore access and a gradual slope to a colourful reef make this the best place to hoist a snorkel.

Best Underground Garden

Gorgonian I Renowned for 16m fan coral and house-sized cabbage coral.

Gorgonian II Spectacular trimming of fire, stony and raspberry corals.

Best Turtle Encounter

Power Station Turtles regularly frequent this dive site. Don't be unnerved by the hammerheads – shark attacks are extremely rare.

Best Watering Holes

Darna Divers Village This is the current favourite to dry your flippers while you wet your whistle.

Bedouin Garden Village Swapping fishy stories under a Bedouin tent is an 'après dive' highlight.

Clear Visibility

Surrounded by desert on three sides, the Red Sea was formed 40 million years ago when the Arabian Peninsula split from Africa, and it is the only tropical sea that is almost entirely enclosed by land. No river flows into it and the influx of water from the Indian Ocean is slight, resulting in minimal tides and high salinity. It is also windy – on average the sea is flat for only 50 days a year. This unique combination of elements means that visibility underwater is usually unfailingly crystal-clear, contributing to the almost surreal sense of encounter with kaleidoscopic marine life.

High Accessibility

Enjoying the wonders of the deep is easy to organise, with many of the dive sites readily accessible to snorkellers. Dive centres offer accommodation close to the shore – handy for those who want to make diving and snorkelling the main focus of their visit to southern Jordan, and fun for those who just want to enjoy a laid-back, sociable time among fellow travellers.

Those who prefer the buzz and amenities of Jordan's seaside city can easily find transport to and from Aqaba, making the dive sites accessible as a day trip from town. Tala Bay nearby offers mid- and top-end resort accommodation.

When, Where & How

When to Go

The water temperature is warm (an average 22.5°C in winter and 26°C in summer), making the in-water experience pleasant at any time of year. That said, it is important to bear in mind the high temperatures of summer, which can make it uncomfortably hot on shore with a high risk of sunburn during the day.

Best Times

Late January–mid-May This is the best time to dive weather-wise. Bear in mind that late winter attracts holidaymakers from Amman, pushing up the price of accommodation in Aqaba. Spring is peak tourist season for international visitors and the busiest time for dive centres.

October–November The second-most popular time to dive but prepare for the odd overcast or rainy day, which makes for comparatively disappointing viewing of marine life.

Times Best Avoided

Mid-May–September The shore is usually miserably hot in the middle of summer and the risk of burning is high both in and out of the water.

RESPONSIBLE DIVING & SNORKELLING

The Red Sea's natural wonders are just as magnificent as Jordan's historical and cultural splendours – and they need just as much protection. To help preserve the ecology and beauty of the reefs for posterity, please heed the following advice:

- Do not touch, remove or stand on coral and avoid dragging equipment across the reef. Reefs are easily damaged by unthinking contact with feet and flippers.
- Minimise your disturbance of marine animals. In particular, do not ride on the backs of turtles or give food to the fish. Yes, sadly, it happens!
- Avoid large surges of water or kicking up sand with your fins; this may smother the delicate organisms of the reef.
- Do not throw rubbish into the sea or leave it on the beach. Plastics in particular are a serious threat to marine life. Turtles often mistake plastic for jellyfish, their favourite food.
- Ensure boats are anchored to buoys, not attached to precious coral, and are not grounded on coral. If your captain is unmindful of this rule, report any misconduct to your dive centre on return to shore.
- Practise and maintain proper buoyancy control. Major damage can be done by divers descending too fast and colliding with the reef.
- Resist taking marine souvenirs, which depletes the beauty of a site and is illegal in Jordan. Remember, too, that shells are the 'castles of the hermit crabs'.

Late December–late January Although usually mild in Aqaba, freezing-cold weather and occasional thunderstorms can sweep in from the desert at any time during winter. Wetsuits are a must and locals will wonder why you're bothering with the sea in chilly weather when you could be just enjoying a mint tea and chatting with friends.

Where to Go

Jordan's short coastline along the Gulf of Aqaba stretches between Israel and the Palestinian Territories and Saudi Arabia. Diving and snorkelling is focused between the port of Aqaba and the Saudi border. This stretch of coast is protected within the Aqaba Marine Park, part of the larger Red Sea Marine Peace Park, run in cooperation with Israel and the Palestinian Territories. Reefs here are in excellent condition, and the soft corals, especially those found on the *Cedar Pride,* are beautiful and varied.

There are about 15 sites worth visiting. The majority can be enjoyed by snorkellers as well as divers as they are easily accessible from either a jetty or the beach. Although you can enter the water at any spot along the coast, snorkellers tend to gravitate towards the private beach at the Royal Diving Club.

Sites are not signposted, nor are they remotely obvious from the road. If you want to dive or snorkel independently, you'll have to ask for directions, or take your chances and search for 'obvious' offshore reefs. On the whole, to avoid wasting half a day trying to find an interesting stretch of water, it's better to take local advice.

How to Go

Dive Centres

Trips are easily organised through specialist operators in Aqaba or along the Red Sea coast and many hotels facilitate diving and snorkelling trips as well. There are a number of dive centres with a long-standing reputation for excellence.

Choosing a Dive Centre

➡ Choose a reputable dive centre that makes safety a priority.

➡ If you have not dived for more than three months, take a refresher dive. The cost is usually applied towards later dives.

Diving & Snorkelling

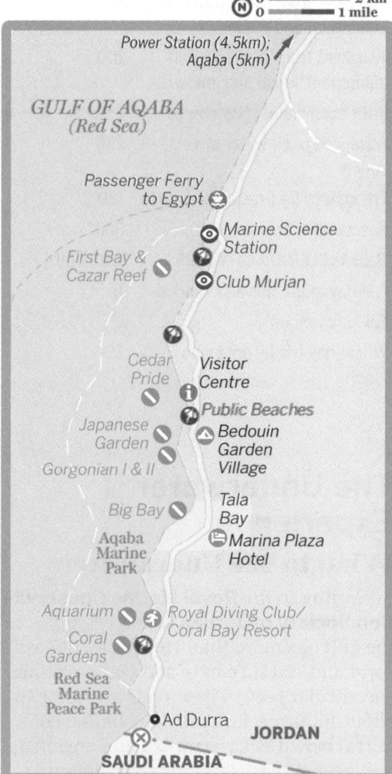

➡ Check hoses, mouthpieces and valves for cuts and leakage.

➡ Choose your wetsuit carefully: it may sound patronising, but in the heat of summer they perish, easily leading to a chilly and unpleasant experience in winter months.

➡ Check that there is oxygen on the dive boat in case of accidents.

Costs

The satisfying part of diving and snorkelling in Jordan is that it doesn't have to cost an arm and a leg. In fact, for under JD10 per day you can bask above fan corals, swim with sardines, tread water among angels and float among clowns. The following table gives a rough idea of what costs to expect. With competitive rates for courses, Jordan is a good place to learn to dive or to enhance your skills at all levels.

DIVING ACTIVITIES	COST (JD)
Two dives from shore with full equipment and guide	60
Two dives from boat with full equipment, lunch and guide	100
PADI open-water diver course	350
Advanced open-water diver course	250
Emergency first-response course	150
Rescue-dive course	350
SNORKELLING ACTIVITIES	**COST (JD)**
Full-day mask, fins and snorkel	15
Full-day wetsuit	5
Whole-day trip by boat with lunch	35

The Underwater Experience

What to See Underwater

According to the **Royal Marine Conservation Society of Jordan** (www.jreds.org), the gulf has more than 110 species of hard coral and 120 species of soft coral forming spectacular reefs. These reefs are home to about 1000 species of fish, including colourful clownfish, parrotfish and angelfish, and a whole variety of life from dolphins to molluscs and sponges. Protected green turtles frequent the dive sites and harmless whale sharks pay a visit in summer.

Buy the plastic *Red Sea Fishwatchers Field Guide,* which can be taken underwater to identify species of fish and coral.

Internet Resources

Among the hundreds of internet references to help inform your underwater experience, the following are recommended.

Wind Finder (www.windfinder.com/forecast/aqaba) Check on current conditions to ensure you pick the best day for your dive.

PADI (www.padi.com/scuba-vacations/jordan) Jordan is a good place to learn to dive and PADI arguably gives the most trusted certification. Its website has details about dive courses and other diving-related information on Jordan.

Reef Check (www.reefcheck.org) A membership organisation working to save coral reefs in the Red Sea and elsewhere in the world.

Hazards of the Sea

It's worth familiarising yourself with the main marine hazards before snorkelling or diving – single-page colour guides to the Red Sea's common culprits can be bought in hotel bookshops around diving areas.

Stonefish A poisonous fish with a nasty habit of lying half-submerged in the sand: wear something on your feet if you're wading out to a dive site. If stung by a stonefish, you should see a doctor immediately.

Lionfish These have poisonous spikes like stonefish. Calamine lotion, antihistamines and analgesics may reduce the reaction and relieve pain. Some swear by the application of urine!

Jellyfish Sometimes occurring in enormous groups, jellyfish can be something of a scourge in warm waters. Depending on the species, their sting can be very painful. The best remedy is to douse the rash with vinegar.

Sharks In this part of the Gulf of Aqaba, you're most likely to encounter white- or black-tipped reef sharks. Tiger sharks and the enormous, plankton-eating whale sharks are generally found only in deeper waters. Attacks from these apex predators are extremely rare in this area but obvious common sense applies if you have a bad cut or bleeding wound.

Coral The cuts from coral are notoriously slow to heal. Make sure you clean wounds thoroughly to avoid infection. Unlike the cold waters of northern seas, subtropical sea water is full of troublesome organisms that can cause serious infection.

RED SEA ROYALS

Sultan Ibrahim, king fish and king soldier bream are not the only royals in the water. Diving in Jordan enjoys support from the very top, with King Abdullah II reported to be an avid diver. In fact, his patronage was instrumental in the establishment of Jordan's premier artificial reef, the wreck of the *Cedar Pride.* Running aground after a fire in the engine room, this Spanish-built cargo ship was towed back out to sea in 1986 by the World Wildlife Fund (WWF) and sunk as an artificial reef. Today, the freighter lies on her port side at a depth of 25m, within easy reach from the shore, and is now one of the premier dive sites in the Red Sea.

BEARACREATIVE/SHUTTERSTOCK ©

Top: Diving in the Red Sea

Bottom: Picasso triggerfish in the Red Sea

THE RED SEA – A SEVENTH WONDER

Ever wondered where the Mare Rostrum (Red Sea) got its name? Some believe it was named after the red sandstone mountain ranges that surround the sea. Others insist it was named after the periodic blooms of algae that tinge the water reddish-brown. But whatever the etymology of the name, the Red Sea is now synonymous with underwater spectacles par excellence – and that's official! In 1989 a panel of scientists and conservationists selected the northern portion of this 1800km-long body of water as one of the Seven Underwater Wonders of the World.

Crown of Thorns Starfish Known as COTS, these invasive starfish feed on and kill local coral. Divers should notify their divemaster if they spot them.

Other Creatures to Avoid Moray eels, sea urchins, fire coral, blowfish, triggerfish and turkeyfish are better left alone.

Safety Advice

Any underwater adventure incurs some element of risk but with planning and a bit of common sense, the risks can be minimised. It's also worth brushing up on key diving tips before you book your trip.

If it's too late for that, the excellent **Princess Haya Hospital** (Map p196; ☎03 201 4111; Ash Sharif Al Hussein Bin Ali St) in Aqaba is well-equipped for diving mishaps, including cuts, bites and stings. It also has a decompression chamber, where the staff is trained to deal with diving accidents. The reputable dive centres are equipped with emergency oxygen tanks, a first-aid kit and a mobile phone.

Jordan's Best Dives

Power Station

Location: Around 500m south of Aqaba

Rating: Intermediate

Access: Shore or boat

From a shallow fringing reef of fire coral, a sloping plateau of coral and sand patches leads to a 200m sheer wall, dropping from 12m to a narrow shelf at 40m.

First Bay

Location: Next to the Marine Science Station

Rating: Novice

Access: Shore or boat

First Bay is a shallow reef plateau with lagoons and sandy channels leading to a fringing reef of fire coral. Just south is **Cazar Reef**, noted for black coral trees.

Diver near the *Cedar Pride* shipwreck (p32)

DIVE SAFE CHECKLIST

Before You Go

Are you insured? If things go wrong underwater, treatment in the decompression chamber can cost thousands of dollars. If you hadn't planned to dive before arriving in Jordan, many of the better dive centres can provide insurance.

Have you informed your doctor? Diving can affect your metabolism and if you're on medication, your dosage of prescription drugs might need to be changed.

Have you been drinking? Alcohol dehydrates, especially in Jordan's dry climate, and increases susceptibility to decompression sickness.

During the Dive

Do you know your diving depth limit? The Red Sea's clear waters and high visibility often lure divers into going too deep. The depth limit for casual divers is 30m – stick to it.

Will you remember what your boat looked like? Some dive sites get crowded and boats can look similar from underneath. It's not unknown for divers to be left behind because they didn't realise that their boat was leaving.

After Care

Have you allowed 24 hours before flying? Divers are in serious danger of decompression sickness if they attempt to fly too soon.

Have you allowed 12 hours before leaving Aqaba? As most routes out of town involve an uphill drive, the change in altitude may trigger decompression sickness. If you're heading for Petra or Wadi Rum, leave your journey until tomorrow.

Cedar Pride

Location: 5km north of the Royal Diving Club

Rating: Intermediate

Access: Shore or boat

Intact and festooned with soft corals, the wreck of the *Cedar Pride* is a true highlight with magnificent sea fans, basket stars and rainbows of fish caught in the sunlight.

Japanese Garden

Location: 4km north of the Royal Diving Club

Rating: Novice

Access: Shore or boat

Just south of the *Cedar Pride,* this reef sports large coral heads, including black coral. Lionfish, angelfish and schools of snapper and butterfly fish inhabit the magnificent colourful reef.

Gorgonian I and II

Location: 3km north of the Royal Diving Club

Rating: Novice

Access: Shore or boat

Gorgonian I and II take their names from large, solitary fan corals. Nearby wonders include giant cabbage corals and green turtles that feed on the sea grass.

Big Bay

Location: 2km north of the Royal Diving Club

Rating: Intermediate

Access: Shore or boat

There are four sites in Big Bay – **Blue Coral**, **Kalli's Place**, **Moon Valley** and **Paradise** – which feature lacy blue and black coral. The 'long swim' (1km) to the Royal Diving Club is popular.

Aquarium & Coral Gardens

Location: Offshore from the Royal Diving Club

Rating: Intermediate

Access: Shore or boat

The Aquarium is home to a spectacular fringing reef with a giant wall of fire corals. Immediately south lies Coral Gardens, home to lots of reef fish, seahorses and moray eels.

Plan Your Trip

Outdoor Activities

With the opening of the Jordan Trail and Jordan Bike Trail, Jordan has become a hot spot for outdoor activities, including guided canyoning organised through the Royal Society for the Conservation of Nature (RSCN; www.rscn.org.jo), camel riding and ballooning in Wadi Rum through Bait Ali Lodge, water sports in Aqaba and driving off-road along the Eastern Badia Trail to Burqu.

Best Land-Based Activities

Best Hike

With its magnificent canyon scenery, the section of the Jordan Trail between Dana and Petra is already gathering an international reputation as a hike of high drama.

Best 4WD Drive

You don't need to be behind the wheel to get a buzz from surfing on sand. Riding shot gun with the Bedouin across the dunes of Wadi Rum is likely to be every bit as exhilarating.

Best Nature Reserve for Outdoor Activities

Wadi Mujib, with its slot canyons and wet river beds, the hint of elusive ibex and the surreal sense of climbing *up* to sea level, offers trails to suit all levels of interest and fitness.

Best Community Engagement

A stroll through the gnarled and aged woodlands of Ajloun Forest Reserve offers opportunities to meet with the soap makers, biscuit bakers and mobile phone forsakers of Jordan's northern hamlets.

Top Activities in Jordan

Hiking & Canyoning

Hiking (and canyoning) are exhilarating activities in Jordan because of the varied quality of the landscape and the historical allusions that underlie each path. While the epic Jordan Trail offers the quintessential hiking route in Jordan, it's not the only trail: smaller routes meet all levels of fitness and challenge.

When to Go

Always check local conditions before setting out as flash floods can occur throughout spring and may make wadis impassable. Bear in mind that GPS units and mobile phones may not function between steep canyon walls.

Best Mid-March to late April when it's not too hot, the rains have finished, the flowers are blooming and wells are full.

Good Late September to mid-October when it's dry but not excessively hot.

Avoid November to March when rains make it dangerous to hike or camp in narrow wadis and flash floods can sweep unheralded out of the hills. Paths are often washed away, so routes change frequently. It's also very cold for camping.

Where to Go

When pondering where to go along the Jordan Trail, the obvious resource to consult is the Jordan Trail website (www.jordantrail.org), which describes individual legs of the route. *National Geographic* voted the Dana to Petra leg of the trail as one of the top 15 hikes in the world.

Among numerous other hiking options, the RSCN-protected areas of Ajloun Forest Reserve, Dana Biosphere Reserve and Mujib Biosphere Reserve offer the most structured routes in some of the most beautiful destinations and provide guides along many of the trails. For more DIY options, there are some exciting hikes in Petra and in Wadi Rum. Bedouin guides also offer accompanied hikes along the old caravan routes that link these two spectacular locations.

What to Bring

Lightweight trousers and long-sleeved shirts are culturally sensitive and best for the terrain. Other essentials include a hat, sunscreen, water bottle, torch (flashlight) and insect repellent. Lightweight walking boots are ideal, and bring a watertight bag for wet wadi walks. Warm layers are essential in winter.

How to Organise a Hike

The best way to organise a trek is through RSCN's Wild Jordan (p65), the visitor centre in Petra (p179) or Wadi Rum (p220), or a private tour company that specialises in hiking. If you engage a Bedouin guide independently, make sure you understand exactly what services are on offer to avoid disappointment on either side. Rates vary (and are negotiable) between JD30 to JD120, depending on the skills required.

Wild Jordan (p65) Wide range of guided hikes in Jordan's nature reserves; can arrange long-distance treks if given prior notice.

Experience Jordan (p59) A recommended tour company for facilitating hikes along part or all of the Jordan Trail.

Terhaal Encounters (www.terhaal.com) For individual or group adventure hikes, including abseiling and canyoning, that minimise environmental impact and bring benefits to local communities.

Tropical Desert Trips (www.tropicaldeserttrips.com) Hiking, climbing and canyoning trips across Jordan.

Desert Guides Company (www.desertguidescompany.com) Specialises in adventure hikes, treks and climbs throughout Jordan.

Yamaan Safady (www.adventurejordan.com) Leads weekly hiking trips to places such as Wadi Yabis and Wadi Hasa as part of the Adventure Jordan Hiking Club.

Resources

It's best to buy both maps and books before arriving as their availability in Jordan is sporadic.

Trekking & Canyoning in the Jordanian Dead Sea Rift by Itai Haviv contains numerous trekking and canyoning routes in the wadis of Central Jordan; its cultural and environmental insights alone make it worth the trouble to find.

British climbers Tony Howard and Di Taylor have spent much of their lives exploring and mapping the hiking, trekking and rock-climbing possibilities in Jordan. Their books include the following:

- *Treks & Climbs in Wadi Rum*
- *Walks & Scrambles in Wadi Rum*

THE JORDAN TRAIL

More than 650km from top to toe, the newly established 36-day **Jordan Trail** (www.jordantrail.org) covers the entire length of Jordan and threads through some of the country's most iconic landscapes, including Petra and Wadi Rum. The trail is segmented into eight legs averaging around 80km each.

Those who have already completed this route recommend taking 42 days to cover the distance, allowing for one or two rest days along the way. The Jordan Trail Association, established to preserve the trail and help ensure its accessibility, maintains a useful website that describes each leg of the trail and recommends tour operators who can facilitate travel along all or parts of its length. These include Experience Jordan (p59). The Dana to Petra stage is particularly rewarding and has been described by *National Geographic* as one of the best 15 hikes in the world.

➡ *Jordan: Walks, Treks, Caves, Climbs & Canyons*
➡ *Walks, Treks, Climbs & Caves in Al Ayoun*

Cycling

With its beautiful and diverse scenery, relatively uncongested roads, short distances between accommodation and minimal worries about bike theft, cycling is becoming increasingly popular in Jordan. This is slightly tempered by the odd stone-lobbing tot, poor road and route maintenance, and lack of spare parts, but the excitement of the new Jordan Bike Trail more than compensates.

For information and costs for cycling tours, contact Bike Rush (p62) in Amman (offers weekly trips), Experience Jordan (p59), founder of the epic Jordan Bike Trail, Baraka Destinations (p104) in Umm Qais (half-/full-day tours) and Feynan Ecolodge (p151), with its locally run Bedouin bike shop.

Jordan Bike Trail

The biking equivalent of hiking's Jordan Trail, the epic **Jordan Bike Trail** (www.jordanbiketrail.com) navigates a path from Umm Qais to the Red Sea. The website has detailed information on the route, including GPS waypoints and elevation charts for each stage, and is highly challenging, even for experienced riders. Described as not very technical, this canyon-crossing trail does, however, include lots of stiff climbs.

A man bathing in mud sourced from the Dead Sea (p113)

Riding

Camel Treks

Camel riding is available for getting around the ancient city of Petra (from JD20). In Wadi Rum, camel trekking costs from JD5 for 30 minutes to JD60 for an overnight camel trip. Choose a mounted rather than a walking guide for a more authentic experience.

Horse Treks

Given the Bedouin horse-owning heritage, Jordan is a great place to ride, offering a rare chance to saddle up an Arabian stallion. As these animals are notoriously highly strung, prior knowledge of horse riding is generally necessary.

GREATER PROFESSIONALISM IN ADVENTURE SPORTS

Adventure tour companies are rising to the challenge of greater demand for their services by providing more professional support for those in their care while being responsible towards the communities and environment in which they work.

The government, in recognising Jordan's potential for excellence in the field of adventure tourism, has matched this initiative by encouraging collectives such as the Jordan Mountaineering Association. The result of this new professionalism towards adventure travel and tourism in Jordan is that the visitor can now hike and climb in stunning landscapes, painstakingly piece together the past on an archaeological dig or engage with the community through community-led activities, safe in the knowledge that there is backup, a structured approach to health and safety and sound infrastructure to support them.

Wadi Rum (p209)

As well as day rides, Rum Horses (p216), a long-established stable in Wadi Rum, offers multiday camping trips (helmets provided). For a more ad hoc experience, horse riding is available in and around Petra from around JD50 for a two-hour trek.

Rock Climbing

There are many routes in **Wadi Rum** (www.wadirum.net) best tackled through Shabab Sahra (p217), the only internationally accredited climbing operator in Wadi Rum. This company belongs to the Jordan Mountaineering Association and represents Wadi Rum in this new national forum designed to uphold standards. In Amman, Climbat (p62) has a good climbing wall for all abilities with instructors on hand. Popular climbs all around Jordan are detailed in excellent books written by Tony Howard and Di Taylor.

Running

Runners can email **Hash House Harriers** (HashemiteHHH-subscribe@yahoogroups.com) to be added to its mailing list for alerts on forthcoming runs. In addition, look out for two annual events: Dead Sea Ultra Marathon (p113) and Petra Desert Marathon (p177). Dubbed 'drinkers with a running problem' on its website, the HHH organises local runs each Monday from Amman.

Spas & Turkish Baths

The sky's the limit when it comes to booking a Dead Sea spa at one of Jordan's best hotels. A cheaper option is to book in for a scrub down at the local hammam (otherwise known as a Turkish bath). Costing

MAKING THE MOST OF JORDAN'S NATURE RESERVES

For hiking and activities in Jordan's nature reserves contact the tourism department of the Royal Society for the Conservation of Nature (www.rscn.org.jo), which can arrange short activity breaks or entire itineraries.

For an extended trip to Wadi Rum it's best to contact a local Bedouin agency, such as the recommended Wadi Rum Mountain Guides (www.bedouinroads.com).

Mujib Biosphere Reserve (p121)

around JD25, including massage, Wadi Musa has the best selection. It's a great antidote for aching muscles. Women should call ahead for a female assistant.

Organising an Activity

DIY Activities

An alternative to a group tour organised from abroad is to arrange your own private mini-tour with a Jordanian travel agency. Many of these can arrange hiking or archaeological itineraries and provide a car and driver. If you're travelling independently, and on a tight budget, jumping on a budget-priced organised tour from Amman (offered by many budget hotels) to a remote destination like the desert castles of eastern Jordan is far easier, and often cheaper, than doing it yourself and some of these cover popular activities such as hiking and canyoning.

Best Tour Agencies for Guided Activities

Atlas Travel & Tourist Agency (www.atlastours.net) Also offers side trips to Israel and the Palestinian Territories and Lebanon.

Desert Guides Company (www.desertguides.net) Trekking, mountain-bike and adventure trips.

Engaging Cultures Travel (www.engagingcultures.com) Highly regarded small group and tailor-made tours from Amman, with strong emphasis on culturally immersive experiences.

Golden Crown Tours (www.goldencrowntours.com) Offers archaeological, religious and adventure tours.

Jordan Beauty Tours (www.jordanbeauty.com) Local tour operator offering archaeological and biblical tours, as well as hiking, camel trips, diving and cross-border tours to Israel.

La Beduina (www.labeduinatours.com) Specialist tours, including hiking, cooking, horse and camel riding, and yoga tours.

Petra Moon Tourism Services (www.petramoon.com) The most professional agency in Wadi Musa for arranging hiking trips inside Petra and around Jordan (including Wadi Rum and Aqaba).

Tropical Desert Trips (www.td-adventures.com) Active tours, including hiking, climbing, canyoning and desert exploration.

Zaman Tours & Travel (www.zamantours.com) Adventure tours, camping, camel treks and hiking.

Plan Your Trip

Travel with Children

Children are universally adored in Jordan, so you'll find that taking the kids adds a welcome dimension to your trip. Children are instant ice breakers and will guarantee contact with local people, especially as foreign families are still something of a novelty.

Jordan for Kids

Expect a Warm Welcome

While few concessions are made for youngsters, except the occasional high chair in a restaurant and baby-changing facilities in modern city malls, you'll find people go out of their way to make your family feel welcome, especially on buses and in shops, hotels and restaurants.

The Jordanian Family Way

Child-oriented activities are still a novel concept in Jordan as normally children are included in adult outings and entertainments. Jordanians enjoy socialising in groups, so there's usually an extra pair of hands to mind the kids. As a result of this child-inclusive approach, most adult highlights are treated as children's highlights too.

Cultural Highlights a Hit

Feedback from parents on Lonely Planet's Thorn Tree forum is very positive about the experience of taking children to Petra, Jerash, Karak and Wadi Rum, although it pays to get the family curious about the destination in advance. Jordan is a gold mine for school projects on the Romans, for example.

Best Regions for Kids

Amman

Don't miss the Children's Museum in Amman. This brilliant interactive centre offers features in English and Arabic and staff are wonderful with the kids.

Northwestern Jordan

Kids studying the Romans will love Jerash, where centurions bring history alive.

Dead Sea Highway

Children can swim with extra buoyancy in the very salty water – if warned to be careful with eyes.

Central Jordan

With tunnels and passageways, there's heaps to explore about the Crusaders at Karak Castle and its Islamic Museum.

Southern Jordan

Teenagers can learn to dive in Aqaba while younger kids paddle in the temperate sea. Camel rides, 4WD adventures and sandboarding make Wadi Rum a hit.

Eastern Desert

Youngsters will enjoy searching for oryx and ostriches on the Shaumari Wildlife Reserve safari.

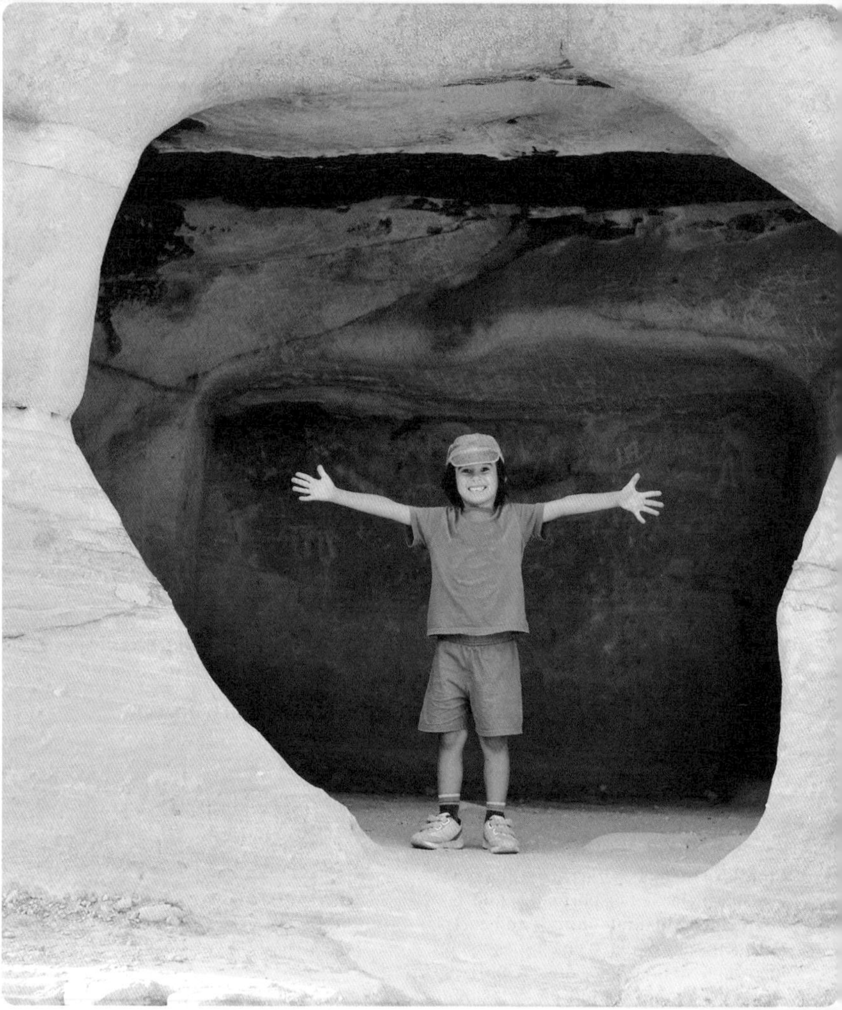

KOLDERAL/GETTY IMAGES ©

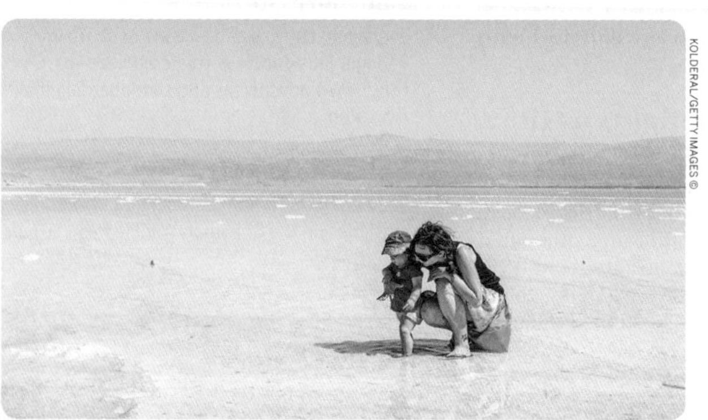

Top: Child in a tomb entrance, Petra (p155)

Bottom: Mother and child in the shallow water of the Dead Sea (p111)

Children's Highlights

Rainy Day Activities

Haya Cultural Centre, Amman (p57) Includes an interactive ecomuseum.

Children's Museum, Amman (p58) This fun and informative interactive centre, with its emphasis on engineering and human biology, is likely to keep mum and dad as engaged as the kids.

Climbat, Amman (p62) Offers a child-friendly introduction to climbing with a starter wall.

Malls A great retreat on a rainy day (or when midsummer temperatures soar), Amman's modern malls, such as Mecca Mall (p75), have cinemas and activity areas for kids.

Amusement Parks

Amman Waves, Amman (p62) A Western-style water park between the airport and Amman that is a hit with all ages.

Luna Park, Amman (p58) Offers rides and amusements for kids.

Al Wadi Resort, Dead Sea (p113) This water park offers lots of slides – kids are measured on entry!

Planning

When to Go

Spring is the best time for a family visit. The weather is great, attractions are open and the peak tourist season brings evening amusements.

The heat of summer (mid-May to mid-September) is difficult for children to tolerate, restricting your activities to early morning and late afternoon. Winter months (mid-November to mid-February) can be freezing and many activities are restricted or too cold to be enjoyable. The risk of flash floods in wadis is an added anxiety.

Coping with High Temperatures

At any time of year, temperatures are comparatively high, particularly around noon. Trips to Petra and Wadi Rum involve long periods of sun exposure, and it's not always easy to find shade: plan visits around early mornings and late afternoons. Follow local custom and take a family nap after lunch: this has the advantage of keeping the kids out of the worst of the sun and ensuring they're fresh for an evening out.

Avoiding Sickness

To prevent stomach complaints, children should stick to bottled mineral water, which is readily available, and avoid peeled fresh fruit and washed salads.

Fresh and powdered milk is available, but it's worth checking that fresh dairy products (such as milk, cream, yoghurt and cream cheese) are made with pasteurised milk. Ice cream is usually best avoided in rural areas where the electricity supply is often unreliable, leading to frozen goods defrosting and refreezing.

General hygiene might not be the priority it is in many Western countries; carrying a hand sanitiser is a good idea in case the local water supply is suspect.

Nursing Infants

Breast-feeding in public is culturally acceptable providing you are reasonably discreet. Carrying an extra garment, like a shawl or a cardigan, to tuck around you and the babe might help keep male curiosity at bay.

What to Pack

Disposable nappies (diapers) are not readily available outside Amman and Aqaba. Come prepared with plastic bags to avoid contributing to Jordan's ubiquitous litter problem.

Mosquito nets and repellent are handy in the warmer months; malaria is not an issue in Jordan, but itchy bites can easily become infected in the heat.

Car seats are not a big thing in Jordan so bring one with you. Pavements, or lack of, will be challenging for most prams, but the locals seem to cope with them!

Jordanians are tolerant of Western norms, but you will earn local respect if the kids dress appropriately. This is particularly the case with teenage girls: provocative clothing, however fashionable elsewhere, will bring unwanted attention and stares.

Safety Check

Travelling in Jordan is generally safe for the family, with low incidences of crime.

Further Reading

For all-round information and advice, check out Lonely Planet's *Travel with Children*.

Regions at a Glance

Petra is the natural focus of a visit to Jordan and for good reason. The Ancient City of the Nabataeans, set in spectacular scenery, is one of the world's wonders. With beautiful Wadi Rum nearby, Red Sea diving and the holiday vibe of Aqaba, southern Jordan is a destination in its own right.

For adventure-seekers, the Jordan Trail winds through Wadi Mujib and Dana, both accessible via the fabled King's Highway. Striking east, the desert castles complement wildlife viewing at Shaumari and Azraq Nature Reserves.

A northern circuit around the semi-arid highlands is lovely in spring when wildflowers bloom at Jerash, Jordan's Roman gem, and at biblical sites around Madaba.

Let's not forget the capital, Amman! With Roman ruins downtown and a youthful cafe culture, the city showcases modern Jordan.

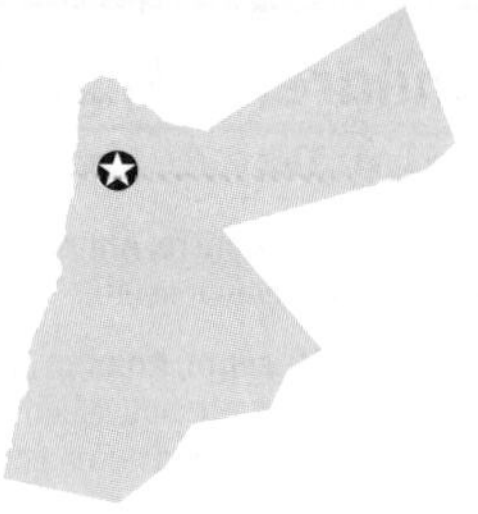

Amman

Roman Ruins
Modern Middle East
Shopping

Ancient Downtown

The Roman antiquities of the Citadel and Roman Theatre define the heart of the city and are well worth exploring. The Jordan Museum gives a thorough context to the country's major historical attractions.

Capital Cafe Culture

Sophisticated malls, buzzing coffee shops and happening nightlife challenge the regional perception of Jordan as a sleepy backwater. Values are conservative and there is plenty of evidence of the traditional Middle East, but for catching the essence of Jordan's youthful, well-educated and tech-savvy population, the capital is the place to be.

Souvenir Hunting

From gold bangles to Iraqi currency, Amman's souqs and streets are full of intriguing souvenirs. To make your spending mean more, root out the neighbourhood cooperatives.

p48

Jerash, Irbid & the Jordan Valley

Roman Ruins
Sustainable Tourism
Scenic Views

Outposts of Empire

No Jordan itinerary is complete without visiting Jerash: this well-preserved outpost of the Roman Empire has been wowing visitors for centuries and is one of the top three highlights of Jordan. Spare time for lesser antiquities at atmospheric Umm Qais. Archaeological buffs will love Pella.

Community Projects

The ecofriendly nature reserve at Ajloun is a byword for sustainable tourism. Community hikes such as Al Ayoun Trail lead through the heartland of rural Jordan and provide an opportunity for village homestays, while basket weaving is on offer at Umm Qais.

Rural Rides

Take any route from the juniper uplands of Jerash, Salt or Umm Qais to the fertile and subtropical Jordan Valley and a natural-history lesson awaits.

p82

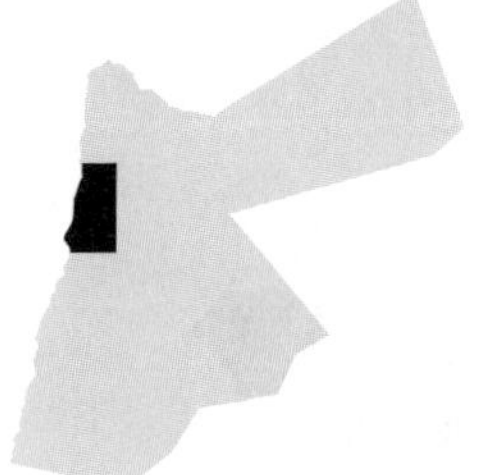

Dead Sea Highway

Spas & Springs
Hiking
Dramatic Drives

Dead Sea Float

Floating in the Dead Sea is one of Jordan's most extraordinary experiences and shouldn't be missed. With luxury spas along the sea's eastern shore, this is the place to schedule some serious R&R. Nearby hot springs complete the opportunity for healthy treatments.

Wild Water

With unexpected waterfalls, oases and glimpses of wildlife, Mujib Biosphere Reserve is a great place for outdoor adventures. Expect to get wet in year-round pools. Further along Wadi Araba, Dana Biosphere Reserve has good sea-level trails and vegetarian feasting at Feynan Ecolodge.

Switchback Drives

Snaking from the vineyards of the King's Highway to the tomato fields and potash plants of the Dead Sea Highway, this region is peppered with exciting drives.

p109

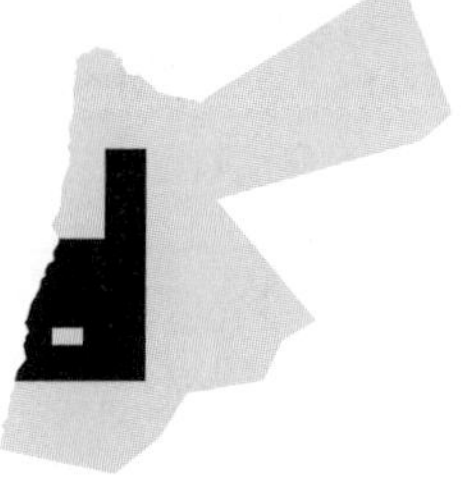

Madaba & the King's Highway

Religious Relics
Handicrafts
Hiking

Soul Searching

Moses, Elijah, Jesus Christ and John the Baptist are some of the many biblical figures said to have blessed Jordan's soil and Mt Nebo remains a place of pilgrimage today. Crusader castles at Karak and Shobak and the Christian town of Madaba show how this inheritance has been embraced over centuries.

Made in Jordan

Some of the best handicrafts in Jordan are made in cottage industries in and around Madaba. Traditional weaving near Mukawir and mosaic-making along the King's Highway are two of many crafts helping sustain rural communities.

Winter Wonders

The best and arguably the most beautiful hikes in Jordan are to be had in the upper wadis of Wadi Mujib and Dana Biosphere Reserve, despite winter snows.

p124

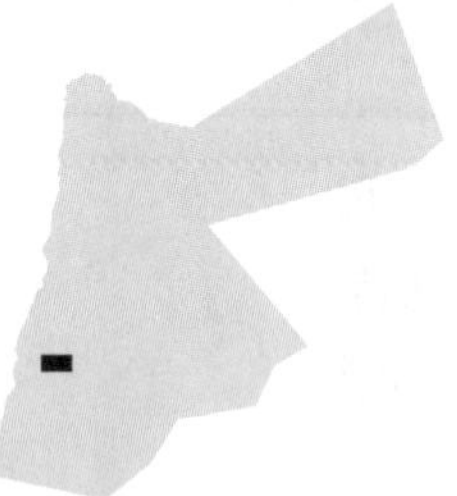

Petra

Ancient Ruins
Hiking
Stunning Scenery

Ancient Architecture

The Ancient City of Petra is a world wonder. Allow enough time to reach the Treasury in the early morning, picnic at a High Place by noon, watch the sunset at the Monastery and walk the Siq by candlelight at night – at least two days in other words.

Hikes to High Places

Petra has some of the best and most accessible hikes in Jordan. Engaging a local Bedouin guide will help bring the recent history of Petra to life. Avoid the oven-baking summer months when the heat is overbearing. Some hikes are restricted after winter rains.

Natural Decor

Outrageously colourful sandstone, wind-eroded escarpments and oleander-trimmed wadis make the landscape of Petra a worthy consort of the ancient architecture.

p155

Aqaba, Wadi Rum & the Desert Highway

Red Sea Diving
Desert Camping
Stunning Scenery

Red Sea Spectacle

Whether you dive, snorkel or simply swim, Jordan's Gulf of Aqaba gives easy access to the delights of the Red Sea. Early spring and late autumn offer the most comfortable temperatures.

Bedouin Encounter

You don't have to be a *Lawrence of Arabia* fan to enjoy hanging up your boots with the Bedouin after a day's camel trek. Desert camps are comfortable but can be freezing in midwinter and stifling in midsummer.

Desert Landscape

Even if you don't stay overnight, it's worth driving as far as the Wadi Rum visitor centre. From here you can see the Seven Pillars of Wisdom and it'll be instantly clear why this particular desert is a highlight of Jordan.

p193

Azraq & the Eastern Desert Highway

Architecture
Wildlife
Remote Travel

Pleasure Domes

The Umayyad bathhouses, hunting lodges and caravan staging posts of the Eastern Desert are collectively known as the 'desert castles'. It's not so much the buildings as the arid desert context that make visiting these outposts of civilisation worth the effort.

Jordan's Wildlife

Safari isn't an activity often associated with desert, but the oryx safari at newly reopened Shaumari Wildlife Reserve helps redefine the concept and showcases other endangered desert species. The nearby oasis at Azraq, while ever-diminishing, is still a top spot for birdwatching.

Extreme Desert

Few make it to the black wastelands of the Badia, but if you're happy to spend some days tackling the extreme desert, then head for Burqu Reserve, which epitomises the term 'remote'.

p224

On the Road

Amman عمان

☎ 06 / POP 3.5 MILLION / ELEV 850M

Includes ➡

Best Places to Eat

➡ Hashem Restaurant (p68)

➡ Jasmine House (p69)

➡ Sufra (p70)

➡ Rosa Damascena (p70)

Best Places to Stay

➡ Jordan Tower Hotel (p65)

➡ La Locanda (p67)

➡ Kempinski Amman (p67)

➡ Hisham Hotel (p67)

➡ Al Qasr Metropole Hotel (p67)

Why Go?

As Middle Eastern cities go, Amman is a relative youth, being mostly a creation of the 20th century. But though it lacks the storied history and thrilling architectural tapestry of other regional capitals, there's plenty here to encourage you to linger awhile before making for Petra, the Dead Sea or Wadi Rum. In fact, Amman is one of the easiest cities in which to enjoy the Middle East experience.

Downtown Amman is a must-see. At the bottom of the city's many hills and overlooked by the magisterial Citadel, it features spectacular Roman ruins, an international-standard museum and the hubbub of mosques, souqs and coffeehouses that are central to Jordanian life.

Elsewhere, urbane western Amman has leafy residential districts, cafes, bars, modern malls and art galleries; and in earthy eastern Amman, it's easy to sense the more traditional and conservative pulse of the capital.

When to Go

➡ The capital's hilly location brings sharp winds during cold winters – and even the occasional day of snow, which brings Amman to an icy halt.

➡ The spring months of March to May and autumnal October to November are the best times for a visit, with warm days and cooler nights.

➡ If you can bear the claustrophobic heat of midsummer, which radiates off densely packed buildings and lurks in breezeless alleyways, then July and August are recommended for the annual Jerash Festival. At this time the Roman Theatre comes alive and the capital's penchant for an evening promenade comes into its own.

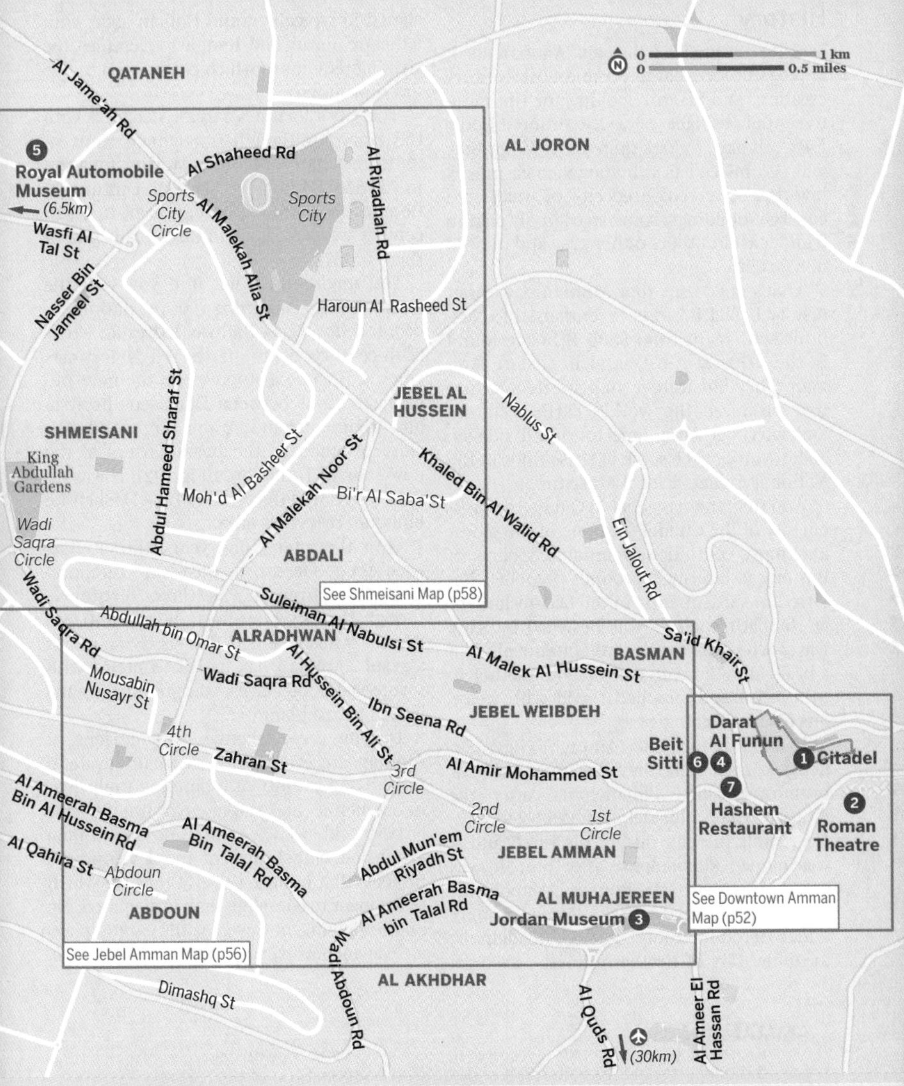

Amman Highlights

❶ **Citadel** (p51) Admiring the ancient ruins with fine hilltop views across Amman.

❷ **Roman Theatre** (p54) Marvelling at the engineering precision of Amman's most spectacular ancient monument.

❸ **Jordan Museum** (p51) Discovering the story of ancient Jordan in this world-class museum.

❹ **Darat Al Funun** (p53) Seeing a contemporary art exhibition and sipping tea amid the Byzantine ruins.

❺ **Royal Automobile Museum** (p59) Driving through Jordan's recent history with some classic cars.

❻ **Beit Sitti** (p65) Learning to cook like a local.

❼ **Hashem Restaurant** (p68) Queuing at downtown's legendary falafel eatery.

History

Despite its ancient lineage, Amman as it appears today is largely a mid-20th-century creation, and visitors looking for the quintessential vestiges of a Byzantine Middle East will have to look quite hard. What they will see instead is a homogeneous, mostly low-rise, cream-coloured city of weathered concrete buildings, some sparklingly clad in white marble, others rather grey and in need of a facelift.

That's not to say that Amman is without history. In fact, impressive remnants of a Neolithic settlement from 8500 BC were found in the 1970s at Ain Ghazal in eastern Amman. They illustrate a sophisticated culture that produced the world's earliest statues and carvings from limestone and plaster. Today, you can see some of these finds at the National Archaeological Museum.

And then there is Jebel Al Qala'a, the present site of the Citadel, and one of the oldest and most continuously inhabited parts of the city, established around 1800 BC. Referred to subsequently in the Old Testament as Rabbath, the city was besieged by King David who burnt many inhabitants alive in a brick kiln. Rabbath continued nonetheless to flourish and supplied David with weapons for his ongoing wars.

Visitors bump into Amman's Egyptian heritage each time they see a company or restaurant called Philadelphia, after the Ptolemy ruler Philadelphus (283–246 BC). He rebuilt the city during his reign and it was named Philadelphia after him. It was one of the cities of the Roman Decapolis before being assumed into the Roman Empire under Herod in around 30 BC. Philadelphia, meaning 'City of Brotherly Love', was redesigned in typically grand Roman style, with a theatre, forum and Temple to Hercules, the striking remains of which can be seen to this day downtown.

The city's fortunes largely declined with the empire, although it regained some of its former glory after the Muslim invasion in AD 636. From about the 10th century little more is heard of Amman until the 19th century when a colony of Circassians settled there in 1878.

You might not think it if you visit the sleepy tracks of Amman train station today, but the Hejaz Railway led to an early-20th-century boom in the city's fortunes when it became a stopover on the new 'pilgrimage route' between Damascus in Syria and Medina in Saudi Arabia. Emir Abdullah chose Amman as the headquarters of the new state of Trans-Jordan in 1921; it was officially declared the capital of the Hashemite kingdom two years later.

Over the intervening years, the city has weathered successive waves of immigration, mostly from the Palestinian Territories, though the city now hosts nearly 440,000 Syrians who have fled due to civil war. As a result, Amman has had to contend with severe water shortages, compounded by the lack of urban planning.

Despite the challenges, the citizens of Amman are ever-optimistic, many grateful for the opportunity of rebuilding their lives in a generous and stable environment. This is best evidenced by the almost continual expansion, embellishment and development projects that besiege the city, most of which take longer to complete than anticipated. No one complains, however, as the capital plays an ever-increasing role on the regional stage.

AMMAN IN ...

Spend the first day in the excitement of downtown Amman. Start at the **Roman Theatre** (p54), checking the ancient acoustics and dropping in on the **Folklore Museum** (p55). Take lunch at the famous **Hashem Restaurant** (p68), before walking it off through the city's souqs. After a drink at a downtown coffee shop, make your way to the excellent **Jordan Museum** (p51). By late afternoon you're ready to take a taxi uphill to watch the sun dip over the hills from the **Citadel** (p51). After sunset, treat yourself to dinner at **Sufra** (p70).

On day two, start with some shopping along **Rainbow Street** (p57), stopping for a bite to eat at the **Wild Jordan Center** (p69). In the afternoon, take in the unexpectedly excellent **Royal Automobile Museum** (p59) for a different take on modern Jordanian history and then make your way to Lweibdeh for a cookery class at **Beit Sitti** (p65), enjoying a local dinner you've made with new friends over a bottle of wine from Jordan's Mt Nebo vineyards.

Only minimally troubled by the 2011 revolutions, it remains a vibrant, open-minded city, famed in the region for its educational institutions and confident about the future.

Dangers & Annoyances

Amman continues to be a safe city for visitors.

Crime is rare and Jordanians take pride in reminding foreigners that their country remains an oasis of peace in a notoriously belligerent region.

Security guards and metal detectors are in place at entrances to top-end hotels.

Sights

A largely modern construction, Amman is home to few vistas that evoke images of grand empires. That said, scattered amid the concrete streetscapes are several spectacular remnants of Philadelphia, particularly the ruins on top of Jebel Al Qala'a, and the Roman Theatre downtown. The most interesting part of this open-hearted city, however, is the chance that it affords to meet its cosmopolitan inhabitants – in the souqs of downtown, for example, or in the coffeehouses and modern malls of its fashionable hilltop neighbourhoods of Jebel Amman and beyond.

Downtown

★Jordan Museum MUSEUM

(Map p56; www.jordanmuseum.jo/en; btwn Omar Matar & Ali Bin Abi Taleb Sts; JD5; ⏲10am-2pm Sat-Mon, Wed & Thu) The Jordan Museum, located next to the City Hall, is one of the best in the Middle East. Housed in a grand modern building, a series of beautifully presented and informative displays tell Jordan's historical epic from the first people through the Nabataean civilisation to the cusp of the modern era. Highlights include the oldest-known human statues (the spookily modern 9500-year-old plaster mannequins of Ain Ghazal), Jordan's share of the Dead Sea Scrolls, and a host of remains from Petra and surrounds.

★Citadel RUINS

(Map p52; ☎06 463 8795; Jebel Al Qala'a; JD2, free with Jordan Pass; ⏲8am-7pm Sat-Thu Apr-Sep, to 4pm Sat-Thu Oct-Mar, 10am-4pm Fri year-round) The area known as the Citadel sits on the highest hill in Amman, Jebel Al Qala'a (about 850m above sea level), and is the site of ancient Rabbath-Ammon. Occupied since the Bronze Age, it's surrounded by a 1700m-long wall, which was rebuilt many times during the Bronze and Iron Ages, as well as the Roman, Byzantine and Umayyad periods. There's plenty to see, but the Citadel's most striking sights are the Temple of Hercules and the Ummayad Palace.

Artefacts dating from the Bronze Age show that the hill was a fortress and/or agora (open space for commerce and politics) for thousands of years.

The two giant standing pillars are the remains of the Roman **Temple of Hercules**. Once connected to the Forum (downtown), the temple was built during the reign of Roman Emperor Marcus Aurelius (AD 161–80). The only obvious remains are parts of the podium and the columns, which are visible from around town. There's also a rather touching remnant of a stone-carved hand, which shows the level of detail that would have adorned the temple in its glory days. Nearby is a lookout with sweeping views of the downtown area.

The Citadel's most impressive series of historic buildings is focused around the **Umayyad Palace**, behind the small (and rather old-fashioned) archaeological museum. Believed to be the work of Umayyad Arabs and dating from about AD 720, the palace was an extensive complex of royal and residential buildings and was once home to the governor of Amman. Its lifespan was short – it was destroyed by an earthquake in AD 749 and was never fully rebuilt.

Coming from the south, the first major building belonging to the palace complex is the domed audience hall, designed to impress visitors to the royal palace. The most intact of the buildings on the site, the hall is shaped like a cross, mirroring the Byzantine

TUNNEL UNDER AMMAN

In ancient Roman Philadelphia, royalty considered it beneath them to mingle with the general public unless they had to. To ease their path between the major sites, an underground tunnel was built to connect the Citadel high on the hill with the Nymphaeum and the Theatre. While modern visitors to Amman might welcome having such access without having to negotiate the streets of downtown, the tunnel's precise location and state of repair is a closely guarded secret.

Downtown Amman

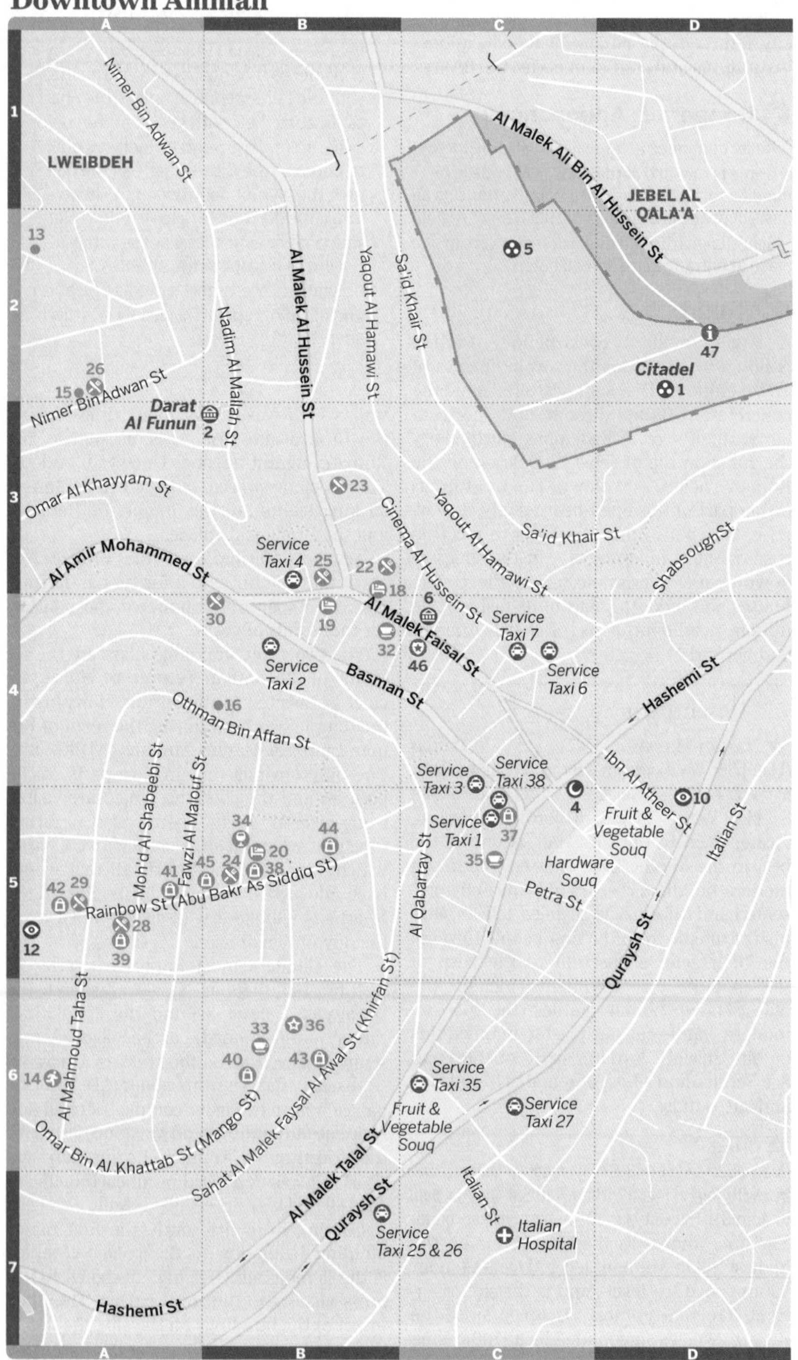

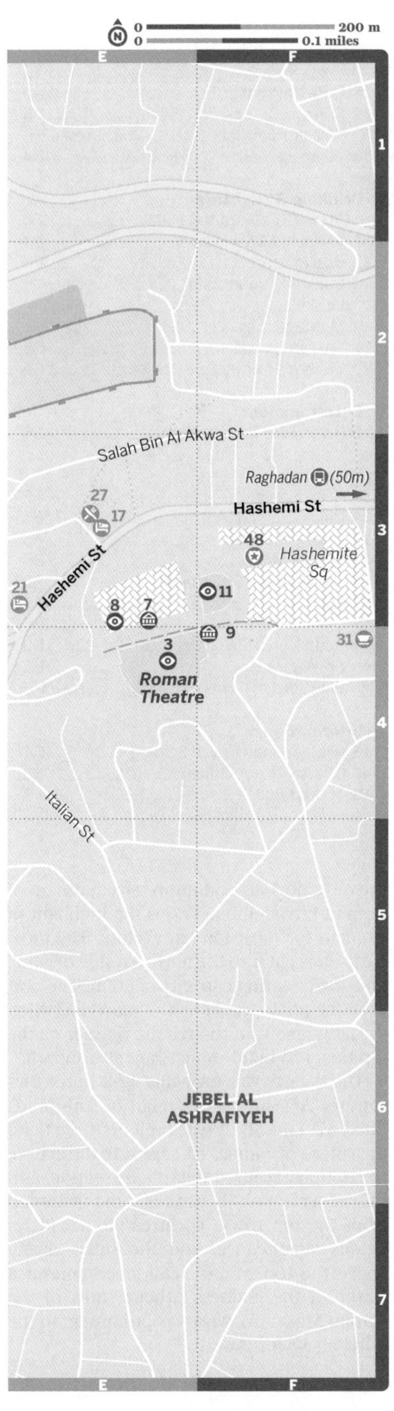

church over which it was built. After much debate as to whether the central space had originally been covered or left open to the elements, consensus came down on the side of the ceiling dome, which was reconstructed by Spanish archaeologists.

A courtyard immediately north of the hall leads to a 10m-wide colonnaded street, lined with numerous arches and columns, and flanked by residential and administrative buildings. Further to the north is the former governor's residence, which includes the throne room.

East of the audience hall is the **Umayyad Cistern**, an enormous circular hole with steps leading down to the bottom, which once supplied water to the palace and surrounding areas. The small disc on the floor in the centre once supported a pillar that was used for measuring water levels.

Near the museum to the south is the small **Byzantine Basilica** (Map p52), most of which has been destroyed by earthquakes. It dates from the 6th or 7th century AD, and contains a few dusty mosaics.

The **Citadel ticket office** (Map p52) is on the road leading up to the Citadel's entrance. Multilingual, fully licensed guides (up to JD15 per hour) usually congregate near the ticket office and can really enhance your visit.

The only access roads to the Citadel are from Al Malek Ali Bin Al Hussein St. It's better to hire a taxi for the trip up (around JD1 from downtown) and save some energy for the recommended walk down. Steps lead from east of the Citadel complex, past a viewing platform to Hashemi St, opposite the Roman Theatre. This makes a fine start to a walking tour of downtown.

★Darat Al Funun GALLERY

(House of Arts; Map p52; ☎06 464 3251; www.daratalfunun.org; 13 Nadim Al Mallah St, Lweibdeh; ⏲10am-7pm Sat-Thu, closed Aug) FREE On the hillside to the north of the downtown area, this cultural haven is dedicated to contemporary art. The main building features an excellent **art gallery** with works by Jordanian and other Arab artists, an art library, and workshops for Jordanian and visiting sculptors and painters. A schedule of upcoming exhibitions, lectures, films and public discussion forums is available on the website.

Almost as significant as the centre's artistic endeavours are the architectural features of the site. At the base of the complex, near the entrance, are the excavated ruins

Downtown Amman

Top Sights
1 Citadel D2
2 Darat Al Funun B3
3 Roman Theatre E4

Sights
4 Al Husseiny Mosque C5
5 Byzantine Basilica C2
6 Duke's Diwan C4
7 Folklore Museum E3
8 Forum E3
9 Museum of Popular Traditions F4
10 Nymphaeum D5
11 Odeon F3
12 Rainbow Street A5

Activities, Courses & Tours
13 Ahlan World A2
14 Al Pasha Turkish Bath A6
15 Beit Sitti A2
16 Wild Jordan B4

Sleeping
17 Amman Pasha Hotel E3
18 Art Hotel B3
19 Cliff Hotel B4
20 Jabal Amman Hotel B5
21 Jordan Tower Hotel E3

Eating
22 Afrah Restaurant & Coffeeshop B3
23 Al Quds Restaurant B3
24 Cantaloupe B5
Habibah .... (see 23)
25 Hashem Restaurant B3
26 Najla's Kitchen A2
27 Pizza Roma E3
28 Q Restaurant A5
29 Sufra A5
Wild Jordan Cafe .... (see 16)
30 Zajal B4

Drinking & Nightlife
31 Al Hail Restaurant & Café F4
32 Al Rashid Court Café B4
33 Books@café B6
Darat Al Funun Café .... (see 2)
La Calle .... (see 24)
Montage .... (see 36)
34 Sekrab B5
35 Shaher's Penthouse Cafeteria C5

Entertainment
36 Royal Film Commission B6

Shopping
37 Al Afghani C5
38 Balian B5
39 Bawabet Al Sharq A5
40 Jacaranda B6
41 Jordan River Foundation A5
42 Mlabbas A5
43 Ola's Garden B6
44 Soap House Trinitae B5
45 Souk Jara B5
Wild Jordan Center .... (see 16)

Information
46 Al Madeenah Police Station C4
47 Citadel Ticket Office D2
48 Tourist Police F3

of a 6th-century Byzantine church. Buildings further up the hill are mostly restored residences from the 1920s in the lovely Mediterranean-Venetian style that was popular in the region in the 1920s. There is also a peaceful cafe and gardens with views over Amman.

Access is easiest on foot. From near the southern end of Al Malek Al Hussein St, head up the stairs under the 'Riviera Hotel' sign. At the top of the stairs, turn immediately right onto Nimer Bin Adwan St and walk uphill for 50m where you need to take the left fork. The entrance gate (no English sign) is on the right after a few metres.

★ **Roman Theatre** THEATRE
(Map p52; JD2, incl Folklore Museum & Museum of Popular Traditions, free with Jordan Pass; 8am-4pm Sat-Thu, 9am-4pm Fri Oct-Mar, 8am-7pm Apr-Sep) This magnificently restored theatre is the most obvious and impressive remnant of Roman Philadelphia, and is the highlight of Amman for most foreign visitors. The theatre itself is cut into the northern side of a hill, and has a seating capacity of 6000. The best time for photographs is the morning, when the light is soft – although the views from the top tiers just before sunset are also superb.

The theatre was probably built in the 2nd century AD during the reign of Antoninus Pius (AD 138–61). It was built on three tiers: the rulers, of course, sat closest to the action, the military secured the middle section, and the general public perched and squinted from the top rows. Theatres often had religious significance, and the small shrine above the top row of seats once housed a statue of the goddess Athena (now in the Jordan Museum), who was prominent in the religious life of the city.

Full restoration of the theatre began in 1957. Unfortunately, non-original materials were used, which means that the present reconstruction is partly inaccurate. However, the final product is certainly impressive, especially considering that the theatre has again become a place of entertainment in recent years. Concerts are sometimes put on here in the summer; check with the tourist office.

Folklore Museum MUSEUM
(Map p52; ☎06 465 1742; Roman Theatre complex; admission incl in Roman Theatre ticket, free with Jordan Pass; ⏰8am-4pm Sat-Thu, 9am-4pm Fri Oct-Mar, 8am-7pm Apr-Sep) Immediately to the right as you enter the Roman Theatre, this small museum houses a modest collection of items illustrating traditional Jordanian life. It includes a Bedouin goat-hair tent complete with tools, musical instruments such as the *rababa* (a one-stringed Bedouin instrument), looms, *mihbash* (coffee grinders), some weapons and various costumes, including traditional Circassian dress.

Museum of Popular Traditions MUSEUM
(Map p52; ☎06 465 1670; Roman Theatre complex; admission incl in Roman Theatre ticket, free with Jordan Pass; ⏰8am-4pm Sat-Thu, 9am-4pm Fri Oct-Mar, 8am-7pm Apr-Sep) This small museum, immediately to the left as you enter the Roman Theatre, has well-presented displays of traditional costumes, jewellery and face masks, along with mannequins dressed in the traditional costumes of Jordan's different ethnic groups. A separate gallery displays mosaics from Jerash and Madaba.

Forum ROMAN SITE
(Map p52) The row of columns immediately in front (north) of the Roman Theatre is all that's left of the forum, once one of the largest public squares (about 100m by 50m) in Imperial Rome. Built in AD 190, the square was flanked on three sides by columns and on the fourth side by the Seil Amman stream, though almost everything lies underneath the modern streets.

Duke's Diwan MUSEUM
(Map p52; Al Malek Faisal St; ⏰8am-dusk) FREE This historic townhouse, built in 1924, has served as a post office (Amman's first), the Ministry of Finance and a hotel. Today, it has been restored with period furnishings by a prominent Jordanian businessman, who is also the duke of the village of Mukhaybeh. The collection of old photos of Amman provide an interesting glimpse of a bygone age. It's all quite underplayed, but rather charming nonetheless.

Odeon THEATRE
(Map p52; ⏰daylight hours) FREE On the eastern side of Amman's Forum stands a 500-seat odeon. Built in the 2nd century AD, it served mainly as a venue for musical performances. It was probably enclosed with a wooden roof or temporary tent roof to shield the performers and audience from the elements. Like its bigger sibling, the nearby Roman Forum, it is seasonally used for performances.

Al Husseiny Mosque MOSQUE
(Map p52; Hashemi St) FREE Built by King Abdullah I in 1924 and restored in 1987, this compact mosque is in the heart of downtown on the site of an earlier mosque built in AD 640. The mosque is possibly more interesting as a hive of activity than for any architectural splendour – the precinct is a popular local meeting place. Respectfully dressed non-Muslims may be admitted – ask at the gate.

Nymphaeum FOUNTAIN, RUINS
(Map p52; Quraysh St; ⏰daylight hours Sat-Thu) FREE Built in AD 191, this elaborate public fountain was once a large, two-storey complex with water features, mosaics, stone carvings and possibly a 600-sq-metre swimming pool – all dedicated to the nymphs. Excavations started in earnest in 1993, and restoration will continue for many years. Except for a few columns, an elegant archway and a few alcoves, there is little to see, though the workers toiling away may yet reveal hidden treasures in the years to come.

Jebel Amman & Around

★Jordan National Gallery of Fine Arts GALLERY
(Map p56; ☎06 463 0128; www.nationalgallery.org; Hosni Fareez St, Jebel Lweibdeh; JD5; ⏰9am-5pm Wed-Mon) This small but impressive gallery is a wonderful place to gain an appreciation of contemporary Jordanian painting, sculpture and pottery. The attractive space highlights contemporary art from around the Middle East and the wider Muslim world. Temporary exhibitions here are of high quality and serve as a valuable introduction (or refresher) to the world of Islamic art. The gallery is signposted from Suleiman Al Nabulsi St, opposite the King Abdullah Mosque.

Jebel Amman

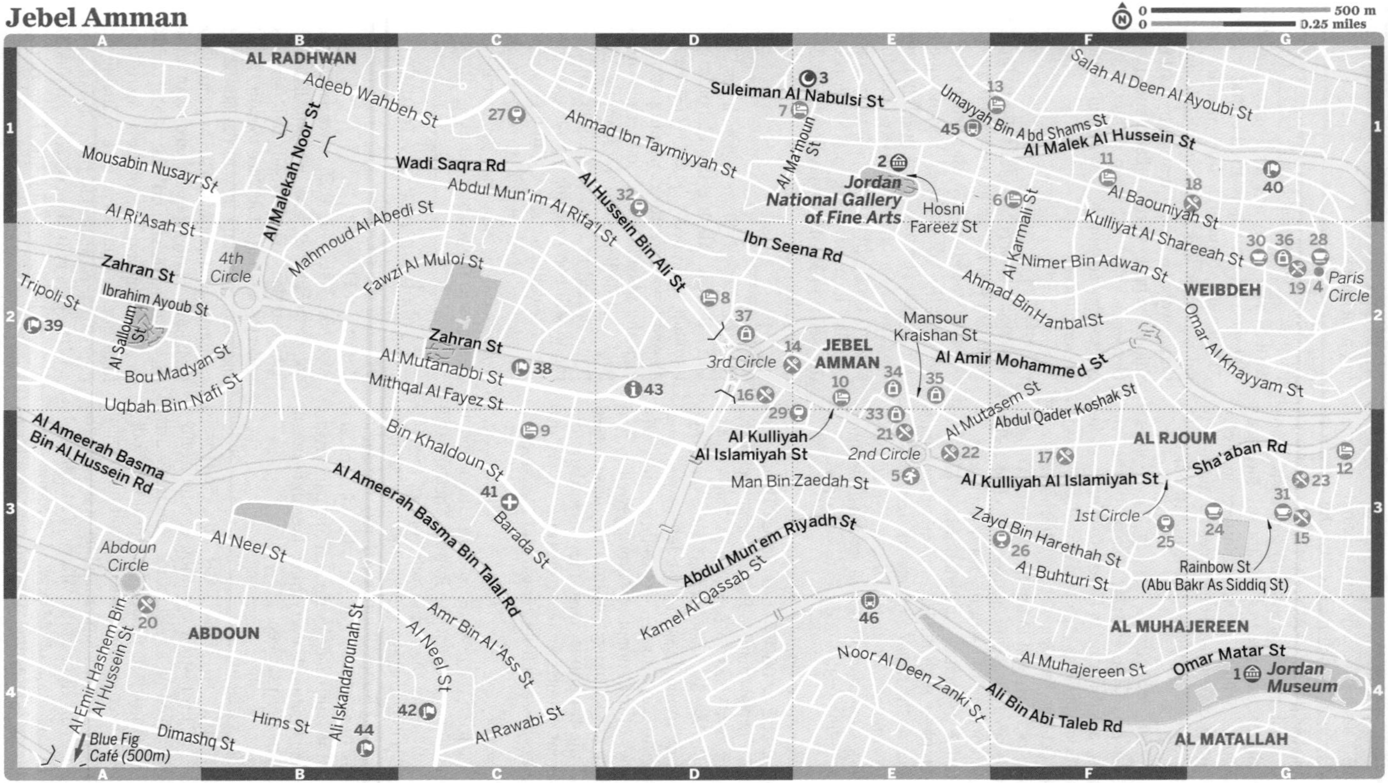

0 500 m
0 0.25 miles

AL RADHWAN
Adeeb Wahbeh St
Al Malekah Noor St
Mousabin Nusayr St
Wadi Saqra Rd
Abdul Mun'im Al Rifa'i St
Al Ri'Asah St
Mahmoud Al Abedi St
4th Circle
Zahran St
Tripoli St
Ibrahim Ayoub St
Al Salloum St
Fawzi Al Muloi St
Bou Madyan St
Uqbah Bin Nafi St
Zahran St
Al Mutanabbi St
Mithqal Al Fayez St
Al Ameerah Basma Bin Al Hussein Rd
Bin Khaldoun St
Al Ameerah Basma Bin Talal Rd
Barada St
Abdoun Circle
Al Neel St
ABDOUN
Al Emir Hashem Bin Al Hussein St
Ali Iskandarounah St
Amr Bin Al 'Ass St
Al Neel St
Hims St
Dimashq St
Blue Fig Café (500m)
Al Rawabi St
Ahmad Ibn Taymiyyah St
Al Hussein Bin Ali St
Suleiman Al Nabulsi St
Al Ma'moun St
Jordan National Gallery of Fine Arts
Hosni Fareez St
Ibn Seena Rd
3rd Circle
JEBEL AMMAN
Mansour Kraishan St
Al Amir Mohammed St
Al Kulliyah Al Islamiyah St
2nd Circle
Man Bin Zaedah St
Abdul Mun'em Riyadh St
Kamel Al Qassab St
Al Mutasem St
Abdul Qader Koshak St
Umayyah Bin Abd Shams St
Al Malek Al Hussein St
Salah Al Deen Al Ayoubi St
Al Karmali St
Al Baouniyah St
Kulliyat Al Shareeah St
Nimer Bin Adwan St
Ahmad Bin Hanbal St
WEIBDEH
Paris Circle
Omar Al Khayyam St
AL RJOUM
Sha'aban Rd
Al Kulliyah Al Islamiyah St
1st Circle
Zayd Bin Harethah St
Al Buhturi St
Rainbow St (Abu Bakr As Siddiq St)
AL MUHAJEREEN
Al Muhajereen St
Omar Matar St
Jordan Museum
Noor Al Deen Zanki St
Ali Bin Abi Taleb Rd
AL MATALLAH

Jebel Amman

Top Sights
1 Jordan Museum G4
2 Jordan National Gallery of Fine Arts E1

Sights
3 King Abdullah Mosque E1

Activities, Courses & Tours
4 Institut Français G2
5 Marrakech Hammam E3

Sleeping
6 Canary Hotel F1
7 Caravan Hotel E1
8 Grand Hyatt Amman D2
9 Hisham Hotel C3
10 Jordan InterContinental Hotel E2
11 La Locanda F1
12 Sydney Hotel G3
13 Toledo Hotel F1

Eating
14 Abu Ahmad Orient Restaurant D2
15 Al Quds G3
16 Bonita Inn D2
17 Fakhr El Din Restaurant F3
18 Jasmine House G1
19 Joz Hind G2
20 Noodasia A4
21 Reem Cafeteria E3
22 Rosa Damascena E3
23 Shams El Balad G3
Volk's Burger ..... (see 19)

Drinking & Nightlife
24 Caffe Strada G3
25 Copas Central F3
26 District F3
27 Ghoroub C1
Jungle Fever ..... (see 2)
28 Kepi G2
29 Living Room E3
Maestro Music Bar ..... (see 11)
30 Rumi G2
31 Turtle Green G3
32 Winemaker D1

Shopping
33 Al Alaydi Jordan Craft Centre E3
34 Al Burgan E2
35 Artisana E2
36 JoBedu G2
37 Oriental Souvenirs Store D2

Information
38 French Embassy C2
39 German Embassy A2
40 Irish Consulate G1
41 Khalidi Hospital C3
42 Lebanese Embassy C4
43 Ministry of Tourism D2
Tourist Police ..... (see 43)
44 UK Embassy B4

Transport
45 Abdali Bus Station E1
46 Muhajireen Bus Station E4

Rainbow Street STREET

(Abu Bakr As Siddiq St; Map p52) This street in Jebel Amman is a destination in itself. Ammanis come here every evening to promenade and to visit the many great cafes and restaurants – to see and be seen. There are plenty of shops if you come in the daytime (the area is good for souvenirs), but either way it's best explored by foot as the narrow one-way street easily clogs with traffic any time of day or night.

King Abdullah Mosque MOSQUE

(Map p56; ☎ext 219, 06 567 2155; Suleiman Al Nabulsi St, Jebel Lweibdeh; admission incl museum JD2; ⏱8-11am & 12.30-2pm Sat-Thu) Completed in 1989 as a memorial by the late King Hussein to his grandfather, this blue-domed landmark can house up to 7000 worshippers, with a further 3000 in the courtyard. There is also a small women's section for 500 worshippers and a much smaller royal enclosure. The cavernous, octagonal prayer hall is capped by a magnificent blue dome 35m in diameter, decorated with Quranic inscriptions. This is the only mosque in Amman that openly welcomes non-Muslim visitors.

The **Islamic Museum** inside the mosque houses a small collection of photographs and personal effects of King Abdullah I. Shards of ancient pottery are also on display together with coins and stone engravings.

A Friday visit may be possible if you avoid prayer time, but call ahead to be sure. Women are required to cover their hair – headscarves are available at the entrance to the mosque together with *abayas* (black full-length dress) to cover bare arms, legs or jeans. Shoes must be removed before entering the prayer hall.

Shmeisani

Haya Cultural Centre CULTURAL CENTRE

(Map p58; ☎06 568 8633; www.facebook.com/hccjo; Ilya Abu Madhi St; ⏱9am-6pm Sat-Thu) FREE Designed especially for children, this centre has a library, a playground, an interactive

Shmeisani

ecomuseum and an inflatable castle. It also organises regular activities and theatre, puppet and music performances for kids.

Military Museum MUSEUM

(Map p58; ☎06 566 4240; ⏱9am-4pm Sat-Thu) FREE The simple and solemn Martyr's Memorial houses a small but interesting collection of documents, chronicling Jordan's recent military history, from the Arab Revolt in 1916 (in which 10,000 Arab fighters were killed) through to the Arab–Israeli wars. The intention, however, is a focus on remembrance rather than historical verisimilitude.

Luna Park AMUSEMENT PARK

(Map p58; ☎06 569 8925; Khaled Bin Al Walid Rd; JD3; ⏱4pm-1am) Rides and amusements for the kids, including Ferris wheels, teacup rides and pedalos.

Other Suburbs

★Children's Museum MUSEUM

(Map p80; ☎06 541 1479; www.cmj.jo; King Hussein Park; JD3; ⏱9am-6pm Wed-Thu & Sat-Mon, 10am-7pm Fri; 👪) This brilliantly designed hands-on museum for kids is a complete joy. In its many zones, young visitors can play and learn about everything from the working of the human body to lasers and rainbows. Particular favourites (possibly because they also involve dressing up) are the building site with its bricks and pulleys, and the mocked-up Royal Jordanian plane and air control tower. There's an outdoor play area and a cafe, plus a lovely library if the children need some quiet time.

Shmeisani

Sights
1 Haya Cultural Centre ... B4
2 Luna Park ... D3
3 Military Museum ... C1

Sleeping
4 Al Qasr Metropole Hotel ... B3
5 Kempinski Amman ... B4

Eating
Vinaigrette ... (see 4)

Entertainment
6 Amman International Stadium ... C1

Information
7 Israeli Consulate ... A2

Transport
8 Avis ... A4
9 Europcar ... C3
Hertz ... (see 8)
10 JETT (Abdali) ... D4
11 National Car Rental ... A3

★ **Royal Automobile Museum** MUSEUM
(Map p80; ☎06 541 1392; www.royalautomuseum.jo; King Hussein Park; JD3, with audio guide JD5; ⏰10am-7pm Wed-Mon, from 11am Fri) You really don't have to be a car enthusiast to enjoy this museum, which displays more than 70 classic cars and motorbikes from the personal collection of King Hussein. It's something of a gem, and a great way to recount the story of modern Jordan. Vehicles range from pre-1950s glories to modern sports cars, taking in chrome-clad American cruisers to regal Rolls-Royces along the way, with accounts of presidential visits, Hollywood stars and defunct Middle Eastern monarchies enlivening the narrative.

The final display of suitably dusty rally cars is a neat rejoinder to the polish and chrome of the rest of the vehicles, while outside Matt Damon's ruggedly cool Martian rover from *The Martian* (filmed in Wadi Rum) gives a vision of possible future road trips. The museum is in the northwestern suburbs, north of 8th Circle.

★ **Qasr Al Abad** RUINS
(Palace of the Slave; Map p80; ⏰daylight hours) FREE The small but impressive Qasr Al Abad, west of Amman, is one of the very few examples of pre-Roman construction in Jordan. Mystery surrounds the palace, and even its precise age isn't known, though most scholars believe that Hyrcanus of the powerful Jewish Tobiad family built it sometime between 187 and 175 BC as a villa or fortified palace. Although never completed, much of the palace has been reconstructed, and remains an impressive site.

The palace was built from some of the biggest blocks of any ancient structure in the Middle East – the largest is 7m by 3m. The blocks were, however, only 20cm or so thick, making the whole edifice quite flimsy, and susceptible to the earthquake that flattened it in AD 362. Today, the setting and the animal carvings on the exterior walls are the highlights. Look for the carved panther fountain on the ground floor, the eroded eagles on the corners and the lioness with cubs on the upper storey of the back side. The gatekeeper will open the interior, as well as a small museum (which includes drawings of what the complex once looked like) for a tip of JD2. If he's not around, ask for the *miftah* (key) at the small shop near the gate.

Qasr Al Abad is best visited by private transport. It's on the outskirts of Iraq Al Amir village, about 10km west of Wadi As Seer, which is served by minibus from Amman's Muhajireen Bus Station (p78). There are only occasional minibuses between Iraq Al Amir and Wadi As Seer.

Hejaz Railway HISTORIC SITE
(Map p80; ☎06 489 4117; www.jhr.gov.jo; King Abdullah I St; JD1; ⏰8am-2pm Sun-Thu) The Hejaz Railway once ferried pilgrims from Damascus in Syria to Amman and then on to Medina in Saudi Arabia, but only the breeze rolls through this historic old station at present. There's a small on-site museum, and you can sit in the elaborately decked Royal Carriage. Very occasionally, there are rumours that a tourist service will start using the splendid steam locomotive, but plans seem forever to run into the buffers. We live in hope.

Activities

The top-end hotels offer a day rate to nonguests for use of their swimming pools and other facilities (from around JD25).

★ **Experience Jordan** ADVENTURE SPORTS
(Map p80; ☎07 7041 7711; www.experiencejordan.com; 44 Ali Nasouh Al Taher St, Sweifieh) High-quality local tour operator offering individual and group tours specialising in

4
جعده
ملوخيه
Cassia
سنامكه
Senna
زهورات شاميه
Zhourat shamia

MBRAND85/SHUTTERSTOCK ©

2

LEONID ANDRONOV/SHUTTERSTOCK ©

1. Citadel, Temple of Hercules (p51) On top of Amman's highest hill is the Citadel where you'll find one of its most striking sights, the Temple of Hercules.

2. Roman Theatre (p54) This magnificently restored theatre is an impressive remnant of Roman Philadelphia, and is the highlight of Amman for most foreign visitors.

3. King Abdullah Mosque (p57) Completed in 1989 as a memorial by the late King Hussein to his grandfather, this landmark can house up to 7000 worshippers.

4. Herbs and spices, Amman markets Jordanian cuisine is known for its use of aromatic herbs and spices, which can be found at many markets around the city.

3

RICHARD YOSHIDA/SHUTTERSTOCK ©

hiking and mountain biking. Every weekend it runs popular day or overnight trips that vary from canyoning to day hikes along sections of the Jordan Trail.

Experience Jordan also mapped out the Jordan Bike Trail (www.jordanbiketrail.com) that reaches from the far north to the Red Sea and is starting to operate vehicle-supported bike tours along its route.

Climbat CLIMBING
(Map p80; ☎06 573 6177; www.climbat.com; 687 Al Quds St; from JD14; ⏰10am-10pm) This excellent and well-equipped climbing centre on the outskirts of Amman has a series of climbing walls for everyone from beginners to experts. Three to four climb sessions cost JD14/19 – great for getting in shape for climbing in Wadi Rum (where it has connections with local guides). The starter walls are suitable for ages six and up.

Bike Rush CYCLING
(Map p80; ☎07 9945 4586; www.facebook.com/bikerush; Al Jafn St, 8th Circle; ⏰noon-9pm Sat-Thu) A respected bike-tour company. Trips cost around JD25, including transport out to the area you'll explore. Most destinations are a short drive from Amman: the Dead Sea, Madaba and Mt Nebo are commonly offered destinations, but they vary according to the time of year – heading north to the green hills is a popular option in spring.

Amman Waves WATER PARK
(Map p80; ☎06 412 1704; www.ammanwaves.com; Airport Rd; adult/child JD23/17; ⏰10am-7pm) This enormous Western-style water park is about 15km south of town on the highway to the airport. There are multiple water slides, a tube ride, artificial beach with wave machine and a children's paddling pool for the little ones. Note that adults should respect local sensibilities and wear appropriate swimwear (no Speedos or bikinis).

JOR Elite Bowling Centre BOWLING
(Map p80; ☎07 9228 3838; Wasfi Al Tal St; game JD3; ⏰noon-midnight) Family-friendly bowling alley.

Courses

Amman is a popular place to take an Arabic language course, attracting students who might have opted for Cairo or Damascus in more peaceful times.

City Walk
Highlights of Amman

START CITADEL
END HASHEM RESTAURANT
LENGTH 3KM; TWO HOURS

The best way to experience the key sights of Amman, which are clustered in downtown, is on foot. Go in the morning, when the light is best for photos, or early evening when the souqs are at their liveliest.

Begin at the hilltop ❶ **Citadel** (p51). The pillars of the Temple of Hercules is the best place to gain a sense of Amman's ancient Philadelphian roots and to survey how the city has spread beyond the original seven hills.

Follow Al Qalat St round the edge of the Citadel walls. A flight of steps (by a school with a flag) leads down to Salah Bin Al Akwa St; this is the shortcut locals take to reach downtown. A ❷ **viewpoint** to the right offers great views of the Roman Theatre. A further flight of stairs leads steeply downtown, past the Amman Panorama Art Gallery.

Head gingerly across the busy main road at the bottom (Hashemi St), cross Hashemite Sq, and climb the hill to the left of the theatre. Take in the view of the Citadel and the hotchpotch of facades that line the main road, most of which date from the mid-19th to the mid-20th centuries. Follow the stairs in front of the coffeehouse and pass by the souvenir shops en route to the theatre complex.

The small building on your right is the Roman ❸ **Odeon** (p55), but it's somewhat overshadowed by the neighbouring ❹ **Roman Theatre** (p54), which seems to extend indefinitely up the hillside. Walk between the Theatre and the Roman columns, all that remains of the ❺ **forum** (p55); the newly rebuilt plaza here provides space for the traditional Ammani evening stroll. From here, you're ready to plunge into the heart of downtown.

Cross the road onto Hashemi St, passing nut shops, perfumeries and a store selling mosque accessories such as brass crescents for minaret tops. Turn left at the traffic lights and you'll come

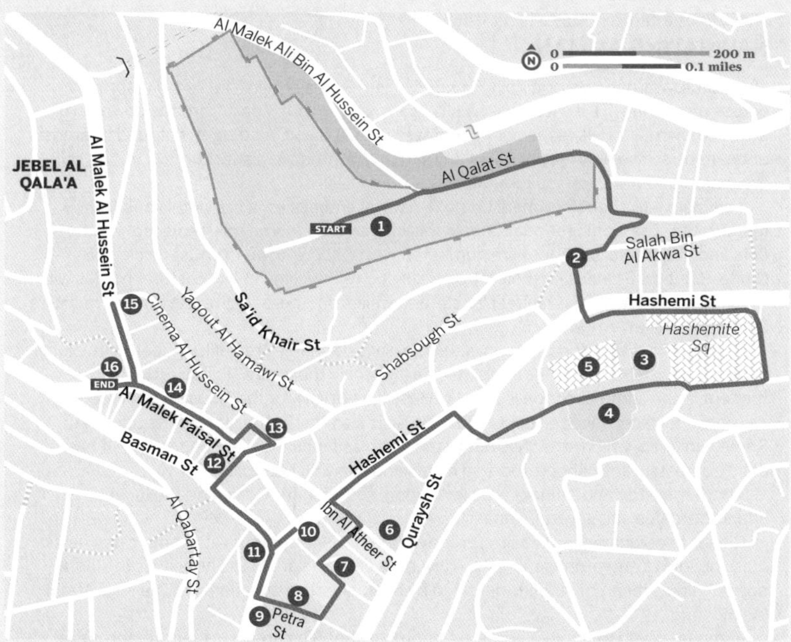

to the **6 Nymphaeum** (p55). It takes imagination to resurrect this Roman fountain complex from the remaining ruins and even more imagination to picture the stream that ran nearby until recently and which now flows under the road.

Pluck up courage and dive into the **7 fruit and vegetable souq** opposite. It's possible to travel the Middle East in this part of the souq as you pass sticky mounds of Saudi dates, Iranian pistachios and Syrian olives.

Turn left at the yellow shop, passing flatbread bakeries, and then right, through the **8 hardware souq** of aluminium kettles and giant ladles. Turn right into Petra St (spelt 'Betra') and take in the gorgeous aroma of spice-grinding and coffee-roasting. On either side of the road are traditional **9 Arabic medicine stalls**, recognisable by the dangling dried lizards, trays of starfish and drawers of herbs and henna.

A right turn onto Hashemi St takes you to **10 Al Husseiny Mosque** (p55). At Friday lunchtime, hundreds of men stream out of the mosque after the weekly sermon.

Cross the street and enter the tiny **11 Al Afghani souvenir store** (p74). Every conceivable space is occupied by chess sets, old postage stamps, plastic mosque clock-radios and odd ephemera.

Turn left into Basman St, passing fine examples of Palestinian embroidered dresses, and turn right down a flight of stairs just before House 22. The **12 women's souq** here challenges any preconceptions about prudish Arab women: the alleyways flutter with risqué lingerie. It may be no accident that the **13 gold souq**, where Arab men are expected to spend a portion of their salary, sits opposite, on the other side of Al Malek Faisal St (King Faisal St).

Continue along Al Malek Faisal St, with its grand central aisle of Washington palms, and you'll come to the **14 Duke's Diwan** (p55). The city is enjoying a renaissance at present and now old establishments like this are being highlighted with signs in English along the length of Al Malek Faisal St. Just past the ornate Arab Bank, for example, a sign indicates a short diversion to **15 Habibah** (p68), the perennially popular sweetmeat store with its brass platters of *kunafa* (shredded wheat and syrup dessert). After stocking up on desserts, return to Al Malek Faisal St and the legendary **16 Hashem Restaurant** (p68), where you can refuel after the walk with Amman's best hummus and falafel platters.

NAVIGATING AMMAN

Like Rome, Amman was originally founded on seven major hills, but today it spreads across more than 20. It's not really a city to explore on foot, apart from the downtown area – known by locals (especially taxi drivers) as Al Balad. A straight, flat road is almost unheard of, so the only way to make any sense of Amman in a short time is to pick out the major landmarks on the hills (jebels).

The main hill is Jebel Amman, home to several embassies, a few hotels and trendy restaurants. The traffic roundabouts in this central area (some now replaced with tunnels and major intersections) are numbered west of downtown from 1st Circle to 8th Circle. Rainbow St leads east off 1st Circle. If you're travelling in a taxi, street names will mean little, so ask for the nearest 'circle' and walk from there or give the driver a nearby landmark (like an embassy or hotel).

Slightly northwest of downtown is the funkily fashionable area of Lweibdeh, with plenty of places to eat, have a coffee in a cool cafe and enjoy the area's slightly arty vibe. Further out in the same direction is Jebel Al Hussein, notable for the Housing Bank Centre; its mossy, terraced facade sticks out a mile. This also marks the start of the upmarket Shmeisani area, which stretches out to the north as far as the leafy Sports City. It has plenty of restaurants, shops, top-end hotels and a few nightclubs.

Another trendy and affluent area is Abdoun, south of 4th Circle and the location of supercool cafes and several embassies.

Closer to downtown is Abdali, currently under redevelopment with some glitzy new glass buildings and promised malls. A few budget hotels are in the area near the large bus terminus. It can be readily identified by the distinctive blue dome of the King Abdullah Mosque.

In the far west is swanky Sweifieh, a booming shopping area. Further out, the city's outlying towns, suburbs and refugee camps have now pretty much merged into one sprawling urban area.

Shababeek LANGUAGE

(Map p80; ☎06 582 2158; www.shababeekcenter.com; Senad Complex 9, 8th Circle, Sweifieh) Highly recommended Arabic language centre. Prices vary according to the number of hours per week you study: 10 hours a week costs JD10 per hour if you're studying on your own, which goes down to JD8 per hour if you go for 25 to 30 hours per week. If you can join a group, lessons are just JD4.500 per hour if you sign up for 30 hours.

Institut Français LANGUAGE

(Map p56; ☎06 461 2658; www.ifjordan.com; Kulliyat Al Shareeah St, Lweibdeh; 40hr course JD190; ⏰9am-6.30pm Sat-Wed, to 3pm Thu) Offers intensive Arabic courses at its centre in Lweibdeh. Private lessons are available from JD29 per hour (JD35 per hour for two people).

Ahlan World LANGUAGE

(Map p52; ☎06 461 5315; www.ahlan-world.org; 8 Fouad Salim St, Lweibdeh; 2-week course from JD140) Comprehensive Arabic courses, with residential options also available.

Tours

The main backpacker hotels all offer a variety of day trips from Amman.

Engaging Cultures TOURS

(☎800 731 0655; https://engagingcultures.com) Engaging Cultures provides customised, community-based tourism experiences with conscious consideration for local people and the environment. Whether you are looking for a day trip or a week-long escape, this outfit can connect you to local culture, people, food and activities for a deeper understanding of Jordan. Harvesting olives, hiking through forests and desert, and cooking in a local family's home are just a few of the possibilities.

Tropical Desert ADVENTURE

(☎07 9543 8708; www.td-adventures.com) If you have a taste for adrenaline, this respected Amman tour company has scheduled trips every weekend, including rock climbing, canyoning and hiking. Adventure specialists with well-trained guides.

Wild Jordan ECOTOUR
(Map p52; ☎06 461 6523; www.wildjordan.com; Othman Bin Affan St, Downtown) There are no nature reserves within the capital area, but Amman is the best place to organise trips to any of Jordan's Royal Society for the Conservation of Nature (RSCN) reserves. Accommodation in most of these reserves has to be booked in advance. Tour destinations include Mujib Biosphere Reserve, Dana Biosphere Reserve, Ajloun Forest Reserve, Shaumari Wildlife Reserve and Azraq Wetland Reserve.

Festivals & Events

Concerts, plays and performances are occasionally held at the Odeon (p55) and the Roman Theatre (p54) in July and August. The Ministry of Tourism office (p76), near 3rd Circle, is the best source of information, but also check out the English-language newspapers and posters in the cafes along Rainbow St.

The Jerash Festival of Culture & Arts (p91) is Jordan's best-known cultural event (generally visited as a day trip from Amman).

Amman Jazz Festival MUSIC
(www.ammanjazzfestival.com; Apr) Regional and international musicians visit and concerts are held in Amman, most notably at Maestro and the Haya Cultural Centre.

Hakaya Cultural Project CULTURAL
(☎06 568 7557; www.hakaya.org/en; Sep) Connects organisations and individuals from around the wider Mediterranean world who believe in the power of storytelling to effect positive cultural change. Its annual festival is held around Amman every September.

Sleeping

There are several areas for hotels. Jebel Amman has a range of top-end and midrange accommodation options close to downtown; downtown itself has most of the budget options. Five-star hotels compete favourably with others in the region and represent reasonable value for money, including in Shmeisani.

Most hotels include breakfast in their room rates. Budget hotels are also big on offering tours to Petra, the Dead Sea and other tourist sites.

Close to the airport, the **Amman Airport Hotel** (☎06 445 1000; r from JD90) is a convenient if unexciting option worth considering if you have an early morning flight.

Downtown

★ **Jordan Tower Hotel** HOTEL $
(Map p52; ☎06 461 4161; www.jordantoweramman.com; 50 Hashemi St; dm/s/d/tr with shared bathroom JD12/18/25/35, s/d/tr JD25/35/45; @) This friendly hotel has a winning location: you couldn't be closer to the key sights without offering beds in the Forum. Rooms are bright and snug with flat-screen TVs, and there's also a big, bright and homely reception-cum-lounge area and rooftop restaurant. Perennially popular, and with good reason.

Sydney Hotel HOTEL $
(Map p56; ☎06 464 1122; www.sydneyhotelamman.com; 9 Sha'aban Rd; dm without breakfast JD7, s/d JD26/37;) Halfway between Jebel Amman and downtown (so you'll keep fit), this hotel has big rooms that have been recently renovated to very welcome effect.

DON'T MISS

COOKING AT GRANDMA'S

If you want to learn the secrets of Jordanian cooking, head for **Beit Sitti's** (Map p52; ☎07 7755 7744; www.beitsitti.com; 16 Mohammad Ali Al Sadi St; lessons JD35), 'Grandmother's House', a villa on the edge of Lweibdeh, where ebullient chef-sisters Maria, Dina and Tania Haddad have opened the kitchen of their old family home to share their love of good eating.

Over two hours you'll tackle a handful of classic and lesser-known recipes and then sit down to a mouth-watering four-course feast at the end of it, prepared by your own hands.

Lessons are available for breakfast, lunch and dinner and you're welcome to take a bottle of wine to enjoy with your meal. Recently, Beit Sitti has started to work with local refugee women to introduce Syrian, Iraqi and Palestinian dishes to their menu to showcase the many regional influences on Jordan's food, as well as arranging occasional visits to organic farms just outside the city for a real farm-to-table experience.

BATHING WITH BRUISERS IN AMMAN'S HAMMAMS

If walking up and down Amman's many hills leaves you sore, then a trip to the local hammam (bathouse) may just put you right. A largely Ottoman creation, based no doubt on the Roman obsession with communal bathing, so-called Turkish baths have existed as places of social gathering and ritual cleansing across the Middle East for centuries. Amman's bathhouses, despite being largely modern affairs, belong to this tradition. They offer what can only be described as a deep steam clean performed by pro-wrestlers, leaving you as pink and dazed as a newborn. Think we're exaggerating? Pay a visit to the **Al Pasha Turkish Bath** (Map p52; ☎06 463 3002; www.pashaturkishbath.com; Al Mahmoud Taha St; JD25; ⏰9am-2am, last booking midnight) or **Marrakech Hammam** (Map p56; ☎06 461 5551; Bldg 45, 2nd Circle; JD15-50; ⏰women 9am-4pm, men 5pm-1am) and you can make up your own mind about this quintessential Middle Eastern experience.

Your session begins with a brief spell in the steam room, sipping ice-cold *karkade* (sweetened hibiscus tea), as your body begins to loosen up in the heat. Further softening takes place in the jacuzzi, getting you ready for the performance to come as an attendant waits to lather you up.

Using what can only be described as a glorified Brillo pad, the attendant will scour every visible inch of your body. Don't expect phrases like 'no' and 'please don't' – uttered in either Arabic or English – to help you. More likely you'll be scrubbed even harder like a recalcitrant child. After five to 10 minutes (which can feel like a lifetime), you'll be led to marble slabs for a soothing olive-oil massage. If you opt for an additional full-body mud pack, then prepare to be pinched as the masseur checks you're still breathing under the caking armour and then kneads out the knots in muscles you didn't even know you had. The more enthusiastic masseurs may pull and twist you like a pretzel, leaving you feeling like you have jelly limbs at the end of it all.

If, by now, the prospect of being bullied in the bath is putting you off the idea altogether, don't let it. The wonderful part about the experience is that the moment you step out of the steaming pools of indistinct water and are laid to rest on the marble platform, or the moment you expose your newly scraped and kneaded flesh to the outside air, you'll feel so rejuvenated that you'll be booking your next appointment before you leave.

Generally speaking, women are welcome during the day, while evenings are men only, though couples sessions can sometimes be booked in advance. Be sure to bring modest swimwear – women may go topless, but it's not the done thing to strip off to absolutely nothing.

There's a huge communal area surrounding reception. Breakfast isn't included for the dorm rate, but it remains a great-value option.

Cliff Hotel HOTEL $

(Map p52; ☎06 462 4273; Al Malek Faisal St; s/d/tr/q with shared bathroom JD7/12/14/21; 📶) This long-standing shoestring option has basic and quite dark rooms and a bit of a grungy entrance, but there's a big bright lounge area that acts as a sociable meeting place. The shared bathrooms have hot water. A popular choice among younger shoestringers.

Amman Pasha Hotel HOTEL $

(Map p52; ☎06 461 8262; www.ammanpashahotel.com; Ash Shabsough St; s/d/tr from JD25/30/37; 📶) Popular budget hotel in downtown Amman. Rooms are pretty basic (wi-fi is only in the common areas), and things could be cleaner, but the fridges are a nice touch, and it's a popular place to meet like-minded travellers. There's a decent restaurant on the ground floor and a roof terrace where some rather sad-looking rabbits run free under foot.

Art Hotel HOTEL $$

(Map p52; ☎06 463 8900; www.arthoteljordan.com; 30 Al Malek Faisal St; s/d/tr JD40/50/70; 📶) Under new management in 2017, this stylish new hotel occupies a good spot in the downtown scene. Rooms are well-finished in crisp white with good fittings, and each is decorated idiosyncratically with fun street art murals. Rooms facing the street have double-glazing to cut down on noise.

Jebel Amman & Around

Canary Hotel HOTEL $

(Map p56; ☎06 463 8353; canary_h@hotmail.com; 17 Al Karmali St; s/d JD25/35; 📶) In the leafy Jebel Lweibdeh area, the cosy B&B-style Canary feels a million miles from the chaos of downtown. The rooms are more comfortable than luxurious, though they're in need of a new paint job and fittings in places. There's a pleasant garden area in front of the hotel.

Caravan Hotel HOTEL $

(Map p56; ☎06 566 1195; www.caravanhotel.net; Al Ma'moun St; s/d/tr/q JD22/28/33/38; 📶) On a quiet side street location near the King Abdullah Mosque, this place has long been a favoured choice, but these days possibly more for its reliable service than its sometimes dated fixtures. The big clean rooms have a bright aspect.

★**La Locanda** BOUTIQUE HOTEL $$

(Map p56; ☎06 460 2020; www.locandahotel.com; 52 Al Ba'ouniyah St, Lweibdeh; r JD75-95; 📶) A lovely themed boutique hotel, with each of the stylish rooms decorated to match an Arabic music icon, from Umm Kulthum to Fairuz. There's keen attention to detail throughout, with fine fabrics and slick modern bathrooms, and a relaxed, comfortable air. If you want to continue the musical theme, you can eat and drink at the hotel's Maestro bar (p71).

Hisham Hotel HOTEL $$

(Map p56; ☎06 464 4028; www.hishamhotel.com.jo; Mithqal Al Fayez St; s/d from JD50/70; @📶) This delightful hotel in a leafy embassy district of Jebel Amman is an excellent choice if you're looking for a hotel removed from the hustle and bustle of the city while still within easy reach of downtown. The rooms are comfortable and modern. The family atmosphere, attractive decor and convivial bar next door make this a worthwhile haunt.

Jabal Amman Hotel HOTEL $$

(Map p52; ☎06 463 7733; www.jabalammanhotel.com; Rainbow St, Bldg 2; s/d from JD58/88; 📶) Formerly the Heritage Hotel, Jabal Amman offers convenient accommodation just off the amenities of Rainbow St. Compact, subtle and modern, it's a useful getaway from city life, with a series of studio apartments in varying sizes. Each comes with a small kitchenette allowing guests to prepare their own food, though breakfast is included in the daily rate.

Toledo Hotel HOTEL $$

(Map p56; ☎06 465 7777; www.toledohotel.jo; Umayyah Bin Abd Shams St; s/d/tr from JD52/62/72; 📶🏊) The Toledo offers a quality experience on the cusp of the top-end sector, even more so since the hotel got a complete refit in 2015. Modern rooms with soft and subdued lighting boast business-friendly amenities, and the bathrooms are pleasingly spacious. The hotel has a restaurant and coffee shop in Moroccan tiling.

Jordan InterContinental Hotel HOTEL $$$

(Map p56; ☎06 464 1361; www.intercontinental.com; Al Kulliyah Al Islamiyah St; r from JD180; @📶🏊) The granddaddy of luxury hotels in Amman, the much-loved InterCon has been hosting foreign dignitaries since the early days of Jordan's founding. A great favourite for local weddings, regular guests can enjoy excellent Lebanese, Indian and Mexican restaurants, quality craft and antique shops, as well as a good gym and pool and modern, comfortable rooms.

Grand Hyatt Amman HOTEL $$$

(Map p56; ☎06 465 1234; www.hyatt.com; Al Hussein Bin Ali St, 3rd Circle; r from JD180; @📶🏊) An enormous complex with hundreds of rooms and suites as well as restaurants, bars, clubs, swimming pools and its own mall, the Grand Hyatt is truly a class act. The majority of the hotel is constructed from polished Jerusalem sandstone, an elegant touch that tones down the sheer extravagance of it all.

Shmeisani

★**Kempinski Amman** HOTEL $$$

(Map p58; ☎06 520 0200; www.kempinski.com; Abdul Hamid Shouman St; r from JD190; 📶🏊) By some way Amman's most chic and sophisticated accommodation option, this European-styled hotel is right at home in Shmeisani with immaculate rooms, designer furnishings and positively regal bathrooms. Offering a wide range of upmarket bars and restaurants, there's also an impressive list of entertainment, including an adjoining bowling alley, a cinema, and a games centre for the kids.

Al Qasr Metropole Hotel HOTEL $$$

(Map p58; ☎06 568 9671; www.alqasrmetropole.com; 3 Arroub St; s/d JD120/150; 📶) Straddling the boundary between midrange and top-end in terms of facilities if not price, is this smart hotel with large contemporary paintings making a splash in the foyer. Located in fashionable Shmeisani, Al Qasr has only 66 rooms, each artistically designed with wood floors, crown moulding and soft lighting, plus a relaxing bar and decent rooftop restaurant in Vinaigrette.

Eating

Amman has a wide range of eating options, with budget places concentrated in downtown, while the more upmarket restaurants serving Arabic and international cuisine are concentrated in Jebel Amman, Lweibdeh and Shmeisani.

Many bars in Amman also serve food. Although there are small grocery stores throughout the capital, you can find larger supermarkets in the major malls.

Downtown

★Hashem Restaurant FALAFEL $
(Map p52; Al Malek Faisal St; falafel JD3; ⏲24hr) You haven't tried falafel until you've eaten here. This legendary eatery, more than 50 years old, is so popular with locals and visitors that there's stiff competition for tables, many of which overflow into the alleyway. Aim for an early lunch or supper if you want to avoid queues, although Hashem does a fantastic job of feeding the multitude in record time.

Habibah DESSERTS $
(Map p52; Al Malek Al Hussein St; pastries from 500 fils; ⏲8am-10pm) This legendary shop is a good bet for Middle Eastern sweets and pastries. Sweet tooths of all ages line up for honey-infused, pistachio-topped and filo-crusted variations on the region's most famous desserts. There is another branch on Al Malek Faisal St.

Pizza Roma INTERNATIONAL $
(Map p52; Ash Shabough St; mains from JD2.500; ⏲7.30am-midnight) This international restaurant downtown aims strongly towards the budget end of the market. Tricked out like the interior of a Bedouin tent lined with black and white photos, it has a nice vibe, and the menu runs from continental breakfasts to Jordanian classics via surprisingly decent pizza.

Zajal JORDANIAN $$
(Map p52; Al Amir Mohammed St; mains JD4-8; ⏲9am-2am) This is a pleasant low-key cafe-restaurant that attracts a young crowd with its open areas and terrace plus good cheap food. Going simple is the best – the *manakeesh* (baked flatbread with toppings like cheese and minced meat) is particularly nice, washed down with fresh juices. Entrance is from the street staircase pleasingly shaded with dozens of suspended umbrellas.

Afrah Restaurant & Coffeeshop JORDANIAN $$
(Map p52; ☎06 461 0046; Al Malek Faisal St; mains JD5-10; ⏲9am-1am) This popular restaurant in the heart of downtown is as much about the ambience as the traditional Jordanian food. Squeezed into every nook and cranny of the upper storeys of this old townhouse, the tables fill up quickly in the evening, particularly those with a balcony view of Al Malek Faisal St below. Live Arab pop entertainment is offered most nights from around 9pm.

Jebel Amman, Jebel Weibdeh & Abdoun

★Al Quds FALAFEL $
(Map p56; Rainbow St; falafel 500 fils) We'll happily vote for this tiny, spotlessly clean place on Rainbow St as one of the best falafel spots in Amman. Tasty sandwiches (with tomato and pickles) have been served up fast for more than 50 years, but watch out for lunchtime queues when the office workers descend.

★Reem Cafeteria MIDDLE EASTERN $
(Map p56; 2nd Circle; shawarma JD1; ⏲11am-late) There are hundreds of shoebox-sized shawarma (meat sliced off a spit and stuffed in a pocket of pita-type bread with chopped tomatoes and garnish) kiosks in Amman but few that have the customers queuing down the street at 3am. Having had one of Reem's delicious shawarmas (and a second and third), we know exactly why. Look for the red-and-white awning (with milling crowds) on 2nd Circle.

Volk's Burger BURGERS $
(Map p56; ☎06 462 2020; www.facebook.com/VolksBurgerJo; Paris Circle, Lweibdeh; burgers with fries/drink from JD4.750; ⏲noon-1am Sat-Thu, from 6pm Fri) Amman's gourmet burger craze of recent years seems to have blown itself out, but Volk's Burger has stood the test of time. Fat juicy patties and good bread with a side of peppery fries. The fillings are uniformly excellent, though we're particularly partial to blue cheese with sautéed onions and honey mustard.

Shams El Balad JORDANIAN $

(Map p56; ☎06 465 1150; 69 Mu'Ath Bin Jabal St; mezze JD2-3, flatbreads JD3-4, salads JD4; ⏲9am-9pm; ☑) A busy cafe-restaurant that just keeps the right side of hipster-dom with a popular Jordanian meat-free menu. The flatbreads piled high with herb, cheese and vegetable toppings are fabulous, along with thick *labneh* (thick yoghurt flavoured with garlic and sometimes with mint), eggs cooked every which way and of course plenty of hummus, *zaatar* (a blend of spices that includes hyssop, sumac and sesame) and halloumi.

★**Jasmine House** MEDITERRANEAN $$

(Map p56; ☎06 461 1879; Al Baouniyah St, Lweibdeh; mains around JD7; ⏲4.30-11.30pm Mon-Sat) Jasmine House is well-named, as the scent of the blooms on the terrace make dining a fragrant experience. The restaurant, in a 1950s villa, takes inspiration from the Italian homes of the period, matching it with the eloquent cooking of its Calabrian chef. Ingredients are fresh and come served in well-balanced dishes. The homemade pasta is superb.

★**Joz Hind** ITALIAN $$

(Map p56; Kulliyat Al Shareeah St, Lweibdeh; mains around JD7; ⏲12.30-9pm Sun-Thu) This tiny restaurant is one of Lweibdeh's gems, and you won't mind sharing at one of the large tables on the communal verandah when the meals come. The freshest of seasonal Italian food is made in a semi-open kitchen and served up with love.

Najla's Kitchen JORDANIAN $$

(Map p52; ☎07 9515 5566; 16 Mohammed Ali Al Saedi St; set meals JD15; ⏲12.30-6pm) This daytime-only menu is a spin-off from the popular Beit Sitti (p65) cooking school next door, but this time the Haddad family cook for you. The set menu changes from day to day according to the seasonal availability of produce, but you can call ahead to advise if you have any special dietary requirements, as well as to book a table.

Blue Fig Café INTERNATIONAL $$

(☎06 592 8800; Al Emir Hashem Bin Al Hussein St; mains JD5-11; ⏲8.30am-1am) If you're wondering where Amman's fashionable set go to escape their own cuisine, look no further than this glass-and-steel restaurant with a lovely terrace near Abdoun Circle. It offers an extensive and imaginative menu, though we've always found the pizzas and salads particularly good. There's beer on tap plus a good wine list.

Noodasia ASIAN $$

(Map p56; ☎06 593 6999; Abdoun Circle; mains JD5-12) The shiny chrome and dark woods of this stylish pan-Asian diner feel like they have been lifted straight from the cooler quarters of Shanghai. However, the menu stretches across the Asian continent and includes Chinese, Thai and Japanese snacks and main dishes such as green curries, sushi combos and Chinese noodles, all prepared by chefs who really know their stuff.

Wild Jordan Center CAFE $$

(Map p52; ☎06 463 3542; Othman Bin Affan St; mains JD7-12; ⏲9am-11pm; ☎☑) At the eco-friendly cafe at Wild Jordan Center, the emphasis is on locally sourced produce, healthy wraps, organic salads and locally plucked herbs. It's not the cheapest place, but the food is great, as are the smoothies. The glass walls and open-air terrace offer unparalleled vistas of the Citadel and the downtown area.

Q Restaurant INTERNATIONAL $$

(Map p52; ☎06 461 9080; Rainbow St; mains from JD7; ⏲4pm-1am Sun-Thu, noon-1am Fri & Sat) This Rainbow St establishment offers something we think is unique for Jordan: camel burgers. They're worth the detour too, along with the novelty of sitting in a fresh open-fronted restaurant on the street and having a cold beer. The rest of the menu leans towards chicken wings and fajitas, plus the expected Middle Eastern standards.

Abu Ahmad Orient Restaurant MIDDLE EASTERN $$

(Map p56; ☎06 352 2520; Al Sharq St, 3rd Circle; mains JD5-11; ⏲noon-midnight) This midrange Lebanese place has a leafy outdoor terrace that bustles with life during the summer months. The standard fare comprises grilled meats, but the real highlights are the hot and cold mezze – try a *buraik* (meat or cheese pie) or the *yalenjeh* (stuffed vine leaves).

Al Quds Restaurant JORDANIAN $$

(Jerusalem Restaurant; Map p52; ☎06 463 0168; Al Malek Al Hussein St; pastries from 800 fils, mains from JD5; ⏲7am-10pm) This place really specialises in sweets and pastries, but it has a large, good-value restaurant at the back that provides an opportunity to try typical Jordanian dishes. The house speciality is

WORTH A TRIP

FUHEIS FOR FINE DINING

Just 15km northwest of Amman, the pleasant village of Fuheis is famous for fruit growing and, somewhat incongruously, cement production. First built in about 2000 BC, Fuheis is now a largely Christian village, with several Orthodox and Catholic churches. The main reason for a visit, however, is to have lunch or dinner in the town's celebrated restaurant or to take a tour of the local microbrewery.

Highly popular with Fuheis locals and discerning expats from Amman, the ambience at **Zuwwadeh Restaurant** (Map p80; ☎06 472 1528; mains JD5-16; ⏲noon-12.30am Fri-Wed, to 1am Thu) is lively and warm. The food is delicious, especially the *fatteh* (fried bread) with hummus, meat or chicken and pine nuts – the 'wedding fatteh' is complemented by tomato and cardamom. You can choose between shady outdoor tables or an intimate indoor dining area. Most nights, an oud (lute) player entertains diners. Alcohol is served.

The bar at the **Carakale Brewery** (Map p80; ☎07 9728 5192; www.carakale.com; ⏲6-10pm Thu, from 2pm Fri & Sat) offers tasting sessions for the ales brewed on-site. Inside, tables overlook the brewing floor, but it's nicer to sit on the terrace to catch the sunset across the valley.

The town of Fuheis is easy to reach by minibus from Abdali bus station (600 fils, 40 minutes). The town is also connected to Wadi As Seer, making it possible to visit both destinations as a day trip from Amman. If you're dining at the restaurant or sampling ale at the brewery, it's best to prearrange a chartered taxi back to Amman for around JD12.

mensaf, a Bedouin dish of lamb on a bed of rice, and *maklubbeh* (upside-down rice and vegetables) is frequently on the menu.

★ **Sufra** JORDANIAN $$$
(Map p52; ☎06 461 1468; www.facebook.com/SufraRestaurant; 28 Rainbow St, Jebel Amman; starters from JD3.350, mains from JD10; ⏲noon-11pm Sun-Thu, from 10am Fri & Sat) Housed in a lovely old villa with a terrace garden, this really is the place to eat well, and Sufra is about as good as it gets when it comes to traditional Jordanian cuisine. The signature *mansaf* (chicken or lamb over rice with a thick, meaty broth) is a delight that will leave you loosening your belt.

★ **Rosa Damascena** SYRIAN $$$
(Map p56; ☎06 461 0010; 2nd Circle; mezze JD2-3, mains JD7-10) Rosa Damascena brings a welcome taste of Syria to Amman. The variety of hot and cold mezze is mouthwatering – make particular space on your plate for dips of *mohammara be jouz* (ground walnuts with pomegranate and chilli), along with tasty mains like *jidi bel zeit* (stewed lamb with cracked wheat) and *musakhan* (baked chicken on bread with sumac).

Cantaloupe INTERNATIONAL $$$
(Map p52; www.cantaloupe.jo; 10 Rainbow St; mains JD10-16; ⏲1pm-1am) A self-styled gastropub, this restaurant-lounge is a lovely place for a splurge. While you can eat inside, the treat here is the rooftop terrace, with breathtaking views over downtown Amman. The menu is largely international (the steaks are quite superb), the wine list broad, and the music softly jazzy.

Fakhr El Din Restaurant LEBANESE $$$
(Map p56; ☎06 465 2399; Taha Hussein St, 2nd Circle; mains JD8-15) Tastefully decorated and with crisp white linen tablecloths, this Lebanese fine-dining restaurant is located in a 1950s house with a beautiful outdoors dining area. Over 10 years, countless guests have visited this establishment in search of what the proprietor terms 'genuine Arabic cuisine and hospitality'. Reservations are essential.

Bonita Inn SPANISH $$$
(Map p56; ☎07 9645 0135; Qays Bin Sayeedah, 3rd Circle; mains JD12-25; ⏲noon-midnight) This primarily Spanish restaurant and tapas bar just off 3rd Circle is a favourite with well-heeled locals, who want a drink and a table of dishes between friends. The outside terrace is very pleasant in the warm evenings. Don't eat too many tapas if you want to do justice to the paella or the steaks that are cooked to absolute perfection.

Shmeisani & Other Suburbs

Seed CAFE $
(☎07 9656 0001; www.facebook.com/SeedAmman; Fawzi Al Kawekji, Abdoun; sandwiches JD3.500-7.500; ⏲8am-10pm Sun-Thu, from 10am Fri & Sat) In a city with limited health food and

gluten-free options, Seed is a quaint oasis offering fruit and vegetable smoothies, salads, soups, sandwiches and a small selection of allergy-friendly groceries. Grab a fresh to-go wrap to take on your road trip, or refuel post-hike with the Dream Date smoothie. Seed's staff is extra friendly and the outdoor seating is perfect for people-watching.

Dina JORDANIAN **$**
(Map p80; Ibn Zanjuwayh St; meals from JD3; 7.30am-3am Mon-Sat, to midnight Sun) A great Jordanian place with a large shaded terrace and swift service in an area that's popular with international aid agencies working in Jordan. The grilled meats are succulent, but you'll be just as happy with big plates of hummus and falafel and the softest pillowy bread straight from the oven.

Pizza Al Reef PIZZA **$$**
(Map p80; 06 568 7087; 244 Medina Al Munawarah St; pizzas JD4-6) Splendid pizza joint with red-checked tablecloths giving an appropriate nod for the decor. Pizza crusts are cooked to thin and crunchy perfection and there is a good variety of toppings. The rocket with *labneh* is our favourite. It's a bit out of the way, but you can always call for delivery.

Vinaigrette FUSION **$$$**
(Map p58; 06 569 5481; Al Qasr Metropole Hotel, 3 Arroub St, Shmeisani; mains JD8-15, sushi from JD3; noon-midnight) Located on the top floor of the Al Qasr hotel, and in keeping with the hotel's boutique theme, this restaurant offers trendsetting Middle Eastern fusion food and gourmet sushi and salads – build your own salad and sushi combo, or let the house choose for you.

Kan Zeman JORDANIAN **$$$**
(Map p80; 06 412 3838; www.kanzamaanjo.com; Airport Rd; mezze from JD2.500, mains from JD8; 12.30pm-2am) Located in a fabulous historic inn with vaulted ceiling, this restaurant is brought to life each night when traditional live music fills the ancient halls. The menu is high-quality Jordanian, with plenty of delicious mezze. In warm weather, enjoy the fine views from the terrace. It's on the outskirts of Amman.

Drinking & Nightlife

Jebel Amman, Abdoun and Shmeisani have numerous fashionable cafes and bars. Downtown specialises in grubby masculine bars. Most places serve food of some description.

Downtown, around Hashemite Sq and along Hashemi St, is good for cafes.

Alcohol is pricey in Jordan, so be aware that many bars operate a half-price happy hour roughly between 5pm and 8pm.

★ **Rumi** CAFE
(Map p56; www.facebook.com/rumicafejo; 14 Kulliyat Al Shareeah St, Lweibdeh; 7am-midnight Sun-Thu, from 9am Fri & Sat;) This cafe goes from strength to deserved strength. There's plenty of excellent coffee on offer, but tea is the thing here: choose from a menu that includes blends from Bahrain (flavoured with rosewater), Iraq (cardamom), Morocco (mint) and more besides. There's a simple breakfast menu, plus cakes and sandwiches throughout the day.

★ **Maestro Music Bar** BAR
(Map p56; www.facebook.com/maestrobaramman; 52 Al Baouniyah St, Lweibdeh; 9am-midnight) Lively bar in Lweibdeh where you can also grab a bite to eat, attached to La Locanda (p67) boutique hotel. The big draw here is the live music, with bands playing every Friday night, open mic jam sessions on Mondays and jazz through the sound system on other nights. Maestro also hosts sessions for the Amman Jazz Festival (p65).

District BAR
(Map p56; 07 7001 7517; www.facebook.com/DistrictAmman; Zayd Bin Harethah St, Jebel Amman; 5pm-1am) Catch the sunset over the old city while sipping a happy hour cocktail (50% off from 5pm to 8pm) on District's rooftop terrace. The casual chic vibe, industrial-modern design, year-round outdoor seating, creative cocktails and well-dressed crowd make this one of Amman's most popular spots to see and be seen.

Ghoroub BAR
(Map p56; 06 560 7100; www.facebook.com/ghoroub.13thfloor; 13th fl, Landmark Hotel, Al Hussein Bin Ali St; 6pm-2am) For an elevated lounge experience, head up to the 13th floor of the Landmark Hotel. Home to Amman's longest bar, Ghoroub is the perfect perch from which to view the setting sun while sipping a cocktail and nibbling tasty tapas. Ghoroub is great for groups, but dress up and call ahead – to maintain the sophisticated vibe, reservations for large parties and smart casual clothing are required.

Copas Central BAR
(Map p56; 9 Al Imam Malek St, Jebel Amman; ⏲4pm-midnight) A lively Latin-styled bar that's popular with the expat set, Copas Central has a laid-back vibe and a great terrace that's perfect for whiling away a couple of hours over a chilled bottle of wine. Go for the happy hour, when there's 25% off food (tapas and bar snacks) and two-for-one drinks.

Jungle Fever CAFE
(Map p56; ☎07 9570 0220; www.facebook.com/JFCoffeeandTeaHouse; National Gallery of Fine Arts, Husni Fareez St, Lweibdeh; ⏲9.30am-11pm Sat-Wed, to midnight Thu, 1pm-midnight Fri) Put your caffeine addiction to good use at this colourful cafe at the National Gallery of Fine Arts, where you can sample locally sourced coffees, teas and sweet treats while relaxing on cushions hand-embroidered by a women's cooperative. It's on the top floor of the gallery and has an outdoor terrace, perfect for views of the park below.

Caffe Strada COFFEE
(Map p56; 15 Mohamed Rasheed Ridha St; ⏲7am-11pm; 📶) Chilled-out coffee shop just off Rainbow St, always popular with the cool laptop crowd. The inside is deliciously air-conditioned, and there's a terrace at the back for smokers. The menu has some good smoothies, and things are kept simple menu-wise, with decent paninis and green salads.

La Calle BAR
(Map p52; ☎07 7726 6928; Rainbow St; ⏲noon-1am) One of the few proper drinking holes on Rainbow St, La Calle has a couple of decent-sized bar areas, and a small but breezy terrace on the 3rd floor that's great for cooling off with a glass of wine or a chilled bottle of local Carakale ale. Food (burgers, pizzas, salads and the like) is available.

Turtle Green CAFE
(Map p56; 46 Rainbow St; ⏲8am-midnight Sat-Thu, from 10am Fri; 📶) Named for the terrapins in the cafe window, this tea shop is a good place to refuel halfway down Rainbow St. As well as hot drinks and juices, the pitchers of iced tea are very refreshing, and Turtle Green does a good line in *manakeesh* (baked flatbread with toppings like cheese and minced meat), salads and sandwiches.

Kepi CAFE
(Map p56; www.facebook.com/CafeKepi; Paris Circle, Lweibdeh; ⏲7.30am-1am Sun-Thu, from 8.30am Fri; 📶) This corner cafe is a refreshing mix of traditional and modern: the old wood and high ceilings give it the air of a place where old Ammani men congregate to play dominoes, but you're just as likely to see trendy young urbanites with laptops. Large windows keep things breezy, and there's a good menu if you fancy lunch (there's even a passable stab at Tex-Mex food).

Darat Al Funun Café CAFE
(Map p52; Nimer Bin Adwan St, Downtown; ⏲10am-7pm Sat-Thu; 📶) In the heart of a cultural centre, this is a peaceful place to escape from downtown, especially as it's surrounded by a garden and the ruins of a Byzantine church. TE Lawrence wrote part of *Seven Pillars of Wisdom* in the neighbouring house, so who knows what creative spirits linger here.

Books@café CAFE
(Map p52; ☎06 465 0457; Omar Bin Al Khattab St; ⏲10am-midnight; 📶) You may need to keep your sunglasses on when you enter this establishment – the retro floral walls in psychedelic colours are a fun throwback to the '70s. This is typical modern Jordanian coffeehouse chic, and the tasty global food is far less interesting than the hip young Jordanians lounging on sofas in corners or typing furiously on their laptops.

Rovers Return PUB
(Map p80; ☎06 581 4844; Ali Nasouh Al Taher St, Sweifieh; ⏲1pm-late) This popular, cosy English pub in Sweifieh has wood panelling and a lively atmosphere. The comfort food includes authentic fish and chips, and roast beef with gravy. The entrance is round the back of the building and can be hard to find – look for the red 'Comfort Suites' sign.

Living Room COCKTAIL BAR
(Map p56; ☎06 465 5988; Mohammed Hussein Haikal St, Jebel Amman; ⏲1pm-1am) Part lounge, part sushi bar and part study (think high-backed chairs, a fireplace and the daily newspaper), the Living Room is pretty understated. It offers quality bar meals, fine music and delicious iced tea with lemon grass and mint. Expertly crafted cocktails are served up strong – take advantage of the happy hour until 6pm to ease the burden on your wallet.

Winemaker WINE BAR
(Map p56; ☎06 461 4125; www.facebook.com/TheWinemakerAmman; 129 Arar St, Wadi Saqra; ⏲9am-7pm Sat-Thu) Shop a selection of local

and international wines or schedule a wine tasting or pairing at one of the largest wine cellars in Jordan. The Winemaker regularly hosts events, but be warned: the vibe may not align with your typical tasting room expectations, as they occasionally cater to the party crowd, with dance music and beer pong.

Montage CAFE
(Map p52; 5 Omar Bin Al Khattab St; ⏲9am-11pm; 📶) The Royal Film Commission's (p74) cafe is a good place to grab a coffee and a toasted sandwich if you've just walked the length of Rainbow St and are looking for somewhere to refuel. It's a stripped-back metal and glass box, with a pleasant shady area outside for eavesdropping on Jordan's fashionably arty types and finding out about upcoming film screenings.

Al Rashid Court Café CAFE
(Map p52; ☎06 465 2994; Al Malek Faisal St, Downtown; ⏲10am-midnight Sat-Thu, 1-11pm Fri) The 1st-floor balcony here is *the* place to pass an afternoon with a *nargileh* (water pipe) and survey the chaos of the downtown area below, though competition for seats is fierce. You won't see any local women here but it's well accustomed to foreign tourists.

Shaher's Penthouse Cafeteria CAFE
(Map p52; Al Malek Talal St, Downtown; ⏲9.30am-11pm) This cosy cafe has a traditionally decorated indoor dining area as well as an outdoor terrace overlooking the street far below. There's frequently someone playing the oud (lute) or violin to provide a cultured counterpoint to the street noise below.

Sekrab BAR
(Map p52; ☎07 9173 5722; www.facebook.com/sekrabjo; off Rainbow St, Bldg 2, Jebel Amman; ⏲5pm-1am) This Rainbow St bar's extensive cocktail list, colourful decor – crafted from discarded items once destined for the scrapyard – and weekly music events make Sekrab a standout as Amman's one and only 'junkyard jewel'. Visit during the summer to enjoy treetop views from the 3rd-floor open-air terrace.

Al Hail Restaurant & Café CAFE
(Map p52; Hashemite Sq, Downtown; ⏲9am-midnight) A glass of mint tea here comes with perhaps the best view of the Citadel on offer downtown. It's an unpretentious place, despite the decorative well in the front garden, and it's popular with locals in the evening when the neighbouring theatre is illuminated.

☆ Entertainment

Various foreign cultural centres organise lectures, exhibitions and musical recitals. Darat Al Funun is the city's premier cultural space and has art exhibitions as well as regular recitals of classical and traditional music. The Jordan National Gallery of Fine Arts has visiting exhibitions of contemporary art. Jacaranda is one of the best private galleries promoting contemporary Arab art, and has regular shows. There is regular live music at Maestro (p71) in Lweibdeh, and during the summer frequent concerts are held at the Roman Theatre downtown. Check programs at the Royal Film Commission and Institut Français (p64) for other cultural events.

ARTISTIC AMMAN

In more ways than one, Amman is a young city. Not only does the capital mostly date from the middle of the 20th century, but around half of its population is aged under 30. A highly educated population combined with high youth unemployment and Jordan's status as a safe haven in a tough regional neighbourhood have all helped give birth to a lively arts scene with a young, cool vibe.

The regeneration of Rainbow Street was a key moment in providing a hub for artistic endeavours in the capital, and there are plenty of cafes where you can spot trendy youth tapping away at laptops while smoking on a hookah, or you can find them at the hipster fashion outlet Mlabbas (p74). There's also the cool movie crowd at the Royal Film Commission (p74). Flyers along Rainbow St will alert you to concerts and art gatherings, as well as events you might not immediately associate with the region, such as video-game and digital-animation events.

Amman's artistic quarter has since migrated over the hill to the quasi-hipster district of Lweibdeh, leaving a great trail of street art behind it. In Lweibdeh, the fashionable arty hang-out is undoubtedly Rumi (p71), but the cool crowd at JoBedu (p74) are welcoming if you want to hook up with the arts and music scene.

Football (soccer) is followed religiously by most locals. The capital's two main teams, playing in Jordan's Premier League, are Wahadat (generally supported by Palestinians, as it was originally formed in a refugee camp), who play at the Amman International Stadium, near Sports City in Shmeisani, and arch-rivals Faisaly, who play at King Abdullah Stadium in Qwesmeh.

Events are advertised in the local English-language newspapers, on flyers posted along Rainbow St and most importantly all over Facebook.

Royal Film Commission CINEMA
(Map p52; ☎06 464 2266; www.film.jo; 5 Omar Bin Al Khattab St) The home of the Jordanian film industry, the commission holds regular screenings and festivals featuring the best of local and international cinema. The outdoor amphitheatre looking over downtown is a great place to see a film, while the stylish on-site Montage (p73) cafe is worth a visit at any time of day.

King Abdullah Stadium STADIUM
(Map p80; Qwesmeh; ticket from JD2) The home ground for Faisaly, Jordan's most successful football club. The games are mostly played on Friday.

Amman International Stadium SOCCER
(Map p58; Sports City, Shmeisani; ticket from JD2) Wahadat, one of Amman's two main football teams, play their matches at Amman International Stadium. They have heavy Palestinian support, as the club was originally formed in a refugee camp. The stadium is near Sports City in Shmeisani.

Shopping

Amman has several quality craft centres, where you can buy handmade items and antiques, on Rainbow St and near the Inter-Continental Hotel. Other souvenir shops are dotted around the tourist sights of downtown.

Mall mania has swept through Amman in recent years. They're incredibly popular among the city's middle classes and are an oddly fascinating reflection of modern Jordanian culture.

JoBedu CLOTHING
(Map p56; www.jobedu.com; 10 Al Baouniyah St; ⏲10am-10pm) Get your cool-for-cats T-shirts and hoodies here and keep up to date with the Amman street-design vibe, with hints of graffiti, hip-hop culture, anime aesthetic and a very Jordanian sense of humour. Funky designs are available in kids' sizes, as well as prints for your wall. The laptop stickers are great.

Al Afghani GIFTS & SOUVENIRS
(Map p52; Talal St; ⏲10am-10pm Sat-Thu, from 2pm Fri) If we call this souvenir shop long-established, we mean it: the original family business goes back to 1870s Palestine. It's jammed to the rafters with shopping delights big and small – if you can't find it here, you probably don't need it.

Balian CERAMICS
(Map p52; www.armenianceramics.com; 8 Rainbow St; ⏲9am-6pm Sat-Thu) The Balian family came to Amman from Jerusalem in the early 1920s, and have been selling their traditional hand-painted tiles ever since. The decor is popular with wealthy Ammanis eager to show off their good taste, and while you might not be able to decorate an entire bathroom, their individual decorative tiles make lovely souvenirs.

Jacaranda ART
(Map p52; ☎06 464 4050; www.facebook.com/JacarandaImages; 18 Omar Bin Al Khattab St; ⏲11am-8pm) One of Amman's leading contemporary art galleries, Jacaranda holds regular exhibitions of excellent regional artists and is particularly strong in its print and photographic offerings.

Mlabbas CLOTHING
(Map p52; www.mlabbas.com; 28 Rainbow St; ⏲10.30am-11pm) Want to look like a hip urban Jordanian? Head to this cool-as-you-like T-shirt shop on Rainbow St for an amazing array of screen-printed tees by local artists. Styles range from big-brand pastiches through to graffiti art, manga and cartoons, as well as a witty line in Arabic puns (ask the staff for translations). Prints, postcards and stickers are also available.

Soap House Trinitae COSMETICS
(Map p52; ☎06 552 3757; www.trinitae.com; 8 Rainbow St; ⏲9am-7pm Mon-Sat, 11am-6pm Sun) There's more to pampering yourself in Jordan than just Dead Sea mud. Up an alley at the bottom of Rainbow St, you'll find this lovely old villa and garden offering the best in organic luxury, with a gorgeous range of soaps and skincare products. Local herbs, fruits and essential oils create a dizzyingly scented atmosphere.

Jordan River Foundation ARTS & CRAFTS

(Map p52; ☎06 593 3211; www.jordanriver.jo; Bani Hamida House, Fawzi Al Malouf St, Jebel Amman; ⏰8.30am-7pm Sat-Thu, 10am-5pm Fri) Supporting top-notch worthy causes by selling equally top-notch crafted items, this shop is an Amman institution. The showroom supports handloomed rugs from Bani Hamida and exquisite Palestinian-style embroidery. Cushions, camel bags, embroidery, baskets and Dead Sea products make it an excellent place to buy stylish decor. Only the highest-quality pieces make it into the showroom – a fact reflected in the prices.

Wild Jordan Center ARTS & CRAFTS

(Map p52; ☎06 463 3718; www.wildjordancenter.com; Othman Bin Affan St, Downtown; ⏰10am-10pm) The nature store at the Wild Jordan Center sells products made in Jordan's nature reserves, including silver jewellery, organic herbs, teas and jams from Dana, and candles made by Bedouin women as part of an income-generating project in Feynan. Decorated ostrich eggs from Azraq are another speciality. All profits are returned to the craftspeople and to nature-reserve projects.

Souk Jara MARKET

(Map p52; www.facebook.com/soukjara; Rainbow St; ⏰10am-10pm Fri) A weekly open-air flea market run by the Jebel Amman Residents' Association selling a variety of handicrafts (though recently there's been a big influx of plastic tat). It's good fun to browse, and there are some great food and drink stalls and occasional live music to add to the atmosphere.

Ola's Garden ARTS & CRAFTS

(Map p52; ☎07 9539 0136; www.facebook.com/ola.garden; Khirfan St; ⏰11am-6pm Wed-Mon) The home of beautiful handcrafted fashion, from clothes to jewellery. Owner-designer Ola Mubaslat showcases her creations in the most welcoming way (we particularly love the scarves and necklaces) and even offers classes in embroidery and jewellery design.

Iraq Al Amir Cooperative ARTS & CRAFTS

(Map p80; ⏰8am-3pm Sat-Thu) This cooperative, west of Amman in the village of Iraq Al Amir, opposite the village caves of the same name, sells handmade pottery, fabrics, foodstuffs, carpets and paper products. The project was founded by the Noor Al Hussein Foundation and employs dozens of women from the surrounding area.

City Mall MALL

(Map p80; www.citymall.jo; Al Malek Abdullah Bin Hussein Thani St; ⏰10am-12.30am) Mall with local and international chain stores, a Carrefour supermarket, restaurants, coffee shops and a cinema. The mall is in west Amman, near King Hussein Park.

Artisana GIFTS & SOUVENIRS

(Map p56; ☎06 464 7858; Mansour Kraishan St, Jebel Amman; ⏰10am-6pm Sat-Thu) This excellent small showroom has a wide mix of traditional and modern Jordanian crafts and souvenirs, ranging from scarves and stools to bottles of holy water from the Jordan River and spooky reproductions of the famous 9500-year-old statues from Ain Ghazal.

Silsal Ceramics CERAMICS

(☎06 593 1128; www.silsal.com; Innabeh St, North Abdoun; ⏰9am-6pm Sat-Thu) Has a small showroom of superb contemporary pottery that make unexpected but stylish souvenirs from today's Jordan. If you're coming along Zahran St from 5th Circle, it's on the third small street on the right.

Al Alaydi Jordan Craft Centre ARTS & CRAFTS

(Map p56; ☎06 464 4555; Jebel Amman; ⏰9am-6pm Sat-Thu) Spread over several floors, just off Al Kulliyah Al Islamiyah St behind the InterContinental Hotel, this vast showroom includes jewellery, Hebron glassware, Palestinian embroidery, kilims, woodcarvings, old kitchen implements and Bedouin tent accessories.

Beit Al Bawadi CERAMICS

(☎06 593 0070; www.beitalbawadi.com; Fawzi Al Qawuqji St, Jebel Amman; ⏰9am-6pm Sat-Thu) Quality ceramics bought here support local artisans, whom you can see working in the basement. Designs are both traditional and modern, some decorated with Arabic calligraphy, and pieces cost around JD50 to JD80.

Mecca Mall MALL

(Map p80; ☎06 552 7948; Makkah Al Mukarramah Rd) The biggest mall in Amman, in the northwestern suburbs, has a cinema, bowling alley, video arcade and dozens of restaurants.

Abdoun Mall MALL

(Map p80; ☎06 592 0246; Al Umawiyeen St, Zahran) Popular mall with local and international chain stores, restaurants, coffee shops and a cinema.

Al Burgan ARTS & CRAFTS
(Map p56; ☎06 465 2585; www.alburgan.com; 12 Talat Harb St, Jebel Amman; ⊙9.30am-6.30pm Sat-Thu) Al Burgan has a small but good selection of handicrafts, but the staff is knowledgeable and prices are reasonable. It's behind the InterContinental Hotel.

Oriental Souvenirs Store GIFTS & SOUVENIRS
(Map p56; ☎06 464 2820; 3rd Circle, Jebel Amman; ⊙9am-7pm Sat-Thu) This family-run store is more rustic than many others, but it's something of an Aladdin's cave if you're prepared to dig for treasure.

Bawabet Al Sharq ARTS & CRAFTS
(Map p52; ☎06 463 7424; Rainbow St, Downtown; ⊙9am-8pm) The 'Gate of the Orient' has locally made home decor items including some interesting contemporary textiles and embroidery sewn by women's cooperatives.

Information

EMERGENCY

The tourist police have an office at the Ministry of Tourism & Antiquities and there is a small **tourist police booth** (Map p52; Hashemi St) near the Roman Theatre. You can lodge visa extension paperwork at **Al Madeenah police station** (Map p52; ☎06 465 7788; 1st fl, Al Malek Faisal St, Downtown).

The emergency number for ambulance, fire and police is ☎911.

GAY & LESBIAN TRAVELLERS

There is not much of an open scene in Amman, although Books@Cafe (p72) is a notably gay and lesbian venue, especially on Thursday evenings.

INTERNET ACCESS

Wi-fi is widely available in Amman, often even in the scruffiest and most unassuming of coffee shops.

MEDICAL SERVICES

Amman has some of the best medical facilities available in the region. The English-language *Jordan Times* lists hospitals and doctors on night duty throughout the capital. It also publishes a list of pharmacies open after-hours. Most pharmacists speak good English.

Italian Hospital (Map p52; ☎06 477 7101; Italian St, Downtown)

Khalidi Hospital (Map p56; ☎06 464 4281; http://khmc.jo; Bin Khaldoun St) One of the best hospitals in the country, with 24-hour facilities.

Palestine Hospital (Map p58; ☎06 560 7071; www.palestinehospital.org.jo; Al Malekah Alia St, Shmeisani) Recommended hospital with emergency ward.

MONEY

Changing money in Amman is quick and easy, especially since there are dozens of banks downtown and in Jebel Amman, the two areas in which most visitors are likely to find themselves.

Banks with ATMs are plentiful, and most accept international cards. You'll usually be charged around JD2 per ATM transaction. Arab Bank, Cairo Amman Bank, Jordan Gulf Bank and Bank Al Etihad are all reliable.

Many moneychangers are located along Al Malek Faisal St in downtown.

POST

There are lots of small post offices around town, including at the Jordan InterContinental Hotel between 2nd and 3rd Circles in Jebel Amman, on Kulliyat Al Shareeah St in Lweibdeh, and in the Housing Bank Centre in Shmeisani.

TOURIST INFORMATION

A useful free map to pick up is *99 Things to Do in Amman*, produced by the Jordan Tourism Board, which has a large city plan. The *Curating the Best Culinary & Cultural Spaces of Amman* map by Plurality (www.facebook.com/pluralityME) is another useful guide.

Ministry of Tourism (Map p56; ☎ext 254 06 460 3360; ground fl, Al Mutanabbi St, Jebel Amman; ⊙8am-9pm) The most useful place for information, southwest of the 3rd Circle. Also the centre for the **tourist police** (Map p56; ☎ext 254 06 460 3360; Ministry of Tourism, ground fl, Al Mutanabbi St, Jebel Amman; ⊙8am-9pm). The staff are friendly and speak good English.

Wild Jordan Center (p65) Provides information and bookings for activities and accommodation in any of Jordan's nature reserves, including Dana and Wadi Mujib.

Getting There & Away

AIR

Amman remains the main arrival and departure point for international flights to Jordan.

Queen Alia International Airport (☎06 401 0250; www.qaiairport.com) Located 35km south of the city. There are two terminals: Terminal 1 is used for most Royal Jordanian flights and Terminal 2 is used by other airlines. The terminals are within easy walking distance, on opposite sides of the airport road. Both terminals have ATMs, foreign-exchange counters, a post office and left-luggage.

WHEN CIRCLES ARE SQUARES

With its endless one-way streets, stairways, narrow lanes and hills, Amman is confusing enough to get around anyway, but the ambiguous names for the streets and circles would challenge the navigational skills of even the most experienced explorer. We try to use the more common names, but if street signs (handily written in English as well as Arabic), directions given by locals and queries from taxi drivers are still confusing, refer to the list below.

Al Malek means King, so King Faisal St is sometimes labelled Al Malek Faisal St. Similarly, Al Malekah is Queen and Al Emir (Al Amir) is Prince. And don't be too surprised that some 'circles' (*duwaar*) are now called 'squares' *(maidan)*...

Circles

- 1st Circle (Duwaar Al Awaal) – Maidan Al Malek Abdullah
- 2nd Circle (Duwaar Al Thaani) – Maidan Wasfi Al Tal
- 3rd Circle (Duwaar Al Thaalith) – Maidan Al Malek Talal
- 4th Circle (Duwaar Ar Raab) – Maidan Al Emir Gazi Bin Mohammed
- 5th Circle (Duwaar Al Khamis) – Maidan Al Emir Faisal Bin Hussein
- 6th Circle (Duwaar As Saadi) – Maidan Al Emir Rashid Bin Al Hassan
- 7th Circle (Duwaar As Saabe) – Maidan Al Emir Talal Bin Mohammed
- Lweibdeh Circle – Duwaar Al Baris (Paris Circle)
- Ministry of the Interior Circle (Duwaar Ad Dakhliyeh) – Maidan Jamal Abdul Nasser
- Sports City Circle – Maidan Al Medina Al Riyadiyah

Streets

- Rainbow St – Abu Bakr As Siddiq St
- Zahran St – Al Kulliyah Al Islamiyah St
- Mango St – Omar Bin Al Khattab St
- Saqf Sayl St – Quraysh St
- Police St – Suleiman Al Nabulsi St

BUS, MINIBUS & SERVICE TAXI

Amman has quite a few different bus stations, and the one you want depends on your destination. Most towns and cities are actually served by minibuses rather than bus, which are white with the route written on the side in Arabic. Service taxis between towns are also available at most stations. Either way, they usually don't follow fixed schedules unless noted, and depart when the driver deems them full enough. All departures are more frequent in the morning, and most dry up completely after sunset.

Alternatively, the private coach company JETT (www.jett.com.jo) runs services to several cities form their own stations, as well as tourist services to Petra and the Dead Sea (a link to Wadi Rum was expected to open in early 2018).

Public Bus Stations

The two main public bus stations are Tabarbour (North Bus Station) and Wihdat (South Bus Station), serving the northern and southern parts of Jordan, respectively.

Tabarbour Bus Station (North Bus Station) Fairly regular minibuses and service taxis depart for Ajloun (JD1, every 30 minutes, two hours), Jerash (JD1, hourly, 1¼ hours) and Irbid (JD1, two hours). Change at Irbid for Umm Qais. You can also get connections to Deir Alla (for Pella; one hour), Fuheis (45 minutes), Irbid (two hours), Ramtha (two hours), Salt (45 minutes) and Zarqa (for Azraq; 30 minutes); all these services cost under JD1. Heading south, Tabarbour also has frequent minibuses to Madaba (800 fils, 45 minutes).

Wihdat Bus Station (South Bus Station) There are minibuses to Aqaba (JD5.500, five hours) leaving every two hours or so until 9pm. For Petra, minibuses and service taxis (JD5, four hours) depart for Wadi Musa when full from the far corner of the lot between about 7am and 4pm (but travel early in the day where possible). There are regular buses to Karak (JD1.800, two hours) until 5pm, Shobak (JD4, 2½ hours) and Ma'an (JD3, three hours). For Dana, take a bus to Tafila (JD2.750, 2½ hours) and change, but note that most accommodation in Dana offers cheap direct transfers from Amman.

For the Dead Sea, minibuses leave from **Muhajireen Bus Station** (Map p56; Al Ameerah Basma Bin Talal St), near 3rd Circle. There are no direct services: the route involves a minibus to Shuneh Al Janubiyyeh (South Shuna; JD1, 45 minutes) and then a wait for another minibus to Suweimeh. At Suweimeh, you'll have to hire a taxi, which is an unreliable option – it's easier to take the JETT bus. There are also services to Madaba (800 fils, 45 minutes) between 6am and 5pm.

Raghadan Bus Station, downtown, has minibuses and service taxis to Salt, Fuheis and Madaba.

Private Bus Stations

Private coach company JETT has two bus stations, in **Abdali** (Map p58; ☎06 566 4146; www.jett.com.jo; Al Malek Al Hussein St, Shmeisani) and at **7th Circle** (☎06 585 4679; www.jett.com.jo). Abdali is slightly busier, with at least six daily services each to Aqaba (four hours, JD7) and Irbid (two hours, JD2), as well as a daily 6.30am departure to Wadi Musa (for Petra; four hours, JD10). You'll need your passport to book a ticket.

For international travellers, Abdali also has a daily 7am departure for the King Hussein Bridge (one hour, JD10). The bus takes you to Israeli immigration, but must be booked no later than a day in advance. Services to Cairo are also offered (around 20 hours, JD35). Schedules vary, so check in advance and ensure your visas are in order before booking.

There are a similar number of Aqaba and Irbid departures from 7th Circle, along with a daily VIP Aqaba service that includes more comfortable seating, drinks and snacks (JD17) and a daily 9am tourist service to the Dead Sea resort area (one hour, JD7), which returns at 5pm.

CAR

There are many car-rental agencies to choose from around King Abdullah Gardens.

Avis (Map p58; ☎06 569 9420, 24hr ☎07 7739 7405; www.avis.com.jo; King Abdullah Gardens)

Budget (☎06 581 4477; www.budgetjordan.jo; 248 Mecca St)

Europcar (Map p58; ☎06 550 4031; www.europcar.jo; Isam Al Ajlouni St)

Hertz (Map p58; ☎06 562 4191; www.hertz.jo; King Abdullah Gardens)

National Car Rental (Map p58; ☎06 559 1731; www.nationalcar.com; Al Sharif Nasir Bin Jamil St)

Reliable Rent-a-Car (☎06 592 9676; www.rentareliablecar.com; 19 Fawzi Al Qawuqji St)

Getting Around

TO/FROM THE AIRPORT

The **Sariyah Airport Express Bus** (☎06 489 1073; www.sariyahexpress.com; JD3.250) runs between the airport and the Tabarbour Bus Station (p77; North Bus Station), passing through the 4th, 5th, 6th and 7th Circles en route. Departures are every 30 minutes in both directions between 6.30am and midnight. The trip takes 45 minutes.

If you're flying with Royal Jordanian, its **booking office** (☎06 550 3870; Ibn Mada St, 7th Circle) at 7th Circle offers a free transfer

SERVICE TAXI ROUTES

Service taxi 1 (Map p52) From Basman St for 4th Circle.

Service taxi 2 (Map p52) From Basman St for 1st and 2nd Circles.

Service taxi 3 (Map p52) From Basman St for 3rd and 4th Circles.

Service taxi 4 (Map p52) From the side street near the central post office for Jebel Lweibdeh.

Service taxi 6 (Map p52) From Cinema Al Hussein St for the Ministry of the Interior Circle, past Abdali station and JETT international and domestic offices.

Service taxi 7 (Map p52) From Cinema Al Hussein St, up Al Malek Al Hussein St, past Abdali station and King Abdullah Mosque, and along Suleiman Al Nabulsi St for Shmeisani.

Service taxis 25 & 26 (Map p52) From Italian St, downtown, to the top of Jebel Al Ashrafiyeh and near Abu Darwish Mosque.

Service taxi 27 (Map p52) From Italian St to Middle East Circle for Wahadat station.

Service taxi 35 (Map p52) From opposite the Amman Palace Hotel, passing close to the Muhajireen Police Station.

Service taxi 38 (Map p52) From Basman St to Makkah Al Mukarramah Rd.

between 8.30am and 10pm – you can also check in here and have your bags transferred.

There are branches of **Avis** (☎06 445 1133; www.avis.com.jo; Queen Alia Airport; ⏲24hr), **Hertz** (☎06 471 1771; www.hertz.jo) and other car-rental companies. Those that don't have an office at the airport will meet you at the airport or otherwise will arrange for you to pick up a car from there.

Airport taxis cost JD18 to JD22 to Amman, JD15 to Madaba and around JD35 to the Dead Sea. Fares are displayed at the rank outside the arrivals terminal.

TAXI

Private Taxi

Private taxis are painted yellow. They are abundant, can be flagged anywhere, have cheap fares and most drivers automatically use the meter. A taxi from downtown to Shmeisani, for example, costs JD2.500, and it's JD3 to Tabarbour.

Careem (www.careem.com/amman), a Middle East–wide ride-hailing company, operates in Amman, and you can book lifts from your phone app. Being able to enter your destination in the app is very convenient if the driver doesn't speak English. Fares are around a third more expensive than a standard yellow cab. **Uber** (www.uber.com) is also in Amman.

Service Taxi

These white cabs are shared taxis that stick to specific routes and are not permitted to leave the city limits. Fares cost around 400 fils per seat, and you usually pay the full amount regardless of where you get off. After 8pm, the price for all service taxis goes up by 25%.

There can be long queues at rush hour (8am to 9am and 5pm to 6pm). The cars queue up and usually start at the bottom of a hill – you get into the last car and unusually the whole line rolls back a car space and so on.

AROUND AMMAN

With the exception of downtown, uncovering remnants of the ancients is no easy task in Amman as the capital is largely a 20th-century creation. However, you don't have to look far beyond the city limits for historical reminders of the country's illustrious past. Indeed, the outskirts of the capital are home to Roman ruins, biblical landmarks, Byzantine churches and Ottoman structures, all of which are set against beautiful landscapes that are a world apart from the streets of Amman. Most destinations can be reached on a half-day trip from Amman.

Wadi As Seer & Iraq Al Amir

وادي السير & عراق الأمير

West of the capital lies the fertile Wadi As Seer, standing in marked contrast to the treeless plateau surrounding Amman. The stream-fed valley is lined with cypress trees, and dotted with fragrant orchards and olive groves. In the springtime, particularly April and May, Wadi As Seer plays host to spectacular wildflower blooms that include the Jordanian national flower, the black iris.

The village itself, which is largely Circassian in origin, is now virtually part of sprawling western Amman. However, there still remains a sense of distinct community, especially in the Ottoman stone buildings and mosque that lie at the centre of the village. The main attractions of the area, however, lie further down the wadi.

About 4km west of Wadi As Seer, on the road to the village of Iraq Al Amir, you can spot part of an ancient Roman aqueduct (p81). Shortly past the aqueduct, look up to the hillside on the left to a facade cut into the rock. Known as Ad Deir (p81), it most likely served as an elaborate medieval dovecote.

The caves of **Iraq Al Amir** (Caves of the Prince) are 6km west of Wadi As Seer. The caves are arranged in two tiers – the upper tier forms a long gallery (partially damaged during a mild earthquake in 1999) along the cliff face. The 11 caves were once used as cavalry stables, though locals have taken to using them to house their goats and store fodder. Steps lead up to the caves from the paved road – keep an eye out for the ancient Hebrew inscription near the entrance.

Opposite the caves is the village of Iraq Al Amir, home to the Iraq Al Amir Cooperative (p75), selling handmade pottery, fabrics, carpets and paper products. The project was founded by the Noor Al Hussein Foundation and employs many women from the surrounding area. Profits are returned to the community.

About 700m further down the road, just visible from the caves, is the small but impressive Qasr Al Abad (p59). Despite appearances and indeed its name, it was most likely built as a fortified villa rather than a military fort. Its precise age isn't known, though it's thought that it was built by Hyrcanus of the powerful Jewish Tobiad family sometime between 187 and 175 BC. Although

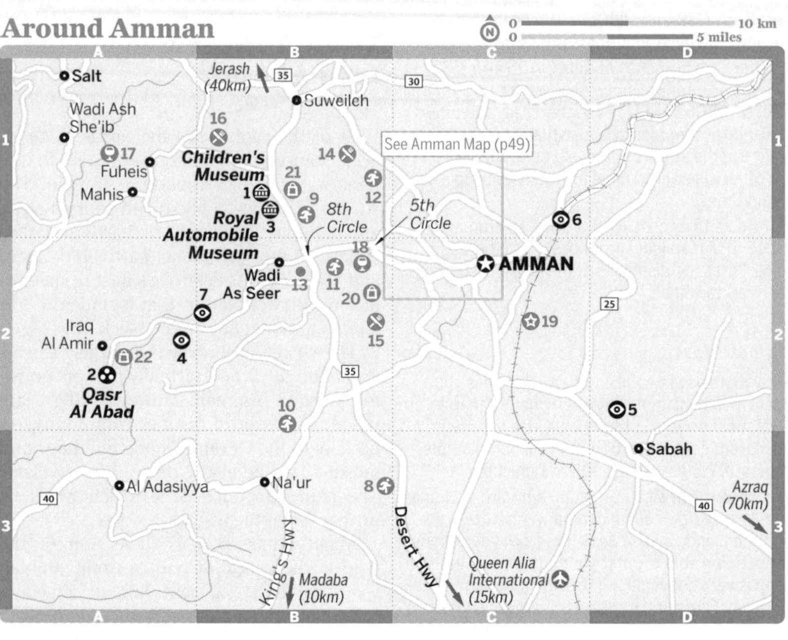

Around Amman

Top Sights
- 1 Children's Museum B1
- 2 Qasr Al Abad A2
- 3 Royal Automobile Museum B1

Sights
- 4 Ad Deir A2
- 5 Cave of the Seven Sleepers D2
- 6 Hejaz Railway C1
- 7 Roman Aqueduct B2

Activities, Courses & Tours
- 8 Amman Waves B3
- 9 Bike Rush B1
- 10 Climbat B2
- 11 Experience Jordan B2
- 12 JOR Elite Bowling Centre B1
- 13 Shababeek B2

Eating
- 14 Dina B1
- 15 Kan Zeman B2
- Pizza Al Reef .... (see 14)
- 16 Zuwwadeh Restaurant B1

Drinking & Nightlife
- 17 Carakale Brewery A1
- 18 Rovers Return B2

Entertainment
- 19 King Abdullah Stadium C2

Shopping
- 20 Abdoun Mall B2
- 21 City Mall B1
- 22 Iraq Al Amir Cooperative A2
- Mecca Mall .... (see 21)

never completed, much of the palace has been reconstructed, and it remains an impressive site.

The palace was built from some of the biggest blocks of any ancient structure in the Middle East – the largest is 7m by 3m. The blocks were only 20cm or so thick, making the whole edifice quite flimsy, and susceptible to the earthquake that flattened it in AD 362. Today, the setting and the animal carvings on the exterior walls are the highlights. Look for the carved panther fountain on the ground floor, the eroded eagles on the corners and the lioness with cubs on the upper storey of the back side.

The gatekeeper will open the interior, as well as a small museum (which includes drawings of what the complex once looked like) for a JD2 tip. If he's not around, ask for the *miftah* (key) at the small shop near the gate.

Minibuses leave regularly from the Muhajireen Bus Station (p78) for Wadi As Seer village (400 fils, 30 minutes) and less frequently from the Raghadan Bus Station (p78) in downtown. From Wadi As Seer, take another minibus – or walk about 10km, mostly downhill – to the caves. Look for the signpost to the Iraq Al Amir Cooperative, which is virtually opposite the stairs to the caves. From the caves, it's an easy stroll down to the *qasr* (castle; but a little steep back up).

If you're driving, head west from 8th Circle and follow the main road, which twists through Wadi As Seer village.

Ad Deir HISTORIC SITE

(Monastery; Map p80) Ad Deir is a facade cut into the rock of a hillside about 4km west of Wadi As Seer on the road to Iraq Al Amir village. It most likely served as an elaborate medieval dovecote.

Roman Aqueduct HISTORIC SITE

(Map p80) About 4km west of Wadi As Seer, on the road to the village of Iraq Al Amir, you can spot part of an ancient Roman aqueduct, testament to Rome's success at irrigating this dry land. Wadi As Seer is served by minibus from Amman's Muhajireen Bus Station (p78), but you'll need to walk or have your own transport to get to the aqueduct.

Cave of the Seven Sleepers اهل الكهف

The legend of the 'seven sleepers' involves seven Christian boys who were persecuted by the Roman Emperor Trajan, then escaped to this **cave** (Ahl Al Kahf; Map p80; ⏲8am-6pm) FREE and slept there for 309 years. This is one of several locations that claim to be that cave. Inside the main cave – also known as **Ahl Al Kahf** (Cave of the People) – are eight smaller tombs that are sealed, though one has a hole in it, through which you can see a creepy collection of human bones.

Above and below the cave are the remains of two mosques. About 500m west of the cave is a large and slightly unkempt Byzantine cemetery. The cave is to the right of a large new mosque complex in the village of Rajib, off the road from Amman to Sabah. Buses from Amman to Sabah pass 500m from the mosque; catch them at Wihdat Bus Station (p77). The journey costs less than 500 fils and takes 15 minutes. Alternatively, take a minibus from Quraysh St in downtown, ask for 'Al Kahf' and the driver will show you where to get off to change for a Sabah bus. The easiest way here is by chartered taxi (around JD8 each way).

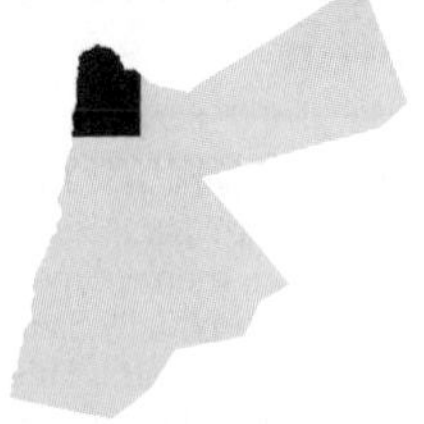

Jerash, Irbid & the Jordan Valley
جرش & اربد & غور الاردن

Includes ➡

Best Places to Eat

- Lebanese House (p92)
- Umm Qais Resthouse (p103)
- Galsoum's Kitchen (p104)

Best Places to Stay

- Olive Branch Resort (p91)
- Beit Al Baraka (p103)
- Al Ayoun Homestays (p96)

Why Go?

The north of Jordan is sometimes overlooked by visitors, but this is a region rich in ancient ruins and biblical associations, all set in rolling countryside that's ablaze with wildflowers in springtime.

The epic Roman city of Jerash is the north's big hitter, a world-class destination without the crowds. Its contemporary, Gadara in Umm Qais, is smaller but has a tremendous setting overlooking the Sea of Galilee in Israel and the Palestinian Territories. Even better, Umm Qais is at the forefront of Jordan's community-tourism scene, with everything from hiking and cooking classes to beekeeping on offer.

Ajloun Castle, atop an imposing hill, and the well-preserved Ottoman town of Salt offer insights into Jordan's Islamic history, while you can get close to nature at Ajloun Forest Reserve, and hike the paths of the locally run Al Ayoun Trail, sleeping in village homestays to meet the people of this fascinating area.

When to Go

- A wonderful time to visit the northern part of Jordan is in spring (March to mid-May), when the black iris, the country's national flower, makes a shy appearance along roadsides and a profusion of knee-high wildflowers spills across the semi-arid hillsides.
- For culture vultures, the hot summer months of July and August bring music and poetry to Jerash's Roman ruins during the town's Festival of Culture & Arts.
- From early November to January, subtropical fruits ripen in the Jordan Valley, while the region's hill towns shiver through winter.

History

The name 'Gilead' crops up from time to time in northwestern Jordan. This was the biblical name of the region, defined by the sculpting waters of the Yarmouk River to the north and the once-mighty Jordan River to the west. The hills of Gilead have been occupied since antiquity and were home to the Roman Decapolis (p88). Largely established during the Hellenistic period, these city states flourished along the boundaries of the Greek and Semitic lands. The Romans transformed them into powerful trading centres – the torch-bearers of Roman culture at the furthest reaches of the empire.

If you're wondering where these cities are today, chances are you're walking on them. Northern Jordan is the most densely populated area in the country, home to the major urban centre of Irbid as well as dozens of small towns and villages that have largely engulfed many of the ancient sites. With a bit of amateur investigation, it's easy to make out the tells (mounds) and archaeological remains of the Decapolis, scattered among Gilead's rolling hills. If you haven't the time or inclination for such sleuthing, head for Umm Qais (Gadara), Pella and especially Jerash, where there are enough clues among the standing columns, amphitheatres and mosaic floors to conjure the full pomp and splendour of the Roman past.

Nature Reserves

There are two reserves in the north of Jordan, both encompassing rare woodland. Ajloun Forest Reserve (p94) is the more developed of the two, with excellent hiking trails and accommodation options. Dibeen Forest Reserve (p93) is a popular spot for weekend picnics. Not strictly a nature reserve, but worth checking out, is the Royal Botanic Garden (p85) at Rumman.

Dangers & Annoyances

This region is bordered by Israel and the Palestinian Territories to the west and by Syria to the north. Given the sensitivity of relations between these countries, a bit of discretion is advised when travelling near the Yarmouk or Jordan Valleys. There are many checkpoints, particularly around the convergence of those two valleys near Umm Qais, so it is imperative to carry your passport and, if driving, your licence and car-rental details. Don't hike too close to either border. Avoid taking photographs near the border area – this includes photographing the Jordan River near checkpoints.

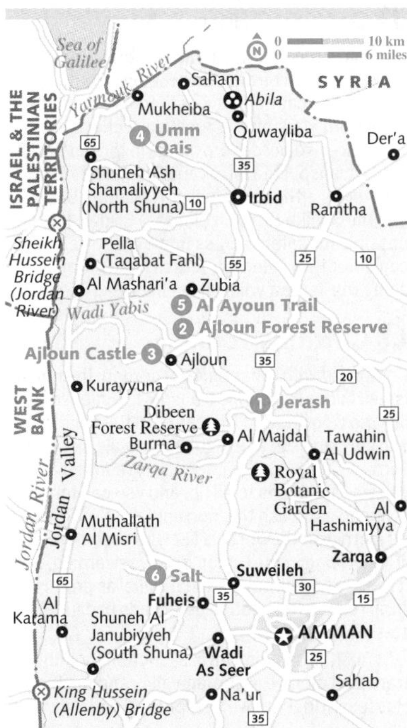

Jerash, Irbid & the Jordan Valley Highlights

1. **Jerash** (p84) Wandering the colonnaded streets and admiring the impressive theatres of a Roman provincial city, one of the most spectacularly well-preserved such sites in the Middle East.
2. **Ajloun Forest Reserve** (p94) Hiking along shady trails in one of the prettiest nature reserves in the country.
3. **Ajloun Castle** (p93) Enjoying the sweeping views from this dramatic hilltop castle, one of Jordan's most impressive Islamic structures.
4. **Umm Qais** (p101) Taking in Roman ruins and enjoying the town's community-tourism projects, from cooking classes and beekeeping to hiking and mountain biking.
5. **Al Ayoun Trail** (p95) Walking through the countryside along this locally run hiking trail and sleeping at village homestays.
6. **Salt** (p106) Ambling by traditional Ottoman houses in this souq town close to Amman.

Getting There & Away

Amman is the gateway to the north, so most public transport from other regions transits through the capital, though there are connections from Madaba and Aqaba directly to Irbid. There are two border crossings in the north with public transport to Israel and the Palestinian Territories – the King Hussein (Allenby) Bridge and the Sheikh Hussein (Jordan) Bridge. It is not possible (or safe) to cross into Syria. By car, you can enter the region via Jerash from Amman or along the Jordan Valley from the Dead Sea.

Getting Around

Compared with other parts of Jordan, the north is well served by public transport. Minibuses link most towns and villages (and the main city of Irbid), and run at irregular intervals along the Jordan Valley. A bit of patience is required as you wait for buses to fill up, and you can forget trying to establish the 'correct fare' (however, no journey in the north is likely to cost more than JD1). Driving in the region is very rewarding, but it requires a few navigational skills, as promising rural roads often lead to dead ends because of steep-sided wadis.

Shuneh Al Janubiyyeh is a junction for public transport along the Jordan Valley and the King Hussein Bridge, as well as for the Dead Sea.

JERASH & AROUND

Often referred to as the 'Pompeii of Asia', the ruins at Jerash (known in Roman times as Gerasa) are one of Jordan's major attractions, and one of the Middle East's best examples of a Roman provincial city. Remarkably well preserved through the centuries by the dry desert air, Jerash cannot fail to impress.

Although the ruins are the undoubted key attraction in the area, there is more to Jerash (which also comprises a thriving modern town) and the surrounding area than just the ruins. Nearby Ajloun, for instance, has a grand castle and offers hiking trails, picnic opportunities, community engagement and places to buy fresh fruit from the surrounding hillside orchards. As such, although Jerash is usually visited as a day trip from Amman, there's more than enough of interest in the area to warrant at least one overnight stop.

Jerash جرش

02 / POP 50,750 / ELEV 618M

Arriving in the modern town of Jerash, with its provincial streets and small market gardens, you see little to suggest its illustrious past. But the moment you cross from the new town into the ancient city, its boundary marked by the imposing Hadrian's Arch, it becomes apparent that this was once no ordinary backwater but a city of great wealth and importance.

While the Middle East contains other surviving Roman cities that boast similar architectural treasures, the ancient ruins at Jerash are famous for their remarkable state of preservation. Enough structures remain intact for archaeologists and historians, and even casual visitors, to piece together ancient life under the rule of an emperor.

History

Although inhabited from Neolithic times and settled as a town during the reign of Alexander the Great (333 BC), Jerash was largely a Roman creation, and the well-preserved remains of all the classic Roman structures – forum, *cardo maximus*, hippodrome, nymphaeum – are easily distinguishable among the ruins.

Following Roman general Pompey's conquest of the region in 64 BC, Gerasa became part of the Roman province of Syria and then a city of the Decapolis (p88). Over the next two centuries, trade with the Nabataeans (of Petra fame) flourished, and the city grew extremely wealthy thanks to local agriculture and iron-ore mining. In the 1st century AD the city was remodelled on the grid system, with a colonnaded main north–south street (the *cardo maximus* – one of the great highlights of the site today) intersected by two side streets running east–west.

The city was further enhanced in AD 106 under Emperor Trajan, and the triumphal arch at the far southern end of the city (through which the site is accessed today) was constructed in 129 to mark the important occasion of Emperor Hadrian's visit. Jerash's fortunes peaked around the beginning of the 3rd century, when it attained the rank of colony and boasted a population of 15,000 to 20,000 inhabitants.

The city declined following a devastating earthquake in 747, and its population shrank to about a quarter of its former size. Apart from a brief occupation by a Crusader garrison in the 12th century, the city was completely deserted until the arrival of the Circassians from Russia in 1878. The site's archaeological importance was quickly recognised, sparking more than a century of excavation and restoration and the revival of a new town on the eastern flank of the ruins.

Sights

Jerash is cleaved in two by a deep, cultivated wadi. Today, as in the days of the Romans, the bulk of the town's inhabitants live on the eastern side. The walled city on the western side, graced with grand public monuments, baths and fountains, was reserved for administrative, commercial, civic and religious activities. The two were once linked by causeways and processional paths, and magnificent gates marked the entrance. Today, access to the remains of this walled city is through the most southerly gate, known as Hadrian's Arch or the Arch of Triumph. There's a ticket office where you can also buy souvenirs, sunhats and cold drinks.

The site covers a huge area and can seem daunting at first, especially as there's virtually no signage. To help the ruins come alive, engage one of the knowledgeable guides (JD20) at the ticket checkpoint (p92) to help you navigate the main complex. Walking at a leisurely pace, and allowing time for sitting on a fallen column and enjoying the spectacular views, you can visit the main ruins in a minimum of three to four hours.

Roman Ruins of Jerash ARCHAEOLOGICAL SITE
(JD8, with Jordan Pass free; 8am-4.30pm Oct-Apr, to 7pm May-Sep) The ruined city of Jerash is Jordan's largest and most interesting Roman site, and a major tourist drawcard. Its imposing ceremonial gates, colonnaded avenues, temples and theatres all speak to the time when this was an important imperial centre. Even the most casual fan of archaeology will enjoy a half-day at the site – but take a hat and sunscreen in the warmer months, as the exposed ruins can be very hot to explore.

★ Hadrian's Arch GATE
There's no better way of gaining a sense of the pomp and splendour of Rome than walking through the triumphal, 13m-tall Hadrian's Arch at the entrance to Jerash, built to honour the visiting emperor. From here you can see a honey-coloured assortment of columns and walls, some delicately carved with acanthus leaves, some solid and practical, extending all the way to a pale view of hills in the distance – just as the Roman architects intended.

The gateway was originally twice this height and encompassed three enormous wooden doors.

★ Temple of Artemis TEMPLE
Dedicated to Artemis, the goddess of hunting and fertility and the daughter of Zeus and Leto, this temple was built between AD 150 and 170, and flanked by 12 elaborately carved Corinthian columns (11 still stand). The construction is particularly impressive given that large vaults, housing temple treasure, had to be built to the north and south to make the courtyard level. The whole building was once clad in marble, and prized statues of Artemis would have adorned the niches.

If you visit on a partly cloudy day, you're in for a treat, as the sandstone pillars of the temple light up like bars of liquid gold each time the sun comes out. It's a magical sight, and magic – or a sense of the world beyond – was exactly what the architects of this gem of a building would have been trying to capture in their design.

Alas, the edict of Theodorius in AD 386, permitting the dismantling of pagan temples, led to the demise of this once-grand edifice, as it was picked apart for materials to construct churches. The Byzantines later converted the site to an artisan workshop for kitchenware and crockery. In the 12th century the structure was temporarily brought back to life as an Arab fortification, only to be destroyed by the Crusaders.

WORTH A TRIP

JORDAN'S ROYAL BOTANIC GARDEN

Aiming to showcase Jordan's surprisingly varied flora, the new **Royal Botanic Garden** (RBG; www.royalbotanicgarden.org; Rumman) highlights best practice in habitat conservation. The site, which overlooks the King Talal Dam, spreads over 180 hectares, with a variation in elevation of 300m, allowing it to reproduce Jordan's main habitat zones – pine forest, oak forest, juniper forest, the Jordan Valley and freshwater wadi. Check the website for access details, as the garden only erratically opens to the public.

Jerash Ruins

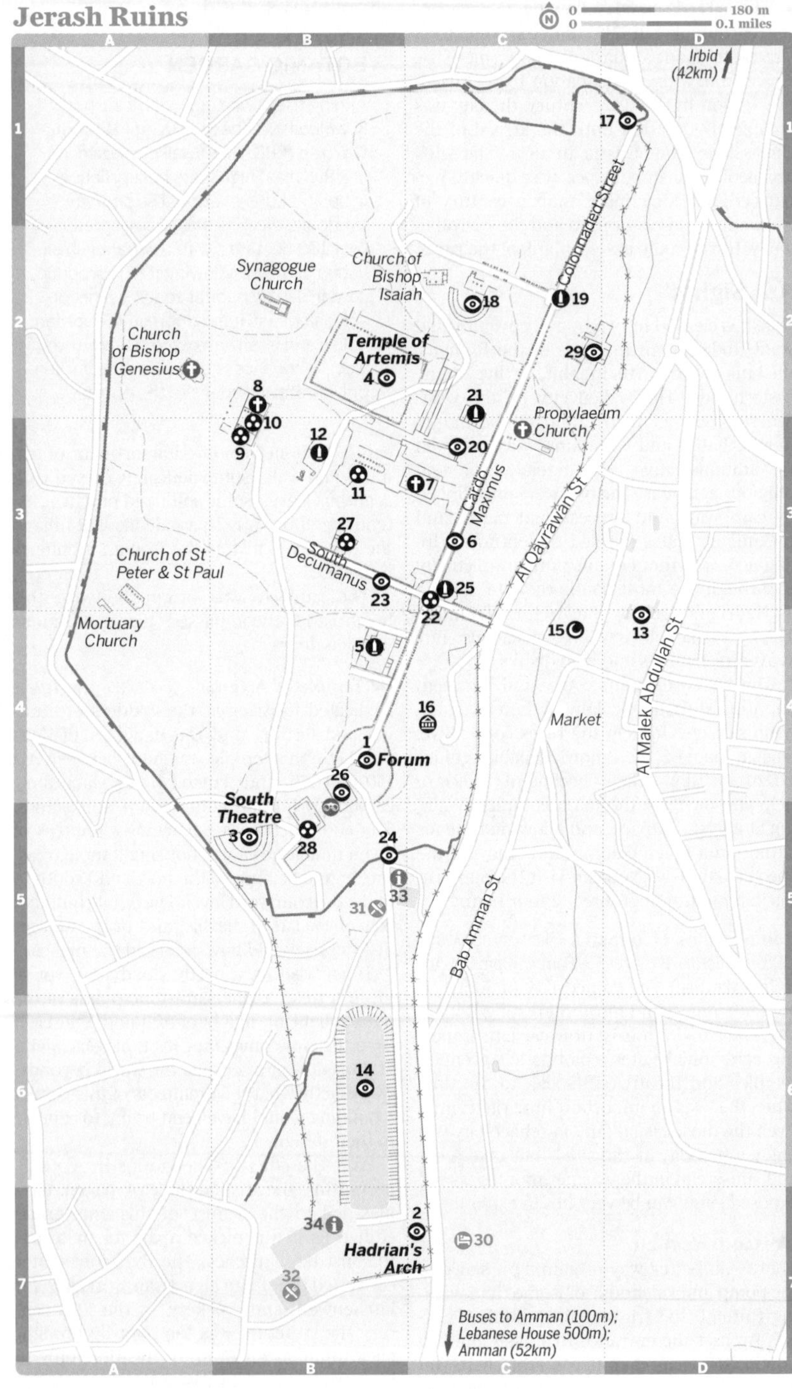

Jerash Ruins

Top Sights
1 Forum ... B4
2 Hadrian's Arch ... C7
3 South Theatre ... B5
4 Temple of Artemis ... B2

Sights
5 Agora ... B4
6 Cardo Maximus ... C3
7 Cathedral ... C3
8 Church of St Cosmos & St Damianus ... B2
9 Church of St George ... B3
10 Church of St John the Baptist ... B3
11 Church of St Theodore ... B3
12 Courtyard of the Fountain ... B3
13 Eastern Baths ... D4
14 Hippodrome ... B6
15 Mosque ... C4
16 Museum ... C4
17 North Gate ... D1
18 North Theatre ... C2
19 Northern Tetrapylon ... C2
20 Nymphaeum ... C3
21 Propylaeum ... C2
22 Roman Ruins of Jerash ... C3
23 South Decumanus ... B3
24 South Gate ... B5
25 Southern Tetrapylon ... C3
26 Temple of Zeus ... B4
27 Umayyad Houses ... B3
28 Upper Temple of Zeus ... B5
Vaulted Gallery ... (see 26)
29 Western Baths ... C2

Sleeping
30 Hadrian Gate Hotel ... C7

Eating
31 Jerash Rest House ... B5
32 Jordan House Restaurant ... B7

Information
33 Ticket Checkpoint ... B5
34 Ticket Office ... B7

If your energy is starting to flag, this is a good place to turn back. You can descend through the temple's gateway, the propylaeum (p89). If you want to get a sense of the complete extent of Jerash, head towards the North Gate (p90) for further views.

★ Forum — ROMAN SITE

Whatever the light and whatever the weather, the forum, with its organ-pipe columns arranged around an unusual oval-shaped plaza, is always breathtaking. It's one of Jerash's undisputed highlights. This immense space (90m long and 80m at its widest point) lies in the heart of the city, linking the main thoroughfare (the *cardo maximus*; p88) with the Temple of Zeus (p89). It served as a marketplace and the main locus of the city's social and political life.

Today it still draws crowds, with Jordanian families picnicking and site guards napping among the columns. And what superb columns they are! Constructed in the middle of the 1st century AD, the forum is surrounded by 56 unfluted Ionic columns, each made from four solid cuts of stone that appear double in number because of their shadow. The plaza itself is just as spectacular, paved with extremely high-quality limestone slabs. The slabs, which increase in size as they radiate from the middle, create a sense of vortex that draws your eye to the centre point. To appreciate this effect fully you need an aerial view, which can be gained from climbing the steps to the Temple of Zeus.

★ South Theatre — ROMAN SITE

As you enter the South Theatre through a wooden door between the arches, there's little to suggest the treasure encased by the plain exterior. But then you emerge into the upper seating area... Built between AD 81 and 96 and once housing 5000 spectators in its two storeys of seating (only one tier of which remains), the theatre is almost perfect.

Sit in row 30 of the 32 rows of seats (if you can read the Greek numbers) and you'll see how the elaborately decorated stage is just a foreground for the backdrop of ancient and modern Jerash. The light at sunset melts the stage surface. Cue music? That's provided by the visitors who whisper experimental choruses and the members of the Jordanian Scottish bagpipe band who, with less subtlety, blast sporadic tunes to the four winds to illustrate the excellent acoustics.

The theatre comes into its own during the Jerash Festival of Culture & Arts (p91), when it proves as worthy a venue today as it was for the ancients 2000 years ago.

Upper Temple of Zeus — RUINS

Though most of it has collapsed, this temple has imposing 15m-high columns that are some of Jerash's most dramatic. The thick walls of the sanctum still stand, giving a

THE DECAPOLIS

The Roman commercial cities within modern Jordan, Syria, and Israel and the Palestinian Territories became known collectively as the Decapolis in the 1st century AD. Despite the etymology of the word, it seems that the Decapolis consisted of more than 10 cities, and possibly as many as 18. The league of cities served to unite Roman possessions and to enhance commerce in the region. In Jordan, the main Decapolis cities were Philadelphia (Amman), Gadara (Umm Qais), Gerasa (Jerash) and Pella (Taqabat Fil), and possibly Abila (Qweilbeh) and Capitolias (Beit Ras, near Irbid).

Rome helped facilitate the growth of the Decapolis by granting the cities a measure of political autonomy within the protective sphere of Rome. Each city operated more like a city state, maintaining jurisdiction over the surrounding countryside and even minting its own coins. Indeed, coins from Decapolis cities often used words such as 'autonomous', 'free' and 'sovereign' to emphasise their self-governing status.

The cities may have enjoyed semi-autonomy, but they were still recognisably Roman, rebuilt with gridded streets and well-funded public monuments. A network of Roman roads facilitated the transport of goods from one city to the next, and the wheel ruts of carriages and chariots can still be seen in the paving stones at Umm Qais and Jerash. The so-called imperial cult, which revolved around mandatory worship of the Roman emperor, helped unify the cities in the Decapolis while simultaneously ensuring that its residents didn't forget the generosity of their Roman benefactors.

Wandering the streets of the ruined cities today, it's easy to imagine life 2000 years ago: the centre bustling with shops and merchants, and lined with cooling water fountains and dramatic painted facades. The empty niches would have been filled with painted statues; buildings clad in marble and decorated with carved peacocks and shell motifs; and churches topped with Tuscan-style terracotta-tiled roofs.

The term Decapolis fell out of use when Emperor Trajan annexed Arabia in the 2nd century AD, although the cities continued to maintain connections with one another for a further 400 years. Their eventual demise was heralded by the conquest of the Levant in 641 by the Umayyads. Political, religious and commercial interests shifted to Damascus, marginalising the cities of the Decapolis to such an extent that they never recovered.

clear view of how the original temple would have looked in its prime.

The tumble of columns in front of the temple speak to the destructive power of the earthquake that levelled Jerash in the 8th century.

Cardo Maximus ROMAN SITE

Jerash's superb colonnaded *cardo maximus* is straight in the way that only a Roman road can be. This is one of Jerash's great highlights, and the walk along its entire 800m length from North Gate to the forum is well worth the effort. Built in the 1st century AD and complete with manholes to underground drainage, the street still bears the hallmarks of the city's principal thoroughfare, with the ruts worn by thousands of chariots scored into the original flagstones.

The 500 columns that once lined the street were deliberately built at different heights to complement the facades of the buildings that stood behind them. Although most of the columns you see today were reassembled in the 1960s, they give an excellent impression of this spectacular thoroughfare.

There are many buildings of interest on either side of the *cardo maximus*, in various states of restoration and ruin. A highlight is the northern tetrapylon (p90), an archway with four entrances.

North Theatre ROMAN SITE

Built about AD 165 and enlarged in 235, the beautiful little North Theatre was most likely used for government meetings rather than artistic performances. Originally it had 14 rows of seats, with two vaulted passageways leading to the front of the theatre, as well as five internal arched corridors leading to the upper rows. Many of the seats are inscribed with the names of delegates who voted in the city council.

Like many of the grand monuments at Jerash, the North Theatre was destroyed by earthquakes and then partially dismantled for later Byzantine and Umayyad building projects. However, in recent years it has been magnificently restored and still maintains a capacity of about 2000 people. The theatre may not have been used for performances, but there's still plenty of rhythm in the design details, with round niches, inverted scallop shells, and exuberant carvings of musicians and dancers at the base of the stairs.

South Gate GATE

Two hundred metres north of the hippodrome is the imposing South Gate, which was likely constructed in AD 130 and originally served as one of four entrances along the city walls. Along the way you can see how the Roman city, then as now, spilt over both sides of Wadi Jerash, with most of the residential area lying east of the wadi. The visitor centre is on the right before the gate; hire a guide here.

One square kilometre of the city is encased by the 3m-thick, 3.5km-long boundary walls. Don't forget to look up as you pass under the South Gate: like Hadrian's Arch, the columns bear elaborately carved acanthus-leaf decorations and would once have supported three wooden doors. Framed by the archway is the first hint of the splendour ahead – the columns of the forum start appearing in ever greater profusion as you walk towards them.

Hippodrome STADIUM

Built sometime between the 1st and 3rd centuries AD, this ancient sports field (244m by 50m) was once surrounded by seating for up to 15,000 spectators, 30 times the current capacity, and hosted mainly athletics competitions and chariot races. Recent excavations have unearthed the remains of stables and pottery workshops, plus indications that the site was used for polo by invading Sassanians from Persia during the early 7th century.

In recent years the hippodrome has hosted chariot races and reconstructions of Roman military manoeuvres, but falling tourist numbers since the Arab Spring have put these on ice for now.

Museum MUSEUM

(☎02 631 2267; ⏲8.30am-6pm Oct-Apr, to 5pm May-Sep) FREE Before you finish exploring ancient Jerash, visit this compact museum and visitor centre just above the forum. It houses a small but worthwhile selection of artefacts from the site, such as mosaics, glass, gold jewellery and coins found in a tomb near Hadrian's Arch. Almost as good as the exhibits is the view the hill affords of Jerash, ancient and modern, spread across either side of the town's defining wadi.

Courtyard of the Fountain MONUMENT

This ancient fountain was once fed by a local reservoir. When it was dedicated to Dionysus, it was alleged that the god would turn its water into wine, the better to celebrate him. The paved portico of the fountain still dominates the scene.

Lookout VIEWPOINT

Near the South Theatre (p87), this viewpoint offers a panorama of the forum and beyond – one of the first opportunities to truly take in the size of Jerash.

Propylaeum MONUMENT

Built in AD 150, this is the monumental gateway to the Temple of Artemis (p85). It was originally flanked by shops.

Temple of Zeus TEMPLE

Built in AD 162 over the remains of an earlier Roman temple, the Temple of Zeus was once approached by a magnificent stairway leading from the *temenos* (sacred courtyard). Today, lizards sun themselves in the cracks of pavement, oblivious to the holy sacrifices that used to take place here. Positioned on the summit of the hill, the temple towers above the city. Despite erosion and earthquakes, enough of this once-beautiful building remains to allow visitors to understand its former importance.

A path leads from the *temenos* to the temple, via a welcome stand of trees. You can pause here for a panorama of the forum (p87) and a small hill of pines. As you walk from the trees to the temple, notice the intricate friezes of floral and figurative motifs unearthed by French excavations. The delicacy of the design contrasts strikingly with the massive size of the building blocks that comprise the temple's inner sanctum.

Nymphaeum FOUNTAIN

On the western side of the *cardo maximus* is the elegant nymphaeum, the main ornamental fountain of Jerash, dedicated to the water nymphs. Built about AD 191, the two-storey construction was elaborately decorated, faced with marble slabs on the lower level, plastered above and topped with a half dome. Water cascaded into a large pool at the front, with the overflow pouring out through seven carved lions' heads.

Although it's been quite some time since water poured forth, the well-preserved structure remains one of the highlights of Jerash. Several finely sculpted Corinthian columns still frame the fountain, and at its foot is a lovely pink-granite basin, which was probably added by the Byzantines. At one point the entire structure was capped by a semi-dome in the shape of a shell, and you can still make out the elaborate capitals lining the base of the ceiling.

Vaulted Gallery RUINS

The vaulted passageway under the courtyard of the Temple of Zeus (p89) is a good starting point in Jerash's ancient city. When your eyes become accustomed to the gloom, you'll see a superb display of columns, pediments and masonry carved with grapes, pomegranates and acanthus leaves. This is the place to brush up on the three main column styles: Doric, Ionic and Corinthian.

Take a look at the model of the Temple of Zeus, as it will help to recreate the ruins in your mind later.

North Gate GATE

Built in about AD 115, the North Gate is an impressive full stop at the northern limit of the Jerash ruins. Commissioned by Claudius Severus, who built the road to Pella, it still makes a fine, if somewhat neglected, frame for the *cardo maximus* (p88), which stretches in all its glory along the entire length of the ancient city.

If you've reached the North Gate, you deserve a pat on the back because very few visitors bother to walk this far.

Southern Tetrapylon MONUMENT

Marking the intersection of the *cardo maximus* with the south *decumanus*, this four-pillared structure is in good repair.

Eastern Baths ROMAN SITE

Jerash's Eastern Baths lie outside the gated city on the other side of the wadi in the modern town. They are lit up at night and are interestingly juxtaposed with a modern mosque, though only real archaeological enthusiasts need seek them out.

Mosque MOSQUE

At the eastern end of the south *decumanus* is a modern mosque, a reminder of how Jordan has embraced many religions over the years and continues to tolerate different forms of worship to this day.

Umayyad Houses RUINS

The unassuming walls of these buildings don't look especially noteworthy, but they're interesting for adding another level of historical accretion in Jerash, this time from the Islamic Umayyad period.

Church of St Theodore RUINS

Little remains of this church apart from the twin colonnades (picturesquely overgrown with wildflowers in spring) and the apse, which overlooks the Courtyard of the Fountain (p89).

Church of St George RUINS

These ruins of a former church are one of the only sites in Jerash to have a few fragments of Byzantine mosaic in situ.

Church of St John the Baptist RUINS

The circular ruins of this church contain patches of original floor mosaics.

Northern Tetrapylon MONUMENT

This archway with four entrances was built over the intersection of Jerash's *cardo maximus* (the main north–south axis) and the north *decumanus* (an east–west street). Rebuilt in 2000, it was probably designed as a gateway to the North Theatre.

Agora MONUMENT

(Macellum) On the western side of the *cardo maximus* is the agora, where people gathered for public meetings around the central fountain.

Western Baths ROMAN SITE

On the eastern side of the *cardo maximus* lie the earthquake-stricken remains of the Western Baths. Dating from the 2nd century AD, the baths were once an impressive complex of hot (*calidarium*), warm (*tepidarium*) and cold (*frigidarium*) baths. In Roman times, public bathing fulfilled the role of a social club and attracted a wide variety of people, who gathered to exchange news and gossip as well as to enjoy music, lectures and performances.

The Western Baths represent one of the earliest examples of a dome atop a square room.

Church of St Cosmos & St Damianus CHURCH

When Christianity became the state religion under Emperor Constantine in 324, all Roman monuments that were tainted by so-called pagan practices were abandoned.

WORTH A TRIP

FESTIVALS & EVENTS

If you happen to be in Jerash in July or August it's worth catching a show in one of its Roman theatres. Since 1981, the city has hosted an annual **Festival of Culture & Arts** (www.facebook.com/Festival.Jarash), which features an eclectic array of performances, including plays, poetry readings, opera and musical concerts from around the world.

Events are listed in English in the official souvenir news sheet, the *Jerash Daily*, printed every day of the festival, and the English-language newspapers published in Amman. Tickets cost around JD10 for events in Jerash. There are also more formal events in Amman, including at the Roman theatre (p54) downtown. Since the events change from year to year, it's best to check online regarding the location of ticketing venues. Several bus companies, including JETT, offer special transport to Jerash, which is useful as public transport usually finishes early in the evening.

These structures were subsequently pilfered for building materials as Roman cities competed with one another to build glorious churches and cathedrals. A total of 15 churches lie among Jerash's ruins, with the Church of St Cosmos & St Damianus (look for a complex with four bulbous columns and a thick outer wall) one of the best preserved.

Consecrated in 533 in memory of twin brothers – both doctors, who devoted themselves to the care of the poor and the needy, and who were martyred during the reign of Diocletian – the church boasts the best-preserved mosaics at Jerash. Stand above the retaining wall and you can clearly make out zoomorphic figures, geometric designs and medical symbols. Some of the mosaics from this church are now housed in the Museum of Popular Traditions (p55) in Amman.

Continue up the hill and just before you reach the great temple in front of you, sit on the stone sarcophagus nearby and survey the view: this is one of the best vantage points in Jerash, showing the extent of the ruins from North Gate to Hadrian's Arch.

Cathedral CHURCH

South of the nymphaeum, an elaborate staircase rises from the *cardo maximus* to Jerash's only cathedral. Little more than a modest Byzantine church, it was constructed in the second half of the 4th century on the site of earlier temples. At the height of its glory the cathedral consisted of a soaring basilica supported by three naves and it boasted a magnificent portal finely decorated with elaborate marble carvings. It's a fascinating insight into the many periods of Jerash's history.

South Decumanus ROMAN SITE

The south *decumanus* at Jerash once served as the Roman town's main east–west axis. At the eastern end is the modern mosque (p90). Take the left fork from the street's western end up to what might be termed 'Church Hill', where a number of ancient churches lie in ruins. The path that runs between the South Theatre (p87) and the Temple of Artemis (p85) offers a good vantage point of the south *decumanus*' double colonnade stretching to the south.

Sleeping

Many people visit Jerash as a day trip from Amman, but an overnight stop is more rewarding. However, with only one hotel in the middle of the town, and only one other place to stay nearby, it's important to book ahead. If you have a car, Ajloun has more accommodation and is only about a 20-minute drive away.

Olive Branch Resort HOTEL **$$**

(02 634 0555; www.olivebranch.com.jo; s/d/tr from JD37/52/63, campsites per own/hired tent JD10/12;) Around 7km from Jerash on the road to Ajloun, this hilltop hotel is situated amid olive groves and pine trees. Refurbished rooms are neat and spacious, some with balconies, others in a separate annexe below the gardens. Country fare is served in the airy restaurant.

Unstructured camping is possible in the grounds. Call ahead for bookings, as the hotel is popular for NGO and business retreats.

Hadrian Gate Hotel HOTEL **$$**

(07 7779 3907; s/d/tr/penthouses from JD25/40/50/70;) The only hotel in Jerash boasts a spectacular location overlooking

Hadrian's Arch (p85). Breakfast is served on the rooftop terraces, boasting a panoramic view of the Temple of Artemis (p85) to the west and Jerash's market gardens to the east. A range of private rooms with shared bathrooms are humble but spotless; the host's hospitality makes up for the simple amenities.

Eating

Modern Jerash is a bustling town with several outdoor markets, as well as a smattering of kebab and falafel shops. There's a string of no-fuss restaurants on the main street opposite the entrance to the ruins, but there's only one place to buy refreshments inside the ruins proper.

Jordan House Restaurant BUFFET **$$**
(buffet JD7; 8am-9pm;) Serving a comprehensive buffet between 11am and 5pm, this friendly establishment at the entrance to the Jerash ruins is a good place for a Turkish coffee before starting out, and a fresh lemon and mint drink over lunch on your return.

Jerash Rest House BUFFET **$$**
(02 635 1437; buffet JD8; noon-8pm) The only restaurant inside the Jerash ruins, this is a welcome stop for weary visitors. Located near the South Gate, it attracts large volumes of tourists, but service is quick and efficient, and it serves alcohol. The lunch buffet and barbecue is more conducive to an afternoon nap than a jaunt round ancient Jerash, but it's tasty nonetheless.

★**Lebanese House** LEBANESE **$$$**
(02 635 1301; www.facebook.com/LebaneseUmKhalil; meals JD10-18; 11am-1am;) Nicknamed 'Umm Khalil', this rambling restaurant, a 10-minute walk from Jerash's centre, has been a national treasure since it opened in 1977. On offer are plenty of sizzling and cold mezze and freshly baked bread, as well as superior salads and mouth-watering grills. If you can't decide what to sample, try the set menu for a selection of the best dishes.

The indoor and outdoor seating gets busy with local families after 9pm.

Drinking & Nightlife

Jerash isn't a place for nightlife, although Lebanese House serves alcohol – a few drinks and plates of mezze make for a very pleasant evening.

Information

MAPS

Published by the Jordan Tourism Board, the free *Jerash* brochure includes a map, some photos and a recommended walking route. It can be found at the visitor centre (p89) in Jerash.

Anyone with a particular interest in the history of Jerash should pick up one of three decent pocket-size guides: *Jerash: The Roman City*, *Jerash: A Unique Example of a Roman City* or (the most comprehensive and readable) *Jerash*. All three are available at bookshops in Amman. *Jerash* by Iain Browning gives a more detailed historical account.

TOURIST INFORMATION

Near the South Gate, the visitor centre has informative descriptions and reconstructions of many buildings in Jerash, as well as a good relief map of the ancient city. The site's **ticket office** (02 635 1272) is in a modern souq with souvenir and antique shops, a post office and a semi-traditional coffeehouse. Keep your ticket, as you'll have to show it at the South Gate.

Toilets are available at the site entrance (inside the souvenir souq), at Jerash Rest House and at the visitor centre.

It's possible to leave limited luggage at Jerash Rest House, for no charge, while you visit the site.

Getting There & Away

Jerash is located approximately 50km north of Amman, and the roads are well signposted from the capital, especially from 8th Circle. If you're driving, note that this route can get extremely congested during the morning and afternoon rush hours.

From the North Bus Station (Tabarbour) in Amman, public buses and minibuses (800 fils, 1¼ hours) leave regularly for Jerash, though they can take an hour to fill up. Leave early for a quick getaway, especially if you're planning a day trip.

Jerash's bus and service-taxi station is a 15-minute walk southwest of the ruins, at the second set of traffic lights, behind the big white building. You can pick up a minibus to the station from outside the visitor centre for a few fils. From here, there are also plenty of minibuses travelling regularly to Irbid (JD1, 45 minutes) and Ajloun (500 fils, 30 minutes) until around 4pm. You can normally flag down the bus to Amman from the main junction in front of the site to save the trek to the bus station.

Transport drops off significantly after 5pm. Service taxis sometimes leave up to 8pm (later during the Jerash Festival) from the bus station, but this is not guaranteed.

A private taxi between Amman and Jerash should cost around JD20 each way. From Jerash, a taxi to Irbid costs around JD15.

Dibeen Forest Reserve
محمية غابات دبين

Established in 2004, this **nature reserve** (www.rscn.org.jo/content/dibeen-forest-reserve) FREE consists of an 8-sq-km area of Aleppo pine and oak forest. Managed by the Royal Society for the Conservation of Nature (RSCN), Dibeen is representative of the wild forests that once covered much of the country's northern frontiers but which now account for only 1% of Jordan's land area. Despite its small size, Dibeen is recognised as a national biodiversity hot spot and protects 17 endangered animals (including the Persian squirrel) and several rare orchids.

There are some short marked (but unmapped) hiking trails through the park. In March and April carpets of red-crown anemones fill the meadows beneath the pine-forested and sometimes snowcapped hills. Most trails are either small vehicle tracks or stony paths, some of which continue beyond the park's boundaries. The area is very popular with local picnickers on Fridays, and litter is a problem. The park is only usefully accessed by car. Follow the signs from Jerash and expect to get lost! Keep heading for the obvious hillside woodland as you pass through nearby hamlets and you'll eventually stumble on the entrance.

Ajloun
عجلون

☎02 / POP 9990 / ELEV 744M

It may look a bit rough around the edges, but Ajloun (or Ajlun) is founded on an ancient market town and boasts a 600-year-old mosque with a fine stone-dressed minaret. Most visitors, however, don't come to experience this chaotic little hub and its limited attractions: they come for the impressive castle perched atop a nearby hill, where it has commanded the high ground for nearly 1000 years.

With the biblical site of Mar Elias and one of Jordan's best nature reserves in the vicinity, Ajloun makes a good base for a couple of days of exploration. It's also reasonably close to Jerash (30 minutes by minibus, 20 minutes by car), offering alternative accommodation and making a rewarding weekend circuit from Amman.

Sights

★Ajloun Castle CASTLE

(Qala'at Ar Rabad; JD3, with Jordan Pass free) This historic castle was built atop Mt 'Auf (1250m) between 1184 and 1188 by one of Saladin's generals, 'Izz ad Din Usama bin Munqidh (who was also Saladin's nephew). The castle commands views of the Jordan Valley and three wadis leading into it, making it an important strategic link in the defensive chain against the Crusaders and a counterpoint to the Crusader Belvoir Fort on the Sea of Galilee in present-day Israel and the Palestinian Territories.

The castle was enlarged in 1214 with the addition of a new gate in the southeastern corner, and once boasted seven towers as well as a 15m-deep dry moat. With its hilltop position, Qala'at Ar Rabad was one in a chain of beacons and pigeon posts that enabled messages to be transmitted from Damascus to Cairo in a single day. The rearing of pigeons is still a popular pastime in the area.

After the Crusader threat subsided, the castle was largely destroyed by Mongol invaders in 1260, only to be almost immediately rebuilt by the Mamluks. In the 17th

THE JORDAN TRAIL: AJLOUN TO FUHEIS

Distance 60km

Duration Four days

Ajloun Castle provides a dramatic starting point for this section of the Jordan Trail. The route begins amid pine forest and olive groves as you hike down along the cliffs of Wadi Mahmoud to the village of Khirbet Al Souq. The following day leads you to the spectacular King Talal Dam and its reservoir. Country tracks take you towards Rmeimeen, a typical village in this area, with its mosque and church side by side. You're briefly shaken from rural life as you rise up from the valley to cross the main highway at Al Ahliyya, but it's a reminder that you're near your reward for finishing this section of the trail: a cold beer at Jordan's only microbrewery, Carakale (p68), in Fuheis.

This section of the trail is particularly good for wild camping. Visit www.jordantrail.org for route maps, GPS waypoints and detailed breakdowns of daily hikes.

century an Ottoman garrison was stationed here, after which it was used by local villagers. Earthquakes in 1837 and 1927 badly damaged the castle, though slow and steady restoration is continuing.

Note that there is a useful explanation in English just inside the main gate, and a small museum containing pots, snatches of mosaics and some intriguing medieval hand grenades. Apart from this, nothing else in the castle is signposted, although not much explanation is needed to bring the place to life, especially given that the views from these lofty heights are nothing short of spectacular.

The castle is a tough 3km uphill walk from the town centre, but minibuses very occasionally go to the top (about 100 fils). Alternatively, take a taxi from Ajloun (JD1 to JD2 each way). The visitor centre and ticket office is about 500m downhill from the castle entrance; there's a small scale model of the castle on display here and, perhaps more usefully, clean toilets.

Mar Elias ARCHAEOLOGICAL SITE

(8am-7pm Apr-Oct, to 4pm Nov-Mar) FREE This little-visited archaeological site, believed to be the birthplace of the prophet Elijah, gives you just the excuse you need to explore the countryside around Ajloun. To be honest, it's not a spectacular site by any stretch of the imagination, though it's worth visiting for its religious and historical significance.

Sleeping

There are two hotels on the road up to the castle, either of which is a good option if you want to enjoy the sunset from the castle ramparts.

Ajloun Hotel HOTEL $

(02 642 0524; s/d JD27/35;) This is a handy option for an early morning visit to the castle (p93), as it's located just 1km down the road. There's a comfortable lounge area in the foyer, and decent basic rooms. Choose a top-floor room for grand views of the countryside.

Mountain Castle Hotel HOTEL $

(07 9565 6726, 02 642 0202; s/d from JD28/38;) This busy little hotel boasts a gorgeous garden terrace of flowering jasmine, grapevines and roses – enjoying your meals here will be a highlight of your stay. The decor is a tad tired and the furnishings on the minimal side, but there are expansive views from many of the rooms.

Eating

There are a few places for a snack and a drink at the entrance to Ajloun Castle. You can pick up supplies in Ajloun's grocery stores, supplement your rations with freshly picked fruit from the many roadside fruit stands, and head into the surrounding hills for a picnic.

Abu Alezz Restaurant JORDANIAN $

(Abdallah bin Hussein St; meals JD2-4; 10am-9pm) Near the main roundabout, this restaurant has cheap and tasty standard Jordanian fare, including grilled chicken, hummus and shawarma (meat sliced off a spit and stuffed in a pocket of pita-type bread with chopped tomatoes and garnish).

Barhoum JORDANIAN $

(Abdallah bin Hussein St; meals JD2-6; 10am-9pm) In central Ajloun, and handy for grilled meats, hummus, salads and the like.

Getting There & Away

Ajloun is approximately 75km northwest of Amman and 30km northwest of Jerash. The castle can be clearly seen from most places in the area – if you're driving or walking, take the signposted road (Al Qala'a St) heading west at the main roundabout in the centre of Ajloun. The narrow streets of the town centre can be horribly congested at times.

From the centre of town, minibuses travel regularly to Jerash (800 fils, 30 minutes), along a scenic road and Irbid (JD1, 45 minutes). From Amman (JD1, two hours), minibuses leave half-hourly from the North Bus Station.

Ajloun Forest Reserve

محمية غابات عجلون

Located in the Ajloun Highlands, this small (just 13 sq km) but vitally important **nature reserve** (02 647 5673; www.wildjordan.com; per day JD2.500) was established by the RSCN in 1988 to protect oak, carob, pistachio and strawberry-tree forests. The reserve also acts as a sanctuary for the endangered roe deer, as well as wild boar, stone martens, polecats, jackals and even grey wolves. The landscape of rolling hills and mixed forest is lovely, especially if you've been spending a few too many hours in Jordan's deserts or congested capital.

The RSCN has developed a good network of **hiking trails**, with a variety of paths suited to hikers of all fitness levels. At the edge of the reserve, the villages of Orjan, Rasoun and Baoun have linked together in a

WORTH A TRIP

COMMUNITY TOURISM ON THE AL AYOUN TRAIL

The villages around Ajloun have been at the forefront of developing community-tourism projects in Jordan. At the heart of this is the 12km Al Ayoun Trail, linking the three villages of Orjan, Rasoun and Baoun to the ruins at Mar Elias, and managed by the cooperative Al Ayoun Society (p95). The scenery is delightful, but the real point is to enable visitors to hike through the villages and interact with the community, stopping for tea, tasting fresh bread and produce, and meeting farmers with their animals. This makes taking a local guide an essential part of the experience; you can expect to pay around JD50, knowing that 100% of the money stays in the community. The Al Ayoun Society has also helped several families set up their houses as homestays. There's no better or more enjoyable way to learn about the local area. Talk to lead organisers Eisa Dweekat and Mohammed Sawlmeh to make arrangements for both walking and homestays.

For extended hikes in the area, including in Ajloun Forest Reserve, to Ajloun Castle and as far away as Pella, pick up a copy of Di Taylor and Tony Howard's excellent *Walks, Treks, Climbs & Caves in Al Ayoun, Jordan*. It offers 20 routes lasting from two hours to two days, with detailed maps and GPS waypoints, as well as information on rock climbing and caving in the area.

community-tourism initiative to promote hiking in the area with their own Al Ayoun Trail; they also offer homestays with local families.

Sights

The Royal Society for the Conservation of Nature (RSCN) supports a number of community projects in and near the reserve to help develop new sources of income for the local population. These small-scale, high-value projects include three workshops that produce olive-oil soap, screen-printed items and traditional Jordanian cuisine, all of which can be purchased on-site or in the reserve's Nature Shop. The three workshops are free to visit. Pick up a map from the visitor centre (p96) before you set out – it'll call ahead to make sure they open up for you.

House of Calligraphy WORKSHOP

(Orjan; by appointment via Wild Jordan) You don't have to be a linguistic scholar to enjoy the dynamic rhythms of Arabic script. Reinforcing Islamic heritage, the women in this workshop aim to educate visitors about Arab culture, and there's even an opportunity to try your hand at calligraphy as you use a reed to write your name in Arabic.

Biscuit House WORKSHOP

(Orjan; by appointment via Wild Jordan) Delicious Jordanian delicacies are prepared for sale in RSCN Nature Shops in this cottage-industry kitchen. With an on-site cafe selling locally produced herbal teas, olive-oil crisps, and molasses and tahini sandwich cookies, it's tempting to stay until morning.

Soap House WORKSHOP

(Orjan; by appointment via Wild Jordan) Ever wondered what pomegranate soap smells like? Local women demonstrate the art of making all kinds of health-promoting soaps using natural local ingredients and comprising 90% pure olive oil. Pomegranate is one of a dozen exotic fragrances.

Activities

Ajloun is great walking country. In addition to a spur of the Jordan Trail, there are lots of local hikes leading from Ajloun Forest Reserve. It's important to arrange return transport at the visitor centre (p96) before you leave on any hike except the Roe Deer and Rockrose Trails. Trails are maintained by the RSCN and each has a specific hiking fee. For most trails, a guide (included in the fee, along with the reserve entrance fee) is compulsory.

An excellent local-tourism cooperative, **Al Ayoun Society** (07 9682 9111, 07 7973 4776; www.facebook.com/alayounsociety), based in Orjan village can arrange guides for the Al Ayoun Trail as well as homestays in Orjan and Rasoun. Taking its guides on the trail is one of the best ways to discover the Jordanian countryside and village life.

Roe Deer Trail

If you're just stopping by for the day, the 2km, self-guided Roe Deer Trail is included in the reserve entrance fee. It starts from the accommodation area, looping over a nearby hill – past a 1600-year-old stone wine press and lots of wildflowers (in April) – and returning via a roe-deer enclosure.

Soap House Trail

This guided 7km trail (three hours, JD16.500) combines a visit to the reserve's oldest strawberry tree with a panoramic vista at Eagle's Viewpoint. Descending from the 1100m lookout, the trail leads through evergreen woodland to the Soap House (p95), where enterprising women make natural olive-oil soap.

Orjan Village Trail

A guide is needed for this rural 12km trail (six hours, JD26 including meal) that weaves alongside a brook, passing poplar trees and orchards. The olive trees at the end of the hike date back to Roman times. The trail is open April to October only.

Rockrose Trail

This scenic 8km trail (four hours, JD16.500) involves some steep scrambling and requires a guide. The route passes through heavily wooded valleys, near rocky ridges and alongside olive groves and offers sweeping views of the West Bank. The trail is open April to October only.

Prophet's Trail

Terminating at the archaeological site of Mar Elias (p94), where it's said the prophet Elijah was born, this 8.5km guided route (four hours, JD22 including packed lunch) winds through fig and pear orchards. At Wadi Shiteau the trail plunges into a dense forest of oaks and strawberry trees.

Ajloun Castle Trail

With prior arrangement, it's possible to continue hiking from Mar Elias for another 9.5km through Wadi Al Jubb to Ajloun Castle (p93) – a tough extra four hours over rough and steep terrain. The trail is 'donkey assisted', which helps considerably on the difficult final ascent towards the castle

Sleeping & Eating

There are two choices: stay in the Ajloun reserve itself, or at a homestay in one of the nearby villages. The Al Ayoun Society can arrange meals with families in the local homestays if you contact it in advance.

★ Al Ayoun Homestays HOMESTAY **$$**
(☎ 07 9682 9111, 07 7973 4776; www.facebook.com/alayounsociety; homestays around JD20-40) The Al Ayoun Society is a local community-tourism initiative that can arrange homestays in the lovely rural village of Orjan near Ajloun, where a stream, olive groves and ancient poplars make a pleasant change from the dusty hills of Ajloun. Several families offer their houses as B&Bs, where you're guaranteed a warm welcome and delicious home-cooked food.

Ajloun Reserve Cabins CABIN **$$$**
(☎ 02 647 5673; s/d/tr with shared bathroom from JD82/93/105, deluxe cabins s/d/tr JD105/116/128) These rustic cabins with terraces overlooking a patch of forest make for a delightful retreat. Regular cabins share environmentally sound composting toilets and solar-heated showers; the stylish deluxe cabins are en suite. Lunch and dinner are available by reservation in the tented rooftop restaurant, though you can always cook for yourself on the barbecues. Bring plenty of mosquito repellent in summer.

Rooftop Restaurant JORDANIAN **$$$**
(☎ 02 647 5673; buffet JD14) Meals are available in this tented rooftop restaurant at Ajloun reserve (p94) if you give them some notice. From the rooftop, check out the great views of snowcapped Jabal Ash Sheikh (Mt Hermon; 2814m) on the Syria–Lebanon border.

Information

At the entrance to the reserve is a modest **visitor centre** (www.wildjordan.com; ⌚ dawn-dusk) with a helpful reception where you'll find information and maps on the reserve and its flora and fauna. There's also a Nature Shop selling locally produced handicrafts.

You should book accommodation and meals in advance with the RSCN through its Wild Jordan Center (p69) in Amman. If you're planning to take a guided hike, you must book 48 hours ahead. Guided hikes require a minimum of four people and start at JD9 per person, depending on the choice of trail.

Getting There & Away

You can reach the reserve by hiring a taxi from Ajloun (around JD6, 9km); ask the visitor centre to book one for your departure. If you're driving, the reserve is well signposted. Take the road from Ajloun towards Irbid and make a left turn by a petrol station 5km from Ajloun towards the village of Ishfateena. About 300m from the junction, take a right and follow the signs to the reserve, which is next to the village of Umm Al Yanabi.

IRBID & AROUND

Jordan's far-flung northern hills were once popular with those heading overland to Syria, but these days see relatively few travellers. This is a shame as the region's rolling hills and verdant valleys are home to characterful rural villages, country lanes overrun by goats, and ubiquitous olive groves among whose ancient trunks lie the scattered remains of forgotten eras.

And then, of course, there is Irbid. This thriving university town is generally overlooked by visitors, despite some national treasures; in this densely populated part of the country, Irbid is a key place in which to feel the pulse of modern Jordan.

All minibuses, in whatever village you find them, appear to make a beeline for Irbid, from where connections can be made to almost anywhere in the country. With a car, it's possible to visit the remote battleground of Yarmouk or the ruins of the Decapolis city of Umm Qais as a day trip from Irbid.

Irbid إربد

02 / POP 502,700 / ELEV 582M

Jordan's second-largest city is something of a glorified university town. Home to Yarmouk University, which is regarded as one of the most elite centres of learning in the Middle East, Irbid is in many ways more lively and progressive than staid Amman. The campus, which is located just south of the city centre, is home to shady pedestrian streets lined with outdoor restaurants and cafes. Since the start of the crisis in Syria, Irbid has taken in large numbers of refugees, who live in the city itself or in the extensive camp on the outskirts.

Historians and archaeologists have identified Irbid as the Decapolis (p88) city of Arbela. The area likely predates the Romans, with significant grave sites suggesting settlement since the Bronze Age. Aside from the tell lying at the centre of town, however, there is little evidence today of such antiquity.

Sights

Dar As Saraya Museum MUSEUM

(02 724 5613; Al Baladia St; JD2, with Jordan Pass free; 8am-6pm) Located in a stunning old villa of basaltic rock that's located just behind the town hall, this museum is an interesting diversion. Built in 1886 by the Ottomans, the building is typical of the caravanserai established along the Syrian pilgrimage route, with rooms arranged around a paved internal courtyard. It was used as a prison until 1994 and now houses a delightful collection of local artefacts illustrating Irbid's long history.

Museum of Archaeology & Anthropology MUSEUM

(02 721 1111; 10am-1.45pm & 3-4.30pm Sun-Thu) FREE This museum features exhibits from all eras of Jordanian history. The collection opens with 9000-year-old Neolithic statuettes found near Amman, covers the Bronze and Iron Ages, continues through the Mamluk and Ottoman occupations, and closes with modern displays on rural Bedouin life. One of the highlights is a reconstruction of a traditional Arab pharmacy and smithy. The Numismatic Hall has some fascinating displays on the history of money over 2600 years. All displays are labelled in English.

Beit Arar MUSEUM

(9am-5pm Sun-Thu) FREE Set up to host occasional cultural events, Beit Arar is located off Al Hashemi St in a superb old Damascene-style house. The rooms are set around a courtyard paved with volcanic black stones, and there are photo displays on Arar, one of Jordan's finest poets, as well as some of his manuscripts.

Sleeping

There's little pressing reason to stay in Irbid, which is fortunate, as the hotel standard is not high.

Omayah Hotel HOTEL $

(02 724 5955; omayahhotel@yahoo.com; King Hussein St; s/d JD24/32) Decent value for money, this budget hotel boasts satellite TV and fridges, as well as large picture windows overlooking the heart of the city. The friendly proprietor is kind and helpful, and solo women will feel comfortable here. Rooms towards the back of the property and away from the main road are a bit quieter.

Al Joude Hotel HOTEL $$

(02 727 5515; s/d/tr from JD35/40/55; @) Located near the campus of Yarmouk University, off University St. Rooms are spacious but tired. The hotel has a popular cafe (p98) and restaurant (p99).

Irbid

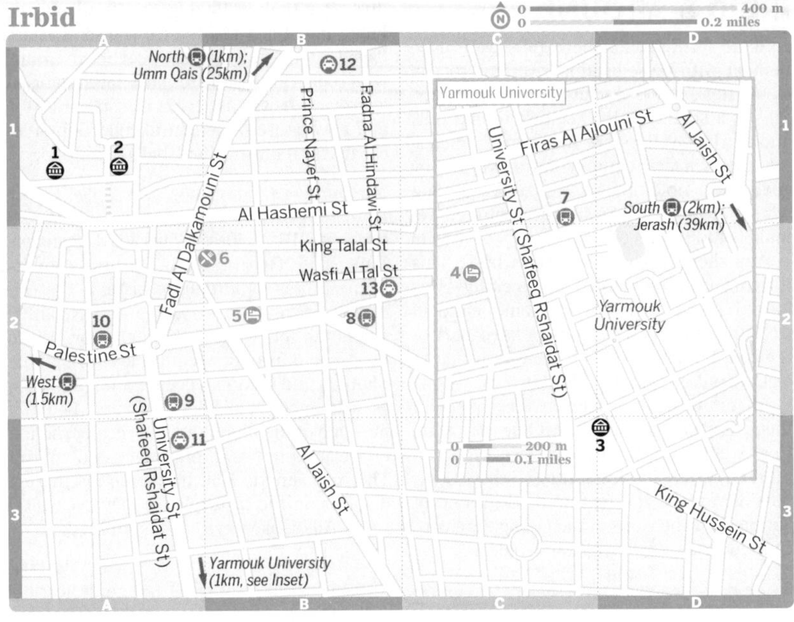

Irbid

Sights

1 Beit Arar A1
2 Dar As Saraya Museum A1
3 Museum of Archaeology & Anthropology D3

Sleeping

4 Al Joude Hotel C2
5 Omayah Hotel B2

Eating

Al Joude Garden Restaurant .... (see 4)
Alia Supermarket .... (see 5)
6 Clock Tower Restaurant B2
News Café .... (see 4)

Transport

7 Minibus & Service Taxis to Downtown C1
8 Minibus to Amman's South Bus Station B2
9 Minibus to Irbid University A2
10 Minibus to West Bus Station A2
11 Service Taxi to Irbid University A3
12 Service Taxis to Amman's North Bus Station B1
13 Service Taxis to Amman's South Bus Station B2

Eating

University St has the greatest congregation of eating spots, all patronised by students. The fare's pretty standard, but the real attraction is the evening vibe: after 9pm the streets swell with crowds looking for a good night out and seeming to find it on the promenade between roundabouts.

The street market sells all manner of fresh fruit from northern orchards.

Clock Tower Restaurant JORDANIAN $
(Al Jaish St; meals JD3-5; ⊙8.30am-11.30pm) The name of this popular local is written in Arabic, but as it's right next to the clock tower and has a huge spit of shawarma roasting in the window, it's hard to miss. There's a family seating area upstairs for a bit of peace and quiet, and the Jordanian staple dishes are cheap, cheerful and delicious.

News Café CAFE $
(pizza JD2.500; ⊙10am-midnight) Downstairs from the Al Joude Hotel, this is one of the most popular gathering places for Irbid's cool set. Styled along the lines of a Western-style coffee shop, the News Café is warm and inviting, offering coffee, milkshakes, pizza and other snacks. It's off University St.

Alia Supermarket SUPERMARKET $
(King Hussein St) Self-caterers and would-be picnickers should head to this supermarket near the Omayah Hotel (p97); it has a good selection of local produce, including the region's justifiably famous olives.

Al Joude Garden Restaurant JORDANIAN $$
(mixed-grill meals JD5-10) Students, visiting parents and local families crowd into the courtyard outside Al Joude Hotel (p97) to sip fresh fruit juices and smoke a strawberry shisha (water pipe). The waiters are kept in a constant state of rush in this teeming venue as they are summoned for hot embers and top-ups of Turkish coffee – expect long waits for food orders. It's off University St.

Drinking & Nightlife

Irbid has its share of grungy bars, where the testosterone is on tap as much as the beer. Stick to the student-friendly coffee shops if you want a more genial night out.

Getting There & Away

Approximately 85km north of Amman, Irbid is home to three main minibus/taxi stations.

From the **North Bus Station** (Tabarbour), there are minibuses to Umm Qais (45 minutes), Mukheiba (for Al Himma; one hour) and Quwayliba (for the ruins of Abila; 25 minutes); fares are between 400 fils and JD1.

From the large **South Bus Station** (new Amman bus station; Wahadat), air-conditioned Hijazi buses (JD2, 90 minutes) leave every 15 to 20 minutes between 6am and 7pm for Amman's North Bus Station. There are also less comfortable buses and minibuses from Amman's North Bus Station (less than JD1, about two hours) and plenty of service taxis (JD1). Minibuses also leave the South Bus Station for Ajloun (45 minutes) and Jerash (45 minutes); fares are around 800 fils.

From the **West Bus Station** (Mujamma Al Gharb Al Jadid), about 1.5km west of the centre, minibuses go to Al Mashari'a (45 minutes) for the ruins at Pella, Sheikh Hussein Bridge (for Israel and the Palestinian Territories; 45 minutes) and Shuneh Ash Shamaliyyeh (North Shuna; one hour); fares are between 800 fils and JD1.200.

Getting Around

Getting between Irbid's various bus stations is easy, with service taxis (200 fils) and minibuses (100 fils) shuttling between them and the centre. Service taxis and minibuses to the South Bus Station can be picked up on Radna Al Hindawi St; for service taxis to the North Bus Station, head to Prince Nayef St. For the West Bus Station, take a bus from Palestine St, just west of the roundabout.

The standard taxi fare from the centre (Al Bilad) to the university (Al Jammiya) is 500 fils; few taxis use meters in Irbid.

A minibus from University St to the university gate costs 200 fils. There are also service taxis, or it's a 25-minute walk. There's a stop on Abdel Qadir Al Tall St for minibuses and service taxis back downtown.

Irbid's traffic is notoriously bad. If you have a car, be aware that the congestion, one-way roads and lack of parking can make driving a stressful experience.

Abila (Quwayliba)

ابيلا (قويلبة)

Lying 10km north of Irbid, between the hills of Tell Abila and Tell Umm Al Amad, are the remains of the Decapolis (p88) city of **Abila** (daylight hours) FREE. Largely unexcavated, the site isn't set up for visitors, but you don't need a guide to find the Roman-Byzantine theatre or the scattered remains of columns from the markets, temples and baths. Buses leave from Irbid's North Bus Station for Quwayliba (less than JD1, 25 minutes), near the site; ask the driver to drop you at the ruins.

Yarmouk Battleground

If you have a car and are intrigued to know why all roads out of Irbid seem to lead to Yarmouk battleground, follow the signs northeast towards the village of Saham Al Kfarat. The site is of great significance to Muslim Arabs, as this was where, on 12 August 636, an army of 40,000 Arabs confronted 125,000 Byzantine fighters and emerged victorious.

A lot of blood was spilled that day, with 4000 Arabs and 80,000 of their adversaries killed, and the battleground remains something of a pilgrimage site even now. The signposted road from Irbid leads not to the battleground itself but to a spectacular viewpoint, high above the Yarmouk River, which marks the border with Syria. The battle took place in the valley below, but from this vantage point it's easy to see how the disciplined, motivated, mobile and homogeneous Arabs, united by faith and good leadership, were able to overcome the mercenary Byzantine groups. The latter, who had no belief in the fight, lacked strategy and were ill-disciplined, and they were particularly disadvantaged by their heavy armour – as can easily be imagined on a hot August day as you look down at the steep, sun-parched hillsides opposite the viewpoint. The viewpoint, which has an interpretative plaque and a monument but no facilities, is not accessible by public transport. By car, it's a 30-minute drive from Irbid; don't give up on the signs – they're just widely spaced. A shortcut to Umm Qais is signposted halfway between the viewpoint and Irbid.

THE JORDAN VALLEY

The Jordan Valley and the hills that surround it are well worth exploring for the scenery, archaeological sites in Pella and Umm Qais, and community-tourism projects in the latter, overlooking the Sea of Galilee in Israel and the Palestinian Territories. The valley has supported human settlement since antiquity, sustained by the rich soil that to this day makes farming a logical pursuit. Visitors will be struck by the contrast between the olive-growing hillsides and the subtropical Jordan Valley; they will also probably note the heavily policed border with Israel and the Palestinian Territories, which runs along the length of the river. The valley has been the site of conflict for centuries and it's still a sensitive area, as disputes about territory give way to concerns over water.

The Jordan Valley is easily accessible from Amman, so many people visit as a day trip. However, Umm Qais has one of the most charming guesthouses in the country, making a longer visit to the area more feasible. Umm Qais has the best eating options in the area. You can also stop at roadside stalls and treat yourself to some fresh local produce straight from the farm.

Getting There & Away

There's plenty of public transport plying the valley from village to village, with Irbid as the main hub. With a car, however, it's considerably easier to make side trips from the valley floor (which is well below sea level) to places of interest above sea level, such as the ruins at Pella or the bustling town of Salt. It takes about 1½ hours to drive the full length of the valley.

The valley has two of Jordan's three border posts with Israel and the Palestinian Territories: at the King Hussein and Sheikh Hussein Bridges. Even if you're not crossing, don't forget your passport to show at the numerous police checkpoints.

THE JORDAN VALLEY

Forming part of the Great Rift Valley that runs from Africa to Syria, the fertile valley of the Jordan River was of considerable significance in biblical times, and is now regarded as the food bowl of Jordan.

The hot, dry summers and short, mild winters make for ideal growing conditions, and (subject to water restrictions) two or three crops are grown every year. The main ones are tomatoes, cucumbers, melons and citrus fruits, many of which are cultivated under plastic.

The Jordan River rises from several sources, mainly the Anti-Lebanon Range in Syria, and flows south into the Sea of Galilee, 212m below sea level, before draining into the Dead Sea. The actual length of the river is 360km, but as the crow flies the distance between its source and the Dead Sea is only 200km.

It was in the Jordan Valley, some 10,000 years ago, that people first started to plant crops and abandon their nomadic lifestyle for permanent settlements. Villages were built and primitive irrigation schemes were undertaken; by 3000 BC produce from the valley was being exported to neighbouring regions, much as it is today.

The Jordan River is revered by Christians, mainly because Jesus is said to have been baptised in its waters by John the Baptist at the site of Bethany-Beyond-the-Jordan. Centuries earlier, Joshua is believed to have led the Israelite armies across the Jordan River near Tell Nimrin (Beth Nimrah in the Bible) after the death of Moses, marking the symbolic transition from the wilderness to the land of milk and honey.

Since 1948 the Jordan River has marked the boundary between Jordan and Israel and the Palestinian Territories, from the Sea of Galilee to the Yarmouk River.

During the 1967 war with Israel, Jordan lost the West Bank, and the population on the Jordanian east bank of the valley dwindled from 60,000 before the war to 5000 by 1971. During the 1970s, new roads and fully serviced villages were built and the population has now soared to more than 100,000.

Mukheiba المخيبة

☎02 / POP 1500 / ELEV -130M

If you're staying in Umm Qais or visiting the Yarmouk Battleground (p99) viewpoint, you may be interested to descend to the hot springs of **Al Himma** in the village of Mukheiba. At the confluence of the Yarmouk and Jordan Rivers, you can gain a good idea of the battle site from the ground, although access to the site proper is currently restricted.

Several of the hikes and bike tours offered by Baraka Destinations in Umm Qais visit Mukheiba and include access to the hot springs.

Getting There & Away

Mukheiba marks the northernmost reach of Jordan's portion of the Jordan Valley, 10km north of Umm Qais. The town can be reached via a scenic road (with checkpoints – carry your passport) giving views of the Golan Heights and the Sea of Galilee across the border in Israel and the Palestinian Territories. Public transport is not reliable here, so you'll need your own vehicle.

Umm Qais (Gadara) أم قيس

☎02 / POP 6100 / ELEV 310M

In the northwestern corner of Jordan, in the hills above the Jordan Valley, are the ruins of the Decapolis (p88) city of **Gadara** (JD3, with Jordan Pass free), now called Umm Qais. The site is striking because of its juxtaposition of Roman ruins with an abandoned Ottoman-era village, as well as its tremendous vantage point, with views of three countries (Jordan, Syria, and Israel and the Palestinian Territories), encompassing the Golan Heights, Mt Hermon and the Sea of Galilee.

According to the Bible, it was here that Jesus performed the miracle of the Gadarene swine: casting the demons out of two men into a herd of pigs.

Today Umm Qais is at the forefront of community-tourism development in Jordan, and it's worth staying a night or two to enjoy an increasing array of options, from hiking and biking to beekeeping, foraging and cooking classes.

History

The ancient town of Gadara was ruled by a series of powerful nations, including the Ptolemies, the Seleucids, the Jews and, from 63 BC, the Romans, who transformed the town into one of the great cities of the Decapolis.

Herod the Great was given Gadara following a naval victory and he ruled over it until his death in 4 BC – much to the disgruntlement of locals, who tried everything to put him out of favour with Rome. On his death the city reverted to semi-autonomy as part of the Roman province of Syria, and it flourished in various guises until the 7th century when, in common with other cities of the Decapolis, it lost its trading connections and became little more than a backwater.

The town was partially rebuilt during the Ottoman Empire and many structures from this period, built in the typical black basaltic rock of the region, remain well preserved alongside the earlier Roman ruins. The Ottomans used the town as a tax-collection centre. They called it M'keis, but a 1960s government census mistook the local accent of residents and transcribed the town's name as Umm Qais, which has stuck with official sanction ever since.

In 1806 Gadara was 'discovered' by Western explorers, but excavation did not commence in earnest until the early 1980s. Considerable restoration of the Roman ruins has taken place, but this involved the removal of families who had lived in the ruins for generations.

Sights

★West Theatre RUINS

Entering Umm Qais from the south, the first structure of interest is the well-restored and brooding West Theatre. Constructed from black basalt, it once seated about 3000 people. This is a place to sing or declaim a soliloquy – the acoustics are fantastic.

Lookout Point VIEWPOINT

This viewpoint offers tremendous vistas over Israel and the Palestinian Territories across the Sea of Galilee and the Golan Heights.

Decumanus Maximus ROMAN SITE

Still paved to this day, the main road through the site once linked Gadara with other nearby ancient cities such as Abila (p99) and Pella (p105). In its heyday, the road extended as far as the Mediterranean coast.

Museum MUSEUM

(☎02 750 0072; 8am-6pm Sat-Thu, to 4pm Fri) FREE Housed in Beit Russan, the former residence of an Ottoman governor, this modest museum is set around an elegant and tranquil courtyard of fig trees. The main mosaic on display (dating from the 4th century

Umm Qais (Gadara)

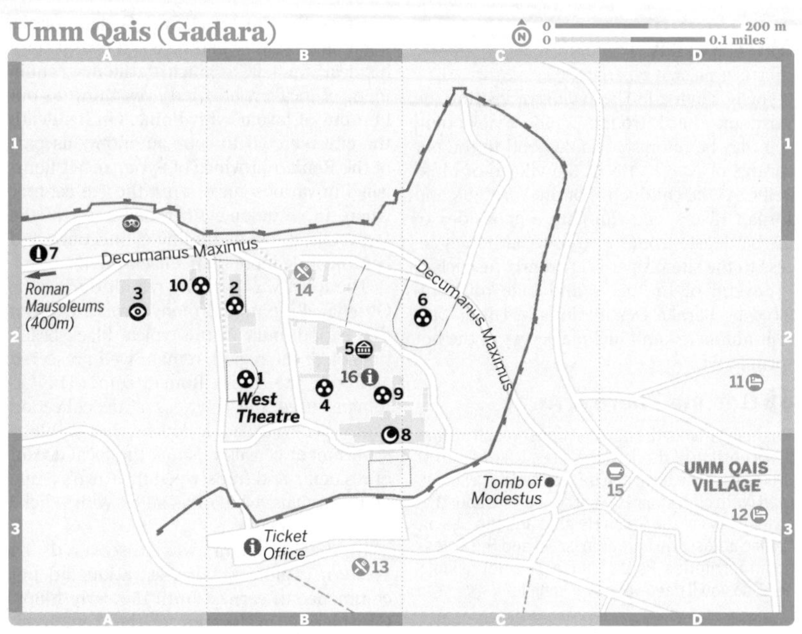

Umm Qais (Gadara)

Top Sights

1 West Theatre ... B2

Sights

2 Basilica Terrace ... B2
3 Baths ... A2
4 Gadara ... B2
5 Museum ... B2
6 North Theatre ... C2
7 Nymphaeum ... A2
8 Ottoman Mosque ... B3
9 Ottoman Village ... B2
10 Shops ... A2

Sleeping

11 Beit Al Baraka ... D2
12 Umm Qais Hotel ... D3

Eating

13 Shine Cottage Grilling ... B3
14 Umm Qais Resthouse ... B2

Drinking & Nightlife

15 Beit Al Baraka Cafe ... D3

Information

16 Baraka Destinations ... B2

and found in one of the tombs) illustrates the names of early Christian notables. Another highlight is the headless white-marble statue of the Hellenic goddess Tyche, which was found sitting in the front row of the West Theatre.

Baths ROMAN SITE

West along the *decumanus maximus* are the overgrown public baths. Built in the 4th century, this would once have been an impressive complex of fountains (like the nearby nymphaeum, statues and baths, though little remains today after various earthquakes.

Tomb of Modestus TOMB

The thick stone doors of this Roman tomb outside the main archaeological area still swing on ancient hinges. Nearby are the less notable tombs of **Germani** and **Chaireas**.

North Theatre RUINS

The North Theatre is overgrown and missing much of its original black-basalt stones, which were recycled by villagers in other constructions, but it's still fun to clamber about.

Shops RUINS

The shells of a row of shops remain in the western section of what was once the colonnaded courtyard of the Basilica Terrace.

Nymphaeum MONUMENT

This public water fountain, once a two-storey complex with a large covered cistern, has niches for statues of the water goddesses.

Ottoman Village RUINS

Surrounding the museum are the comprehensive ruins of an Ottoman village dating from the 18th and 19th centuries. Two houses, **Beit Malkawi** (now used as an office for archaeological groups) and the nearby **Beit Heshboni**, are still intact. An Ottoman mosque and the remains of a **girls' school** are also worth a cursory visit if you choose to amble around the derelict lanes. The village was inhabited until the 1980s, when the residents were evicted to allow archaeological excavations at Gadara.

Basilica Terrace RUINS

A bit of imagination is needed to reconstruct the colonnaded courtyard of the Basilica Terrace, the western section of which housed a row of shops. The remains of a 6th-century **church**, with an unusual octagonal interior sanctum, are marked today by the remaining basalt columns. The church was destroyed by earthquakes in the 8th century.

Ottoman Mosque MOSQUE

This small mosque, no longer consecrated, is at the heart of the old Ottoman village of Umm Qais.

Roman Mausoleums TOMB

The *decumanus maximus* continues west of the main site for 1km or so, leading to some ruins of limited interest, including **baths**, **mausoleums** and **gates**. Japanese and Iraqi archaeologists are currently excavating here. Most interesting is the basilica built above one of the Roman mausoleums. You can peer into the subterranean tomb through a hole in the basilica floor. The sarcophagus of Helladis that once lay here can be seen in the Museum of Anthropology & Archaeology (p97) in Irbid.

Sleeping

Umm Qais has one of Jordan's most appealing guesthouses. Baraka Destinations (p104) can arrange camping in the area as part of its hiking package.

Umm Qais Hotel HOTEL $

(☎02 750 0080; s/d from JD15/20) With modest rooms above a bakery (guess where the bread for breakfast comes from?), and located a stone's throw from the ruins, this is a friendly, family-run hotel. Home-cooked Jordanian meals are available on request from the landlady. Half-day trips into the countryside can be organised from here.

★**Beit Al Baraka** B&B $$

(☎07 9661 5738; www.barakadestinations.com; tw with shared bathroom JD70) This friendly, charming B&B offers simple rooms sharing two bathrooms (with some nice toiletries). The roof terrace has great views over the hills, but the particular treat is the breakfast spread, piled high with jams, cheeses, olives and other locally sourced foods.

In winter, tuck yourself up on a sofa in the lounge next to the quirky animal-shaped wood-burning stove.

Eating

The ruins of Gadara host one of Jordan's loveliest restaurants.

North Jordanian food is distinct from Bedouin cuisine. Foodie options run by Baraka Destinations (p104) include joining in the olive harvest, making pomegranate molasses, foraging for wild herbs and vegetables, and learning local recipes.

Shine Cottage Grilling CAFE $

(meals JD2-4; ⏲9am-9pm) With great views from the terrace, this small open-air cafe with a grill is one of only two places for casual refreshments near the ruins. It's opposite the parking lot.

★**Umm Qais Resthouse** JORDANIAN $$

(☎02 750 0555; mezze JD1.500-3, mains around JD7; ⏲10am-7pm Oct-May, to 10pm Jun-Sep; 🍷) Without doubt one of the best parts of visiting the Gadara (p101) site is pausing to take refreshment at the Umm Qais Resthouse, perched atop a small hill in the heart of the ruins. With stunning views over the Sea of Galilee, the Golan Heights and the peaks of Lebanon, it's the perfect venue for lunch or an early dinner.

Located inside a converted Ottoman house, the restaurant is part of a famed consortium of top-notch restaurants in Jordan and offers an impressive seasonal menu highlighting fresh produce, regional wines and locally raised meats. In spring the open-air terrace is surrounded by flowers.

THE JORDAN TRAIL: UMM QAIS TO AJLOUN

Distance 80km

Duration Four days

The Jordan Trail's 650km path to the Red Sea kicks off in fine style amid the olive-tree-clad hills of northern Jordan. From Umm Qais, the route takes in the Roman city of Gadara, overlooking the Sea of Galilee in Israel and the Palestinian Territories. Heading south, hills skirt Ziglab Lake at the edge of the Jordan Valley, softening to rolling meadows around the ancient ruins of Pella. Wooded countryside leads to the villages of Rasoun and Orjan, where there are local homestays, and finally through the Ajloun Forest Reserve to the imposing Islamic castle of Ajloun.

This route is particularly pretty in spring, when the hills are green and covered with wildflowers. Umm Qais and Ajloun are both connected to the transport network, and have good accommodation options. Baraka Destinations in Umm Qais and the Al Ayoun Society (p95) near Ajloun can help with local guides.

See www.jordantrail.org for route maps, GPS waypoints and detailed breakdowns of daily hikes.

Galsoum's Kitchen JORDANIAN **$$$**
(☎07 9661 5738; www.barakadestinations.com; meals JD15) Book ahead to enjoy a traditional north Jordanian meal using locally sourced produce, served up in cook Galsoum's home in Umm Qais. It's a great taste of regional culture. Menus depend on the season. Directions to Galsoum's house are given after you book.

Drinking & Nightlife

Beit Al Baraka Cafe CAFE
At the time of research this cafe near the ruins was due to open in early 2018. It will offer tea, coffee and fruit juices, and will serve as an information hub and bike shop for Baraka Destinations.

Information

There are minimal signs in Gadara, so it's worth collecting the brochure about Umm Qais from the ticket office. *Umm Qais: Gadara of the Decapolis* (JD3), published by Al Kutba, is ideal for anyone who wants further information. Guides (JD10) are available at the ticket office.

Baraka Destinations (☎07 9661 5738; www.barakadestinations.com) has an office near the ruins offering information about the various community-tourism projects in the area.

There are no ATMs in Umm Qais.

Getting There & Away

Umm Qais village, and the ruins 200m to the west, are about 25km northwest of Irbid and about 110km north of Amman. Minibuses leave Irbid's North Bus Station (800 fils, 45 minutes) on a regular basis. There's no direct transport from Amman.

With a car, you can descend to the Jordan Valley road via the village of Adasiyyeh. The occasional minibus runs down this road to Shuneh Ash Shamaliyyeh (North Shuna), but if you're relying on public transport to get to Pella from here, it's easier to backtrack via Irbid.

Umm Qais is a 25-minute drive from the Sheikh Hussein Bridge border crossing with Israel and the Palestinian Territories.

Pella (Tabaqat Fahl) طبقة فحل

In the midst of the Jordan Valley are the ruins of the ancient city of Pella, one of the cities of the fabled Roman Decapolis (p88). Centred on a large tell and surrounded by fertile valleys that together comprise a rich watershed, Pella has fostered human civilisation from the Stone Age to medieval Islamic times. The ruins lie a few kilometres away from the modern Arab village of Tabaqat Fahl. Many of the ruins are spread out and in need of excavation, so some walking and a bit of imagination are required to get the most from the site.

History

Pella was inhabited a million years ago by hunters and gathers who followed herds of game through the Stone Age forests and savannah. By 5000 BC permanent Neolithic farming villages had sprung up around the tell and attracted the attention of the Egyptians, who referred to the site in written texts in the 2nd millennium BC.

Pella thrived because of its strategic position on the trade routes running between Arabia, Syria, Egypt and the Mediterranean.

Luxury items, including ivory sculpture and gold jewellery, have been excavated from the site, suggesting that Pella was a prosperous settlement throughout the Bronze and Iron Ages.

Under the Greeks, the settlement earned the name 'Pella' after the birthplace of Alexander the Great. The Jews largely destroyed Pella in 83 BC, as the inhabitants were not inclined to adopt Jewish customs. Twenty years later, the legions of Roman general Pompey swept into the Levant and rebuilt it, along with neighbouring cities in the Decapolis. Life under the Romans was embraced in Pella and the city enjoyed an era of political autonomy and economic stability; it even had the power to mint its own coins.

Christians fled to Pella in 66 to escape persecution by the Roman army in Jerusalem. Although they later returned to Jerusalem, they left a strong mark on Pella, helping to ease the city's adoption of Christianity a few centuries later.

Pella reached its peak during the Byzantine era, and by 451 the city was influential enough to warrant its own bishop. The population at this time may have been as high as 25,000, and there is evidence that Pella was part of an expansive trade route that encompassed most of Asia Minor as well as North Africa.

The city was virtually destroyed by the earthquake that shook the whole region in 747. The last occupiers of Pella were the Mamluks of the 13th and 14th centuries. While Pella enjoyed a brief renaissance, the defeat of the Mamluks by the Ottomans caused the residents of Pella to flee, ending more than 6000 years of continuous settlement.

Sights

Pella ROMAN SITE

(8am-6pm) FREE Pella, near the modern Arab village of Tabaqat Fahl, was one of the cities of the fabled Roman Decapolis (p88). It's of great importance to archaeologists because it reveals evidence of 6000 years of continuous settlement. Many of the ruins are spread out, and a bit of imagination is required to get the most from the site, but the superb setting just above the Jordan Valley can be reward enough, particularly when the land blooms in spring.

At the base of the main mound (on your right as you pass through the entrance) are the limited remains of a **Roman gate** to the city. Atop the hill are the ruins of an **Umayyad settlement**, which consisted of shops, residences and storehouses. The small, square **Mamluk mosque** to the west dates from the 14th century. Carved into the southern side of the hill is the recently excavated **Canaanite temple**; constructed in around 1270 BC, it was dedicated to the Canaanite god Baal.

The main structure, and indeed one of the better preserved of the ruins, is the Byzantine **civic complex church** (or middle church), which was built atop an earlier Roman civic complex in the 5th century, and modified several times in the subsequent two centuries. Adjacent is the **odeon** (a small theatre used for musical performances). It once held 400 spectators, but you will need considerable imagination to picture this now. East of the civic complex church are the low-lying remains of a Roman **nymphaeum** (public fountain).

Pella (Tabaqat Fahl)

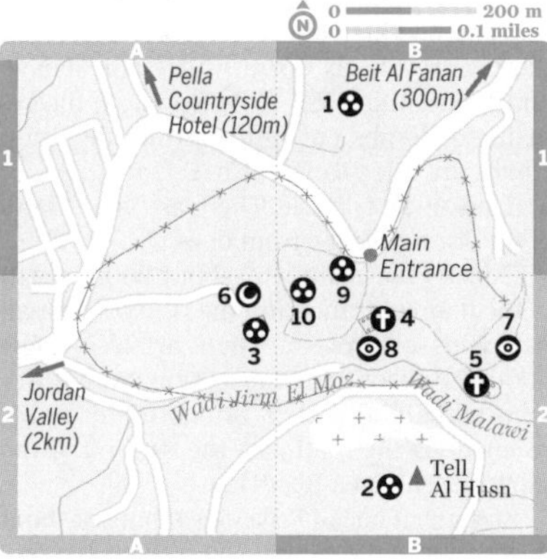

Pella (Tabaqat Fahl)

Sights

1 Abbasid Settlement.....B1
2 Byzantine Fort.....B2
3 Canaanite Temple.....A2
4 Civic Complex Church (Middle Church).....B2
5 East Church.....B2
6 Mamluk Mosque.....A2
7 Nymphaeum (Baths).....B2
8 Odeon (Theatre).....B2
9 Roman Gate.....B1
Roman Temple.....(see 2)
10 Umayyad Settlement.....B2

Up the hill to the southeast is the 5th-century **east church**, which has a lovely setting perched high above the lower city. From there a trail leads down into Wadi Malawi and then climbs Tell Al Husn (note the remains of tombs cut into the hillside), atop which are the stones of a **Byzantine fort** and a **Roman temple**. There are good views of the Jordan Valley from here.

Outside the main site, about 200m north of the main entrance, are the ruins of a small **Abbasid settlement**. There are also a few limited Palaeolithic ruins (4km away), Roman baths and a rock bridge (3km away), reached via the road past the turn-off to the (now closed) Pella Rest House.

Enquire at one of Pella's guesthouses about how to get to the rubble of a Hellenistic temple high on Jebel Sartaba to the southeast. From there, Jerusalem is visible on a clear day. The return hike takes a good couple of hours.

Sleeping & Eating

There are a couple of simple sleeping options in Pella. The only places to eat are at the guesthouses. The countryside here is dotted with perfect picnic spots.

Pella Countryside Hotel B&B **$**
(07 7618 4337; www.pellacountrysidehotel.com; r JD45) This B&B has lovely rural views from a shared guest lounge, and the comfortable rooms have plenty of country-style flourishes. It's a good place to relax for a couple of nights. The owners can arrange picnics in the surrounding hills; lunch is available for JD7. From February to May, black irises, the national flower of Jordan, bloom in the garden.

The hotel is signposted off the road to the Pella ruins.

Beit Al Fanan B&B **$$**
(07 7666 7660; www.barakadestinations.com) At the time of research, this small guesthouse overlooking the Pella site was due to open in late 2017. The property was once owned by artist-architect Ammar Khammash, who designed Wild Jordan's iconic buildings, and who visited Pella for inspiration for his paintings. Expect cosy rooms, sublime views from the terrace, and art materials for guests to indulge their own muse.

Information

The site can be entered for free at several points, including next to the (closed) Pella Rest House on the hill.

Anyone with a specific interest should buy *Pella* (JD3), published by Al Kutba and available in major bookshops around Jordan.

Getting There & Away

From Irbid's West Bus Station, minibuses go to Al Mashari'a (800 fils, 45 minutes), though be sure to get off before Al Mashari'a at the junction. Pella is a steep 2km walk uphill from the signposted turn-off, but you might be offered a lift by passing traffic. Minibuses and service taxis travel regularly from Amman's North Bus Station to Deir Alla (800 fils, one hour), close to the Pella junction.

With your own car, the ruins are an easy day trip from Irbid, Jerash or Amman. Exploring the scenic back roads to Ajloun (25km) takes a bit of a nose for navigation, but is worthwhile for the insights into rural life among the olive groves that it affords.

Salt السلط

05 / POP 99,800 / ELEV 814M

During Ottoman rule, Salt was the region's administrative centre, but it was passed over as the new capital of Trans-Jordan in favour of Amman. Consequently, Salt never experienced the intense wave of modernisation that swept across Amman and it has retained much of its historic charm. Today, much of Salt's downtown is a living museum of Ottoman-period architecture.

Salt is visited by few foreign tourists and remains one of the undiscovered highlights of the Jordan Valley. A number of international aid packages awarded to the city have been used to preserve many of its old buildings. While tourist infrastructure is largely still lacking, it's heartening to see that the residents of Salt have embraced their city's architectural heritage.

History

While you'd be forgiven for thinking that the town's moniker derives from the table condiment, Salt was actually named after the Greek word *saltus*, meaning 'forests' (although these are long gone), or from *sultana*, for the grapes that were once abundant in the region.

Construction began on Salt's characteristic limestone buildings in the late 19th century, thanks to the arrival of merchants from Nablus. Over several decades, Salt began to thrive as trade networks sprang up between the city and neighbouring Palestine.

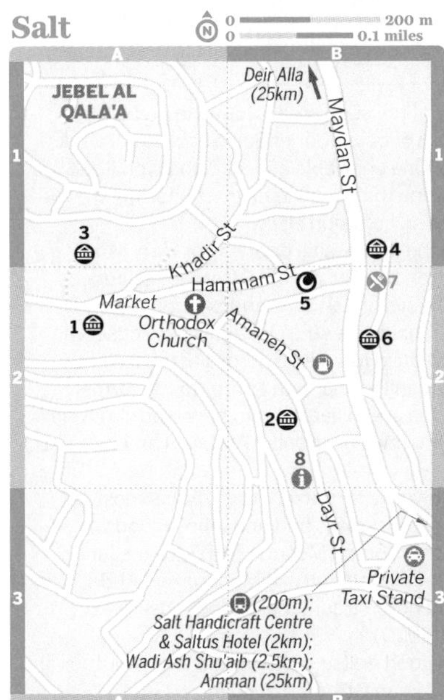

Salt

Sights

1 Beit Abu Jaber....................A2
Beit Mismar....................(see 8)
2 Beit Muasher....................B2
3 English Hospital....................A1
4 Muhammed Al Bashir's House....................B1
5 Ottoman Mosque....................B2
6 Salt Archaeological Museum....................B2

Eating

7 Al Salam Restaurant....................B2

Information

8 Tourist Office....................B2

Following the establishment of Trans-Jordan, the new emir chose Amman as his capital because of its proximity to the railway. Almost overnight, Salt went into decline. War with Israel separated Salt from the port of Haifa in 1948, and later from its trading partner of Nablus in 1967, ending Salt's significance as anything more than a rural town above the Jordan Valley.

Sights

There are some fine examples of **Ottoman architecture** in town dating from the late 19th and early 20th century. Few of these gracious limestone buildings are open to the public, but some of the elegant facades are worth viewing. Stairways lead to fine views from atop Jebel Al Qala'a.

Orthodox Church CHURCH

(donations welcome) Salt's historic Orthodox church is dedicated to St George. The vaulted stone interior is rich with icons, and the rood screen is carved with dragons being vanquished by the saint. The church isn't always unlocked, so ask around for the key holder if it's shut.

Ottoman Mosque MOSQUE

A gorgeous Ottoman mosque, overlooking the traditional market area of Souq Hammam. Non-Muslims are not allowed inside, but anyone can enjoy its traditional stone facade.

Muhammed Al Bashir's House HISTORIC BUILDING

An Ottoman house with colonnaded entry, built between 1890 and 1910. It's now a traditional coffeehouse (with a tree in front).

Salt Handicraft Training Centre WORKSHOP

(05 355 0279; Nageb Al Daboor; 8am-3pm Sun-Thu) Visitors can watch weaving, pottery, mosaics and other handicrafts being made at this women's cooperative, 3km out of town in Nageb Al Daboor district. The centre specialises in both training and production and has a showroom displaying the finished products.

Salt Archaeological Museum MUSEUM

(05 355 5651; JD1, with Jordan Pass free; 8am-6pm May-Oct, to 4pm Nov-Apr) This delightful little museum is located in a well-restored Ottoman-era building and covers the history of the Jordan Valley area with excellent information boards in English. The downstairs rooms focus on glass and pottery (some dating back 5000 years) from the Roman, Byzantine and Islamic eras, mostly from around Salt but also from Deir Alla and Tell Nimrin. Upstairs are some examples of local traditional dress, displays on farming activities and mosaic fragments from churches around Salt.

Activities

Wadi Ash Shu'aib HIKING

If you have a car, it's worth exploring Wadi Ash Shu'aib, a refreshing valley named after the prophet Jethro (called Shu'aib in Arabic). There are some hiking opportunities here and interesting caves.

DISCOVERING SALT ON FOOT

Salt is one town that really rewards a bit of on-foot exploration, as much of the old quarter can only be accessed by stairways and the best of the souq area is found in pedestrian-only alleyways. The following route leads you on a circular tour of Salt's backstreets, taking in its bazaars and old Ottoman architecture. One enjoyable aspect is that you'll see the restored wooden shop fronts and creamy stone that give the town its charm – they're a pleasing contrast to the plastic and neon signs so common elsewhere.

From Salt bus station, walk up Dayr St, past the impressive doorway of **Beit Mismar** and the lovely balcony columns of **Beit Muasher**, both grand old Ottoman residences. Continue along Dayr St as it passes the curved walls of Salt's Orthodox Church (p107) to the recently restored **Beit Abu Jaber**, which houses a small local-history museum. Its arched facade makes it one of Salt's loveliest buildings. Head across the plaza and take the stairs up to the right of the mosque, curving round to the entry to the former **English Hospital** (look for the letters 'EH' on the green gate). From here, you can wind your way uphill for particularly fine views over the town from Jebel Al Qala'a and descend along a neighbouring staircase.

Alternatively, return to the plaza and head down **Hammam Street**, Salt's most atmospheric backstreet. The market here, selling food, spices and household goods, is a compact delight. The souq leads past the ornate Ottoman Mosque (p107) to the junction with Maydan St. Across the street is the colonnaded entry of Muhammed Al Bashir's House (p107), built between 1890 and 1910, and now a traditional coffeehouse. Next door is **Beit Al Sulibi** (built between 1920 and 1930).

Break for lunch at Al Salam Restaurant, with good grilled options, and end your tour at the Salt Archaeological Museum (p107), housed in an Ottoman building.

Sleeping & Eating

Salt has one decent sleeping option, although the city's proximity to Amman means that most visitors come just for the day. The northern end of Maydan St is lined with traditional cafes, full of patrons drinking tea and smoking *nargileh* (water pipes). Basic restaurants along the same street and by the bus station sell kebabs.

Saltus Hotel HOTEL $$
(07 9542 1790; www.saltushotel.com; r JD45-58) Salt's only hotel, the Saltus sits on the outskirts of town and operates in part as a vocational school for the hospitality industry. The hotel itself is a comfortable if modest affair, with simple contemporary rooms, a restaurant and views across the hills.

Al Salam Restaurant JORDANIAN $
(05 355 2115; Maydan St; meals JD3-5; 7am-10.30pm Sat-Thu) The best place in town for cheap Arabic food, the Al Salam Restaurant serves up good shish kebabs and other offerings from the grill.

Information

The **tourist office** (05 355 5652; Dayr St; 8am-3pm Sun-Thu) is upstairs in the impressive old residence of Beit Mismar, but it's not always open during its advertised hours. Try to pick up a copy of the excellent *Salt Heritage Trail* pamphlet, which has a useful map and guide to the town's history and architecture.

Getting There & Away

The bus station is on the main road south of the town centre. There are minibuses from Amman's North Bus Station via the University of Jordan (JD1, 45 minutes) and occasional service taxis from Raghadan. From Salt, minibuses head fairly regularly down the Jordan Valley to Shuneh Al Janubiyyeh (South Shuna; 800 fils, 45 minutes). Minibuses also go to Wadi As Seer (600 fils, 30 minutes) and Fuheis (600 fils, 30 minutes), with which Salt can be combined as a day trip from Amman. Taxis can be chartered to Amman for around JD12 to JD15.

The drive to Salt from the Jordan Valley, along either the road south of Deir Alla or from Shuneh Al Janubiyyeh, is spectacular. The 30-minute route winds through Bedouin encampments to the coniferous and windswept hillsides of Zay National Park (little more than a municipal picnic spot) and affords many panoramic views of the Jordan Valley. If you're heading into the countryside, it's a good idea to fill your tank at a Salt petrol station, as they're few and far between further north.

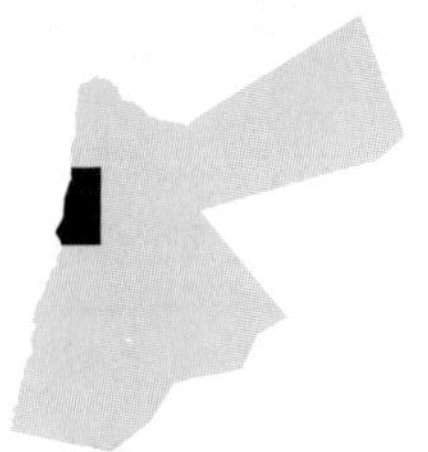

Dead Sea Highway
طريق البحر الميت

Includes ➡

Best Places to Stay & Eat

- Mövenpick Resort & Spa (p114)
- Dead Sea Marriott (p114)
- Mujib Biosphere Reserve (p121)
- Hilton Dead Sea Resort & Spa (p114)
- Kempinski Hotel Ishtar (p114)

Best Places for a Spa

- Zara Spa (p113)
- Resense Spa (p113)
- Dead Sea Marriott Spa (p113)
- Ma'In Hot Springs Resort & Spa (p121)

Why Go?

Sometimes you've got to get down low to find the real highlights. The Dead Sea is the example par excellence – to be found quite literally at the lowest point on earth. Taking a dip takes on a new meaning here, as the intensely salty water keeps you so buoyant you'll be bobbing about like a cork rather than gracefully swimming a few strokes. Dead Sea mud famously doubles as a skincare product, and you can take things to a more luxurious level at one of the many high-end spas that line the coast.

There are more waters to take than just the Dead Sea, however. Nearby is Bethany-Beyond-the-Jordan, the site where Jesus Christ is said to have been baptised, and a magnet for religious and secular tourists alike. More worldly attractions can be found at the nature reserve of Wadi Mujib, where you can splash your way through watery canyon trails.

When to Go

- Blisteringly hot and humid from May to October and chilly from December to January, the best time to enjoy the Dead Sea pleasure domes is around February and November – perfect for sunny swims and balmy dining alfresco. Catering to the peak tourist season at this time, resorts offer live entertainment.
- Those looking for adventure should aim for spring: the Dead Sea Ultra Marathon brings physical activity to a seashore more famous for sunning than running, and hikes along water-bound Wadi Mujib are free from the danger of flash flooding.

Dead Sea Highway Highlights

1 **Dead Sea** (p111) Descending to the depths for a bob in the incredibly salty water at the lowest point on earth.

2 **Dead Sea Spas** (p113) Relaxing mind and body and applying mud used for cosmetic purposes since the time of the biblical King Herod.

3 **Bethany-Beyond-the-Jordan** (p115) Making a pilgrimage to the holy spot on the Jordan River where it's said that John the Baptist baptised Jesus Christ.

4 **Hammamat Ma'in** (p121) Wallowing in hot springs at one of the region's thermal oases.

5 **Mujib Biosphere Reserve** (p121) Splashing through the canyon pools, keeping an eye open for ibex.

6 **Zikra Initiative** (p123) Getting a taste of traditional village life at this community-tourism project.

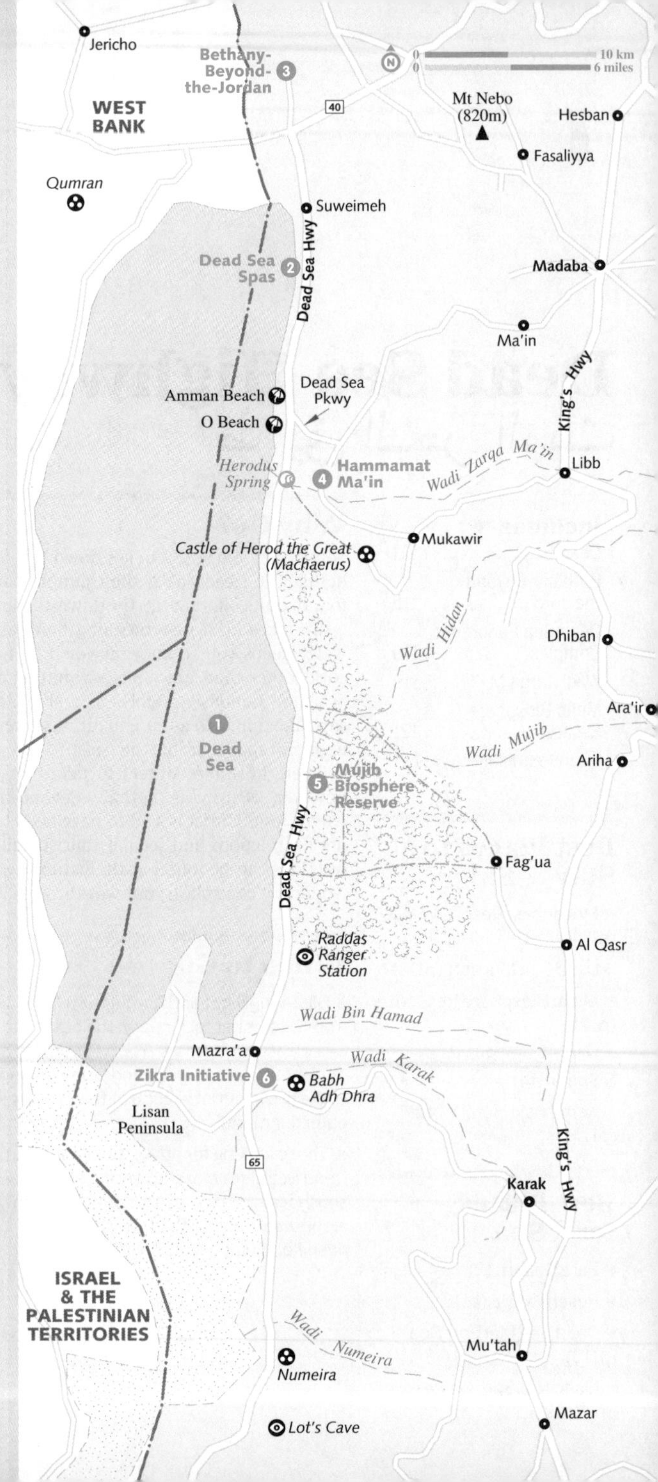

History

It's easy to sense the antiquity of a region that has supported human endeavour for thousands of years. All along the highway, freshwater springs bring a hopeful abundance of life (as at Wadi Mujib) in vivid contrast to the surrounding barren escarpment. In season, the parched soil is threaded with crates of blood-red tomatoes and glossy-coated aubergines (eggplants), proving the unexpected fecundity of a region that looks to all intents and purposes like a desert.

Belying its name, even the Dead Sea has contributed to the pattern of human civilisation. Known to the ancients as the Sea of Asphalt, it produced bitumen, creating a nascent oil industry, as it was harvested by the Nabataeans and sold to neighbours for embalming processes.

Travel along the Dead Sea Highway today, with its proximity to the Israel and Palestinian Territories, and you'll quickly feel how division defines the territory to this day. Police checks, border posts, cautious eyes across the Rift Valley – this is disputed soil, a land cleaved in two, geologically, historically and politically. You may try to float in peace in a Dead Sea spa, but you can't help but be aware that the calm has been bought at a high price.

Nature Reserves

One of the most delightful wilderness areas in Jordan, Mujib Biosphere Reserve (p121), lies just around the corner from the Dead Sea resorts. Unfortunately, this is partially why there are concerns for the long-term viability of the reserve, as the water that flows through the wadi is siphoned off to supply the demands of tourism. Whatever the future of the reserve, for now the area offers waterfalls, canyon adventures and a chance to catch sight of the elusive ibex.

The Dead Sea Highway also gives secondary access to the spectacular Dana Biosphere Reserve and to Dana's Feynan Ecolodge (p151). The main entrance to Dana Biosphere Reserve, however, is via the village of Dana off the King's Highway.

Dangers & Annoyances

There are few petrol stations in the area, and little accommodation (except at the Dead Sea resorts and within the national parks of Wadi Mujib and Wadi Dana). It's therefore important to honour the desert code and fill up every time you see a petrol station, otherwise you stand a very real chance of getting stranded.

Because of the proximity to the border with Israel and the Palestinian Territories, there are numerous police checkpoints in the area. Keep your passport, driver's licence, rental contract and *ruksa* (car registration card) handy when driving.

There is very little shade at the Dead Sea, or indeed anywhere along the Dead Sea Highway, so it is important to bring a hat and plenty of water, particularly in the summer when temperatures can soar to an intolerable 50°C.

Getting There & Away

The Dead Sea Highway is most easily reached by road from Amman, but other access points include Madaba, Karak and Wadi Musa, all of which make suitable bases for exploring the region. Although the Dead Sea Highway (Hwy 65) ends in Aqaba, there's not much to see or explore along the southern reaches of the highway, and there's no public transport. It's just about possible to get to the Dead Sea resorts with a frustrating and unreliable combination of minibuses and taxis, but tours offer the most realistic way of reaching the area.

Getting Around

Pretty much the only way to explore the Dead Sea Highway (Hwy 65) is with a car; there are effectively no public transport options. The Dead Sea Highway runs along the edge of the Dead Sea, between the honey-coloured Moab Mountains and the distant cliffs of Judaea on the West Bank, and offers an interesting alternative to the Desert Highway between Amman and Aqaba.

There are some spectacular roads that link the Dead Sea Highway with the King's Highway, which are ideal if you're not in a hurry. With the intimate insight these roads afford into Bedouin communities and striking desert landscapes, they are almost destinations in their own right.

DEAD SEA HIGHWAY

Dead Sea البحر الميت

ELEV -408M

At 408m below sea level – the lowest point on earth – the Dead Sea is a body of intense blue water, polished smooth like oiled skin on a windless day in winter and ruffled into whitecaps by the summer winds.

Dead Sea salts and minerals have long been exploited for their skin-friendly properties. While swimming, the extreme salinity will help you discover cuts you never knew you had (don't shave beforehand), and be prepared for a few minutes of agony if any water gets in your eyes. 'Swimming' is actually a misnomer – the buoyancy makes it difficult to do much more than happily bob.

The northeast coast is lined with luxury resorts. Here you can enjoy a spa treatment, watch the sunset across the water and look across to the West Bank and the distant lights of Jerusalem.

The Dead Sea is also an easy day trip from Amman or Madaba.

History

The Dead Sea has been called many names in its time, including the logical 'Salt Sea' and the less flattering 'Stinking Sea' (slap a little Dead Sea mud on your face and you'll soon see why). A Greek traveller, Pausanias, first gave it the current name in the 2nd century AD, noticing that the extreme brackishness of the water made it unsupportive of life. The high salinity is due to the fact that the sea has no outlet and the high summer temperatures evaporate the fresh water more quickly than it is replenished. Each year, because of intensive irrigation in the Jordan Valley, the sea shrinks. This, together with the potash industry on the southern shore, has caused many environmentalists to lament the imminent death of this extraordinary stretch of water.

Sights

Amman Beach BEACH

(05 356 0800; Dead Sea Hwy; adult/child JD25/15, restaurant buffet JD14; 9am-8pm, restaurant 11am-5pm) This public facility goes under the full title of Amman Beach Tourism Resort, Restaurant & Pools. The beach, 2km south of the main resort strip, gives affordable access to the Dead Sea. The grounds are attractively landscaped and the beach is clean, with sun umbrellas and freshwater showers.

Locals generally swim fully clothed, though foreigners shouldn't feel uncomfortable in a modest swimming costume. Solo women may attract less unwanted attention in shorts and a T-shirt.

There are also a number of swimming pools, a restaurant, some drinks stalls, basketball courts and a small amusement park. It gets very busy at weekends (especially Friday afternoon and Saturday morning).

FAST FACTS

- The Dead Sea is part of the Great Rift Valley; it is the lowest spot on earth at 408m below sea level and more than 390m deep.
- It is not actually a sea but a lake filled with incoming water with no outlet.
- It is the second-saltiest body of water on earth (after Lake Aral in Djibouti), with a salt content of 31%.
- Egyptians used Dead Sea mud (bitumen) in their mummification process; the last lump of floating bitumen surfaced in 1936.
- The majority of Dead Sea minerals (including calcium and magnesium) occur naturally in our bodies and have health-giving properties.
- The Dead Sea is three million years old but has shrunk by 30% in recent years (half a metre per year) because of evaporation and the demands of the potash industry, one of Jordan's most valuable commodities.

Oh Beach BEACH

(05 349 2000; www.ohresort.net; Dead Sea Hwy; adult/child JD15/10, with lunch JD40/25; 9am-6pm) This private beach, stepped down the hillside in a series of landscaped terraces and infinity pools, is a great way to enjoy the Dead Sea in comfort without paying for a night in one of the neighbouring hotels. The rocky beach area was still being remodelled when we visited and should be much improved. There are several restaurants and bars, and a weekend buffet. A range of spa treatments are also available.

Activities

Many people go to the Dead Sea area for the therapeutic treatments on offer in the spas. The low levels of UV rays and high oxygen levels are good for the health, and Dead Sea mud contains high concentrations of minerals. These include calcium and magnesium, helpful remedies against allergies and bronchial infections; pungent bromine, which promotes relaxation; iodine, which alleviates certain glandular ailments; and bitumen, which has skin-rejuvenating properties. Many of these Dead Sea minerals are made into easy-to-use preparations such as soaps, shampoos and lotions, and are sold at the Dead Sea spas and in tourist shops throughout Jordan.

Of course, you don't need to be under-the-weather to enjoy the benefits of a spa treatment. If you feel like a scrub or a massage, or just a bit of pampering, it's easy to book in for an hour or two.

Swimming

Although technically you can take a dip anywhere along the Dead Sea coast, unless you are staying at one of the resorts it can be surprisingly difficult to reach the sea. This is especially the case as each year the sea retreats further from the shore, making it less and less accessible from the cliffs. Second, after a dip in the Dead Sea, you'll find yourself coated in uncomfortable encrustations of salt that are best washed off as soon as possible. Third, there's the utter lack of privacy to consider: the road follows the shoreline closely, and so do the border police. For these reasons, it's better to reserve your swim for the comfort of the Dead Sea resorts or private day beaches where freshwater showers are available and where access to the sea is generally cleared of sharp and potentially lethal slippery rocks.

As well as the hotel resorts, there are two day beaches with paid facilities.

Al Wadi Resort WATER PARK
(☎05 349 3333; www.alwadideadsea.com; Dead Sea Resort Zone; adult/child JD25/18; ⊙9am-6pm Sat-Thu, to 7pm Fri) This huge water park has a giant pool with a wave machine and epic slides, in pleasantly landscaped surroundings. There are two restaurants, one poolside offering light food, and a larger buffet restaurant. Children are measured on entry: those under 95cm are admitted free.

Mud Bathing

Most beaches have mud pots by the sea's edge where you can self-administer a full-body mud pack. Leave it in place to bake under the sun for five to 10 minutes and then wash it off in the sea. It tightens the skin and leaves it feeling smooth, tingly and refreshed.

Spa Treatments

People come to the Dead Sea to engage with the sea and its mineral properties, either by taking a dip or by wallowing in a spa. About the only other activity on offer is a chance to ride on a camel or a horse (around JD2).

★**Resense Spa** SPA
(☎05 356 8888; www.kempinski.com; Kempinski Ishtar Hotel, Dead Sea Resort Zone; day spa JD68; ⊙10am-10pm) This highly luxurious and architecturally striking spa is currently the largest in the Middle East. Among the many offerings, its signature experience is the Royal Hammam Ritual (JD130, 90 minutes), touted as 'pure bliss for mind and body'. It includes massage, body scrub and body wrap applied with traditional Jordanian-style vigour.

Zara Spa SPA
(☎05 349 1310; www.movenpick.com; Mövenpick Resort & Spa, Dead Sea Resort Zone; guests/nonguests JD20/50; ⊙8.30am-8.30pm) Offering a range of facilities and treatments in a beautiful environment; entry includes access to a gym, private beach, pool, sauna, steam room and foot-massage pool, plus an infinity pool and aqua-pressure pool. A day package costs JD190 for 3½ hours of treatments; a three-day package is JD365.

Extra services include a mud wrap (JD60, one hour), dry flotation, hot-stone therapy, shiatsu and other massages (from JD60 for 50 minutes).

Dead Sea Marriott Spa SPA
(☎05 356 0400; Dead Sea Marriott, Dead Sea Resort Zone; guests/nonguests JD20/30; ⊙8.30am-8.30pm) This stylish hotel spa has a heated pool, Dead Sea saltwater pool, Jacuzzi, steam room and sauna. Treatments include massages (JD75, 55 minutes), body wraps, salt scrubs, phytomer and mud facials, dry flotation and hydrobaths. An Arabic loofah experience (JD95, 75 minutes) has to be tried to be believed – expect your skin to glow by the end.

Dead Sea Spa SPA
(☎05 356 1000; www.dssh.jo; Dead Sea Spa Hotel, Dead Sea Resort Zone; weekdays/weekends JD25/30; ⊙9am-8pm) This spa focuses on medical as well as recreational treatments. Entry includes the beach, pools, spa, a fitness room, solarium and Dead Sea saltwater pool. Mud wraps cost JD35, massages JD35 to JD85 (Thai and Balinese massages available).

Festivals & Events

Dead Sea Ultra Marathon SPORTS
(www.deadsea.runjordan.com; ⊙Apr) The Dead Sea is home to the lowest marathon on earth, held every April. The finishing line is Amman Beach.

DON'T MISS

BRAVING LUXURY IN A DEAD SEA SPA

You can't come to the Dead Sea and not try a spa. Even if you're a die-hard, old-school traveller who feels that sleeping on a bed with a soft mattress is a sign of weakness, there's a certain gratification to succumbing to the spa experience. You'll be in good company: Herod the Great and Cleopatra, neither noted as wimpy types, both dipped a toe in spa waters.

The spa experience (from around JD30 to JD40) usually begins with a mint tea and a spa bag to stow your worldly goods – this isn't going to be a chlorinated swim in the municipal pool back home. You'll then be shown to the mirrored changing rooms, with Dead Sea soaps and shampoos and more towels than you'll have body to dry off. This marks the point of no return: the silent-padding assistants waft you from here along marble corridors to the opulent bathhouses.

All the spas offer a range of cradling Dead Sea waters with different levels of salinity. There's usually a foot spa and a float in a Damascene-tiled Jacuzzi. Outside pools assault visitors with a variety of bullying jet sprays. Best of all are the little Jacuzzis that bubble when you sit in them and ought to be X-rated.

Luxury of this kind is an extreme sport, and by the time you reach the spa's private infinity pool you'll be so seduced by the ambience you won't have the energy to try the saunas, steam rooms or tropical sprays, let alone the gym. Lie instead under an oleander by the pool, sip a chilled carrot juice and wonder why you resisted the spa experience for so long.

Sleeping & Eating

Along the Dead Sea Highway, about 5km south of Suweimeh, there are a number of first-class resorts. They don't look much from the highway, but once you're inside you'll see that they tumble into landscaped gardens, terraced sun spots, cascading pools and pristine Dead Sea beaches.

There are no budget sleeping options along the Dead Sea coast.

Eating options are all contained within the resort hotels – you need to be a guest or visiting on a day pass to dine at them.

★Mövenpick Resort & Spa RESORT **$$$**
(☎05 356 1111; www.moevenpick-hotels.com; Dead Sea Resort Zone; d JD180; P 📶) This pleasantly green haven boasts a river that ambles through the village-style complex of rustic two-storey apartments. Wooden screens and balconies allow guests to enjoy sea or garden views in private, while secluded seating areas around a superb infinity pool add to the ambience. The Zara Spa (p113) is particularly well-regarded.

Culinary high points include the Al Saraya buffet restaurant, a Thursday night barbecue and a prodigious Friday brunch. The Mövenpick charges nonguests JD50 for access to the pools, beach and buffet (couples and families only) and an extra JD50 for access to the spa.

Hilton Dead Sea Resort & Spa RESORT **$$$**
(☎05 349 3000; www.hilton.com; Dead Sea Resort Zone; d JD145; P 📶 🏊) The new Hilton opened in 2017 and is an impressive addition to the area. Rooms are expansive, in several discrete blocks, looking down to the swish pool area. The floating pontoon on the beach is a nice addition. Expect a high-end spa when the hotel is finally finished, and seven restaurants.

Dead Sea Marriott RESORT **$$$**
(☎05 356 0400; www.marriott.com; Dead Sea Resort Zone; s/d from JD145/170; P 📶 🏊) Polished marble floors, brass fixtures and fittings, and spacious rooms contribute to the general opulence of this much-loved resort. Eating spots include sea-view cafes and a brasserie-style French restaurant. A cinema, high-speed internet access, a jungle playground, mini-waterfall and family pool ensure the kids are kept happy while parents luxuriate in the spa.

Marriott charges nonguests JD60 for use of its pools and access to the beach, with JD25 of that redeemable against food and drink in its restaurant.

Kempinski Hotel Ishtar RESORT **$$$**
(☎05 356 8888; www.kempinski.com; Dead Sea Resort Zone; s/d JD200/220; P 📶 🏊) This grand resort isn't shy in its bid to be the best. Floor-to-ceiling windows stretch the length of the Dead Sea vista, a Sumerian-style lobby

overlooks a spectacular, circular infinity pool, and a series of water features tumble down to the Dead Sea. Each of the modern rooms has a semi-shaded balcony and semi-sunken bath. A palace among hotels.

Crowne Plaza RESORT **$$$**
(☎05 349 4000; www.crowneplaza.com/deadsea jordan; Dead Sea Resort Zone; d JD90; P ☎ ≋) The Crowne Plaza feels more like a small town, with several blocks of rooms circled around the immense central pool area and great facilities for kids. Rooms are large and comfortable, if you can drag yourself away from the spa, four restaurants and three bars.

Holiday Inn Resort Dead Sea RESORT **$$$**
(☎05 349 5555; www.ihg.com; Dead Sea Resort Zone; s/d JD120/145; P ☎ ≋) This excellent resort with a series of epic pools stretching down to the beach will appeal to families, as its access to the Dead Sea is quicker and easier than the steep descent at other resorts. It charges nonguests JD25 on weekdays and JD45 at weekends and holidays for access to its beach and pools.

Dead Sea Spa Hotel RESORT **$$$**
(☎05 356 1000; www.dssh.jo; Dead Sea Resort Zone; d JD90; P ☎ ≋) This hotel is pleasant, if not quite as refined as others on the Dead Sea. It has a medical/dermatological spa, private beach access, a big pool and a separate kids' pool with slides. Choose from rooms in the main block or bungalows. The restaurant complex at the northern end of the hotel has sea views and some chain outlets.

The Dead Sea Spa Hotel charges nonguests JD25 for day entrance to its resort and beach facilities, with a snack and a drink thrown in.

Getting There & Away

BUS & MINIBUS

JETT buses offer a daily service to the resort strip south of Suweimeh from Amman (JD8 return) at 9am, returning at 5pm. The bus leaves from the JETT office near 7th Circle. Check with the JETT office (p315) in Amman for the latest timetable. Minibuses from Muhajireen bus station only run as far as Suweimeh.

CAR

From Amman, it takes just under an hour to reach the Dead Sea resorts, along Hwy 40 and Hwy 65. Alternatively, you can drive from Madaba via Mt Nebo. If you choose this route, your first view of the Dead Sea will be a spectacular blue lozenge beyond the iron-coloured hills.

TAXI

A return taxi from Amman to Amman Beach costs about JD50 including three hours' waiting time (minimum required to make the trip worthwhile) or JD20 for a one-way journey.

Some budget hotels in Amman and most hotels in Madaba organise day trips via Mt Nebo, the Dead Sea Panoramic Complex and Hammamat Ma'in.

Bethany-Beyond-the-Jordan المغطس

Whatever one's religious persuasion, it's hard not to be moved by this minimal pile of ruins lying at the end of the Jordan Valley near the Dead Sea. This is the site, archaeologists assure us, where John the Baptist preached, where Jesus was baptised, where the first five apostles met, and where, thereby, the foundations of the early Christian faith were laid. They chose an auspicious spot, as many also believe this was the place from where prophet Elijah (who was born in Mar Elias in north Jordan) ascended to heaven in a whirlwind.

History

The name Bethany comes from the Aramaic Beit Anniya (House of the Crossing). As you stand by the near-stagnant river, Israel and the Palestinian Territories are almost within arm's reach. Pilgrim churches, guesthouses and a 6th-century pilgrim road developed around the crossing as pilgrims broke their journey between Jerusalem and Mt Nebo. Today, there's little visible evidence of the early passage of pilgrims, but the sense of crossing is still apparent: the site is close to contested land – on the opposite bank of the river from Jordan, an Israeli flag flies over the West Bank.

The sense of fight and flight at this point is captured in the famous mosaic map of Madaba where a gazelle turns towards a lion (identifiable only by its tail) in hot pursuit. They're running through the Jordan Valley towards the Dead Sea, just above the place where John baptised Jesus, and are symbolic, perhaps, of the human flight that has marked this poignant patch of land for centuries.

The site has only relatively recently been identified. Some ancient ruins were discovered in 1899, but it wasn't until the clearing of landmines (following the 1994 peace treaty with Israel) that the remains of churches,

DRIVING BELOW ZERO

The switchback roads that link the high ground with the low ground (often below sea level) are a highlight of Jordan, especially if you are driving and can stop to admire the panoramic views. The roads twist through terraced fields of onions, hug contours of sheep-cropped hills and edge past nomadic communities of Bedouin with their black tents and attendant goats, before spiralling into a painted desert, vermilion with iron ore, olive green with copper oxides and laced with hanging gardens. You won't find the roads indicated on all maps, but they are all well paved, suitable for a 2WD car (beware sharp bends) and usually marked 'Dead Sea' or 'Wadi Araba' on signs. Remember to carry your passport with you as there are numerous checkpoints along the roads to the Jordan Valley and Dead Sea Highway.

Salt to the Dead Sea

1½ hours, 23km descent and 60km along the Jordan Valley

A varied drive along a busy road of Aleppo pines, red-barked strawberry trees and gardens of early-summer hollyhocks, giving way to tamarisks and acacias. Let your brakes cool at the sea-level marker and enjoy the view of the fertile Jordan Valley, lit up with flowering flame trees in May.

Follow signs for Zay National Park and Deir Alla on Hwy 30 from Salt. Watch out for truck drivers on their mobile phones on the hairpin bends! Add a 14km detour (well signposted) to Mountain Breeze Country Club for a tea break. Notice the humidity and heat as you approach the Dead Sea.

Mt Nebo to the Dead Sea

30 minutes, 21km

An easy drive, passing wildflowers and clumps of prickly pear, going through Bedouin grazing grounds before descending to a colourful, semi-arid desert with spectacular Dead Sea views.

The start of the descent is to the left of the Mt Nebo entrance gate. After 14.5km, turn left for the Dead Sea resorts or right for Bethany-Beyond-the-Jordan.

Madaba to the Dead Sea Panoramic Complex

50 minutes (half-day with stops), 30km plus 5km return trip to Hammamat Ma'in

The best of the Dead Sea drives, through avenues of windswept junipers and firs, vines and olive groves, and alongside a wadi decorated with flowering oleander. Don't miss the steep descent of the sulphurous hillside to Hammamat Ma'in. Recover at the aptly named Panorama Restaurant (p119). Follow signs for Hammamat Ma'in from King's Highway, 1km

caves, extensive wells and several baptism pools were unearthed. After much debate, scholars identified the site of John the Baptist's mission and Jesus' baptism from descriptions in the Bible and from 3rd- to 10th-century pilgrim accounts. Pope John Paul II sanctified the claim with an open-air mass at the site in the spring of 2000.

Sights

Entry to the Baptism Site includes a one-hour tour (in up to seven languages) of all the sites, as well as the shuttle bus from the ticket office at the main gate to the start of the tour. Tours run every 30 minutes. The complex is close to the sensitive border with Israel and the Palestinian Territories – security is tight and you should bring your passport. The last admission is one hour before closing.

The flies here can be of plague proportions in spring, so it's a good idea to bring repellent, along with a hat as the site is very exposed to the sun.

Jordan River RIVER

A walking trail passes a golden-roofed Greek Orthodox church and leads to a shaded wooden platform by the river, which here is little more than a creek lined with reeds. You can be baptised in the Jordan if accompanied by a priest; there's also a font accessible to all that is filled with water from the river (but note that, despite its holy status, south of Madaba. The road, sometimes referred to as the 'Dead Sea Parkway', is incorrectly shown on most maps. Use low gear if you're making a detour to Hammamat Ma'in. Continue to the Dead Sea resorts (7km), Bethany-Beyond-the-Jordan (25km) or Amman (60km).

Karak to Safi

30 minutes, 40km

This is an easy drive along a steep-sided wadi, with expansive views of potash production. Take a side trip to Lot's Cave (p123).

Time this drive for mid-afternoon, when the sunset turns the sandstone to molten gold. Follow signs from the King's Highway in Karak to Mazra'a or 'Dead Sea' along Hwy 50. Turn left at the Dead Sea Highway for Safi.

Tafila to Fifa

40 minutes, 26km

Descend from cypress woodland, through weather-beaten rock formations and palm oases to tomato fields at Fifa.

Give extra time to this trip – it's a veritable geography lesson in habitats at different altitudes. Take Hwy 60 from the centre of Tafila, following signs for Wadi Araba; take care on the sharp bends.

Little Petra to Wadi Araba

One hour 15 minutes (half-day with stops), 45km plus 2km return to Little Petra and 20km return to Feynan Ecolodge

This fantastic drive begins with Nabataean sites such as the Elephant Rock and a side trip to the Siq at Little Petra. Look out for rock-cut wine presses and dams through Siq Umm Al Alda, decorated with ancient carob trees. Pass through the psychedelically green landscape surrounding a reclaimed-water project and visit a pre-pottery Neolithic tell (ancient mound) – look for a wire fence on the left of the road – at Shkarat Msaiad. The mountain road thereafter twists through magnificent rainbow rocks before gliding into Wadi Araba, dotted with Bedouin camps, acacia trees and sand dunes.

Head through Umm Sayhoun to Little Petra. Turn right to Hesha and Bayder and immediately left, following signs to Wadi Araba. The road, which doesn't appear on most maps and isn't numbered, is damaged but not impassable at the bottom. At the junction in Wadi Araba, turn right to Qurayqira to stay at Feynan Ecolodge (p151) or left to reach the Dead Sea Highway. From the highway junction, it is 130km to Aqaba.

the river itself is quite polluted, so the water shouldn't be drunk).

This is the only place where civilians can currently touch the Jordan River in Jordan, as the remainder runs through a military no-man's land. Across the river is the Israeli-run complex of Qasr Al Yahud in the Palestinian Territories, where you can often see large groups of religious tourists being baptised.

Spring of John the Baptist SPRING

Accessible on foot (hot in summer so take a hat and water), this is one of several places where John is believed to have carried out baptisms. Most baptisms were conducted in the spring-fed waters of Wadi Al Kharrar rather than in the Jordan River. The path leads through thickets of tamarisk and *argul* (wild cherry), and the yellow rose of Jericho in spring.

Site of Jesus's Baptism RUINS

The main archaeological site comprises the remains of three churches, one on top of the other. Steps lead down to the original water level and a building nearby marks the likely site of Jesus's baptism. Byzantine churches were built to mark the site during the 5th and 6th centuries, and rebuilt on the same site after they were destroyed by flooding. All that remains today are traces of original mosaic.

IN SEARCH OF SODOM

Say the words 'Sodom and Gomorrah' and dens of iniquity spring to mind. The Book of Genesis (Gen 19:24–25), responsible for the wicked reputation of these two terrible towns, describes the last straw – namely, when local Sodomites demanded to have sex with the angels sent by God to visit Lot. In response 'the Lord rained upon Sodom and upon Gomorrah brimstone and fire...and he overthrew those cities, and all the plain, and all the inhabitants of the cities, and that which grew upon the ground...'

Fanciful legends of a fevered biblical imagination? Not necessarily. The edge of Wadi Araba is located on a major fault line, and it's possible that the towns were swallowed up by collapsing soil. Another possibility is that an earthquake released large amounts of underground flammable gas and bitumen (the infamous 'slime pits' referred to in the Old Testament), which were ignited by fire or a lightning strike.

Whatever the cause of their demise, archaeologists have long speculated about the location of the world's most sinful cities. Many archaeologists favour the southern shore of the Dead Sea. But there's also the Bronze Age site of Babh Adh Dhra, on the edge of Wadi Karak. This town (population roughly 1000) was destroyed in 2300 BC, but intriguingly it holds the remains of 20,000 tombs, containing an estimated half a million bodies – as such it's odds-on favourite for Sodom. Both Babh Adh Dhra and the nearby site of Numeira, believed to be Gomorrah, are covered in a 30cm-deep layer of ash, suggesting the cities ended in a great blaze.

Natural disaster or the wrath of God? Some believe it amounts to the same thing.

Rhotorios Monastery HISTORIC BUILDING
The hill behind the House of Mary the Egyptian holds the presumed cave of John the Baptist, a 5th-century monastery (built around the site) and the ruined Rhotorios Monastery, which has a mosaic floor with Greek inscriptions. In the 3rd to 4th century, the plaster-lined pools were used by pilgrims for bathing. In the early years of Christianity, John was a more celebrated figure than Jesus and this was the more important pilgrimage site at Bethany.

Tell Elias RUINS
Tell Elias is where Elijah is said to have ascended to heaven, although there is little to see here. The rebuilt arch marks the 5th- to 6th-century pilgrim chapel, where Pope John Paul II authenticated the site in 2000. The nearby 3rd-century rectangular prayer hall is one of the earliest Christian places of worship ever discovered, dating from a period when Christianity was still illegal.

House of Mary the Egyptian RUINS
Mary the Egyptian was a 'reformed sinner' who lived and died in a two-room house in the 4th century, now a ruin. The trail continues left, up some wooden stairs to a two-room **hermit cave** burrowed into the soft rock.

Eating

Bethany Touristic Restaurant SEAFOOD **$$**
(07 9607 6060; fish JD6-12; 10am-midnight) Attached to a thriving fish farm, this restaurant specialises in excellent tilapia (*talloubi* in Arabic), locally known as baptism fish. The fish is fried or baked with sweet peppers and fresh coriander. It's a popular spot at weekends, particularly at dusk when the sun sets over distant Jerusalem. It's halfway between the Baptism Site and the Amman–Dead Sea road.

Information

Collect a brochure and map at the **ticket office** (www.baptismsite.com; 8.30am-4pm Nov-Mar, to 6pm Apr-Oct) to the baptism site, where there are toilets and cold drinks for sale.

Getting There & Away

The site is near Shuneh Al Janubiyyeh, at the southern end of the Jordan Valley. Coming from Amman, follow signs to the Baptism Site along the main road to the Dead Sea. Tours from budget hotels in Amman and Madaba often include this site in a trip that also takes in the Dead Sea and Mt Nebo (from around JD60 for a taxi carrying four people).

There is no public transport to the Baptism Site; the closest you can get is 5km away at the Al Maghtas junction, on a Suweimah-bound minibus from Amman.

Dead Sea Panoramic Complex بانوراما البحر النيت

Walk among cacti to this lookout, high above the Dead Sea, and then watch raptors wheel in the wadis below, and you will have to pinch yourself to think that you are standing at sea level. This museum and restaurant **complex** (JD2; ⊙8am-10pm) offers breathtaking views, especially on a crisp day in winter when the Judaea Mountains across the water seem as if they are just an arm's stretch away.

For a solid introduction to the geology, history and environment of the Dead Sea, spare an hour for the **Dead Sea Museum** (☎08 771 2999; ⊙9am-4pm) FREE. Drive the roads in the area and you'll notice the rich pattern, texture and hue of the exposed rocks alongside the road. This is particularly the case on the Dead Sea Parkway, which extends above the Dead Sea Panorama to Hammamat Ma'in and Madaba, and below to the Dead Sea Highway. Along the cut of the steepest section of road, rich layers of sedimentary rock create natural murals that add to the beauty of the journey. You can identify and touch specimens of this geological treasure in the museum.

A short hiking trail called the **Zara Cliff Walk** (1.4km; easy) follows the edge of the wadi from the complex and highlights local flora and fauna. You will hear the Tristram's Grackles before you see these birds as they screech across the wadi. Hyrax can also be spotted here. The complex is clearly signposted off the Dead Sea Highway, about 10km south of the Dead Sea resorts. The Dead Sea Panorama makes a worthwhile stop on a day circuit from Madaba, Mt Nebo, Bethany, the Dead Sea and Hammamat Ma'in, either by hired car or taxi (JD50 through Charl at the Mariam Hotel). There is no public transport.

Panorama Restaurant MIDDLE EASTERN $$$
(☎05 324 5500; Dead Sea Panorama Complex; mains JD7-18; ⊙noon-10pm; ✍) The Panorama Restaurant more than lives up to its name and is a popular venue for weekend lunch and dinner. Try the ground walnut paste or the *shanklish* (local cheese, rolled in thyme and mixed with tomatoes, onion and parsley), and follow with marinated lamb chops or *sawda dajaj* (chicken livers with grenadine syrup and lemon), which are a meal in themselves.

Wadi Zarqa Ma'in وادي الزرقاء ماعين

ELEV -90M

Drive anywhere in the hills above the Dead Sea, and you'll notice occasional livid-green belts of vegetation, a trickle of water as it catches the sunlight, or a curtain of ferns across a disintegrating landscape of sulphurous rock. On closer inspection, you may catch a puff of steam and the hiss of underground water. These hills are alive with the sound of thermal springs – about 60 of them suppurate below the surface, breaking ground with various degrees of violence.

THE JORDAN TRAIL: FUHEIS TO ZARQA MA'IN

Distance 78km

Duration Four days

This four-day section of the Jordan Trail hike offers a great illustration of Jordan's many contrasting landscapes, from rolling green hills to the sparse, rocky crags overlooking the Dead Sea.

From the town of Fuheis, you strike out into fertile countryside dotted with small farms, following the paths of Roman roads towards the ancient ruins at Iraq Al Amir. After staying here one night, the hike takes you southwest down the soft landscapes of the Jordan Valley to the Kafrain Dam where you camp. Over the next day, the landscape grows increasingly stark as you head towards the Dead Sea Plateau. Shepherd's paths take you past old Mukawer, always with views to the sea and the hills in Israel and the Palestinian Territories beyond. Finally, you descend to the springs of Wadi Zarqa Ma'in, where the hike concludes.

This is a moderate hike, but it is best done with support as there is no water available on the last two days. For route maps, GPS waypoints and detailed breakdowns of daily hikes visit Jordan Trail (www.jordantrail.org).

THE DEAD SEA IS DYING

The Dead Sea is the lowest place on earth, and probably one of the hottest. The resulting evaporation produces an astonishing salinity of 31%, about nine times higher than the oceans. The high mineral concentrations mean incredible buoyancy and great photo opportunities – get a snapshot of your travel companions happily sitting upright on the water reading newspapers. The water's oily minerals also contain salubrious properties. German health insurance covers periodic visits to the Dead Sea for psoriasis patients to visit and luxuriate in the healing waters.

Sadly, no natural resource in the Middle East shows more signs of relentless population growth and economic development than the Dead Sea. Technically, the sea is a 'terminal lake' into which the Jordan River, along with other more arid watersheds, deposit their flow. Despite the folk song's characterisation of the River Jordan as 'deep and wide', in fact it has never been much of a gusher. When Israeli and Jordanian farmers began to divert its water to produce a new agricultural economy in the 1950s, the flow was reduced to a putrid trickle, and the Dead Sea began to dry up.

In 1900, the river discharged 1.2 trillion litres a year into the Dead Sea, but water levels in the river today are hardly 10% of the natural flow. The Jordanian and Israeli potash industries in the southern, largely industrial Dead Sea region exacerbate the water loss by accelerating evaporation in their production processes. The impact is manifested in sink holes, created when underground salt gets washed away by the infiltrating subsurface freshwater flow. Particularly ubiquitous on the western (Israeli side) of the sea, the ground literally opens up – with people, farming equipment and even trucks falling in. Perhaps the most acute environmental consequence though is the 27m drop in the sea's water level, and the long and discouraging walks now required to reach the retreating waters.

Several solutions have been considered to bring back water to the Dead Sea. A 'Med-Dead' canal utilising the height drop from the Mediterranean Sea was discarded because of the prohibitively expensive price tag. But a similar pipeline from the Red Sea is currently under consideration, to pipe water from the Gulf of Aqaba to the Dead Sea's southern shore, producing hydroelectricity as well as a desalination plant that would provide water to Amman. Environmentalists question the anticipated mixing of different salinities of sea water, while noting that it would ultimately not do enough to replace the water already being lost. Nevertheless, the US$1.1 billion 'Red-Dead' project has been put out to tender, and Jordan expects to break the first ground in 2018.

Activities

Hiking

It's possible to hike the 8km from the Hammamat Ma'in springs through Wadi Zarqa Ma'in to Herodus Spring on the Dead Sea Highway. The moderate to hard trail involves negotiating deep pools, reed beds and slippery surfaces and is closed after rains. The hike requires a guide (JD120 for a minimum of two people), which can be organised through the resort reception if you book one day ahead. The fee includes the price of transport to collect you from the end of the trail.

Another small trail leads from the security guard hut to a spot above the main waterfall. It is an easy hike and there is no need for a guide, but you are requested to let the Ma'in Hot Springs Resort reception know that you are attempting it. If you would prefer a guide to help manage the small, steep section, it costs JD35 per person (minimum two people); for JD65, you can also have breakfast, which is winched across the wadi in a basket to a shaded picnic spot in full view of the main waterfall.

Thermal Bathing

Ma'in Hot Springs Spa SPA

(☎05 324 5500; www.mainhotsprings.com; Hammamat Ma'in; ⌚9am-8pm) The resort's exquisite spa offers a range of different treatments and experiences. There are two thermal pools naturally hovering at 42°C and a natural sauna cave (65°C to 70°C) buried discreetly in the heart of the wadi. It's a beautiful place to relax, with grouse scuttling over the rocks and eagles wheeling above.

In addition, there is a dry sauna and treatment rooms, each with a private garden. Use of the facilities costs JD38 including towels and green tea. The range of treatments includes a one-hour Dead Sea body wrap, Swedish massage and Dead Sea Salt Body Polish. If you book in at the spa, the JD15 entry fee to Hammamat Ma'in is waived.

Hammamat Ma'in BATHHOUSE
(JD15; 9am-9pm) The most famous thermal spring in the hills above the Dead Sea is Hammamat Ma'in, 18.5km from the Dead Sea resorts. Here the water, ranging from 45°C to a blistering 60°C, tumbles off the hillside in a series of waterfalls and less assuming trickles, and is collected in a variety of pools for public bathing. It contains potassium, magnesium and calcium. The entrance fee permits use of the **Roman baths** at the base of the waterfall closest to the entrance.

The Roman baths have clean, indoor hot baths (separate for men and women). There is also a small family pool beside a waterfall (turn left after the entrance), restricted to women, families and couples. The large, clean, cold-water swimming pool closes around 4pm. A steaming waterfall downstream makes a striking backdrop for tea on the terrace of the hotel.

Visitors are requested not to bring their own picnic, but this is rarely enforced. The springs are hugely popular on Friday during spring and autumn.

Sleeping & Eating

Ma'In Hot Springs Resort & Spa RESORT $$$
(05 324 5500; www.mainhotsprings.com; Hammamat Ma'in; r from JD130;) This luxurious resort is shaded by mature trees and boasts extravagant arabesque features. Many of the rooms – which have sumptuous bathrooms – share a view of the steaming, sulphurous hillsides. Windows onto the waterfalls from the restaurant bring the hot springs to your table. Fine dining includes herbs and vegetables from the hotel's organic garden.

The hotel organises daily excursions to the Dead Sea, but chances are you'll find it hard to leave the sanctuary of its intimate spa.

Getting There & Away

The resort at Hammamat Ma'in is 18.5km from the Dead Sea resorts and 27km from Madaba, and well signposted in either direction. If you're driving, the 2.5km descent into Hammamat Ma'in is scenic (with bands of green, yellow and red streaking the hillside) but very steep, so use low gear.

A taxi from Madaba costs around JD25 for a return journey, including waiting time. There is no public transport.

Mujib Biosphere Reserve
محمية الموجب

This **reserve** (06 461 6523; Dead Sea Hwy) – the lowest on earth – was originally established by the Royal Society for the Conservation of Nature (RSCN) for the captive breeding of the Nubian ibex. It now supports a surprising variety of more than 400 species of plants (including rare orchids), 186 species of birds and 250 animal species, including Syrian wolves, striped hyenas, caracals and Blandford's fox. It's also an important staging post for migratory birds travelling between Africa and Europe.

The reserve encompasses the canyonesque landscape of Wadi Mujib, and is a great destination for day hikes. There are several guided routes, including a number that involve scrambling over rocks and then wading through chest-high pools of water.

Activities

Hiking and splashing your way through Mujib's canyons are the main reason to visit the reserve. Different trails are open at different times of year – the wet trails are only accessible between April and October as water levels outside of this period can make them too dangerous.

Siq Trail

The most popular hike on offer, this exciting self-guided 2km wade and scramble into the gorge ends at a dramatic waterfall. Fees are JD21 per person; the trail is open from 1 April to 31 October.

HIKING HINTS IN WADI MUJIB

- The best months for hiking are April and May.
- Guided treks usually begin early in the morning.
- For the wet trails, bring a swimming costume, towel, walking shoes that can get wet, and a waterproof bag. Spare clothes are also recommended. Life jackets are provided.
- There's a minimum group size of three on some trails.
- Under 18s are not allowed on the trails.

The wadi is decorated with outrageously banded rock, scooped out and smoothed by the water. Late spring and summer are the perfect times for hiking this 'wet trail'. And by wet, we really do mean it – at some point you may need to wade waist or chest deep, and the hike culminates in a spectacular waterfall with a large pool where you can swim. After rains, rising water can make the wadi dangerous and inaccessible, so it is closed between November and March.

You don't need a guide for the Siq Trail, but there are three or four points where you need a steadying hand to help cross fast-moving water or to pull yourself up the steps set into boulders.

Wear hiking sandals rather than leather hiking boots.

Malaqi Trail

This guided wet trail is one of the reserve's most popular hikes (per person JD44). It's a half-day trip involving a hot and unremitting climb into the wadi, a visit to the natural swimming pools of Wadi Hidan and a descent (often swimming) through the siq (gorge). The finale involves rappelling down an 18m waterfall (not suitable for nonswimmers or vertigo sufferers). Open from 1 April to 31 October.

Ibex Trail

This dry winter trail (per person JD21) is a half-day guided hike that leads up to a Nubian ibex enclosure at the Raddas ranger station, along a ridge with views of the Dead Sea, and an optional excursion to the ruined Qasr Riyash. Open from 1 November to 31 March.

Canyon Trail

If you have limited time at Wadi Mujib, tackle the guided wet Canyon Trail (JD31). The trail starts 3km south of the visitor centre and takes around four hours. Open from 1 April to 31 October.

Sleeping & Eating

★Mujib Chalets CHALET **$$**

(☎07 9720 3888; www.wildjordan.com; s/d/tr JD52/64/75; 📶) Wild Jordan operates 15 stylish and modern en-suite chalets overlooking the Dead Sea. You need to book in advance, either by calling the chalet manager directly or when booking your hike through the RSCN. The chalets have double or twin beds, a fridge and a shaded patio overlooking the Dead Sea, in a plot that is still under development.

There are freshwater showers by the beach. The small restaurant serves an early breakfast for hikers; guests can also order a simple lunch or dinner in advance.

Information

The **visitor centre** (☎07 9720 3888; ⏰8am-8pm) is along the Dead Sea Highway, about 20km south of the Dead Sea resorts, beside a suspension bridge across Wadi Mujib. Guides are compulsory for all but the Siq Trail and should preferably be booked in advance through the RSCN's Wild Jordan Center (p69), though they can be booked at the visitor centre if any are available on the day. There are a few information boards about the reserve, but few facilities. Children under 18 years are not allowed on the trails.

Getting There & Away

There's no public transport to the reserve: hire a car or take a taxi from Amman, the Dead Sea resorts, Madaba or Karak.

Lisan Peninsula

شبه جزيرة اللسان

The Lisan Peninsula lies at the southern end of the Dead Sea. It's worth a detour for the community tourism project of the Zikra Initiative, along with Lot's Cave and the appropriately named Lowest Point on Earth Museum. The region was settled during the early-Byzantine period and a number of minor ruins are scattered across the landscape.

The area, together with the shallow waters of the Southern Ghor (Depression), is now dominated by a giant potash plant. Huge quantities of potassium chloride (Jordan's most valuable commodity), calcium and bromine are reclaimed from the Dead Sea through solar evaporation.

The fields to the south of the Lisan Peninsula are highly fertile and produce vegetables in biblical quantities, making it a particularly colourful region to visit during the January harvest.

Sights

Lowest Point on Earth Museum MUSEUM

(☎03 230 2845; Safi; JD2, free with Jordan Pass; ⏰8am-4pm) Near the start of the climb up to Lot's Cave is the literally titled Lowest Point on Earth Museum. Shaped like a giant stone comma, it contains beautifully displayed remains excavated from the site, including mosaics, 4500-year-old pottery and ancient

WORTH A TRIP

A DAY AMONG THE DEAD SEA RESIDENTS

While luxury spas are the face of Dead Sea tourism, the **Zikra Initiative** (www.zikrainitiative.org) has been pioneering an alternative approach: community-exchange tourism. Visitors can arrange to spend the day in the farming community of Ghor Al Mazra'a at the southern tip of the Dead Sea, learning how to tend gardens, make handicrafts and bake bread, or how to cook the delicious local dish *galayat bandora* ('tomato in a pan'). Locals can also take you on hikes in the surrounding hills.

It's a relaxed and low-key approach to tourism, allowing you to make a direct personal connection with rural Jordanians and learn about their lives. The visitor fees (usually around JD35) are ploughed directly back into the community in the form of microloans for local families, and social development projects. Visits must be arranged in advance through the website.

textiles. Other displays explain the area's importance for sugar production during the Mamluk period, and artefacts that bring the region's story up to the Bedouin tribes of today.

Lot's Cave CAVE

(daylight) FREE Lot's Cave, a stiff 10-minute climb up a steep flight of steps, is surrounded by the ruins of a small Byzantine church (5th to 8th centuries), a reservoir and some mosaics, which were excavated by the British Museum. Remains from the cave date to the early Bronze Age (3300–2000 BC) and an inscription in the cave mentions Lot by name.

Lot, the nephew of Abraham, features repeatedly in the colourful annals of the Dead Sea's southern shores. Lot's Cave, just past the Lisan Peninsula, is where he and his daughters are said to have lived after fleeing the destruction of Sodom and Gomorrah; Lot's wife is famously believed to have turned into a pillar of salt after looking back at the smouldering city.

In an eyebrow-raising incident that's remarkable even for the Bible, it's said that Lot's two daughters spiked their father's drink, had sex with him and then nine months later gave birth to his grandsons/sons Moab and Ben Ammi, the forefathers of the Moabite and Ammonite peoples.

The cave is 2km northeast of Safi and well signposted from the Dead Sea Highway. Look for the circular museum building on the hillside. Regular minibuses run between Karak and Safi (800 fils, one hour). If you're relying on public transport, be prepared for a 2km walk from the highway.

Getting There & Away

Your own vehicle is essential for exploring around the Lisan Peninsula and southern Dead Sea area. Fill your tank before setting out – there are no petrol stations in the area.

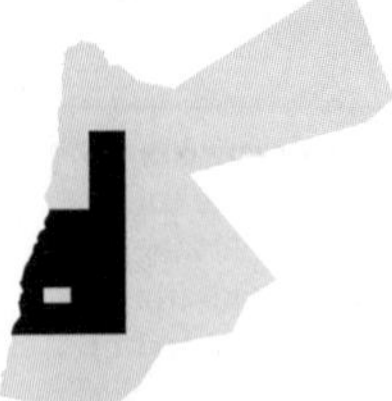

Madaba & the King's Highway
مأدبا & الطريق الملوكي

Includes ➡

Best Places to Eat

- Haret Jdoudna (p134)
- Adonis Restaurant & Cafe (p133)
- Al Mandi (p133)

Best Places to Stay

- Black Iris Hotel (p131)
- Mariam Hotel (p131)
- Al Nawatef Camp (p150)
- Dana Guest House (p152)
- Feynan Ecolodge (p151)

Why Go?

The King's Highway runs down the spine of Jordan's central highlands, bisected by the mighty canyon of Wadi Mujib. With panoramic sites of biblical importance, exquisite Roman mosaics and well-preserved Crusader castles, there's something fascinating to see along the entire length of this central region.

Madaba, with mosaic-decorated churches reflecting its rich Christian heritage, is the perfect base for exploring the area. From here you can visit the castles of Karak and Shobak, and the spot where it's said Moses first saw the Promised Land at Mt Nebo. You're also just a short hop from Amman and the Dead Sea.

The Dana Biosphere Reserve is one of Jordan's best natural areas, with ample opportunities to hike, camp, birdwatch and otherwise get close to nature. It's easy to engage with both town and country in a region that's still surprisingly off the beaten track for most visitors.

When to Go

- Enjoyable year-round, the higher-altitude towns in the central highlands often see snow in winter, providing a spectacular backdrop to Crusader castles. The cold air brings cut-glass clarity to the region's sweeping panoramas by day, and chilly nights inspire huddles around wood fires in true Arabian fashion.
- For hiking, the season extends from March (when trail-side flowers are at their best) until 30 October. While Jordan's lowlands shrivel in the heat, this region's uplands offer relative cool, grapes and figs in abundance, raptor migration and grand sunsets.

Madaba & the King's Highway Highlights

1 Madaba
(p126) Piecing together early Christian history while exploring Jordan's best collection of Byzantine mosaics, housed in a series of still operating churches.

2 Mt Nebo
(p136) Surveying the view that Moses is said to have gazed upon when he saw the Promised Land.

3 Wadi Mujib
(p141) Enjoying the eagle's-eye vista from the lookout over a dramatic Grand Canyon–esque landscape.

4 Karak Castle
(p143) Seeing Jordan's Crusader and Mamluk history carved into the stones of the country's most impressive castle complex.

5 Dana Biosphere Reserve (p148)
Hiking from the temperate uplands to the scorching desert floor of Wadi Araba, while staying at some of the Middle East's most ecofriendly guesthouses.

History

The landscape either side of the great yawning gap of Wadi Mujib is identical. There are neat olive groves, avenues of poplars, prickly-pear fences, gently undulating hills, sheep being driven along a network of paths, villages of flat-roofed houses and occasional piles of fallen masonry from antiquity. North and south of the divide, the rural communities seem to form part of a seamless continuum along the surface of the upper plateau and, unless you've driven along the King's Highway, you might never guess at the great hiatus that divides the region in two.

There is surely no better metaphor for the continuity of human life along this ancient trade route. During the past 3000 years, the King's Highway has been traversed by the Israelites en route to the Promised Land; by Nabataeans to and from their sacred city at Petra; by Christian faithful on pilgrimages to Mt Nebo (where Moses is said to have seen the Promised Land); by Crusaders to their castle fortifications; and by Muslim pilgrims heading to and from Mecca. Travel the road today, with all its difficulties, and you follow in the path of history.

Nature Reserves

The Royal Society for the Conservation of Nature (RSCN) manages two nature reserves straddling the central plateau, wedged between the King's Highway and the Dead Sea Hwy. Mujib Biosphere Reserve is more usually accessed from the Dead Sea. Dana Biosphere Reserve (p148) is accessed via the small upland village of Dana, just off the King's Highway. Protecting a rich diversity of flora and fauna, Dana Biosphere Reserve offers the visitor a chance to camp and hike in the reserve's striking landscape. Note that the Feynan Ecolodge (p151) inside the reserve is only accessible by vehicle from the Dead Sea Hwy (it's a day's hike from Dana village).

Dangers & Annoyances

Hiking and canyoning in any of the wadis that criss-cross the region should be approached with caution, if not avoided, from November to February because of the danger of flash floods. After rains, walls of water roll out of the canyons without warning, even on a cloudless day, uprooting trees and strewing boulders in their wake. Take advice before setting out and inform your accommodation where you are heading.

It can get seriously cold in winter, with snow and hail. Many visitors get caught without adequate clothing, as the daytime temperatures may still be beguilingly warm.

There is no public transport that crosses Wadi Mujib on the King's Highway, making it easy to get stranded – especially dangerous in high summer temperatures.

Getting There & Away

Of Jordan's three highways running north to south, the King's Highway, little more than a rural road for most of its length, is by far the most interesting, with a host of historical attractions lying on the road or nearby. The King's Highway is connected with the Dead Sea Hwy via spectacular hairpin roads that are a highlight in their own right. Most public transport, however, connects with the King's Highway via the Desert Hwy.

A border crossing at King Hussein (Allenby) Bridge north of the Dead Sea gives access to Israel and the Palestinian Territories.

Madaba is directly accessible from the main international airport (without the need to enter Amman).

Getting Around

It's not possible to travel the length of the King's Highway by public transport. This is because Wadi Mujib gets in the way. Minibuses serve the communities on either side of the wadi, but through traffic uses the Desert Hwy. Chartering a taxi for the day, however, is feasible. If you need to change minibuses, you're likely to do that in Tafila.

The most convenient way to explore the King's Highway is to hire a car. You can drive the whole route from Madaba to Petra in a day. Allowing time to stop at all the places of interest and then returning along the Dead Sea Hwy takes four to five days.

Hotels in Madaba and downtown Amman run minibus tours that stop in Wadi Mujib and Karak (and sometimes Dana and Shobak) en route to Petra.

CENTRAL JORDAN

Madaba مأدبا

☎05 / POP 105,350 / ELEV 800M

The amiable market town of Madaba is best known for a collection of Byzantine-era mosaics. The most famous of these is the map on the floor of St George's Church, but there are many others in different parts of the town, several of them even more complete and vibrantly colourful.

Madaba has one of Jordan's largest Christian communities. The town's long tradition of religious tolerance is joyfully – and loudly – expressed on Friday, when imams (religious teachers) summon the faithful to pray before dawn, and bells bid Orthodox Christians to rise at first light.

The town remains one of the most traveller friendly in Jordan, and it's an alternative to Amman as a base for exploring the King's Highway and Dead Sea highlights. By taxi, you can even travel directly from Queen Alia International Airport in around 20 minutes, bypassing Amman altogether.

History

The region around Madaba has been inhabited for around 4500 years and is said to be one of the towns divided among the 12 tribes of Israel at the time of the Exodus. The region passed from the Ammonites to the Israelites, the Nabataeans and eventually, by AD 106, the Romans, under whom Madaba became a prosperous provincial town with colonnaded streets and impressive public buildings. The prosperity continued during the Christian Byzantine period, with the construction of churches and the lavish mosaics that decorated them.

The town was abandoned for about 1100 years after a devastating earthquake in 747. In the late 19th century, 2000 Christians from Karak migrated to Madaba after a bloody dispute with Karak's Muslims. The new arrivals found the town's signature mosaics when they started digging foundations for houses. News that a mosaic map of the Holy Land had been found in St George's Church in Madaba reached Europe in 1897, leading to excavation work that continues to this day.

Sights

The most interesting part of town is the old quarter on top of the hill, rather than the new developments along the King's Highway. Follow signs for the 'Visitors Centre', or any of the hotels, to reach the centre of town.

NAVIGATING THE MADABA MAP

It takes some orientation to be able to 'read' the Mabada Map spread across the floor of St George's Church. Chances are you will intuitively look at the mosaic expecting north to be in front of you, towards the altar. In fact, the map, and indeed the church itself, is oriented towards the east. Imagine, therefore, as you approach the map, that you are in the hills west of Jerusalem, looking over the crenulated tops of the great city residences towards the Dead Sea, and follow the guide below for the highlights.

North (Top Left)

In the most touching part of the mosaic, fish in the Jordan River swim upstream from the lethal waters of the Dead Sea, making their way under the cable-drawn ferries of the river crossing (marked today by King Hussein Bridge). A bodiless lion pursues a gazelle just above Bethany, said to be the site of Jesus's baptism (marked as 'Sapsafas' on the map).

East (Straight Ahead)

The most exquisitely detailed part of the map depicts Jerusalem, complete with city walls, gates and the central road (*cardo*). Becalmed on the waters of the Dead Sea, their oars at the ready, lie two boats going nowhere. Perhaps they were trying to ferry Herod to the spa at Callirhöe (Zara), marked by three springs and two palm trees. Lot's Cave, where the old man is said to have been seduced by his two daughters, lies just above the oasis of Safi (Balak or Zoara). The walled town of Karak appears in the uppermost portion of the map, at the end of vertical Wadi Al Hasa.

South (Far Right)

Mt Sinai is recognisable by the multicoloured mountains from which Moses is believed to have descended with the Ten Commandments. Look for fish in the mosaic fingers of the Nile Delta; they swim towards the Mediterranean, only a snippet of which remains. Almost fragmented from the rest of the Holy Land by damage, but resolutely connected to Egypt and the Mediterranean Sea, is Gaza. This accident of history gives the map a kind of presentiment that matches its historical vision.

Madaba

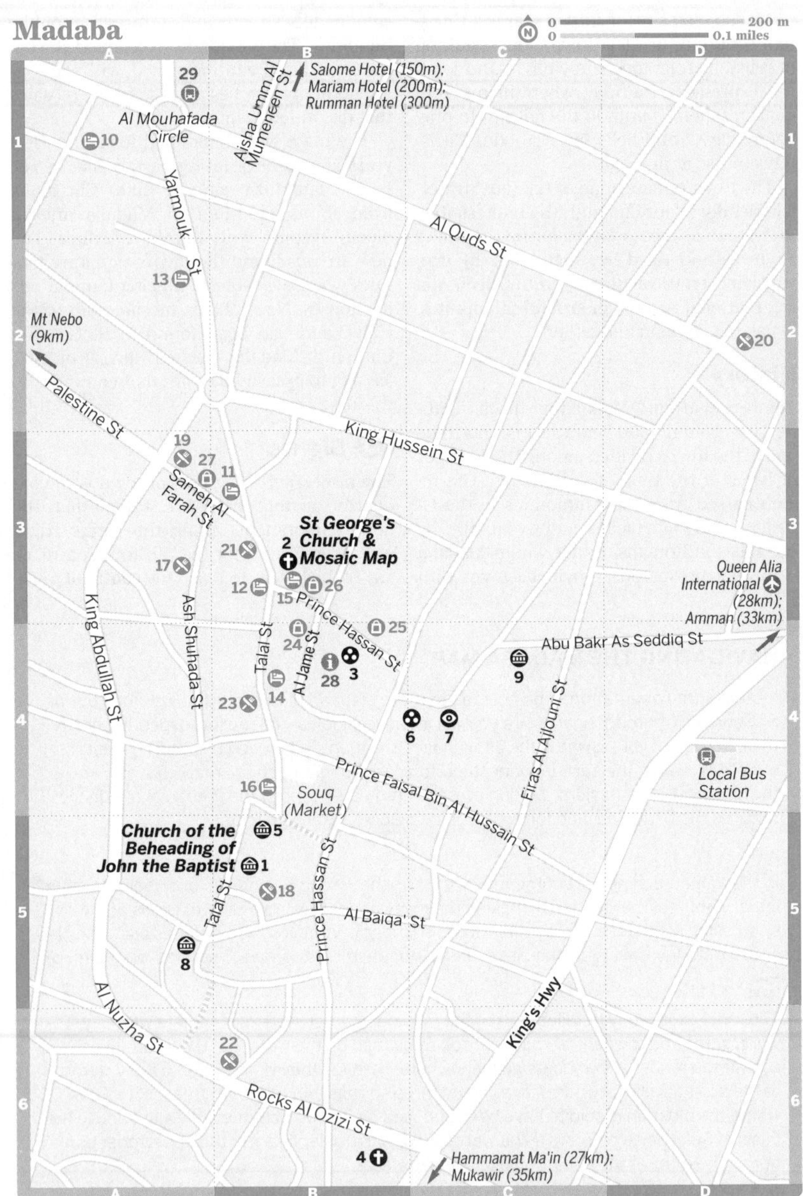

Many tourists file dutifully into and out of St George's Church and pay scant attention to the rest of Madaba. This is good news for those with the time to pore over the town's other stunning mosaics, as they'll be untroubled by crowds.

You can buy a combined ticket (JD3) at Archaeological Parks I and II, Madaba Museum and the Church of the Apostles that will cover admission to all four sights.

Madaba

Top Sights
1 Church of the Beheading of John the Baptist B5
2 St George's Church & Mosaic Map B3

Sights
3 Archaeological Park II B4
4 Church of the Apostles B6
5 Dar Al Saraya B5
6 Madaba Archaeological Park I & Virgin Mary Church C4
7 Madaba Institute for Mosaic Art & Restoration C4
8 Madaba Museum A5
9 Visitors Centre C4

Sleeping
10 Black Iris Hotel A1
11 Madaba 1880 Hotel B3
12 Moab Land Hotel B3
13 Mosaic City Hotel A2
14 Queen Ayola Hotel B4
15 St George's Church Pilgrim House B3
16 St John Hotel B4

Eating
17 Abu Yousef A3
18 Adonis Restaurant & Cafe B5
19 Al Baraka Sweets A3
20 Al Mandi D2
21 Ayola Coffeeshop & Bar B3
Bowabit Restaurant .... (see 21)
22 Dana Restaurant B6
23 Haret Jdoudna B4

Shopping
24 Carpet City B4
25 Hanania Silver Shop & Rafidi for Silver B4
Haret Jdoudna Complex .... (see 23)
Holy Treasures Centre .... (see 12)
26 Lawrence Arts & Crafts B3
27 Spice A3

Information
28 Ministry of Tourism & Antiquities B4

Transport
29 Minibuses to Amman A1

★ Church of the Beheading of John the Baptist — MUSEUM

(Latin Church; ☎05 324 4065; Talal St; adult/child under 12yr JD1/free; ⏰9am-5pm Oct-Apr, to 7pm May-Sep) This operational early-20th-century Roman Catholic church has been transformed into an intriguing destination for visitors and pilgrims by the restoration of the ancient sites upon which it sits. The gem of the complex is the **Acropolis Museum**, housed in the vaulted underbelly of the church. Here a well dating to the Moabite era, 3000 years ago, is still operational.

The church facade was built with stones from antiquity, and Roman columns with Corinthian capitals dot the courtyard. In the 19th-century chapel, which now acts as a visitor centre and gift shop, there's a fascinating exhibition of photographs dating from 1902 to 1911 and an excellent replica of the mosaics at Umm Ar Rasas. Spare some time and energy to scale the belfry. The last section involves steep metal ladders with handrails and a bit of dexterity manoeuvring around the bells and bell ropes, but it's worth the effort for the best panorama in Madaba. Vertigo sufferers, however, should definitely avoid the climb.

The church is closed to visitors during Mass and for occasional Sunday events.

★ St George's Church & Mosaic Map — CHURCH

(Talal St; adult/child under 12yr JD1/free; ⏰9.30am-5pm Fri year-round, 8am-5pm Sat-Thu Nov-Mar, to 6pm Sat-Thu Apr-Oct) This rather modest 19th-century Greek Orthodox church houses a treasure of early Christianity. Imagine the excitement in 1884 when Christian builders came across the remnants of a Byzantine church on their construction site. Among the rubble, having survived wilful destruction, fire and neglect, the flooring they discovered wasn't just another mosaic but one with extraordinary significance: to this day, it represents the oldest map of Palestine in existence and provides many historical insights into the region.

Crafted in AD 560, the map has 157 captions (in Greek) depicting all the major biblical sites of the Middle East, from Egypt to Palestine. It was originally around 15m to 25m long and 6m wide, and once contained more than two million pieces. Although much of the mosaic has been lost, enough remains to sense the complexity of the whole.

On Friday and Sunday mornings the church opens at 7am for Mass (visitors are welcome); viewing the map at these times is not permitted. A shop by the exit sells copies of the map and reproduction Orthodox icons.

The ticket office doubles as a small interpretative centre, and has excellent displays recounting the history of the mosaics and the church – it's well worth spending some time here before viewing the map, as it will make it easier to spot the details that you want to focus on in the church.

Church of the Apostles CHURCH

(King's Hwy; adult/child under 12yr JD3/free, with Jordan Pass free; ⏲9am-4pm Oct-Apr, 8am-5pm May-Sep) This insignificant-looking church contains a remarkable mosaic dedicated to the Twelve Apostles. The embroidery-like mosaic was created in AD 568 and is one of the few instances where the name of the craftsman (Salomios) is included. The central portion shows Thalassa, a female personification of the sea, surrounded by fish and slippery marine creatures. Native animals, birds, flowers, fruit and cherubic faces decorate the corners.

Madaba Archaeological Park I & Virgin Mary Church ARCHAEOLOGICAL SITE

(☎05 324 6681; Abu Bakr As Seddiq St; adult/child under 12yr JD3/free, with Jordan Pass free; ⏲8am-4pm Oct-Apr, to 5pm May-Sep) Some careful restoration and excavation in the early 1990s led to the creation of this open-air museum, which houses a collection of ruins and fine mosaics from the Madaba area. The Church of the Virgin Mary is also included in the site; built in the 6th century and unearthed beneath the floor of a private house in 1887, the church boasts a central mosaic, thought to date from 767, that is a masterpiece of geometric design.

As you enter the complex you'll see a 1st-century-BC mosaic from Machaerus, which is believed to be the oldest mosaic found in Jordan. Follow the walkway to the right, above the Roman street. This street once ran east to west between the Roman city gates and was lined with columns. Continue past the faded but elegant mosaics of the Church of the Prophet Elias (built AD 607), pausing to enjoy the details (such as the fine green bird), and then descend to the crypt (built AD 595).

The large roofed structure in front of you contains some of the most impressive mosaics on the site, including those of Hippolytus Hall, an early-6th-century Byzantine villa. Spot the four seasons in each corner and notice the beautiful depictions of flowers and birds. The middle section shows figures from the classic Greek tragedy of Phaedra and Hippolytus. The upper image shows Adonis and a topless Aphrodite spanking naughty, winged Eros, while the Three Graces (daughters of Zeus representing joy, charm and beauty) float nearby.

Visitors Centre HISTORIC BUILDING

(☎05 325 3563; Abu Bakr As Seddiq St; ⏲8am-6pm Oct-Apr, to 7pm May-Sep) This helpful interpretative centre makes a good starting point for visiting the highlights of Madaba. It's worth a visit in its own right, as it's housed in a beautifully restored traditional house from the late 19th century, belonging to the Al Batjali family. Two of the rooms contain interesting information panels in English on the history of Madaba, and there's a 10-minute film that sets the town in its historical context.

The shady courtyard of plumbago and geraniums offers respite from a hot day's sightseeing; there are clean toilets next to the centre's car park.

Archaeological Park II ARCHAEOLOGICAL SITE

(Burnt Palace; Prince Hassan St; adult/child under 12yr JD3/free, with Jordan Pass free; ⏲8am-3pm Sun-Thu Oct-Apr, to 5.30pm Sun-Thu May-Sep) FREE Walkways lead around the ruins of this late-6th-century luxury private mansion, destroyed by fire and earthquake around 749. The walkways offer a good view of assorted mosaics, the best of which are the hunting sequences in the east wing, and the lion attacking a bull in the west wing. It's fair to say that the site takes more imagination than most.

Look out for the continuation of the ancient Roman road that runs through what is now the Archaeological Park, as well as the 6th-century Martyrs Church, which was destroyed in the 8th century. If the guard on duty is willing, you may be able to see the buried mosaics of the church: protected from the light by sand until restoration takes place, the few tesserae (squares) of mosaic that he'll expose for you are astonishing in the vibrancy of their colour.

Madaba Institute for Mosaic Art & Restoration WORKSHOP

(MIMAR; ☎05 324 0723; Abu Bakr As Seddiq St; ⏲8am-3pm Sun-Thu) FREE Originally set up as a school in 1992 by the Jordanian government, this institute trains Jordanian artists in the production and restoration of mosaics, spreads awareness of mosaics in Jordan and actively preserves mosaics throughout the country. The restoration work of the school's artisans is evident in the Archaeological Park, the Church of the Apostles and at Khirbet Mukhayyat. Visit the administration office to arrange a workshop visit to enhance your appreciation of the painstaking nature of mosaic making.

Madaba Museum MUSEUM
(☎05 324 4189; Haya Bint Al Hussin St; adult/child under 12yr JD3/free, with Jordan Pass free; ⏲8am-5pm Oct-Apr, to 7pm May-Sep) Housed in several old Madaba residences, this museum features a 6th-century mosaic depicting a naked satyr; a saucy (and partly damaged) mosaic of Ariadne dancing with cymbals on her hands and feet; and a mosaic in the courtyard depicting two rams tied to a tree – a popular image recalling Abraham's sacrifice. A small, dusty Folklore Museum is included in the admission price; it features jewellery, traditional costumes and a copy of the Mesha Stele (p141).

The museum is a little below par if you've toured the rest of the Madaba mosaics, but the open courtyard with grapevines, palms and a view makes a pleasant place to sit.

Dar Al Saraya HISTORIC BUILDING
(Talal St) Built in the late 19th century as the administrative centre of the Ottomans, this grand old building was subsequently used as the headquarters of the British administration in 1922. It's been well restored and there are plans for it to become a restaurant. In the meantime, the adjacent hillside plaza makes a good place to catch the breeze.

Sleeping

Madaba has a good range of hotels, almost all within easy walking distance of the town's main sights.

★**Black Iris Hotel** GUESTHOUSE $
(☎05 324 1959; www.blackirishotel.com; s/d/tr JD25/35/48; 📶) For a home-away-from-home feeling, it's hard to beat this tidy hotel near Al Mouhafada Circle. The rooms are cosy and there's a spacious communal sitting area. The breakfast spreads are notably excellent (try the date molasses with tahini). The kindly and knowledgeable travel assistance makes the Black Iris ever popular with readers; women travelling alone will feel comfortable here.

Rumman Hotel HOTEL $
(☎05 325 2555; www.rummanhotel.com; Aisha Umm Al Mumeneen St; s/d/tr JD23/30/38; @📶) With a friendly owner, spacious contemporary rooms and the only bathtubs in town, Rumman lives up to the Twal family reputation for hospitality and visitor assistance.

Moab Land Hotel GUESTHOUSE $
(☎05 325 1318; www.moablandhotel.com; Talal St; s/d/tr JD26/32/40) With grand views of St George's Church (p129) and beyond, this family-run hotel couldn't be more central. The prize draw, apart from the welcome, is the glorious rooftop terrace where breakfast is served in summer. Reception is on the upper floor.

St George's Church Pilgrim House GUESTHOUSE $
(☎07 7536 4218; pilgrimshousemadaba@gmail.com; Talal St; s/d/tr JD25/35/45; 📶) Although this guesthouse receives mainly Christian pilgrims, all travellers can expect a warm welcome here. Rooms are ascetically simple. If you encounter the patron, the urbane and charming Father Innocent (self-described as 'Innocent by name, guilty by every other means'), your stay will be extra blessed. Guesthouse profits are invested in the neighbouring church school. Entry is via Prince Hassan St.

Queen Ayola Hotel HOTEL $
(☎05 324 4087; Talal St; r JD20, with shared bathroom JD18; 📶) This once-popular travellers' haunt has seen better days. The rooms are extremely basic, but they're clean, and two have balconies onto the street – fun for people-watching in the heart of town. The restaurant was mothballed at the time of research, but guests might still be able to get a drink at the bar.

★**Mariam Hotel** HOTEL $$
(☎05 325 1529; www.mariamhotel.com; Aisha Umm Al Mumeneen St; s/d/tr/q JD26/38/46/55; @📶🏊) The well-regarded Mariam offers good facilities, including a bar, a pool-side restaurant and a cheerful communal area. There's also a restaurant-bar on the 5th floor offering views across town. Reservations are recommended. The hotel arranges transport and tours for guests.

St John Hotel HOTEL $$
(☎05 324 6060; www.saintjohnmadaba.com; Talal St; s/d/tr JD45/55/65; 📶) 🍃 Don't be put off by the slightly dusty lobby; this central hotel has cosy, modern rooms, many with balconies. The hotel has been designed with ecofriendly features such as solar panels and energy-efficient bathrooms. In addition, the

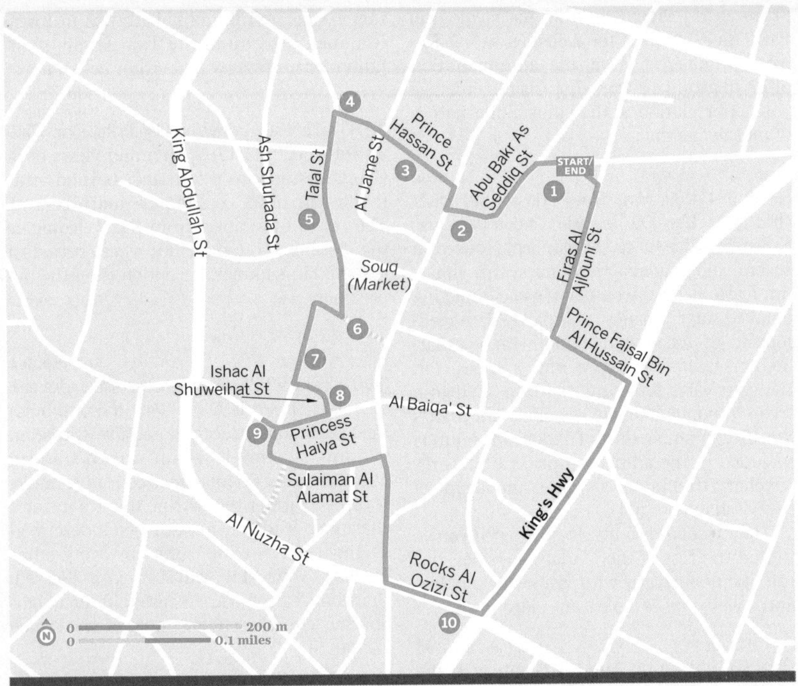

Walking Tour
Mosaics & Museums in Madaba

START VISITORS CENTRE
END VISITORS CENTRE
LENGTH 3KM; THREE HOURS

From the 1 **visitors centre** (p130), leave via Abu Bakr As Seddiq St, pausing at the bend to admire the town view. Call in at 2 **Archaeological Park I** (p130), catching topless Aphrodite spanking Eros. Turn right and immediately left along colourful, pedestrianised 'Artisan St' (Prince Hassan St), with its flapping kilims. Duck into 3 **Archaeological Park II** (p130) for a preview of yet-to-be-restored mosaics. The antiques shop opposite is an Aladdin's cave of copper coffee pots.

At the T-junction with Talal St, turn right for 4 **St George's Church** (p129), famed for its mosaic map, and visit cosy Ayola Coffeeshop opposite. Backtrack along Talal St, passing clothing shops with their ancient mannequins. The renowned restaurant 5 **Haret Jdoudna** (p134) is tucked into a traditional Madaba residence on the right; the craft shop here supports good causes. Continue uphill along Talal St towards the grand 6 **Dar Al Saraya** (p131), planned to become a restaurant. The road curves uphill to the 7 **Church of the Beheading of John the Baptist** (p129), a Catholic church constructed with Roman fragments. Compare the modern town vista from the belfry with the photographs exhibited in the gallery.

From the church, turn left along Ishac Al Shuweihat St, passing 8 **Adonis Restaurant** (p133), atmospherically housed in a dignified old residence. Turn right onto Princess Haiya St to the 9 **Madaba Museum** (p131) – a shady spot in which to absorb Madaba's layered history.

Backtrack to Sulaiman Al Alamat St and pass an unexcavated cathedral and fine houses. Turn right at the T-junction and head downhill, turning left onto Rocks Al Ozizi St. Call into the tiny 10 **Church of the Apostles** (p130) to see imagined marine creatures in mosaic.

Walk north along the King's Highway past hardware stores abuzz with Bedouin shoppers in traditional headdresses. Turn uphill along Prince Faisal Bin Al Hussain St, noting the mosque's minaret rising majestically above Madaba's skyline.

Skybar and Restaurant offers wonderful views and a convivial atmosphere. A gym and free bicycle use help balance out a night on the roof.

Mosaic City Hotel HOTEL $$
(☎05 325 1313; www.mosaiccityhotel.com; Yarmouk St; s/d JD42/52; 📶) This well-kept, central, family-run hotel has bright and spacious rooms. Some have balconies overlooking lively Yarmouk St, but windows are double glazed, keeping street noise to a minimum. The reception staff is ever amiable and facilities include a bar and mini gym. A family room with double-size bathroom sleeps four (JD87).

Madaba 1880 Hotel HOTEL $$
(☎05 325 3250; www.madaba1880.com; Talal St; s/d/tr JD48/72/85; 📶) Reopened in 2016 after a complete refurbishment and under new management, this central hotel punches well above its price range, with modern, comfortable rooms and a plush lobby. The San George bar is a good place for an evening drink, whether you're a guest or not.

Salome Hotel HOTEL $$
(☎05 324 8606; www.salomehotel.com; Aisha Umm Al Mumeneen St; s/d/tr JD30/45/55; @📶) With the appeal of a small, family-run residential hotel, the Salome is a good choice for a quiet stay. It has a welcoming reception-lounge, a licensed restaurant and helpful staff. It's an easy five-minute walk from the town centre.

Eating

Madaba is a good place to sample traditional Jordanian food. Snack shops selling falafel, shawarma and roast chicken line Yarmouk St and the King's Highway. For Arabic bread, head for the ovens opposite the Church of the Apostles. There are grocery stores in the centre of town. Fresh fruit and veg for a picnic can be bought along King Abdullah St.

★**Al Mandi** JORDANIAN $
(☎05 325 3256; Al Quds St; meals JD3; ⏰11am-9pm) Al Mandi knows the adage: do one thing and do it well. Come for an enormous plate of *mandi* – delicious barbecued chicken with portions of different types of rice, topped with nuts and dried fruit and served with broth and a salad – for around JD3 including a soft drink. Light eaters might prefer to share a plate between two.

Note that hours are flexible – if they sell out the day's offerings early, they shut up shop for the night.

Abu Yousef JORDANIAN $
(Ash Shuhada St; mains JD1-2; ⏰8am-1pm; 🌿) Little more than a hole in the wall, Abu Yousef's establishment is part of the fabric of the town, serving fresh hummus and falafel daily to those in the know. Found opposite the parking lot of Haret Jdoudna restaurant (p134), this modest place has supported owner Abu Yousef (now very elderly) and his family for more than 30 years.

Al Baraka Sweets BAKERY $
(cnr Sameh Al Farah & King Abdullah Sts; ⏰10am-10pm) A classic Arabic bakery, Al Baraka Sweets offers round trays of honey-drizzled pastries. Nuts and sugar abound, though there's also the toothsome *kunafeh* (a warm, syrupy cheese-based pastry).

Ayola Coffeeshop & Bar CAFE $
(☎05 325 1843; Talal St; snacks around JD2.500; ⏰8am-11pm; 📶🌿) If you want a toasted sandwich (the steak and cheese option is unexpectedly good), Turkish coffee, a cold beer or a glass of arak (Middle Eastern spirit) with the locals, or simply a comfortable perch on which to while away some time with fellow travellers, then this is the place to come.

Adonis Restaurant & Cafe JORDANIAN $$
(☎05 325 1771; Ishac Al Shuweihat St; mixed grill JD7; ⏰11am-2am) Housed in a beautifully restored typical Madaba residence and run by one of the town's returning sons, this excellent restaurant has quickly become the place to be at weekends. Serving typical Jordanian fare in a space that expands almost magically into unseen corners, Adonis has the added charm of live music on Thursday and Friday nights.

Bowabit Restaurant CAFE $$
(☎05 324 0335; Talal St; mains JD7.500; ⏰10am-midnight) With two tables overhanging the road opposite St George's Church (p129), photographs of old Madaba on the wall and excellent Italian-style coffee, this is a number-one place to relax after strolling around town. Alternatively, make a night of it over a dish of Madaba chicken and a beer.

Dana Restaurant BUFFET $$
(☎05 324 5452, 05 324 5749; Rocks Al Ozizi St; lunch buffet JD10; ⏰noon-3pm) Popular with tour groups, this restaurant serves a quality

buffet in a pleasant dining hall. It makes a reasonable stop if you've worked up an appetite on a walking tour.

★ Haret Jdoudna JORDANIAN **$$$**
(05 324 8650; Talal St; mains JD8-15; noon-midnight;) Popular with locals and discerning diners from Amman, and set in a restored Ottoman house, this restaurant is always worth a visit. Sit indoors by a roaring fire in winter or in the leafy courtyard in summer and sample traditional Jordanian dishes such as *mutaffi bethanjan* (fried eggplant with sesame).

Other popular dishes include *fatteh* (fried bread with garlic-laced yoghurt and hummus, sometimes with chicken) and *sawani* (meat or vegetables cooked on trays in a wood-burning oven).

Drinking

Many of Madaba's restaurants serve beer, some interesting wines and the local firewater, arak. Madaba's licensed restaurants, notably Haret Jdoudna and Ayola Coffeeshop & Bar (p133), are the best option for those who want an evening drink. Hotels with bars include the Mosaic City Hotel (p133) and the Madaba 1880 Hotel (p133).

Shopping

You can visit private mosaic workshops (with no obligation to buy) and purchase your own artwork. Madaba's famous hand-loomed kilims can be found between the Burnt Palace (Archaeological Site II) and St George's Church on a pedestrianised street lined with artisans' shops. The town has several quality jewellery shops, including locally renowned silversmiths along Prince Hassan St.

Haret Jdoudna Complex ARTS & CRAFTS
(05 324 8650; Talal St; 10.30am-11pm) Selling an extensive range of crafts, including mosaics, ceramics, textiles and clothing, this shop, attached to the restaurant of the same name, stocks particularly exquisite embroidery. Many of the items are sponsored by the Arab Cultural Society. Indeed, most items come from local nonprofit organisations, including the Jordan River Foundation.

Lawrence Arts & Crafts GIFTS & SOUVENIRS
(07 9550 4121; Prince Hassan St) Visit this private workshop for an insight into the painstaking process of laying out mosaics. You can purchase your own copy of the Madaba map or a more modest Tree of Life (from JD8, depending on size).

Carpet City ARTS & CRAFTS
(05 324 4397; Al Jame St; 10am-1pm & 4-7pm) Be warned: it's notoriously difficult to leave a carpet shop in Jordan empty-handed. This is partly due to the skill of the salesmen and partly because the rugs are so desirable. This family-run enterprise made the camel bags that feature in the film *Lawrence of Arabia*; if their rugs don't win your favour, the stories they weave surely will.

Hanania Silver Shop & Rafidi for Silver JEWELLERY
(Prince Hassan St; 10am-1pm & 4-7pm) There's little on display in the windows, but every piece in this shop is handcrafted to the highest standards.

Spice FOOD
(Sameh Al Farah St; 8am-8.30pm) For an unusual present, take home a selection of spices or freshly ground coffee beans from this aromatic grocer.

Holy Treasures Centre GIFTS & SOUVENIRS
(05 324 8481; Talal St; 10am-1pm & 4-7pm) Opposite St George's Church (p129), this shop has an extensive range of Dead Sea products. It also sells consecrated holy water from the Jordan River.

Information

MONEY

Madaba has plenty of banks with ATMs. There's a useful cluster around Sameh Al Farah St.

TOURIST INFORMATION

Ministry of Tourism & Antiquities (05 325 2687; www.tourism.jo; 8am-3pm Sun-Thu) Has an office above the Burnt Palace for specialised information about Madaba's preservation efforts.

Visitors Centre (p130) Collect a brochure called *Madaba and Mount Nebo*, summarising Madaba's attractions, here. Other good Jordan Tourism Board brochures include *Madaba Mosaic Map* and *Mount Nebo*. Also available are the definitive *Madaba: Cultural Heritage* (American Center of Oriental Research; around JD20); the more portable *Mosaic Map of Madaba* (Herbert Donner; JD10), with a fold-out reproduction of the map and detailed text; and the recommended, pocket-size *Madaba, Mt Nebo* (Al Kutba; JD3).

Ask to see the 10-minute film that sets Madaba in the context of the surrounding highlights. The centre has toilets and a handy car park.

Getting There & Away

The bus station is about 15 minutes' walk east of the town centre on the King's Highway. Most

OFF THE BEATEN TRACK

CANYONING

The central part of Jordan is riven with wadis and canyons, some only coming alive during a flash flood and others home to permanent watercourses that push their way through the rocky landscape to the Dead Sea. Along the way the presence of water creates beautiful semi-tropical oases of palms, oleander and ferns. Often hidden from the road, these secret gardens are one of the treasures of Jordan.

While the most spectacular canyons (such as those of the lower Wadi Mujib) are protected and made safely accessible by the Royal Society for the Conservation of Nature (RSCN; www.rscn.org.jo), there's nothing to stop a visitor from exploring other canyons off the beaten track. The Upper Hidan Gorge and Wadi Zarqa Ma'in near Madaba, together with Wadi Ibn Hammad and Wadi Labun near Karak, offer a range of outdoor adventures, from casual splashing through shallow pools to technical routes involving abseiling and swimming across deep pools with points of no return.

It's worth bearing in mind with any veering off the beaten track in Jordan that canyoning is not yet an established sport here and you're more likely to bump into shepherds than fellow adventurers. You must be self-sufficient and aware of the potential dangers.

To go it alone, the essential companion for canyoning is the widely available *Jordan: Walks, Treks, Caves, Climbs & Canyons*, by Di Taylor and Tony Howard (4th edition 2007). For escorted trips (recommended, given the unpredictability of flash flooding), contact the RSCN at Wadi Mujib or Dana, Feynan Ecolodge (p151), or Black Iris Hotel (p131) or Mariam Hotel (p131) in Madaba.

attractions around Madaba (with the exception of Mt Nebo and Mukawir) are time-consuming, if not impossible, to reach by public transport. It's easy, however, to charter a taxi in Madaba or take one of the well-thought-out tours or transport options from the Black Iris Hotel or the Mariam Hotel. Both of these hotels have a wealth of experience in organising trips for independent travellers. **Ammar Damseh** (☎ 07 9727 1688, 07 7640 3515; lanatours2017@gmail.com) is also a recommended independent English-speaking operator who can arrange taxi tours locally and as far afield as Petra and Jerash.

TO/FROM THE AIRPORT

If you want to bypass the bustle of Amman, it's possible to reach Madaba from Queen Alia International Airport by private taxi (set fare JD20) in under half an hour. Most hotels in Madaba can arrange a taxi from the airport (JD17) if you contact them in advance. Taxis from Madaba to the airport cost a couple of dinars less.

TO/FROM AMMAN

Minibuses leave throughout the day from Madaba's bus station to Amman's south and north bus stations. Minibuses depart when full. There's also a useful stop at Al Mouhada Circle where Amman minibuses congregate. Taxis cost a minimum of JD15 during the day, JD20 at night.

TO/FROM THE DEAD SEA

It's really not feasible to rely on public transport to reach the Dead Sea, as the route involves two minibus rides, which are unreliable at best, and a taxi ride from Suweimah that can cost almost as much as a taxi from Madaba. If you're determined, check with your hotel for the latest information on these ad hoc services. To visit the Dead Sea by taxi with enough time for a swim, you need to factor in three hours' waiting time – taxis charge around JD28 for this.

One popular trip from Madaba to the Dead Sea is via Mt Nebo and Bethany, returning via the Dead Sea Panoramic Complex (around JD35).

With your own transport, you can drive to the Dead Sea via Mt Nebo and return along the Dead Sea Panoramic Complex road. Branch off to Hammamat Ma'in and the new Mukawir road for a spectacular detour. Alternatively, you can make a longer but equally stunning drive via Karak.

TO/FROM MUKAWIR

From the local bus station in Madaba, minibuses go to Mukawir (for Machaerus castle; JD1, one hour) several times a day except Friday. The last minibus leaves at around 5pm. The service isn't wholly reliable – it will only run if there are enough passengers. A taxi costs JD20 with one hour of waiting time.

SOUTH ALONG THE KING'S HIGHWAY

There's no public transport linking Madaba with Karak along the King's Highway, as there's not enough demand for minibuses to make crossing Wadi Mujib worthwhile. Trying to get there via a sequence of local minibuses and taxi hire is made problematic by the lack of taxis to charter across Wadi Mujib from Dhiban to Ariha. Even if you find a taxi, the fare is likely to be as much as the fare from Madaba to Karak, so you gain little by the enterprise.

MA'AN NOT AMMAN!

If you're brave enough to try travelling by public transport in the region, be careful how you pronounce the transport hub of Ma'an. If you don't get your gutturals worked out, you may just find yourself heading back to the capital – no laughing matter if you've just spent a day of your trip trying to edge along the King's Highway.

From Karak, minibuses run to Tafila, where you can find transport to Qadsiyya (for access to Dana). Public transport south of Qadsiyya is infrequent, so you may need to take a minibus to Ma'an and then another to Wadi Musa (Petra).

Madaba hotels charge around JD20/40 per car for a one-way/return taxi to Karak, with stops en route to enjoy the panoramas at Wadi Mujib. They can also arrange drop-offs in Petra or Dana. This service requires a minimum of three people (the hotels will link you with other passengers) and a maximum of four, and costs JD20 per person. A normal taxi fare for this service is JD90 to JD120 per car.

Getting Around

Madaba is small enough to explore on foot, though the walk from the bus station to the centre of town is quite a hike with bags. Taxis (around JD1) are plentiful. If you're driving, note that it's not possible to park outside some of the cheaper hotels, as they're on busy, narrow streets.

Mt Nebo جبل نيبو

Mt Nebo is where Moses is said to have seen the Promised Land, a land he was himself forbidden to enter. It's believed that he died aged 120 and was later buried in the area, although the exact location of the burial site is the subject of conjecture.

The Mt Nebo region features several rocky outcrops, including Siyagha (the local name of the site, meaning 'monastery'). The Moses Memorial Church is perched on the summit, commanding sweeping views of the Dead Sea and Israel and the Palestinian Territories beyond. A pleasant side trip from Madaba, just 9km away, the church with its magnificent mosaics is the centrepiece of a small hilltop complex, signposted from the Madaba–Dead Sea road.

History

A Roman nun, Etheria, stumbled across the original three-apsed church on this site during a pilgrimage in 393. A nave was added in the 5th century, the first baptistery chapel in 530, and the main basilica (with its masterpiece mosaic) in 597, together with a large monastery.

By this time Nebo had grown into an important pilgrimage site, even earning a signpost off the main Roman road through the region (a Roman mile marker lies in the museum). Pilgrims would travel to Jerusalem, Jericho, Bethany, Ayoun Musa and Mt Nebo, before descending to Hammamat Ma'in for post-pilgrimage bathing.

Sights

★ Memorial Viewpoint VIEWPOINT
(JD2, with Moses Memorial Church free; 8am-4pm Oct-Apr, to 6pm May-Sep) Moses' view of the Promised Land towards ancient Gilead, Judah, Jericho and the Negev is marked by an Italian-designed bronze memorial next to the Moses Memorial Church. The ironwork, symbolising the suffering and death of Jesus on the cross and the serpent that 'Moses lifted up' in the desert, stands in the middle of an invariably windy viewing platform. Markers indicate notable points in the often-hazy distance, including the Golan Heights, Jerusalem (just 46km away) and the Dead Sea.

To enjoy similar views away from the crowds, pack a picnic and hike along the road downhill from Mt Nebo (towards the Dead Sea) for 100m and take the track to the left to the nearby hilltop.

Moses Memorial Church CHURCH
(Mt Nebo; JD2; 8am-4pm Oct-Apr, to 6pm May-Sep) On top of Mt Nebo, this modest church, or more accurately basilica, was built around 4th-century foundations in 597 and has just undergone major reconstruction. It houses some of the best (and best presented) mosaics in Jordan, dating from around 530. The masterpiece is a hunting and herding scene interspersed with an assortment of African fauna, including a zebu (humped ox), lions, tigers, bears, boars, zebras, an ostrich on a leash and a camel-shaped giraffe.

The church was abandoned by the 16th century and only relocated in the 20th century, using 4th- and 5th-century pilgrim travelogues. The Franciscans bought the site in 1932 and were responsible for excavating most of the ruins of the church and the monastery, as well as reconstructing much of the basilica.

The church is part of a functioning monastery, off limits to visitors. There's a small but fascinating museum presenting the history of the site.

La Storia Tourism Complex MUSEUM
(Ethnographic Diorama; ☎05 324 1119; www.lastoria-nebo.com; JD2; ⏲9am-5pm) This new ethnographic diorama, 2km before Mt Nebo on the Nebo–Madaba road, features an exhibition of tableaux billed as depictions of the religious, historical and cultural highlights in the heritage of Jordan. The scenes border on the kitsch (Noah's Ark is populated by a variety of soft toys and badly stuffed animals), but the experience improves considerably with the folkloric and ethnographic scenes, including a recreation of a traditional souq with its many tradespeople.

A large handicraft shop sells some quality items, such as mosaics and olive-wood carvings, some of which are produced by artisans attached to the complex.

Eating

★Nebo Restaurant & Terrace BUFFET $$
(☎05 324 2442; buffet JD10; ⏲11.30am-6pm Sat-Thu, to late Fri) The spectacular view and warm welcome from the owners make this restaurant worth a trip to Mt Nebo in its own right. The panoramic windows and the roof terrace make the very best of the vista, and the restaurant has its own ovens for baking fresh Arabic bread.

Asa Moses Restaurant BUFFET $$
(Siyagha Restaurant; ☎05 325 0226; buffet JD10; ⏲noon-4.30pm; 🍃) This trestle-tabled restaurant opposite the Ayoun Musa junction produces a daily lunch buffet of traditional Jordanian dishes, including *makloubeh* (chicken, rice, vegetables and spices cooked together and turned 'upside down') if ordered an hour ahead. The stone pillars and reed ceiling add to the been-here-forever ambience. Try a local Mt Nebo wine and sink into the *majlis* (Arab-style sitting area) cushions for a nap.

Shopping

Jordan Jewel ART
(☎05 324 1364; Mt Nebo Rd; 10am-1pm & 4-7pm) This handicraft centre specialising in mosaics is located 1km before Mt Nebo on the road from Madaba. The owner employs a large number of locals with physical disabilities.

Information

The authoritative *Town of Nebo* by Fr Sylvestre J Salter and Fr Bellarmiro Bagatti details Mt Nebo and other Christian sites in Jordan. More portable is *Mount Nebo* by Michelle Piccirillo. Both are usually available for sale inside the church. The Jordan Tourism Board publishes an excellent pamphlet entitled *Mount Nebo*, which summarises the site's significance. The encyclopedic *Mosaics of Madaba* is on display inside the church.

Getting There & Away

From Madaba, shared taxis to Mt Nebo cost around JD1; a private taxi from Madaba costs JD5 (JD8 return, with one hour waiting time). It's common for Madaba drivers to offer trips to Mt Nebo, in conjunction with the Baptism Site at Bethany, for around JD20.

From Mt Nebo the road continues for 17km into the Jordan Valley to meet the main Dead Sea Hwy, offering grand views of the Dead Sea. The drive takes you from the tree line of olives and root vegetables past a rocky landscape of prickly pears to the ochre-coloured hills of the Dead Sea depression. The yellow turns to red as the road twists past iron-rich escarpments and finally descends to the extreme green of the Jordan Valley, dotted with greenhouse plastic.

There's no reliable public transport along this route.

Around Mt Nebo

The hills and wadis (dry valleys) around Mt Nebo are peppered with ancient sites that are seldom visited except by archaeologists, sheep, goats and the occasional lost rambler. Though needing a bit of perseverance to find, and imagination to make the ruins and their historical context come alive, these sites are intimations of the complexity of this region's multilayered past. They also show the rural beauty that lies just off the beaten track.

Church of SS Lot & Procopius CHURCH

(Khirbet Mukhayyat; ⏱daylight hours) FREE Originally built in 557, this church houses a remarkable mosaic with scenes of daily life such as agricultural work, fishing and wine-making (in particular the cutting and carrying of grapes). The mosaics have recently been painstakingly restored after damage by rainwater. Look for the on-site caretaker to unlock the door for you; a tip of JD1 is appropriate in return.

The church is near the village of Khirbet Mukhayyat, the original site of ancient Nebo village, as mentioned on the 9th-century-BC Mesha Stele (p141) and in the Bible. The turn-off to Khirbet Mukhayyat is signposted 'Al-Makhyt' about 6km from Madaba and 3km before reaching the church complex at Mt Nebo. A sealed road leads 2.5km along the edge of the village to a rugged car park surrounded by juniper trees. There's no public transport.

Moses' Spring RUINS

(Ayoun Musa; ⏱24hr) This spring is one of two places where Moses is believed to have obtained water by striking a rock. Six giant eucalyptus trees mark the spot, and there's an occasional waterfall over the lip of the rocks if it's been raining, but there's little to see except the low-lying ruins of a couple of churches nearby. There's no public transport to the site. Walking down from the main road is easy; coming back up is the killer.

To reach the site from Madaba, turn right at the sign about 1km before the church at Mt Nebo. A 2.4km switchback road to the spring is steep (but sealed) and offers a close-up view of Bedouin encampments, hunkered down against the elements. Arums grow in abundance among the rocky patches of tilled ground, and small, fertile wadis bristle with citrus and olive trees. Sadly, the littered site is disfigured by discarded concrete buildings and is badly in need of a clean-up.

Tell Hesban RUINS

(Hesban; ⏱daylight hours) FREE Amateur archaeologists will like Tell Hesban, 9km north of Madaba. Over the centuries this strategic hill has been a Bronze Age settlement, a Hellenistic fortress (198–63 BC), a Roman settlement called Esbus (63 BC–AD 350), a Byzantine ecclesiastical centre (AD 350–650), an Umayyad market town (650–750), a regional capital of the Abbasids (750–1260) and the Mamluks (1260–1500) and, finally, an Ottoman village. All these layers of history are on view, albeit faintly.

The site is well signed, indicating the remains of a Byzantine church (the mosaics are displayed in Madaba), a Roman temple and a Hellenistic fort. There are lots of caves and cisterns both here and in neighbouring Wadi Majar. The largest Bronze Age cave can be explored with a torch (flashlight). Minibuses run frequently from Madaba (300 fils, 20 minutes) to Hesban; otherwise, take a taxi for JD6. Coming from Madaba, the tell is on the left side of the road; if you're driving, turn left at the first set of traffic lights after the pedestrian bridge in the modern town of Hesban and follow your nose up the hill.

Wadi Jadid Dolmen Field ARCHAEOLOGICAL SITE

(⏱24hr) More terraced fields than wadi, Wadi Jadid is locally renowned for its remarkable collection of early Bronze Age burial chambers and stone memorials. Known as dolmens ('dolmen' means stone table), the latter date to between 5000 and 3000 BC and consist of two upright stones capped by a bridging stone. How the huge bridging stones were winched into position remains unknown: it's little wonder that social anthropologists regard them as proof of early social cohesion.

There are about 40 dolmens scattered across this unmarked site, with at least 12 in good condition, though some are badly graffitied. Some locals know the site as Beit Al Ghula ('House of Ghosts'). There are thousands more scattered across Jordan, especially around Ar Rawdah.

From the road, it takes about 30 minutes to walk to the nearest dolmen and an hour to reach more distant groups. The site is near the village of Al Fiha, 10km southwest of Madaba, but you need to be in the know to find it. The best way to visit is by checking on directions with the Mariam Hotel (p131) in Madaba, downloading a map from the hotel's website or joining a tour (JD12, plus JD3 for each hour spent at the site).

With your own vehicle, you can continue downhill to the Dead Sea (30 minutes) after Wadi Jadid. The road is narrow and potholed towards the end, but it threads through beautiful and varied terrain, with Bedouin camps, green valleys of grapevines, olive groves and citrus orchards. As it descends to the desert floor, the road passes a spring with a small waterfall – almost miraculous in the arid landscape.

Mukawir (Machaerus)

مكاور (مكاريوس)

☎05 / POP 5000 / ELEV 700M

Just beyond the village of Mukawir (pronounced mu-*kar*-wir) is the spectacular 700m-high hilltop perch of Machaerus: the Castle of Herod the Great and the place where Salome is said to have danced for the head of John the Baptist.

The pudding basin of a hill was first fortified in about 100 BC, and expanded by Herod the Great in 30 BC. The ruins themselves are of minor interest, but the setting, with the wind blowing through the columns like one of Salome's seven veils, is both haunting and beautiful. Most days you'll be alone.

Sights

Castle of Herod the Great CASTLE

(Machaerus; JD1.500, with Jordan Pass free; 8am-6pm) Machaerus is known locally as Qala'at Al Meshneq (Castle of the Gallows), a fitting name given that it is renowned as the place where John the Baptist was beheaded by Herod Antipas, the successor of Herod the Great. The castle is about 2km past Mukawir village and easy to spot. If you don't feel in the mood for a climb, it's worth coming this way just to see the hilltop fortress framed by sea and sky.

From the car park, a stone staircase leads down to the main path, which climbs the hill in a clockwise direction. Near the base of the climb, a small track leads around the main hill to the right, past a number of caves. Legend has it that the gruesome execution took place in one of these caves. Flocks of choughs wheel through the air in suitably ominous fashion.

The main path climbs eventually to the castle. At the top, the modest ruins are unlabelled, but you can just about make out the low-lying remains of the eastern baths and defensive walls.

The reconstructed columns southwest of the deep cistern mark the site of Herod Antipas' palace triclinium; this is the site where Salome reputedly danced. According to the Bible, John the Baptist had denounced Herod Antipas' marriage to his brother's wife, Herodias, as Jewish law forbade a man to marry his brother's wife while he lived. Bewitched by his stepdaughter Salome's skill as a dancer, the king promised to grant her anything she wished. To take revenge on the Baptist, Herodias told her daughter to ask for John's head on a platter.

So, at the request of Salome, John was killed at Herod's castle, Machaerus. Provocative Salome has inspired painters and writers ever since.

The Romans built a siege ramp on the western side of the hill when taking the fort from Jewish rebels in AD 72; the remains are still visible.

WEAVING A FUTURE: THE WOMEN OF BANI HAMIDA

The Bani Hamida rug-making initiative was established in 1985, with help from Save the Children, to bring paid work to the newly settled Bedouin women of Mukawir district. The project began with only 12 women, all experienced hand-loom weavers. Ten years later, the cooperative involved 1500 women from the surrounding hillsides washing, carding, spinning and dyeing sheep's wool, and weaving the rugs. All these activities took place around the usual business of looking after husband, family and home. Now supported by the Jordan River Valley Foundation, the initiative employs 24 full-time staff who are responsible for the coordination of the project, carrying out international marketing and promoting the vision of the enterprise.

There have been challenges (such as competition, cheap imports and failing tourism), but the project continues to be a success, empowering women in proportion to their involvement. Earning even a little extra money has brought independence and social manoeuvrability, allowing women to change their lives and, most significantly, those of their children. When asked what the project meant for her family, one weaver at the showroom in Mukawir explained that she could afford to buy new pans from Madaba; another had funded a university education for her son.

These changes have been achieved by harnessing, rather than rejecting, the traditional skills that have been handed from mother to daughter since the days of Abraham, and which have helped define the Bedouin identity. As such, buying a Bani Hamida rug is more than just making a purchase; it is affirming an ancient but evolving way of life.

Activities

Dead Sea & Hammamat Ma'in Trails HIKING

(with guide from JD50) Mukawir is a great area for hiking, with plenty of shepherds' trails snaking around the hilly contours. One particularly worthwhile track leads steeply down the western side of the castle hill (p139) from the top and along a ridge towards the Dead Sea. It's also possible to follow shepherds' trails (or the 4WD road) to the hot springs at Hammamat Ma'in.

You must exercise extreme caution if taking any of these trails as the terrain falls steeply away and many paths are only for the sure-footed; you should not hike alone. You can arrange with a private tour operator to hike from Mukawir to Herodus Spring, a strenuous three- to four-hour trek. On any of these trails the views are magnificent, particularly at sunset.

Shopping

★ **Bani Hamida Weaving Centre & Gallery** ARTS & CRAFTS

(www.jordanriver.jo; 8am-3pm Sun-Thu, 10am-6pm Fri, to 4pm winter) This women's cooperative in Mukawir village (by the side of the road leading to the castle; p139) is run by the Bani Hamida Centre and is a good place to buy gorgeous, colourful kilims and cushions. Designs reflect contemporary tastes and traditional Bedouin patterns. The kilims aren't super cheap, but the fixed prices fairly reflect the labour that went into their weaving.

The women who run the centre speak little English but welcome you to the workshop. For an excellent anthropological take on the Bani Hamida story, it's worth picking up a copy of *A Bedouin Perspective* (JD5) by Sue Jones, who worked with the Jebel Bani Hamida women in the early 1990s. This booklet is for sale in the showroom. Hours are extremely erratic.

Getting There & Away

Frequent minibuses (600 fils, one hour) leave from outside Madaba bus station for Mukawir village, via Libb (the last is at around 5pm). From there, it's a 2km downhill stroll to the foot of the castle. There's no traffic between the castle car park and the village.

By car, the road from the King's Highway snakes along a ridge with spectacular views. An impressive sealed road links the site with Hammamat Ma'in and the Dead Sea.

Umm Ar Rasas أم الرصاص

Like many places along the King's Highway (and, indeed, in Jordan), Umm Ar Rasas is an unassuming spot that's hiding a lot of history – enough, in fact, to earn it a World Heritage Site designation from Unesco.

Umm Ar Rasas was once the Roman garrison town of Lehum, built in AD 300 to house the 4th Roman Legion, and forming part of a line of forts called the Limes Arabicus, which defended Rome's most remote borders. It houses several ruined Byzantine churches, including the Church of St Stephen, which has some notable mosaics.

About 1.5km north of the ruins is an enigmatic 15m-tall **stone tower**, which baffles archaeologists as there are no stairs inside but several windows at the top. It was most likely a retreat for stylites (early Christian hermits who lived at the top of pillars). Crosses decorate the side of the tower and some ruined monastery buildings lie nearby.

Sights

Church of St Stephen CHURCH

(JD2, with Jordan Pass free; 8am-4pm) The ruined Church of St Stephen, protected by a large hangar, is one of four churches in the original village of Umm Ar Rasas. Inside, the magnificent **mosaics** date back to about AD 785. Even if you have mosaic fatigue after Madaba and Mt Nebo, try to muster one last flurry of enthusiasm for this well-preserved masterpiece.

There are depictions of hunting, fishing and agriculture; scenes of daily life (such as boys enjoying a boat ride, a man astride an ostrich); and the names of those who helped pay for the mosaic. A panel consisting of 10 cities in the region includes Umm Ar Rasas, Philadelphia (Amman), Madaba, Esbounta (Hesban), Belemounta (Ma'in), Areopolis (Ar Rabba) and Charac Moaba (Karak). A northern panel depicts Jerusalem, Nablus, Caesarea, Gaza and others.

Kastron Mefaa RUINS

(8am-4pm) FREE The Umm Ar Rasas site spans the expansive ruins of Kastron Mefaa (mentioned in the Bible as the Roman military outpost of Mephaath). The ruins encompass four churches (including the Church of Lions, with impressive namesake mosaics) and the city walls. Arches rise up randomly from the rubble like sea monsters and you can spot cisterns and door lintels everywhere,

THE MESHA STELE

If you're travelling along the King's Highway, you'll keep coming across references to the Mesha Stele, but chances are you'll find little opportunity to discover what it is. Here's a quick ready reference to this significant artefact.

What is a stele? It's an ancient upright stone, usually decorated in some way.

And the Mesha Stele? It was a chest-high, black basalt tablet of stone carved with inscriptions.

Who discovered it? It was found by a missionary at Dhiban in 1868.

Why was it so famous? It provided historical detail of the battles between the Moabites and the kings of Israel and was also the earliest example of Hebrew script to be unearthed at that time.

Why was it made? It was commissioned by King Mesha of Moab to advertise his successes against Israel.

What happened to it? After surviving intact from about 850 BC to AD 1868, it quickly came to a rather unfortunate end. After finding the stele, the missionary reported it to Charles Clermont-Ganneau at the French consulate in Jerusalem, who made a mould of the tablet and returned to Jerusalem to raise the money to buy it. While he was away, local families, arguing over who was to benefit from the sale, lit a fire under the stone and poured water over it, causing it to shatter. Although most pieces were recovered, inevitably some were lost.

Where is it now? The remnants were collected and shipped off to France, and the reconstructed stone is now on display in the Louvre in Paris. Copies can be seen in museums at Amman, Madaba and Karak.

although a lack of signposts makes it hard to grasp the structure of the ancient town.

Getting There & Away

As with many sites in this region, the easiest way to get to Umm Ar Rasas is to drive or charter a private taxi from Madaba, 32km north. The turning is clearly signposted off either the King's Highway or the Desert Hwy (Umm Ar Rasas lies halfway between the two).

A few minibuses go directly to Umm Ar Rasas via Nitil from the local bus station in Madaba. Alternatively, catch anything going to Dhiban, and try arranging a taxi (if you can find one) from there. It costs around JD12/20 one way/return, including waiting time.

Wadi Mujib وادي الموجب

Stretching 70km from the Desert Hwy to the Dead Sea is the vast Wadi Mujib, proudly called the 'Grand Canyon of Jordan'. The spectacular chasm is also significant as the historic boundary between the ancient Amorites (to the north) and the Moabites (to the south). Moses is believed to have walked through Wadi Mujib, then known as the Arnon Valley. The King's Highway crosses the wadi's upper reaches, while its lower reaches fall within the Mujib Biosphere Reserve – normally accessed from the Dead Sea Hwy.

The canyon measures 1km deep and 4km wide, but it takes the King's Highway 18km of road to switchback down one wall of the wadi, across the dam at the bottom and up the other side. From the picturesque olive groves of the upper plateau, on either side of the wadi, there's no hint of the upheaval that splits the land in two.

Sights

The grandest views of the canyon are on its northern rim, 3km beyond the small town of Dhiban. Some enterprising traders have set up a tea stall here, and an assortment of fossils and minerals from the canyon walls are for sale. This is the best point on the road to stop, absorb the views and take photographs.

Getting There & Away

Your own transport (driving or hiring a private taxi) is necessary to explore Wadi Mujib: due to lack of demand, public transport rarely crosses the canyon. If you do have transport, the landscape here makes driving between Madaba and Karak (and even on to Petra) particularly spectacular.

THE JORDAN TRAIL: THREE WADIS TO KARAK

Distance 75km

Duration Four days

This is one of the most scenically dramatic legs of the Jordan Trail, as it involves traversing three of the great canyons that bisect the country and reveal its geological history as the uppermost tip of the Great Rift Valley.

The trek begins in Wadi Zarqa Ma'in, which you ascend to enjoy views of the Dead Sea, before crossing the gorgeous Wadi Hidan, where there's the chance to bathe in its waterfalls. The second day sees you climbing the gorge to hike to Wadi Mujib, which at nearly 1km deep is the most spectacular of Jordan's canyons. You'll overnight near the river at the bottom, before rising the next day for the stiff half-day hike back to the plateau and eventually the rim of Wadi Ibn Hammad. From here, the final day is a relatively easy stroll, crossing the King's Highway and concluding at Karak under the imposing gaze of its Crusader castle.

The Three Wadis hike is probably the most physically challenging stage of the Jordan Trail, as the days are particularly long, with some steep descents and climbs. It's wild camping, and you'll need filters to access water sources, particularly at Wadi Hidan and Wadi Mujib.

Visit www.jordantrail.org for route maps, GPS waypoints and detailed breakdowns of daily hikes.

Ar Rabba الربة

The minimal **ruins** (daylight hours) FREE of this Roman temple date from the end of the 3rd century AD (two niches contained statues of the Roman emperors Diocletian and Maximilian), and you'll also find other Roman and Byzantine buildings here. None of the ruins are signposted. The site is accessible by minibus from Karak, 16km south, but is best visited as a 15-minute stop en route between Madaba and Karak.

The holy and historic city of Ar Rabba came under the rule of King Mesha (9th century BC), then Alexander the Great (mid-4th century BC) and later the Nabataeans (from the 2nd century BC to the 2nd century AD). The Greeks named it Areopolis after Ares, the god of war, and the Romans based their Arab governorate here.

Karak الكرك

03 / POP 32,200 / ELEV 1000M

The ancient Crusader stronghold of Karak (or Kerak) lies within the walls of the old city and is one of the highlights of Jordan. The fortified castle that dominates the town was a place of legend in the battles between the Crusaders (Franks) and the Islamic armies of Saladin (Salah ad Din). Now one of the most famous Crusader castles, in its day Karak was just one in a long line of Frank defences, stretching from Aqaba in the south to Turkey in the north.

In late 2016, Islamist terrorists tried to take hostages at Karak, resulting in 10 deaths. The attack had the effect of galvanising the community, with residents pulling together to refurbish the town's mosques and churches and creating volunteer groups to improve local services.

History

Karak lies on the ancient caravan routes between Egypt and Syria, and was used as a stopover by the Greeks and Romans. The city is mentioned several times in the Bible as Kir, Kir Moab and Kir Heres, capital of the Moabites, and later emerges as a Roman provincial town, Charac Moaba. The city also features in the famous mosaic map in St George's Church in Madaba.

The arrival of the Crusaders gave the city renewed prominence, especially after King Baldwin I of Jerusalem built the castle in 1142. As it stands midway between Shobak and Jerusalem, Karak's commanding position and strategic value are obvious even today: unsurprisingly, it soon became the capital of the Crusader district of Oultrejourdain and, with taxes levied on passing caravans and food grown in the district, helped Jerusalem to prosper.

Saladin's Muslim armies took the castle in 1183 after an epic siege. Mamluk sultan

Beybars took the fort in 1263 and strengthened the fortress, deepening the moat and adding the lower courtyard, but three towers collapsed in an earthquake in 1293.

Little more is known of the castle until Jean Louis Burckhardt (the Swiss explorer who rediscovered Petra) passed through Karak in 1812, describing the fortress as 'shattered but imposing'.

In the 1880s, religious fighting compelled the Christians of Karak to flee north to resettle in Madaba and Ma'in; peace was only restored after thousands of Turkish troops were stationed in Karak.

Sights

Karak's friendly, chaotic town centre radiates out from the statue of Saladin (p144). The plaza near the entrance to the castle has been redeveloped, and it's in the surrounding streets that you'll find most of the tourist hotels and restaurants. Al Qala'a St is also known by its English name, Castle St.

Karak Castle CASTLE

(☎03 235 1216; JD2, with Jordan Pass free; ⏰8am-4pm Oct-Mar, to 7pm Apr-Sep) This fantastic Crusader stronghold, and later Mamluk fortress, is the reason to visit Karak. Throughout the castle, boards give detailed descriptions of the history and function of particular structures. Reconstruction and excavation work is ongoing: bring a torch (flashlight) to explore the darker regions, and watch your head on low doorways. The ticket office (p146) – and guides, charging around JD10 for a tour – can be found near the entrance.

You enter the castle via the **Ottoman Gate**: on a windy day, high above the dry moat, it's a struggle and a relief to reach the gate's shelter.

The **Crusader Gallery** functioned as the castle stables. Near the far end of the gallery, steps lead down to the **Crusader's Gate**. This would once have been the main castle entrance, but it is currently awaiting restoration and remains closed to the public. Those entering the castle here did so via a narrow, winding passage, separated from the Crusader Gallery by a wall. This restrictive access ensured that the entrance could be easily defended and is typical of Crusader castles.

On the north wall of the gallery is a (now headless) carved figure that local legend claims to be Saladin, but which actually dates from the 2nd century AD and is believed by scholars to be a Nabataean funerary carving. A small staircase leads up to the site of the ruined **northeast tower**, while a long passageway leads southwest to the **barracks**, notable for the small holes used for light, the walls of limestone and straw, and a few Byzantine rock inscriptions on the walls. Across the corridor is the **kitchen**, which contains large, round stones used for grinding olives, and huge storage areas for oil and wheat. In a dark tunnel (only visible with a torch) are some **Greek inscriptions** of unknown meaning. A door from the kitchen leads to a giant oven.

Beyond the parapet is the **glacis**, the dizzyingly steep rocky slope that prevented invaders from climbing up to the castle and prisoners from climbing down. This is where Renauld de Châtillon delighted in expelling his enemies.

The overgrown upper court has a large cistern and the mostly unexcavated **domestic residences**. At the northern end of the castle is the terrace, directly above the Crusader Gallery, with fine views. Above the far (southern) end of the castle rises Umm Al Thallaja (Mother of Snows), the hill that posed the greatest threat to the castle's defences during a siege. To the west is the village of Al Shabiya, which was once called Al Ifranj because many Crusaders (Franks) settled here after the fall of the castle.

The castle's main Crusader **church** was built with a sacristy down the stairs to the right (north). Note how in this lowered room there are arrow slits in the walls, suggesting that this originally formed part of the castle's outer wall. The neighbouring tower is believed to have been a Mamluk mosque.

Two corridors lead from the church. The left (east) corridor leads past seven **prison cells** and the prison administration office. The right (west) corridor leads from the foot of the stairs through the **Rosette Gallery**, named after the carved rosette at the bottom of the staircase.

Also from the church, you can take a passage to the left of the steps that leads northwest through the bowels of the castle, roughly underneath the church. The corridor turns right (north) and emerges into the better-lit areas of a delightful underground **marketplace** with various shops and cellars.

At the southern end of the castle is the **keep** – the refuge of last resort. It was here that Karak's defences were strongest, with 6.5m-thick walls, arrow slits on all four levels and a crenellated section at the top. The keep was built from 1260 by Mamluk sultan Beybars.

Karak

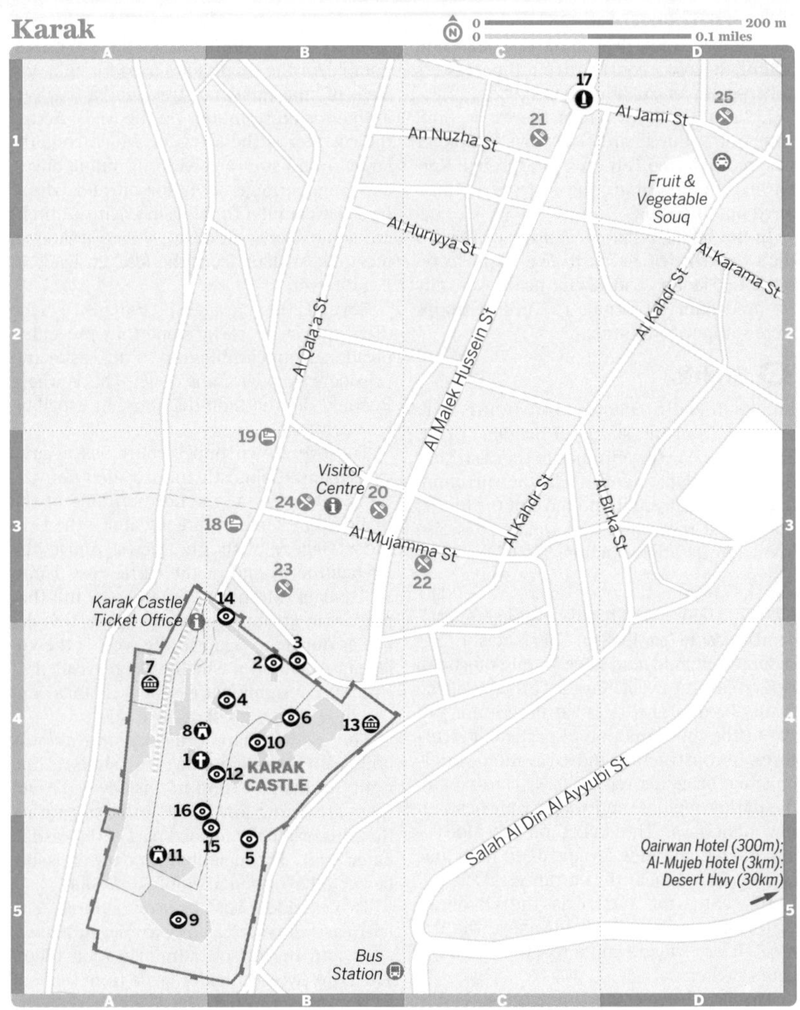

From the keep, stairs lead down to the **Mamluk Palace**. Built for Sultan Al Nasir Muhammad in 1311, the palace has an open-air reception hall that is a variation of the classic Islamic design of four *iwans* (chambers) off the main hall; there are barrel-vaulted rooms on two sides. The mosque here, with a clearly visible *mihrab* (niche in mosque indicating direction of Mecca), was probably reserved for palace notables. Pause near the top of the stairs for good views of Wadi Karak and the site said to be that of the condemned cities of Sodom and Gomorrah.

Down the hill is the excellent **Islamic Museum**. In a semi-subterranean part of Karak Castle, with a vaulted ceiling, this evocatively lit collection houses some of the finds from the castle and excavations in the surrounding area.

Statue of Saladin MONUMENT

This fine statue of the Muslim hero Saladin (Salah ad Din) sits in the middle of a roundabout at the bottom of the town's main shopping street. Astride a rearing horse, sword in hand, this helmeted bronze figure is beloved by locals, who use the plinth as a popular meeting place.

Karak

Sights

1	Crusader Church	A4
2	Crusader Gallery	B4
3	Crusader's Gate	B4
4	Domestic Residences	B4
5	Glacis	B5
6	Greek Inscriptions	B4
7	Islamic Museum	A4
8	Karak Castle	A4
9	Keep	A5
10	Kitchen	B4
11	Mamluk Palace	A5
12	Marketplace	B4
13	Northeast Tower	B4
14	Ottoman Gate	B3
15	Prison Cells	B5
16	Rosette Gallery	A4
17	Statue of Saladin	C1

Sleeping

18	Karak Rest House	B3
19	Towers Castle Hotel	B3

Eating

20	Al Fid'a Restaurant	B3
21	Al Motaz Sweets	C1
22	Al Shubba	C3
23	King's Castle Restaurant	B3
24	King's Restaurant	B3
	Kir Heres Restaurant	(see 19)
25	Shawarma Stands	D1
	Shehab Restaurant	(see 19)

Sleeping

Qairwan Hotel BOUTIQUE HOTEL $

(Cairwan Hotel; ☎03 239 6022; King's Hwy; s JD27, with shared bathroom JD10, d/tr JD30/40, 5-bed Jacuzzi ste with kitchen JD45; wi-fi) This homely family-run establishment has plenty of personality. Each of the nine rooms is unique, with quirky decoration. Unexpectedly, stairs lead to a cavernous disco. The hotel is 500m from the bus station, just outside Karak town. Breakfast costs an extra JD4, and dinner is available on request.

Towers Castle Hotel HOTEL $

(☎03 235 4293; Al Qala'a St; s/d/tr JD20/30/35) Near Karak Castle (p143), this friendly hotel is a good option. The reception area is unassuming, but the floral rooms are clean, and many open onto balconies with views across Wadi Karak. Staff can help with onward travel.

Al Mujeb Hotel HOTEL $$

(☎03 238 6090; almujeb_hotel@yahoo.com; King's Hwy; s/d/tr JD30/45/60) This sprawling three-storey hotel has good facilities but is let down by its location. The hotel is around 5km south of Karak, by the junction on the road to Ar Rabba. If you're driving, consider parking here and taking a taxi (JD5 to JD6 one way) into town.

Karak Rest House HOTEL $$

(☎03 235 1148; moaweyaf@gmail.com; Al Qala'a St; s/d JD28/47) Next door to Karak Castle, with sweeping views of Wadi Karak from many of the rooms, this tired hotel with its faded lobby is at least conveniently located.

Eating

Most restaurants are near the castle on Al Mujamma St or near the statue of Saladin. Shawarma (meat sliced off a spit and stuffed in a pocket of pita-type bread with chopped tomatoes and garnish) stands are clustered around Al Jami St.

Shawarma Stands STREET FOOD $

(shawarma JD1; ⊙4-10pm) These popular shawarma stands are in a busy part of town, and offer a quick, filling meal.

King's Restaurant JORDANIAN $

(☎03 235 4293; Al Mujamma St; mezze 500 fils, mains from JD4; ⊙8am-10pm) This boulevard restaurant with tables on the pavement attracts travellers at all times of the day and night. It offers grills, pizzas and sandwiches, and local, home-cooked Jordanian dishes like *makloubeh* (chicken, rice, vegetables and spices cooked together and turned 'upside down').

Al Fid'a Restaurant JORDANIAN $

(☎07 9503 7622; Al Mujamma St; mains JD5; ⊙8am-10pm) This unsophisticated but popular eatery sells the standard local fare of grilled chicken, hummus and salad.

Al Shubba SUPERMARKET $

(Al Mujamma St; ⊙10am-10pm) Stock up here on supplies for the next leg of the King's Highway.

Al Motaz Sweets BAKERY $

(☎03 235 3388; An Nuzha St; ⊙8am-10pm) This Arabic pastry shop is a must for those with a sweet tooth.

King's Castle Restaurant JORDANIAN $$
(☎03 239 6070; mains JD5, buffet JD10; ⏲noon-4pm) At busier tourist times, groups come here for the daily lunch buffet. With pleasant outdoor seating, castle views and a host of salads to choose from, it's easy to understand why. At quieter times, there's no buffet, so order off the menu. The eastern building is worth a visit for its impressive relief display of the castle.

Shehab Restaurant JORDANIAN $$
(☎03 951 3803; Al Qala'a St; mains JD6; ⏲noon-8pm) A reasonable option for standard Jordanian cuisine. Note that if unrequested mezze is brought out and you eat it, it'll be added to the bill.

Kir Heres Restaurant JORDANIAN $$
(☎03 235 5595; Al Qala'a St; mains JD5-7; ⏲noon-10pm; ✎) This restaurant serves steak, chicken with local herbs, fried halloumi and mushrooms with garlic and thyme, as well as standard Jordanian fare. There's a decent upper gallery, or sit at the tables out the front to watch the world go by.

Shopping

For an idea of how the people of Karak like to spend their money, take a walk down Al Malek Hussein St – the road that leads from Castle Plaza to the Saladin statue (p144). Here you will find tailors stitching fake fur to collars; leather jackets and red woollen sweaters dangling in the wind; vendors with rakishly tied headscarves and broken-backed shoes (the local answer to slip-ons); bushy green bundles of coriander hanging from butchers' shops; fennel, turnips and shaggy-mopped carrots begging to be bought for a picnic; and locally gathered herbs in textile bags flagging the outside of spice and coffee-bean shops. There's even a small gold souq – selling mostly silver.

Information

MONEY

There are at least four banks that change money on An Nuzha St, one block south of the Saladin roundabout, and most have an ATM for Visa and MasterCard.

TOURIST INFORMATION

Visitor Centre (☎03 235 4263; Al Qala'a St; ⏲8am-4pm Sat-Thu) Active in high season only.

Karak Castle Ticket Office (⏲8am-4pm Oct-Mar, to 7pm Apr-Sep)

Getting There & Away

BUS & MINIBUS

From the bus station – outside the town, at the bottom of the hill by the junction of the King's Highway – several daily buses go direct to Amman's South Bus Station (JD2, around two hours) via the Desert Hwy. Minibuses also run about every hour along the King's Highway from Karak to Tafila (JD1.500, one hour), the best place for connections to Qadsiyya (for Dana Biosphere Reserve) and Shobak. To Wadi Musa (for Petra), take a minibus to Ma'an (JD2.500, two hours), which leaves around 1pm daily, and change there. Alternatively, leapfrog on minibuses to Tafila, Shobak and Wadi Musa.

Buses to Aqaba (JD5, three hours) travel in the mornings via the Dead Sea Hwy about four times a day. In the afternoon it's better to take the Amman bus to Qatrana on the Desert Hwy and change to a southbound bus to Aqaba.

THE JORDAN TRAIL: KARAK TO DANA

Distance 83km

Duration Four days

This is a dry stretch of the Jordan Trail through rocky and only sparsely green landscapes, but with a few hot springs and great wild camping.

Leading out from the shadow of Karak Castle, you follow the geologically striking Wadi Ed Dab'a to a series of abandoned villages. There are more canyons on the subsequent days, with unexpected cave houses in the cliffs near Taboun. The landscape greens around the hot spring at Burbeita (where you can camp), before the track gently rises to a ridge that takes you to the village of Ais. There are views of the Dead Sea again past Tafila and then the trek runs through olive groves to Ma'tan, sitting dramatically above Wadi Labun. The last day takes you to the pretty Ottoman village of Dana, at the edge of the Dana Biosphere Reserve, where there are good accommodation options.

Visit www.jordantrail.org for route maps, GPS waypoints and detailed breakdowns of daily hikes.

CAR & MOTORCYCLE

If you're driving, the highly scenic Rte 50 leads from Karak down to the Dead Sea.

TAXI

From Amman it's possible to charter a taxi to Karak via the Desert Hwy for about JD50 one way. From Amman via the King's Highway, with a stop at Madaba and Wadi Mujib, it costs at least JD80.

From Karak, taxi fares are around JD50 to Amman or Madaba, JD45 to Dana and JD65 to Petra. There's a taxi stand near the vegetable market.

Getting Around

The old city of Karak is easy to get around on foot but has a maddening system of narrow one-way streets. If you're driving, consider parking outside town and taking a taxi.

Khirbet Tannour خربة التنور

The King's Highway south of Karak gradually descends from a brooding piece of black volcanic hillside into the impressive but arid Wadi Hasa (the biblical Zered Valley). Attempts at tomato growing are in evidence, but it's hard to encourage the rocky topsoil into production in an otherwise wild and thermally active landscape. However, water does bubble up in other places, most notably the nearby hot springs of Hammamat Burbita and Hammamat Afra.

The highway skirts a reservoir, above which looms a small, conical hill. A steep 15-minute hike leads off the highway to the top of the hill for panoramic views and the ruined temple of Khirbet Tannour.

Sights

Khirbet Tannour Temple RUINS

(daylight hours) FREE The neglected ruins of the 2000-year-old Nabataean temple of Khirbet Tannour are worth the hike up the hill for the view, if nothing else. A famous statue of Nike was found here, a copy of which is housed in the Jordan Museum in Amman; the original is in Cincinnati (USA). A statue of the goddess Atargatis (also currently in Amman) was also unearthed at this auspicious little hilltop.

There's not much to see here except for column bases and the outlines of a temple courtyard with adjoining rooms. Despite this, most visitors will relish the windswept site and epic location.

The turn-off to the ruins is 36km south of Karak town, at the crest of the hill – a dam is clearly visible at the bottom. The turn-off is marked as 'AT TA NO I QUI ES SI', which isn't a Latin inscription but a weather-beaten version of 'At Tannour Antiquities Site'. The 1.5km access road is potholed, but you can park off the track quite easily. Walk up to the communication tower and the path up the hill becomes obvious.

Activities

Hammamat Burbita BATHHOUSE

(Hammamat Burbayta; JD5; 8am-8pm, closed Ramadan) This modest pool complex is fed from natural hot springs at the bottom of a reed-filled wadi. Popular with locals, especially at weekends, the oasis is a welcome sight amid the arid landscape. There are changing facilities and a separate pool for women. The spring is 13km off the King's Highway; the turning is signposted about 23km north of Tafila.

There's no public transport, but the complex is adequately signposted if you're driving. A chartered taxi from Karak costs around JD30 return, including waiting time.

Hammamat Afra BATHHOUSE

(JD7; 8am-10pm) Facilities at this large thermal spring include private pools for men and women, changing rooms and picnic areas. Admission is paid at the entry gate, 5km from neighbouring Hammamat Burbita. You must show your passport before continuing the 1km to the rock pools, built against the canyon walls. You can't see the springs from the road. Solo women are likely to feel conspicuous.

There's quite a rowdy atmosphere at weekends and there's little chance of escaping the party as wardens prohibit you from exploring the wadi upstream.

Getting There & Away

Access to the whole area is only feasible with private transport.

Dana ضانا

03 / ELEV 1250M

One of Jordan's hidden gems, the charming 15th-century stone village of Dana dangles beneath the King's Highway on a precipice, commanding exceptional views of the valley below. That valley and the surrounding area make up the Dana Biosphere Reserve. It's a wonderful place to escape Jordan's cities and spend a few days hiking, enjoy some village atmosphere and look for wildlife.

Sights

★Dana Biosphere Reserve NATURE RESERVE

(adult/student per day JD8/4, with RSCN lodging or hikes free) The Dana Biosphere Reserve is the largest in Jordan and includes a variety of terrain, from sandstone cliffs more than 1700m high near Dana to a low point of 50m below sea level in Wadi Araba. Sheltered within the red-rock escarpments are protected valleys that are home to a surprisingly diverse ecosystem. About 600 species of plant (ranging from citrus trees and junipers to desert acacias and date palms) thrive in the reserve, together with 180 species of bird.

More than 45 species of mammal (25 of which are endangered) also inhabit the reserve, including caracals, increasing herds of ibex, mountain gazelles, sand cats, red foxes and wolves. The installation of night traps has given reserve wardens a better understanding of the movement of these rarely spotted animals.

The best time to visit Dana is in spring, when the hillsides bloom with flowers, or during autumn, when the auburn foliage thins out, making it easier to spot wildlife. While winter can be bitterly cold in the upper part of the reserve (some of the trails will close), it's a good time to explore the Feynan area in the lower part of the reserve. Similarly, when it's sweltering in summer in the lower reaches of the wadi, there's seldom need for air-con in Dana.

Dana Museum MUSEUM

(www.rscn.org.jo; 8am-3pm) FREE Spare some time for the Royal Society for the Conservation of Nature's wonderful little museum. It illustrates the various wildlife at 1500m on the King's Highway, at 1100m at Dana Village and 50m below sea level in Wadi Araba. It also explains the particular ecological challenges in a reserve that experiences 350mm of rain per year in winter on the mountaintops, and soaring desert temperatures and 10mm of rain per year at sea level.

This is a good place to begin an exploration of the area, providing context for the various treasures to look out for during a hike.

Activities

Dana Biosphere Reserve begs to be explored on foot. It's only by getting out into the thick of it that you feel the special beauty of the terrain and invite chance encounters with Dana's diverse wildlife.

THE JORDAN TRAIL: DANA TO PETRA

Distance 73km

Duration Four days

The hike from Dana to Petra is the crown jewel of the Jordan Trail, hiking through one of Jordan's best and most scenic nature reserves along the back route to one of the Middle East's most iconic sights at Petra. It's a truly world-class hike.

Day one takes you down the sandstone cliffs of Dana through the long valley of Wadi Dana. It's a biologically diverse area and a historically important one, too – you'll pass ancient copper mines before arriving at Feynan Ecolodge, where you can spend the night. The next day you'll follow the open valley of Wadi Al Malaqa to Ras Al Feid, passing local Bedouin camps along the way. After camping here, you'll enter rocky sandstone terrain and pass more Bedouin camps until you reach a narrow canyon, through which you'll wind your way to Beihdah, the site of Little Petra. The last day follows Nabataean tracks out of the valley to the dramatic chasm of Siyyagh. When you emerge, you'll be rewarded with your first view of Petra's Monastery, where you can have a hard-earned cold drink at a tourist cafe and enjoy the fruits of reaching the site the long way round. Explore Petra on foot, walking towards the Treasury and the Siq to the town of Wadi Musa, where soft beds and refreshing showers await.

Reserve entrance fees are payable to hike through Dana. You'll also need a reserve guide – they're extremely knowledgeable about the local flora and fauna. Unless you have a Jordan Pass, you'll need to arrange your Petra ticket in advance, as you'll be entering through the back door.

Visit www.jordantrail.org for route maps, GPS waypoints and detailed breakdowns of daily hikes.

The Royal Society for the Conservation of Nature (RSCN) organises a series of established hikes ranging from a couple of hours of easy ambling to strenuous overnight trips. In addition, there are hikes taking in the wadis adjacent to the reserve, including a two-day hike to Feynan Ecolodge, via Wadi Ghuweir, overnighting at the lodge and returning via Wadi Dana. The visitor centre (p153) can give information on the full range of hikes. The trails from Al Barra require a short drive to get to the trailhead (the RSCN can arrange a transfer).

RSCN guides are available (and compulsory on most hiking trails) to give visitors a deeper understanding of the reserve. If you're staying at Feynan, all guides and hikes are included in the price.

Hotels in Dana can help organise longer treks to Shobak (two days) via Wadi Feynan, Wadi Ghuweir and the village of Mansourah, and even on to Petra. Guides typically cost JD30/60 for a half/full day. Ask about Ali's Walk, a three-day hike to Petra (around JD200 per person for a minimum of two people), including guide, camping facilities, all meals and transportation of luggage.

Easy Hiking Trails

Rummana Campground Trail HIKING

This spectacular one- to two-hour, self-guided trail traces the fluted edge of Wadi Dana's canyons, circling through the trees and rock formations around the campground, and giving plenty of opportunities for a quiet sit among untroubled wildlife.

Look out for griffon vultures wheeling above the stone turrets of Wadi Dana, brilliant turquoise agamas (a type of lizard) basking on rocks, jewel beetles and, if you get really lucky, an early-morning ibex in the creases and folds of neighbouring canyons.

The trail is open from 15 March to 31 October. Guides cost JD12.

Wadi Dana Trail HIKING

Although the Wadi Dana Trail is the most popular trek, you're still likely to have this long hike through majestic Wadi Dana to yourself. The 16km, six-hour trail is easy to follow, running partly along a disused road and partly via Bedouin grazing paths. Although no scrambling is involved, be aware that there's a relentless one-hour descent at the beginning that gives toes, calves and knees a good bruising.

The trail is open year-round. Guides cost JD20.

Moderate Hiking Trails

Rummana Mountain Trail HIKING

From Rummana Campground to the nearby Rummana (Pomegranate) Peak, the 2.5km, one- to two-hour Rummana Mountain Trail provides great views over Wadi Araba.

The trail is self-guided (if you want a guide, the price is JD12) and is open from 15 March to 31 October.

Nawatef Trail HIKING

The Nawatef Trail is a great 2.5km hike from Al Barra to the luscious springs and Nabataean ruins of Nawatef. It involves a steep uphill walk back to Dana.

The trail is open year-round, requires a guide (JD15) and takes about 2½ hours.

White Dome Trail HIKING

Taking you past dramatic wadi escarpments surrounding Rummana Campground and past the beautiful terraced gardens of Dana village, the 8km White Dome Trail leads through waist-high vegetation to Dana Guesthouse.

The walk takes about three hours, and a guide (JD15) is required. You can go out only from 15 March to 31 October.

Strenuous Hiking Trails

Fida Canyon Trail HIKING

The short but strenuous Fida Canyon Trail leads from Al Barra to Shaq Al Reesh and is not for the faint-hearted.

A guide (JD15) is required, but the trail is open year-round. Count on the 2.5km taking about two hours.

Hamman Al Dathnah Trail HIKING

The spectacular but rugged Hammam Al Dathnah Trail leads from Al Nawatef, crossing Hamra Valley and Palm Tree Valley to Feynan Ecolodge over 17km.

A guide (JD20) is required for the nine-hour journey. The trail is open year-round, and even in summer most of the hike is in the shade.

Wadi Ghuweir Trail HIKING

The demanding 16km Wadi Ghuweir Trail leads along river beds and through a gorge and a valley of palm trees to arrive at Feynan Ecolodge. Avoid the hike if rain is expected or has recently fallen because of the risk of flash floods. Transport to the start of the trail, near Shobak, costs JD25.

The hike should take six to seven hours, and a guide (JD20) is required.

WORTH A TRIP

ANCIENT DANA

There's something rather magical about coming across a pile of smelted fragments and realising that this is evidence of industry, not from any industrial revolution but from the activities of communities 6000 years ago.

There are almost 100 archaeological sites in the Dana Biosphere Reserve, most still being excavated by British teams. The ruins of **Khirbet Feynan**, at the mouth of Wadi Feynan and Wadi Ghuweir, are particularly interesting: the 6000-year-old copper mines here were once the largest metal-smelting operations in the Near East and are mentioned in the Bible. The Romans later worked the mines using Christian slaves.

The hills of Dana still contain copper, but despite lobbying from mining companies, the Jordanian government has agreed not to allow mining in the reserve. A growing cement factory that quarries along the rim of the reserve is the nearest incursion permitted in this wildlife haven.

You can explore the slag heaps of the main mines of Umm Al Amad, together with the ruins of three churches, Iron Age sites and a Roman tower, on a fascinating three- to four-hour **hike** (☎07 9959 9507; www.ecohotels.me/feynan; ⏲Sep-Jun) FREE offered most days from Feynan Ecolodge. The tour is very hot for much of the year, so carrying water and wearing a hat are essential.

Cycling

Mountain Bike Trail CYCLING
(☎07 9959 9507; www.ecohotels.me/feynan; ⏲Sep-Jun) FREE This mountain-bike trail in the lower Dana area starts at Feynan Ecolodge, uses gravel tracks past the archaeological site of Khirbet Feynan, and ends at the villages of Rashaydeh and Greigra. There are opportunities to stop en route to hike or have tea with the Bedouin people who live here. The lodge has 10 bikes available for guests.

Sleeping & Eating

There are several sleeping options around Dana. You can stay at one of the guesthouses in the village proper or at one of the permanent tented camps at the edge of the reserve (camping is not permitted inside the reserve itself). Finally, the delightful Feynan Ecolodge sits inside the reserve, but note that it only has vehicle access from the Dead Sea Hwy; from Dana, it's a five-hour hike.

All accommodation options in Dana offer food to guests, but you usually need to advise in advance which meals you'll need. Otherwise, there's just the one restaurant in Dana.

Dana Hotel HOTEL $
(☎07 9559 7307, 02 227 0537; www.suleimanjarad.webs.com; half board per person in villas JD25, s/d JD12/20) A warm welcome is assured at this hotel, run by the Sons of Dana, a local tourism cooperative. Deservedly popular, and the oldest established hotel in Dana, it has very simple rooms in its original building, but it has also expanded across the square into an attractively built house with villas and a terrace overlooking the valley.

Al Nawatef Camp CAMPGROUND $
(☎02 227 0413, 07 9639 2079; www.alnawatefcamp.com; half board in tented chalets with shared shower block JD15) Perched at the edge of an escarpment, this wonderful camp is run by a hospitable local who knows the area 'because', he says, 'it runs in my blood'. The goat-hair chalets with beds, linen and blankets boast balconies with exceptional views. The camp is signposted 2km off the King's Highway, 5km south of the Dana turning in Qadsiyya.

Tea and coffee are available all day, and delicious dinners are rustled up from the ground oven. A free transport service is offered to Dana village. You can set your own tent up in the grounds for JD5 and order dinner (JD5) or breakfast (JD2) to suit. The owner can collect you from the main road. He also organises onward travel via local buses and will drop you at the relevant junction. The camp organises some excellent hiking opportunities.

Dana Tower Hotel GUESTHOUSE $
(☎07 7751 4804, 07 9568 8853; www.dana-towerhotel.com; half board per person JD15, with shared bathroom JD11, summer rooftop camping JD3;) Free transfers to/from the main road, a quirky warren of small, unheated rooms called 'Flying Carpet' and 'Crazy Camel', leafy courtyards, a *majlis* (Arab-style sitting area)

draped in memorabilia, and rooftop seating with a view make this a popular choice. Added perks: a dinner of 27 dishes, plus free tea and laundry.

Onward 4WD transport (JD17 to Petra, JD45 to Feynan) is available, as is hiking in the Dana Biosphere Reserve (p148).

Dana Moon Hotel GUESTHOUSE **$**
(☎07 9753 3581; dana.moonhotel@hotmail.com; half board per person JD15) Simple rooms with shared bathrooms make up this no-frills guesthouse, with an attractive seating area under the pine trees. The guesthouse runs the nearby Feynan Way Restaurant (p152).

Rummana Campground CAMPGROUND **$$**
(☎06 461 6523; www.wildjordan.com; s/d/tr/q tent JD53/64/76/87, deluxe tent JD70/82/93/105; ⏲15 Mar-31 Oct) Prices at this camp may seem steep, but when you wake up to the sound of Dana's wildlife, it's easy to see why reservations are necessary. Views from the campsite down the valley are incredible, and with great hiking trails just beyond the tents, you've got easy access to the reserve. Tents have comfy beds and a shared bathroom block.

You can drive here in 20 minutes or hike in three hours from Dana village, but you have to park your vehicle at the reserve entrance – call ahead, or drop into the Dana Visitor Centre (p153), to arrange a transfer (10 minutes) to the campsite. Barbecue grills are available (bring your own food and fuel). Dinner (JD15) and breakfast are whipped up by a jolly cook intent on beefing you up for another day's exertions.

★ **Feynan Ecolodge** LODGE **$$$**
(☎06 464 5580; www.ecohotels.me/feynan; Wadi Feynan; full board incl park entrance fee from s/d/tr JD101/127/170; ⏲Sep-Jun) Owned by the RSCN, this unique ecolodge – frequently rated one of the world's best – is accessible on foot from Dana (a day's hike) or by 4WD from the Dead Sea Hwy. Powered by solar energy (including the hot water), and with its mud-rendered architecture lit entirely by locally made candles, Feynan has a magical caravanserai ambience.

The lodge lives up to its mantra of 'helping nature, helping people' through its commitment to the environment and community-based projects. Local people are directly involved (as drivers, guides, bakers and candle makers), benefiting 80 local families; around half of all revenue from tourism is returned to the community. Waste is recycled and the use of traditional water filtration saves the equivalent of 15,000 plastic bottles a year.

Feynan Ecolodge runs a number of hiking, canyoning and special-interest tours that allow guests to experience the best of the lower reaches of the reserve, as well as providing unique opportunities to engage with the semi-nomadic Bedouin people. There can't be too many hotels where you can learn bread making, coffee pounding and kohl crushing. Better yet, pack a knapsack of supplies and some water, and spend the day with a shepherd or hike to the ancient copper mines and then enjoy guided stargazing on the roof. All activities are

FROM VILLAGE TO RESERVE

Dana village dates from the Ottoman period but was abandoned less than a generation ago as locals moved to nearby Qadsiyya in search of jobs. Farmed by only a handful of remaining residents, the neighbouring terraces, which once grew pistachios, almonds, walnuts, pomegranates, lemons and apples, almost slipped back to nature. Thanks in part to the persistent efforts of the Royal Society for the Conservation of Nature (RSCN; www.rscn.org.jo) and the tourism it promotes, many old houses have been renovated and people are slowly returning.

About 50 Bedouin families drift into and beyond the lower reaches of the reserve. To allow the vegetation to recover, they are only permitted to herd their livestock in the Dana Valley at certain times of year.

The RSCN assumed control of the reserve in 1993 in an integrated project to promote ecotourism, protect wildlife and improve the lives of local villagers. The reserve directly or indirectly employs locals from nearby villages, and income from tourism is helping to sustain a number of families beyond the reserve and provide environmental education in local schools.

Dana is unique because it has four ecosystems, ranging in altitude from 1700m to minus 50m, all of which occur within a very compact area. For this reason, Dana has now achieved official 'biodiversity reserve' status.

THE WADI DANA TRAIL

One of the most popular trails at Dana is the 'easy hike': the 16km Wadi Dana Trail from Dana to Feynan Ecolodge. As it's downhill all the way, it ought to be a mere walk in the park, but don't be deceived – it's not as easy as it sounds! Start the walk after lunch: that way you'll reach the hotter part of the walk in the cooler part of the day. Take more water than you think you'll need and wear a hat. Don't forget in your planning that it takes three hours, partly by 4WD, to return to Dana by road.

The Bad Bits

- Interminable initial descent on a potholed vehicle track, wishing you'd worn thicker socks
- Blazing heat with little shade (there's only one tree in the first hour)
- Not having time to stop to chat with the Bedouin (some JD1 notes for tea would've been handy)
- The end of the wadi is nowhere near where you think it is
- Being overtaken by an encouraging old couple on a donkey saying '*Funduq* (hotel) – only five minutes', when you're still an hour's walk from Feynan
- The prospect of no beer and no meat at the inn – Feynan Ecolodge is dry and vegetarian only

The Good Bits

- A lizard sunning itself in the ash of an old fireplace
- A crest of goats marshalled into camera by an entrepreneurial herdsman
- Carnival-pink oleander flowers, waving like bunting along the entire lower wadi
- Secret gardens of reeds and oleander and huge, spreading trees
- A barefoot race by local lads conducted for the sheer fun of running
- A Sinai agama (a type of lizard), whose brilliant turquoise livery demanded a second look
- The same encouraging couple returning on the donkey saying '*Funduq* – only five minutes'
- The sampling of delicious cool water and superb vegetarian food at Feynan Ecolodge

So is it worthwhile? Without doubt! Chances are that even in peak season you'll have the reserve to yourself. Anyone who has hiked main trails in other popular destinations will know what a treat that is.

included in the accommodation package, so you're free to explore the area as much as you like.

★Dana Guest House LODGE $$$
(☎02 227 0497; www.rscn.org.jo; incl park entrance fee s/d/tr/q JD87/99/110/122, with shared bathroom JD64/76/87/90) With panoramic views across the reserve, a roaring fire in winter and enthusiastic park rangers, this ecolodge is run by the RSCN. All but two of the minimalist, stone-walled rooms have a balcony. Heating and hot water are provided by solar panels. The newer deluxe rooms are tremendous; few showers can offer such amazing vistas.

Breakfast and delicious local suppers (JD14; order in advance) are shared around trestle tables.

Feynan Way Restaurant JORDANIAN $
(dinner JD3-10; 7am-midnight) Occupying a tree-shaded terrace, this simple restaurant provides an opportunity for breakfast or lunch after the long hike from the campground, or a welcome chance to 'go out' from your hotel in the evening.

Shopping

Nature Shop ARTS & CRAFTS

(Dana Guest House; ⌚9am-5.30pm) With a wide range of quality crafts inspired by nature, workshops and a food-drying centre for making organic food, this shop is well worth a visit. Villagers are given the opportunity to make quality local crafts (organic herbs, fruit rolls, jams, olive-oil soaps, candles and silver jewellery) that are sold by the RSCN throughout Jordan.

The leather goods and candles produced by local Bedouin women at Feynan Ecolodge (p151), in particular, give the women a degree of economic independence and an incentive to move away from goat rearing, which is detrimental to the fragile environment. The workshops close by 3.30pm.

Information

The **visitor centre** (☎03 227 0497; www.rscn.org.jo; ⌚8am-3pm) at Dana is the first port of call for a visit to the reserve, unless you're staying at Rummana Campground (though it can call ahead to arrange your transfer). The ticket office closes at 3pm, so if you're planning a sunset hike, make sure you arrive before then. Stop here for further information about the reserve and its hiking trails and to arrange a guide. Reservations for guides are advisable in spring and autumn, as there's a daily maximum of people permitted on certain trails.

Admission fees are included in the price of Royal Society for the Conservation of Nature (RSCN) accommodation.

Getting There & Away

BUS

The easiest way to get to Dana by public transport is from Tafila. Minibuses run every hour or so between Tafila and Qadsiyya (JD1, 30 minutes). The turn-off to Dana village is 1km north of Qadsiyya; from here it's a steep 2.8km downhill walk to the village (there's no bus).

There are three early-morning buses to Amman (JD3, three hours); the first leaves Qadsiyya at 4.30am, the next at 5am and the third at around 6am.

CAR & MOTORCYCLE

If you're driving from Tafila or Karak, the first signpost you'll see off to the right points to Rummana Campground. The turn-off to the Dana Biosphere Reserve is signposted just before Qadsiyya. Beware the steep descent: use low gear instead of relying on your brakes.

To get to Rummana Campground from Dana village, head 4.5km north of Qadsiyya along the King's Highway and turn left at the signpost. The campground is 6km along a road partly shared by cement-factory traffic.

TAXI & GUESTHOUSE TRANSFER

You can take a private car to Dana with one of the locals in Qadsiyya for JD3.

The non-RSCN Dana guesthouses all offer transfers to/from Dana village (usually free) and can arrange pick-ups. Minibus transfers from Amman's South Bus Station cost JD5 if you book with your guesthouse in advance.

A taxi to Dana from Karak costs around JD40 one way.

A taxi from Dana to Petra costs JD36, or JD12 per person in a shared taxi from your hotel.

Shobak الشوبك

Semi-arid for most of the year, the striking white-stone hills and wadis of Shobak make for a dramatic landscape, particularly on a crisp winter's day when the sky is cobalt blue. Most people visit Shobak for its grand eponymous castle, but it's also the start or end point of some spectacular hikes towards Dana in the north and Petra in the south.

Sights

★**Shobak Castle** CASTLE

(Mont Real, Montreal; JD1, with Jordan Pass free; ⌚daylight hours) Perched in a wild, remote landscape, Shobak Castle wins over even the most castle-weary visitor, despite being less complete than its sister fortification at Karak (p143). It's especially imposing when seen from a distance, as it sits on a dramatic hill (formerly called Mons Realis, or the Royal Mountain), imposing its might on the surrounding countryside. Local guides, who really know their stuff, are available at the gate for around JD10.

Shobak was built by the Crusader king Baldwin I in 1115. Its defenders withstood numerous attacks from the armies of Saladin (Salah ad Din) before succumbing in 1189 (a year after Karak), after an 18-month siege. It was later occupied in the 14th century by the Mamluks, who built over many of the Crusader buildings. As you climb up from the entrance, there are some **wells** on the left. Soon after passing these, you'll see the reconstructed **church**, one of two in the castle, down to the left. It has an elegant apse supported by two smaller alcoves. The room leading off to the west was the **baptistery**; on the north wall there are traces of water channels leading from above.

Return to the main path and turn left. After you pass under the arches, a door leads into the extensive **market**. Turn left and descend 375 steps into an amazing secret passageway that leads to a subterranean spring, finally surfacing via a ladder outside the castle, beside the road to Shobak town. Tread carefully, use a torch and don't even think about coming down here if you're claustrophobic. Alternatively, continue past the tunnel for 50m and you'll pass a large two-storey building with archways, built by the Crusaders but adapted by the Mamluks as a school. At the northern end of the castle is the semicircular **keep** with four arrow slits. Outside, dark steps lead down to the **prison**. Head to the northeastern corner of the castle to see Quranic inscriptions, possibly dating from the time of Saladin, carved in Kufic script around the outside of the keep.

Following south along the eastern perimeter, you'll pass the **entrance to the court** of Baldwin I, which has been partly reconstructed. Continuing south, you'll pass some baths on the right. Off to the left is a reconstructed **Mamluk watchtower**. Just past the tower is the second church. In a room to the left as you enter, you can see above a door in the east wall a weathered carving of a Crusader cross. In the **church** proper, the arches have been reconstructed. Beneath the church are **catacombs**, which contain Islamic tablets, Christian carvings, large spherical rocks used in catapults and what is said to be Saladin's very simple throne. From the catacombs, the path leads back to the gate.

There have been long-standing plans to bring the history of Shobak Castle to life with a local re-enactment company, but the tourism doldrums seem to have put this on hold. In the interim, staff dressed as Saladin's soldiers guard the entrance to Shobak sweetly and will happily pose for photos or engage visitors in mock sword fights.

Activities

Jaya Tourist Camp offers day trips and overnight camping trips from Shobak to Feynan Ecolodge or to Little Petra, with longer trips possible. Guided trips cost JD70 per day and the camps can arrange the transportation of luggage (JD70 per day). Visits to a local Bedouin family (JD5, overnight stay JD30) are also available.

Sleeping

Jaya Tourist Camp CAMPGROUND **$**
(☎07 9595 8958; www.jayatouristcamp.yolasite.com; half/full board per person JD20/25) With a variety of basic tents in a tranquil spot on high ground opposite Shobak Castle (p153), this friendly campground set in a garden of hollyhocks has a clean shower block and Bedouin goat-hair tents for relaxing. Hiking, including to Dana, can be arranged in advance. The campground is poorly signed but is downhill from the larger Montréal Hotel.

Montréal Hotel HOTEL **$$**
(☎07 7695 1714; www.jhrc.jo; r/ste JD50/90; wi-fi) This hotel, with a spectacular view of the castle (p153), has some lovely features including a stylish lounge around a central gas fire. The rooms are simple but comfortable. The hotel takes a sustainable approach and has solar panels for hot-water heating and electricity. Dinner (JD9) is available.

Information

Situated at the bottom of the castle hill, the **visitor centre** (⌚9am-5pm Nov-Mar, to 7pm Apr-Oct) has limited information, but you can get hot and cold drinks in the attractive courtyard, and there are functioning toilets.

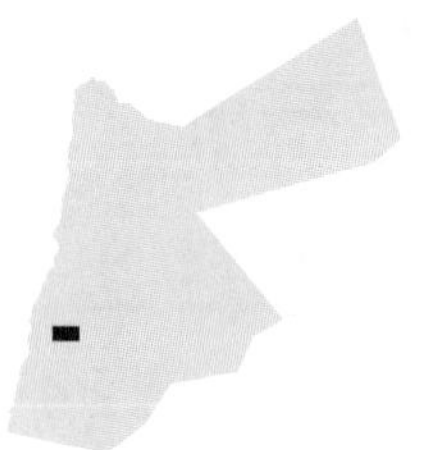

Petra البتراء

Includes ➡

Best Places to Eat

- Al Saraya Restaurant (p187)
- Petra Kitchen (p183)
- Oriental Restaurant (p187)
- Basin Restaurant (p177)

Best Places to Stay

- Mövenpick Hotel (p186)
- Rocky Mountain Hotel (p184)
- Cleopetra Hotel (p184)
- Peace Way Hotel (p184)
- Petra Guest House Hotel (p185)

Why Go?

Petra, the great Ancient City that lies half-hidden in the wind-blown landscape in southern Jordan, is one of the world's most treasured Unesco Heritage Sites. Voted by popular ballot in 2007 as one of the 'New Seven Wonders of the World', it has retained its magnetism even through times of strife in the wider region.

A visit to Petra when it was rediscovered for the wider world by Jean Louis Burckhardt in the 19th century meant going in disguise, speaking in local dialect and engaging the trust of surrounding tribespeople. Today visitors are welcomed both by the Bedouin who still relate to the Ancient City as home, and by the townspeople of neighbouring Wadi Musa whose facilities make a several-day visit to the Ancient City a pleasure. With nearby Nabataean attractions at so-called Little Petra, desert camping and numerous hiking opportunities, at least two days should be allowed to do Petra justice.

When to Go

- March to May is peak tourist season in Petra and for good reason. Hiking is at its safest, the wadis are seamed with prolific pink-flowering oleander, and climbs to the High Places are accompanied by spears of flowering aloe.
- Mid-October to the end of November, Petra's second high season, offers a last chance to visit in good weather before rains make some routes off limits.
- Bitterly cold by night with bright blue skies by day, Petra is almost empty in winter, allowing for a more intimate engagement with the 'Pink City'. This is a good time to catch the best bargains in Wadi Musa hotels.

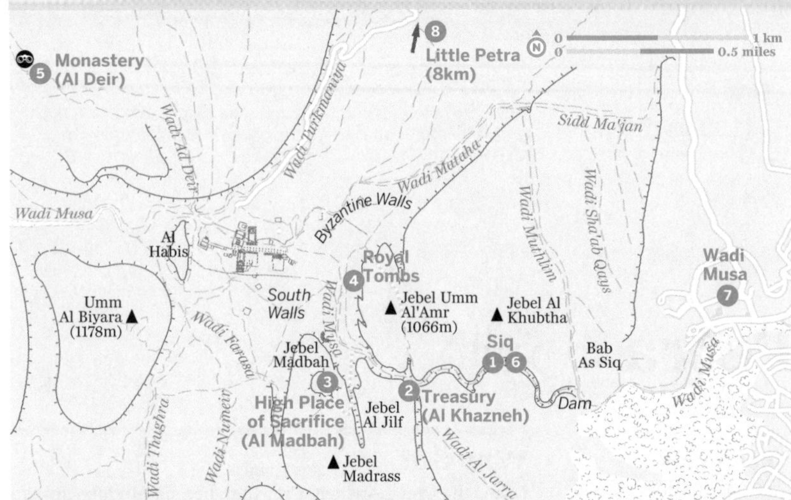

Petra Highlights

1 **Siq** (p159) Following the path of pilgrims through the sheer-sided chasm that leads to an ancient world.

2 **Treasury** (p160) Catching the early-morning sun slanting off the pillars of this Petra icon at the end of the Siq.

3 **High Place of Sacrifice** (p160) Climbing the processional way, pausing for tea with the Bedouin in the gardens of wildflowers.

4 **Royal Tombs** (p161) Searching for spirits lurking in the rainbow-coloured hollows.

5 **Monastery** (p165) Watching the weather-burnished stones catch alight at sunset from this celebrated Petra High Place.

6 **Petra by Night** (p176) Letting the soul glide through the Siq's shadows, guided by music and candlelight.

7 **Petra Kitchen** (p183) Preparing a traditional Jordanian supper in the company of fellow travellers, guided by experts, in Wadi Musa.

8 **Little Petra** (p190) Enjoying Nabataean tombs and temples in a miniature siq outside the Ancient City often overlooked by tour groups.

History

Petra: An Ancient Land

Petra is inextricably linked with the Nabataeans, the nomadic tribe from western Arabia who built most of the monuments in the Ancient City that are visible today. They were not the first inhabitants of the region, however. In fact, Neolithic villages dating from around 7000 BC are in evidence in the surrounding wadis and hillsides of Petra. Remains of the most famous of these, excavated in the 1950s, can be seen at Al Beidha, just north of the Ancient City near Little Petra. Built at the same time as Jericho on the West Bank, Al Beidha is one of the earliest known farming communities in the Middle East.

Nabataean Heyday

The Nabataeans arrived in the region around the 6th century BC. They were organised traders, and over the next 500 years they used their wealth to build the city of Petra. In its heyday, under King Aretas IV (8 BC–AD 40), the city was home to around 30,000 people, including scribes (the Nabataeans created their own cursive script, the forerunner of Arabic) and expert hydraulic engineers who built dams, cisterns and water channels to protect the site and its magnificent buildings.

The Romans in Petra

By AD 106, as trade routes shifted from Petra to Palmyra and new sea trade routes via the Red Sea to Rome bypassed Petra altogether, the Romans assumed control of the weakened Nabataean empire. Far from abandoning the declining city of Petra, however, the invaders recast the Ancient City with familiar Roman features, including a colonnaded street and baths. The city was honoured by a visit from Emperor Hadrian in AD 131, and in the 3rd century Petra once again became a capital – this time of the newly created province of Palaestrina Tertia. It was a short-lived second glory as an earthquake in 363 brought ruin.

Petra's 19th-Century Rediscovery

By the time of a second devastating earthquake in 551 Petra had became a forgotten outpost, a 'lost city' known only to local Bedouin who preferred to keep its whereabouts secret. In 1812, however, the young Swiss explorer, Jean Louis Burckhardt, ended Petra's splendid isolation, riding into the abandoned Ancient City disguised as a Muslim holy man, bringing in his wake a series of explorers, fortune hunters and curious travellers.

Throughout the 19th century, Petra became the focus of the Western European obsession with the Arabic Orient and the site was pored over by numerous archaeologists, poets and artists (including the famed British painter David Roberts in 1839).

Ongoing Exploration

The first English archaeological team arrived in 1929 and excavations have continued unabated to the present day. In 1992 the mosaics of the Petra Church were unveiled and in 2003 a tomb complex was found underneath the Treasury. Part of the continuing allure of the 'Pink City' is that despite years of scrutiny, Petra still has many secrets yet to be discovered.

Nature Reserves

Petra and the immediate vicinity is a protected area, although it is administered differently from Jordan's other nature reserves. Given the number of visitors it hosts each year, the area has its own challenges, particularly erosion and damage to antiquities. Visitors must avoid littering, wandering off paths, picking flowers, marking the monuments or disappearing behind a rock instead of using the toilet facilities.

Dangers & Annoyances

Petra has a few specific issues related to its geography and the large volume of visitors received each year.

- From September to March, dangerous flash floods (walls of water that pulse along the narrow defiles) can catch hikers unaware. Checking the forecast is essential.
- Hotel touts, traders and animal handlers (including children) can be over-persistent in the competitive high season, sometimes overcharging and employing hard-sell techniques. Deciding on a choice of hotel in advance of arrival at the bus station and engaging would-be traders in conversation are the best antidotes.
- Women are especially vulnerable to unwanted romantic advances in remote parts of Petra. A firm 'no thank you' is generally a sufficient deterrent. In budget hotels in Wadi Musa, it's worth making sure doors lock properly and that there are no peepholes.
- The Ancient City is strewn with High Places, once used for sacrifice or other rituals. These locations, all of which afford magnificent views and are a highlight of a visit, usually involve a steep hike up steps to a hilltop where there is no railing or other safety features. Some readers have expressed dismay at this.

Getting There & Away

Petra is a four-hour drive from Amman, two hours from Aqaba and 1½ hours from Wadi Rum. If driving to or from the Dead Sea, consider travelling along the spectacular and seldom-used road that links Little Petra with Wadi Araba through Namleh. Signs stating that this route is closed are outdated, but flash floods often cause damage to the road, so it's worth checking locally before attempting the drive.

Getting Around

There are usually plenty of yellow taxis with green plates travelling up and down the main road of Wadi Musa towards the entrance for Petra, especially in the early morning and late afternoon. They congregate outside Petra Visitor Centre. It's best to stick with these taxis as other cars offering taxi services are unlicensed and often uninsured.

Within Petra, the only way to reach most sites is by walking (strong, comfortable shoes are essential!) or by taking a camel, donkey or mule to more distant and uphill sites.

The Ancient City

The ancient Nabataean city of Petra, with its myriad tombs scooped out of the sandstone cliffs, is not just the leading highlight of a country blessed with more than its fair share of top sights: it's a world wonder. It lay forgotten for centuries, known only to the Bedouin who made it their home, until Swiss explorer Jean Louis Burckhardt happened upon it in 1812. Built partly in honour of the dead, the Petra necropolis retains much of its sense of mystery thanks to its inaccessible location in the heart of a wind-eroded landscape. Reached via the Siq, a narrow rift in the land whose cliffs cast long shadows across the once-sacred way, the path suddenly slithers into sunlight in front of the Treasury – a spectacle that cannot fail to impress. Add to this the cheerfulness of the Bedouin, and it's easy to see what makes a visit to Petra a must.

Sights

There are more than 800 registered sites in Petra, including some 500 tombs, but the best things to see are easy to find and easy to reach. From the main gate, a path winds 800m downhill through an area called **Bab As Siq** (Gateway to the Siq), punctuated with the first signs of the old city.

There are signs in English throughout Petra, helping to identify the main monuments, but a guidebook is useful to interpret what each site represents.

Start your visit to Petra at the Petra Visitor Centre plaza in Wadi Musa, across the road from the Mövenpick Hotel. This is where you buy tickets, get leaflets and a map, and use the toilets (although there are several toilets inside the Ancient City).

The sights are listed in this chapter in the order in which they are most usually encountered. The key places of interest are marked with a star.

Djinn Blocks MONUMENT

(Map p162) About halfway between Petra Visitor Centre and the entrance to the Siq, look out for three enormous, squat monuments, known as Djinn Blocks or God Blocks. Standing guard beside the path, they take their name from the Arabic word for spirit, the source of the English word 'genie'. Other than the fact they were built by

'IBRAHIM' BURCKHARDT: EXPLORER EXTRAORDINAIRE

There can't be many explorers in history who can match the remarkable exploits of Jean Louis Burckhardt. Born in 1784 in Lausanne, Switzerland, he studied Arabic and attended lectures on science and medicine at Cambridge University in the UK before moving to Aleppo (Syria) in 1809. Here, he converted to Islam and took the name Sheikh Ibrahim Bin Abdullah. Over the next two years, he became a master of disguise, adopting local customs and putting his alias to the test among local Bedouin.

In 1812, travelling between Damascus and Cairo, he heard locals tell of fantastic ruins hidden in the mountains of Wadi Musa. Determined to see for himself, he had to think of a ploy to allay the suspicions of his guide and porters and decided to disguise himself as a pilgrim on a mission to pay his respects at the tomb of Haroun. This was an ingenious strategy because the tomb lies at the furthest end of the valley, allowing him cautious glances at the wonders he passed en route.

Although he tried hard to hide his astonishment, his guide wasn't fooled for long and imagined that the pale Syrian had come hunting for treasure. To avoid occasioning more suspicion, Burckhardt therefore had to confine his curiosity to the briefest examination of the ancient monuments – enough, however, to conclude that this was Petra, a place which he understood no European traveller had ever visited. Despite being a man not given to literary flourishes, his journal, *Travels in Syria and the Holy Land,* reveals something of the excitement of his discovery and he describes emerging from the subterranean gloom of the Siq in terms that have inspired generations of future travellers.

For many an explorer, this expedition would have been a lifetime's achievement – but not for Burckhardt. He went on to find the source of the Niger, stumbled on the magnificent Ramses II temple at Abu Simbel in Egypt, and still under disguise explored Mecca and Medina. In 1815 he contracted dysentery in Cairo, which returned with fatal consequences in 1817. He was buried as a Muslim in the Islamic Cemetery in Cairo. He was only 33 years old.

Nabataeans in the 1st century AD, little is known about their why or wherefore.

Many visitors miss the blocks in their hurry to reach the Siq but they are worth a pause to speculate about their purpose. Some suggest they represent the start of tombs, or were associated with funerary dedications or the worship of water and fertility. Whatever their intended function, they are the lodestar for the modern visitor – a tantalising taste of the monuments to come, or announcing journey's end on the weary return.

Obelisk Tomb & Bab As Siq Triclinium — TOMB

(Map p162) Between the Petra Visitor Centre and the entrance to the Siq (south side of the path), there is a fine tomb with four pyramidal obelisks, built as funerary symbols by the Nabataeans in the 1st century BC. The four obelisks, together with the eroded human figure in the centre, probably represent the five people buried in the tomb.

The obelisk tomb at first appears to be multistorey. In fact, it was built on top of a much earlier structure, with a Doric columned facade. This building is known as a triclinium (dining room), and is one of several in Petra. This is where annual feasts were held to commemorate the dead, although it's hard to imagine the conviviality of a banquet in the silent hollow that remains.

If you miss it on the way down to the Ancient City (easily done if you're riding a horse to the Siq), look out for it on the way back: the monument comes into its own at sunset when the obelisks are thrown into relief.

Near the Obelisk Tomb, further down the track towards the Siq, a signposted detour to the right leads to several stepped tombs carved into the tops of domed hills. It's a secret little place, missed by almost everyone in their rush to get to the Siq.

★Siq — CANYON

(Map p162) The 1.2km Siq, or canyon, with its narrow, vertical walls, is undeniably one of the highlights of Petra. The walk through this magical corridor, as it snakes its way towards the hidden city, is one full of anticipation for the wonders ahead – a point not wasted on the Nabataeans, who made the passage into a sacred way, punctuated with sites of spiritual significance.

The Siq starts at an obvious bridge, beside a modern dam. The dam was built in 1963, on top of a Nabataean dam dated AD 50, to stop floodwater from Wadi Musa flowing through the Siq. To the right, Wadi Muthlim heads through a Nabataean tunnel – the start (or finish) of an exciting hike. The entrance to the Siq was once marked by a Nabataean monumental arch. It survived until the end of the 19th century, and some remains can be seen at twin niches on either side of the entrance. Many people charge through the Siq impatient to get to Petra. That's a pity because the corridor of stone is worth enjoying for its own sake and the longer you take to travel through it, the more you can savour the final moment of arrival.

Technically, the Siq, with its 200m-high walls, is not a canyon (a gorge carved out by water), but a single block that has been rent apart by tectonic forces. At various points you can see where the grain of the rock on one side matches the other – it's easiest to spot when the Siq narrows to 2m wide. The original channels cut into the walls to bring water into Petra are visible, and in some places the 2000-year-old terracotta pipes are still in place. A section of Roman paving was revealed after excavations in 1997 removed 2m of soil accumulation.

Some historians speculate that the primary function of the Siq was akin to the ancient Graeco-Roman Sacred Way. Some of the most important rituals of Petra's spiritual life began as a procession through the narrow canyon, and it also represented the end point for Nabataean pilgrims. Many of the wall niches that are still visible today along the Siq's walls were designed to hold figures or representations (called *baetyls*) of the main Nabataean god, Dushara. These small sacred sites served as touchstones of the sacred for pilgrims and priests, offering them a link to the more ornate temples, tombs and sanctuaries in the city's heart, reminding them that they were leaving the outside world, and on the threshold of what was for many a holy city.

At one point the Siq opens out to reveal a square tomb next to a lone fig tree. A little further on, look for a weathered carving of a camel and caravan man on the left wall. The water channel passes behind the carving. Hereafter, the walls almost appear to meet overhead, shutting out the sound and light and helping to build the anticipation of a first glimpse of the Treasury. It's a sublime introduction to the Ancient City.

FINDING YOUR OWN PACE IN PETRA

Instead of trying to tick off all the top spots in the Ancient City (the quickest way to 'monument fatigue'), it's better to personalise Petra by sparing time to amble among unnamed tombs, have a picnic in the shade of a flowering oleander or sip tea at a stall on the valley floor and watch everyone else toiling to 'see it all'.

The following suggestions combine some of the obvious highlights with off-the-beaten-track exploration.

Half Day (five hours) Amble through the Siq, absorbing its special atmosphere and savouring the moment of revelation at the Treasury. Resist the temptation to head for the Theatre; instead, climb the steps to the High Place of Sacrifice. Pause for tea by the Obelisk and take the path into Wadi Farasa, enjoying wildflowers and the Garden Tomb en route. The path reaches the Colonnaded Street via a paintbox of rock formations. If there's time, visit the Royal Tombs and then return to the valley floor for a chat with Bedouin stallholders and a hunt for the perfect sand bottle.

One Day (eight hours) Spend the morning completing the half-day itinerary, but pack a picnic. After visiting the Royal Tombs, walk along to Qasr Al Bint and hike along the broad wadi that leads to Jebel Haroun as far as Snake Monument – an ideal perch for a snack and a snooze. Return to explore Qasr Al Bint but save some energy for the climb to the Monastery, a fitting finale for any visit to Petra.

Two Days Spend the second day scrambling through exciting Wadi Muthlim (if open) and restore your energy over a barbecue in the Basin Restaurant. Walk off lunch exploring the hidden beauty of Wadi Siyagh with its pools of water before strolling back along the Street of Facades. Sit near the Theatre to watch the sun go down on the Royal Tombs opposite – the best spectacle in Petra.

★ Treasury — TOMB

(Al Khazneh; Map p162) Known locally as the Treasury, this tomb is where most visitors fall in love with Petra. The Hellenistic facade is an astonishing piece of craftsmanship. Although carved out of iron-laden sandstone to serve as a tomb for the Nabataean King Aretas III (c 100 BCE–CE 200), the Treasury derives its name from the story that an Egyptian pharaoh hid his treasure here (in the facade urn) while pursuing the Israelites.

Some locals clearly believed the tale because the 3.5m-high urn is pockmarked by rifle shots. As with all rock-hewn monuments in Petra, the interior is unadorned. The Treasury is at its most photogenic in full sunlight between about 9am and 11am.

Street of Facades — RUINS

(Map p162) From the Treasury, the passage broadens into what is commonly referred to as the Outer Siq. Riddling the walls of the Outer Siq are more than 40 tombs and houses built by the Nabataeans in a 'crow step' style reminiscent of Assyrian architecture. Colloquially known as the Street of Facades, they are easily accessible, unlike many tombs in Petra.

A couple of tombs are worth exploring here. The first tomb (number 67) is unusual in that it has a funeral chamber in the upper storey. The low entryway highlights how the valley floor has risen over the centuries thanks to the debris washed down during flash floods. Nearby, tomb 70 is unusual in that it is freestanding, with a ziggurat-style top that makes it look like a miniature fort.

★ High Place of Sacrifice — VIEWPOINT

(Al Madbah; Map p162) The most accessible of Petra's High Places, this well-preserved site was built atop Jebel Madbah with drains to channel the blood of sacrificial animals. A flight of steps signposted just before the Theatre leads to the site: turn right at the **obelisks** (Map p162) to reach the sacrificial platform. You can ascend by donkey (about JD10 one way), but you'll sacrifice both the sense of achievement on reaching the summit and the good humour of your poor old transport.

The obelisks are more than 6m high; they are remarkable structures because they are carved out of the rock face, not built upon it: looking at the negative space surrounding them, you can understand the truly epic scale of excavation involved. Dedicated to the Nabataean gods Dushara and Al 'Uzza, their iron-rich stone glows in the sun and they act like totems of this once-hallowed ground.

The altar area includes a large rectangular triclinium, where celebrants at the sacrifice shared a communal supper. In the middle of the High Place, there's a large stone block preceded by three steps. This is a *motab* (repository), where the god statues involved in the procession would have been kept. Next to it is the circular altar, reached by another three steps; stone water basins nearby were used for cleansing and purifying.

The faint bleat of sheep or the clunk of a goat bell evokes the ancient scene – except that no ordinary person would have been permitted to enter this holy of holies at that time. Cast an eye across the superb panorama in front of you – far above the mortal goings-on of both ancient and modern city – and it's easy to see how this site must have seemed closer to the sky than the earth.

The steps to the High Place of Sacrifice are well maintained, if unremitting, and it takes about 45 minutes up through the crevices and folds of the mountain to reach the obelisks from the Theatre. From here you fork right to reach the altar area. The route is steep but not unduly exposed, so is manageable (unless you suffer from severe vertigo) even without a head for heights. From the altar area, descend the shelves of rock to a broad rim: about 50m down are regal views of the Royal Tombs.

It's worth sitting here for a while. From this lofty vantage point you can watch the everyday dramas of camel handlers arguing with their mounts, young children moving goats from one patch of sparse vegetation to the next and Bedouin stallholders regaling the unsuspecting traveller. They each move beyond the languishing tombs of ordinary folk, far too mindful of the needs of the living to worry much about the forgotten hopes of the ancient dead.

From the obelisks it's possible to continue to the city centre via a group of interesting tombs in beautiful Wadi Farasa.

★Theatre — THEATRE

(Map p162) Originally built by the Nabataeans (not the Romans) more than 2000 years ago, the Theatre was chiselled out of rock, slicing through many caves and tombs in the process. It was enlarged by the Romans to hold about 8500 (around 30% of the population of Petra) soon after they arrived in 106 CE. Badly damaged by an earthquake in 363 CE, the Theatre was partially dismantled to build other structures but it remains a Petra highlight.

The seating area had an original capacity of about 3000 in 45 rows of seats, with three horizontal sections separated by two corridors. The orchestra section was carved from the rock, but the backdrop to the *frons scaenae* (stage, which is no longer intact) was constructed, as opposed to carved, in three storeys with frescoed niches and columns overlaid by marble. The performers entered through one of three entrances, the outlines of which are still partially visible.

To make room for the upper seating tiers, the Romans sliced through more tombs. Under the stage floor were storerooms and a slot through which a curtain could be lowered at the start of a performance. From near the slot, an almost-complete statue of Hercules was recovered.

With a backdrop worthy of a David Roberts canvas, the Theatre now offers a vantage point from which to watch a modern tragicomedy of the ill-costumed, cursing their high-heeled footwear; the ill-cast, yawning at tedious tour guides; and the ill-tempered – mainly in the form of irritable camels and their peevish owners.

★Royal Tombs — TOMB

(Map p162) Downhill from the Theatre, the wadi widens to create a larger thoroughfare. To the right, the great massif of Jebel Al Khubtha looms over the valley. Within its west-facing cliffs are burrowed some of the most impressive burial places in Petra, known collectively as the 'Royal Tombs'. They look particularly stunning bathed in the golden light of sunset.

The Royal Tombs are reached via a set of steps that ascends from the valley floor, near the Theatre. A worthwhile hike from the Royal Tombs leads up to the numerous places of worship on the flattened High Place of Jebel Khubtha, together with a spectacular view of the Treasury. The steps are easily visible between the Palace Tomb and the Sextius Florentinus Tomb. The Royal Tombs can also be reached via the adventurous hike through Wadi Muthlim.

➡ ★Urn Tomb

(Map p162) The most distinctive of the Royal Tombs is the Urn Tomb, recognisable by the enormous urn on top of the pediment. It was built in about AD 70 for King Malichos II

Petra

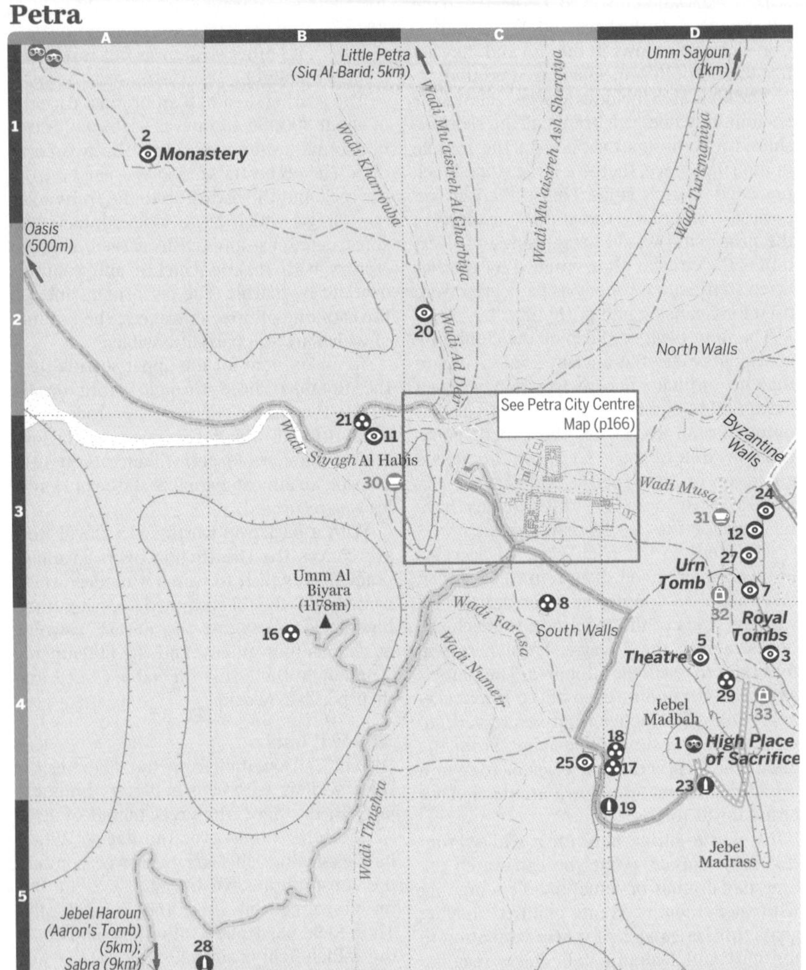

(AD 40–70) or Aretas IV (8 BC–AD 40). The naturally patterned interior of the Urn Tomb measures a vast 18m by 20m.

Part of what makes the Urn Tomb such a grand structure is the flanking Doric portico cut into the rock face on the left of the tomb, and the huge open terrace in front of it – a feature that encouraged its use, according to a Greek inscription inside the tomb, as a cathedral in AD 447. The double layer of vaults was added at a later date by the Byzantines. Look towards the top of the building and you'll see three inaccessible openings carved between the pillars. These are also tombs, the central one of which still has the closing stone intact, depicting the king dressed in a toga.

➡ Silk Tomb

(Map p162) Next to the distinctive Urn Tomb in the Royal Tomb group is the so-called Silk Tomb, noteworthy for the stunning swirls of pink-, white- and yellow-veined rock in its facade.

➡ Corinthian Tomb

(Map p162) The badly damaged Corinthian Tomb is something of a hybrid, with Hellenistic decorative features on the upper level

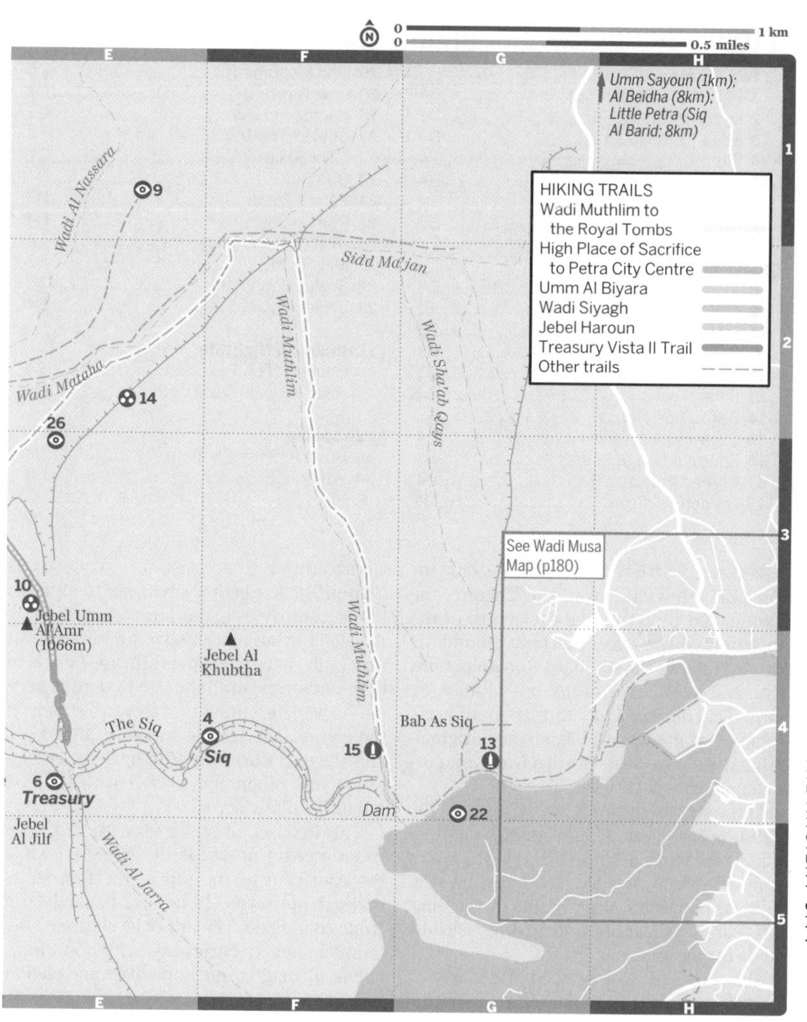

and a Nabataean portico on the lower level. The tomb gets its name from the Corinthian capitals adorned with floral motifs.

➡ Palace Tomb

(Map p162) The delightful three-storey imitation of a Roman or Hellenistic palace, known as the Palace Tomb, is distinctive among the Royal Tombs for its rock-hewn facade, the largest in Petra. The doors lead into typically simple funerary chambers while the 18 columns on the upper level are the most distinctive and visually arresting elements of the tomb. Notice the top-left corner is built (rather than carved) because the rock face didn't extend far enough to complete the facade.

Sextius Florentinus Tomb — TOMB

(Map p162) A few hundred metres around the hill from the Royal Tombs is the seldom-visited Sextius Florentinus Tomb, built from AD 126 to 130 for a Roman governor of Arabia, whose exploits are glorified in an inscription above the entrance. Unlike many other tombs, the interior is worth a look for the clearly discernible *loculi* (graves); there are five carved into the back wall and three on the right as you enter.

Petra

Top Sights
1 High Place of Sacrifice D4
2 Monastery A1
3 Royal Tombs D4
4 Siq F4
5 Theatre D4
6 Treasury E4
7 Urn Tomb D3

Sights
8 Az Zantur C3
9 Christian Tombs E1
10 Cistern E3
11 Convent Group B3
12 Corinthian Tomb D3
13 Djinn Blocks G4
14 Dorotheos' House E2
15 Eagle Monument F4
16 Edomite Village Ruins B4
17 Garden Tomb D4
18 Garden Triclinium D4
19 Lion Monument D5
20 Lion Tomb C2
21 Nabataean Quarry B3
22 Obelisk Tomb & Bab As Siq Triclinium G4
23 Obelisks D4
24 Palace Tomb D3
25 Roman Soldier's Tomb C4
26 Sextius Florentinus Tomb E3
27 Silk Tomb D3
28 Snake Monument A5
29 Street of Facades D4

Drinking & Nightlife
30 Bdoul Mofleh Tea Shop B3
31 Have a Break Tea & Coffee D3

Shopping
32 Umm Raami's Shop D3
33 Why Not Shop D4

Colonnaded Street ARCHAEOLOGICAL SITE
(Map p166) Downhill from the Theatre, the Colonnaded Street marks the centre of the Ancient City. The street was built around AD 106 and follows the standard Roman pattern of an east–west *decumanus,* but without the normal *cardo maximus* (north–south axis). Columns of marble-clad sandstone originally lined the 6m-wide carriageway, and covered porticoes gave access to shops.

At the start of the Colonnaded Street is the **Nymphaeum** (Map p166), a public fountain built in the 2nd century AD and fed by water channelled from the Siq. Little can be seen today, although it's recognisable by the huge 450-year-old pistachio tree, giving welcome shade in summer.

Also along the Colonnaded Street are the limited remains of the market area and the unrecognisable ruins of the **Royal Palace** (Map p166).

The street ends at the **Temenos Gateway** (Map p166). Built in the 2nd century AD, the gateway originally had huge wooden doors and side towers. It marked the entrance to the **temenos** (Map p166; sacred courtyard) of the Qasr Al Bint, separating the commercial area of the city from the sacred area of the temple. Look closely for the few remaining floral friezes and a figure with an arrow, which suggest that this was once a very grand structure. Opposite are the minimal ruins of the **Nabataean baths** (Map p166).

Great Temple TEMPLE
(Map p166) A major Nabataean temple of the 1st century BCE, this structure was badly damaged by an earthquake not long after it was built, but it remained in use (albeit in different forms) until the late Byzantine period. A *theatron* (miniature theatre) stands in the centre. The temple was once 18m high, and the enclosure was 40m by 28m. The interior was originally covered with striking red-and-white stucco.

The first set of stairs was fronted by a **monumental propylaeum** (gateway) while the courtyard at the top of the first stairs marked the **lower temenos**, flanked by a triple colonnade. The upper level housed the temple's sacred enclosure, with four huge columns (made from stone discs and clad in marble) at the entrance.

Archaeologists debate the function of this so-called temple, some suggesting that it may have been used by the Nabataeans as a royal audience hall. The Romans appear to have used it in later times as a civic centre.

Qasr Al Bint TEMPLE
(Map p166) One of the few free-standing structures in Petra, Qasr Al Bint was built in around 30 BCE by the Nabataeans. It was later adapted to the cult of Roman emperors and destroyed around the 3rd century CE. Despite the name given to it by the local Bedouin – Castle of the Pharaoh's Daughter

– the temple was originally built as a dedication to Nabataean gods and was one of the most important temples in Petra.

The temple once stood 23m high and its features included marble staircases, imposing columns, a raised platform for worship, and ornate plaster and stone reliefs – examples of which are housed in the display at the Petra Visitor Centre. The central 'holy of holies', known as an *adyton*, would have housed an image of the deities. The sacrificial **altar** (Map p166) in front, once overlaid with marble, indicates that it was probably the main place of worship in the Nabataean city and its location at street level suggests that the whole precinct (and not just the temple interior) was considered sacred.

Temple of the Winged Lions TEMPLE

(Map p166) The recently excavated Temple of the Winged Lions, built around AD 27, is named after the carved lions that once topped the capitals of each of the columns. The temple was probably dedicated to the fertility goddess, Atargatis, the partner of the male god Dushara. Fragments of decorative stone and painted plaster found on the site of this once important temple are now on display in Petra Visitor Centre.

Petra Church CHURCH

(Map p166) An awning covers the remains of Petra Church (also known as the Byzantine Church). Inside the church are some exquisite Byzantine floor **mosaics**, some of the best in the region. The mosaics originally continued up the walls. A helpful map and explanations in English are also located inside the church.

Al Habis VIEWPOINT

(Map p166) Beyond Qasr Al Bint is the small hill of Al Habis (the Prison). From the Nabataean Tent Restaurant, steps lead up the hill past a disused museum around the back of Al Habis, with striking views of fertile Wadi Siyagh and the junction with Wadi Numeir.

The path soon skirts the tea shop and comfortable **cave home** of Bdoul Mofleh, one of the last residents of Petra. Asked why he didn't leave when the rest of his family were relocated to Umm Sayoun, he replied, 'Why would I? This is my home; I've always lived here.' With a view to die for and a garden of flowering jasmine, it's easy to see why this hardy resident chose to stay. Notice the red-capped aloe, standing to attention in early summer, billeted across the cliffs opposite.

The path continues around the hill, past the **Convent Group** (Map p162) of tombs to a flight of steps. These lead in turn (via a wooden plank bridge) to the top of Al Habis, another of Petra's many High Places. At the summit (allow 10 to 15 minutes to reach the top) are the limited ruins of a small **Crusader fort** (Map p166), built in AD 1116 by Baldwin I. The ruins are not impressive, but the views across the city certainly are.

From here you can either hike via the Pharaun Column (p172), which is a good landmark, to Snake Monument in Wadi Thughra, or along Wadi Farasa to the High Place of Sacrifice.

Alternatively, complete the circuit of Al Habis by descending the hill behind Qasr Al Bint. On your way down, look out for the **Unfinished Tomb** (Map p166). It offers a rare glimpse of the way the Nabataeans constructed their rock tombs, starting at the top on a platform of scaffolding and working their way down. Nearby is the enigmatic **Columbarium** (Map p166), whose multiple niches remain a mystery; some suppose they housed votive images or urns, others say this was a dovecote for pigeons.

Basin Area AREA

(Map p166) The Basin is an area just beyond Qasr Al Bint where the main wadi widens at the bottom of the valley. The area, which houses the two restaurants (Basin Restaurant and Nabataean Tent Restaurant), makes a handy pause point before the ascent to the Monastery. This is also the access point for the so-called backdoor to Petra and is where most of the four-legged transport congregates for further-flung points of the Ancient City.

★ Monastery TOMB

(Al Deir; Map p162) Hidden high in the hills, the Monastery is one of the legendary monuments of Petra. Similar in design to the Treasury but far bigger (50m wide and 45m high), it was built in the 3rd century BCE as a Nabataean tomb. It derives its name from the crosses carved on the inside walls, suggestive of its use as a church in Byzantine times. The ancient rock-cut path of more than 800 steps starts from the Basin Restaurant and follows the old processional route.

The cave tea shop opposite is a good vantage point for admiring the Monastery's Hellenistic facade. The courtyard in front of the Monastery was once surrounded by columns and was used for sacred ceremonies.

Petra City Centre

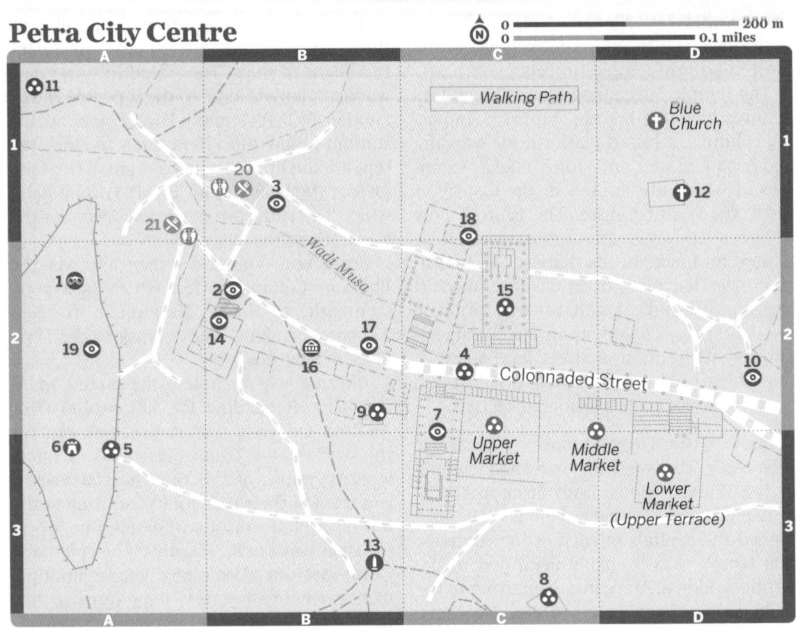

Petra City Centre

Sights

1 Al Habis....A2
2 Altar....B2
3 Basin Area....B1
4 Colonnaded Street....C2
5 Columbarium....A3
6 Crusader Fort....A3
7 Great Temple....C2
8 Nabataean & Roman Houses....C3
9 Nabataean Baths....B2
10 Nymphaeum....D2
11 Painted House....A1
12 Petra Church....D1
13 Pharaun Column....B3
14 Qasr Al Bint....B2
15 Royal Palace....C2
16 Temenos....B2
17 Temenos Gateway....B2
18 Temple of Winged Lions....C1
19 Unfinished Tomb....A2

Eating

20 Basin Restaurant....B1
21 Nabataean Tent Restaurant....A1

Behind the tea shop, tomb 468 is worth exploring for another fine facade, some defaced carvings and excellent views. A trail leads up to stunning **viewpoints** over Wadi Araba, Israel and the Palestinian Territories and south to the peak of Jebel Haroun, topped by a small white shrine.

The easy-to-follow trail from the Basin Restaurant to the Monastery takes about 40 minutes (if in doubt as to the trailhead, look for weary hikers coming down). Alternatively, donkeys (with a guide) can be hired for about JD20 return depending on your negotiation skills; you're better off walking coming down as the donkeys travel fast and the way is steep and slippery, making for an uncomfortable and at times dangerous journey for both you and your mount. The trip is best started in mid-afternoon when there is welcome shade and the Monastery is at its most photogenic. The path follows the old processional route and is a spectacle in its own right, with flights of eroded steps scooped out of the weird and wonderfully tortured stone. There are several side paths to explore, including a detour to the **Lion Tomb** (Lion Triclinium; Map p162), set in a gully. The two weather-beaten lions that lend the tomb its name face each other at the base of the monument.

An exciting 6km hike leads from the Monastery to Siq Al Barid (Little Petra; it takes about 2½ hours and involves a newly paved path and steps). Ask at Petra Visitor Centre (p179) or at local travel agencies for a guide as the route is difficult to find.

Activities

Hiking

Anyone wanting to see some stunning landscapes, explore unexcavated tombs and meet the Bedouin should pack an extra bottle of water and go hiking – preferably with the contoured *Map of Petra,* available from shops in the Petra Visitor Centre complex.

Most hikes are not that strenuous and none are overnight trips (camping is not permitted within Petra). Only the hikes along Wadi Muthlim (which is often closed) and to Sabra or Little Petra require a guide. Note that the approximate hiking times are just that and do not include time for pottering.

Experienced multilingual guides can be hired from the Petra Visitor Centre from JD50 (for one to nine people) for a simple route to the Basin, or from local travel agencies. It costs an extra JD20 for a guide to either the High Place of Sacrifice or to the Monastery. Unofficial Bedouin 'guides' may charge considerably less than the official rates: occasionally they are very good, but there's no guarantee. Women on their own should be cautious about hiking with unregistered guides, particularly as most of the hikes involve spending time in isolated parts of Petra.

Stick to trails, use only the toilets provided and remove your litter to avoid degradation of the area.

Short Hikes

Wadi Muthlim to Royal Tombs HIKING

This adventurous 1½-hour canyon hike is an exciting alternative route into Petra if you've already taken the main Siq path. Flash floods are a serious issue in the area and, as a result, the trail is often closed and a guide is mandatory. The hike is not difficult or too strenuous, but there are several boulder blockages, and in winter you may need to wade through pools of water.

The trail starts from the dam, just before the entrance to the Siq. Before entering the ancient, 88m-long Nabataean tunnel, it's possible to make a short detour (veer right and double-back over the top of the tunnel) to the **Eagle Monument** (Map p162), with its eponymous carvings.

Back on the hike, walk through the tunnel and you'll emerge into the sunlight of Wadi Muthlim with its thick ribbon of oleander. The wadi gradually narrows into a 1m-wide siq, and in three places, you'll have to lower yourself down 2m-high boulder blockages. The first is easy enough to negotiate; the other two take a bit more strategy – not impossible if you have someone to lean on, but tricky if you attempt it on your own. If you're not comfortable on the second boulder, turn back or you could get stuck between boulder blockage two and three!

After 25 minutes from the start of the hike, look for the remains of a Nabataean dam above the trail. Five minutes later, you'll meet a T-intersection where the trail joins Wadi Mataha. Follow the painted arrow to the left. This is the most exciting part of the hike as the canyon narrows to little more than a crack in the rock. You can see here how treacherous this hike would be in a flash flood as there is little space between you and the parallel walls. At certain times of the year you may have to splash through residual pools of water here until at length you pass into the perfect picnic point. Surrounded by Nabataean niches, and shaded on two sides almost all day, this little square of ancient Petra has a presence far bigger than its dimensions.

NAVIGATING PETRA

The town of Wadi Musa is the transport and accommodation hub for the Ancient City of Petra, as well as for other attractions in the vicinity, such as Little Petra. The town is split roughly into three parts. The upper part comprises a few top-end hotels lining the main road, each of which has spectacular views of the weathered sandstone landscape (although not of Petra itself). The town centre is where most of the cheaper hotels, the bus station and shops are located. The lower part of town, a 10-minute walk from the town centre, is where most of the top-end and midrange hotels, together with souvenir shops, tourist restaurants and the famed Cave Bar, are located.

Beyond this is the Petra Visitor Centre (p179) and the main entrance to Petra. From here the Ancient City is reached on foot via the Siq, or gorge, which begins after a 15-minute walk (or horse ride) from the entrance and takes a further 20 minutes on foot. There is another seldom-used entrance near the village of Umm Sayoun, but tickets (p178) can only be bought from Petra Visitor Centre.

Petra

A WALKING TOUR

Splendid though it is, the Treasury is not the full stop of a visit to Petra that many people may imagine. In some ways, it's just the semicolon – a place to pause after the exertions of the Siq, before exploring the other remarkable sights and wonders just around the corner.

Even if you're on a tight schedule or worried the bus won't wait, try to find another two hours in your itinerary to complete this walking tour. Our illustration shows the key highlights of the route, as you wind through Wadi Musa from the ❶ **Siq**, pause at the ❷ **Treasury** and pass the tombs of the broader ❸ **Outer Siq**. With energy and a stout pair of shoes, climb to the ❹ **High Place of Sacrifice** for a magnificent eagle's-eye view of Petra. Return to the ❺ **Street of Facades** and the ❻ **Theatre**. Climb the steps opposite to the ❼ **Urn Tomb** and neighbouring ❽ **Silk Tomb**: these Royal Tombs are particularly magnificent in the golden light of sunset.

Is the thought of all that walking putting you off? Don't let it! There are donkeys to help you with the steep ascents and Bedouin stalls for a reviving herb tea. If you run out of steam, camels are on standby for a ride back to the Treasury.

TOP TIPS

- ➡ From around 7am in summer and 8am in winter, watch the early morning sun slide down the Treasury facade.
- ➡ Stand opposite the Royal Tombs at sunset (around 4pm in winter and 5pm in summer) to learn how Petra earned its nickname, Pink City.
- ➡ Petra's oleanders flower in May.

Treasury
As you watch the sun cut across the facade, notice how it lights up the ladders on either side of Petra's most iconic building. These stone indents were most probably used for scaffolding.

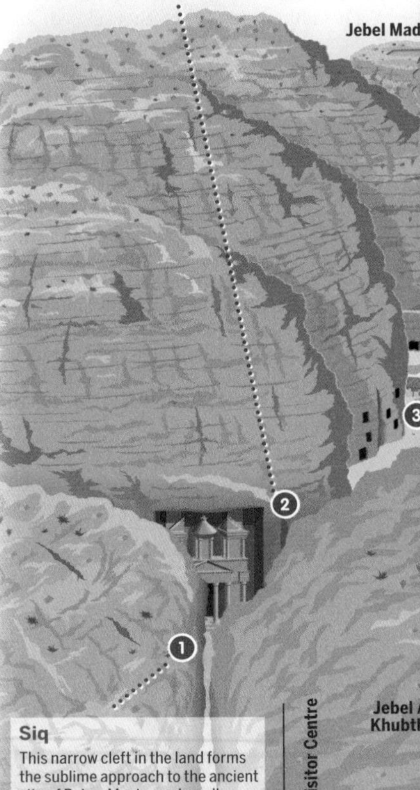

Siq
This narrow cleft in the land forms the sublime approach to the ancient city of Petra. Most people walk through the corridor of stone but horse carts are available for those who need them.

ANOTHER WAY DOWN

A superb walk leads from the High Place of Sacrifice, past the Garden Tomb to Petra City Centre.

ˈligh Place of ˈacrifice

ˈnagine the ancients ˈeading the stone ˈteps and it'll take ˈour mind off the steep ˈscent. The hilltop ˈlatform was used for ˈcense-burning and ˈbation-pouring in ˈonour of forgotten ˈods.

CHRISTOPHE CAPPELLI/SHUTTERSTOCK ©

Outer Siq

Take time to inspect the tombs just past the Treasury. Some appear to have a basement but, in fact, they show how the floor of the wadi has risen over the centuries.

CLAUDIOVIDRI/SHUTTERSTOCK ©

Street of Facades

Cast an eye at the upper storeys of some of these tombs and you'll see a small aperture. Burying the dead in attics was meant to deter robbers – the plan didn't work.

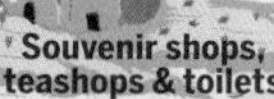

5

6

Souvenir shops, teashops & toilets

Wadi Musa

Wadi Musa

To Ancient City Centre →

7

8

Royal Tombs

Jebel Umm al'Amr (1066m)

Royal Tombs

HEAD FOR HEIGHTS

For a regal view of Petra, head for the heights above the Royal Tombs, via the staircase.

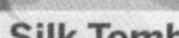

ˈrn Tomb

ˈarning its name ˈom the urn-shaped ˈnial crowning the ˈediment, this grand ˈdifice with supporting ˈrched vaults was ˈerhaps built for the ˈan represented by ˈhe toga-wearing bust ˈ the central aperture.

Silk Tomb

Perhaps Nabataean builders were attracted to Wadi Musa because of the colourful beauty of the raw materials. Nowhere is this more apparent than in the weather-eroded, striated sandstone of the Silk Tomb.

Theatre

Most stone amphitheatres are freestanding, but this one is carved almost entirely from the solid rock. Above the back row are the remains of earlier tombs, their facades sacrificed in the name of entertainment.

NAEBLYS/SHUTTERSTOCK ©

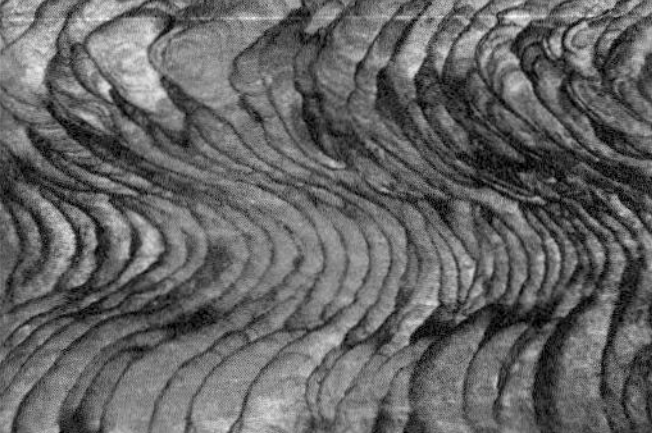

ALBERT H. TEICH/SHUTTERSTOCK ©

DON'T MISS

PETRA UNDER THE STARS

Like a grumbling camel caravan of snorting, coughing, laughing and farting miscreants, 200 people and one jubilantly crying baby make their way down the Siq 'in silence'. Asked to walk in single file behind the leader, breakaway contingents surge ahead to make sure they enjoy the experience on their own. And eventually, sitting outside the Treasury, the collected company shows its appreciation of Arabic classical music by lighting cigarettes from the paper bag lanterns, chatting energetically, flashing their cameras and audibly farting some more.

Welcome to public entertainment in the Middle East! If you really want the Siq to yourself, come during winter, go at 2pm or take a virtual tour on the internet.

Despite the promotional literature to the contrary, silence and solitude is not what the Petra by Night tour (p176) is all about. What this exceptional and highly memorable tour does give you is the fantastic opportunity to experience one of the most sublime spectacles on earth in the fever of other people's excitement. Huddles of whispering devotees stare up at the candlelit God Blocks, elderly participants are helped over polished lozenges of paving stones, the sound of a flute wafts along the neck hairs of fellow celebrants – this is surely much nearer to the original experience of the Ancient City of Petra than walking reverentially through the icy stone corridor alone.

From here, follow the cliff face to the left, past a series of little-visited tombs, including **Dorotheos' House** (Map p162) and the Sextius Florentinus Tomb (p163), until you reach the Royal Tombs. Alternatively, you can turn northeast on a small track that begins from the wadi almost opposite the Tomb of Sextius Florentinus, and explore the interesting so-called **Christian Tombs of Moghar Al Nassara** (Moghar Al Nassara; Map p162) where excavations are ongoing.

Some parts of the canyon may be impassable if it's been raining. Flash floods occur along Wadi Muthlim because the dam at the start of Petra's main Siq deliberately diverts water along this wadi. As such, it's imperative that you don't start this trek if it has been raining, is raining or is likely to rain soon. Your guide should have the latest information on the condition of the route.

High Place of Sacrifice to Petra City Centre HIKING

This moderate one-hour hike starts from the High Place of Sacrifice (p160) and passes through a less visited but beautiful part of Petra. It's also possible to do this hike in reverse, making for a grand afternoon exit from the site.

From the top of the High Place path, near the obelisks, a trail with steps heads down towards Wadi Farasa. The start of the trail is not obvious, so look for the helpful piles of stones indicating the trail, or ask for directions at the drinks stand. The hike is immediately rewarding with magnificent veined rock formations and wild gardens of flowers. After about 10 minutes of descent, you'll come to the 5m-long **Lion Monument** (Map p162), where water was channelled to pour out of the lion's mouth from the rock face above – an example of Nabataean engineering at its most sophisticated. A stone altar diagonally opposite suggests the fountain had some religious function. The steps wind further down the side of the cliff to the **Garden Tomb** (Map p162), which was more likely to have been a temple, and the remains of a giant water cistern.

A little further down, on the left, is the elegant **Roman Soldier's Tomb** (Map p162), named after the statue over the door. Almost opposite is the **Garden Triclinium** (Map p162), a hall used for annual feasts to honour the dead placed in the Soldier's Tomb. The hall is unique in Petra because it has carved decoration on the interior walls. The tomb and triclinium were once linked by a colonnaded courtyard.

Hereafter, the trail branches to the right, above the dry wadi floor. A tea shop here sells handmade strings of cloves, a good sniff of which is surprisingly reviving. The path forks at the ridge ahead. The right fork leads past some outrageously colourful but dilapidated tombs and descends eventually to the Colonnaded Street (p164). The left fork passes **Az Zantur** (Map p162), a 1st-century-AD palace that's still under excavation. Nearby is a collection of ruined **Nabataean and Roman houses** (Map p166), one of the few traces of habitations so far discovered in Petra. The trail continues west along the ridge to the Pharaun Column (p172), the lone surviving column of another Nabataean temple. From here you can turn left to Snake Monument (p172) for a longer hike or go straight on for Qasr Al Bint (p164) and Al Habis (p165). If you're disoriented, look for Petra Church, north of the Colonnaded Street: its pale roof makes a good landmark.

Wadi Siyagh HIKING

For an easy one-hour leg-stretcher that doesn't require a vertical take-off, try the trail that follows the dry riverbed of Wadi Siyagh beneath Al Habis hill. Once a residential suburb of Petra, the wadi and the nearby slopes have unexcavated tombs and residences to explore and offer some peaceful picnic spots once you pass the noisy restaurant generator.

Enter Wadi Siyagh opposite the Basin Restaurant. You'll soon see steps on the right leading to the **Painted House** (Map p166), one of the very few tombs in Petra that still has traces of Nabataean frescoes. Further down, at a bend in the valley, is a **Nabataean quarry** (Map p162).

The main attraction further along the valley is the dense oasis of green bushes, water pools and even waterfalls (in winter). In spring, the flowers are beautiful and in May and June it's worth making the hike just to enjoy the oleander and seams of aloe.

The trail along Wadi Siyagh is easy to follow, but becomes a bit rough in parts as it ascends the wadi walls. Don't attempt the hike if rain is imminent because flash floods are possible.

Treasury Vista I HIKING

Leading steeply up from the trailhead opposite the Treasury, this strenuous trail (about one hour return) is generally closed to casual visitors as the handkerchief-sized lookout above the vertical cliff is extremely dangerous. Check with the Petra Visitor Centre to see if the trail is currently open.

If the trail is open, a guide is required. Don't be tempted to accompany an ad hoc guide whose goat-like facility on the rock is unlikely to match your own and who may be less than sympathetic to your discomfort on the descent. Fatalities have been recorded on this trail.

THE TOMBS OF PETRA

There are more tombs dotted around Petra than any other type of structure; for years visitors assumed that the city was a vast necropolis. One plausible reason why so few dwellings have been discovered is that many of the Nabataeans lived in tents, much like some Bedouin do today.

Petra's earliest rock tombs date from the 3rd century BC. The size and design of the tombs depended on the social status and financial resources of the deceased, ranging from simple cave-like tombs to the ornate facades of the Royal Tombs, the high point of Nabataean funerary architecture.

More sculptors than architects, the Nabataeans quickly realised that it was easier to carve tombs out of the soft sandstone rock than to build freestanding structures that were vulnerable to earthquakes. The larger tombs were carved out of the rock from the top down, using scaffolding support, and the facades were then plastered and painted (almost none of this decoration remains).

The dead were buried in *loculi* (small, separate cavities) carved from the plain walls inside the tomb, while the exterior decoration was made to represent the soul (and sometimes likeness) of the deceased. All but the most simple tombs contained banqueting halls where funerals and annual commemorative feasts were held. Some rooms were frescoed and traces of coloured decoration can still be seen in Wadi Siyagh's Painted House and in Siq Al Barid (Little Petra).

The Nabataeans were a nomadic desert people without an architectural heritage of their own, but as traders they were cosmopolitan enough to borrow elements of art and architecture from their neighbours. Egyptian, Assyrian, Mesopotamian, Hellenistic and Roman styles can all be spotted throughout Petra, as well as unique local architectural inventions, such as the Nabataean horned column. Combine this eclecticism with the organic nature of Petra's cave-like tombs, the stunning natural colour of the rock and natural grandeur of the landscape, and it's easy to see how Petra has captured the imagination of generations of travellers.

Treasury Vista II HIKING

Offering a dramatic and unusual view of the Treasury, this moderate self-guided hike (about 1½ hours return) ascends processional steps about 150m northeast of the Palace Tomb (the steps are signposted). The stiff climb takes about 20 minutes and flattens out at a hilltop Nabataean **cistern** (Map p162) and a dramatic lookout about 200m above the entrance to the Siq. Start this hike in the early morning to catch the Treasury in sunlight. Along the way, there are wonderful views of the Theatre.

Continue south from the cistern (currently occupied by a helpful Bedouin tea shop owner) along a less obvious dirt path. Descend through the dry wadi for about 15 minutes and then pass into a small ravine; suddenly, you will reach a dramatic lookout about 200m above the Treasury, with fantastic views of its mighty facade. Watch your step and look out for landmarks on the way down as it is hard to find the path back to the top of the steps.

Back at the cistern, a tiny cleft in the rock reveals worn steps leading down a gully and along the rock face to a point next to the Urn Tomb (p161). The trail isn't all that clear (and is rather dirty at the outset), but it is navigable with a bit of common sense. The writer, lacking in this quality, ended up on a Nabataean drain dangling over a vertical drop. Of course, you can always return the way you came.

Long Hikes

Umm Al Biyara HIKING

The strenuous self-guided hike (about six hours return) from Qasr Al Bint (p164) to Umm Al Biyara (1178m) offers stunning mountaintop views. Legend has it that the flat-topped mountain was once the Edomite capital of Sela, from where the Judaean king Amaziah (r 796–781 BC) threw 10,000 prisoners to their deaths over the precipice.

There are ruins of a 7th-century-BC **Edomite village** (Map p162) at the top as well as several cisterns. There are also many unexcavated tombs along the base of the eastern cliffs.

The return trip from Qasr Al Bint to Umm Al Biyara (the Mother of Cisterns) offers stunning mountaintop views over Petra (you can even spot the Monastery). It's a fairly strenuous hike up hundreds of steps, but the trail is easy to follow. Start the hike in the mid-afternoon when most of the path is in shade but don't leave it too late as you don't want to be coming down in poor light.

From behind Qasr Al Bint, head to the Pharaun Column and descend to the road that leads along Wadi Thughra towards Snake Monument. The path up the rock face starts from the left of the largest of the rock-cut tombs on the southeast face of the mountain.

Jebel Haroun HIKING

This strenuous self-guided hike (about six hours return) via Snake Monument starts from Qasr Al Bint (p164). Jebel Haroun (1350m) is thought to be the biblical Mt Hor – the burial site of Moses' brother Aaron; a white **shrine** built in the 14th century marks the site.

Some people (Muslims as well as Christians) consider the shrine as a place of pilgrimage. For many, however, the big drawcard of Jebel Haroun is the superb panoramic view from the top.

It's possible to hire a guide with a donkey or even a camel for the trip, but if you're reasonably fit and not fazed by working out your own route from the network of goat tracks that head in the general direction, then this really isn't necessary.

The trail to Jebel Haroun starts at **Pharaun Column** (Map p166), and follows the dirt road past Bedouin settlements to **Snake Monument** (Map p162), a curled stone that resembles a snake on a rock pedestal. Continue to the southwest towards the obvious white shrine (which looks deceptively close); the trail is not as steep as it looks. At the bottom of the mountain, find the caretaker if you want to enter the shrine.

Sabra HIKING

The strenuous trek (about five hours return – guide recommended) starts from Qasr Al Bint (p164) and leads to the remote Nabataean suburbs of Sabra. It follows the path of ancient trade caravans that once unloaded their precious cargoes at the fringes of the main city.

The remains at Sabra include some ruined walls, temples, bridges and a small Roman theatre. A guide is needed even to find the trail from Snake Monument. A return trip on donkey costs from around JD100, depending on your powers of negotiation.

An exciting option offered by some travel agencies is the adventurous two-day hike from Tayyibeh, through the Siq-like Wadi Tibn to Sabra, camping overnight and continuing on to Petra the next day.

TREATMENT OF ANIMALS IN THE ANCIENT CITY

If there's one area of complaint that understandably upsets visitors more than others in the Ancient City, it's the mistreatment of animals. Indeed, many visitors are now quick to admonish any incidents of animal mishandling, particularly from the younger boys, some of whom mete out the kind of treatment to animals that a harsh environment often delivers to them. This, of course, is no excuse, and the local community, together with the Petra administration, have come together over recent years to try to improve the welfare of the animals who form an essential part of the Bedouin family livelihood and whose presence helps to greatly enhance the pleasure of the site for visitors. These efforts are beginning to bear fruit, and animals appear generally in better condition, are better nourished and are on the whole better treated than in former times. While most owners take responsibility for their animals very seriously, incidents of ill treatment still occur. Some visitors have suggested a ban on animal use, but this is more likely to encourage neglect of the family assets as Bedouin incomes are extremely limited and don't stretch to supporting a redundant 'family member'. And in all likelihood, this would lead to the dispiriting prospect of a Petra without the people and animals who have been minding this valley for centuries, replaced by technological alternatives, such as golf buggies and electric carts.

While some Bedouin animal handlers resent tourists interfering in the way they treat their animals, most are now sensitive to the fact that their actions are under scrutiny. A word of encouragement to the animal handler about an alternative way of cajoling their charges into action is appreciated more than a diatribe against animal cruelty. All ill treatment should be reported to the tourist police at the Petra Visitor Centre, preferably with photographic or video evidence. This approach is already having a positive impact, and the attitudes of handlers towards the various animals at work in Petra are slowly changing. Tourists can also play an important part in encouraging the humane treatment of animals by ensuring they are not too heavy for their mount. They should also pay the appropriate fare (as given at the Petra Visitor Centre) for the services they commission. It is largely as a result of cut-price fares that handlers feel pressured to return more quickly to base (thereby putting their animals at risk) to recoup the loss with an additional fare.

Horse Riding

For those who know how to ride, it costs from around JD50 for a two- to three-hour horse ride around the surrounding hills. A particularly exciting ride leads across a plateau at the top of the Treasury – definitely not one for the faint-hearted as the horses pull up from a gallop to a stop at the vertiginous cliff edge. Book a ride through one of the tourist agencies in town or, for more of an adventure, ask the animal handlers near the entrance to Petra to take you to their favourite haunt.

Tours

Experienced licensed guides (identifiable by their photo ID badges) are available for private tours to a number of different destinations in the Ancient City and their depth of knowledge – not to mention their sense of humour – brings a different dimension to a visit. These guides can be hired from a kiosk opposite the ticket office inside the Petra Visitor Centre complex. Their rates are standardised and displayed inside the kiosk.

Typical rates for one of these official private guides (who speak English, Spanish, French, German, Russian, Arabic and Hebrew) cost JD50 to JD150, for one to nine people. For the three-hour private tour from Petra Visitor Centre to the Basin it costs JD50; it costs an additional JD35 to take a guide to any of the High Places, a further JD25 to engage the guide for the descent through Wadi Farasa.

Guides are also available for hikes further afield. To the Monastery from the Basin it costs JD50 via the Back Door from Wadi Sayoun, JD90 from the Petra Visitor Centre and JD150 for the Back Trail from Little Petra. It costs JD50 to engage a guide along Wadi Muthlim (a guide is mandatory for this hike) and JD150 to Sabra.

1. Petra (p155)
Chiselled into out-of-the-way cliffs, the buildings of Petra lay forgotten for centuries.

2. Camels
Riding a camel is a good way to pace through the heart of Petra.

3. Treasury (Al Khazneh; p160)
The Treasury, an astonishing piece of craftsmanship, served as a tomb for the Nabataean King Aretas III, and is now where most visitors fall in love with Petra.

4. Rock tombs (p171)
Petra's rock tombs were carved into the sandstone and date back to the 3rd century BC.

3

JPRICHARD/SHUTTERSTOCK ©

MAKING THE MOST OF PETRA

Petra at Dawn The Treasury is sunlit in the morning; it is a much-photographed sight, but the real thing is indescribably magical.

Tip: Tour groups arrive at 8am, leaving Petra at dawn for the early birds.

Photogenic Petra Mid-afternoon and most of Petra's weary guests have returned to base. Those who linger catch the Royal Tombs turning pink at sunset.

Tip: The sun sets around 6pm in summer and 5pm in winter.

Petra on High The Siq, Street of Facades and museum all lie brooding in the wadi bottom. Climb a few steps, hike to a high place, sit on a camel and a whole new dimension to Petra opens up.

Tip: The Theatre seats give grandstand views.

Hidden Petra Petra doesn't give up its secrets easily and most visitors leave without discovering the Monastery, at the top of 800 hand-hewn steps.

Tip: Best seen in the full sun of afternoon, beautiful views of Wadi Araba are just a 15-minute stroll from the Monastery. Using the 'backdoor' from Umm Sayoun saves walking time and distance.

Green Petra A parallel world begs to be explored along the hidden wadis that lie outside the Ancient City; lizards, snakes and scorpions are common but shy residents beside the rocky pools.

Tip: Pink oleander blossoms stripe surrounding wadis in profusion in May.

Living Petra Petra may be a pile of ruins to some, but for others it's home; Raami Tours from Umm Sayoun shows how the Bdoul Bedouin interact with their famous monuments.

Tip: Saying yes to tea with the Bedouin involves participating in one of Petra's age-old rituals.

Petra by Night Three times per week, the spirit of Petra is chased down the Siq by candlelight, often in the company of merry hoards.

Tip: Warm coat needed in winter.

Specialist guides available at Petra include **Mohammed Twaissi**, who is one of only 13 guides in Jordan licensed to lead ornithological trips. He is able to help visitors spot Jordan's national bird, the Sinai rose finch, and identify the other flora and fauna within the Petra vicinity. Ask for him at Petra Visitor Centre, or track him down through his brother Mahmoud Twaissi (p183).

★ **Petra by Night** TOURS

(Petra Visitor Centre, Tourism St; adult/child under 10yr JD17/free; ⏲8.30-10.30pm Mon, Wed & Thu) The extremely popular Petra by Night tour was introduced in response to numerous requests from visitors wanting to see the Siq and Treasury by moonlight. The 'tour' starts from the Petra Visitor Centre (cancelled if raining) and lasts two hours.

Readers express a mixed response to the experience, which leads along the Siq (lined with 1500 candles) as far as the Treasury in as much silence as is possible given the crowds. Here, traditional Bedouin music is played and mint tea served. Clearly, given the popularity of the tour, this isn't going to be the moment to commune with history in awed solitude, but night brings a different perspective to the Siq that many feel is worthwhile. The performance of Bedouin storytelling at the Treasury depends on the mood of the raconteur. Tickets are available from travel agencies in town, or from the Petra Visitor Centre before 6pm.

Festivals & Events

★History of Petra PERFORMING ARTS
(Jordan Heritage Revival Company; ☎06 581 0808; www.jhrc.jo; ⏲Sat-Thu) Included in the price of the entry ticket to Petra is a chance to see the Jordan Heritage Revival Company in action. Dressed as Roman centurions, some in full armour on horseback, their steel helmets glinting in the sun, the actors in this dramatic re-enactment cut quite a dash against the normally imperturbable Ancient City monuments.

Ask at the Petra Visitor Centre about the current schedule or look out for tunic-clad centurions around the entrance to the Siq for a fun photo opportunity. There are no shows on Friday or during Ramadan.

Petra Desert Marathon SPORTS
(www.albatros-adventure.com/petra-desert-marathon) A full and a half-marathon is run annually starting at the Street of Facades in the Ancient City of Petra. The route leads punishingly up near-vertical slopes and crosses patches of open desert in the neighbouring vicinity and finishes in Wadi Musa.

Eating & Drinking

It's not possible to stay overnight in the Ancient City. Some Bedouin scammers might entice travellers (especially lone women) to stay in a cave with them but this is strictly forbidden by the management of Petra and is not recommended. If nothing else, scorpions are not uncommon bedfellows!

Most people visiting the Ancient City either take a box lunch from their hotel or head for one of the two restaurants near Qasr Al Bint. A simple buffet is available from Nabataean Tent Restaurant, or a more lavish lunch is served outdoors or in an air-conditioned dining room at the Basin Restaurant. Water, tea and snacks are sold at kiosks with outside seating throughout the main parts of the site.

Nabataean Tent Restaurant BUFFET $$
(Map p166; lunch buffet JD10, lunchbox JD7; ⏲10am-3.30pm) With simple Jordanian dishes and one or two international favourites, this casual restaurant occupies a lovely spot under blue-flowering jacaranda trees (they flower in May). The proprietors rustle up a generous packed lunch with bread, cheese, cucumber, falafel, yoghurt and cake for a bargain JD7; it can be eaten on the spot with a Turkish coffee if you wish.

★Basin Restaurant BUFFET $$$
(Map p166; lunch buffet JD16, fresh orange juice JD4; ⏲noon-4pm; 🍷) The Basin serves a wide spread of international dishes, including a healthy selection of salads, fresh falafel and barbecued spicy sausage. Lots of desserts are also on offer, including fruit and *umm ali* (dessert of filo pastry, butter, raisins and nuts baked in milk). There's a fully air-conditioned interior seating area or groups sit by the ravine under canvas while independent travellers are given tables under the trees.

★Bdoul Mofleh Tea Shop TEAHOUSE
(Map p162; ☎07 7609 4797; Al Habis; tea by donation; ⏲10am-4pm) Long-term Petra resident Bdoul Mofleh rustles up ad hoc tea for those passing his 'unofficial' cave house on Al Habis. This is the best tea shop in Petra with a view over remote, little visited tombs on the other side of the Al Habis hill in the heart of the Ancient City. Access is from near the Nabataean Tent Restaurant.

Have a Break Tea & Coffee CAFE
(Map p162; ⏲9am-6pm) With a view of the Royal Tombs, this Bedouin-run establishment can muster sandwiches, snacks and milkshakes. It has a permanent awning and nascent garden, and is in just the right spot to enjoy sunset.

Shopping

Ad hoc stalls run by local Bedouin are scattered throughout the Ancient City of Petra selling items for the ubiquitous 'one JD'. Most are cheap imports, but some of the Bedouin jewellery is authentic.

WHAT TO WEAR

The Ancient City of Petra is strewn over a vast area of mountains and wadis and it's easy to underestimate the amount of time it takes to walk between sights, and especially the uphill return journey when you're tired. Sturdy footwear, a hat, sunscreen and water are essential at any time of year and a warm coat is needed in winter.

LOVING PETRA TO DEATH

It seems ironic that after 1000 years of obscurity, if not neglect, Petra owes its current fragility to a renaissance of interest. In a 'good' year, half a million people visit, putting a huge strain on the management of one of the world's best-loved antiquities. The combination of thousands of footprints a day, increased humidity levels from the breath of tourists in tombs, and erosion caused by adventurous travellers clambering over monuments and steep hillsides combine to threaten Petra's longevity.

Acutely aware of the problems, a number of local, national and international bodies have been cooperating for more than a decade to protect and enhance the 853-sq-km site. For the most part, Petra is now spotlessly clean, thanks to constant maintenance, improved toilet facilities and a shift in attitude from visitors, who largely carry their rubbish back out with them.

Other improvements include the use of an invisible mortar to conserve fragile masonry and replace unsightly cement used in previous restoration attempts; major shoring up of the Siq; and ongoing conservation of tomb facades. Urban expansion in Wadi Musa has also been checked, an infrastructure of drainage and sewerage systems installed, and a moratorium enforced on the building of unsightly hotels that impinge on the sense of seclusion in Petra. Better signage and trail markers are appearing, and there are new plans afoot to remove the Bedouin stalls from the Ancient City to a special tourism complex near Little Petra.

These conservation measures, however, will only save Petra for future generations with the cooperation of visitors. Each visitor can play an important part by sticking to trails, not clambering over the monuments, resisting the temptation to touch crumbling masonry, removing litter and using designated toilet facilities. These things sound obvious, but judging by a piece of graffiti that reads 'Ahmed & Liza 2017' on top of one of the High Places, responsible tourism may still be a long time coming.

★**Umm Raami's Shop** JEWELLERY
(Map p162) Marguerite van Geldermalsen, of *Married to a Bedouin* fame, sells silver jewellery from this stall nearly opposite the cave in which she once lived with her Bedouin husband and in which she raised her eldest son, Raami. The jewellery is inspired by ancient Nabataean designs and crafted by local women originally trained through a Noor Al Hussein Foundation project.

Why Not Shop GIFTS & SOUVENIRS
(Map p162) Selling a collection of souvenirs and with an ever-friendly greeting for those with the energy to walk beyond the Treasury, this Bedouin shop also sells refreshments. It is also a useful landmark as it marks the entrance to the stone staircase for the High Place of Sacrifice.

ℹ Information

TOILETS

There are reasonable toilets at Petra Visitor Centre, near the Theatre and outside the Basin Restaurant. Teahouses provide clean portable toilets throughout the site – most people give a tip of JD1 to the caretakers who maintain them. Please keep to these facilities to avoid spoiling the site for others.

TOURIST INFORMATION

The **ticket office** (☎03 215 6044; Tourism St; ⏰6am-4pm, to 6pm in summer) is in the Petra Visitor Centre, just before the entrance to Petra at Wadi Musa. Although tickets are not sold after 4pm, you can remain in Petra until sunset (7pm in summer, 5pm in winter).

Entry fees are JD50/55/60 for one-/two-/three-day passes (payable in Jordanian currency or by credit card). If visiting Petra as a day trip, including from Israel and the Palestinian Territories, the entry fee is JD90. Children aged under 12 and visitors with disabilities are admitted free. The Jordan Pass, which represents great value for money, gives free entry to Petra.

The ticket includes the price of a horse ride along the Bab Al Siq (the pathway between the Visitor Centre and the opening of the Siq) and a guided tour for a minimum of five people. The tour is not mandatory but is recommended; it runs on the hour between 7am and 3pm and lasts for two hours, helping to highlight the key points of interest along the main trail to Qasr Al Bint (near the Basin Restaurant).

If you're contemplating trying to enter Petra without paying, don't. The preservation of Petra depends on the income from tourists, and this is where responsible tourism begins. Tickets are nontransferable between visitors, and you have to show your passport when buying a ticket. Multiday tickets must be used on consecutive days, and they don't include the cost of the Petra by Night experience.

Information is available on the Ancient City at the **Petra Visitor Centre** (☎03 215 6044; www.visitpetra.jo; Tourism St; ⏱6am-6pm May-Sep, to 4pm Oct-Apr). Besides housing the ticket office, this complex has a helpful information counter and is surrounded by souvenir shops that are useful for a hat and last-minute supplies.

WEBSITES

American Museum of Natural History (www.amnh.org/exhibitions/petra) See an online Petra exhibition.

Go 2 Petra (www.go2petra.com) For background and general travel info on Petra.

Nabataea Net (http://nabataea.net) Everything you could want to know about the Nabataean empire.

ℹ Getting There & Away

MAIN ENTRANCE

The main entry point for the Ancient City of Petra is at the bottom of Tourism St, at the lower end of the town of Wadi Musa. This is the location of the Petra Visitor Centre and the ticket office. From here, it is a two-minute walk to the main entry gate that marks the beginning of the path that slopes downhill towards the Siq – the ancient gateway to the site.

BACK DOOR TO PETRA

In the 1980s many of the Bdoul Bedouin, who had lived in Petra for generations, were resettled in villages such as neighbouring Umm Sayoun. At the end of this village is an access road into the old city of Petra. It would be a pity to enter Petra this way on your first day, as the Siq is Petra's most spectacular highlight. But if you want a shortcut to the Monastery thereafter, take a taxi to the gate at the top of this road and walk down to the Basin Restaurant (20 minutes). From there it's a 40-minute walk to the Monastery. This is 45 minutes shorter than the alternative walk via the Siq. Note that you can't buy tickets here, and you can't enter without one, so don't forget to bring your ticket with you.

There is another back trail to Petra that leads from Little Petra along a picturesque path and ascends steps (far less than 800!) to the Monastery. The walk takes around 1½ hours and currently requires a guide as it is remote and can be hard to find the way. Ask for details at the Rocky Mountain Hotel (p184), which organises this trek from its camp nearby.

ℹ Getting Around

If you buy your ticket at the Petra Visitor Centre, a return horse ride for the 800m stretch between the main entrance and the start of the Siq is included in your ticket (arrange a return time with the handler). A tip of JD4 is appreciated. If you walk down, you can usually find a ride back to the entrance for around JD4. Horses and carriages with drivers travel between the main entrance and the Treasury (2km) for JD20 per carriage (which seats two people), plus JD5 per person in tips.

Unofficial donkey and mule rides (with handlers) are available all around Petra for negotiable prices. Donkeys can reach the High Place of Sacrifice (one way from JD10) and the top of the Monastery (return JD20). Mules can also be rented for longer trips to the Snake Monument (from JD25), Jebel Haroun (JD50) and Sabra (JD100).

Magnificently bedecked camels are available for rides between Qasr Al Bint and the Treasury (one way/return about JD20/30), and they will pause for a photograph near the Theatre. You may be able to hitch a ride on something four-legged back along the Siq for a few dinars at the end of the day.

Leading donkeys, mules and camels is a genuine occupation for local Bedouin, who prize their animals as an important part of their livelihood; that said, some of the younger animal handlers can be seen using a stick or whip with unnecessary aggression – perhaps in a misguided bid to look manly. If you have hired animal transport, don't feel shy to intervene if you feel the treatment is inappropriate. Report mistreatment of animals to the Tourist Police at the Petra Visitor Centre and to the official Petra government complaints site at www.pdtra.gov.jo. It may not feel as if your complaint is taken seriously, but over the years, the prevailing attitude towards the humane treatment of animals has begun to change for the better. This is partly because of the complaints registered by visitors (see box on p171).

Wadi Musa وادي موسى

☎03 / POP 18,000 / ELEV 1150M

The town that has sprung up around Petra is called Wadi Musa (Valley of Moses). It's an easygoing assemblage of hotels, restaurants, shops and houses stretching about 5km from Moses' Spring ('Ain Musa) to the main entrance of Petra near the bottom of the wadi.

Wadi Musa's fortunes depend almost entirely on tourism. Dozens of new hotels were hastily erected in the late 1990s (after the peace treaty with Israel), often with no

Wadi Musa

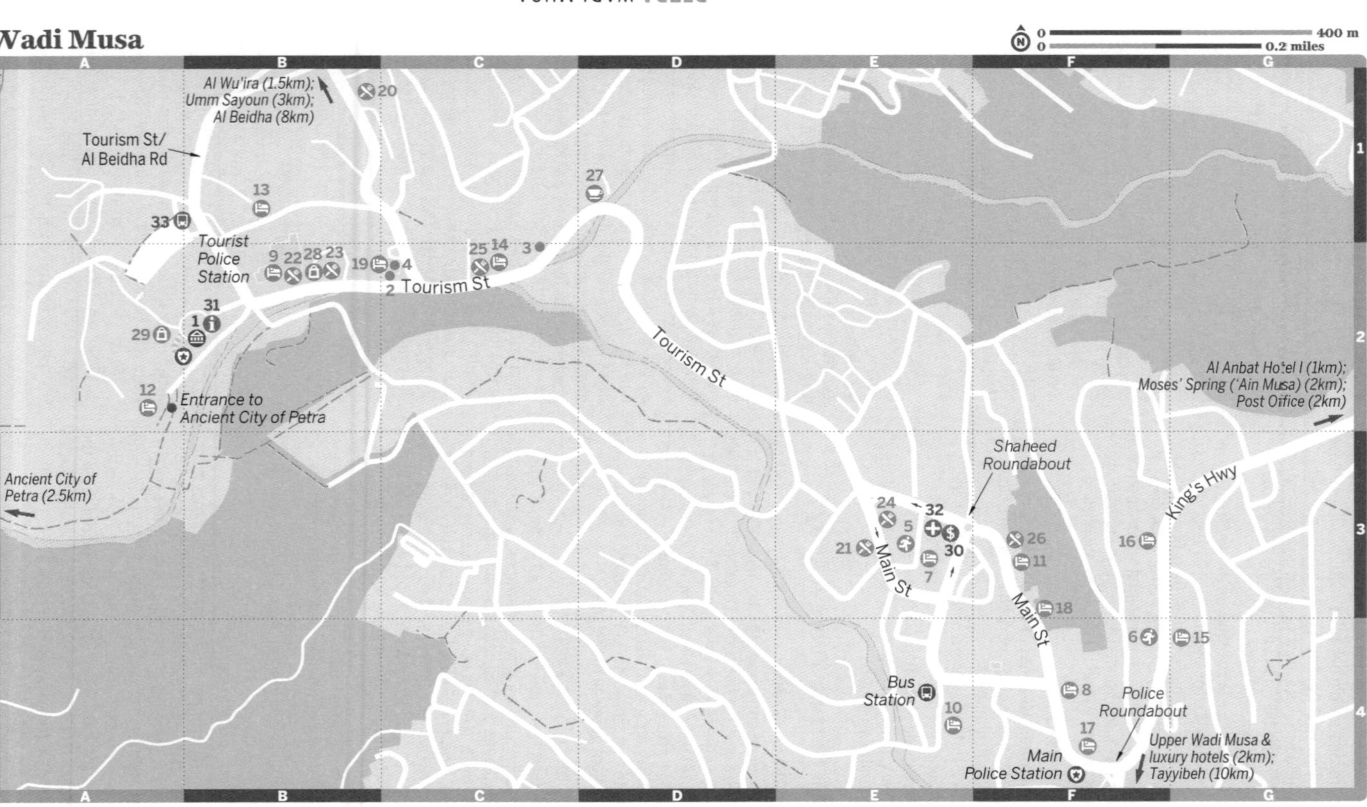

0 400 m
0 0.2 miles
Al Wu'ira (1.5km);
Umm Sayoun (3km);
Al Beidha (8km)
Tourism St/
Al Beidha Rd
Tourist
Police
Station
Tourism St
Entrance to
Ancient City of Petra
Ancient City of
Petra (2.5km)
Tourism St
Main St
Main St
Shaheed
Roundabout
King's Hwy
Al Anbat Hotel I (1km);
Moses' Spring ('Ain Musa) (2km);
Post Office (2km)
Bus
Station
Police
Roundabout
Main
Police Station
Upper Wadi Musa &
luxury hotels (2km);
Tayyibeh (10km)

Wadi Musa

aesthetic or social sensitivity. Many locals bought into the new opportunities that mass tourism offered only to be stung in the tourism slumps that have followed hostilities among Jordan's neighbours. A moratorium on hotel building remains in place in an effort to curb rampant expansion and to shift the focus to improving services rather than simply 'packing them in' – a strategy that has largely worked in a town that takes its custodianship of Petra seriously.

Sights

Petra Exhibition MUSEUM

(☎03 215 6020; www.visitpetra.jo; Petra Visitor Centre, Tourism St; ⏲6am-6pm May-Sep, to 4pm Oct-Apr) FREE Awaiting the completion of a new home (currently being built across from the Petra Visitor Centre), this excellent exhibition makes the most of more than 200 artefacts that were formerly housed in the now-defunct Al Habis and the Basin Museums in the Ancient City. The exhibition is divided into different display areas, including Petra through the ages, art and architecture, religion, politics and society, and trade, and help give a tangible context to the site itself.

Allow an hour to do the displays justice.

Moses' Spring SPRING

('Ain Musa; King's Hwy; ⏲dawn-dusk) FREE Moses' Spring is one of two possible locations in Jordan for the site where Moses supposedly struck the rock with his staff and water gushed forth to the thirsty Israelites (the other possible site is near Mt Nebo). The spring still flows but is now housed within a simple modern three-domed building occasionally visited by local pilgrims. The site is located near the King's Way Hotel, at the main junction into Wadi Musa from the north.

Activities

While pretty much the only reason to come to Wadi Musa is to visit Petra, the town does have a few activities of its own, one of which is enjoying a Turkish bath, of which there are many scattered all over town.

A Turkish bath is the perfect way to ease aching muscles after a long day's walk in Petra. This time-honoured bathing experience is enjoying a current resurgence in popularity and many new baths have appeared in Wadi Musa, most attached to hotels, including the Amra Palace Hotel and the Petra Palace Hotel. The service on offer at a hammam (bathhouse) typically includes steam bath, massage, hot stones, scrubbing and 'body conditioning'. The baths are popular with tourists and locals alike, so it's best to book ahead, especially if requesting a female attendant (women only). Prices typically cost JD15 to JD30, depending on the combination of services on offer. Hotels often offer their residents discounts to their own baths or the baths they patronise.

WALKING TIMES TO KEY SIGHTS IN PETRA

To make the most of Petra you need to walk. The good news is that you don't have to be a serious hiker with a week to spare to have a 'Burckhardt moment' in the Ancient City – you just need to know where to go and when. Times in the following table indicate one-way walks (unless stated otherwise) at a leisurely pace. At a faster pace without stopping, you can hike from the Petra Visitor Centre to the Treasury in 20 minutes and the Basin Restaurant in 40 minutes along the main thoroughfare. Don't forget to double the time for the uphill return journey, particularly if you're tired after a day's sightseeing. A variety of animal transport is usually on hand to get you back to base if you're seriously flagging; for example, you can take a donkey from the Monastery to the Basin Restaurant, a camel to the Treasury, a horse carriage to the Siq entrance and a horse to Petra Visitor Centre.

DIRECT ROUTE	TIME	DIFFICULTY	ALTERNATIVES & INTERESTING DETOURS
Visitor Centre to Siq Entrance	15 min	Easy	**Horse ride** Ponies are for hire to help you reach the dam near the Siq entrance – useful on the uphill return journey.
Siq Entrance to Treasury	20 min	Easy	**Hike** Clamber above the Royal Tombs to a Treasury viewpoint and look down on everyone else looking up (one hour; strenuous).
Treasury to Royal Tombs	20 min	Easy	**Hike** Climb the steps between the Royal Tombs and Sextius Florentinus tomb for a regal-eyed view of Petra. Continue to the cistern and descend to the Urn Tomb (one to 1½ hours; strenuous). **Hike** As an alternative to the Siq, squeeze through sinuous Wadi Muthlim to reach the Royal Tombs (1½ hours; moderate, guide required).
Treasury to Obelisk at High Place of Sacrifice	45 min	Moderate	**Walk** Go beyond the High Place altar onto the solitary edge of the escarpment for a wide-angle view of Petra (15 minutes from Obelisk; easy).
Obelisk to Basin Restaurant (via main thoroughfare)	45 min	Easy	**Hike** Instead of returning down the steps you ascended, hike via enchanting Wadi Farasa, passing rainbow-coloured rocks, Lion Monument and Garden Tomb (one hour from Obelisk; moderate).
Treasury to Basin Restaurant	30 min	Easy	**Walk** Trace the path around the base of the Royal Tombs to Dorotheos' House, explore the rarely visited Christian Tombs and follow Wadi Mataha to the Basin Restaurant (one hour; easy).
Basin Restaurant to Monastery	40 min	Moderate	**Walk** Get a head start to the Monastery via Umm Sayoun access road (one hour; moderate), pausing at Turkmaniya Tomb, famous for its long Nabataean inscription (20 minutes from Umm Sayoun to Basin Restaurant; easy). **Hike** For a rare glimpse of how tombs like the Monastery were cut, walk around Al Habis to see the Unfinished Tomb (40 minutes return to Basin Restaurant; moderate).

Salome Turkish Bath HAMMAM
(☎03 215 7342; opposite Al Anbat II Hotel; bath, body scrub & massage JD24; ⏰3-10pm) Entered via a grotto displaying old farming implements, this bathhouse has an atmospheric sitting area for relaxing with herbal tea. Offering mixed bathing with body scrub and massage, this traditional little hammam makes a virtue out of staying the same while the rest of the town celebrates change.

Sella Turkish Bath HAMMAM
(☎03 215 7170; www.sellahotel.com; King's Hwy; ⏰5.30-10pm) The Sella bathhouse has a comprehensive list of services, including sauna, and separate baths for men and women. Dead Sea products are on sale here.

Petra Turkish Bath HAMMAM
(☎03 215 7085; Tourism St; steam room, massage & scrub 1hr JD30; ⏰3-10pm) In the passage under the Silk Road Hotel, near the entrance of Petra, this hammam has a completely separate bath area for women, with female attendants.

Courses

★Petra Kitchen COOKING
(☎03 215 5900; www.petrakitchen.com; Tourism St; cookery course per person JD35; ⏰6-9pm) For those wanting to know how to prepare wonderful hummus or bake the perfect baklava, Petra Kitchen offers a practical course, delivered in a single evening. Located 100m up the main road from the Mövenpick Hotel, it offers nightly cookery courses for those wanting to learn from locals how to cook Jordanian mezze, soup and main dishes in a relaxed family-style atmosphere.

A local Jordanian chef is on hand to make sure that apprentices don't make a goat's ear of the authentic Jordanian dishes. The menu, which includes delicious vegetarian fare, changes daily. The price includes the printed recipes, food and soft drinks. Better still, it's possible to buy a bottle of St George to share with fellow learners – a great way to mask any less than perfect results. Reservations (with a deposit) are recommended.

Course times might change slightly from season to season.

Tours

Jordan Experience TOURS
(☎03 215 4343; www.jordan-experience.com; Tourism St) Focuses on religious tours, including an 'In the Footsteps of Jesus in Jordan' tour. It can help chart the Christian presence in the Petra area for those with a historical or religious interest in this dimension.

Zaman Tours & Travel ADVENTURE
(☎03 215 7723; www.zamantours.com; Tourism St; ⏰9am-5pm) Adventure tours, camping, camel treks and hiking.

Mohammed Al Hasanat TOURS
(☎07 7738 0884; explorerone69@yahoo.com) Mohammed Al Hasanat has been a licensed national guide since 1979. He has a love of hiking and has had plenty of practise. Reliable, knowledgeable both of the historical and cultural contexts of the areas he covers, and experienced in catering to the needs of individuals or groups with special interests. He can organise camping tours over several days, including camel and horse safaris.

Petra Moon Tourism Services TOURS
(☎07 9617 0666; www.petramoon.com; Tourism St; all-day horse rides to Jebel Haroun US$100, min 3 people) Petra Moon is the most professional agency in Wadi Musa for arranging trips inside Petra and around Jordan (including Wadi Rum and Aqaba). It can arrange horse riding, fully supported treks to Dana (three nights), hikes from Tayyibeh to Petra, and camel treks in Wadi Rum. It also runs a popular 14-day tour around Jordan for 10 to 26 people.

Petra Night Tours TOURS
(☎03 215 4010; www.pntours.com; off Tourism St) Not to be confused with the Petra by Night tour, this well-established, family-run agency organises a variety of tours in Petra and beyond. It also sells tickets for the candlelit tour of the Siq.

Mahmoud Twaissi TOURS
(☎07 7725 4658; mat65petra@yahoo.com) Mahmoud Twaissi has a well-earned reputation not just as a guide but also as a fixer for large-scale projects throughout the country.

La Beduina CULTURAL
(☎06 554 1631; www.labeduinatours.com; off Tourism St) Specialist tours including hiking, horse and camel riding, and yoga tours.

Jordan Travel & Tourism TOURS
(☎03 215 4666; www.jordantours-travel.com; King's Hwy) Local tours and longer trips around Jordan. Near the Petra Sella Hotel.

Sleeping

Visitors have a choice of more than 70 hotels (none of which are inside the Ancient City itself) catering to most budgets. Prices

WORTH A TRIP

A DOZEN UNUSUAL WAYS TO ENJOY PETRA

- Enter Petra via the narrow Wadi Muthlim (p167) instead of the Siq (best kept for the second day of a visit; often closed).
- Gain an eagle's-eye view of the Treasury from a path above the Royal Tombs (p172).
- Gallop across a plateau on horseback, high above the Treasury.
- Descend from the High Place of Sacrifice (p170) via the garden valley of Wadi Farasa.
- Take tea with one of the few remaining residents of Petra behind Al Habis (p165).
- Unfurl a portable feast in a triclinium, a banqueting hall for honouring the dead.
- Hike with a guide from Little Petra (p191) along the back trail to the Monastery.
- Find a secret garden beyond the Siq at Little Petra (p191).
- Saddle up a donkey for the two-day hike to Sabra (p172) via Wadi Tibn.
- Leave Petra with the Bdoul Bedouin via the road to Umm Sayoun.
- Walk between Umm Sayoun and Wadi Musa for a sublime view of Petra at sunset.
- Stop at the viewpoint on the scenic road to Tayyibeh for the ultimate Petra panorama.

generally include a private bathroom, breakfast, free wi-fi and tax; they sometimes include a free transfer to the Petra Visitor Centre. Outside high season (April to mid-May and October to November) prices drop substantially from official rates, especially for stays of three nights or more.

Most top-end and midrange hotels are located at the bottom end of town, within walking distance to the entrance to Petra and well supplied with restaurants and souvenir shops. Their proximity to the Petra Visitor Centre can be a boon after a long day's hiking in the Ancient City.

The hotels in the town centre are most convenient for the bus station, cheaper cafes and supermarkets. It's possible to walk downhill to the Petra Visitor Centre from here, but it won't leave as much energy for exploring the Ancient City itself.

Some good budget and midrange options are available on the King's Highway between Moses' Spring and the start of Main St, all of which have panoramic views. The luxury hotels of Upper Wadi Musa are located on the scenic road that leads from the town centre to Tayyibeh, a 10- to 15-minute drive from the Petra Visitor Centre. Perched at around 1400m above sea level, they offer fine views over the Rift Valley and most have beautiful terraces for a sunset drink. On the downside, they feel very much removed from the Petra experience.

★ Peace Way Hotel BOUTIQUE HOTEL $
(☎03 215 6963; peaceway_petra@yahoo.com; Main St; s/d/tr JD16/22/35; [wi-fi] [pets]) This hotel has undergone the most remarkable transformation from budget to boutique. The impressive makeover includes blue-lit ceilings, carved wooden doors and a handsome chocolate brown theme to the corridors and rooms, contrasted with cream-coloured marble. Even more remarkable is that the hotel has kept its budget prices, making this central option very good value. Unusually, it's pet-friendly too.

★ Rocky Mountain Hotel HOTEL $
(☎03 215 5100, 07 9694 1865; www.rockymountainhotel.com; King's Hwy; s/d/tr/q JD26/39/50/60; @ [wi-fi]) This backpacker-friendly hotel has caught just the right vibe to make it Petra's most successful travellers' lodge. There's a cosy communal area with free tea and coffee and the *majlis*-style roof terrace makes the most of the impressive sweeping views. A free shuttle service to the Petra entrance leaves at 7.30am and 8.30am, returning at 4pm and 5pm.

The Anglo-Jordanian couple who run the hotel advise on onward travel and overnight trips to Wadi Rum. They also operate the peaceful Seven Wonders Bedouin Camp (p191).

Lunch boxes are available for JD4.

★ Cleopetra Hotel HOTEL $
(☎03 215 7090; www.cleopetrahotel.com; Main St; s/d/tr JD18/25/32; @ [wi-fi]) One of the friendliest and most efficiently run budget hotels in town, Cleopetra has bright, fresh rooms. There's a communal sitting area in the lobby where wi-fi is available for JD2. The hotel

can arrange overnight 4WD trips to Wadi Rum (JD50 per person for a minimum of three) and the ever-helpful Mosleh can organise other transport.

Al Anbat Hotel I HOTEL $
(03 215 6265; www.alanbat.com; King's Highway; s/d/tr JD25/35/50;) Located some way out of town, this hotel features large rooms with sunset views, and an attractive lobby and restaurant (buffet lunch or dinner JD10) with a magnificent view. There's a Turkish bath (guests JD15) and free transport to/from Petra. Campers can pitch a tent (JD7 per person with showers and kitchen access); campervans are welcome (JD5 per van plus JD7 per person).

Al Anbat Hotel II HOTEL $
(07 7809 3113, 03 215 7200; www.alanbat.com; off Main St; s/d/tw/tr JD17/23/25/38; 5-bed f JD50;) This hotel has recently undergone a refurbishment and rooms are now luxurious with new soft furnishings. There are good views across Wadi Musa and the surrounding hills from many of the rooms and the roof terrace. In high season the neighbouring building offers less attractive accommodation but with similarly large and comfortable rooms. There's an excellent Turkish bath opposite.

★**Petra Guest House Hotel** HOTEL $$
(03 215 6266; www.guesthouse-petra.com; off Tourism St; r from JD75;) Guests can't get closer to the entrance to Petra without sleeping in a tomb – and indeed the hotel's famous Cave Bar (p187) is located in one. Accommodation ranges from spacious, motel-like chalets or sunny (if cramped) rooms in the main building. The staff are unfailingly delightful and the breakfast buffet is superior to most. Offers excellent value for money.

P Quattro Relax Hotel HOTEL $$
(03 215 6577; www.p4hotel.com; opposite bus station; s/d from JD40/50;) This new hotel, whose owner has worked in Italy, reveals a European character in its choice of black-and-white decor. Surprisingly for the region, there are three pet-friendly rooms. Piles of luxurious linen, an on-site mini gym, a small roof garden and a restaurant serving authentic Italian fare help contribute to the quality experience at this small, often fully booked hotel.

Seven Wonders Hotel HOTEL $$
(03 215 5156; www.sevenwondershotel.com; junction of Main St & King's Hwy; s/d JD60/85;) The rooms at this hotel are decked out with thick carpets and some have balconies with good views over the town and surrounding landscape. There's a terrace with a 'dry' bar (no alcohol served). Book two hours ahead for the hotel's Afra Turkish bath (JD35 per person). Open from 5pm to 10pm, the baths offer sauna, Jacuzzi, steam room and massage.

Petra Sella Hotel HOTEL $$
(03 215 7170; www.sellahotel.com; King's Hwy; s/d/tr JD45/65/85;) This newly renovated hotel has luxurious rooms, decked in stylish stone tiles with split ceilings and marble sinks in the bathrooms – almost boutique for Wadi Musa. There are good views from front rooms but rooms at the back are bigger. The hotel runs the spotless Sella Turkish Bath (p183) opposite.

Lunch boxes are available for JD8.

Petra Palace Hotel HOTEL $$
(03 215 6723; www.petrapalace.com.jo; Tourism St; s/d/tr/q JD41/55/76/96;) Located 500m from the entrance to Petra, this attractive and well-established hotel, with its palm-tree entrance, big bright foyer and helpful management, offers rooms around a swimming pool. Corridors and grounds are looking tired but the sociable English Bar and a good restaurant compensate. A mixed Turkish bath (JD20 per person) is open from 8am to 10pm.

Petra Moon Hotel HOTEL $$
(03 215 6220; www.petramoonhotel.com; off Tourism St; s/d/tr JD50/65/75;) On a hill at the bottom of Wadi Musa, near the entrance to Petra, this hotel with its distinctive pink exterior features modern rooms, big bathrooms and a rooftop swimming pool. A large terrace is a good place to enjoy splendid sunset views and a popular nightly barbecue (JD15, 7pm to 11pm).

Sharah Mountains Hotel HOTEL $$
(03 215 7294; www.sharahmountains.com; Main St; s & d JD35, tr/q JD45/55;) A large marble foyer with leather sofas makes an impressive entrance to this newly refurbished hotel. Corridors are simple enough but the quality of new fixtures and furnishings in the rooms and bathrooms makes this a good-value choice. There are views from most rooms and a terrace.

Silk Road Hotel HOTEL $$
(03 215 7222; www.petrasilkroad.com; Tourism St; s/d/tr JD35/45/55;) Hand-painted panels

DAVID ROBERTS: PAINTING PETRA

Stand in certain parts of Petra and Little Petra and it's almost impossible not to imagine striped-robed Arabs from the 19th century lounging languidly in the foreground. Sit in the cafes and hotel lobbies of Wadi Musa and you'll see the same characters and landscapes writ large across otherwise vacant walls. And who do we have to thank for this 'picturesque' peopling of ancient Petra? The culprit is one David Roberts: artist, Scot and much-beloved topographer of the late Romantic era.

Given the continuing popularity of his images with tourists, it's safe to say that Roberts (1796–1864) had the common touch. This may have had something to do with his seven-year apprenticeship as a house painter, or perhaps his stint as a scenery painter at the Theatre Royal in Edinburgh. Whatever the reason, his compositions are full of human interest – an unloaded caravan, friends waving across a wadi, a quarrel between traders cast against a backdrop of exaggerated landscape.

Roberts visited the region in 1839 dressed as an Arab, in the tradition of Burckhardt just two decades earlier, and travelled with a caravan of 20 camels and local bodyguards. Petra was the high point of his journey, despite having to cut short his visit because of trouble with local tribes. On his return to Britain, his watercolours, magnificently interpreted in lithograph by the Belgian engraver Louis Haghe, were exhibited in 1840 and won instant critical acclaim.

Roberts' images have now passed into the visual vocabulary of one of the world's most treasured sites. For a shoemaker's son with no formal art training who began life painting houses, that's a formidable legacy.

of Bedouin camps stretch across the foyer and restaurant walls of this old favourite, 300m from the entrance to Petra. The rooms in lavender hues may not be to everyone's taste, but they are large with big bathtubs, and most have a view. The buffet lunch (JD10) is popular with tour groups.

★ Mövenpick Hotel HOTEL **$$$**
(☎03 215 7111; www.moevenpick.com; Tourism St; r from JD500; P@) This beautifully crafted Arabian-style hotel, 100m from the entrance to Petra, is worth a visit simply to admire the inlaid furniture, marble fountains, wooden screens and brass salvers. As the hotel is in the bottom of the valley there are no views, but the large and super-luxurious rooms all have huge windows regardless. The buffet breakfast and dinner are exceptional.

Petals are floated daily in the jardinière, a roaring fire welcomes winter residents to the Burckhardt Library (a lounge on the upper floor) and there's a pleasant ambience on the roof garden in summer. Big discounts possible in low season.

Petra Panorama Hotel HOTEL **$$$**
(☎03 215 7393; www.petrapanorama.com; King's Hwy; from s/d JD90/120;) Popular with European tour groups, this hotel was designed for the package tourist with its cavernous corridors, unsubtle touches and an abandoned ship atmosphere during the day. That said, the rooms, which cascade in tiers down the mountain, are bright and spacious, if dated. Each room has its own terrace with uninterrupted views for a private sunset.

Nabataean Castle Hotel HOTEL **$$$**
(☎03 215 7201; www.moevenpick.com; King's Hwy; r incl half board from JD300;) Mövenpick runs this opulent choice as a sister hotel (p186) to the one near the entrance to Petra. Most rooms have views over the valley, but the windows are surprisingly small and the hotel is often fully booked. There's a free daily shuttle bus to and from Petra.

Petra Marriott HOTEL **$$$**
(☎03 215 6407; www.marriott.com; King's Hwy; r from JD135; @) One of the most elegant hotels in the area, though remote in every sense from the experience of Petra. Services include a pool, several restaurants, a Turkish bath and even a cinema for free use by guests.

✕ Eating

The cheapest eating options are around Shaheed roundabout and Sanabel bakery. Most offer similar menus with falafel and shawarma (meat sliced off a spit and stuffed in a pocket of pita-type bread with chopped tomatoes and garnish) as staples. Midrange options with a wider selection of Jordanian dishes are near the Petra entrance. International dining with alcohol is largely confined to five-star hotels. Wadi Musa has many grocery stores for picnic supplies and most hotels arrange snack boxes.

Mövenpick Hotel Ice Cream Parlour ICE CREAM **$**
(Mövenpick Hotel, Tourism St; 1 scoop JD2.400; ⏲2-11pm) After a hot day's hiking in Petra, it's hard to resist a Swiss ice cream from the hotel's foyer cafe. The ice creams are also dispatched through the window on Tourism St.

Bin Bukhara Restaurant KEBAB **$**
(off Main St; mains JD4; ⏲11am-midnight) Selling rotisserie-style barbecued chicken and kebabs, this popular restaurant on the one-way loop round the centre of Wadi Musa is just the place to satisfy an appetite after the long slog up from Petra.

Sanabel Bakery BAKERY **$**
(off Main St; ⏲5am-midnight) Good for putting together a picnic, the Sanabel Bakery sells a delicious range of Arab sweets.

Sunrise Supermarket SUPERMARKET **$**
(Tourism St; ⏲7.30am-11pm) This handy shop near the entrance to Petra sells all the necessary ingredients of a picnic for a day's walking in the Ancient City, including fruit and bottled water.

★ **Oriental Restaurant** JORDANIAN **$$**
(☎03 215 7087; Tourism St; mains JD6; ⏲11am-9.30pm) This main-street favourite offers tasty grills and Jordanian fare, such as *mensaf* (Bedouin dish of lamb on a bed of rice). The outdoor terrace, bedecked with Doric columns, makes a sociable hang-out after the long hike back from Petra.

Zawaya Restaurant INTERNATIONAL **$$**
(☎07 7763 8373, 03 215 6055; Main St; mains JD6; ⏲8am-midnight; 📶) With a coffee shop atmosphere, this new restaurant in the heart of Wadi Musa looks set to become a travellers' meeting place with tables outside and a fashionable interior. The chefs are from Jordan and the US, and the theme of the menu is Mediterranean, Jordanian and Italian.

Red Cave Restaurant JORDANIAN **$$**
(☎03 215 7799; Tourism St; mains from JD5; ⏲9am-10pm) Cavernous and friendly, this restaurant serves local Bedouin specialities, including *mensaf* and *makloubeh*. It's a popular travellers' meeting point.

Sandstone Restaurant JORDANIAN **$$**
(☎07 9554 2277; Tourism St; mains JD9, large beer/small bottle of wine JD7/15; ⏲9am-11pm; 📶) This popular restaurant offers simple fare of tasty mixed grills, salad and mezze and has an outdoor terrace that is particularly popular at lunchtime. Beer and wine is discreetly served outside or served with greater aplomb for an indoor party over tasty Jordanian dishes.

★ **Al Qantarah** JORDANIAN **$$$**
(☎03 215 5535; www.al-qantarah.com; Lower Wadi Musa; lunch/dinner JD10/12; ⏲lunch 11.30am-4.30pm, dinner 7-10pm; P 🌶) Wadi Musa's best restaurant specialises in Jordanian food and serves up to 500 people in one lunch sitting. There is no menu – lunch and dinner are buffet style with 15 kinds of salads and mezze, eight meat and soup dishes and eight kinds of dessert. There's a cooking station and live music every day in the delightful, traditional dining rooms.

★ **Al Saraya Restaurant** INTERNATIONAL **$$$**
(☎03 215 7111; www.moevenpick.com; Mövenpick Hotel, Tourism St; buffet dinner JD20; ⏲lunch 11am-3pm, dinner 7-10pm; P 🌶) Serving a top-notch international buffet in an elegant banquet hall, this fine-dining restaurant offers a quality of dishes that matches the general opulence of the Mövenpick Hotel in which it is located. It's worth leaving time for a nightcap in the grand, wood-panelled bar afterwards, which sports a roaring fire in the hearth in winter or a rooftop cocktail in summer.

Drinking & Nightlife

There is generally a lively buzz in town from around 4pm to 7pm as visitors drift wearily back into town after extended hikes in the Ancient City. This is the most sociable part of the day when an early supper at one of Wadi Musa's Tourism St restaurants phases seamlessly into happy-hour drinks at a rooftop bar. Some hotels organise films or other entertainment, but only when there are enough takers.

★ **Cave Bar** BAR
(☎03 215 6266; www.guesthouse-petra.com; Petra Guesthouse, near Petra Visitor Centre; ⏲3-11pm) It's almost a crime to visit Petra and miss the oldest bar in the world. Occupying a 2000-year-old Nabataean rock tomb, this atmospheric Petra hot spot has been known to stay open until 4am on busy summer nights. Sitting among the spirits, alcoholic or

otherwise, gives a flavour of Petra that's in animated contrast to the bar's ancient origins.

The menu includes a small range of cocktails and simple fare, such as burgers, salads and pasta. The restaurant and bar are next to the entrance to Petra Guest House Hotel, behind the Petra Visitor Centre. Tax and service of 17% are added to the bill.

Al Maqa'ad Bar BAR
(☎03 215 7111; www.moevenpick.com; Mövenpick Hotel, Tourism St; ⌚4-11pm) The Mövenpick Hotel bar has a superb Moroccan-style interior with carved wooden grills and a grand chandelier. It's worth having a cocktail or an ice-cream special just to enjoy the ambience. A 26% tax and service charge is applied. There's another bar called the Roof Garden in the same hotel if weather allows.

English Bar BAR
(☎03 215 6723; Petra Palace Hotel, Tourism St; ⌚2-11pm) The Petra Palace Hotel runs this sociable bar, decorated with assorted local memorabilia. It is one of the few dedicated bars in town, and it makes for a particularly cosy spot in winter when the alternative rooftop bars are closed.

Al Qaysar Restaurant CAFE
(Tourism St; ⌚10am-midnight) If you're climbing the hill between Petra Visitor Centre and Shaheed roundabout, you might like to stop at the Al Qaysar Restaurant, a halfway house with a small craft shop, cafe with seating on the pavement, and clean toilets. It's also a popular place to try shisha (water pipe).

Shopping

There are many souvenir shops near the entrance to Petra selling scarves, hats and fridge magnets. Throughout Wadi Musa, craftsmen patiently pour coloured sand into glass bottles; they will write a name in the sand if given enough time. Books on Petra can be found in the shops at the visitor centre and along Tourism St in lower Wadi Musa.

Indiana Jones Gifts Shop GIFTS & SOUVENIRS
(☎03 215 5069; ⌚8am-10pm) This old timer of a store is now one among many in the outdoor shopping complex that arcs around the Petra Visitor Centre. It remains a good place to buy a video of the main sites in Petra or a *shamag* (headscarf), which works well as a hat in the heat of a summer visit.

Made in Jordan ARTS & CRAFTS
(☎03 215 5900; Tourism St; ⌚8.30am-11pm) This shop sells quality crafts from local enterprises. Products include olive oil, soap, paper, ceramics, table runners, nature products from Wild Jordan in Amman, jewellery from Wadi Musa, embroidery from Safi, camel-hair shawls, and bags from Aqaba as well as Jordan River Foundation goods. The fixed prices reflect the quality and uniqueness of each piece; credit cards are accepted.

Andalusia Bazaar GIFTS & SOUVENIRS
(Tourism St; ⌚8am-10pm) Has a good selection of hand-blown glass bottles displayed in the window. Prices cost JD10 to JD40 depending on the complexity of the design.

Rum Studio & Labs PHOTOGRAPHY
(Tourism St; ⌚10am-10pm) Some pocket-sized cameras and a range of digital accessories are available here; the shop is located in front of the Silk Road Hotel on the main street.

ℹ Information

BOOKS

There is some interesting literature about Petra, together with beautiful souvenir books, available at shops and stalls around Wadi Musa and Petra.

One of the best guidebooks, *Petra: A Traveller's Guide* by Rosalyn Maqsood, covers the history and culture of the site and describes several hikes. The pocket-sized *Petra: The Rose-Red City* by Christian Auge and Jean-Marie Dentzer provides excellent historical context. Jane Taylor's *Petra* is another good paperback introduction to the site. Taylor also wrote the authoritative *Petra & the Lost Kingdoms of the Nabataeans*. There's a chapter on hiking in Petra in Tony Howard and Di Taylor's *Jordan – Walks, Treks, Climbs & Canyons*.

For an engaging account of the Bdoul Bedouin who once lived in the caves surrounding the Petra valley and who now live on the rim of the Ancient City, *Married to a Bedouin* is a recommended read. The author, Marguerite van Geldermalsen, raised three children among the Bdoul and ran the local health clinic. Since the book's publication in 2006, Marguerite has become a local celebrity in Jordan, has received the Queen of England and Queen Noor in her cave, and her son now runs tours for those wanting to gain an understanding of Bedouin life in the area. She continues to live in the Bdoul community at Umm Sayoun.

MAPS

Signposting is steadily improving within the Ancient City, but a map and guidebook remain essential to identifying and interpreting sights.

The best map for hiking without a guide is the Royal Jordanian Geographic Centre's contoured 1:5000 *Map of Petra* (2005; JD5), available at bookshops in Wadi Musa.

A free *Petra* map published by the Petra Development & Tourism Region Authority is given on purchasing tickets and includes a few photographs that help identify certain monuments. There's also a plan of hiking trails on the wall of the Petra Visitor Centre (p179), a photograph of which may make a useful, portable supplement to other available maps.

MEDICAL SERVICES

The **Queen Rania Hospital** (☎03 215 0635; off King's Hwy) offers high-standard health care and is open for emergencies without referral. It's located 5km from the police roundabout on the road to Tayyibeh.

The **Wadi Musa Pharmacy** (Main St; ⏲24hr), located near the Shaheed roundabout, has a wide range of medications and toiletries.

MONEY

There are several ATMs dotted around town, including at the **Arab Bank** (Main St) in central Wadi Musa and at the Mövenpick Hotel near the Petra Visitor Centre. Many hotels will change money, albeit at a poor rate. The banks are open from about 8am to 2pm Sunday to Thursday and (sometimes) 9am to 11am on Friday.

TOURIST INFORMATION

Information and tickets are available at the Petra Visitor Centre (p179), just before the main entrance to the Ancient City.

Tourist Police Station (☎03 210 6044; info@visitpetra.jo; ⏲8am-midnight) Within the Petra Visitor Centre complex. This is the place to register complaints about misconduct on behalf of guides (an unlikely occurrence) or mistreatment of animals by their handlers.

Getting There & Away

Public transport to and from Wadi Musa is less frequent than may be expected, given that it's the top tourist attraction in Jordan. The best place to find information about minibuses and other transport is to ask at any of the hotels or one of the restaurants around the Shaheed roundabout.

BUS

A daily JETT bus connects Amman with Petra, largely designed for those wanting to visit on a day trip. The service leaves at 6.30am from the JETT office, near Abdali Bus Station (JD10 each way, four hours) and drops off passengers at the **JETT bus stop** (☎06 566 4141; www.jett.com.jo; Tourism St), just up the Al Beidha Rd, a two-minute walk from the Petra Visitor Centre in Wadi Musa. The return bus leaves at 5pm in summer, 4pm in winter.

MINIBUS

Minibuses leave from the bus station in central Wadi Musa. Most minibuses won't leave unless they're at least half full, so a wait is almost inevitable. If there are insufficient passengers, they may not leave at all. It's possible the driver may suggest payment for the empty seats. This is not a scam: it's just an attempt by the driver to cover the cost of the journey. As such, passengers should establish the fare before departing. There are far fewer services on Fridays. Passengers may well be charged extra for luggage (around JD3), especially if it takes up a seat that could be used for a paying customer.

The following services run when full from Wadi Musa Bus Station:

Amman (JD5 to JD6, four hours) Regular minibuses travel daily between Amman's South Bus Station (Wihdat) and Wadi Musa via the Desert Highway. These buses leave Amman and Wadi Musa when full every hour or so

PETRA: PUBLIC TRANSPORT AT A GLANCE

TO/FROM	DURATION	FREQUENCY	NOTES
Amman (210km) via Desert Hwy	4hr	1 bus daily/ 11 minibuses daily	**JETT Bus** Leaves 6.30am from the JETT bus office near Abdali Bus Station. Returns 4pm (summer 5pm) from Petra Visitor Centre. **Minibus** Leaves (only when full) between 6am and noon to/from the South Bus Station (Wihdat) in Amman and Wadi Musa Bus Station.
Wadi Rum (90km)	2hr	1 daily	**Minibus** Leaves 6am from Wadi Musa bus station. Leaves 8.30am from Petra Visitor Centre. May only leave if full: ask hotel/camp owner to contact bus driver in advance.
Aqaba (120km)	2½hr	4 daily	**Minibus** Leaves between 6.30am and 8.30am, with one mid-afternoon to/from Wadi Musa Bus Station and Aqaba Minibus Station. Leaves only when full.

THE JORDAN TRAIL: PETRA TO WADI RUM

Distance 90.6km

Duration Five days

The route joining the two iconic destinations of Petra and Wadi Rum lies across some of the wildest stretches of desert in Jordan.

The trek begins by meandering out of the Ancient City of Petra via Sabra. There's a side trip up Jebel Haroun on offer for those who are hankering after the steep challenges of the previous leg. For the more sane hiker, the route climbs to a plateau and then leads gradually down to the desert floor near the little-visited ruins of Humeima. From here, the hike into Wadi Rum gives rise to magnificent views of the wind-eroded landscape that made such an impression on Lawrence of Arabia.

The hike is marked by a couple of relatively easy days – an opportunity to shore up energy needed to tackle walking on soft sand towards the end of the five-day leg. Wild camping here is accompanied by some of the best show of stars along the trail.

Visit the Jordan Trail (www.jordantrail.org) for route maps, GPS waypoints and detailed breakdowns of daily hikes.

between around 6am and noon. From Amman there are services until around 4pm; from Wadi Musa there may be an additional journey or two depending on demand. Schedules change frequently but hotels in Wadi Musa can give up-to-date advice.

Ma'an (JD0.500, 45 minutes) Minibuses leave fairly frequently throughout the day (more often in the morning), stopping briefly at the university, about 10km from Ma'an. From Ma'an there are connections to Amman, Aqaba and the Wadi Rum junction.

Aqaba (JD5, 2½ hours) These leave at about 6am, 8.30am and possibly at 3pm – timings can be checked through a hotel the day before.

Wadi Rum (JD7, two hours) There is a daily minibus around 6am. It's necessary to reserve a seat the day before – hotels normally contact the driver on guests' behalf. If the service isn't operating, an alternative is to take the minibus to Aqaba, get off at the Ar Rashidiyyah junction and catch another minibus (hitching is not recommended though possible) the remainder of the journey to Rum. Cleopetra Hotel, among other hotels, organises competent overnight tours to Wadi Rum as an alternative to the patchy public transport.

Karak (JD7, two hours) A minibus sometimes leaves at around 7am and sometimes at noon, but demand is low so it doesn't leave every day and there is no service on Fridays. Alternatively, travel is possible via Ma'an.

CAR

Petra and Wadi Musa are well signposted along the main highways. The road from Petra to Little Petra extends to the Wadi Musa to Shobak road, offering a scenic alternative route out of town. A spectacular road winds into Wadi Araba for direct access to the Dead Sea Highway that has just been rebuilt after flood damage. The road to Tayyibeh is also particularly scenic.

TAXI

Private (yellow) taxis are easy to find in Wadi Musa. One-way taxi fares cost JD45 to Wadi Rum (one hour) or JD80 return with a one-hour wait. A few 4WD taxis are available for much the same cost, but they are not of much benefit as Wadi Rum visitors still have to join a 4WD tour from the Wadi Rum Visitor Centre to explore the protected area.

The one-way fare to Aqaba (1½ hours) is JD45; to Shobak (40 minutes) it is JD30 or JD60 return including a one-hour wait; and to Karak (1½ hours) it's JD75 or JD150 return including a one-hour wait. To travel to Madaba or Amman via the scenic King's Highway, with stops at Shobak, Dana and Karak, the fare is JD120 to JD150. Nonstop to the airport, Madaba and Amman along the dull and badly surfaced Desert Highway, the fares are JD70, JD75 and JD100, respectively.

Getting Around

Taxis are unmetered, but the fares are kept pretty much standard. Between lower and central Wadi Musa it costs JD4; between lower and upper Wadi Musa (Moses' Spring) it costs JD7.

Siq Al Barid (Little Petra)

سيق البيضاء (البتراء الصغيرة)

Siq Al Barid (Cold Canyon) is colloquially known as Little Petra and is well worth a visit. It was thought to have served as an agricultural centre, trading suburb and resupply post for camel caravans visiting Petra. The surrounding area is picturesque and fun to explore, especially as it is home to some of the oldest settlements in the world, including Al Beidha.

Sights

★Little Petra Siq RUINS

(Siq Al Barid; daylight hours) FREE An obvious path leads through the 400m-long Siq Al Barid, opening out into flat, sandy areas. The first open area boasts a **temple** while four **triclinia** – one on the left and three on the right – are in the second open area. These were probably used as dining rooms to feed hungry merchants and travellers. About 50m further along the siq is the **Painted House**, another small dining room reached by some exterior steps.

The Painted House is worth a closer look as faded but still vivid frescoes of vines, flowers and birds on the underside of the interior arch are a rare example of Nabataean painting, though the walls have been blackened by Bedouin campfires. Cut into the rock opposite the room is a large cistern; there are also worn water channels at various points along the siq.

Climbing the steps at the end of Siq Al Barid affords great views of the wind-eroded landscape and plenty of picnicking opportunities. With extra time and interest the Nabataean quarries and cisterns of Umm Qusa, located just before the entrance to Siq Al Barid, are worth a look.

There are guides, souvenirs, drinks and snacks available in the stands clustered near the entrance to the siq, beside the car park.

Al Beidha RUINS

(daylight hours) FREE The neolithic ruins of Al Beidha date back 9000 years and, along with Jericho, constitute one of the oldest archaeological sites in the Middle East. The remains of around 65 round (and later rectangular) structures are especially significant because they pinpoint the physical transition from hunter-gatherer to settled herder-agriculturalist communities. The settlement was abandoned around 6000 BCE, keeping the site intact. A 15-minute walking trail, starting to the left of the entrance to Little Petra, leads to the site.

It's important to keep to the marked trails at Al Beidha as the site is fragile. It's fair to say that for the casual visitor, the ruins require imagination, but the location among wind-eroded cliffs is an inspiring one. Broken tablets leading from Little Petra to the site helpfully mark key points in world history that put the mind-stretching antiquity of Al Beidha into context.

Activities

There's a rewarding hike from Siq Al Barid to the Monastery (Al Deir) inside Petra. Often referred to as the 'back trail to Petra', this beautiful concealed route takes two hours combining 4WD and hiking (three hours hiking only) and costs JD60 for two people. Along the route, which is paved for much of the way and has steps that help with the steep section, there are wonderful views into Wadi Araba. This is one of the routes that Rocky Mountain Hotel (p184) in Wadi Musa specialises in, either from its hotel or from its Seven Wonders Bedouin Camp. Another route leads from Petra centre via Wadi Mu'aisireh Al Gharbiya. Both hikes require a guide as it can be hard to find the way. A valid ticket to Petra (not available from Siq Al Barid) is required, and ticket validity is checked along the route.

Sleeping & Eating

There are several simple camps in the area that make a delightful rural retreat from the slightly claustrophobic atmosphere of Wadi Musa. If travelling with family, ask about discounts for children – some camps offer half price for kids aged under 12.

A cluster of stands around the entrance to Siq Al Barid sell tea, coffee, soft drinks and snacks. Other than these, the camps all offer half-board accommodation with breakfast and dinner.

Seven Wonders Bedouin Camp CAMPGROUND $

(07 9795 8641; www.sevenwondersbedouincamp.com; off Al Beidah Rd; tent incl half-board per person JD30, B&B JD20) Signposted along a track off the road to Little Petra and tucked discreetly into a hillside, this relaxed and good-value camp looks particularly magical at night when the open fires are burning and the rocks behind the camp are illuminated. Accommodation is in simple but cosy tents with electric light, carpets and mosquito nets. Hot water and towels are available.

A range of tasty traditional fare is prepared by locals and sometimes includes dishes from a *zerb* oven (buried in the ground) and *mehndi* (barbecue) pits. The camp offers both a guided visit to Little Petra (JD15) and the back trail guided 4WD-hike to the Monastery in Petra (from JD60). Other trips include a two-hour 4WD and hiking excursion (JD60) to a local wadi with impressive rock formations. The camp is run by the same management as the popular Rocky Mountain Hotel (p184) in Wadi Musa.

Little Petra Bedouin Camp CAMPGROUND **$**
(☎ 07 7867 4953, 07 7716 2453; www.lpbcamp.com; Al Beida Rd; B&B/half board per person JD20/25, for 2 people JD25/30) Signposted just off the main road to Little Petra, this secluded complex in a tree-filled basin surrounded by mountains offers a rural retreat. Accommodation is in army tents that sport proper beds with linen and mattresses with segregated bathroom blocks for women and men. Romantic settings for dinner are dotted around the campsite, including in a cave.

Ammarin Bedouin Camp CAMPGROUND **$$**
(☎ 07 9975 5551; www.bedouincamp.net; half board per person in tent JD52) A 10-minute walk from Little Petra (signposted off the approach road), this camp is in Siq Al Amti, hidden in a spectacular amphitheatre of sand and hills, and run by the local Ammarin tribe. Accommodation comprises mattress and blankets in a sectioned Bedouin tent with concrete floors, with a clean shower and toilet block. Reservations (booked by email) are essential.

It's possible to pitch a tent here and use the camp's facilities (JD20 per person) and there's space to park a campervan (JD32 per night per vehicle, with power). Special *zerb* dinners (meat cooked in a pit in the ground) can be prepared on request (JD25 extra – ordinary dinner is JD35). The camp offers guided hikes and camel trips in the surrounding hills. A Bedouin guide is JD100 per day or JD50 for the back trail to Petra (for up to five people).

There's also a wonderful little ethnographic museum on-site, spotlighting the local Ammarin tribe. In particular, it's interesting to read the story of Torfa Bint Saleh Al Ammarin for an idea of the everyday hardships of life on the desert fringe.

The camp offers transfers from Petra Visitor Centre in Wadi Musa (JD10 one way).

Getting There & Away

Some hotels in Wadi Musa organise tours to Little Petra. Private taxis cost JD10 in one direction and between JD20 and JD25 return, including an hour's wait. An accompanying guide costs JD50 from the Petra Visitor Centre.

The road to Little Petra is an extension of Tourism St. which loops north of the Mövenpick Hotel. After 8km there's a left turn signposted 'Beda' or 'Al Beidha', from where it's just under 1km to the car park.

Alternatively, it's a pleasant walk following the road. The route passes the village of Umm Sayoun, the 'Elephant Rock' formation and then 'Ain Dibdibah, which once supplied Petra with much of its water. A shortcut across fields to the left about 1km before the junction to Al Beidha cuts off the corner.

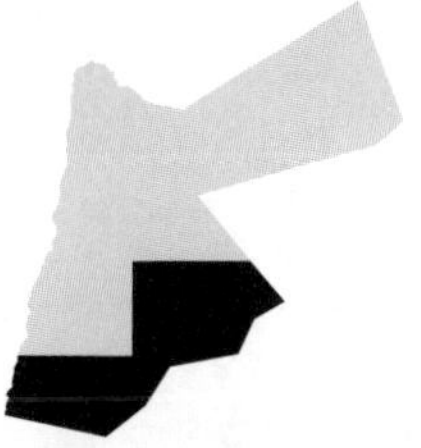

Aqaba, Wadi Rum & the Desert Highway العقبة وادي رم & الطريق الصحراوي

Includes ➡

Best Places to Eat

- Captain's Restaurant (p204)
- Romero at Royal Yacht Club (p204)
- Al Mohandes (p202)
- Formosa Restaurant (p204)

Best Places to Stay

- Darna Divers Village (p208)
- Bait Ali Lodge (p219)
- Captain's Hotel (p201)
- Mövenpick Resort Hotel (p202)

Why Go?

Welcome to the home of the Bedouin, a people of legendary courage and bravado who inhabit a landscape of sand dunes, oases and weathered escarpments.

Wadi Rum is at the heart of any visit to southern Jordan, a landscape so magnificent that it leaves all but the most unromantic at heart dreaming of casting everything aside to lead the life of a nomad. And that's possible – at least for a day or two amid the area's camps, as you explore by foot, camel or 4WD, scramble up mountains or fly above them in a hot-air balloon.

The modern city of Aqaba and the neighbouring diving centres give access to another of Jordan's natural splendours: the coral gardens of the Red Sea. Even if wetsuits aren't your thing, Aqaba is a relaxed and pleasant destination in which to wash off the desert dust.

When to Go

- Aqaba enjoys year-round warmth, even in winter, and a crystal-clear sea. This brings holidaymakers from the chilly uplands to the shore in large numbers – especially during national holidays and religious festivals.
- The desert springs to life after rain, making February to May and October to November the perfect time for a desert adventure in Wadi Rum. With temperate days and balmy nights, camping is blissful.
- Everyone bakes in the summer, with temperatures pushing 40°C not unusual.
- Beware! Midwinter brings bitter evening temperatures to the desert.

History & Culture

There is a magnificent road (A35) that leads from Wadi Musa, with westerly glimpses across expansive Wadi Araba, to the escarpment of Jebel Batra. Here the road joins the Desert Highway and hand in hand they sweep onto the majestic floor of what is commonly called the Southern Desert. For centuries this has been the home of the Bedouin, whose tribes rallied together in the most convincing expression of the pan-Arab ideal during the 20th-century Arabic Revolt. The cry of 'to Aqaba' still rings between the towering walls of Wadi Rum, carried in the whistle of the freight train as it winds along the now-placid tracks of the Hejaz Railway.

As romantic as the nomadic life may seem, in the past two or three decades many of the Bedouin tribes have turned to a settled life. The desert, much of which is characterised not by the picturesque features of Wadi Rum but by inhospitable plains, doesn't take prisoners. Life to this day is hard here, even for the Bedouin. Take the journey along the Desert Highway, along the edge of the mighty Badia, and you'll quickly learn a new respect for this extreme environment – and for the people and wildlife who have adapted to its privations.

Nature Reserves

There are two reserves in southern Jordan. On land, the **Wadi Rum Protected Area**, run by the Aqaba authorities, offers desert adventures such as camping, camel treks, hiking, ballooning and off-road driving, amid beautiful sand dunes and sandstone landscapes.

Offshore, the **Aqaba Marine Park** (part of the bigger, cross-border Red Sea Marine Peace Park) was established in 1997 to protect the complex marine environment of the Red Sea south of Aqaba. It is best accessed through one of the diving clubs in the area. The park stretches from the Marine Science Station to the Royal Diving Club and extends about 350m off the coast. Enforced by rangers, there's a ban on fishing, and boating is limited within the park. Jetties enable divers and snorkellers to jump into the water rather than wade out over coral from the beach.

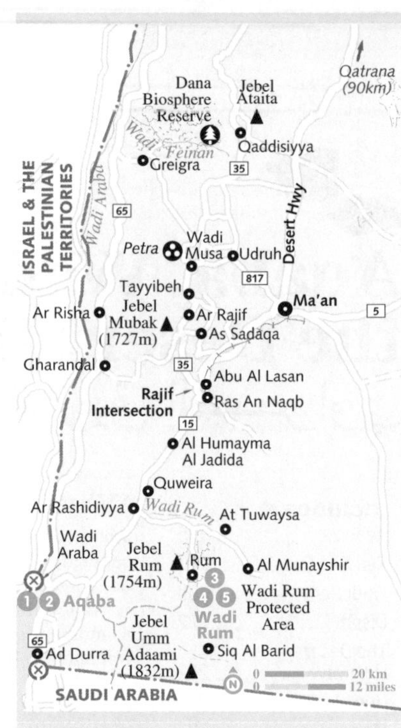

Aqaba, Wadi Rum & the Desert Highway Highlights

1. **Red Sea Coast** (p207) Donning mask and flippers and hovering with the fish over spectacular coral gardens.
2. **Aqaba** (p195) Eating out in the relaxed port city, a stone's throw from Egypt and Israel and the Palestinian Territories.
3. **Wadi Rum** (p209) Camping with the Bedouin in a goat-hair tent and experiencing the night sky in all its glory.
4. **Camel Trekking** (p214) Taking a 'ship of the desert' into the dunes of Wadi Rum.
5. **Rock Climbing** (p217) Roping yourself up or just scrambling in the terrific mountains and crags of Wadi Rum.

Dangers & Annoyances

Scuba divers should note that most roads out of Aqaba lead uphill. This means that 'the bends' are a serious concern if you fail to acclimatise in Aqaba before heading on to Wadi Rum or Petra.

Getting There & Away

Aqaba is well served by public transport from Amman and even has an international airport. The city is a gateway to Egypt, by boat to Nuweiba and Sharm El Sheikh. Aqaba also accesses Israel and the Palestinian Territories through the blissfully straightforward Wadi Araba border crossing. There are only limited onward transport options from Eilat, many of which involve transiting through Jerusalem. Given the volatility of regional politics, always check the current security situation before planning any international crossings.

Wadi Rum is not as easy to get to without your own transport or without taking a tour from Aqaba or Petra. With a car it's possible to link this region with the Eastern Desert via Hwy 5.

Getting Around

It's possible to make a round trip of this most southerly part of Jordan by public transport from Aqaba in three to four days. Hiring a car from Aqaba makes accessing the South Coast and Wadi Rum much easier. You don't need a 4WD for Wadi Rum as you can drive to the Visitors Centre on tarmac. From there, unless you are an expert sand driver, it's advisable to take an excursion with a Bedouin driver.

AQABA & AROUND

Aqaba العقبة

☎03 / POP 148,400

Aqaba carries the relaxed small-town atmosphere of a popular local getaway. The town offers a sociable stopover en route to the diving and snorkelling clubs to the south and the big destinations of Wadi Rum and Petra. It's also an obvious place to break a journey to or from Israel and the Palestinian Territories or Egypt.

The winter temperature in Aqaba rarely goes below 20°C and is often quite a few degrees warmer. In summer the weather is hot, with daytime temperatures often the other side of 35°C, but the sea breezes make it bearable. It also helps to follow the traditional siesta: everything shuts down around 2pm and reopens after the afternoon nap, around 6pm.

History

In the 10th century, a Muslim traveller described Aqaba as 'a great city' and a meeting place for pilgrims en route to and from Mecca. Indeed, from as early as the 10th to 5th centuries BCE, it was at the heart of ancient trade routes transporting copper ore, smelted from mines in Wadi Araba, and transported by King Solomon's fleets to far-flung destinations. Ceramics from China and coins from Ethiopia highlight the cosmopolitan nature of the port throughout its early history. Thereafter the Egyptians, Nabataeans and Romans all found their uses for 'Ayla', as it came to be known, and the discovery of a late-3rd-century purpose-built church – one of the oldest in the world – is suggestive of a prosperous community, embracing of change.

In AD 1068 the town's fortunes changed when a huge earthquake split the old city of Ayla in two. The shifting of trade routes to Baghdad in the middle of the 16th century led to the final eclipse of the port, which dwindled to an insignificant fishing village for the next 500 years.

Aqaba returned to the spotlight during the Arab Revolt in the early 20th century when Ottoman forces were ousted after a raid by the Arabs (and TE Lawrence) in 1917. Thereafter the British used the town as a supply centre from Egypt to support the assault on Damascus.

After WWI, the border between TransJordan and Saudi Arabia had not been defined, so Britain arbitrarily drew a line a few kilometres south of Aqaba. The Saudis disputed the claim but took no action. As the port of Aqaba grew, the limited coastline proved insufficient, so in 1965 King Hussein traded 6000 sq km of Jordanian desert for another 12km of coastline with Saudi Arabia. Today, with the value of tourism to the gross national product, that has proven to be a very foresighted deal.

Sights

Aqaba isn't overburdened with sights of its own – most people come to Aqaba to relax by the beach or go snorkelling or diving. The one or two sights here are best enjoyed as part of a stroll around town.

King Hussein St (sometimes known simply as the Corniche) is the main axis of Aqaba. It follows the languid gulf from the border with Israel and the Palestinian Territories to the border with Saudi Arabia. In the centre of town, a walking path parallels King Hussein St along the beach, ending at a huge flag – the location of Aqaba Fort and the tourist office. The disappointingly obtrusive port is a few kilometres south of the centre of Aqaba.

Aqaba Bird Observatory BIRD SANCTUARY
(☎03 205 8825; www.facebook.com/aqababirds; Wadi Araba Border Rd; JD7; ⏲8am-3pm Sun-Thu) Run by the Royal Society for the Conservation of Nature, this bird sanctuary is an

Aqaba

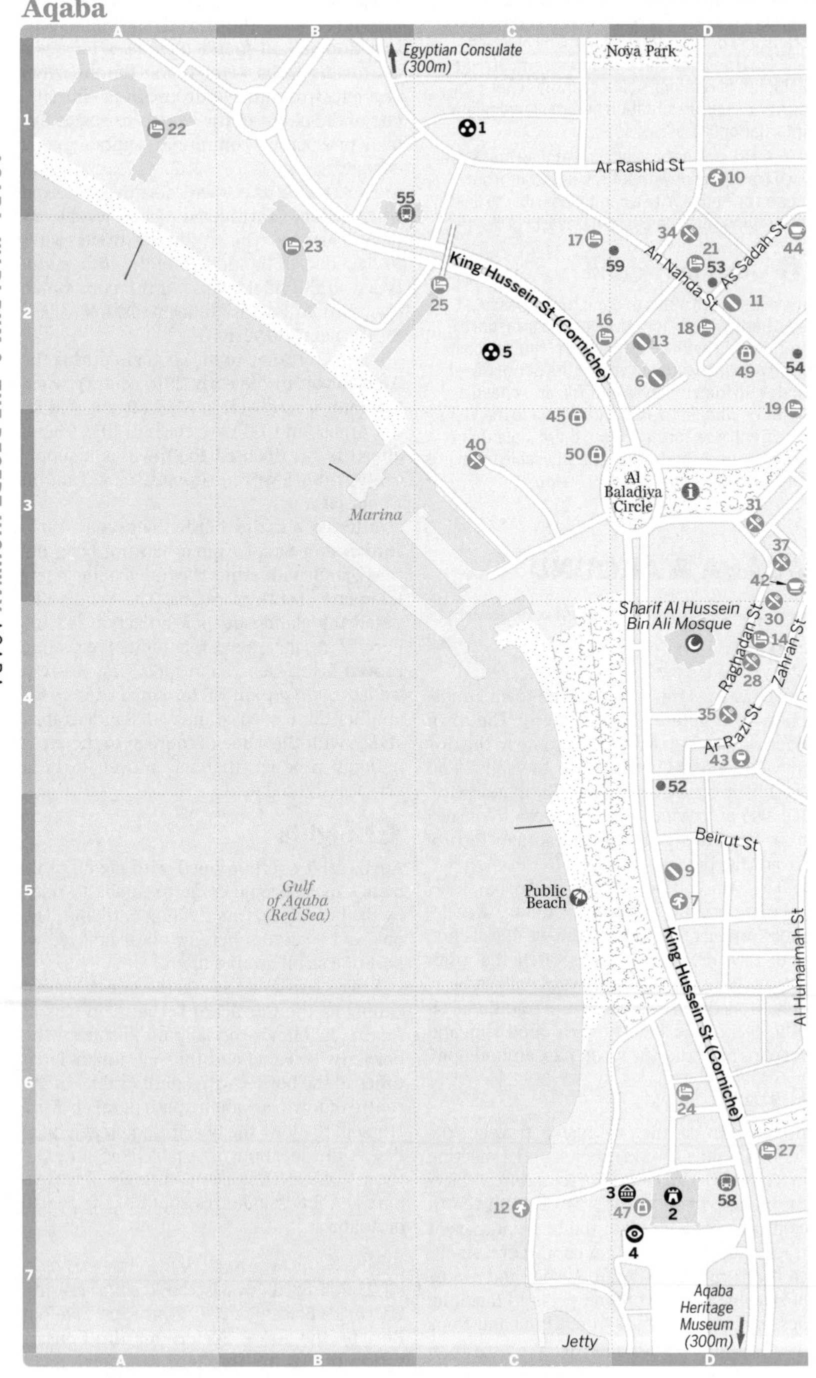
Egyptian Consulate
(300m)
Noya Park
Ar Rashid St
King Hussein St (Corniche)
An Nahda St
As Sadah St
Marina
Al Baladiya Circle
Sharif Al Hussein Bin Ali Mosque
Raghadan St
Zahran St
Ar Razi St
Beirut St
Gulf of Aqaba (Red Sea)
Public Beach
Al Humaimah St
Aqaba Heritage Museum
(300m)
Jetty

artificially created wetland that's become host to a variety of species that use the area as a stopping-off point on the great bird migrations between Africa, Europe and Asia. There's a 1.5km walking trail around the cluster of lakes, and in winter especially the place is thick with ducks and waders.

Birders will get particular pleasure from the concentration of white-eyed gulls – the Gulf of Aqaba has the largest population in the world.

Aqaba Fort FORT

(off King Hussein St) The fort (currently closed for renovation with no set reopening date) was built between 1510 and 1517, as attested by the Arabic inscriptions inside the monumental gateway, and was used as a khan (travellers' inn) for pilgrims on their way to Mecca. The Ottomans occupied the castle until WWI when, in 1917, the fortress was substantially destroyed by shelling from the British Royal Navy. The Hashemite coat of arms above the main entrance commemorates the Arab Revolt that swept through Aqaba, ousting the Turks.

Aqaba Aquarium AQUARIUM

(near Aqaba Port; JD7; 8am-4pm Sun-Thu, 8am-5pm Fri-Sat) This aquarium is part of the Aqaba Marine Science Station, although its location in the shadow of the ferry terminal doesn't make you feel particularly close to nature. Over a series of large and small tanks, you're introduced to the variety of fish and corals in the Gulf of Aqaba, and get a good picture of what you might see when snorkelling or scuba diving, from colourful parrotfish to reef sharks.

Public Beach BEACH

FREE Packed at the weekend and on public holidays, this stretch of rather minimal sand beneath the palm trees offers a fun and sociable way to engage with Jordanians at play. During *eids* (Islamic feasts), the family parties extend well into the night. Note that women on the beach here should remain fully clothed – keep the swimsuits for the hotels and private beaches.

Arab Revolt Flagpole LANDMARK

Standing a massive 137m high and with a flag measuring 20m by 40m, this is Aqaba's most easily spotted landmark by some degree. Look closer, however, and you'll see the flag isn't Jordanian as you might expect. Instead, it's the banner of the Great Arab Revolt, whose centenary was celebrated in

Aqaba

Sights

1 Ancient Church at Ayla C1
2 Aqaba Fort D7
3 Aqaba Museum D7
4 Arab Revolt Flagpole D7
5 Ayla C2

Activities, Courses & Tours

Aqaba Adventure Divers Office .... (see 13)
6 Aqaba International Dive Centre Office D2
7 Aqaba Turkish Baths D5
8 Aquamarina Sea Breeze E1
9 Arab Divers D5
10 Bab Al Hara D1
11 Dive Aqaba Office D2
12 Glass-Bottom Boat Dock C7
13 Red Sea Dive Centre Office D2
Sindbad .... (see 45)

Sleeping

14 Al Shula Hotel D4
15 Amir Palace Hotel F2
16 Aqaba Gulf Hotel C2
17 Aquavista Hotel C2
18 Captain's Hotel D2
19 Doubletree by Hilton D2
20 Dweik 3 Hotel E2
21 Golden Tulip D2
22 InterContinental Hotel A1
23 Kempinski Hotel B2
24 Moon Beach Hotel D6
25 Mövenpick Resort Hotel C2
26 Shweiki International Hotel E2
27 Yafko Hotel D6

Eating

28 Al Mabrouk Beach Touristic Restaurant D4
29 Al Mohandes E2
30 Al Tarboosh Restaurant D3
31 Ali Baba Restaurant D3
32 Baba Za'atar E2
Captain's Restaurant .... (see 18)
33 Carrefour F1
34 Floka Restaurant D2
Formosa Restaurant .... (see 45)
35 Fruit & Vegetable Souq D4
36 Gelato Uno E2
37 Hani Ali D3
38 Humam Supermarket F3
39 Rakwet Kanaan Restaurant E2
40 Romero at Royal Yacht Club C3
41 Route 65 .... E2
Syrian Palace Restaurant .... (see 14)

Drinking & Nightlife

42 Al Fardos Coffee Shop D3
43 Juice Stands D4
Rovers Return .... (see 45)
Royal Yacht Club Bar .... (see 40)
44 Wisalak Cafe D2

Shopping

45 Aqaba Gateway C3
46 Eibal Coffee E1
47 Noor Al Hussein Foundation D7
48 Redwan Bookshop E3
49 Souk by the Sea D2
50 South Kingdom Bazaar C3
51 Yamani Library E3

Transport

52 Avis D4
53 Europcar D2
54 Hertz D2
55 JETT Bus Office B1
56 Main Bus & Minibus Station E4
57 Minibus & Service Taxi Station to Karak E5
58 Minibuses to Ferry Terminal, Southern Beaches & Royal Diving Club D7
59 Thrifty D2

2017. The capture of Aqaba was a key moment in the revolt against Ottoman rule in the Middle East.

Aqaba Museum MUSEUM

(Museum of Aqaba Antiquities; west of King Hussein St) FREE The museum, closed in 2017 for renovation of the Aqaba Fort complex, was previously the home of the great-great-grandfather of the present king, Abdullah II. The collection of artefacts includes coins, ceramics and 8th-century Islamic stone tablets. Anyone who has travelled the King's Highway may be interested to see an inscribed milestone from the Trajan Rd (the Roman incarnation of this famous thoroughfare). No date has been announced for the museum's reopening.

Aqaba Heritage Museum MUSEUM

(off King Hussein St; 8.30am-2pm Sun-Tue, to 4pm Wed, Thu & Sat) FREE This free museum, in the shadow of the giant flagpole, is moderately diverting. There are some fascinating period photos of Aqaba, including at the time of the Arab Revolt, and a reproduction of a letter from the Prophet Mohammed to the inhabitants of the city. There are some tatty replica traditional fishing boats and a folklore display with mannequins portraying traditional Aqaba life.

Ancient Church at Ayla RUINS
(daylight hours) FREE To the untrained eye, these ruins look unprepossessing to say the least, but archaeologists maintain that the remains of this ancient mud-brick complex represent the oldest purpose-built church in the world. The foundations date back to the late 3rd or early 4th century, and the church was probably in use for about a century before an earthquake devastated the region. Layers of sand have helped preserve the walls, some of which are more than two meters high.

Sharif Al Hussein Bin Ali Mosque MOSQUE
(King Hussein St) This grand and beautiful gleaming white mosque – an icon of Aqaba – is named for the great-great-grandfather of the current king, the emir of Mecca who proclaimed the Arab Revolt.

Ayla RUINS
(Corniche; 24hr) FREE Located along the Corniche and incongruously squeezed between the marina and the Mövenpick Resort Hotel, Ayla is the site of the ancient port of Aqaba. Fading noticeboards in English pinpoint items of interest. Archaeological enthusiasts will appreciate the imagination needed to turn the jumble of foundations and columns into a living city – start at the old street leading from the Egyptian gate and let your mind do the rest.

Activities

InterContinental Hotel (p201) and Mövenpick Resort Hotel (p202) open their pools to nonguests for a day-use fee (around JD30).

Water Sports

The top-end hotels are well equipped for various water sports (prices start from around JD15 per hour). Waterskiing, jet-skiing, windsurfing and kayaking are some of the water sports on offer between March and October. All hotels can organise snorkelling and diving, although these activities are best carried out from the diving clubs south of town.

Cruises

Each of the big hotels has a cruise boat for swimming and lunch by day, or sundowners and belly dancing by night. In addition, several boats moor by the harbour office in the marina waiting for sufficient customers to leave. A popular option is to visit **Pharaoh's Island**, just off the Egyptian coast, which has some great snorkelling, as well as a historic Crusader castle. As the cruise operators need to organise a permit to visit Egyptian waters, you'll need to provide your passport when booking.

Aquamarina Sea Breeze CRUISE
(07 9950 0731; www.aquamarina-aqaba.com; Shwaikini Bldg, Princess Haya Sq; 1hr sunset cruise per person JD15) With four or five boats operational in Aqaba, this company is leading the way in boat trips. It offers trips to Pharaoh's Island (adult/child under 12 years JD45/20), three-hour glass-bottom boat rides between 3pm and 6pm (30 minutes/one hour JD25/40) and popular one-hour sunset trips at 6pm. Prices include soft drinks.

Sindbad CRUISE
(07 7543 4150; www.sindbad.jo; Aqaba Gateway) Operates a number of popular cruises around the Gulf of Aqaba either from the marina or from Berenice Beach Club (p205). Popular trips include a four-hour snorkelling cruise (adult/child under 12 JD25/12), and a sunset cruise from 6pm to 9.30pm including a BBQ dinner on the beach (adult/child JD25/12).

Glass-Bottom Boats

If you don't have time to go diving or snorkelling, the next best thing is a glass-bottom boat. The ride is fun, but the amount of fish and coral on view is usually disappointing unless you get away from central Aqaba, which entails hiring a boat for at least two to three hours.

Neptune Submarine Vision BOATING
(07 7722 3375, 07 7943 0969; www.facebook.com/pg/NeptuneBoat) A glass-bottom boat with a difference, the *Neptune* has a glass hull that is fully submerged allowing for a 360-degree view in what the company describes as a dry-dive experience. The self-styled 'underwater observatory' leaves daily from the Tala Bay marina, on the south coast.

Discounts are available from the Tala Bay Beach Club.

Glass-Bottom Boat Dock BOATING
(30min/1hr JD25/40; 6am-sunset) Boats, which operate between 6am and sunset, congregate along the jetty in front of Aqaba Fort. The rate charged is per boat, which hold about 10 people. Prices reflect demand so be prepared to bargain when it's busy. During any of the trips, you can swim, snorkel or fish (bring your own equipment).

WORTH A TRIP

ON A WINTER'S DAY SOUTH OF AQABA YOU CAN ...

- Snorkel or dive in safe hands at the dive clubs near Tala Bay. All offer a day rate and snorkel hire, or around JD35 for an introductory scuba session.
- Learn about what's under the sea without getting your feet wet at the Aqaba Aquarium (p197). Part of the Marine Science Station complex (7.5km south of Aqaba), the ageing and dated tanks nonetheless provide a colourful glimpse of coral, moray eels, turtles and stonefish.
- Laze under a sunshade on the free public beach at the **Marine Park Visitors Centre** (☎03 203 5801; www.aqabamarinepark.jo). As the headquarters of the Aqaba Marine Park (12km south of Aqaba), it has a jetty, museum, cafe, gift shop and park office. It gets busy on Friday and overrun on public holidays.
- Mull over fishermen's tales and a mint-and-lime juice at Berenice Beach Club (p207). This diving centre (13.5km south of Aqaba) offers a good beach, swimming pools, showers, bar and restaurant.
- Explore a Crusader castle on **Pharaoh's Island**. Hotels can book day trips to the island (off Egypt's coast) for around JD40 per person, which includes the entrance fee to the island, Egyptian visa, lunch and transport.

Scuba Diving & Snorkelling

Scuba diving and snorkelling in the Red Sea are a big draw for visitors. Most operators are based south of Aqaba on the road to Tala Bay for quicker access to the sea, but some have offices in the city. Expect to pay around JD35 for an introductory dive, and JD45/55 for a two-/three-tank. Most operators also offer full PADI certification.

Aqaba Adventure Divers Office DIVING
(☎07 9584 3724; www.aqaba-diving.com; King Hussein St) Well-regarded scuba outfit.

Aqaba International Dive Center Office DIVING
(☎07 9694 9082; www.aqabadivingcenter.com) Popular, well-equipped scuba operator.

Arab Divers DIVING
(☎03 203 1808; www.aqabadive.com; King Hussein St) Recommended scuba operator.

Darna Divers Village DIVING
(☎07 9671 2831; www.aqabadivers.com) Scuba operator based at the south beach near Tala Bay.

Dive Aqaba Office DIVING
(☎03 210 8883; www.diveaqaba.com; An Nahda St) A highly professional training centre known for its high-quality teaching staff.

Red Sea Dive Centre Office DIVING
(☎03 202 2323; www.aqabascubadiving.com; King Hussein St) One of the most established dive centres in Aqaba.

Hammams

Bab Al Hara HAMMAM
(☎07 9966 3800; Ar Rashid St; JD25; ⏲9am-10pm) This spotlessly clean, friendly establishment offers steam bath, Jacuzzi, foot and body massage, sauna and a separate pool for women and families.

Aqaba Turkish Baths HAMMAM
(☎03 203 1605; King Hussein St; JD15; ⏲10am-10pm) Offers the full hammam experience massage, steam bath and scrubbing. The bath caters mainly for men, but keeps erratic women-only hours – call in advance.

Sleeping

Aqaba is a popular place for Jordanian and Saudi tourists from October to March, with the season and hotel rates peaking in April, May, October and November. Book in advance.

Dive enthusiasts should consider staying at one of the camps along the beach south of Aqaba.

Most hotels are on the free shuttle bus route to the Berenice Beach Club (p207).

Yafko Hotel HOTEL $
(☎03 204 2222; www.yafko.com; cnr Corniche & Prince Mohammed St; s/d without breakfast JD27/38; 📶) Set back from the Corniche you can sit in bed at this slick hotel and enjoy the sea views. Some rooms are an odd shape, but the furnishings and stone trim make this an attractive choice. It is conveniently located near the fort and transport hubs.

Shweiki International Hotel HOTEL $
(☎03 202 2657; shweiki_hotel@yahoo.com; Amman Hwy; s/d JD25/35) This budget option on the main street is well-placed, though it won't win any prizes for excitement. Rooms are decent and spacious, but avoid the ones at the back of the hotel, which are rather dark.

Al Shula Hotel HOTEL $
(☎03 201 5153; alshulahotel@yahoo.com; Raghadan St; s/d/tr JD25/30/35; 📶) With its black-and-white marble reception desk and painted mirrors, the Al Shula makes quite a statement. Rooms are very simple, but most have balconies and views to the sea across the Sharif Al Hussein Bin Ali Mosque. The hotel is in the heart of one of Aqaba's busiest restaurant streets.

Moon Beach Hotel HOTEL $
(☎03 201 3316; ashrafsaad77@yahoo.com; King Hussein St; s/d/tr with sea view JD18/30/35) Near the fort, this budget option is long past its best. Most rooms have sea views, though the faded furnishings and dodgy decor won't be to everyone's liking. The friendly management just about manage to be the saving grace, but it's a close-run thing.

★**Captain's Hotel** BOUTIQUE HOTEL $$
(☎03 206 0710; www.captains.jo; An Nahda St; s/d/tr JD55/65/85; 📶🏊) Aqaba's version of a boutique hotel, the Captain's began life as a fish restaurant (p204) – still flourishing on the ground floor – and slowly evolved into this stylish accommodation. With copper-tiled flooring and compact rooms with Arabian-style furniture, sauna and jacuzzi, this is an upmarket choice for a midrange price.

Dweik 3 Hotel HOTEL $$
(☎03 203 5919; atalla_dweik@yahoo.com; Amman Hwy; s/d/tr JD50/60/70; 📶) An excellent midrange hotel with a great location close to all the action. Rooms are generously sized and well kept, and those at the front have pleasant balconies. Not to be confused with the nearby Dweik 1 and Dweik 2 Hotels.

Amir Palace Hotel HOTEL $$
(☎03 206 3113; www.amirpalacehotel.com; Al Petra St; r JD25-45; 📶) Unpretentious but reliable hotel just off the main thoroughfare in Aqaba, with helpful staff and comfortable spotless rooms. Rooms facing the side street are slightly cooler, as they avoid the full day-long blast of the sun.

Aquavista Hotel HOTEL $$
(☎03 205 1620; humanehabco@gmail.com; An Nahda St; s/d JD45/55; 📶) The rooms in this functional, nondescript hotel are clean and comfortable. The staff are helpful and the hotel is well located for Aqaba's restaurants and nightlife, though you get the impression the builders forgot to put in an intended swimming pool.

Golden Tulip HOTEL $$
(☎03 205 1234; www.goldentulipaqaba.com; As Sadah St; s/d/tr JD50/75/85; 📶) This hotel in the centre of town is pretty standard but is nevertheless comfortable and modern. The foyer comes complete with a vocal African grey parrot. The rooms are cosy and bright but beware knees and elbows in the surprisingly small bathrooms.

Aqaba Gulf Hotel HOTEL $$
(☎03 201 6636; www.aqabagulf.com; King Hussein St; s/d JD60/70; @📶🏊) This tired old favourite is just across the road from the Aqaba Gateway complex. The first hotel to be built in Aqaba, it has quite an honour roll of guests. The stained-wood, split-level dining room looks thoroughly dated, like the rest of the common-use areas, but rooms themselves are pleasant enough, and the location is great.

★**Kempinski Hotel** RESORT $$$
(☎03 209 0888; www.kempinski.com; King Hussein St; r from JD245; P@🏊) Lavish, multilayered swimming pools, six restaurants and bars (including the renowned Fish Inn and Black Pearl) and a spa make this super-luxury hotel worth top dollar. The beachfront set-up is tremendous, and the service, naturally, is flawless.

★**InterContinental Hotel** RESORT $$$
(☎03 209 2222; www.intercontinental.com; King Hussein St; r from JD134; P@🏊) An imposing full stop at the end of the bay, the InterCon boasts less of an infinity pool than an infinity sea: on a calm day, the Gulf of Aqaba stretches in one seamless ripple all the way to Egypt. With exceptional landscape gardening, pools and a lazy river, the InterCon has stolen the top spot in Aqaba's luxury accommodation.

Providing the kind of practical service that has made this chain a favourite throughout the Middle East, and with six restaurants and a shopping arcade among its many amenities, you won't want to move on in a hurry.

Doubletree by Hilton HOTEL $$$

(03 209 3209; http://doubletree3.hilton.com; An Nahda St; r from JD165; P) This Hilton franchise has become an instant Aqaba landmark, if only for its location. Rooms and service are of the expected high standard, though the place can feel a bit boxy and cramped because of the building's relatively small footprint; it would be nice if there were proper space for a pool instead of squeezing it onto an upper floor.

Mövenpick Resort Hotel RESORT $$$

(03 203 4020; www.movenpick-hotels.com; King Hussein St; r from JD185; P@) Spread-eagled across the main road, this stylish hotel has a palatial interior decorated with mosaics and Moroccan lamps. The huge pool and beach complex has three pools, a gym, lovely gardens and the Red Sea Grill. Other dining options include Italian and Lebanese restaurants, both with outdoor terraces.

Eating

Aqaba offers a wide choice for food. For grills and snacks, the stalls and restaurants along King Hussein St and Raghadan St are the places to go. There are plenty of modern and sophisticated restaurants in the newer part of town, especially along either side of As Sadah St. Note that many restaurants do not have a licence to sell alcohol.

★ **Al Mohandes** JORDANIAN $

(At Tabari St; mains JD1; 7am-1am) This canteen restaurant is as unpretentious as they come, but it's always busy whatever the time of day. Super-cheap bowls of hummus, falafel and *fuul* (fava bean paste) are quickly served up to be washed down with mint tea, maybe with some eggs if you're feeling fancy. Takeaway sandwiches are also available. Female diners will be directed to the family salon upstairs.

Baba Za'atar JORDANIAN $

(As Sadah St; mains JD1.250-4.500; 8am-1am) If you like bread and cheese, come here. The speciality is *manakeesh* (baked flatbread with toppings like cheese and minced meat), served piping hot from the oven. There's a long list of *kaskhowan* breads (with cheese), plus pizzas. The shaded seating area outside provides respite even on a hot summer's day. Particularly excellent for breakfast and lunches.

Route 65 BURGERS $

(As Sadah St; burgers JD4.500; noon-2am) This burger joint brings a decent slice of America-na to Aqaba. Patties are cooked just how you like them, and there are a variety of options to fill your sandwich. Meals come with fries and drink, plus optional sides of onion rings, mozzarella sticks and the like. Sit in icy air-con under the framed black-and-white gaze of American icons.

Al Tarboosh Restaurant BAKERY $

(03 201 8518; Raghadan St; pastries from 200 fils; 7.30am-midnight) A handy pastry shop that offers a great range of meat, cheese and vegetable *sambusas* (samosas). Order a bag for taking away or sit and eat them straight from the oven at the tables outside.

Fruit & Vegetable Souq MARKET

(Raghadan St; 10am-7pm Sat-Thu) The fruit and vegetable souq, hidden at the southern end of Raghadan St, is the best place to buy healthy, locally grown items for a picnic.

Syrian Palace Restaurant SYRIAN $

(03 201 4788; Raghadan St; mains JD3-10; 10am-midnight) A good option for Syrian and Jordanian cuisine, including grilled meat and fish. It's next to the Al Amer Hotel.

Hani Ali ICE CREAM $

(Raghadan St; ice cream from JD1; 10am-10pm) On a hot day, stop by Hani Ali, a sugar addict's paradise of traditional sweets and delicious ice cream.

Gelato Uno ICE CREAM $

(off An Nahda St; ice cream from JD1.250; 10am-11pm) Another popular spot for a cooling ice cream.

Carrefour SUPERMARKET $

(Amman Hwy; 6am-midnight) Useful, well-stocked supermarket.

Humam Supermarket SUPERMARKET $

(Al Petra St; 8.30am-2.30pm & 4pm-midnight) Reasonably well-stocked supermarket, with an alcohol shop next door.

★ **Ali Baba Restaurant** JORDANIAN $$

(03 201 3901; Raghadan St; mains JD9; 8am-midnight) No longer quite the star draw with locals that it once was, this evergreen restaurant still pulls in the tourist crowd. The outdoor seating area is a good vantage point for people-watching, though

Town Walk
Discovering Aqaba on Foot

START MÖVENPICK RESORT HOTEL
END MÖVENPICK RESORT HOTEL
LENGTH 3KM; TWO HOURS

Gain a sense of Aqaba's antiquity in the 1 **ruins of Ayla** (p199): there has been a port at the mouth of the gulf for many centuries. From the Corniche, enter the 2 **marina** to understand the town's strategic location, with Egypt and Israel and the Palestinian Territories just across the water and Saudi Arabia 14km to the south.

Returning to the Corniche, walk to the majestic 3 **Sharif Al Hussein Bin Ali Mosque** (p199), recently renovated by the current king, and take the path opposite through the carefully tended allotments of spinach and radish to the 4 **beach** (p197). During holidays, the beach comes alive with picnicking locals; off season, you'll have the sand to yourself. Continue south to the large plaza at the base of the giant flag and cut inland to the 5 **Aqaba Fort** (p197). Catch the cry of 'To Aqaba' as you pass through the giant wooden gates: this is where the Arab Revolt memorably ousted the Turks, with TE Lawrence in tow. Stand in the big man's shoes (or at least in his celebrity sandals) under the courtyard tree and watch the mountains turn ruby red at sunset.

Turn left onto the busiest section of the Corniche, dodging the invitations to snack at the town's popular shawarma vendors. Turn right up Ar Razi St and first left, doglegging through the 6 **fruit and vegetable souq** (p202) selling monumental mounds of eggplants. Turn left on Zahran St – or be led by your nose to the spice shops. 7 **Trinket shops** punctuate the parade. Duck left through one of the alleyways and turn right onto Raghadan St for desserts from the famous 8 **pastry shops** at the bend in the road.

Cross the busy Amman Hwy to An Nahda St, the teeming centre of modern Aqaba. Choose a fish restaurant for the catch of the day or share 9 **coffee** and shisha (water pipe) with locals along As Sadah St. Turn left onto Ar Rashid St by the ruins of an 10 **ancient church**; a few paces will bring you to the Mövenpick Resort Hotel – a grand place for an end-of-tour ice cream.

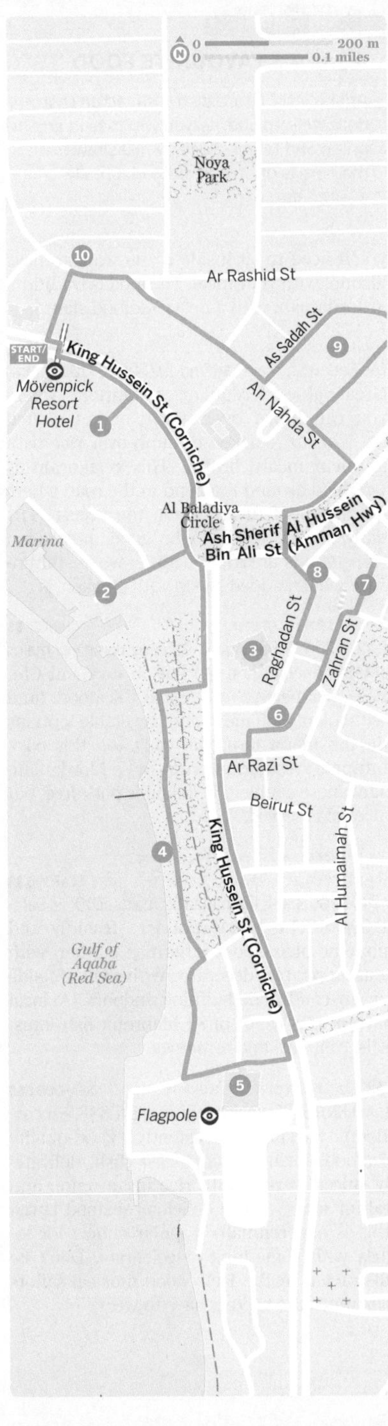

DON'T MISS

AQABA'S FAVOURITE FOOD

Aqaba's signature dish is *sayadieh* (fish, delicately spiced, served with rice in an onion and tahini sauce), while shawarma here is often cooked horizontally over coals.

you'll need to sit inside if you want to have alcohol with your meal. The food is traditional Jordanian, with a heavy seafood slant.

Rakwet Kanaan Restaurant JORDANIAN **$$**
(As Sadah St; mains around JD7.500; ⏲10am-1am) Great-value Jordanian restaurant where you can linger over mezze or get stuffed on *mansaf* (chicken or lamb over rice with a thick, meaty broth). This restaurant is wrapped around the bend in the road where its pavement divans catch the breeze. The daily special tends to be good, but menu translations are idiosyncratic: we're still unsure what 'padded sheep with chicken' is.

Formosa Restaurant CHINESE **$$**
(☎03 206 0098; Aqaba Gateway complex; mains JD6-9; ⏲noon-11pm; ✍) For an excellent Chinese perspective on Aqaba's seafood (and with plenty of meat and vegetable options on the menu too), you can't top this cosy, intimate restaurant run by a Jordanian-Taiwanese couple. The menu is pork-free, but alcohol is served.

Al Mabrouk Beach Touristic Restaurant SEAFOOD **$$**
(☎03 206 3304; Raghadan St; mains JD10; ⏲9am-11.30pm) This restaurant is a friendly and popular place for a large fish supper, with glass-top tables decorated with shells outside or air-conditioned dining indoors. A local favourite is a pot of Al Mabrouk fish, mussels, calamari and tomatoes.

★**Captain's Restaurant** SEAFOOD **$$$**
(☎03 201 6905; An Nahda St; mains JD8-18; ⏲noon-11pm) Serving consistently good-quality seafood, including *sayadieh* (fish, delicately spiced, served with rice in an onion and tahini sauce) and a delicious seafood curry, this is a perennially popular choice for locals with something to celebrate. Don't be distracted by the Hollywood musical sailors costumes the waiters have to wear.

★**Romero at Royal Yacht Club** ITALIAN **$$$**
(☎03 202 2404; www.romero-jordan.com; Royal Yacht Club; mains JD7-16; ⏲noon-11pm; ✍) With views of the marina, this elegant, wood-panelled restaurant is the place to savour a romantic sunset and mingle with Aqaba's nouveau riche. The mostly Italian menu includes Mediterranean flavours, homemade vegetarian pasta, seafood salads – and an unexpected line in sushi. Wash it down with a glass of crisp white wine.

Floka Restaurant SEAFOOD **$$$**
(☎03 203 0860; An Nahda St; mains JD8-15; ⏲12.30-11.30pm) A friendly, unpretentious establishment, where you choose from the catch of the day (which normally includes sea bream, silver snapper, grouper and goatfish) and select how you would like it cooked. Service can be a little slow, but there's indoor and outdoor seating.

Drinking & Nightlife

Many of the midrange and all the top-end hotels have bars, and most offer some kind of happy hour from 6pm to 8pm. Aqaba also has a higher than average number of alcohol shops. Around the As Sadah St loop are a number of open-air coffeehouses with armchairs on the pavement, selling shisha (water pipe), coffee and soft drinks.

There are popular but interchangeable beachfront cafes along the Corniche between Aqaba Fort and the marina. The front-row seats are so close to the water that you can wet your toes while you whet your appetite. No alcohol is served at these public places. Some close in the hot summer low season.

Royal Yacht Club Bar BAR
(☎03 202 2404; ⏲5-11pm) Above the Romero Restaurant in the marina, this is an elegant rendezvous with a delightful harbourside view of the sunset.

Rovers Return PUB
(☎03 203 2030; Aqaba Gateway complex; ⏲12.30pm-12.30am) This 'English' pub attracts a young crowd, plus those curious to see how the iconic pub of soap opera *Coronation Street* has ended up by the Red Sea (check the wall of fame and then order Betty's Hotpot to find out). There's a traditional English pub menu and Guinness on tap. The interior can get smoky, but there's an outdoor terrace.

Al Fardos Coffee Shop COFFEE
(off Zahran St; 10am-midnight) Just off Zahran St, this is a traditional coffeehouse where local men sip *qahwa* (coffee), play backgammon and smoke shisha. It has a pleasant outdoor setting, and foreign women are welcome.

Juice Stands JUICE BAR
(Ar Razi St; 9am-1am) These juice stands are popular for thirst-quenching refreshments.

Wisalak Cafe CAFE
(03 202 2600; As Sadah St; 3pm-midnight) This is a good cafe for sweetened tea and desperately black coffee. There's an upstairs seating area.

Shopping

Some of the best shopping in Aqaba is in the souq in the older part of town, where shops are bulging at the seams with loofahs, colourful Arab headscarves, Dead Sea products and nuts and spices. Aqaba is also a good place to buy jewellery, with a few gold and silver shops in the souq and several shops between King Hussein St and An Nahda St selling beads of turquoise, amber and lapis lazuli.

Aqaba's special economic status also makes it a good place to pick up duty-free goods.

Souk by the Sea MARKET
(Fri evenings Oct-May) A fun tourist market with local handicrafts, carpets and the like.

Noor Al Hussein Foundation ARTS & CRAFTS
(03 560 7460; www.nooralhusseinfoundation.org; Aqaba Fort) The Noor Al Hussein Foundation is a national vocational training organisation, with one of its arms making handicrafts with local cooperatives. The fruits of their labours are on sale here – the needlework products are particularly fine.

Eibal Coffee FOOD
(As Sadah St; 10am-midnight) For upmarket nuts scooped from wooden drawers and great coffee beans, this is the place to come. Try the smoked nuts: the mixed pistachio, cashew and almonds are irresistibly tasty.

Aqaba Gateway MALL
(03 201 2200; Al Baladiya Circle; 10am-midnight) There's not too much in the way of entertainment in Aqaba, but this mall at least offers a popular meeting point in the evening with a bar, a collection of restaurants, fast-food outlets and shops.

Redwan Bookshop BOOKS
(Zahran St; 8am-12.30pm & 4-9pm) A bookshop with a decent selection of English-language books, including titles on Jordan, Lonely Planet guidebooks and a few international newspapers.

Yamani Library BOOKS
(03 201 2221; Zahran St; 9am-2.30pm & 6-10pm) Bookshop with a relatively good range of English novels.

South Kingdom Bazaar GIFTS & SOUVENIRS
(Aqaba Gateway complex; 9am-midnight) One of several tourist souvenir shops along this stretch of road, selling all the local favourites from ostrich eggs and camel bone boxes to Dead Sea products.

Information

DANGERS & ANNOYANCES

Women travellers have reported varying degrees of harassment from local lads on the public beaches. Foreign women may feel less conspicuous wearing loose shirts and baggy shorts over a swimsuit, or, better still, using the facilities of one of the beach-side hotels in town or along the southern coast. Bikinis are acceptable in either of the latter locations.

EMERGENCY

Police Station (191, 03 201 2411; Ar Reem St) Opposite the bus station.

Princess Haya Hospital (p34) Well equipped and modern. It's just north of Princess Haya Square roundabout.

MONEY

There are dozens of banks and ATMs around the city. Many are located along the southern side of Amman Highway, near Baladiya Circle.

Numerous moneychangers are congregated around the corner of Zahran and Ar Razi Sts. They keep longer hours than the banks.

AQABA CUSTOMS

The Aqaba Special Economic Zone covers both Aqaba and the port area. Because of this (and its proximity to sensitive borders), there are customs points on the highways into Aqaba. Whether travelling by private vehicle or bus, always have your passport handy and be prepared for security checks, including having your luggage X-rayed.

TOURIST INFORMATION

The **tourist office** (☎ 03 201 3363; Al Baladiya Circle; ⊙ 8am-2.30pm Sun-Thu) is located in a kiosk in the middle of a new park just east of the roundabout and has lots of leaflets and friendly staff.

VISAS FOR EGYPT

Egyptian Consulate (☎ 03 201 6171; cnr Al Isteglal & Al Akhatal Sts; ⊙ 8am-3pm Sun-Thu) Issues visas for Egypt, usually on the spot for JD12. Take a passport photo for the form. Free 'Sinai only' visas are also issued if you're only travelling as far as Sharm El Sheikh.

ℹ Getting There & Away

AIR

Aqaba has Jordan's only commercial airport, **King Hussein International Airport** (☎ 03 203 4010; www.aac2.info), outside Amman. Royal Jordanian (www.rj.com) flies twice daily between the two cities. One-way tickets cost around JD49.

BOAT

AB Maritime (☎ 03 209 2000; www.abmaritime.com.jo; Amman Hwy) runs two services to Egypt: a fast catamaran to Taba and a slower ferry to Nuweiba. Western governments warn against travel to some parts of the Sinai; check the latest advisories before travelling.

BUS

There are buses to Amman and Irbid from Aqaba. It's worth paying for the comfort, speed and air-conditioning of a JETT private bus. Ordinary public buses travel between the main bus and minibus station in Aqaba and Amman's South Bus Station (Wahadat; JD6, four hours) about every hour between 7am and 5pm.

From the **JETT Bus Office** (☎ 03 201 5222; King Hussein St) next to the Mövenpick hotel, coaches run six times daily to Amman (JD8, four hours) between 7am and 5pm. Different departures go to different bus stations in Amman – Abdali, Tabardour or the JETT station on 7th Circle, so check before booking. There's also a twice-daily VIP service to 7th Circle (JD17, four hours), which includes complementary snacks and more comfortable seating. Book a day in advance (take your passport). JETT also has three coaches a day to Irbid (JD10, five hours).

CAR

Aqaba has branches of all the major car-hire agencies, including **Avis** (☎ 03 202 2883; www.avis.com.jo; King Hussein St), **Europcar** (☎ 03 201 9988; www.europcar.com.jo; An Nahda St), **Hertz** (☎ 03 201 6206; www.hertz.com.jo; An Nahda St) and **Thrifty** (☎ 03 203 0313; An Nahda St). Most charge a 'drop fee' (JD35) if you wish to leave the car in Amman or at Queen Alia International Airport. The cost of car hire is between JD35 and JD45 for a small- or medium-sized car per day, plus a collision damage waiver (average JD10 to JD12 per day). Booking in advance often earns discounts.

MINIBUS

To Wadi Musa (for Petra), two minibuses (JD5, 2½ hours) leave when full, departing between 6am and 7am and between 11am and noon; the exact departure times depend on the number of passengers, and you may have a long wait as very few locals use this service. Drivers often offer passengers the option, however, to leave with a minimum of four to five people providing each passenger pays extra.

There's one daily minibus to Wadi Rum (JD2, one hour), around 1.30pm.

Minibuses to Amman's South Bus Station (JD6, five hours) leave when full, approximately every three hours throughout the day.

All of the above minibuses leave from the **main bus and minibus station** (Ar Reem St). Minibuses to Karak and Tafila (JD3.500, three hours), via Safi and the Dead Sea Highway, are the exception, leaving from the small station next to the mosque on Al Humaimah St.

TAXI & SERVICE TAXI

From the main bus and minibus station, service taxis head to Amman (JD10, five hours), but far less regularly than buses and minibuses. To Karak (JD6, three hours), they leave from the small station on Al Humaimah St. Service taxis start lining up at either station at 6am, and many have left by 8am, so get there early. Chartering a taxi costs around JD45 one way to Petra and JD25 to Wadi Rum.

Chartering a taxi to the south coast beaches costs JD10. Between Aqaba and the Israel and the Palestinian Territories border is also JD10.

ℹ Getting Around

TO/FROM THE AIRPORT

Aqaba's King Hussein International Airport is located 10km north of town, close to the border with Israel and the Palestinian Territories. There's no bus to the airport, so take service taxi 8 (around JD2, 15 minutes) from the main bus and minibus station, or take a taxi for around JD10.

TO/FROM THE FERRY TERMINAL & SOUTHERN COAST

Minibuses (JD1) leave from near the entrance to Aqaba Fort on King Hussein St and go by the southern beaches, camps, dive sites and Royal Diving Centre, passing the ferry terminal for boats to Egypt. A taxi from central Aqaba to the ferry terminal costs JD8.

THE JORDAN TRAIL: WADI RUM TO THE RED SEA

Distance 64.9km

Duration Three days

Hiking and scrambling opportunities abound in Wadi Rum, and it's tempting to add extra days to this itinerary to fully explore the desert. From Rum village (or a Bedouin camp in the protected area), you head south in the shadow of Jebel Rum past Lawrence's Spring to the dunes around Wadi Waraqa. You'll wild camp with a local Bedouin guide, and hopefully enjoy dinner cooked in a *zarb* (buried sand oven) under the stars. From Wadi Waraqa, you turn east towards the tiny village of Titin, past quartz mountains to another campsite. This is at the last line of hills before you reach the Red Sea. From here, you follow another dry wadi towards a pass that gives you your first view of the Gulf of Aqaba. Descending through scree, you briefly come across an industrial depot before veering back on to sandy ridges and your last taste of solitude on the hike. As you approach the highway, there's a tunnel you pass through; you know you've reached your final destination when you reach the cluster of hotels and dive shops that dot the beaches south of Aqaba. If you've done this as the final section of a through hike, congratulate yourself as you cool your feet in the Red Sea – you've just completed the most epic hike in the Middle East.

Visit the Jordan Trail (www.jordantrail.org) for route maps, GPS waypoints and detailed breakdowns of daily hikes.

TAXI

Hundreds of green taxis cruise the streets beeping at any tourist silly enough to walk around in the heat rather than take an air-conditioned taxi. Taxis are unmetered, so prices are entirely negotiable, and the drivers in Aqaba enjoy the sport. Most rides cost from JD1 to JD2. A one-way ride to Tala Bay/Berenice is a set fare of JD10.

Red Sea Coast

Jordan has just 27km of coastline, wedged between Israel and the Palestinian Territories and Saudi Arabia, and looking across to the Sinai Peninsula in Egypt. Nationally, the coast's most important feature is the large container port south of Aqaba, but internationally it's better known for the superb diving opportunities the Red Sea offers. Resorts and dive centres are scattered along this precious seaside, and the reefs here are in good condition. The Red Sea in this northern end of the Gulf of Aqaba is protected in the Red Sea Marine Peace Park and is run in cooperation with Israel and the Palestinian Territories; it is managed locally by the Aqaba Marine Park. The water is more saline than the open ocean; this, together with winds from the north and minimal tides, means the water stays crystal clear, while the average water temperature is 22.5°C in winter and 26°C in summer.

Activities

★ Berenice Beach Club WATER SPORTS

(www.berenice.com.jo; JD15; 9am-sunset) The only dedicated, private beach club on the south coast, Berenice has pools, a jetty giving access to a coral reef, a dive centre, water sports, restaurants and spotless changing rooms. It attracts record crowds on Fridays. It offers a 50% discount for guests of many Aqaba hotels and operates a regular free shuttle bus service (check the website for the current schedule).

As part of the Sindbad Group, it also organises a variety of boat trips, including to Pharaoh's Island.

Tala Bay Beach Club WATER SPORTS

(03 943 0949; www.aqababoat.com; JD10) With three pools, a pool bar, restaurants, waterskiing, jet-skiing, parasailing, windsurfing, kite boarding, kayaking, sailing, diving and snorkelling, this beach club within the Tala Bay complex caters to all levels of energy. Day entry to the beach includes transport on the shuttle bus from Aqaba.

Sleeping & Eating

There are two main types of accommodation along the south coast: the budget-friendly dive camps clustered around the Bedouin Garden Village and the luxury hotels of the Tala Bay complex. All include breakfast and

STONE CORALS: UNIQUE TO AQABA

A quick peek at the Aqaba Aquarium (p197) quickly establishes the pedigree of underwater wildlife along this part of the **Red Sea**. It won't come as any surprise that this part of the coast attracts international underwater photographers, drawn to the clarity of a sea with almost no current, and the relative ease of filming colourful sea slugs, frog fish and seahorses while standing in the shallows.

What is less anticipated is that this part of the coast attracts those in the know for another reason: it is home to a great diversity of stone corals. According to local experts, there are more than 100 different varieties of these marine creatures visible in local dive sites.

Corals, which are generally classified into two main categories, hard and soft, are living marine invertebrates whose exoskeletons fuse together to form coral reefs. Stone corals have been used in the crafting and carving of jewellery for thousands of years, and it remains a respected occupation of local master jewellers. The trade in this natural gem, however, is on the decline as attention turns towards preservation and protection of corals in their natural habitat. Growing in dark shady places on the ocean floor, these remarkable corals take some skill to spot – but your dive operator should help with identification.

have on-site bars and restaurants. They usually provide a free daily shuttle service into Aqaba for their guests.

The beach clubs at Berenice and Tala Bay have plenty of eating options, and the hotels and dive operators also have restaurants. Otherwise, you're pretty close to Aqaba's diverse eating scene.

★Darna Divers Village HOTEL **$**
(www.darnavillage.com; South Beach Hwy; s/d/tr JD25/35/45;) A welcoming hotel–cum–dive camp, with a selection of neat rooms, pleasant pool area and knowledgeable staff. The beach is opposite the hotel, with snorkelling and scuba diving available from the shore. Good lunches and dinners are available.

★Bedouin Garden Village HOSTEL **$**
(07 9560 2521; www.aqaba-hotels.com; South Beach Hwy; campsite per person JD15, s/d/tr/q JD26/40/50/60;) Only a 50m walk from a dive site, this funky little spot offers a clutch of cosy rooms and chalets. There's a very traveller-friendly vibe. Meals are available, plus there's a good on-site dive shop.

International Arab Divers Village GUESTHOUSE **$$**
(03 203 1808; www.aqabadive.com; South Beach Hwy; dm/s/d/tr/f JD15/35/45/60/80;) Up the hill from the coast and with great views across the Gulf of Aqaba from the rooftop terrace, this homely establishment attracts those with a serious interest in exploring below the Red Sea (there's a good dive shop) and returning to relax over a beer in the garden.

★Mövenpick Tala Bay RESORT **$$$**
(03 209 0300; www.movenpick.com/en/middle-east/jordan/aqaba/resort-aqaba-tala-bay/overview; South Beach Hwy; r from JD120) This large resort feels like a small village with its landscaped grounds and many accommodation blocks all painted in dark chocolate shades. Rooms and service are of a uniformly good quality, there's a variety of restaurants and water-sports options plus a dive shop. Particularly family-friendly, with lots of children's activities, a kids' club and plenty of safe sand and water.

Getting There & Away

If you're staying in Aqaba and planning on diving, most operators will arrange transport to the dive sites and there are free shuttle buses to Berenice Beach from many hotels.

Minibuses (King Hussein St; JD2) leave from near the entrance to Aqaba Fort on King Hussein St for the southern beaches, camps, dive sites and Royal Diving Club, passing the ferry terminal for boats to Egypt. A taxi from central Aqaba to the ferry terminal costs JD8, or JD10 to the beach hotels.

WADI RUM & AROUND

Wadi Rum وادي رم

Wadi Rum is everything you'd expect of a quintessential desert: it is extreme in summer heat and winter cold; it is violent and moody as thc sun slices through chiselled siqs (canyons) at dawn or melts the division between rock and sand at dusk; it is exacting on the Bedouin who live in it and vengeful on those who ignore its dangers. For most visitors, on half- or full-day trips from Aqaba or Petra, Wadi Rum offers one of the easiest and safest glimpses of the desert in the region. For the lucky few who can afford a day or two in their itinerary to sleep over at one of the desert camps, it can be an unforgettable way of stripping the soul back to basics.

History

With its many wells and springs, Wadi Rum has been inhabited since prehistoric times. Petroglyphs and burial mounds appear throughout the area, indicating its importance as a hunting and meeting point in ancient times. It was referred to by the Greeks and Romans, who noted its vineyards (now gone), and olive and pine trees (some of which remain on the mountaintops). Some Islamic scholars claim that this is the location of an ancient Arab tribe, the Ad, described in the Quran.

About 30,000 inscriptions decorate Wadi Rum's sandstone cliffs. They were made first by tribes from Southern Arabia and later by the Nabataeans who settled in Wadi Rum around the 4th century BC. The two tribes lived peacefully side by side, honouring the same deities of Lat and Dushara.

The region owes its fame, however, to the publicity of TE Lawrence, who stayed here in 1917 during the Arab Revolt – a campaign led by King Hussein bin Ali against the Ottoman Turks in a bid to establish an independent Arab nation. The king's camel- and horse-mounted troops passed through Wadi Rum on their way to conquer Aqaba and some units (including that of Lawrence) returned to use the area as a temporary base before moving north towards Damascus.

The discovery of a Nabataean Temple (behind the Rest House) in 1933 briefly returned the spotlight to the desert. A French team of archaeologists completed the excavations in 1997.

Flora & Fauna

Despite its barren appearance, Wadi Rum is home to a complex ecosystem. Small medicinal plants dot the desert and are used to this day by the Bedouin, and during the infrequent rains parts of the desert bloom with more than 200 species of flowers and wild grasses. Around the perennial springs, hanging gardens of fig, fern, mint and wild watermelon topple over the rocks, creating shaded lairs for small mammals, birds and reptiles.

For most of the year, the extreme heat and lack of ground water mean that animals only venture out at night. If you sit tight, you may well see a hedgehog, hare or hyrax (a small furry animal implausibly related to the elephant). If you're extremely lucky, you could catch a glimpse of a jackal, wolf, caracal or giant-horned ibex. Sadly, you are not likely to see the highly endangered Arabian oryx. Repeated attempts to reintroduce this beautiful antelope have fallen on rocky ground, though attempts to found a small herd from stock brought from the Untied Arab Emirates are ongoing.

This is big-bird country, and there is usually a raptor or two (including sooty falcons, kestrels and eagle owls) circling on the thermals above the desert floor, on the lookout for the desert's plentiful geckos, agamas and other lizards. If you see a scorpion, snake or camel spider, count yourself lucky, as they are all shy residents of Rum.

Sights

Admission to Wadi Rum Protected Area is controlled and all vehicles, camels and guides must be arranged either through or with the approval of the visitor centre (p220) – where you also pay your entrance fee (adult/child under 12 JD5/free, free with Jordan Pass). Essential items to bring include a hat (preferably with a brim to keep the sun off your neck and face), sunscreen, sturdy footwear and water. Warm clothing, including gloves, is essential in winter.

Rum village, in the middle of Wadi Rum, houses a small community of Bedouin who have chosen to settle rather than continue a more traditional nomadic life. The village has a rest house, restaurants and a couple of grocery shops. It also has the last piece of tarmac before the desert proper. The small, squat Rum Fort is closed to the public.

Wadi Rum

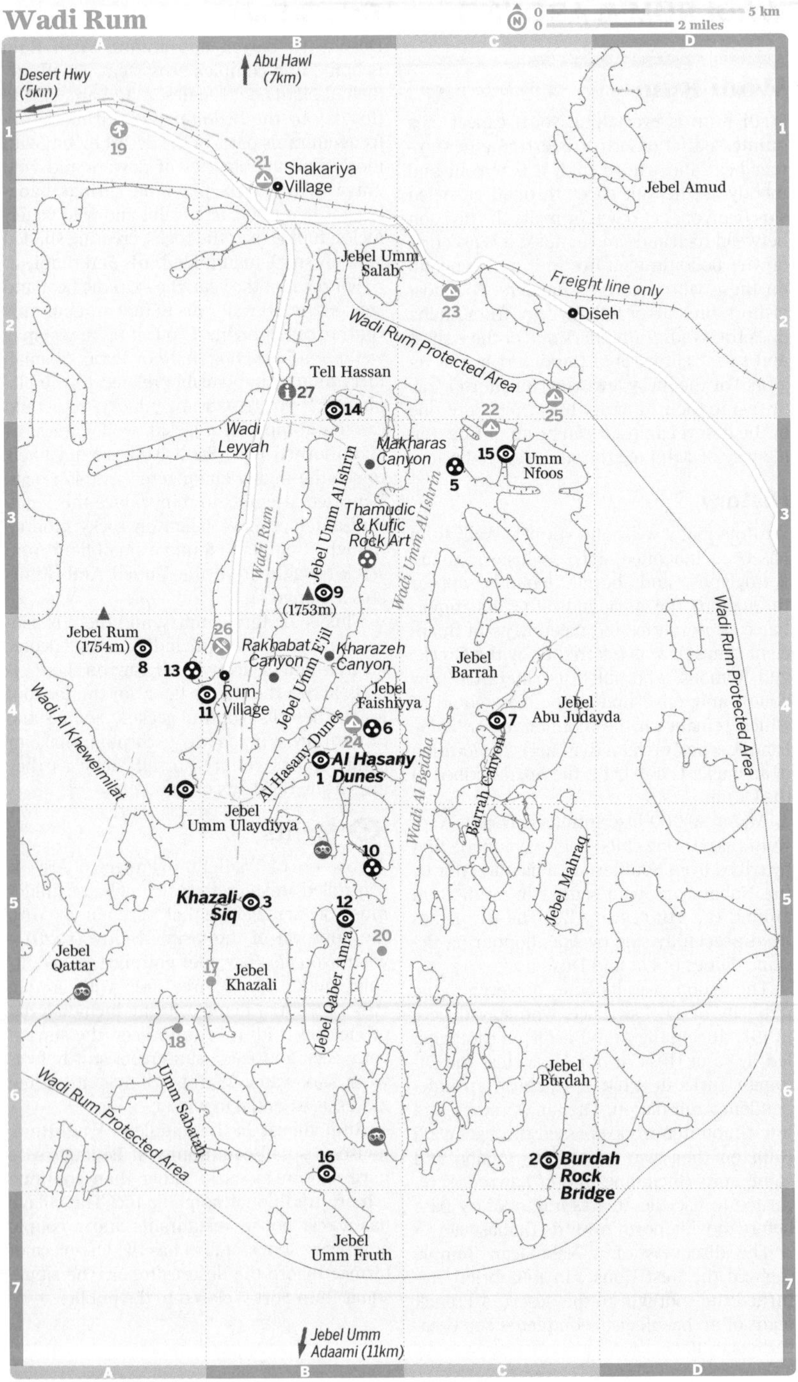

0 — 5 km
0 — 2 miles

Desert Hwy (5km)
Abu Hawl (7km)
19
21
Shakariya Village
Jebel Amud
Jebel Umm Salab
Freight line only
23
Diseh
Wadi Rum Protected Area
Tell Hassan
27
14
25
22
Wadi Leyyah
Makharas Canyon
15
Umm Nfoos
5
Jebel Umm Al Ishrin
Wadi Umm Al Ishrin
Thamudic & Kufic Rock Art
Wadi Rum
9
(1753m)
Wadi Rum Protected Area
Jebel Rum (1754m)
8
26
Rakhabat Canyon
Kharazeh Canyon
13
Jebel Umm E'jil
Jebel Faishiyya
Jebel Barrah
Jebel Abu Judayda
7
Rum Village
11
Wadi Al Kheweimilat
24
6
Al Hasany Dunes
1
Al Hasany Dunes
Barrah Canyon
Wadi Al Bgidha
4
Jebel Umm Ulaydiyya
Jebel Mahraq
10
Khazali Siq
3
12
20
Jebel Qaber Amra
Jebel Qattar
17
Jebel Khazali
18
Wadi Rum Protected Area
Umm Sabatah
Jebel Burdah
16
2
Burdah Rock Bridge
Jebel Umm Fruth
Jebel Umm Adaami (11km)

Wadi Rum

Top Sights
1 Al Hasany Dunes.......... B4
2 Burdah Rock Bridge.......... C6
3 Khazali Siq.......... B5

Sights
4 Ain Abu Aineh.......... A4
5 Alameleh Inscriptions.......... C3
6 Anfaishiyya Inscriptions.......... B4
7 Barrah Canyon.......... C4
8 Jebel Rum.......... A4
9 Jebel Umm Al Ishrin.......... B3
10 Lawrence's House.......... B5
11 Lawrence's Spring.......... B4
12 Little Rock Bridge.......... B5
13 Nabataean Temple.......... A4
14 Seven Pillars of Wisdom.......... B2
15 Siq Umm Tawaqi.......... C3
16 Umm Fruth Rock Bridge.......... B6
Visitor Centre Museum..........(see 27)

Activities, Courses & Tours
17 Bedouin Lifestyle.......... B5
18 Mohammed Mutlak.......... A6
19 Rum Horses.......... A1
20 Rum Stars.......... B5

Sleeping
21 Bait Ali Lodge.......... B1
Captain's Camp..........(see 25)
22 Rahayeb Camp.......... C3
23 Sun City Camp.......... C2
24 Wadi Rum Night Luxury Camp.......... B4
25 Zawaideh Desert Camp.......... C2

Eating
26 Rest House.......... B4
Rum Gate Restaurant..........(see 27)

Shopping
Visitor Centre..........(see 27)

Information
27 Visitor Centre.......... B2

★ Al Hasany Dunes — DESERT

While there are dunes in several places around Wadi Rum, the most striking are the red sands that bank up against Jebel Umm Ulaydiyya. If you are on a 4WD or camel tour, drivers will stop near a pristine slope for you to plod your way to the crest of the dune. They're particularly lovely at sunset.

Ain Abu Aineh — SPRING

Often mistaken for Lawrence's Spring, the 'Father of Aineh Spring' is piped down the mountain into a large tank for Bedouin sheep, goats and camels. Look out for a large boulder near the tank: it is covered with Thamudic inscriptions, proving the spring has been used for a similar purpose for millennia. To reach Ain Abu Aineh, head south from the Rest House and follow the eastern side of Jebel Rum for 3km (a 1½-hour walk in soft sand).

The site in itself is not particularly special, but the views across to Jebel Khazali are wonderful, especially at sunset when the whole amphitheatre of stone and sand turns orange.

Jebel Rum — MOUNTAIN

The western flank of Wadi Rum is formed by Jebel Rum (1754m), which towers over Rum village. It is a popular destination for scramblers and climbers who tackle parts of the ancient Thamudic Way to the summit (guide required – ask at the visitor centre). Similar pathways, once used for hunting ibex and collecting medicinal plants, link one massif to another throughout the area, giving limitless scope for hiking, scrambling and climbing.

Jebel Umm Al Ishrin — MOUNTAIN

The deeply crevassed 'Mother of Twenty', a 20-domed mountain forming the east flank of Wadi Rum, is connected to the Seven Pillars of Wisdom formation. The mountain acquired its name, according to local legend, after a woman killed 19 suitors; she was outwitted by the 20th, so she married him. The whole range turns a magnificent white-capped auburn during sunset.

Alameleh Inscriptions — ARCHAEOLOGICAL SITE

Thamudic and Nabataean inscriptions, depicting camel caravans, hunting warriors and various animals, are common throughout the Wadi Rum area. The Alameleh inscriptions, near the Seven Pillars of Wisdom and on the edge of the Diseh district, are some of the most comprehensive and best preserved.

Thamudic & Kufic Rock Art — ARCHAEOLOGICAL SITE

Adorning the west-facing vertical rock face of Jebel Umm Al Ishrin, this wonderful set of petroglyphs is worth the detour on a 4WD excursion. While the animal forms are easy to interpret, a guide is helpful to make sense of the ancient Kufic inscriptions.

LAWRENCE OF ARABIA

You can't visit Wadi Rum and fail to bump into TE Lawrence. The legacy of the esoteric Englishman is everywhere – there's even a mountain named Seven Pillars of Wisdom, after his famous account of the Arab Revolt. Lawrence's ubiquitous local evocation is something of a cynical one, mind, designed to cash in on the chiefly foreign fascination with this legendary figure.

Lawrence the Legend

It was largely thanks to the promotion of *Seven Pillars of Wisdom* by an American journalist in 1926 that the Lawrence legend was born. In this adventurous account of derring-do, much of which takes place in the desert in and around Wadi Rum, Lawrence casts himself in the role of trusted adviser, brave soldier and ultimately a messiah figure of the Arab cause. However, that was not necessarily how he was regarded from an Arab perspective. Indeed for some he was 'Lawrence who?' – one among 100,000 Arabs, 10% of whom died in their epic struggle to build a nation.

The Man Behind the Myth

So what are the facts? Born in 1888 into a wealthy English family, Thomas Edward Lawrence ('TE' to his friends) nurtured an early passion for the Middle East. He studied archaeology at Oxford and became bewitched by the region in 1909 while researching his thesis on Crusader castles. With the outbreak of WWI, Lawrence was a natural choice for the intelligence service in Cairo, where he became attached to the Hejaz Expeditionary Force. Lawrence felt a natural sympathy towards the fomenting Arab Revolt, the objective of which was to oust the Turks and create an Arab state. Learning to ride camels with the best of them, and wearing Arab clothing like so many other English adventurers before him, Lawrence accompanied the armies of the great Arab warrior (and later statesman) Emir Faisal in 1917 and learned a respect for his comrades that lasted a lifetime. Lawrence died in a motorcycle accident in 1935 – a lone and isolated figure, by all accounts, who never fully found in peacetime the sense of purpose and passion he experienced with his Arab comrades in the desert.

Lawrence's Legacy

It can be argued that Lawrence did little to put his contribution into a more historically accurate perspective. His part in the Arab Revolt certainly sits awkwardly with Britain's subsequent colonial division of the Middle East. To his credit, his writings helped introduce a wider audience to the hallowed names of Auda and Faisal that already rang out of the desert at Wadi Rum, and describes with tenderness the ordinary foot soldiers of the Arab cause who gave their lives for a brave new world. David Lean's epic 1962 film *Lawrence of Arabia* lionises the eccentric and brave accomplishments in grand cinematic style, but his memory in Jordan is much more equivocal, and he is regarded as much an imperialist as an ally of the Arabs.

Sunset Viewing Point VIEWPOINT

One of several spots on the 4WD tour route from which to enjoy the spectacular colours of sunset across the sands of Wadi Rum, here at the dunes close to Lawrence's House.

Sunset Viewing Point VIEWPOINT

On the longer 4WD tour routes, you can enjoy the spectacular views across the sands of Wadi Rum here in the shadow on Jebel Abu Khsheibah, near the Umm Fruth Rock Bridge.

Sunset Viewing Point VIEWPOINT

The slopes of Jebel Qattar are one of several spots on the 4WD tour route from which to enjoy the spectacular colours of sunset across the sands of Wadi Rum.

Lawrence's Spring SPRING

(Ain Ash Shallalah) This spring, on the edge of the open sands, is a regular stop on the 4WD circuit. Alternatively, it can be reached on a soft sand hike from the Rest House; the walk takes about 1½ hours return. Look for a white water tank at the opening of Wadi

Shallalah. After the tank, a path climbs the hill to the spring.

The spring was named in honour of Lawrence's evocative description in the *Seven Pillars of Wisdom:* 'In front of us a path, pale with use, zigzagged up the cliff-plinth… From between [the] trees, in hidden crannies of the rock, issued strange cries; the echoes, turned into music, of the voices of the Arabs watering camels at the springs which there flowed out three hundred feet above ground'.

Together with other springs in the area, this natural water spout that tumbles into a leafy 'paradise just five feet square' allowed Rum to become an important waterhole for caravans travelling between Syria and Arabia. Look out for a small shrine dedicated to Lat, an aqueduct used to channel the water from the spring and inscriptions on the rock face. Notice too the aroma of mint in the air: it grows wild among the ferns and trees of this shady place.

Lawrence's House RUINS

(Al Qsair) There is little left of this building, erected on the Nabataean ruins of a water cistern. Nonetheless, legend has it that Lawrence stayed here during the Arab Revolt and that makes it a must on the regular 4WD circuits of the area. Near the building is a Nabataean inscription that mentions the area's ancient name of Iram. The remote location and uninterrupted view of the **red sand dunes** are the main attractions.

Visitor Centre Museum MUSEUM

(8am-6pm) FREE While you are buying your ticket to enter Wadi Rum, spare half an hour to visit the informative museum (next to the restaurant), which helps to give a human context to the desert. The displays also explain environmental issues through information panels in English and natural history exhibits. Ask to see the 10-minute film on some of the highlights of Wadi Rum, shown in the purpose-built cinema.

Seven Pillars of Wisdom NATURAL FEATURE

Named in honour of Lawrence's book, this large rock formation, with seven fluted turrets, is easy to see from the road near the Wadi Rum visitor centre. If you fancy a closer look, a rewarding hike circumnavigates the mountain via Makharas Canyon (p214).

Nabataean Temple RUINS

On a small hill in Rum village, about 400m behind the Rest House (p219; follow the telephone poles), are the limited ruins of a 2000-year-old temple, dedicated to the deity Lat. Inside the Rest House an information board describes the temple and its excavation. The ruins are important because they are evidence of a permanent Nabataean settlement, built on the earlier foundations of a temple built by the Arab tribe of Ad.

The baths in a villa behind the temple are the earliest so far discovered in Jordan. Near the temple are some inscriptions by hunters and nomads dating back to the 2nd century BC.

Anfaishiyya Inscriptions ARCHAEOLOGICAL SITE

The Anfaishiyya inscriptions are scratched into the smooth surface of a huge, vertical rock face.

Rock Bridges

There are many chiselled rock formations in the area, where the wind has whittled away the softer parts of the sandstone, leaving the tortured forms of harder rock behind. The most striking of these formations are the natural bridges that arch from one rock mass to another. You can see several of these bridges around the area, but there are three famous ones known as Burdah, Umm Fruth and Little Rock Bridge.

★**Burdah Rock Bridge** NATURAL FEATURE

The largest of Rum's three arches is the Burdah Rock Bridge, precariously perched about 80m above surrounding rock. There's a precipitous hike to the summit.

Little Rock Bridge NATURAL FEATURE

(Rakhabat Al Wadak) Easy to climb, this bridge offers great views across a broad expanse of desert.

Umm Fruth Rock Bridge NATURAL FEATURE

Best seen in the late afternoon light, Umm Fruth Rock Bridge is tucked away in a remote corner of the desert and can be easily climbed without gear or a guide.

Siqs & Canyons

★**Khazali Siq** CANYON

An easy siq to explore is the narrow fissure that cuts into Jebel Khazali. You can explore on foot for about 150m, far enough to appreciate the cool shade and to see inscriptions made by the ancients who used the siq for the same purpose. Look out for drawings of ostriches, pairs of feet and a woman giving birth. You need ropes and a guide to penetrate further and 4WD transport to reach the siq.

Barrah Canyon CANYON

One of the most visited of numerous canyons that riddle Wadi Rum, this 5km-long corridor of rock through the mountains offers opportunities for hiking, camel trekking, climbing or simply napping in the shade and absorbing the special atmosphere of Wadi Rum's hidden heartland.

Makharas Canyon CANYON

This attractive canyon threads through the rock massive known as Seven Pillars of Wisdom (p213) and makes for an interesting hike from the visitor centre.

Kharazeh Canyon CANYON

Kharazeh Canyon, one of the mighty incisions in Jebel Umm Al Ishrin, is a popular hiking destination. Guides and agencies offer a day hike (around seven hours) from the Rest House in Rum village combining Rakhabat Canyon with Kharazeh Canyon. A head for heights and an ability (or at least willingness!) to abseil for 40m is necessary to complete the route through Kharazeh Canyon. Path finding through the myriad branches of these canyons is challenging, so a guide is recommended.

Siq Umm Tawaqi CANYON

A popular destination by 4WD is Siq Umm Tawaqi, a beautiful area with mature trees sprouting apparently from the rock face. Locals have carved the humorous likeness of TE Lawrence (complete with Arab headdress) and two other prominent figures of the Arab Revolt into a stone plinth in the middle of the siq.

Rakhabat Canyon CANYON

Close to Rum village, the labyrinthine siqs of Rakhabat Canyon give access to the heart of Jebel Umm Al Ishrin (p211).

Activities

Although you could have a pleasant day out in the Wadi Rum area by calling in at the visitor centre and ambling along to the village of Rum, you will have a more interesting experience if you penetrate deeper into the desert. This requires leaving the tarmac behind and going off-road. You can do this most effectively by hiring a 4WD vehicle with a driver; by hiring a camel or a horse with a mounted escort; or by hiking, scrambling or climbing with or without a guide.

4WD Excursions

The easiest way to see the largest number of sights in the least amount of time is to arrange a 4WD trip. This is easily done on arrival at the excursion office at the visitor centre.

Rates for 4WD excursions are fixed and listed on a board outside the excursion office. The prices are per vehicle, not per person, so it can help with costs if you put together a group in Wadi Musa or Aqaba (not easy to do on arrival at Wadi Rum). Most 4WDs seat six people; some have bench seats in the back offering better views than the closed-in cabs, but they are fearfully cold or boiling hot in extreme seasons.

If you take the vehicle for a day, don't forget to pack food and water for you and your driver. You can buy the basics of a rudimentary picnic in Rum village on your way into the desert.

It's unlikely that anything will go wrong with your trip as the drivers are highly experienced in the desert terrain. Some of the vehicles, however, have seen better days, so if you are involved in a breakdown, try to avoid heated confrontation: the Bedouin take their responsibility towards visitors very seriously, and they will quickly arrange for a replacement – this is easier if everyone remains amicable!

You may be approached by the odd freelance guide in Rum village. Prices may be cheaper, but there are no guarantees regarding the safety or quality of the trip and, more importantly, it cheats the drivers waiting patiently in line for a fare. In addition, 60% of the profit from excursions goes back to the cooperative: someone who jumps the queue robs the community of that revenue. Rangers tour the Wadi Rum area, checking people have tickets. Entering without one is not only unethical, it is also illegal.

You can easily add on an overnight stay at a Bedouin camp (book in advance or ask at the visitor centre when arranging your vehicle). Your driver will simply drop you off in the afternoon and pick you up the next morning.

Camel Trekking

Travelling around Wadi Rum by camel is highly recommended. Apart from being ecologically sound, it enables you to experience Wadi Rum as the Bedouin have for centuries and to appreciate the silent gravitas of the desert. That said, a ride of more than about four hours will leave you sore in places you never knew existed.

Rates for camel-trekking excursions are fixed and listed on a board outside the excursion office in the visitor centre. The prices are per person. You'll enjoy your ride much more if you ride yourself rather than being led. This will cost a bit more as you need to pay for your guide's camel, but it's well worth the extra cost.

You can easily add on an overnight stay at a Bedouin camp (ask at the visitor centre when booking your camel). If you want to return by 4WD, then you have to pay the price of returning the camel to where you collected it from. If you have a lot of gear, it's better to hire an additional camel (at the same rate) to bear the load. It is also possible to arrange longer camel excursions from Wadi Rum to Aqaba (three to six nights depending on the route); or towards Wadi Musa (for Petra; about five nights).

The camel is no longer a common form of transport for Bedouin; most now prefer the ubiquitous pick-up truck – in fact, it's not unusual to see a Bedouin transporting a prized camel in the back of a Toyota. These grumpy but loyal animals, however, are still very much part of the Bedouin culture, and camel races are held weekly in winter, generally on a Friday, at the camel track near Diseh. Ask at the visitor centre for details.

Horse Trekking

An alternative and memorable mode of four-legged transport through Wadi Rum and surrounding areas is by horse. These trips are for people who have riding experience –

4WD EXCURSIONS AROUND WADI RUM

When booking a 4WD excursion at the Wadi Rum visitor centre you can either hire a driver for a whole day (make sure you agree on the destinations before leaving), or you can select a destination from two prescribed routes. 'Operator 1' routes cover the central areas of Wadi Rum; 'Operator 2' routes cover outlying (and equally beautiful) areas. Distances are measured from the visitor centre. Maximum times are given below: you could rush round the main sights of Wadi Rum in a few hours, but the trip will be much more rewarding if you get out of the vehicle and explore each of the sights on foot, or simply sit on a dune or rocky outcrop and enjoy the peace and quiet. Drivers are assigned in strict rotation, so you may get a driver who speaks English and is knowledgeable about the desert or you may not. If you want a guide to accompany you, ask at the visitor centre or book one in advance.

Lawrence's Spring, the Nabataean temple and Khazali Canyon are all included in Operator 1 routes longer than three hours.

SITE	DISTANCE	TIME (HR)	PRICE PER VEHICLE
Operator 1 Routes			
Lawrence's Spring	14km	1	JD25
Khazali Canyon & Little Rock Bridge	30km	2	JD35
Sunset sites of Rum	35km	2½	JD44
Red Dunes	40km	3½	JD51
Lawrence's House	45km	3½	JD59
Umm Fruth Rock Bridge	50km	4	JD67
Burdah Rock Bridge	60km	5	JD75
Burdah Canyon	65km	8	JD80
Operator 2 Routes			
Alameleh inscriptions	15km	1	JD25
Siq Umm Tawaqi	18km	2	JD35
Sunset sites of Diseh	20km	2½	JD44
Barrah Canyon	49km	3	JD51
Burdah Rock Bridge	50km	4	JD67
Full-day tour	60km	8	JD80

novices should not underestimate the challenge of riding high-spirited Arab horses in open country.

★Rum Horses HORSE RIDING

(☎07 9580 2108; rumhorses@yahoo.co.uk; from per hr JD25) The highly recommended and long-established Rum Horses is the best horse-trekking agency in the region. The owner, Atallah Swillheen, trained and qualified in horse management and endurance racing in Europe, and currently stables 11 horses. Riders must be experienced – beginners aren't catered for. As well as short rides, fully supported multiday treks can also be arranged, from around JD130 per day.

The stables are located on the approach road to the Wadi Rum visitor centre, about 10km from the Desert Highway.

Hiking

There are many wonderful places to explore on foot, and you can walk to several of the main sights. Always register your route at the visitor centre before embarking.

Makharas Canyon Hike HIKING

This worthwhile canyon hike includes open vistas, canyon hiking and grand dune views. It begins at the visitor centre (p220). It's a moderate, unguided hike that should take about 2½ hours return.

Hike southeast across the plain towards the Seven Pillars of Wisdom and then head up Makharas Canyon (take the left-hand wadi at the branch). The wadi narrows after about an hour from the visitor centre and then emerges onto a patch of gorgeous red sand with grand views of Jebel Barrah and Umm Nfoos to the east. From here, cut north over the sand dunes and plod around the northern tip of Jebel Umm Al Ishrin to return to the Seven Pillars of Wisdom.

Jebel Rum Round Trip HIKING

This route offers stunning 'big country' scenery and begins at Rum village. Pass Lawrence's Spring and Ain Abu Aineh and circumambulate the southern half of Jebel Rum. It's a strenuous hike that will take about eight hours; a guide is recommended.

Jebel Umm Adaami Ascent HIKING

This route scales Jebel Umm Adaami (1832m), Jordan's highest peak on the rarely visited southern border with Saudi Arabia. It starts at Wadi Saabet, a 45-minute 4WD trip from the visitor centre. It should take about two hours return and is moderately difficult. You'll need a guide.

WADI RUM ITINERARY BUILDING

Even with only a few hours to spend, you can enjoy some of what Wadi Rum has to offer. Below are some suggestions for what you can do in a given time under your own steam. Obviously, the longer you stay, the more your eyes (and heart) open to the desert.

WITH THIS TIME...	YOU CAN GO THIS FAR...	AND DO THIS MUCH...
En route to elsewhere	Visitor Centre	Have a panoramic view of Wadi Rum (lit up magnificently at sunset).
1hr	Visitor Centre	Enjoy a leisurely lunch overlooking Wadi Rum and then visit the museum.
2hr	Rum Village	Walk through Wadi Rum on the tarmac road (7km) as far as Rum village, snack at the Rest House then get a lift back to the Visitor Centre.
3hr	Lawrence's Spring	Take a ride to Rum village and hike through the sand to the Nabataean Temple and Lawrence's Spring.
Half day	Al Hasany Dunes	Time your hike from Rum village to the sands to coincide with sunset.
Overnight	Desert Camp	Book your accommodation at a Wadi Rum camp through the visitor centre (4WD transport included) or pay extra to ride there by camel.
2 days	Wadi Rum & Diseh Area	Choose a Wadi Rum camp near Barrah Canyon and then hike through the canyon (5km) to a Diseh camp for the following night.

The hour-long uphill hike is marked by cairns and offers sweeping views of Wadi Rum to the north and Saudi Arabia to the south and it can be unnerving in parts if you don't have a head for heights. On the way back, stop off at the rock carvings of nearby Siq Al Barid, a lovely spot for a picnic.

Scrambling

Scrambling lies somewhere between hiking and climbing. No technical skills are required, but you may have to pull yourself up short rock faces. Local climbing operator Shabab Sahra also offers scrambling tours.

Burdah Rock Bridge Ascent SCRAMBLING
This popular but strenuous scramble leads to the top of the bridge and fine views. There's nothing technical involved, but you'll need a guide to find the route and a head for heights on one spot just before the bridge. To continue beyond the bridge, you'll need ropes and some climbing skills. The hike should take about two hours return.

Rakhabat Canyon SCRAMBLING
With a local guide or a copy of Di Taylor and Tony Howard's *Walking in Jordan*, you can navigate the labyrinthine siqs of Rakhabat Canyon for an exciting half-day trip through the heart of Jebel Umm Al Ishrin. The route starts at the western mouth of the canyon, just by Rum village.

At the far (eastern) end of the canyon you can hike across the valley to the Anfaishiyya inscriptions and then return to Rum village via the southern point of Jebel Umm Al Ishrin, with a possible detour to Ain Abu Aineh en route. Alternatively, if you have abseiling (rappelling) experience, you can head west through the mountain ridge along the Kharazeh Canyon for a great loop route.

Rock Climbing

Wadi Rum offers some challenging rock climbing (up to Grade 8). Although the Bedouin have been climbing in the area for centuries, climbing as a modern sport is still relatively undeveloped. That said, there are now several accredited climbing guides, most of whom have been trained in the UK. Costs start at around JD200 for one to two days' climbing.

Guides often suggest Jebel Rum for less experienced climbers: minimal gear is needed and it's close to the Rest House. Another popular climbing location is Jebel Barrah.

Quad Biking

Bait Ali Lodge (p219) rents out quad bikes (ATVs), along with maps of possible routes in the dry mudflats north of the camp and outside the Wadi Rum Protected Area. Prices are JD45 per hour.

Other Activities

Royal Aero Sports Club of Jordan BALLOONING
(☎03 205 8052; www.rascj.com) For a magnificent eagle's eye view of Wadi Rum, take to the air by balloon (JD140 per person for a minimum of two people). Trips take a minimum of two hours and are dependent on the weather. Bait Ali Lodge (p219) acts as the local facilitator for this company, and the easiest way to book is through the lodge.

Tours

If you want to combine a tour of Wadi Rum with camping in the desert, it's best to use a local guiding company, which will be able to provide you with a guide and vehicle as well as accommodation – whether that's in a permanent tented camp or a simple night under the stars.

Expect to pay around JD70 per person per day (including transport, food and entrance fee), which can include an overnight stay in the desert (JD25 for facilities and breakfast).

Note that some tours (particularly those sold in Amman, Wadi Musa or Aqaba) overnight at Diseh and do not even enter the main protected area of Wadi Rum. Diseh has some good camps in beautiful scenery, but it is not part of the reserve area so you should be clear about what the tour entails to avoid disappointment.

★Shabab Sahra ADVENTURE
(☎07 7697 6356, 07 7724 7899; www.shababsahra.com; climbing JD50-70, overnight camping JD20) Wadi Rum's only climbing outfit with internationally trained and accredited guides. The guides are all from the Rum area so have excellent knowledge of the best climbing and scrambling areas, and offer packages for everyone from beginners to the highly experienced. Keen attention is paid to equipment maintenance and climber safety. Prices vary according to the number of climbers.

Shabab Sahra has created a handful of bolted climbing routes near Rum village, and offers overnight camping to access more remote climbing and scrambling areas.

★Rum Stars OUTDOORS
(☎07 9512 7025; www.rumstars.com) Camel rides, 4WD trips, hiking and scrambling, led by the erudite Ahmed Ogla Al Zalabey, who was born in a tent near the Rum Stars campsite.

Wadi Rum Nomads OUTDOORS
(www.wadirumnomads.com) Run by the personable Fawaz Mohammad Al Zalabieh, offering hiking, 4WD and camel tours.

Rahayeb Desert Camp Activities OUTDOORS
(☎07 9690 9030; www.rahayebdc.com; per person from JD50) Brush up on your desert skills by being a 'Bedouin for a Day'. This camp arranges a day with a local family, sampling bread and coffee and learning how to milk sheep, goats and camels. It's harder than it looks and, unless you're a dairy farmer, is likely to elicit guffaws of laughter from your expert hosts.

Animal print tracking, stargazing and Bedouin cooking lessons are also on offer.

Mohammed Mutlak OUTDOORS
(☎07 7742 4837; www.wadirum.org; half board in tent per person JD30) Hiking, jeep and camel tours, with a campsite near the merging of red and white sand dunes.

Bedouin Lifestyle OUTDOORS
(☎07 7913 1803; www.bedouinlifestyle.com) Run by Atalla Ablawi, offering tented camps, hiking and camel and jeep tours.

Bedouin Adventures OUTDOORS
(☎Ahmed 07 9512 7025; www.bedouinadventures.com) Hiking, scrambling, camel trekking and three- to seven-night camping trips.

Bedouin Roads OUTDOORS
(☎07 9589 9723; www.bedouinroads.com) Well-respected adventure guide with many years of experience, with camel, jeep and hiking tours, as well as family itineraries.

Sleeping

Campsites are the order of the day around Wadi Rum. Camping can range from a goat-hair blanket under the stars at an isolated Bedouin camp to a luxury air-conditioned pod. You can even pitch your own tent in designated areas (enquire about locations at the visitor centre). Despite the online marketing literature, the camps all offer a very similar experience with a similar level of comfort and activities.

The sky's the limit for those who stay in one of the Bedouin camps in Wadi Rum, and this is definitely the best way to experience

CAMEL TREKS AROUND WADI RUM

Camel routes are sorted into two circuits for operational purposes. Camel excursions normally begin from Rum village and distances are measured from the Rest House. Prices rise with the price of fodder, and the routes on offer change from time to time.

SITE	DISTANCE	TIME	PRICE
From Rum village			
Nabataean Temple	1km	30min	JD5
Lawrence's Spring	6km	2hr	JD10
Khazali Canyon	14km	4hr	JD20
Sunset sites	18km	5hr	JD25
Red Dunes	25km	5hr	JD20
Burdah Rock Bridge	40km	Overnight	JD60
Full-day tour	Unlimited	8hr	JD30
Luggage camel		8hr	JD30
From Alameleh			
Short trip	2km	1hr	JD10
Sunset sites	8km	2hr	JD15
Siq Lawrence	9km	3hr	JD20
Full-day tour	Unlimited	Overnight	JD60
Luggage camel		8hr	JD30
Sunset sites	14km	4hr	JD25

the desert. Unfurl your mat under the stars and let singing youths, together with the snorts of camels and the whistle of mint tea heating over the fire, lull you to sleep.

The Bedouin camps all conform to certain standards and are checked regularly. There are two types of camps – permanent (which usually have toilet-shower blocks and operate year-round) and temporary (used only occasionally by Bedouin groups or tourists). The camps are only permitted in certain areas and these fall either within Wadi Rum or within neighbouring Diseh. The Wadi Rum camps are best booked through the visitor centre or through local guide operators, either in advance (especially if you want to stay at a particular camp) or on arrival.

Accommodation in temporary camps is generally a mattress under the stars or a small two-person tent with a sewn-in ground sheet. Accommodation in permanent camps is in Rum tourist tents. These are tall enough to walk into and are made of goat-hair or other local fabric. The tents, which are like small cabins, usually come with a camp bed, mattress and linen.

One or two camps offer en-suite toilets attached to a larger version of the typical Rum tourist tent. These are probably the best bet if travelling with small children. There are also a couple of luxury camps with air-conditioned tents.

The price of accommodation in the standard permanent camp, including food, tents and bedding, is generally around JD25 per person per night and often includes transport by 4WD to the camp if you don't visit anywhere en route.

Camps advertising half board generally provide a barbecue supper with salads and Arabic bread, coffee or tea, plus breakfast. For groups staying in a temporary camp, there is an additional charge for the transportation of camping items to the campsite each day. If you have your own sleeping bag, tent and food, all you should have to pay is the cost of your four-wheeled or four-legged transport.

Tour operators (p217) run their own camps scattered around the desert, all offering similar services in similarly beautiful parts of the desert – it is hard to recommend one over another.

★ Bait Ali Lodge CAMPGROUND $$
(☎07 9925 7222, 07 9554 8133; www.baitali.com; tent per person from s/d JD35/70, cabin from s/d JD53/84, deluxe chalet s/d JD100/137; 📶 🏊) If you want to stay in the desert but are not wild about roughing it, Bait Ali is a recommended compromise. Tucked behind a hill, with a fine view of the wilderness, this eco-friendly camp is clearly signposted just off the road, 15km from the Desert Highway and 9km before the Wadi Rum visitor centre.

Accommodation is in comfortable air-conditioned chalets, twin-bed cabins or in army tents with a shared shower block, and facilities include swimming pool, restaurant with nightly barbecue produced from an open *zerb* (an oven buried in the sand), a circular meeting hall with a central fire, a bar and a comfortable, cushion-filled Bedouin tent that add an Arabian Nights atmosphere to the camp. The chef prepares delicious local, unleavened bread over a hot stone.

You can pitch your own tent (JD10) or park a camper van (JD10) and use the shower block. Advice is available on quad-bike rides, hikes, ballooning, skydiving (February and March) and other activities in the local area. The hike around Lion Mountain (12km, three hours) is particularly recommended.

Wadi Rum Night Luxury Camp TENTED CAMP $$$
(☎03 215 7070; www.wadirumnight.com; tent with half board JD120-160) The tents here look like nothing on earth, rather as if they've just beamed down from Mars to the base of a Wadi Rum cliff face. Surreal silvery white inflated globes have their own airlocks to gain access; inside bed and bean bags plus an en suite add to the rather dislocating sensation.

Shade covers come off the see-through roof at night to let you enjoy the stars, though the plastic membrane and air-con shield you from enjoying the desert breeze. Instead, relax on your decking or in the more traditionally styled dining tent. The camp also has regular tents, covered in Bedouin goat wool but still containing air-con, a large bed and bathroom.

Eating

There are limited eating options in Wadi Rum. The small grocery stores along the main road through Rum village have basic supplies and mineral water. The area around Diseh has some of the cleanest aquifer water in Jordan. While out in the desert you may be lucky enough to try a *zerb*.

Rest House BUFFET $$
(breakfast JD5, lunch JD12, dinner buffet JD12; ⏰8am-6pm) Dining here is open-air and buffet-style, though if tourist numbers are

low (at hotter times of the year, for example), selections are restricted to what's in stock for the à la carte menu. Late afternoon with food and a cold drink while watching the sun's rays light up Jebel Umm Al Ishrin is the perfect way to finish the day.

Rum Gate Restaurant BUFFET $$
(☎03 201 5995; Wadi Rum visitor centre; snacks JD5, buffet lunch JD12; ⊙8am-5pm;) The buffet at this restaurant at the visitor centre is popular. Outside lunchtime, the restaurant is a meeting place for guides, weary hikers and independent travellers who congregate over a tea and a chicken sandwich.

☆ Entertainment

Film Bus CINEMA
(www.film.jo; JD7) Jordan's Royal Film Commission has been piloting cinema under the stars in Wadi Rum, showing films connected to the area. If you ever wanted to see *Lawrence of Arabia* in situ (or *The Martian* – also filmed in Wadi Rum), this is for you. The open-air screenings are preceded by short films made by local children – part of the RFC's outreach work.

Schedules or locations weren't fixed during research, but details and tickets should be available at the visitor centre.

Shopping

Visitor Centre ARTS & CRAFTS
(☎03 203 2918; ⊙8am-5pm) This is a good place to look for local souvenirs. Most items are made by local women to whom most of the profits are returned. It's possible to visit the workshop in Rum village (closed Friday and Saturday) – ask for directions at the Rest House. There are also ceramics, textiles and Bedouin goat-hair rugs on sale.

ℹ Information

If you are camping (including at the Rest House), bring along a torch (flashlight), a book to read and a padlock (many tents are lockable).

The Bedouin are a conservative people, so dress appropriately. Long shorts and sleeveless T-shirts for men and women are just about acceptable around the Rest House, but baggy trousers/skirts and modest shirts/blouses will save you sunburn and earn you respect from the Bedouin, especially in the desert.

The **visitor centre** (☎03 209 0600; www.wadirum.jo; ⊙7am-7pm) is situated at the entry to the protected area, about 30km east of the Desert Highway and 7km north of Rum village. This is where you buy your entry ticket, book a 4WD or camel excursion, organise accommodation at a camp and book a guide. There are no ATMs or credit card payment facilities in Wadi Rum, nor is there a petrol station. There is a restaurant, craft shops, an excellent museum, clean toilets and parking area. You can also ask to see a 10-minute film on some of the highlights of Wadi Rum, shown in the purpose-built cinema.

ℹ Getting There & Away

BUS

There's at least one minibus a day to Aqaba (JD3, one hour) at around 7am. A second sometimes runs a little later in the morning, but check with your camp operator first. To Wadi Musa (JD7, 1½ hours), there is a fairly reliable daily minibus at 8.30am. Check current departure times at the visitor centre, Rest House or camp operator when you arrive in Wadi Rum.

For Ma'an, Karak or Amman, the minibuses to either Aqaba or Wadi Musa can drop you off at the Ar Rashidiyya crossroads with the Desert Highway (JD2, 20 minutes), where it is easy to hail onward transport.

A JETT bus link from Amman was rumoured to be starting in February 2018. It's expected to cost JD10 to JD12. Check JETT's website for the latest (www.jett.com.jo).

CAR

The most convenient way to get to Wadi Rum as an independent traveller is by car. You can hire a car in Aqaba, and if you intend to continue to Petra, you are well advised to keep it for the round trip. This will save considerable time and frustration trying to fathom the limited public transport.

Off-road driving and navigation in the desert's sandy conditions can be extremely dangerous and isn't recommended unless you have prior knowledge of desert driving and a well-maintained 4WD. Even then, it's strongly recommended to take a local guide from the visitor centre.

Note that unless you book a 4WD excursion to Wadi Rum through the visitor centre, you can't guarantee that the vehicle (with or without a driver) is insured.

HITCHING

Hitching is never entirely safe, and we don't recommend it. Travellers who hitch should understand that they are taking a small but potentially serious risk. You'll see some travellers follow local custom and hitch from the main road to the visitor centre.

TAXI

Occasionally taxis hang around the visitor centre (and very occasionally the Rest House) waiting for a fare back to wherever they came from –

NAVIGATING WADI RUM

Highway to Visitor Centre

Wadi Rum is accessed from a tarmac road off the main Desert Highway, an hour's drive from Aqaba. The road is flanked at first by fields of watermelons, but shortly after crossing the Hejaz railway line the splendid scenery begins, becoming increasingly spectacular as you reach the mouth of Wadi Rum. The road passes a police post and the junction for the small village of Diseh and continues towards the visitor centre. This is where all visitors to Wadi Rum must report before venturing further into the valley.

Even if you don't have time to spend a whole day at Wadi Rum, it is worth coming as far as the visitor centre. From this attractive complex, you can see Lawrence's Seven Pillars of Wisdom (p213; a striking rock formation at the head of the valley), visit the museum, watch a short film about the desert, have lunch and get an idea of what Rum is all about. This is also where you pay the admission fee if you want to proceed further into the valley.

Visitor Centre to Rum Village

Beyond the visitor centre, the road is initially lined by a battered set of 4WDs, accompanied by their Bedouin drivers awaiting the next fare in rotation. The tarmac road continues for 7km to the village of Rum. The village, wedged between the towering dome-capped pillars of Wadi Rum, has a scruffy transient feel – exactly the sort of place you'd expect a nomadic people to build – and spurs you on to want to explore the desert proper.

If you don't have much time or can't afford one of the 4WD tours, consider at least reaching the village (you can drive in your own car or walk after paying the entrance fee). In the village, there's a pleasant Rest House with an outside terrace and basic camping facilities.

Rum Village to the Desert Interior

To penetrate the desert beyond the village of Rum, you must either have organised a 4WD trip from the visitor centre, booked a camel or be prepared for an exhausting hike through soft sand. With your own 4WD, you can make your own way in, provided you know how to drive and navigate off-road in sand.

Beyond the village of Rum, the tarmac runs out and numerous tracks take over, slithering through the soft sand of Wadi Rum to an open area of converging valleys. From here, tracks lead to various points of interest such as rock bridges, desert mushrooms and yardangs. Most 4WD and camel tours make a circular route through the intersecting wadis of the area before returning to the visitor centre.

Outside this heavily visited area is a portion of desert known as the **Wilderness Area**. It is forbidden to take a 4WD into this protected zone but you can hike there with a guide.

For overnight stays, there are several Bedouin campsites with rudimentary facilities within Wadi Rum and the neighbouring Diseh area, on the rim of the reserve.

Books & Maps

If you are planning any hikes and scrambles, bring a detailed guidebook and map; if you plan to do some serious hiking and rock climbing, it's essential to organise a guide in advance.

British climber Tony Howard has spent a lot of time exploring Wadi Rum, and has co-written with Di Taylor the excellent and detailed *Treks & Climbs in Wadi Rum, Jordan* and a pocket-sized version called *Walks & Scrambles in Wadi Rum*. Treks and climbs around Wadi Rum are also mentioned in Howard and Taylor's *Walking in Jordan*. Buy these books before arriving in Wadi Rum.

The free Wadi Rum brochure has a map showing the major sites and is available from the visitor centre. The 1997 *Map of Rum* is contoured and detailed for a small section of northern Wadi Rum (ie around Rum village). The most detailed and informative map is *Wadi Rum Tourist Plan*, published by International Traditional Services Corp, but it's not widely available.

DESERT DANGERS

Before striking out alone, it's worth taking precautions against the following:

- Temperatures (cold as well as hot) can be extreme in midsummer (May to September) and midwinter (January).
- It's easy to get disoriented amid the craggy peaks and maps are often inaccurate.
- Passing traffic is rare.
- Natural water supplies are not common and sometimes undrinkable.
- Walking in sand is particularly exhausting.

normally Aqaba, Wadi Musa or Ma'an. It costs JD20 to Aqaba, and JD35 to Wadi Musa (Petra). A taxi jeep from Rum village to the Ar Rashidiyya crossroads with the Desert Highway costs around JD10. Some camps organise onward transport at competitive rates for their guests.

Diseh الديسة

Recent years have seen the marketing of Diseh as 'Wadi Rum 2'. A lively village, Diseh is outside the Wadi Rum Protected Area. It has a selection of good formalised accommodation options, and some interesting desert landmarks, including Nabataean and Roman dams, artificial rock bridges, rock carvings and inscriptions. Some budget operators claim the area is Wadi Rum, but for the truly spectacular landscapes, you'll need to head into the protected area.

Sleeping & Eating

A number of camps near Diseh are popular and are mostly wrapped around a large hill with the first few camps adjacent to each other and accessible by 2WD (unless there's been heavy rain). They all offer traditional sitting areas with cushions and beds either in cramped individual tents or larger partitioned Bedouin tents. If you are looking for a quieter, more tranquil experience, the camps located in more isolated parts of the desert and requiring 4WD for access are a better bet – to avoid disappointment, make sure you check on the location before you book.

Zawaideh Desert Camp CAMPGROUND **$**
(☎07 9584 0664; zawaideh_camp@yahoo.com; Diseh; half board per person JD20) Close to the road and accessible by car, this basic camp is in the undercliff of the escarpment, on the edge of a wide plain. It has a reputation for providing a sociable experience around the lively campfire and is popular with Jordanians from the city looking to reconnect with the desert.

Rahayeb Camp CAMPGROUND **$$**
(☎07 9690 9030; www.rahayebdc.com; Diseh; half board per person JD35, deluxe tents JD60) Wedged into a secluded bend of the rocks, well away from the other Diseh camps, this is a great establishment. Two professional chefs rustle up traditional fare in the *zerb* oven while guests lounge under the stars around a central fireplace. Deluxe tents are upmarket versions of the typical Rum tourist tent, with their own bathrooms.

The toilet and shower blocks are spotless.

Captain's Camp CAMPGROUND **$$**
(☎07 9551 0432, 03 201 6905; captains@jo.com.jo; Diseh; half board s/d JD45/85) A well-run midrange camp with hot showers, lots of snug seating areas and good buffets, this camp is popular with tour groups, especially as it's easily accessible from the road. The camp also offers a romantic tent for two (JD90 per person) in the middle of the desert, with a candlelit supper delivered to the tent flaps.

Sun City Camp TENTED CAMP **$$$**
(☎07 9566 6673; www.suncitycamp.com; near Diseh; tent JD100, ste tent JD100-200, dome JD210) Diseh's move into the luxury Wadi Rum market offers a variety of tented options. The cheapest are well set-up tents, with air-con and bathrooms; larger ones are divided into suite rooms with their own decking for families. More extravagant by far are the futuristic geodesic domes, completely self-contained right down to the mini-bar.

For total relaxation, the camp has its own hatha yoga instructor. All rates are half board; lunches can be arranged.

THE DESERT HIGHWAY

The Desert Highway, which follows the legendary tracks of the Hejaz Railway and a water pipeline, connects Aqaba in the south of Jordan with Damascus in Syria. The section between Amman and Aqaba is a road of very limited interest, poorly maintained and usually bearing heavy traffic. As such, it hardly ranks as one of Jordan's highlights. It is, however, the shortest route between Amman and southern Jordan and it's likely that you'll end up using the highway in one direction or another. This is the only road in Jordan that actually looks like a highway, with dual carriageway for most of its length and lighting at main intersections.

There are very few places to sleep or eat along the Desert highway but if you make it to Ma'an, you may as well continue on to Wadi Musa, Wadi Rum or Aqaba, all of which are well served with facilities for visitors.

Humaiyma الحميمة

Pressed up against the cliffs on the opposite side of the highway to Wadi Rum is the seldom-visited Bedouin district of Humaiyma. Curious visitors who notice the brown sign off the main Aqaba Highway and struggle along the badly potholed access road are rewarded with a surprisingly large archaeological site.

The largely Nabataean site includes 27km of covered aqueducts, some of which are visible today; they are evidence of the Nabataean attitude towards water that it could be brought in channels from the mountains or held in reservoirs on the plains. King Aretas III built Humaiyma around 80 BCE as a trading post designed, according to archaeologists, to help settle nomadic tribes. His efforts, judging by the nomads camping nearby some 2000 years later, were not wholly successful. Trajan's army built a fort here in AD 106, and settlement continued into the Byzantine and early Islamic periods. In AD 750 the site was eventually abandoned. There is a small visitor centre, but it was unstaffed at the time of writing, and there was no legible information at the site.

Ma'an معان

☎03 / POP 41,500

With little of specific interest to visitors, Ma'an, a useful transport junction, is one of the larger towns in southern Jordan. It has fulfilled this function for centuries as it lies on the main pilgrimage route from Jordan and Syria to Mecca in Saudi Arabia. The main north–south thoroughfare is King Hussein St, centred somewhere around the mosque and the communication tower. To get here from the bus station, head two blocks west and then one block north (a five-minute walk) to the southern end of King Hussein St, where it meets Palestine St.

There's nowhere to stay in town but there are a few grill and chicken restaurants along King Hussein St if you get hungry waiting for the bus.

Getting There & Away

If you can't get a direct bus to where you want to go in Jordan, there's a good chance that you will find a connection in Ma'an.

The station for buses, minibuses and service taxis is a five-minute walk southeast of the centre. Departures from Ma'an start to peter-out around 2pm and stop completely around 5pm.

There are regular minibuses (JD3.500, three hours) and less frequent service taxis (JD8, three hours) to/from Amman's South Bus Station (Wihdat). To Aqaba, minibuses (JD3, 90 minutes) and service taxis (JD3) are also frequent. For Wadi Rum, take an Aqaba-bound minibus to the junction at Ar Rashidiyya (JD2) and then take a minibus. For Petra, minibuses to Wadi Musa (JD2, 45 minutes) leave fairly frequently when full and stop briefly at the university en route. To Karak, there are occasional service taxis (JD3, two hours) and three minibuses a day, via Tafila (JD2.500).

A chartered taxi to Petra/Wadi Musa costs around JD20, and JD35 to Aqaba.

Qatrana القطرانة

One of the few towns along the Desert Hwy is Qatrana, a couple of kilometres north of the turn-off to Karak and a former stop on the pilgrim road between Damascus and Mecca. The only reason to stop here (if you have your own transport) is to have a quick look at Qatrana Castle FREE, built in 1531 by the Ottomans. It has been nicely restored, but there are no explanatory boards.

Azraq & the Eastern Desert Highway
الازرق & الطريق الصحراوي الشرقي

Includes ➡

Best Castles

- Qasr Al Azraq (p230)
- Qusayr Amra (p233)
- Qasr Kharana (p235)
- Umm Al Jimal (p236)

Best Views

- Qasr Burqu (p241)
- Qasr Usaykim (p240)
- Qasr 'Uweinid (p231)
- Azraq Wetland Reserve (p229)

Why Go?

Imagine a space so desolate that not even a boulder or a bush troubles the 360-degree horizon. Now add a carpet of ancient black volcanic rock, unnavigable even by camels. And finally, factor in a ravaging heat so overpowering in the summer that the ground pulses before your eyes and mirages appear in the distance. Welcome to the Eastern Desert!

Look closer and there are treasures to be found here. At Azraq, there are swaying oasis reeds of an improbable wetland beloved of migratory birds. At Shaumari, you can go on safari to spot oryx, returned from the brink of extinction. Throughout the region, a string of intriguing ruined forts, hunting lodges and caravanserai (large merchant's inn enclosing a courtyard, providing accommodation and a marketplace), collectively known as the 'desert castles', wait to be discovered by the intrepid. There's a lot more to Jordan's far east than first meets the eye.

When to Go

- The best time to visit the remote plains of eastern Jordan is October to mid-April when temperate weather means getting stuck at a remote desert castle is merely inconvenient, not life-threatening.
- With proper planning (including reliable transport, sufficient water supplies and a hat), May is another good time to visit. At this time, large numbers of raptors soar above the shimmering heat haze on their annual migration.
- In winter, dust devils spiral on the plains as birds stop over in the Azraq wetlands en route between Europe and sub-Saharan Africa.

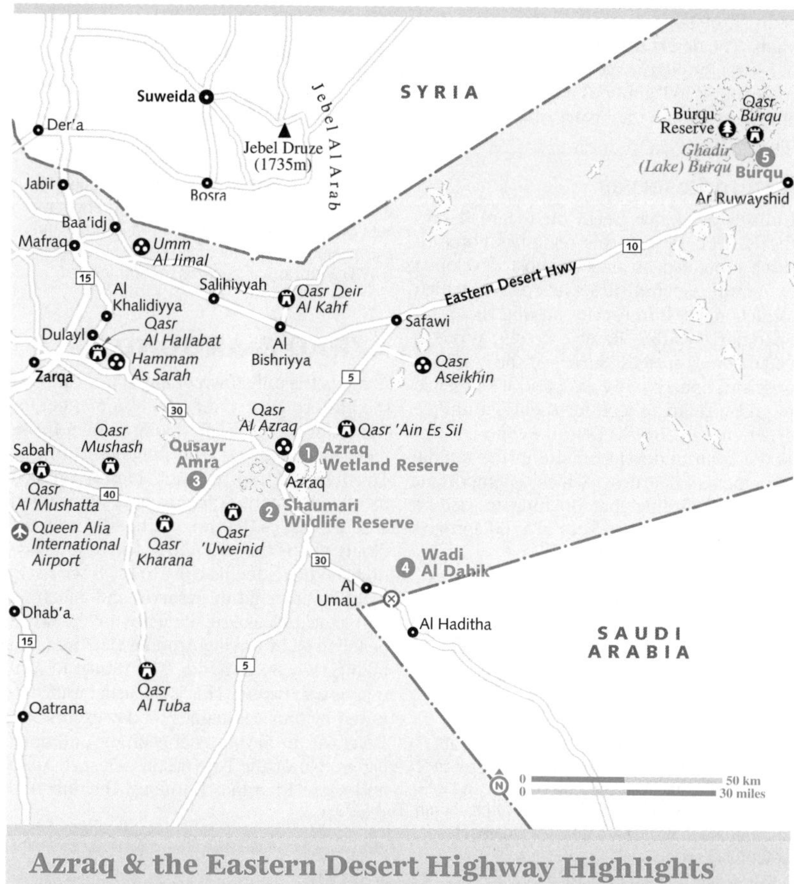

Azraq & the Eastern Desert Highway Highlights

1. **Azraq Wetland Reserve** (p229) Hunkering down in a bird hide and watching the drama of a waterhole unfold.
2. **Shaumari Wildlife Reserve** (p229) Going on safari to spot Arabian oryx, slowly being reintroduced to the area after being hunted to extinction.
3. **Qusayr Amra** (p233) Admiring the risqué frescoes in the bathhouse at this Unesco World Heritage Site.
4. **Wadi Al Dahik** (p240) Hiking through dizzyingly white canyons close to the Saudi border.
5. **Burqu** (p240) Using your off-road driving skills to find an ecotourism resort in the wilderness.

History

A string of ruined pavilions, caravanserai hunting lodges and forts peppers the deserts of eastern Jordan and is one of the country's most surreal attractions. Dating back to the Umayyads (AD 661–750) in the earliest years of Islam, the desert castles were once richly decorated with mosaics, frescoes, marble, plaster and painted stucco, providing oases of rest and refreshment in the harsh and inhospitable desert. Here, the elite could pursue their pastimes of hawking, hunting and horse racing during the day, while evenings were spent in wild festivities with wine, poetry and song.

The early Arab rulers were still Bedouin at heart, and their love of the desert may have led them to build these pleasure palaces, which once teemed with orchards and wild game. Or they may have come to avoid epidemics in the big cities, or to maintain links with, and power over, the Bedouin – the bedrock of their support in the conquered lands. The desert castles also served as staging posts for pilgrimages to Mecca and along trade routes to Damascus and Baghdad; never underestimate the luxury of a hot bath in the desert!

Nature Reserves

Unlikely as it may seem on the road into the Eastern Desert, this region is home to three protected areas. The most developed is Azraq Wetland Reserve (p229), which attracts many bird species around the oasis. Shaumari Wildlife Reserve (p229) protects endangered species such as the Arabian oryx and onager (wild ass), and it's possible to take a safari to look for them – a unique experience in Jordan. **Burqu Proposed Reserve** is an undeveloped site in the middle of remote wilderness, which is important for desert birdlife, but opening to visitors in 2018 under the auspices of Wild Jordan's Eastern Badia Trail.

Dangers & Annoyances

At the time of writing, the intensification of the civil war in Syria and the conflict in Iraq made straying too close to either border unwise. Take local advice (for example, through your consulate or from your hotel in Amman or Madaba) before venturing into this area. It is inadvisable to hitch or pick up hitchhikers along this route at present. Hitching is never entirely safe, and we don't recommend it. Travellers who hitch should understand that they are taking a small but potentially serious risk.

The desert doesn't take prisoners. At any time of year, but particularly in the middle of summer, dehydration and the threat of heat exhaustion and heat stroke – a serious condition that requires immediate medical attention – are hazards of visiting remote desert locations. Minimise the risk by carrying and drinking plenty of water, wearing a hat, avoiding exertion in the middle of the day and planning an exit route if travelling by public transport. If driving off-road, be aware that you will have to be totally self-sufficient in the event of a puncture or mechanical failure.

During the spring, flies and mosquitoes are an annoyance. Bring repellent if visiting the oases.

Getting There & Away

The easiest point of entry to the region is Amman and the towns of Zarqa and Mafraj. Desolate Hwy 5 from the south also leads into the area via Azraq. Trucks and some buses use the border crossing at Al Umau with Saudi Arabia.

Getting Around

Although minimal and intermittent minibuses ply the route to Azraq from Amman, it is very difficult to travel around this region by public transport, which is unreliable. A better option is to take a tour from the capital, covering the main desert castles in a day trip. An even better bet is to hire a car for two days, which will allow for a stopover in Azraq. To make a comprehensive tour of the region, including Umm Al Jimal and Burqu along the remote Eastern Desert Highway, a 4WD with camping gear is recommended.

AZRAQ & AROUND

Azraq is the only town of any significance in the Eastern Desert and acts as a magnet for transcontinental traffic looking for refreshment and company after long desert drives. The name 'Azraq' is often loosely applied to all settlements directly east of Amman and the castles that are scattered across the desert plains there. Some of the best attractions of the region lie close to the town itself, including two nature reserves and a fort.

A logical, clockwise sequence for sights can be followed by leaving Amman via Zarqa and taking Hwy 30 to Azraq. The return to Amman is via Hwy 40. This is the usual route followed by tour companies on day excursions. Don't use up all your energy on the outbound leg as two of the best castles, Qusayr Amra and Qasr Kharana, lie along the inbound Hwy 40.

Zarqa الزرقاء

09 / POP 635,200 / ELEV 620M

The third-largest city in Jordan after Amman and Irbid, Zarqa is now virtually part of the continuous urban sprawl of northern Amman. There's not much to this gritty working-class city that merits anything more than a passing glance, but you may have to change buses here if you're trying to visit the Eastern Desert on public transport.

In Zarqa, there are two terminals for buses, minibuses and service taxis. Transport to/from the north bus station (Tabarbour) in Amman (JD1, 30 minutes) uses the new (Amman) station. From the old station in Zarqa, there is public transport to smaller villages in the region, such as Hallabat (for Qasr Al Hallabat and Hammam As Sarah) and Mafraq. Minibuses also leave intermittently for Azraq (JD1.500, 1½ hours). Minibuses shuttle between the two terminals in Zarqa every few minutes.

Hallabat الحلابات

The modest farming area of Hallabat is home to a fort of the same name and offers the first encounter with Umayyad architecture on the Desert Castle Loop.

Sights

Qasr Al Hallabat Fort CASTLE

(daylight hours) FREE With a fair proportion of masonry still standing, some beautifully restored archways and a desolate perch on the edge of the Eastern Desert, this fort is a good introduction to the history of the region. Hallabat once boasted elaborate baths, intricate frescoes and mosaics, a mosque and several reservoirs, and served as a focus for a thriving farming community. Restoration of a substantial part of the site under Spanish direction has restored an inkling of the castle's former stature.

As with all the castles in Jordan, it takes a bit of sleuthing to peel back the layers of history. In the case of Hallabat, you need only focus on three main eras – Roman, Byzantine and Umayyad.

Look first for a fine mosaic. This sits above a large central cistern and the ruins of the original fort. Built by the Romans during the reign of Emperor Caracalla (AD 198–217), the fort, like many in the region, was originally built as a defence against raiding desert tribes. As you survey the land from the castle hill, you can see why they picked this location, as it would have been easy to spot men on horseback darting across the rocky plain.

Now look for additions in basaltic rock, easily distinguished by its black colour. If you venture further into the Eastern Desert, you'll find this volcanic rock scattered across vast plains providing a ready supply of building materials. In the 6th century the fort was converted by the Byzantines into a monastery for a short period, using the basalt blocks to expand the Roman structure.

Lastly, admire the decorated finesse of limestone walls (distinguished by their white colour), carved niches, reassembled arches and an elaborate porch with pillars. This is the work of the Umayyads (AD 661–750) who revisited the structure under the reign of the hedonistic caliph Walid II and transformed the modest fort into an imposing three-storey complex with four large towers. Look for the remains of a large mosque with cusped arches, an agricultural enclosure fed by an elaborate irrigation system and the ruins of a village for palace servants that were included in the Umayyads' ambitious expansion project. Wondering where the baths are? You'll have to travel 3km east to see the remains of these, at Hammam As Sarah.

Hammam As Sarah RUINS

(daylight hours) FREE Part of the neighbouring fort complex in Hallabat, this hammam (bathhouse) has been extensively restored, revealing the underfloor piping system that was used to heat the bathing rooms. The hammam is located along the main road to Hallabat village, about 3km east of Qasr Al Hallabat and 5km from the main road. The minibus to Hallabat village drives past Hammam As Sarah and can drop you off on request. The site is unlocked – just push open the gate.

There might have been considerably more to see at this hammam and hunting lodge complex if locals hadn't taken a liking to the high-quality limestone blocks in the 1950s. It's hard to complain, though, as this kind of recycling has been traditional in the region since well before the Romans. Outside the main building is a well, nearly 20m deep, an elevated tank and the remains of a nearby mosque.

Information

The courtyard of the **visitor centre** (daylight hours) is adorned with reconstructed pillars and archways that give an idea of the decorative

TOURING THE DESERT CASTLES

Jumping on an organised tour of the desert castles from Amman makes a lot of sense, especially if you're short of time or on a tight budget. Tours can be arranged at the Palace, Farah and Cliff hotels in Amman, which charge about JD20 per person for a full-day trip with an hour at each site. You're unlikely to get a better deal by negotiating directly with the driver of a service taxi or private taxi in Amman, and regular taxi drivers are rarely keen on leaving the city. Tours by car (around JD45 for maximum of four people) can also be arranged from the Black Iris and Mariam hotels in Madaba.

UNICORNS OF THE DESERT

The last time the Arabian oryx was seen in the wild in Jordan was in 1920 when hunting drove this magnificent, straight-horned antelope to local extinction. In 1972 the last Arabian oryx was killed by hunters in Oman, which led officials to declare the oryx extinct in the wild. However, in a remarkable conservation effort, the nine oryx left in captivity (known now as the 'World Oryx Herd') were pooled together and taken to the Arizona Zoo for a captive breeding program.

In 1978, 11 oryx bred in Arizona were transported to Jordan in an effort to help re-establish the country's wild population. Under the auspices of the Royal Society for the Conservation of Nature (RSCN), the first calf, Dusha, was born at the Shaumari Wildlife Reserve (p229) the following year. Today, their numbers have risen to more than 200. Some have been released into the wild at Wadi Rum – a not altogether successful enterprise. The next step is to introduce oryx in other protected areas throughout the country.

The return of the oryx to Jordan was the occasion of great national pride, which prompts the question: what is it about this antelope that provokes such emotion? Perhaps it's the uncanny resemblance of a mature bull, with rapier-like antlers, to the mythical unicorn. This is not as far-fetched as it seems. The ancient Egyptians used to bind the antlers of young oryx so they would fuse into one. Seeing a white, summer-coated herd-bull level up to a rival in profile, it's easy to confuse fact with fiction.

details bestowed on Qasr Al Hallabat by the Umayyads. There is a small museum next door, but it is just as likely to be closed as open. Toilets are available here.

Arabic-speaking guides, most of whom were involved in the restoration work and are knowledgeable about the castle, are available at the gate. Even without a common language, they can point you towards details otherwise missed, and their enthusiasm for the project is infectious.

ℹ Getting There & Away

Close enough to Amman to be visited on a half-day excursion, Qasr Al Hallabat and Hammam As Sarah are located near the village of Hallabat and are one of the few sites in the Eastern Desert that can be easily reached by public transport. From Amman's north bus station, take a minibus to the new (Amman) station in Zarqa, another minibus to the old station in Zarqa, and another to Hallabat village. To get from here to Azraq by public transport, your best bet is to return to Zarqa.

If you're driving, the castle takes a bit of liberal navigating off Hwy 30 (it is at least signposted) and makes a good first stop on the Desert Castle Loop. It's a good hour's drive from here to Azraq, the main destination on the circuit.

Azraq الأزرق

☎05 / POP 15,750 / ELEV 510M

Azraq is the gateway to the Eastern Desert, which makes it all the more surprising that it's home to a small but important wetland reserve, where you can spot migrating water-birds. The area also hosts Shaumari, where you can go on safari to see the once locally extinct Arabian oryx, as well as having one of the best of the eastern castles, Qasr Al Azraq.

Azraq's shimmering lake and extensive wetlands were once famed throughout the entire region as both a refuge for wildlife and a beacon for pilgrims and caravans plying the trade routes between Baghdad and Jerusalem. Unfortunately, the draining of the wetlands has reduced the town's appeal; it is now perhaps more famous for the refugee camp on its outskirts, hosting those who have fled the Syrian civil war.

History

As the region's most important permanent body of water and as a source of malachite, Azraq has been settled since Neolithic times. The Romans, Mamluks and Ottomans each had turns controlling the area, and in 1917–18 the town served as a staging post for the soldiers of Faisal's Arab Revolt. Lawrence of Arabia spent the winter in the fort, using it as a temporary headquarters.

The town is home to two distinct communities. After WWI Druze refugees fleeing Syria settled in north Azraq, earning a living from salt production. South Azraq, meanwhile, was founded by Chechens fleeing Russian persecution, who eked out a living by farming and fishing on the shores of the oasis. Azraq Lodge is run by people from this community and the restaurant produces robust Chechen meals.

Influxes of Palestinian and Syrian immigrants diluted ethnic distinctions, and the virtual death of the oasis in the 1990s caused much of the local population to seek a living elsewhere. Though the wetlands are now being slowly restored, the region is more concerned with shoring up the new refugee camp. The prefabricated huts of Azraq Camp, which can be seen extending near the western approaches to the town, were built by the United Nations in 2014 to house Syrian refugees fleeing the conflict to the north. In mid-2017, more than 35,000 refugees were resident in the camp.

Sights

★Shaumari Wildlife Reserve WILDLIFE RESERVE

(Mahmiyyat Ash Shaumari; www.rscn.org.jo; JD4; ⌚8am-4pm) Established in 1975 by the Royal Society for the Conservation of Nature (RSCN), this 22 sq km reserve was created with the aim of reintroducing wildlife that has disappeared from the region, most notably the highly endangered Arabian oryx, Persian onagers (wild ass), Dorcas gazelles and houbara bustards. The reserve has recently undergone a radical overhaul to make it an excellent and singular Jordanian tourism experience.

The startlingly modernist visitor centre provides a mass of information on the area's ecosystems, as well as the biology of its most celebrated inhabitants. Enclosures allow you to get a good view of oryx, onagers, gazelles and bustards before leaving for the safari experience (JD20). You ride in special safari jeeps with raised seats, and the guides are fonts of knowledge on the flora and fauna, as well as being experts at picking out distant wildlife (onagers in particular are very skittish and require the provided binoculars to spot).

A special area is set aside for the oryx captive breeding program that has helped rescue the species from extinction. It's often possible to see calves. Near the entrance is a reserved aviary, which houses falcons that have been confiscated by rangers from Gulf Arabs who visit the region to illegally hunt. After rehabilitation the birds are reintroduced to the wild. Another bird likely to make a return to Shaumari soon is the ostrich, as the RSCN is currently looking at plans to reintroduce the species, which had been hunted to oblivion in the area.

The turning for Shaumari is well signposted, 7km from the Azraq T-junction, along the road to the Saudi border. A minimum of four people is required for the safari, which lasts up to three hours.

★Azraq Wetland Reserve NATURE RESERVE

(☎05 383 5017; JD2.500; ⌚9am-6pm Mar-Aug, to 4pm Sep-Feb) For several millennia, the Qa'al Azraq (Azraq Basin) comprised a huge area of mudflats, pools and marshlands, which led to the establishment of Azraq as one of the most important oasis towns in the Levant. Since the mass pumping of water to thirsty Amman, however, the wetlands have almost disappeared. Thankfully, the RSCN has worked to preserve and restore the remainder, and they remain a fascinating place to visit.

Although just 10% of the original wetlands remains, about 300 species of resident and migratory birds use the wetlands during their winter migration from Europe to Africa, including raptors, larks, warblers, finches, harriers, eagles, plovers and ducks. A few buffaloes also wallow in the marshy environs, and jackals and gerbils are occasionally spotted in the late evening. The best time to see birdlife is in winter (December to February) and early spring (March and April). Large flocks of raptors steadily arrive in May. Ultimately, however, bird populations are dependent on the water levels in the reserve, and as the water continues to be pumped out quicker than it is pumped in, the future of the oasis remains in jeopardy.

An environmental recovery project of this magnitude is certainly worth support, and the on-site visitor centre has well-documented exhibits detailing the history of the basin's demise and rebirth.

A 1.5km **Marsh Trail** through the reserve, which takes about 30 minutes to walk, gives an idea of the former beauty of the wetlands. The trail follows natural paths made by water buffalo, which still roam through the wetlands. Take a pair of binoculars and stop at the bird hide to spot ducks squabbling between the seasonal reed beds. A viewing hide overlooking the Shishan springs is worth noting: these springs once watered the entire wetlands, and the cooling sound of the wind amid thick reeds makes you forget how close the desert is.

In 2017 a project to restore a new basin (dubbed the Swiss Pond because of the source of the project's funding) began, pumping water back into the land. When we visited, hordes of tiny frogs were already massing on its banks; within a year it was expected to be packed with reeds and other marsh plants, and attracting birdlife again.

The Azraq Wetland Reserve is located 500m east of Azraq and is signposted off the main road.

★ **Qasr Al Azraq** CASTLE

(JD1, ticket also valid for Qusayr Amra & Qasr Kharana, free with Jordan Pass; ⌚daylight hours) On the edge of dusty Azraq, this imposing fort is where TE Lawrence and Sharif Hussein bin Ali based themselves in the winter of 1917–18 during the Arab Revolt against the Turks. Lawrence set up his quarters in the room above the southern entrance, while his loyal followers braved the elements in other areas of the fort. They were holed up here for several months in crowded conditions with little shelter from the intense cold – gaping holes in the roof were patched up with nothing but palm branches and clay.

Despite the hardships endured during his stay at Azraq, TE Lawrence writes fondly about the time spent with his men at arms. In the evenings everyone would assemble before a great fire in the open courtyard and break bread while swapping stories of war, peace and love. At the time, the castle also

AZRAQ: AN OASIS REBORN?

The Azraq Oasis and surrounding wetlands originally fanned out over 12,710 sq km, and was once regarded as the most important source of water in the region. Today, it is considered one of the region's largest ecological disasters. The diary of this catastrophe makes for tragic reading.

200,000 BCE Human settlement and herds of elephants, cheetahs, lions and hippos are evident around the Azraq Oasis.

8000 BCE Age of the 'fossil water' collected in Azraq.

1950 Around 3000 cu metres of water fills the wetlands per year.

1960s Extraction of fossil water from the wetlands to the expanding cities of Amman and Irbid begins.

1967 On 2 February, 347,000 birds are recorded in the wetlands.

1975 To supply Amman's water demands, twice as much water is pumped than is replenished.

1977 The Jordanian government signed an international wetlands protection treaty that led to the establishment of the Azraq Wetland Reserve.

1980 Only 10 cu metres per year of water (compared with 3000 cu metres in 1950) fills the wetlands, exacerbated by the sinking of private illegal wells for farming.

1991 The water table drops to more than 10m below the ground, and the wetlands dry up almost completely.

1994 Funding and commitment from the UN Development Program (UNDP), Jordanian government and RSCN tries to halt the pumping of water from the wetlands to urban centres.

Mid-1990s Over-pumping destroys the natural balance between the freshwater aquifer and the underground brine, resulting in brackish water unpalatable for wildlife.

1998 Species of killifish *(Aphanius sirhani)*, a small fish of only 4cm to 5cm in length and unique to Azraq, is brought to the edge of extinction.

2000 On 2 February, only 1200 birds are recorded in the wetlands.

2011 Around 1.5 million cu metres of fresh water is pumped back into the wetlands every year by the Jordanian Ministry of Water.

2015 Around 10% of the original wetlands is restored.

2017 Work begins on rehabilitation of the 'Swiss Pond', a new habitat adjacent to the restored wetlands.

commanded sweeping views of the nearby palm-fringed oasis at Azraq.

Constructed out of black basalt stone, Qasr Al Azraq was originally three storeys high. Some paving stones in the main entrance have small indentations, carved by former gatekeepers who played a board game using pebbles to pass the time. By the courtyard entrance, look for the carvings of animals and various inscriptions.

Comparatively little is known about the history of Qasr Al Azraq, and there's been little excavation and renovation. Greek and Latin inscriptions date earlier constructions on the site to around AD 300, coinciding with Roman occupation.

The fort was renovated by the Umayyad caliph Walid II, who used it for hunting and as a military base. Its present form dates to 1237 when it was fortified by the Ayyubids as a defence against the Crusaders. The Turks subsequently stationed a garrison here in the 16th century. In a turn of the tide in 1918, it was from this building that the Arab Revolt launched an attack on Damascus that proved successful in ousting the Turks from the region.

Above the entrance is **Lawrence's Room**, strategically overlooking the entry and offset with arrow slits for defence. Opposite the entrance, and just to the left, are the remains of an **altar**, built in the 3rd century AD by the Romans. In the middle of the courtyard is a small **mosque**, angled to face Mecca – it dates from the Ayyubid period (early 13th century) but was built on the ruins of a Byzantine church. In the northeast corner of the courtyard, a hole with stairs leads down to a **well**, full of water until about 20 years ago. In the northwest corner are the ruins of the **prison**.

The northern sections are residential areas with barely discernible ruins of a kitchen and dining room, and nearby storerooms and stables. The **tower** in the western wall is the most spectacular, and features a huge door made of a single massive slab of basalt. Lawrence describes in his book *Seven Pillars of Wisdom* how it 'went shut with a clang and crash that made tremble the west wall of the castle'.

The fort is situated on the edge of Azraq Ash Shomali (north Azraq), about 5km north of the Azraq T-junction. From the town centre, a taxi to the fort costs around JD2 (JD5 with a one-hour wait) – if you can persuade a taxi to bother with such a small commission.

Qasr 'Uweinid CASTLE

(24hr) FREE If you can find this little scrap of history near the Shaumari Wildlife Reserve, you deserve a medal! Once a robust and practical structure, built by the Romans in the 3rd century AD to protect the source of Wadi As Sirhan (now in Saudi Arabia), this fort was abandoned less than 100 years later. All that remains now are the outline of the fort in broken walls and a couple of ruined wells and cisterns.

You don't come to a fort like this to look at the pile of old stones, strewn across the wadi bottom – even though some of those stones have evocative inscriptions and even though you may well be one of only a handful of people to have stepped over the threshold in centuries. No, you come to a castle like this to enjoy the excuse it provides to encounter the desert.

A shallow wadi runs alongside the fort, home to stunted tamarisk trees and shrubs of stick-tight (a type of herb). From the top of the ruins, a vast sky opens up across the almost entirely flat horizon. The silence is almost audible as the nothingness pulses in your ears. This is why you attempt a visit to a castle like Qasr 'Uweinid, to experience the absence of all the usual clutter and noise. If you don't find it, it doesn't matter, but you will have gained a greater understanding of why for centuries visitors have been beguiled by the desert, sand or no sand!

Qasr 'Uweinid is a pile of greyish ruins on a small tell (ancient mound) about 8km southwest of Azraq, though it's probably fair to say that you'll never find it without asking locally for directions. Be aware of driving off-road too close to the military airbase. A 4WD isn't strictly necessary as the gravel plain is firm, and when it stops being firm, you can get out and walk the last 500m.

Activities

Azraq Lodge (p232) can arrange a variety of activities alongside visits to the wetland and Shaumari. Bicycles can be hired for JD12. Bike tours are also offered (JD21, minimum three people) that include a visit to the castle, wetland and lunch with a local Druze family.

Sleeping & Eating

Azraq is one of the only places in the whole Eastern Desert where accommodation is available. To get a real sense of the desert, it is best to plan a trip around an overnight stop that allows at least for a picnic in the wilderness and a walk off-trail between castle-spotting.

Call ahead at Azraq Lodge to arrange one of their delightful lunches or dinners (JD10 to JD14), which showcase the best of local Chechen food. Meals are served buffet style – look out for *mantish* (Chechen lamb dumplings served with yoghurt) and *zalabia*, a dessert local to Azraq flavoured with aniseed and caraway. There are a handful of cheap places selling falafel, shawarma and other standards near the main T-junction in Azraq.

★ Azraq Lodge HOTEL $$

(☎05 383 5017; s/d/tr from JD70/82/93; P ᯤ) This former British 1940s military hospital in south Azraq has been atmospherically renovated by the Royal Society for the Conservation of Nature (RSCN) as a base from which to explore the Eastern Desert. The RSCN has succeeded in preserving the historic building while adding a modern extension, so thankfully there's no need to rough it on bare stretchers.

There's an old field ambulance parked under a canvas porch and some period photographs (worth a visit in their own right) hung alongside paraffin lamps and gas masks to while away the hour before supper. While anyone raving about hospital food could normally expect to be admitted – or committed – at Azraq Lodge, the traditional Chechen dishes served from the modernised hospital **canteen** are likely to be some of the best you'll sample in Jordan. Ring ahead to request lunch or dinner (around JD15) and come with a healthy appetite: the pomegranate salads and thyme-scented meat dishes arrive in generous portions on shared platters.

Azraq Palace Restaurant JORDANIAN $$

(☎07 9503 0356; buffet JD10; ⊙11am-4pm & 6-11pm) This busy restaurant attracts tour groups on desert-castle excursions. The standard Jordanian fare of rice, grills, salads and dips is tasty and filling, and the management is helpful.

Shopping

Azraq Lodge is one of Wild Jordan's main handicraft **workshops** (9am to 4pm Saturday to Thursday), where women from the local community produce and sell silk-screen prints, ostrich-egg paintings and recycled paper products, which are sold at the lodge's shop alongside other Wild Jordan products.

Getting There & Away

Minibuses run up and down the road along northern and southern Azraq in search of passengers before joining the highway to Zarqa (JD1.500, 1½ hours). If you are driving, you have the choice here of joining Hwy 5, which leads south after at least three or four hours of utter desolation to southern Jordan. The drive to Amman along either Hwy 30 or Hwy 40 takes around two hours. Make sure you obey the rules of desert driving and fill up with petrol when you see a station, as pumps are few and far between.

Qusayr Amra قصر عمرة

Today, Qusayr Amra appears randomly rooted on the parched desert plain, but in ancient times the location was carefully chosen for its proximity to a lush wadi famed for its wild pistachio trees. It's the site of an ancient mural-bedecked bathhouse and caravanserai (large merchant's inn enclosing a courtyard, providing accommodation and a marketplace) that's well worth the detour to get out here.

The main three-vaulted structure is well restored, but what would otherwise be a fairly modest site is made remarkable by the high state of preservation of the floor-to-ceiling frescoes decorating the interior of Qusayr Amra. An impressive restoration effort has returned much of the vividness of colour to the Bacchanalian scenes of hunting, nude bathing and revelry.

Adjacent to a 36m-deep well that supplied the bathhouse, a restored *saqiyah* (a contraption activated by the circular pacing of a donkey) shows how the water would have been pumped to a cistern and either diverted to the baths or siphoned off and traded to passing caravans.

History

The Umayyads built Qusayr Amra around AD 711 during the reign of Walid I (AD 705–15). Walid is most famous for launching a building campaign across the Umayyad empire that was crowned by the Umayyad Mosque in Damascus and the Dome of the Rock in Jerusalem.

In contrast to the religious solemnity of these grand projects, the bathhouse at Amra is devoted to more carnal subjects. Walid's disapproving successor ordered the destruction of all such imagery. Fortunately for Amra, the far-reaching hand of Damascus spared this remote outpost of the Eastern

THE FRESCOES OF QUSAYR AMRA

The information boards in the visitor centre at Qusayr Amra assure the visitor that 'none of the paintings of Qusayr Amra portray scenes of unbridled loose-living or carryings-on'. Given the context of early Islam's prohibition of any illustrations of living beings, it's difficult to agree.

Just how far these boundaries were pushed is evident on the western wall of the audience hall, where there is a depiction of a nude woman bathing. Some historians speculate that she may have been modelled on the favourite concubine of the ruler of Amra. The more your eyes roam the walls, past images of musicians, naked dancers, cherubs, baskets of fruit (and even a bear playing a lute!), the more the heresy of the frescoes becomes apparent.

And the purpose of all these paintings? Some Islamic scholars blame the Ghassanids, a pagan Arab tribe that ruled the region at the time of Rome; others mumble about rogue rulers who were not true to Islam. But most admit privately that it seems as though the rulers were simply enjoying themselves on a boys' night out, away from the confines of the court.

Desert, allowing the modern visitor to appreciate a humour not normally associated with the early expressions of Islamic society.

Excavation at the site began in the mid-1970s under a team of Spanish archaeologists, and the frescoes were restored with funding from Austria, France and Spain. In 1985 the frescoes were formally recognised as a 'masterpiece of human creative genius', and Qusayr Amra became a World Heritage Site.

Sights

★Qusayr Amra CASTLE

(JD1, ticket also valid for Qasr Al Azraq & Qasr Kharana, free with Jordan Pass; 8am-6pm May-Sep, to 4pm Oct-Apr) One of the best-preserved desert buildings of the Umayyads, the Unesco World Heritage Site of Qusayr Amra is the highlight of a trip into the Eastern Desert. Part of a much greater complex that served as a caravanserai, bathhouse and hunting lodge, the *qusayr* (little castle) is renowned for its rather risqué 8th-century frescoes of wine, women and wild times.

Walking downhill from the visitor centre towards the modest little structure, it's hard not to wonder what all the fuss is about. Even entering the main building into the **audience hall**, where meetings, parties, exhibitions and meals were once held, is decidedly underwhelming as the searing light of the surrounding desert all but obliterates the frescoes within.

But then your eyes grow accustomed to the light, and you are greeted by two bare-breasted women painted on the arches, holding bowls of food (or money) against a blue background, draped in richly detailed cloth. Five centuries before the Early Renaissance in Europe, these frescoes depict a touchingly human quality – wrestlers warm up before the contest, a woman dressed in a mere strip of cloth bathes without coyness in a hinted patch of sunlight, the ear of a gazelle twitches as the herd surges ahead of the hunt, dogs pant as they race across the **west wall**, driving wild onagers into a trap of nets. Even the mundane construction of the baths is immortalised in the frescoes – in the compartmentalised images on the ceiling, depicting quarrying, moving the stones by camel, carpentry and plastering of the walls.

These are not the normal stylised images of the day, belonging to a religious canon of signs and symbols. Instead they appear to be a unique attempt to capture daily reality – quite unlike the geometric imagery that has come to be associated with early Islamic art.

That's not to say the frescoes fail to pay homage to more weighty subject matter. Look for the defaced image of the Umayyad caliph, and you'll see he is surrounded by **six great rulers**, four of whom have been identified – a Byzantine emperor, Caesar; the Visigoth king, Roderick; the Persian emperor, Chosroes; and the Negus of Abyssinia. The fresco either implies that the Umayyad ruler was their equal or better, or it is simply a pictorial list of Islam's enemies.

And if the frescoes pay lip service to concerning matters of the day, they also encompass their own mostly forgotten symbolism too. A small doorway leads to the left through the three small rooms that made up the baths. The **apodyterium** (changing room) has three blackened faces on the ceiling, said to depict the three stages of man's life. Local Christians believe the central figure to be a depiction of Christ. The left wall has a hallucinogenic painting of an exuberant bear playing the lute, egged on by an applauding monkey, which no doubt would have suggested some political vanity of the day.

In the **tepidarium** (where warm water was offered and warm air circulated beneath the floor), naked women bathe a child while in the neighbouring hot-water **calidarium**, which is closest to the furnace outside, a whole Dome of Heaven spirals around the ceiling. This map of the northern hemisphere sky, accompanied by the signs of the zodiac, is among the earliest known attempts to represent the universe on anything other than a flat surface. Centaur-like Sagittarius, the Great Bear and several other zodiac signs (see the map in the visitor centre for details) would have been a fitting ultimate subject of contemplation for contemporary bathers.

Information

Tickets and public toilets are available at the **visitor centre** (8am-6pm May-Sep, to 4pm Oct-Apr). A relief map of the site, descriptions of the site's history and the plan of the frescoes help in identifying some of the key highlights that are hard to discern without an idea of what to expect.

Photography of the interior of Qusayr Amra is still unregulated, but bear in mind that flash photography and touching the walls will harm the frescoes.

Getting There & Away

Qusayr Amra is on the north side of Hwy 40, 26km from Azraq. It is only signposted coming from Amman, so keep an eye out if you are approaching in the other direction as the small dune-coloured buildings are easy to miss. No minibuses travel this route, and buses will not stop at Amra, making it impossible to visit by

WHICH CASTLES TO VISIT?

There are dozens of ruins belonging to the Umayyad dynasty scattered across the gravel plains of the Eastern Desert, so how do you choose which ones to visit?

Below is a list of the main castles and a guide to their accessibility. The castles fall into two convenient sets. The most famous ones lie on the so-called Desert Castle Loop. These are accessible on a day trip from Amman via Azraq, by tour or by car. Individual castles can be reached with more difficulty by a combination of minibus and taxi.

The other set lies on the so-called Eastern Desert Highway, or Hwy 10, which leads from the town of Mafraq to the Iraqi border. These are much more time-consuming to visit.

Each of the two sets takes a long, full day to cover. You can combine the two sets by staying the night in Azraq and using Hwy 5 to cut between the two.

Set 1: Desert Castle Loop

CASTLE NAME	PUBLIC TRANSPORT	4WD REQUIRED	BY TOUR	RECOMMENDED
Qasr Al Hallabat	Yes	No	Sometimes	☑☑
Qasr Al Azraq	Yes	No	Yes	☑☑☑
Qasr 'Uweinid	No	Yes	No	☑
Qusayr Amra	Taxi from Azraq	No	Yes	☑☑☑
Qasr Kharana	Taxi from Azraq	No	Yes	☑☑☑

Set 2: Castles of the Eastern Desert Highway

CASTLE NAME	PUBLIC TRANSPORT	4WD REQUIRED	BY TOUR	RECOMMENDED
Umm Al Jimal	Yes	No	Sometimes	☑☑
Qasr Deir Al Kahf	No	No	No	☑
Qasr Aseikhin	No	No	No	☑
Qasr Burqu	No	Yes	No	☑☑

VISITING THE DESERT CASTLES BY PUBLIC TRANSPORT

Although this is a region that really repays extra expenditure on a tour or on car hire, that doesn't mean the Eastern Desert is off limits to independent travellers on public transport. What it does mean is that you have to be selective about the castles you want to visit and be realistic about the time it takes to get there. There's no accommodation in the region except at Azraq, so early-morning trips are best, giving you enough time to return to base. If you leave Amman (or Irbid) in the afternoon for the Eastern Desert, you run the risk of getting stranded.

You can visit the castles at **Umm Al Jimal**, **Hallabat** and **Azraq** by public transport, although it's almost impossible to travel between these sites without returning to Amman – or at least Zarqa. You shouldn't rely on hitching as there's little traffic. Hitching is never entirely safe, and we don't recommend it.

Probably the most rewarding itinerary is to take the bus to Azraq (via Zarqa) and stay two nights. On the day of arrival you can walk from the town to **Qasr Azraq** and the following morning you can visit the **Azraq Wetland Reserve**. Take a taxi in the afternoon of the second day to **Qusayr Amra** and **Qasr Kharana**, and return to Azraq in the evening. On the third day, you can head back to Amman.

public transport. Without a car, the only option is to hire a taxi from Azraq (from JD15 return if you can persuade one to take you).

Qasr Kharana قصر خرانه

Located in the middle of a vast, treeless plain, the imposing thick-walled structure of **Qasr Kharana** (JD1, ticket also valid for Qusayr Amra & Qasr Al Azraq, free with Jordan Pass; 8am-6pm May-Sep, to 4pm Oct-Apr) was the most likely inspiration for the 'desert castle' moniker and is arguably the most photogenic of all the desert castles. There is controversy about its function and purpose, but this important Umayyad structure remains an interesting sight for visitors, off the main Azraq–Amman road.

Although it clearly isn't a castle, Kharana was a vital building for the Umayyads as evidenced by its dramatic size and shape. Despite the fact that it has the appearance of a khan (travellers' inn), Kharana wasn't located on any major trade route, and there appears to be a total absence of structures for water storage. That just leaves the supposition that the building served as a meeting space for Damascus elite and local Bedouin. Named after the harra (surrounding gravel plains), Kharana lords imposingly over a harsh and barren moonscape that appears inhospitable for human habitation. Inside, however, the internal courtyard provides a calm, protected space that even the wind fails to penetrate.

Despite its castle-like appearance, there is no evidence that the intimidating two-storey building, with what appear to be round, defensive towers and narrow arrow slits, was ever intended as a fort. In fact, the towers are completely solid, which means that they couldn't be manned by armed soldiers and it would be impossible to fire bows from the bizarrely shaped 'arrow slits', meaning that they most likely served as air and light ducts.

About 60 rooms surround the courtyard inside the castle, and probably served as meeting spaces for visiting delegations. The long rooms either side of the arched entrance were used as stables, and in the centre of the courtyard was a basin for collecting rainwater. Remarkably, the interior is much smaller than you'd imagine as the walls are deceptively thick.

Climb the broad stairways and you'll find rooms on the upper storeys with vaulted ceilings. Some carved plaster medallions, set around the top of the walls, are said to indicate Mesopotamian influence. Also in one of the rooms on the 2nd floor are a few lines of Arabic graffiti, which were crucial in helping to establish the age of the fortress. Above the door in simple black script is an inscription that says 'Abd Al Malik the son of Ubayd wrote it on Monday three days from Muharram of the year 92'.

Stairs in the southeast and southwest corners lead to the 2nd floor and the roof (closed to visitors). Very little is known about the origins of Qasr Kharana, although a painted inscription above one of the doors on the upper floor mentions the date AD 710, making it one of the earliest forts of the Islamic era. The presence of stones with Greek inscriptions in the main entrance also suggests it was built on the site of a Roman or Byzantine building, possibly as a private residence.

Information

Entrance to Kharana is through the visitor centre, which has some displays on local history. Public toilets are available. The hospitable owner of the adjacent Bedouin tent, which doubles as the site coffeehouse and souvenir stall, will brew you fresh mint tea and take time to discuss the issues of the day. Your patronage will be much appreciated if the current absence of tourism continues.

Getting There & Away

Kharana is 16km further west along Hwy 40 from Qusayr Amra. There's no viable public transport along the highway (although it could be included in a round trip by taxi from Azraq, from JD20) and the castle is only signposted coming from Amman. It's easier to spot than neighbouring Amra, especially as it's disappointingly close to a power station.

EASTERN DESERT HIGHWAY

Umm Al Jimal أم الجمال

Umm Al Jimal is one of the region's most captivating sites, the ruins of a seemingly lost city in black basalt, rising out of the grey and tan of the surrounding desert.

It's best to visit early in the morning, or late in the afternoon, when the black basalt isn't too hot. Allow at least an hour or two to visit the site, although its enormous size (800m by 500m) invites lengthier exploration.

History

Supposedly founded in 1 BCE by the Nabataeans, Umm Al Jimal (meaning 'Mother of Camels') is notable for the inverted V-shaped roofs, constructed from black basalt. The town was taken over by the Romans, who used it as part of their defensive cordon against the desert tribes, and it prospered as an important trading station for Bedouin and passing caravans. From Umm Al Jimal, roads led north to Bosra (in present-day Syria) and southwest to Philadelphia (modern Amman), which firmly established the town on most of the region's major trade routes.

The city grew during the Byzantine period, when churches were constructed and Roman buildings demilitarised. At the peak of growth, this thriving agricultural city boasted some 3000 inhabitants. The key to Umm Al Jimal's prosperity lay in its sophisticated method of storing water, which was a necessity for surviving the long periods between rainfall and for irrigating staple crops. Even today, many of the ancient town's reservoirs are still virtually intact.

Umm Al Jimal declined in the early 7th century AD, coinciding with an outbreak of the bubonic plague and an earthquake in 747, which forced the remaining inhabitants to flee the city.

The ruins of Umm Al Jimal were briefly occupied by Druze refugees fleeing persecution in Syria in the early 20th century. Today, a small modern village has sprung up around the impressive ghost town, which is now home to only a few stray dogs and visited by children trotting through the ruins on a shortcut to school with their notebooks tucked under their arms.

Sights

★Umm Al Jimal Ruins RUINS

(daylight hours) FREE The unpretentious urban architecture of Umm Al Jimal, near the Jordanian–Syrian border, encompasses more than 150 buildings standing one to three storeys above ground, including 128 houses and 15 churches. Together, these buildings provide a fascinating insight into rural life during the Roman, Byzantine and early Islamic periods. Compared to other archaeological sites in the region, Umm Al Jimal was rarely looted or vandalised, which has left much of the original layout intact.

Comparatively little is known about the ruined city, referred to by archaeologists as the 'Black Gem of the Desert'. An extensive rural settlement in the lava lands east of Mafraq, the ruins are located on the edge of a series of volcanic basalt flows that slope down from Jebel Druze, providing high-quality building materials.

The large structure just past the southern entrance is the **barracks**, built by the Romans. The towers were added later and, like the castle at Azraq, it has a swinging basalt door that still functions. The **barracks**

Umm Al Jimal

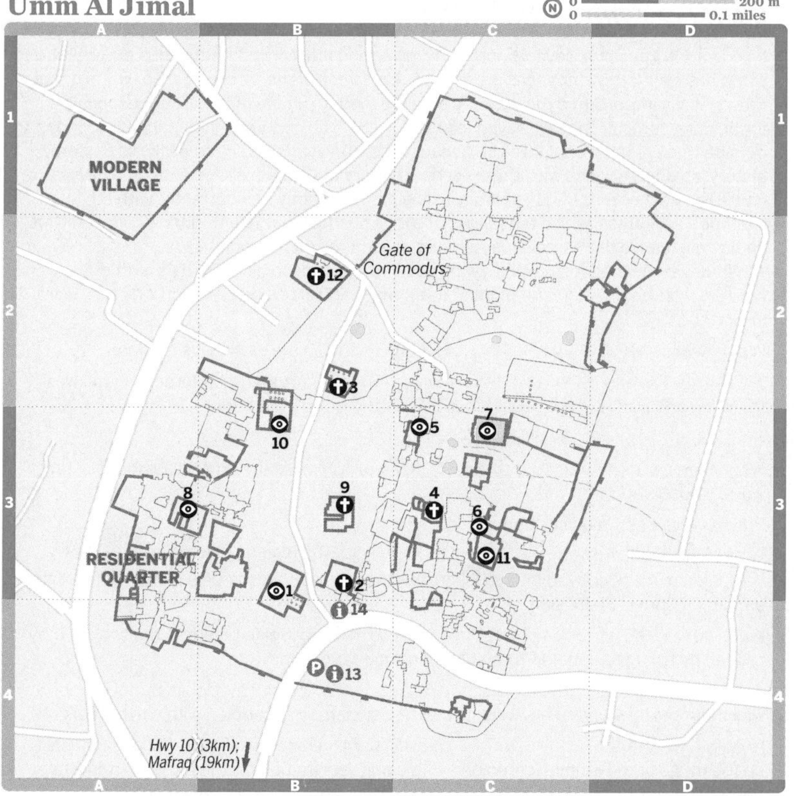

Umm Al Jimal

Sights

Information

chapel was added to the east of the barracks during the Byzantine period (around the 5th century) and is inscribed with the names of the archangels Gabriel, Raphael, Michael and Uriel.

About 150m to the left (west) of the barracks is what some archaeologists believe is a **Nabataean temple** because of the altar in the middle. About 100m north of the barracks is the **Numerianos church**, one of several ruined Byzantine churches. Another 100m to the east is the **double church**, recognisable by its two semicircular naves, a wonderful structure that was renovated and extended several times over the centuries. About 80m to the right (east) is **house XVII**, whose double-door entrance, interior courtyard, fine corbelled ceilings, decorated doorways and carved pillars indicate that it was built by a wealthy family.

A few metres to the south is the **sheikh's house**, notable for its expansive courtyard, stables, black basalt door and stairways. Look for the gravity-defying stairs to the north and the precarious corner tower. You

UMAYYADS? WHO WERE THEY?

If you had to guess the seventh-largest empire (and fifth-largest contiguous empire) the world has ever known, chances are you wouldn't think of the Umayyads. So why is it that this critically important dynasty, central to the modern shape of Islam and responsible for building some of the best-loved expressions of Arab culture, is so unfamiliar to those outside the region? It could well be because the Umayyads belong to a Middle Eastern history, so often at odds with the crusading history of Western nations. It could be because the 8th century AD is generally associated, correctly or incorrectly, with the unenlightened Dark Ages, which tends to cast a long shadow over neighbouring cultures. Or it could be because the name Umayyad just doesn't roll off the tongue.

Whatever the reason, the Umayyads deserve the odds to be evened up a little. So here are a few fast facts to help understand who the Umayyads were and why they were important.

When were the Umayyads around? AD 661–750, in the early days of Islam.

This huge empire of theirs, where was it? From Portugal and Morocco in the west to Arabia and Persia in the east – about 9% of the world's land area.

So how big is that? 13 million sq km.

How many people were governed by this empire? At the time, around 30% of the world's population.

Where was the capital? Damascus.

What was their impact on Islam? Both positive and negative: they implemented a campaign of mass conversions to Islam, but their dynasty was largely responsible for the damaging Sunni–Shiite split.

How were they regarded in their day? The minority Shiite resented the schism they caused by failing to uphold Prophet Muhammad's bloodline.

But the Sunnis supported them, presumably? Not exactly. Public Sunni opinion was that the Umayyad rulers were dim-witted sinners, preoccupied with earthly delights.

Is this what caused their demise? Partly. In 747 a rebellion of dissatisfied subjects on the fringe of the empire, combined with a huge earthquake in the region, led to a takeover of the empire by Shiite forces (known as the Abbasids) from Persia in 750.

Are the Umayyads remembered today? Yes! They established Arabic as the administrative language of the Middle East, their pan-Arab approach is used by nationalists to evoke an Arab Golden Age, and their association with the colour white is reflected in most modern flags of Arab countries.

Any other cultural legacies? They built the Dome of the Rock in Jerusalem and the Umayyad Mosque in Damascus, two of the great icons of Islamic art.

What was their significance in the area we now call Jordan? The string of hunting lodges, bathhouses and pleasure palaces known collectively as the 'desert castles' were built by the Umayyads – festive expressions of their creative and exuberant reign.

can just make out a double stairway to the east of the courtyard. After exiting the building you get a good view of the lovely arched window and vaulted semicircular basement in the exterior eastern wall.

About 150m north of the double church, steps lead down to the **main reservoir**, one of several around the city. Less than 100m to the left (west) is **house XIII**, originally a stable for domestic goats and sheep, and later renovated and used as a residence by Druze settlers. Here, take notice of the stone ventilation screen, which was used to separate the manger from the living space.

To the west (about 100m) is the **cathedral**, built in about AD 556, but now mostly in ruins – look for the lintel stone detailing the Roman emperors that ruled over the region. The **praetorium** (military headquarters) is less than 100m to the southwest. Built in the late 2nd century AD by the Romans, it was extended by the Byzantines and features a triple doorway. About 200m to the north through one of the old city gates is the **west church**, easily identifiable by its four arches and ornate Byzantine crosses.

Information

Visitor Centre (daylight hours) More of a warden's post than a visitor centre, there are at least toilets at the entrance to Umm Al Jimal. For more details about the site, look for the hard-to-find booklet *Umm el-Jimal* (JD3), published by Al Kutba and available sporadically at bookshops in Amman.

Archaeological Office If someone hears your arrival, you'll be expected to sign the visitors' book. So few visitors come this way, however, you can excuse the warden for wandering off post now and again. While it is tempting to slip into the site incognito, it's probably worth letting someone in this office know that you have stepped into the site, just in case you break an ankle walking over the rubble. The site is so big and so deserted, you might not be discovered for days!

Department of Antiquities This is the place to address any technical queries about the ruins, although the office is often closed.

Getting There & Away

Umm Al Jimal is about 20km east of Mafraq and only 10km from the Syrian border. With an early start, it is possible to do a day trip from Amman by public transport. From the Abdali or Raghadan bus stations in Amman, catch a bus or minibus to Bedouin station in Mafraq (possibly with a connection in Zarqa), and from Mafraq catch another minibus to Umm Al Jimal.

If you're driving, head 16km east of Mafraq along Hwy 10 towards Safawi, then take the signed turn-off north for 3km to Umm Al Jimal. If you have chartered a taxi from Amman for a day trip around the desert castles, it is possible to include Umm Al Jimal on the itinerary for a little extra (about JD10) – but start early to fit it all in.

Qasr Deir Al Kahf

قصر دير الكهف

Built in the 4th century, the '**Monastery of Caves** FREE' is a purpose-built Roman fort that primarily served as a sentry post. Like its famous neighbour Umm Al Jimal, Deir Al Kahf is also constructed of black basalt, though the scattered ruins here are not nearly as extensive. There is an access road north of Hwy 10, or look for the signs along the back roads east of Umm Al Jimal.

One of the highlights of Qasr Deir is approaching it along the back roads that lead for 30km or so from Umm Al Jimal. Several Druze settlements dot the way with traditional basalt buildings still in use and small farms with active dovecotes staving off the northern reaches of the Eastern Desert.

The change in scenery is quite dramatic from here as the last of the irrigated farms are left behind on the rolling high ground, replaced by occasional Bedouin tents and herds of livestock. By the time you reach Hwy 10, the dust devils take over the plains, and the land extends as far as the eye can see in an uninterrupted flat disc of nothingness.

Getting There & Away

There's no reliable public transport to make a day trip from Amman or Irbid via Mafraq feasible.

By car, the easiest way to be sure you are on the right road is to return to Hwy 10 and turn north at Salihiyyah. After around 5km, veer right at the intersection with the road from Umm Al Jimal. There are intermittent signposts to Deir Al Kahf or follow your nose east for a further 25km, running parallel to the Syrian border. The fort is behind a police station. An access road leads for 10km south of the ruins to Al Bishriyya on the Eastern Desert Highway.

Safawi

الصفاوي

05 / POP 2300 / ELEV 700M

The small town of Safawi is a welcome sight along the Eastern Desert Highway. It offers the chance to fill up with petrol, buy water and a snack en route to Burqu. Ar Ruwayshid, the junction for Burqu, lies at least another hour and a half to the east (a round trip of 4½ hours from Safawi if you factor in the off-road visit to the lake).

If you have a 4WD, the Tree of Biqawiyya and Qasr Usaykim are south of Safawi, and form part of the Jordan Eastern Badia Trail.

Sights

Tree of Biqawiyya LANDMARK

Despite the surrounding desert, a semi-permanent water pool persists here in a depression surround by black lava stones. Its unmissable feature is the large pistachio tree – literally the only one for miles – that the Prophet Muhammad is said to have rested under when travelling between Damascus and Mecca.

WORTH A TRIP

BADIA GEMS

Wadi Al Dahik

In the southern corner of the Badia desert and nestled close to the Saudi border off the main highway is the alien landscape of Wadi Al Dahik. The area's name refers to its gleaming chalk cliffs that resemble a laughing white smile, and which make a dramatic contrast to the black basalt of the surrounding desert. Time and wind have sculpted the cliffs into dramatic forms, and the area is perfect for hiking.

Around 55 million years ago the region was part of the ancient Tethys Sea, and the erosion of the soft limestone turns up plenty of fossil sea life – keep an eye out for shells and shark teeth.

The Jordan Eastern Badia Trail

The newest ecotourism development from Wild Jordan (www.wildjordan.com), the Jordan Eastern Badia Trail (JEBT) is a self-guided off-road trail for 4WD vehicles in the Eastern Desert.

The two hubs for the trail are Azraq Lodge and Burqu Ecolodge, Wild Jordan's two properties in the area. From Azraq, which also hosts its wetland reserves and the oryx breeding program at Shaumari, you can quickly access the desert in its wildest forms. There are several 'trails' taking in dramatic landscapes, hiking in the white canyons of Wadi Al Dahik, Neolithic petroglyphs, birdwatching, camel riding and even learning to herd sheep with local Bedouin communities, as well as the best of the Eastern Desert castles.

When we visited, the last touches were being put to the trail, which was due to open in 2018. Visit Wild Jordan for more information, including tour packages from Amman.

Qasr Usaykim CASTLE

(24hr) FREE This small Roman fort, built from basalt in the 3rd century over the ruins of a 1st-century Nabataean building, is between Azraq and Safawi. The small structure is worth a visit for the commanding view of the plains, framed by a basaltic Roman arch. The sealed access road to the ruins lies about 10km southwest of Safawi along Hwy 5.

For some reason, the 10km access road stops about 1km short of the hilltop fort. The graded track thereafter is just about navigable in a 2WD vehicle, but the walk is more rewarding if you want to get a sense of the utter remoteness of this former military outpost. From the junction with the main road, it is just 22km to Azraq.

The surrounding vista gives you an idea of the struggle for survival endured by the Bedouin of the Badia – the local name for the Eastern Desert that stretches into Saudi Arabia; even camels are reluctant to pick their way across this rocky, basaltic plain.

Getting There & Away

Public transport to Safawi is virtually nonexistent, but you can fill your car with petrol here.

Burqu بورقو

Burqu is deep in Jordan's desert east; if you travel any further you'll end up in Iraq, which we don't recommend. It's the perfect place for a desert adventure, which is why the Royal Society for the Conservation of Nature (RSCN) has been fighting to establish Burqu as a protected reserve. The Burqu Ecolodge is due to open in 2018 to serve as a base for local tourism as part of the development of the Jordan Eastern Badia Trail – check with Wild Jordan (www.wildjordan.com) for more information. Tours to the castle and lake, along with birdwatching and visits with local Bedouin are all planned.

South of Burqu are the mysterious remains of Bronze Age settlements of Khirbet Abu Hussain in the Harra Desert, known as the black desert.

Sights

Khirbet Abu Hussain ARCHAEOLOGICAL SITE

Deep in the Harra Desert are the peculiar ruins of the ancient settlement of Khirbet Abu Hussain. It's a hill fort on a small peak, and part of a dozen giant stone circles in the area, some of which date back as far as the Neolithic period. Arranged with spokes and other unusual shapes, they can perhaps only be best appreciated from the air, giving rise to the moniker of Jordan's Nasca Lines – though they predate their Peruvian relations by some 6000 years.

The stones are reached by passing near the surreal dried mudflat of Qa'a Abu Hussain, which has a dinner-plate surface that creates wild mirages. Be aware that it forms a seasonal lake after spring storms.

Qasr Burqu & Lake CASTLE
(24hr) FREE The Romans built the small fort at Burqu to protect a seasonal lake that provided precious water in a highly arid region. They helped conserve the water (run-off from the Haurun-Druze Plateau) by building a dam in the 3rd century, thereby securing water for caravans heading between Syria and Arabia. The fort became a monastery during the Byzantine period and was later restored by the Umayyads in about AD 700.

Remarkably, an inscription on one of the walls of the fort suggests that it may have been occupied as late as 1409.

The lake, which often dries out in summer, is home to a number of bird species (including finches, storks, sandpipers, larks, cranes, buzzards, eagles and vultures) that come to roost because the water level rarely changes, even in summer. The harshness of the surrounding landscape, as well as the lack of properly graded roads, has acted as a strong deterrent against poaching, although the Bedouin occasionally fly their birds of prey in the area. Home to gazelles, desert hares, foxes, hyenas and even caracals, this remarkable little oasis has all the makings of a national reserve.

Sleeping & Eating

Burqu Ecolodge offers the only formal accommodation in the Burqu area. The RSCN also plan to offer camping in Bedouin tents in the more temperate months – March to May and October.

Wild camping is possible out here (don't pitch too close to the lake because of biting insects). The local Bedouin are bound to find you and wonder what you are doing here, and likely invite you to tea.

You'll need to be self-sufficient at Burqu, unless you are staying at Burqu Ecolodge, which is full board.

★**Burqu Ecolodge** GUESTHOUSE $$
(www.wildjordan.com) Due to open in 2018, this purpose-built ecolodge from the RSCN will served to anchor tourism in the Badia desert. The architecture echoes the eastern castles with cool inner courtyards, thick walls and high ceilings to protect against the desert environment, while solar power and grey water recycling brings facilities up to date.

On offer at the lodge are walks to Burqu Lake and the Byzantine-era castle, birdwatching, stargazing and Bedouin cultural experiences from making local coffee to learning how to herd sheep. Expect rooms to cost around JD70 to JD90.

FOR THE COMMITTED QASR-SPOTTER

If the castles of the Zarqa–Azraq–Amman loop have whetted your appetite for Umayyad architecture, then you can earn your *qasr*-spotting badge by searching out one or two of the lesser *qasr* sites.

Qasr Al Tuba (24hr) FREE Easily the most impressive of the lesser-known castles, Tuba lies approximately 75km southeast of Amman and captures the sense of a staging post on long-forgotten incense routes. Tuba was erected by Caliph Walid II in about AD 743 and abandoned following his sudden assassination. Tuba is only accessible by 4WD along dirt tracks 50km south of Hwy 40, or 35km west of the Desert Highway. The structure is unique for its sun-baked mud bricks and you can see an imposing doorway from the site at Amman's National Archaeological Museum. The sole nesting place in Jordan of the rare houbara bustard is at nearby Thalathwat.

Qasr Mushash (24hr) Once a grand Umayyad settlement, today Mushash lies in ruin. However, it's still possible to get a sense of the original layout, and there are a number of impressive buildings left standing including the remains of a palace, a large courtyard surrounded by a dozen rooms, baths, cisterns and walls built to protect against possible flooding. Only accessible by 4WD, Mushash can be reached via an access road along Hwy 40.

WINSTON'S HICCUP

When Winston Churchill was serving as British Colonial Secretary in the early 1920s, he once boasted that he had 'created Trans-Jordan with the stroke of a pen on a Sunday afternoon in Cairo'. As Churchill had something of a reputation for enjoying 'liquid lunches', a rumour started to fly that he had hiccuped while attempting to draw the border, and stubbornly refused to allow it to be redefined. The resulting zigzag in Jordan's eastern border subsequently became known as Winston's Hiccup.

Of course, Churchill was anything but drunk and foolish. The zigzag was precisely plotted to excise Wadi Sirhan, an age-old Incense Route and vital communication highway between French-controlled Syria and Arabia, from Jordan. The pen stroke also created a panhandle between Azraq and Iraq, which meant that the British now controlled an unbroken corridor between the Mediterranean Sea and Persian Gulf.

Today, Jordan's erratic boundaries with Syria, Iraq and Saudi Arabia are of little political consequence, at least in comparison to the heightened emotions surrounding the border with Israel and the Palestinian Territories. However, Winston's Hiccup does stand as testament to a time when little to no lip service was given to the colonial division of occupied foreign lands.

Getting There & Away

Burqu is only accessible by 4WD. The lake and castle lie 22km northwest of Ar Ruwayshid, a 45-minute drive across the desert on unmarked and unclear tracks from Hwy 10. The turn-off is about 3km west of Ruwayshid at a sign for Burqu spelt as 'Boarg'a'. Wild Jordan has a reception centre at Manishiyet El Gheyyath on the main highway where it's possible to arrange transfers to the Burqu Ecolodge, courtesy of the local Bedouin community – a policy aimed at spreading the economic benefits of tourism in the area.

Although the driving is fairly straightforward, with a hard surface to within a few metres of the lake, you should not attempt to find the site without a guide unless you are confident of navigating off-road. If you have experience of desert driving, and provided you stick to the most obvious track, which is often routed between piles of white stone, the lake is fairly easy to find, although it takes quite a bit of nerve to stay your course across the barren land. More difficult is finding your way back to the highway from the lake – almost impossible if you haven't taken note of any reverse landmarks on the outbound journey (the pylons are helpful and so is the hint of a low, metre-high embankment of a modern reservoir, which you should keep on your left heading towards Burqu). The sense of satisfaction in finding this remarkable little oasis is worth all the anxiety and effort of getting there.

Understand Jordan

Jordan Today

For a country that only came into existence in its present form less than 100 years ago, Jordan has come far in terms of establishing an independent identity, distinct from neighbouring countries. Its citizens are proud of their nationality and the progress made, with relatively few resources, in developing modern infrastructure, health care and a regionally esteemed education system. It is this investment in human resources that has given Jordan the strength to thrive in a region of troublesome neighbours.

Best in Print

The Desert and the Sown (Gertrude Bell; 1907) The 'brains behind Lawrence's brawn'.

Seven Pillars of Wisdom (TE Lawrence; 1926) The desert revolt classic.

Nine Parts of Desire: The Hidden World of Islamic Women (Geraldine Brooks; 1995) One of the better books in a genre dominated by sensationalist writing.

Married to a Bedouin (M van Geldermalsen; 2006) The story of how the author initially brought her family up in a Petra cave.

Into the Wadi (Michele Drouart; 2000) An account of an Australian woman's marriage to a Jordanian man.

Best on Film

Lawrence of Arabia (1962) David Lean's classic.

A Dangerous Man: Lawrence after Arabia (1991) Starring a young Ralph Fiennes.

Indiana Jones and the Last Crusade (1989) Harrison Ford in Petra caper.

Jordan Circa 2018

With so much history wrapped up in this tiny desert kingdom, it's easy to overlook the modern face of Jordan – something the government is trying to address by improving productivity, making Jordan a more attractive country for foreign investment, promoting Jordan as a high-tech service centre and by planning ambitious tourist developments. The current economic hardship and high unemployment, however, has led to many of these plans, including the 74-hectare astrarium theme park near Aqaba, being put on hold.

Home to a Seventh Wonder

When Petra was voted by popular ballot as one of the seven 'new' wonders of the world in 2007, it was a large accolade for a small country. But Jordan – straddling the ancient Holy Land of the world's three great monotheistic religions, and once an important trading centre of the Roman Empire – is no stranger to punching above its weight. Stand on Mt Nebo, consecrated by Pope John II, and survey the land allegedly promised to Moses; unfurl a veil at Mukawir, where Salome is said to have cast a spell over men in perpetuity; walk along the King's Highway in the footsteps of legionnaires – go just about anywhere in Jordan, and you'll find every stone bares a tale. Jordan's economic emphasis on tourism endeavours to find new ways to harness the attraction of its ancient treasures for the benefit of Jordan today.

The Arab Spring & Benign Dictatorship

For a brief moment in the spring of 2011, it looked as though Jordanians were set to join fellow protesters in Egypt, Tunisia, Libya and Syria in demonstrations popularly dubbed as the Arab Spring. Comprised largely of young students, and peaceful in their approach, Jordanian protesters argued on the streets of Amman for higher wages and a fuller embracing of democracy. The demonstrations soon petered out, however, leaving only weekly gatherings of diehards after Friday prayers.

Democratic reforms have long been in place in Jordan. In November 1989 the first full parliamentary elections since 1967 were held, and women were allowed the vote. Four years later most political parties were legalised and able to participate in parliamentary and municipal elections.

Despite these concessions, democracy in Jordan is still something of an alien concept. Perceived as promoting the interests of the individual over those of the community, it runs against the grain of tribal traditions where respect for elders is paramount. In common with other parts of the Middle East, Jordan traditionally favours a strong, centralised government under an autocratic leader – what might be called benign dictatorship.

Of course, benign dictatorship is only as good as the leader. King Abdullah II is widely regarded at home and abroad as both wise and diplomatic in his role – a modernising monarch in touch with the sensibilities of a globalised world, supportive of social and economic reform, and committed to stamping out corruption.

Jordan's Troublesome Neighbours

Like his father, Abdullah II has proved adept at handling foreign affairs – imperative, considering the neighbourhood Jordan shares. Occupying the calm eye of the storm in the Middle East, the country has a long tradition of absorbing the displaced peoples of its troubled neighbours – so much so, in fact, that the demography of the country has changed forever with a majority population now comprising people of non-Jordanian origin.

While refugees of Palestinian origin now belong to a prospering 'middle class' and wealthy refugees from the conflict in Iraq have mostly returned home, the country continues to contend with its fourth major influx of refugees in 50 years – this time from the civil war in Syria. Most of the more than 620,000 registered Syrian refugees are war-weary subjects, with little chance of repatriation in the foreseeable future, confined to camps such as Za'atari. As if these numbers were not headache enough, a government census at the end of 2015 showed that the refugee problem may be considerably larger than the registered figures suggest, with another 780,000 unregistered refugees trying to get by in the community, supported by already over-burdened local infrastructure.

According to a World Bank report in 2016, Jordan has spent in excess of $2.5 billion a year (6% of its GDP and a quarter of government spending) in supporting refugees, pushing up public borrowing to 95%. Little

POPULATION: **10 MILLION**

POPULATION GROWTH RATE: **2.1%**

INFLATION: **1.8%**

GDP: **US$38.6 BILLION**

UNEMPLOYMENT: **15.8%**

AVERAGE ANNUAL INCOME: **LESS THAN US$5000**

if Jordan were 100 people

98 would be Arab
1 would be Circassian
1 would be Armenian

belief systems

(% of population)

population per sq km

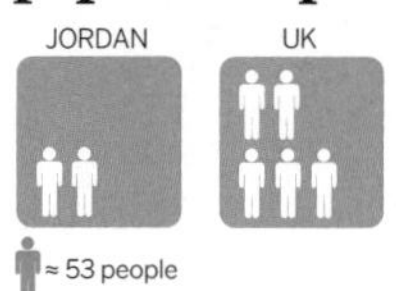

wonder, then, that stellar projects such as the astrarium in Aqaba have been put on hold as Jordan's economy struggles under this onerous responsibility.

Relationship with the West

During the most recent influx of refugees, provoked by the ongoing civil war in Syria, Jordan has repeatedly appealed for international aid to cope. This call to alms was taken up by Pope Francis during his visit in 2014, but there has been little appetite among those in the international community to help share the burden, although the US, among other countries, contributes aid to Jordan.

Jordan remains a staunch ally of the West, however, and it continues its role in the coalition of forces targeting Isis militants. A number of skirmishes have tested Jordan's resolve, the most significant of which occurred at the end of 2016 when a terrorist cell in Karak was flushed out, leading to the death of 10 people, including one Canadian tourist.

Since Jordan is seen as having a key role in potential future peace negotiations with Israel over the Palestinian Territories, it remains to be seen how discussions with US President Donald Trump, held twice in 2017, will impact on the prevailing political stalemate in the region.

A Bright Future?

The former characteristic optimism of Jordanians has been somewhat dented under pressure from the Syrian refugee crisis. According to one international poll (www.iri.org) carried out in January 2017, 71% of Jordanians describe the economy as 'bad' or 'very bad' while more than half feel the country has lost its direction. Many favour closing the border to Syrian refugees. Despite this, Jordanians remain implacably proud of their country and the modernisation it has achieved on minimal resources.

Best in Music

Hashemi, Hashemi (Omar Al-Abdallat; 2014) A traditional patriotic song rendered by a singer-songwriter credited with popularising Bedouin music.

The Square (El Morabba3; 2012) An album of Arab modern pop with poetical and political lyrics produced by the popular group of the same name.

The System (Zaed Naes; 2016) Experimental dance music with interesting visuals from a three-member Amman-based band.

Jerash (Tareq Al Nasser; 2016) A fusion track composed by the founder of Rum music group and composer of Arab film scores.

Best Blogs

Beyond the Wall (https://beyond-the-wall.co/roadtrip-jordan-travel-itinerary) Helpful tips from a couple's travels through Jordan.

Wanderlust Chloe (www.wanderlustchloe.com/petra-jordan-travel-guide-tips) Chloe's top tips for visiting Petra.

Breathe with Us (https://breathewithus.com/jordan-travel-itinerary) A couple on a quest to travel and explore the world shares some insights on Jordan.

Her Packing List (https://herpackinglist.com/2017/02/solo-female-travel-jordan-as-a-woman) An interesting blog from the perspective of a solo female traveller.

Divergent Travellers (https://www.divergenttravelers.com/is-jordan-safe-to-visit) A useful blog that covers safety aspects of travel in Jordan.

History

By default, a visit to Jordan involves engaging with history. But history in Jordan has a habit of coming alive and being instantly relevant to the present. Stub your toe on a ruin, find a Roman coin or hear the call to prayer, and you may just be glad to have a context in which to place that experience. Find out how the major events of the past have shaped Jordan's present.

Blending of Past & Present

Climbing off his donkey, a shepherd in a terraced field near Madaba tethers the animal to a giant thistle and seeks refuge from the noon heat under a dolmen. Stretched full length under the cold stone roof of this ancient burial chamber, he almost blends into the landscape – until his mobile phone erupts in a rendition of 'We wish you a merry Christmas'.

In Jordan, history is not something that happened 'before'. It's a living, breathing part of everyday life, witnessed not just in the pragmatic treatment of ancient artefacts but also in the way people live. Jordanians value their heritage and are in no hurry to eschew ways of life that have proved successful for centuries. The familiar linear approach to history, therefore, where one event succeeds another in an expectation of so-called progress, is almost irrelevant in a country where past and present merge together so seamlessly.

The very entity of Jordan is a case in point. The political state within its current borders is a modern creation, but it encompasses territory (east of the Jordan River) that has hosted the world's oldest civilisations. Egyptians, Assyrians, Babylonians, Greeks, Nabataeans, Romans, Crusaders and Turks all traded, built cities and fought wars here, leaving behind rich cultural influences – leaning posts upon which modern Jordanians have built a proud identity.

Books on Jordan's History

A History of Jordan (Philip Robbins; 2004)

The Modern History of Jordan (Kamal Salibi; 1998)

Global Security Watch – Jordan (W Andrew Terrill; 2010)

Main Periods of History

With some creativity, the abundant historical clues scattered across Jordan can be shuffled into several distinct blocks of time. Each period of history features in the experiences of a visitor to the country, not only

TIMELINE

c 250,000 BC

With the aid of hand axes made of flint, early humans hunt elephants across the plains in the mild, wet climate of the Jordan Valley.

c 100,000 BC

The Red Sea, lying in a branch of the Great Rift Valley, retreats from Wadi Araba, leaving the Dead Sea and the Sea of Galilee as two separate lakes.

c 20,000 BC

Hunters and gatherers live in seasonal camps and rear their own livestock, with goats forming a substantial part of the diet in the early communities at Wadi Madamagh, near Petra.

through a pile of fallen columns by the side of the road, but in the taking of tea with old custodians of the desert or the bargaining for a kilim with designs inherited from the Byzantine era.

In fact, just step foot in Jordan and you begin your encounter with history. Visit the dolmens near Madaba, for example, and you enter the cradle of civilisation; dating from 4000 BC, the dolmens embody the sophistication of the world's first villages. The era of trading in copper and bronze helped bring wealth to the region (1200 BC); you can find forgings from Jordan's ancient copper mines near Feynan Ecolodge in the Dana Biosphere Reserve. Travel the King's Highway and you'll not only be stepping in the path of royalty, but you'll see how this route helped unify city-states into a recognisable Jordan between 1200 BC and 333 BC.

From the earliest settlements, *badawi* (desert nomads) devoted themselves to animal husbandry, sustained by the meat, milk and wool of livestock, while *fellaheen* (farmers) chose to till the land, planting olives and grains. This distinction between the 'desert and the sown' is apparent to this day.

The Greeks, Nabataeans and Romans dominated Jordan's most illustrious historical period (333 BC–AD 333), leaving the magnificent legacies of Petra and Jerash. The arrival of Islamic dynasties is evident from the 7th century onwards – in fact, the evidence is literally strewn over the deserts of eastern Jordan in the intriguing Umayyad structures that dot the stark landscape. The conflict between Islam and Christianity, evident at Jordan's Crusader castles in Ajloun, Karak and Shobak, is a defining feature of the next thousand years.

British imperialism dominates Jordan's history before the Arab Revolt of 1914. Ride a camel through Wadi Rum and cries of 'To Aqaba' hang in the wind – and so does the name of Lawrence, the British officer whose desert adventures have captured the imagination of visitors to such an extent that whole mountains are named after him! Jordan's history is about independence, modernisation and cohabitation with difficult neighbours.

Life in the 'Fertile Crescent' (10,000–4000 BC)

Early Settlements

Stand on top of the knoll at Shkarat Msaiad, on the seldom-used road from Siq Al Barid (Little Petra) to Wadi Araba, and survey the minimal mounds of stone and you could be forgiven for wondering what all the fuss is about. Despite the isolated beauty of the place, there isn't much to see but some stone walling. Yet this is the kind of place that archaeologists rave about because what you are looking at, they will solemnly tell you, is a 'PPN'.

A PPN, for the uninitiated, stands for Pre-Pottery Neolithic and is significant because such sites indicate a high degree of organisation among early communities. In fact, at this sheltered spot in the hills, you are looking at the very dawn of civilisation. If nothing else, the traces of shelter, water collection and farming demonstrate the basic immutability of life.

c 8000 BC

Some of the world's earliest settlements are established at Ain Ghazal, Al Beidha and neighbouring Jericho. Inhabitants tame, breed and cook domestic animals.

c 6000 BC

The Ain Ghazal fertility sculptures (among the world's oldest sculptures) and wall paintings at Teleilat Ghassul in the Jordan Valley show that early inhabitants of the region value cultural activity.

c 5000 BC

Monumental stone dolmen near Ar Rawdah indicate that burials are now linked to concepts of afterlife. The ingenious engineering involved in their construction is a wonder – and a mystery.

c 4000 BC

Permanent settlements are established in modern-day Amman and in the south, while copper is mined at Khirbet Feynan. Arts, such as pottery, illustrate the influence of powerful neighbours in Egypt.

Jordan has a remarkable number of early settlements, largely thanks to its location within the fertile crescent – the rich arc of lands that included Mesopotamia, Syria and Palestine. The fecundity of the soil in this region allowed early humans to move from a hunter-gatherer existence to settlement in the world's earliest villages, dating between 10,000 and 8500 BC.

One such village in Jordan is Al Beidha, near Petra. It's tempting to think of our ancient forebears as simple people living simple lives, but the inhabitants of villages such as Al Beidha built houses of stone and wood; they tamed, bred and cooked domestic animals; they planted wild seeds, grew crops, crushed grains and kept food in mud vessels hardened

THE RIFT VALLEY & THE BIOGRAPHY OF A SEA

You can't think about history in Jordan without factoring in its position on the edge of the ancient Rift Valley. Standing beside the apologetic trickle of water that runs through Bethany-Beyond-the-Jordan today, it's hard to imagine that some 100,000 years ago the entire Jordan Valley was under the fertile waters of the Red Sea. When the sea retreated it left two landlocked stretches of water – the Sea of Galilee (known in Jordan as Lake Tiberias) and the Dead Sea.

Despite its name – given by the Greek geographer and historian Pausanias, who noticed its life-defying salinity – the Dead Sea has long been associated with health-giving properties. Book into a Dead Sea spa and you will be part of a tradition begun in biblical times. Herod visited the spa at Callirhöe near Herodus Spring to treat itching skin, and Byzantine Christians followed suit along pilgrim roads to Bethany-Beyond-the-Jordan, Mt Nebo and Lot's Cave.

Useful in extending life, the Dead Sea has been useful in death, too. The Greeks and Romans named the Dead Sea the 'Sea of Pitch' on account of the bitumen that used to float to the surface. For thousands of years bitumen has been used in funerary functions and it can be seen ringing the haunting eyes of the Ain Ghazal statues in the Jordan Museum in Amman; dated from around 6000 BC, they're reputedly the oldest sculptures in the world. Bitumen was harvested by the Nabataeans who sold it to the Egyptians, who in turn used it for waterproofing funeral boats and for mummification. Ships laden with bitumen regularly crossed the sea in ancient times, as illustrated in the 6th-century Madaba mosaic map. The last piece of bitumen surfaced in 1936.

Today, the area continues to contribute to health and wealth with important revenues from tourism and potash. Part of the western shore belonged to Jordan when the famous Dead Sea Scrolls were discovered by a Bedouin shepherd at Qumran in 1947. Israel took control of the entire western shore in 1967 after the Six Day War, giving the term 'Rift Valley' a particularly modern resonance.

c 2900 BC

City-states emerge across the Middle East. Towns at Amman, Pella, Deir Alla and Tell Irbid are fortified and trade develops with neighbouring powers in Syria, Palestine and Egypt.

c 2300 BC

Sodom and Gomorrah, among the five so-called Cities of the Plain, are destroyed in a cataclysmic disaster on the southeast corner of the Dead Sea.

c 1500 BC

The Middle East enters a period of turmoil as Egypt's influence declines. The Philistines arrive west of the Jordan River, giving the land its current name of Palestine.

c 1200 BC

Ammon (Amman), Moab (Dhiban) and Edom (Buseira) emerge as the dominant kingdoms east of the Jordan River. According to the Bible, Moses and the Israelites are refused entry to Edom.

under the sun; and they began forming decorative items – such as the astonishing fertility sculptures from Ain Ghazal dated around 6000 BC. These early settlers even left a record of their existence through wall paintings, such as those at Teleilat Ghassul in the Jordan Valley.

Complexity of Early Society in Jordan

If you have lingering doubts about the sophistication of the ancients, ponder the fields of dolmens (constructed between 5000 and 3000 BC) that are scattered throughout the country. Come across the local shepherds and they may well ask you: 'Why are you here? Is anything good here?' That would be a great question to pose to the ancients who carefully aligned their last resting places along the shoulders rather than the ridges of the semi-arid hills.

As for us moderns, these highly charged sites force a reconsideration of these early people: how did they lever the monumental bridging stones into place and what power of belief prompted such laborious, collaborative effort? Many of Jordan's archaeological treasures provoke more questions than they answer in our human quest to understand more about our origins.

According to a German survey, 15,000 to 20,000 tonnes of copper were produced from Feynan's copper-smelting sites – some of the oldest such sites in the region. This has left 150,000 to 200,000 tonnes of slag dotting the arid landscape.

From Metals to Massacres (4000–1200 BC)

Invest enough importance in an object and someone else will inevitably want one as well. There's evidence that Jordan's first farmers swapped desirable items among themselves well before 4000 BC, perhaps triggering the rivalry to make and trade more accurate tools and more beautiful adornments. One commodity useful for both tools and adornments was copper – of which Jordan has plenty. A visit to Khirbet Feynan in present-day Dana Nature Reserve, with its vast areas of black copper slag, illustrates the importance of copper mining for the ancient people of the region.

Within a thousand years, experimentation with metalwork led to the mixing of copper and tin to create bronze, a hardier material that allowed for the rapid development of tools and, of course, weapons.

During the Bronze Age (3200–1200 BC) the region's settlements showed greater signs of accumulated luxury items, growing rich on indigo, sulphur and sugar (which was introduced into Europe from the Dead Sea area). It is not by chance that the greater wealth coincided with a preoccupation with security, with defensive walls built around towns such as Pella. Early invaders included the Amorites, whose arrival in the area is often associated with the violent destruction of the five Cities of the Plain (near the southern end of the Dead Sea), including the settlements of Sodom and Gomorrah.

850 BC

The divided Israelite empire is defeated by Mesha, king of Moab, who recorded his victories on the famous Mesha Stele in the Moabite capital of Dhiban.

582 BC

Ammon, Moab and Edom enjoy brief unity after near annihilation by the Israelites under King David and King Solomon. The union is short-lived; they become Babylonian provinces under King Nebuchadnezzar II.

c 500 BC

The innovation of the camel saddle transforms the lives of Arab nomads and eventually brings new caravans to Jordan's southern deserts en route to Damascus.

333 BC

Alexander the Great wins the Battle of Issus, defeating Persian King Darius III. He moves on Syria and Palestine, which come under the expansive empire of Greece.

Invasion was not confined to the boundaries of modern-day Jordan. By the late Bronze Age (1500–1200 BC), the whole of the Middle East appeared to be at war. Wealthy city-states in Syria collapsed, Egyptians retreated within their own borders from outposts in the Jordan Valley, and marauding foreigners ('Peoples of the Sea') reshaped the political landscape of the Eastern Mediterranean. The latter also brought the Philistines, who settled on the west bank of the Jordan River and gave the land the name of Palestine.

Unity in Adversity (1200–333 BC)

Emergence of a Recognisable 'Jordan'

It is difficult to talk about Jordan as a single entity for most of the country's history. That's because, at least until the latter part of the 20th century AD, its borders expanded and retreated and its peoples came and went, largely driven by the political ambitions and expediencies of more powerful regional neighbours.

Around 1200 BC, however, something akin to a recognisable 'Jordan' emerged from the regional mayhem in the form of three important kingdoms: Edom in the south, with its capital in Bozrah (modern Buseira, near Dana); Moab near Wadi Mujib; and Ammon on the edge of the Arabian Desert, with a capital at Rabbath Ammon (present-day Amman). It is unlikely that any of the three kingdoms had much to do with each other until the foundation of the new neighbouring city-state of Israel.

Succumbing to Powerful Neighbours

Israel quickly became a military power to be reckoned with, dominating the area of Syria and Palestine and coming into inevitable conflict with the neighbours. Under King David the Israelites wrought a terrible revenge on Edom, massacring almost the entire male population;

THE CITY-STATE OF ISRAEL

The kingdoms of Edom, Moab and Ammon are mentioned in the Bible, especially in connection with the wandering Jews of the Exodus. According to the Old Testament, Moses and his brother, Aaron, led their people through Sinai in Egypt looking for a permanent territory to inhabit. They were forbidden entry to southern Jordan by the Edomites but managed to wind their way north, roughly along the route of the modern King's Highway, towards the Jordan River. Moses died on Mt Nebo, in sight of the Promised Land, and it was left to his successor Joshua to lead the Israelites across the river to the West Bank where they conquered the city of Canaan, which led to the establishment of the city-state of Israel in around 1436 BC.

c 323 BC

Alexander dies in Babylon. The Greek inheritance gives access to the treasures of classical learning, and the cities of Philadelphia (Amman), Gadara, Pella and Jerash blossom under Hellenistic rule.

c 100 BC

Greek generals squabble over who rules which parts of the Trans-Jordan while a tribe of nomadic Arabs quietly makes money from passing caravans. They establish their capital at Petra.

30 BC

Herod the Great expands the castle at Mukawir, which in a few years' time is said to set the stage for Salome's dance and the beheading of John the Baptist.

9 BC–AD 40

Aretas IV, greatest of the Nabataean kings, presides over Petra, a city of wealth and beauty. The hidden cluster of tombs, temples and houses is adapted from Greek and Roman architecture.

Moab also succumbed to Israelite control and the people of Ammon were subject to forced labour under the new Jewish masters. However, Israelite might proved short-lived and, after King Solomon's brief but illustrious reign, the kingdom split into Israel and Judah.

By the middle of the first millennium BC – perhaps in response to Israelite aggression – Ammon, Moab and Edom became a unified entity, linked by a trade route known today as the King's Highway. The fledgling amalgam of lands, however, was not strong enough to withstand the might of bullying neighbours, and it was soon overwhelmed by a series of new masters: the Assyrians, Babylonians and Persians. It would be centuries before Jordan achieved a similar distinct identity within its current borders.

The Middle Men of the Middle East (333 BC–AD 324)

War and invasion were not the utter disaster that they might have been for the people of the region. Located at the centre of the land bridge between Africa and Asia, the cities surrounding the King's Highway were particularly well placed to service the needs of passing foreign armies. They also profited from the caravan routes that crossed the deserts from Arabia to the Euphrates, bringing shipments of African gold and South Arabian frankincense via the Red Sea ports in present-day Aqaba and Eilat. The Greeks, the Nabataeans and the Romans each capitalised on this passing bounty, leaving a legacy of imported culture and learning in return.

The Greeks

By the 4th century BC the growing wealth of Arab lands attracted the attention of a young military genius from the West known as Alexander of Macedon. Better known today as Alexander the Great, the precocious 21-year-old stormed through the region in 334 BC, winning territories from Turkey to Palestine.

At his death in 323 BC in Babylon, Alexander ruled a vast empire from the Nile to the Indus, with similarly vast dimensions of commerce. Over the coming centuries, Greek was the lingua franca of Jordan (at least of the written word), giving access to the great intellectual treasures of the classical era. The cities of Philadelphia (Amman), Gadara, Pella and Jerash blossomed under Hellenistic rule, and prospered through growing trade, particularly with Egypt, which fell under the same Greek governance.

AD 26

Jesus Christ is said to be baptised in Bethany-Beyond-the-Jordan by John the Baptist. The first church is built soon after at Rihab, reputedly protecting Jesus' disciples from persecution in Jerusalem.

106

Roman emperor Trajan absorbs the Nabataean empire into the province of Arabia Petraea, signalling the end of Petra's heyday.

111–14

The Romans build the Via Traiana Nova, following the path of the ancient King's Highway between Bosra and the Red Sea, bringing new life to an ancient thoroughfare.

c 200–300

The golden age for Roman Arabia is marked by grand monuments in the cities of the Decapolis. Emperor Hadrian honours Jerash with a visit en route to Palestine.

The Nabataeans

Trade was the key to Jordan's most vibrant period of history, thanks to the growing importance of a nomadic Arab tribe from the south, known as the Nabataeans. The Nabataeans produced only copper and bitumen (for waterproofing boat hulls) but they knew how to trade in the commodities of neighbouring nations. Consummate middlemen, they used their exclusive knowledge of desert strongholds and water supplies to amass wealth from the caravan trade, first by plundering and then by levying tolls on the merchandise that traversed the areas under their control.

The most lucrative trade involved the transportation, by camel, of frankincense and myrrh along the Incense Route from southern Arabia to outposts further north. The Nabataeans were also sole handlers of

GATEWAY TO THE AFTERLIFE: THE NABATAEAN RELIGION

A young family, arriving early for the Petra Night Tour, were waved on alone through the candlelit Siq (gorge). Haunted by the sound of their own footsteps, they soon began to feel there was something amiss. Halfway, the young daughter, overwhelmed by the towering shadows of this sacred way, begged her parents to turn back. A few moments later, all three were hastily beating a retreat. Only those who have ever been in Petra's Siq alone will understand the power this extraordinary passage has on the soul. It was chosen surely for exactly this reason, for it was no ordinary passage: it was a gateway to the afterlife.

Surprisingly little is known about Nabataean religion, considering that their preoccupation with the afterlife dominates much of their capital at Petra. It is known, however, that the early desert polytheistic religion of the original Arabian tribe absorbed Egyptian, Greek and Roman, and even Edomite and Assyrian beliefs, to create a unique faith.

The main Nabataean god was Dushara, the mountain god, who governed the natural world. Over the years he came to be associated with the Egyptian god Osiris, Greek god Dionysus and the Roman god Zeus. For fertility, the Nabataeans prayed to the goddess Al 'Uzza (the Very Strong), who became associated with Aphrodite and Isis. Al Kutba was the god of divination and writing, linked to Hermes and Mercury. Allat (literally 'Goddess') was associated with Athena.

Early representations of the Nabataean gods were nonfigurative. Divine stones known as *baetyls* marked important wadis, junctions, canyons and mountaintops, representing the presence of the divine. Religious processions to Petra's spiritual 'High Places' were an important part of the community's religious life, culminating in a sacrifice (perhaps human) and ritual purification.

Though the secrets of Nabataean religious ceremonies are hidden in history, there is a strong sense of what one might call 'spiritual presence' enveloping Petra's high places of sacrifice: the god blocks, carved niches, altars and sacrificial basins all indicate that the hilltops were holy ground, used by the priests for mediating between heaven and earth.

c 284–305

The Romans build the Strata Diocletiana linking Azraq with Damascus and the Euphrates. A string of forts in the Eastern Desert shores up the rim of the empire.

324

Emperor Constantine converts to Christianity. Christianity becomes the dominant religion of the Byzantine Empire and many churches are built. Madaba becomes the focus of pilgrim trails to Jerusalem.

560

The so-called Mosaic Map is crafted in Madaba; found under rubble by church builders in 1884, it remains the oldest map of Palestine found to date.

614

Emperor Heraclius forces invading Persians to make peace; despite this victory Byzantine Christian rule in the Trans-Jordan soon ends. A storm is brewing in Arabia, bringing Islam in its wake.

spices shipped to Arabia by boat from Somalia, Ethiopia and India. Suburbs at the four corners of their capital, Petra, received the caravans and handled the logistics, processing products and offering banking services and fresh animals before moving the goods west across the Sinai to the ports of Gaza and Alexandria for shipment to Greece and Rome.

The Nabataeans never possessed an 'empire' in the common military and administrative senses of the word; instead, from about 200 BC, they established a 'zone of influence' that stretched from Syria to Rome. As the Nabataean territory expanded under King Aretas III (84–62 BC), they controlled and taxed trade throughout the Hejaz (northern Arabia), the Negev, the Sinai, and the Hauran of southern Syria. Nabataean communities were influential as far away as Rome, and Nabataean tombs still stand at the impressive site of Madain Saleh in Saudi Arabia.

Key Nabataean Sites

- *Petra (Jordan)*
- *Siq Al Barid (Little Petra; Jordan)*
- *Madain Saleh (Saudi Arabia)*

The Romans

You only have to visit Jerash for five minutes, trip over a fallen column and notice the legions of other columns nearby, to gain an immediate understanding of the importance of the Romans in Jordan – and the importance of Jordan to the Romans. This magnificent set of ruins is grand on a scale that is seldom seen in modern building enterprises and indicates the amount of wealth the Romans invested in this outpost of their empire. Jerash was clearly worth its salt and, indeed, it was the lucrative trade associated with the Nabataeans that attracted the Romans in the first place. It's perhaps a fitting legacy of their rule that the Jordanian currency, the dinar, derives its name from the Latin *denarius* (ancient Roman silver coin).

The Romans brought many benefits to the region, constructing two new roads through Jordan – the Via Traiana Nova (AD 111–114) linking Bosra with the Red Sea, and the Strata Diocletiana (AD 284–305) linking Azraq with Damascus and the Euphrates. A string of forts in the Eastern Desert at Qasr Al Hallabat, Azraq and Umm Al Jimal was also built to shore up the eastern rim of the empire.

The 2nd and 3rd centuries were marked by a feverish expansion of trade as the Via Traiana became the main thoroughfare for Arabian caravans, armies and supplies. The wealth benefited the cities of Jerash, Umm Qais and Pella, members of the Decapolis, a league of provincial cities that accepted Roman cultural influence but retained their independence.

With the eventual demise of the Roman Empire and the fracturing of trade routes over the subsequent centuries, Jordan's entrepreneurial leadership of the region never quite regained the same status.

Jordan's Roman Spectacles

- *Citadel (Amman)*
- *Roman Theatre (downtown Amman)*
- *Forum (Jerash)*
- *Decumanus maximus (Umm Qais)*
- *Hint of former glories at Pella*
- *Refurbished colonnaded street (Petra)*

629

Muslim forces lose the Battle of Mu'tah against Christians. After Prophet Muhammad's death (632), they win the decisive Battle of Yarmouk (636) and Islam becomes the region's dominant religion.

c 700

The Umayyads from Syria overtake the region and build some extraordinary bathhouses, hunting lodges and fortified meeting places (known today as the 'desert 'castles) in the arid desert east of Amman.

747

An earthquake shatters northern Jordan and Syria, weakening the Umayyads' hold on power. They're replaced by the Abbasids, signalling a period of Persian cultural dominance and less tolerance towards Christianity.

1095

Pope Urban II sparks a 'holy war' in revenge for church destruction by Seljuks and to protect pilgrim routes to the Holy Land. Crusaders soon capture Jerusalem, slaughtering countless inhabitants.

Spirit of the Age (AD 324–1516)

For 1500 years after the birth of Jesus, the history of Jordan was characterised by the expression of organised faith in one form or another. Under the influence of Rome, Christianity replaced the local gods of the Nabataeans, and several hundred years later Islam took its place – but not before a struggle that left a long-term legacy and a string of Crusader forts.

The discovery in 2008 of the world's oldest church in Rihab, near the Jordanian–Syrian border, was described by senior Orthodox clerics as an 'important milestone for Christians all around the world'.

Conversion to Christianity

Think of the history of the Christian religion and most people understandably focus on the 'Holy Land' to the west of the Jordan River. And yet, if recent evidence is to be believed, the Christian church may never have evolved (at least not in the way we know it today) if it hadn't been for the shelter afforded to the early proponents of the faith on the *east* bank of the Jordan.

In 2008, 40km northeast of Amman, archaeologists uncovered what they believe to be the first church in the world. Dating from AD 33 to AD 70, the church, which was buried under St Georgeous Church in Rihab, appears to have sheltered the 70 disciples of Jesus Christ. Described in the mosaic inscriptions on the floor of the old church as the '70 beloved by God and Divine', these first Christians fled persecution in Jerusalem and lived in secrecy, practising their rituals in the underground church. Pottery dating from the 3rd to the 7th century shows that these disciples and their families lived in the area until late Roman rule.

The conversion by Emperor Constantine to Christianity in AD 324 eventually legitimised the practice of Christianity across the region. East of the Jordan River, churches were constructed (often from the building blocks of former Greek and Roman temples) and embellished with the elaborate mosaics that are still visible today at Madaba, Umm Ar Rasas and Petra. Christian pilgrims began to search for relics of the Holy Land, building churches en route at biblical sites, such as Bethany, Mt Nebo and Lot's Cave. It was the archaeological rediscovery of these churches 1400 years later that confirmed the lost location of these biblical sites to a forgetful modern world.

Prophet Muhammad's son-in-law, the caliph Ali, was assassinated in 660. He was succeeded by Mu'awiyah, who established the Umayyad dynasty (661–750). The bitter dispute over this succession split Islam into two factions, the Sunnis and the Shiites.

The Rise of Islam

Reminders of Christianity are scattered across Jordan today, for instance in the observance of the faith in towns such as Madaba. But listen to the bells peal on a weekend and moments later they will be replaced by the muezzin's call to prayer from the neighbouring mosque. Islam is present not just in Jordan's mosques but in the law, in social etiquette and at the very heart of the way people live their lives – in Bedouin camps as well

1115

Crusader King Baldwin I builds Montreal (Mount Real or the Royal Mountain) – the picture-perfect castle in Shobak. It withstood numerous attacks from the armies of Saladin.

1142

The imposing Karak Castle is built to withstand Saladin's armies; in 1148 it is inherited by the sadistic Renauld de Châtillon of France who delights in torturing prisoners.

1187

Despite stout defences at Shobak and Karak, Karak is overrun after an epic siege in 1183; Saladin goes on to beat the Crusader armies in the decisive Battle of Hittin.

1193

Saladin dies and the ensuing family in-fighting enables the Crusaders to recapture much of their former territory.

as in modern city centres. So how did Islam reach here and how did it replace Christianity as the dominant religion?

From 622 (10 years before the death of the Prophet Muhammad) the armies of Islam travelled northwards, quickly and easily spreading the message of submission (Islam) well beyond the Arabian Peninsula. Although they lost their first battle against the Christian Byzantines at Mu'tah (near Karak) in 629, they returned seven years later to win the Battle of Yarmouk. Jerusalem fell in 638 and Syria was taken in 640. Islam, under the Sunni dynasty of the Umayyads, became the dominant religion of the region, headquartered in the city of Damascus, and Arabic replaced Greek as the main language. Within 100 years Muslim armies controlled a vast empire that spread from Spain to India.

The Umayyads' rich architectural legacy included the Umayyad Mosque in Damascus and the Dome of the Rock in Jerusalem. In eastern Jordan, the Umayyads' close attachment to the desert led to the construction of a string of opulent 'desert castles', including the brooding Qasr Kharana (built in 710) and Qusayr Amra (711).

HISTORY OF A HIGHWAY

When pondering the King's Highway, a fair question to ask is, 'Which king?' In fact, the highway was never the personal project of royalty: it gained its name through the sense of major thoroughfare, often referred to in the region as 'royal road'.

The highway has great religious significance for both Christians and Muslims. Today the highway runs for 297km between Madaba and Petra but for a thousand years before Christ, it linked the kingdoms of Ammon, Moab and Edom. One of the earliest mentions of the highway is in the biblical episode in which Moses was refused passage along the highway by the King of Edom. The Nabataeans used the route to transport frankincense, originating in southern Arabia, and other exotic commodities to the important trading posts of Syria. In later times, the highway received a suitably Roman makeover under Emperor Trajan, who widened and rerouted part of the highway to facilitate the passage of troops.

Attracted by the holy sites of Mt Nebo and protected by the Crusader forces, Christians used the route for pilgrimage, building and embellishing many shrines along the way, such as the Church of St Stephen at Umm Ar Rasas. Muslims used the route on pilgrimage to Mecca until the Ottomans developed the Tariq Al Bint in the 16th century – the approximate path of the Hejaz Railway, built in 1900, and the modern Desert Highway.

Inevitably, the importance of the King's Highway declined and it was only in the 1950s and 1960s that it was upgraded to a tarmac road. Today, it's a rural, often potholed route, sadly beleaguered by litter, which despite ambling through some of the loveliest and most striking landscape in Jordan betrays little of its former status as a road fit for kings.

1258

Mongols storm Baghdad and the armies of Genghis Khan's son reach Ajloun and Salt. They are repelled by Mamluks who rebuild the castles at Karak, Shobak and Ajloun.

1453

Ottoman rule is established in Constantinople (modern-day İstanbul), creating one of the world's largest empires that extends throughout the Middle East.

c 1516–1916

The Ottomans lavish their attentions on Jerusalem and Damascus while the area east of the Jordan River becomes a cultural and political backwater.

1798

Napoleon Bonaparte invades Egypt, bringing the Middle East within the sphere of Western political rivalry – a rivalry that influences the political landscape of Trans-Jordan over the next 150 years.

Despite the blossoming of Islamic scholarship in medicine, biology, philosophy, architecture and agriculture over the next three centuries, the area wedged between Jerusalem and Baghdad remained isolated from the sophisticated Arab mainstream. This is one reason why Jordan possesses relatively few demonstrations of Islamic cultural exuberance.

The Crusades & Holy War

The armies of Islam and Christianity have clashed many times throughout history and the consequences (and language of religious conflict) resonate to this day both within the Middle East and across the world at large.

The Crusades of the 12th and 13th centuries are among the most famous of the early conflicts between Muslims and Christians. By surveying the mighty walls of the great Crusader castles at Karak and Shobak, it's easy to see that both sides meant business: these were holy wars (albeit attracting mercenary elements) in which people willingly sacrificed their comfort and even lives for their faith in the hope of gaining glory in the hereafter – ironically, according to Islam at least, a hereafter shared by Muslims and the 'People of the Book' (Jews, Christians and so-called Sabians).

Built by King Baldwin I in the 12th century, the castles were part of a string of fortifications designed to control the roads from Damascus to Cairo. They seemed inviolable, and they may have remained so but for Nureddin and Saladin, who between them occupied most of the Crusader strongholds in the region, including those of Oultrejordain (meaning 'across the Jordan'). The Damascus-based Ayyubids, members of Saladin's family, squabbled over his empire on his death in 1193, enabling the Crusaders to recapture much of their former territory along the coast.

The Ayyubids were replaced by the Mamluks, who seized control of the area east of the Jordan River and rebuilt the castles at Karak, Shobak and Ajloun. They used these strongholds as lookouts and as a series of staging posts for message-carrying pigeons. Indeed, thanks to the superior communications that this unique strategy afforded, you could argue that the Crusaders were defeated not by the military might of Islam but on the wings of their peace-loving doves.

Western Love Affair with the Middle East (1516–1914)

The Ottoman Turks took Constantinople in 1453 and created one of the world's largest empires. They defeated the Mamluks in present-day Jordan in 1516, but concentrated their efforts on the lucrative cities of the region, such as the holy city of Jerusalem and the commercial centre of Damascus. The area east of the Jordan River once again became a forgotten backwater. Forgotten, that is, by the Ottoman Empire, but not entirely

Maalouf's lively *The Crusades Through Arab Eyes* recasts the West's image of knights in shining armour as ruthless barbarians who pillaged the Middle East, the horrors of which incursion still reside in the collective Arab consciousness.

Nureddin (literally 'Light of the Faith') was the son of a Turkish tribal ruler. He united the Arab world and defeated the Crusaders in Egypt. His campaign against the Crusaders was completed by Saladin (Restorer of the Faith), a Kurdish scholar and military leader.

1812
Burckhardt rediscovers Petra for the Western world, sparking an enduring fascination with the fabled Pink City, and the region in general, among Western travellers, archaeologists, writers and artists.

1839
The British artist David Roberts (1796–1864) visits the region and immortalises Petra in lithographic prints that are still popular today.

1908
The Ottoman Empire, now 'the sick man of Europe', builds the Hejaz Railway linking Damascus with the holy city of Medina, via Amman, in an effort to reassert regional influence.

1914–18
During WWI Jordan sees fierce fighting between Ottoman Turks (allied with the Germans) and the British, based in Egypt. By 1917 British troops occupy Jerusalem, and Syria thereafter.

ignored by Western interests. Indeed, the period of gradually weakening Ottoman occupation over the next few centuries also marked an increasingly intense scrutiny by the Europeans – the British and the French in particular.

In the preface to *Les Orientales* (1829), Victor Hugo wrote that the whole of the European continent appeared to be 'leaning towards the East'. This was not a new phenomenon. Trade between the West and the East was long established and stories of the 'barbaric pearl and gold' of Arabia soon aroused the interests of a wider public. By the late 18th century Europeans were making pleasure trips to the Syrian desert, adopting articles of Albanian and Turkish dress, carrying pocket editions of Persian tales and penning their own travelogues.

The Qala'at Ar Rabad at Ajloun was built by the Ayyubids. In 1250 they were ousted by the Mamluks, a group of foreign, adolescent warriors serving as a soldier-slave caste for the Ayyubids. The Mamluks ruled for the next 300 years.

Swiss explorer Johann Ludwig Burckhardt's monumental rediscovery of Petra in 1812 led to a further explosion of interest in the region. Societies were founded for the purpose of promoting Middle East exploration, and scholars began translating Persian, Arabic and Sanskrit texts. Many aspects of the Orient were explored in Western fiction, much of which attracted a wide and enthusiastic readership. Indeed, by the end of the 19th century the fascination with the Arabian East was, to use Edward Said's phrase, no 'airy European fantasy' but a highly complex relationship defined by scientists, scholars, travellers and fiction writers.

This is the cultural backdrop upon which the political manoeuvrings of the 20th century were played out.

Fighting for an Arab Land (1914–46)

Writing of the Arab Revolt that passed through the heart of Jordan in the early 20th century, TE Lawrence described the phenomenon as 'an Arab war waged and led by Arabs for an Arab aim in Arabia'. This is a significant statement as it identifies a growing sense of political identity among Arab people throughout the last half of the 19th century and beginning of the 20th century. This pan-Arab consciousness grew almost in proportion (or at least coincidentally) to the territorial interest of Western powers in Arab lands. Slowly, in place of loose tribal interests, Arabs came to define themselves as a single, unified entity – an Islamic 'other' perhaps to the Christian European threat pulsing around the Suez.

Between 1775 and 1825, 87 volumes on aspects of the Near East were published in Britain alone, and 46 reviews of the same books appeared in leading journals between 1805 and 1825.

Arabs were prepared to fight for this new Arab nationalism, as Lawrence describes in the *Seven Pillars of Wisdom,* his account of the Arab Revolt and the way in which it was inspired by idealism. History shows, however, that it was to take more than just 'spur and rein' to create viable Arab states; indeed complex diplomacy, both within Arab countries and in their relationship with the West, characterised the pursuit of nationalism throughout the 20th century.

1916

The Arab Revolt, led by Faisal and backed by the British with the famous assistance of TE Lawrence, storms Aqaba, disrupts the Hejaz Railway and marches on Damascus.

1917

The Balfour Declaration giving Jews a home in Palestine is not the reward the Arabs are promised. In a reluctant compromise, Faisal's brother, Abdullah, becomes ruler of Trans-Jordan.

1923

Britain recognises Jordan as an independent emirate under its protection. A small defence force, the Arab Legion, is set up under British officers and the nominal control of Emir Abdullah.

1930s

The Nazi persecution of Jews accelerates Jewish immigration to Palestine, fuelling more violence between Jews and Arabs. A 1939 proposal to create a binational state is rejected by both sides.

The Arab Revolt

Ironically, the new Arab nationalist movement cut its teeth not on a Western Christian enemy but on the Ottomans, the apathetic Muslim rulers who dominated most of the Middle East, including the area on either side of the Jordan River. The revolt was fought by Arab warriors on horseback, loosely formed into armies under Emir Faisal, the ruler of Mecca and guardian of the Muslim holy places, who had taken up the reins of the Arab nationalist movement in 1914. He was joined by his brother Abdullah and the enigmatic British colonel TE Lawrence, known as Lawrence of Arabia. Lawrence helped with coordination and securing supplies from the Allies, as well as attacking the Turkish-controlled Hejaz Railway, in a campaign that swept across the desert from Arabia, wrested Aqaba from the Ottomans and eventually ousted them from Damascus. By 1918 the Arabs controlled modern Saudi Arabia, Jordan and parts of southern Syria. Faisal set up government in Damascus and dreamed of an independent Arab realm.

Glad of the help in weakening the Ottoman Empire (allies of Germany during WWI), the British promised to help Faisal. The promise was severely undermined, however, by the 1917 Balfour Declaration which gave stated and practical support to the establishment of a 'National Home for the Jewish people' in Palestine. This contradictory acceptance of both a Jewish homeland in Palestine and the preservation of the rights of the original Palestinian community lies at the heart of the seemingly irreconcilable Arab–Israeli conflict.

The betrayal of the Arab cause by Western allies was underlined by the secret Sykes-Picot Agreement of 1916 in which 'Syria' (modern-day Syria and Lebanon) came under French control, and 'Palestine' (an area including modern Israel, the Palestinian Territories and Jordan) came under British control.

The Creation of Jordan

The Arab Revolt may not have immediately achieved its goal during peace negotiations, but it did lead directly (albeit after more than two decades of wrangling with the British) to the birth of the modern state of Jordan.

THE HEJAZ RAILWAY

The Hejaz Railway was built between 1900 and 1908 to transport pilgrims from Damascus to the holy city of Medina, reducing the two-month journey by camel and on foot to as little as three days. For Jordan, and Amman in particular, this meant a boom in trade. The 1462km line was completely funded by donations from Muslims – but functioned for less than 10 years. The trains and railway line were partially destroyed in the Arab Revolt of 1917 during WWI. The line was rebuilt as far south as Ma'an but is now only used for cargo. There is occasional talk of introducing a tourist passenger service between Aqaba and Wadi Rum, but for now the only hint of the line's former glory is through the occasional re-enactment courtesy of the Jordan Heritage Revival Company.

1931

The colourful Desert Camel Corp is set up by a British officer, Major Glubb, as a branch of the Arab Legion; it is comprised mostly of nomadic Bedouins.

1946

Jordan gains full independence from the British; Emir Abdullah, who took a leading role in the Arab Revolt, is crowned the king of Jordan.

1947

The UN votes for the partition of Palestine but the proposal is rejected by the Arab League on the grounds that the whole territory should remain Arab.

1948

The State of Israel is proclaimed, the British withdraw immediately and renewed hostilities break out between Arabs and Jews. Half a million Palestinians flood into the 'West Bank'.

At the 1919 Paris Peace Conference the British came to an agreement with Faisal, who was given jurisdiction over Iraq, while his elder brother Abdullah was proclaimed ruler of Trans-Jordan, the land lying between Iraq and the east bank. A young Winston Churchill drew up the borders in 1921, and Abdullah made Amman his capital. Britain recognised the territory as an independent state under its protection in 1923, and a small defence force, the Arab Legion, was set up under British officers. A series of treaties after 1928 led to full independence in 1946, when Abdullah was proclaimed king.

Troubles with Palestine (1946–94)

If there is one element that defines the modern history of Jordan, it's the relationship with the peoples on the other side of the Jordan River – not just the Jews but also (and perhaps more especially) the Palestinians, who today make up the majority of the population of Jordan.

Much of the conflict stems from the creation of a Jewish national homeland in Palestine, where Arab Muslims accounted for about 90% of the population. Their resentment was understood by Arabs across the region and informed the dialogue of Arab–Israeli relations for the rest of the 20th century.

Jordan has two recognised ethnic minorities, though most have integrated through marriage. Circassians (Muslims from the Caucasus who fled Russian persecution in the late 19th century) live near Amman. Chechens, related to the Circassians historically and ethnically, live near Azraq. Together they comprise around 2% of Jordan's population.

New Hashemite Kingdom of Jordan

In 1948 resentment escalated into conflict between Arab and Israeli forces, with the result that Jordan won control of East Jerusalem and the West Bank. King Abdullah, reneging on assurances regarding Palestinian independence, annexed the territory and proclaimed the new Hashemite Kingdom of Jordan (HKJ). The new state won immediate recognition from Britain and the US, but regional powers disapproved of the annexation, added to which the unprecedented immigration of Palestinian refugees placed a strain on limited domestic resources.

In July 1951 King Abdullah was assassinated outside Al Aqsa Mosque in Jerusalem. The throne eventually passed to his beloved 17-year-old grandson, Hussein, in May 1953. Hussein offered a form of citizenship to all Palestinian Arab refugees in 1960, but refused to relinquish Palestinian territory. Partly in response, the Palestine Liberation Organisation (PLO) was formed in 1964.

The Six Day War

After a period of relative peace and prosperity, conflict between Arab and Israeli forces broke out again in the 1960s, culminating in the Six Day War, provoked by Palestinian guerrilla raids into Israel from Syria. When the Syrians announced that Israel was amassing troops in preparation for an assault, Egypt responded by asking the UN to withdraw

1950

King Abdullah annexes the West Bank and east Jerusalem, despite paying lip service to Arab declarations backing Palestinian independence and expressly ruling out territorial annexations.

1951

King Abdullah is assassinated at Al Aqsa Mosque (Jerusalem), ending his dream of a single Arab state encompassing Syria, Lebanon, Jordan, Israel and Palestine – a dream that antagonised Arab neighbours.

1953

Hussein becomes king of Jordan after his father is diagnosed with schizophrenia. Despite his British education, Hussein makes his mark by ousting remaining British troops.

1958

King Hussein's gesture of independence doesn't last long as British troops are invited to return after Hussein's failed attempt at union with Iraq.

its Emergency Force from the Egypt–Israel border. Egyptian President Gamal Abdel Nasser then closed the Straits of Tiran (the entrance to the Red Sea), effectively sealing off the port of Eilat. Five days later Jordan and Egypt signed a mutual defence pact, dragging Jordan into the oncoming hostilities.

On 5 June 1967 the Israelis dispatched a predawn raid that wiped out the Egyptian Air Force on the ground. In the following days they decimated Egyptian troops in Sinai and Jordanian troops on the West Bank, and overran the Golan Heights in Syria.

The outcome for Jordan was disastrous: it lost the whole of the West Bank and its part of Jerusalem, which together had supplied Jordan with its two principal sources of income – agriculture and tourism. It also resulted in yet another huge wave of Palestinian refugees.

When it was founded, the Palestine Liberation Organization had the blessing of the Arab League to represent the Palestinian people and train guerrilla fighters. The Palestine National Council (PNC) became the executive body of the PLO, with a remit to govern Palestine.

Black September

After the 1967 defeat, the frustrated Palestinians within Jordan became increasingly militant, and by 1968 Palestinian *fedayeen* (guerrilla) fighters were effectively acting as a state within a state, openly defying Jordanian soldiers.

In 1970 Palestinian militants fired on King Hussein's motorcade and held 68 foreigners hostage in an Amman hotel, while the rogue Popular Front for the Liberation of Palestine hijacked and destroyed three Western planes in front of horrified TV crews. Martial law and bloody fighting (which claimed 3000 lives) followed. Yasser Arafat was spirited out of Amman disguised as a Kuwaiti sheikh to attend an Arab League summit in Cairo. A fragile ceasefire was signed, but it was not until midway through 1971 that the final resistance (around Ajloun) was defeated. The guerrillas were forced to recognise Hussein's authority and the Palestinians had to choose between exile and submission. Most chose exile in Lebanon.

Queen Noor, King Hussein's first wife, is not the mother of the present king. That distinction belongs to Hussein's second wife, Princess Muna, who was from England. They were married for 10 years (1961–71), having met on the film set of *Lawrence of Arabia*.

Relinquishing Claims to Palestinian Leadership

In 1974 King Hussein reluctantly relinquished Jordan's claims to the West Bank by recognising the PLO as the sole representative of Palestinians with the right to set up a government in any liberated territory. By 1988 the King had severed all Jordan's administrative and legal ties with the West Bank.

In the meantime profound demographic changes, including a sharp rise in population, particularly of young people, had reshaped Jordan. Economic migration, both from the countryside to the city and from Jordan to the increasingly wealthy Gulf States, together with improved education, changed social and family structures. Most significantly, Palestinians no longer formed an edgy minority of refugees but instead took their place as the majority of Jordan's population.

1960

Jordan offers partial citizenship to Palestinian Arab refugees but refuses to relinquish Palestinian territory. In response, the Palestine Liberation Organisation (PLO) is formed in 1964, backed by the Arab League.

1967

Israel wins Jerusalem and the West Bank in the Six Day War resulting in another influx of Palestinians. Al Fatah dominates the PLO under Yasser Arafat, training guerrillas for Israeli raids.

1970

Black September results in thousands being injured in clashes between the Jordanian government and Palestinian guerrillas. Three hijacked aircraft are blown up by the PLO.

1988

King Hussein relinquishes remaining ties with the West Bank. The focus turns to home where women are now allowed to vote (from 1989) and political parties are legalised thereafter.

The complete integration of Palestinian refugees into all aspects of mainstream Jordanian life is due in no small part to the skilful diplomacy of King Hussein. The numerous assassination attempts (there were at least 12) that dogged the early years of his reign were replaced with a growing respect for his genuine, deep-rooted concern for the Palestinians' plight – which is significant in a region where few other countries were willing to shoulder the burden.

Peace with Israel

On 26 October 1994, Jordan and Israel signed a momentous peace treaty that provided for the removal of all economic barriers between the two countries and closer cooperation on security, water and other issues.

But there is a twist to the final chapter of relations between Jordan and Palestine in the 20th century. There was a clause in the treaty recognising the 'special role of the Hashemite Kingdom of Jordan in the Muslim holy shrines in Jerusalem'. This inclusion aroused the suspicions of some Palestinians regarding the intentions of King Hussein, who at the outset of his long career had enjoyed more than just a 'special role' on the west bank of the Jordan. The treaty made Jordan unpopular within the region at the time, but in the longer term barely cast a shadow over the illustrious reign of one of the Middle East's most beloved rulers.

A PLO–Israeli declaration of principles in September 1993 set in motion the process of establishing an autonomous Palestinian authority in the Occupied Territories. With this declaration, the territorial question was virtually removed as an obstacle to peace between Jordan and Israel.

Relations with Israel & the Palestinian Territories Today

It has been a long time since the historic 1994 peace treaty and the long-term effect of peace with Israel is still being assessed. While the treaty was branded by some Palestinians as a betrayal, the world at large regarded it as a highly significant step towards vital East–West ties. Flare-ups between the two nations continue to occur, not just over the fate of the Palestinian people but also over issues such as water supply, which many predict will replace oil as the issue of conflict of the next few decades, and more recently over the custodianship of and access to Al Aqsa Mosque in Jerusalem.

The Iraqi Dilemma (1990–2017)

Arab Federation

For the past two decades Jordan has been preoccupied with its neighbours to the East rather than the West – a shift in focus necessitated firstly by the Gulf War and subsequently by the US-led invasion of Iraq.

Given that the founding fathers of the modern states of Iraq and Jordan were brothers, it is not surprising that the two countries have

1990

Saddam Hussein's invasion of Kuwait, supported by the Palestinians, requires careful diplomacy by King Hussein, who publicly supports Baghdad while suing for peace. Palestinian Gulf workers flood into Jordan.

1994

A historic peace treaty between Israel and Jordan ends 46 years of war and gives Jordan a 'special role' over Muslim holy shrines in Jerusalem – straining relations with Arab neighbours.

1999

King Hussein dies. His funeral is attended by former and current presidents of Israel and major powers, honouring his role as peace mediator. His son, Abdullah, becomes king.

2000

Jordan accedes to the World Trade Organisation, and the European Free Trade Association (2001). Trade significantly increases under the free-trade accord with the US and Jordanian Qualifying Industrial Zones (QIZ).

enjoyed periods of close collaboration over the years. In 1958 King Hussein tried to capitalise on this dynastic dimension by establishing the Arab Federation, a short-lived alliance between Jordan and Iraq that was intended to counterbalance the formation of the United Arab Republic between Egypt and Syria. Although the alliance did not last long, the connection between the neighbours remained strong, especially in terms of trade.

The Gulf War

When Saddam Hussein invaded Kuwait in 1990, Jordan found itself in a no-win situation. On the one hand, the Palestinian majority in Jordan backed Saddam's invasion, having been given assurances by Saddam that the showdown would result in a solution to the Palestinian question on the West Bank. On the other hand, King Hussein recognised that siding with Iraq would antagonise Western allies and risk Jordan's US trade and aid. As a solution, he sided publicly with Baghdad while complying, officially at least, with the UN embargo on trade with Iraq. As a result, although US and Saudi aid were temporarily suspended, loans and help were forthcoming from other quarters, particularly Japan and Europe.

Despite these new streams of income, the Gulf War exacted a heavy financial penalty on the small and relatively poor, oil-less state of Jordan. Ironically, however, Jordan's third wave of refugees in 45 years brought some relief as 500,000 Jordanians and Palestinians returned from the Gulf States. They brought with them a US$500 million windfall that stimulated the economy throughout the 1990s and helped turn Amman, in particular, into a cosmopolitan, modern city.

Growing Tensions with Iraq

Ongoing resentment about the outcome of the Iraqi refugee crisis is one reason for a cooling of relations between Jordan and Iraq; another reason is concern over the weakened state of Iraq, resulting in a general vulnerability of the region to radical terrorism – the reason behind Jordan's reintroduction of capital punishment in 2014. Anxiety over Iraq's porous borders and incursions from Isis militants continues, and many in Jordan also fear that a weak Iraq leaves Jordan vulnerable to increased Iranian and Shiite influence.

The heightened tensions between Jordan and Iraq was further exacerbated in 2014 when more than 150 Sunni leaders from various groups opposed to the official government in Iraq met for a two-day meeting in Jordan's capital, pledging to depose Nouri Al Maliki, the Iraqi prime minister. Although nothing came of it, and the Jordanian government

UN assessments put the total cost to Jordan of the Gulf War (mid-1990 to mid-1991) at more than US$8 billion. The UN naval blockade of Aqaba alone, aimed at enforcing UN sanctions against Iraq, cost Jordan US$300 million a year in lost revenue between 1991 and 1994.

Modern History of Jordan

The Middle East: A Brief History of the Last 2000 Years (Bernard Lewis; 1996)

History of the Arabs (Philip Hitti; 1937)

2001

The US invasion of Iraq is strenuously protested by Arab countries. King Abdullah sides publicly with Baghdad while complying, officially at least, with the UN embargo on trade with Iraq.

2005

Three hotels in Amman are blown up in coordinated suicide attacks, masterminded by Al Qaeda. Tourism, booming since the 1994 peace treaty, takes an immediate hit.

2007

As part of the country's political, economic and social modernisation, 20% of seats in municipal councils are reserved for women. Petra is voted one of the new seven wonders of the world by popular ballot.

2008

Iraq contributes to the maintenance of the 500,000 Iraqi refugees in Jordan. The Iraqi influx is the fourth major inflow of refugees in the modern history of this geographically small country.

KING HUSSEIN

Since his death, King Hussein has become a legend. On succeeding to the throne on 2 May 1953 at the age of 17, the youthful, British-educated Hussein was known more for his love of pretty women and fast cars. Forty-five years later he was fêted as one of the Middle East's great political survivors, king against the odds and the de facto creator of the modern state of Jordan.

King Hussein's loyalty to his people was notable. In a role emulated by his son decades later, Hussein would disguise himself as a taxi driver and ask passengers what they thought of the king. Hussein's lasting legacy, however, extends beyond his successful domestic policy. Throughout his reign he maintained close and friendly ties with Britain and courted trade with the West. From his sustained efforts at diplomacy to avert the 1991 Gulf War to his peace agreement with Israel in 1994, the urbane and articulate king of a country in one of the world's toughest neighbourhoods came to be seen as a beacon of moderateness and stability in a region known for neither attribute. This reputation was secured in 1997 when a Jordanian soldier shot and killed seven Israeli schoolgirls in northern Jordan. King Hussein personally attended the funeral in a public display of grief and solidarity with the Israeli families.

Married four times and father to 11 children, Hussein was a highly popular man with many interests and was an accomplished pilot. After a long battle with cancer, during which time he continued his role as peace negotiator between Israel and Palestine, he died in Jordan in February 1999. He was greatly mourned not just by those who knew him personally but by the people of Jordan and the region at large.

Hussein is now regarded as a man who firmly steered the nascent country of Jordan through potentially devastating crises, balancing the demands of Arab nationalism against the political expedience of cooperation with Western interests. In so doing, he helped pave the way for Jordan's modern role in the world as a bridge between two ideologies.

denied involvement in promoting the opposition alliance, the Iraqi government retaliated by threatening to revisit agreements regarding fuel prices. Thankfully for Jordan this did not happen, but the country has been hit by the instability over the last few years occasioned by Isis control of much of Iraqi Anbar province, which lies just across the Iraqi border from Jordan. This resulted in a substantial drop in export revenue arising from Jordanian Free Zones as Isis forces levied high taxes on all Jordanian trucks passing through Anbar province. It remains to be seen what effect on Jordanian–Iraqi trade the apparent demise of Isis in Mosul in 2017 will bring.

2011

Protests in Amman mark the 'Arab Spring', a period of uprising against the establishment across the region and expressed in Jordan in a series of mass demonstrations.

2012

Protests continue, largely as a response to rising costs of living, and result in the unsuccessful demand for the end of the monarchy and the abdication of King Abdullah II.

2012–13

Jordan experiences its fifth major wave of immigration as a result of civil war in Syria. Some 600,000 refugees pour into the north creating the world's second-largest refugee camp.

2017

Two deaths occur at the Israeli embassy in Amman – an incident prompted by tensions over restricted access to Al Aqsa Mosque. Ten terrorists are executed, resulting from the reintroduction of capital punishment in 2014.

Amateur Archaeology

Jordan has been the site of intense archaeological scrutiny for decades, but you don't have to be Indiana Jones to take an interest – anyone can gain pleasure in rummaging around Jordan's many ancient sites. If just looking isn't enough, however, and you can't resist the temptation to get physical with the past, then here are a few ideas on how to join an amateur dig, with some of the key archaeological sites to focus on.

Digging Up the Past

Take any path off the beaten track in central Jordan and you will be sure to stumble on something ancient – a fallen column with poppies dancing on the capital, coloured *tesserae* from a broken mosaic, a coin of indiscriminate currency. Look more carefully, and you'll probably see the remains of a fence enclosing a patch of land fast returning to wilderness – evidence, if any were needed, that human habitation extends back to the very earliest periods of human history.

Two Centuries of Archaeology in Jordan

In many respects, the modern study of Western archaeology was founded in what we now call Jordan, arising out of a fascination with tracing the traditions of the Bible to the unearthed ruins of the Holy Land – on both sides of the Jordan River – and setting them in a historical context.

For decades, this was an occupation that attracted largely foreign interest as the people of the region were more focused on the demands of the present than on digging up remnants of the past.

Today this is no longer the case, as Jordanians have the time and the means to take a greater interest in their heritage, and education helps new generations to come to a better appreciation of the country's position within the cradle of civilisation. Each year more funding is put aside for archaeological exploration, with the result that some of the greatest finds, involving teams from universities in Jordan and abroad, have been made within the last 30 years, culminating in 2008 with the world's oldest church – a befitting discovery for a discipline that arose largely out of Christian curiosity.

1812

Swiss explorer Jean Louis Burckhardt, aged 27, 'rediscovers' Petra for the West, stimulating a fascination with ancient history in the region that endures for the next two centuries.

1868

The precious Mesha Stele, one of the earliest examples of Hebrew script, is discovered by a missionary at Dhiban – and promptly shattered by bickering neighbours.

1900s

Jordan and the Levant are explored by British, American, French and German surveyors, including a young archaeology student from Oxford by the name of TE Lawrence (of Arabia).

1920s

Following the British mandate of Jordan, modest excavation projects aimed at consolidating the main standing monuments begin throughout Jordan.

1930s

Remarkable mosaics, regarded today as some of the finest in the Levant, are unearthed in Madaba.

1940s

The Dead Sea Scrolls are discovered by a Bedouin shepherd in Qumran at a time when parts of the western shore of the Dead Sea belong to Jordan.

1950s–60s

The Arab–Israeli wars and the aftermath of WWII lead to a rare lean period in archaeological study in Jordan.

VLADJ55/SHUTTERSTOCK

Ain Ghazal statue, Jordan Museum (p51)

Getting Involved

Volunteering on a Dig

> **Digs on the Web**
>
> **Madaba Plains Project** *(www.madabaplains.org/hisban) Excavation at Tell Hesban.*
>
> **Popular Archaeology** *(www.popular-archaeology.com) Excavation around the world, including Jordan.ding Jordan.*

Archaeological fieldwork is a painstaking process but the rewards are great, particularly if you uncover something special like a coral bead worn by an ancient, a piece of copper cast 6000 years ago or a shard of pottery with the design intact. It's not so much the finding of an object as the sense of connection with a bygone age that makes archaeology so compelling.

In Jordan, there are numerous sites across the country, from ancient Pre-Pottery Neolithic (PPN) sites to more contemporary excavations in and around the Crusader castles. Archaeologists, not known for consensus on many things, have at least agreed that there remains huge potential for major finds despite the intensive work in the field for the past three decades.

If you fancy being part of an archaeological team and you have the patience and discipline to spend long hours in a dusty hole tickling dirt off a lump of masonry, it's not too difficult to become a volunteer on one of these digs. Here are some guidelines:

- There are usually only a limited number of volunteer positions available on each site, so find out who is conducting which digs and apply early.
- Make contact with the project leader and be sure to emphasise any special skills (like photography or drafting) you may have.
- Mention any travels in the region or Arabic-speaking skills.
- Emphasise your experience on group projects (archaeology is all about teamwork, despite the way it's presented in films).
- Ask how much your volunteer placement will cost. This fee helps cover the costs of adding your name to the team.
- Allow plenty of time. To gain access to sites, project leaders must obtain permits and security clearance, which can take up to six months to complete.
- Don't be put off if you don't succeed with your first application; it takes persistence to find a placement – a quality you'll need when you're on your first field trip!

Fieldwork Opportunities in Jordan

American Center for Oriental Research (www.acorjordan.org) Prepares an extensive annual listing of fieldwork opportunities in Jordan and the Middle East.

American Schools of Oriental Research (www.asor.org) This organisation supports the study of the culture and history of the Near East.

Archaeological Institute of America (www.archaeological.org) The largest and oldest archaeology organisation in the USA is a valuable resource for information.

Biblical Archaeological Society (www.biblicalarchaeology.org) Produces the magazine *Biblical Archaeological Review*, runs archaeological tours and lists volunteer openings.

Council for British Research in the Levant (www.cbrl.org.uk) British Academy–sponsored institute with research centres in Amman and Jerusalem.

University of Jordan (www.ju.edu.jo) The archaeology department at this Amman-based university is a good contact point.

University of Sydney (www.sydney.edu.au/arts/archaeology) This prestigious Australian university runs a highly reputable field project at Pella.

1970s

Excavations near Amman unearth the oldest statues in the world, the 8500-year-old, life-size Ain Ghazal figures, now in the Jordan Museum.

1980s

Projects around Jordan unearth the remains of the Temple of Hercules at the Citadel in Amman, a Greek manuscript library at Petra and ancient temple complexes in the Jordan Valley.

1990s

Early mining sites west of Karak and the reputed baptism site of Jesus Christ at Bethany-Beyond-the-Jordan are just two of many discoveries marking the end of the century.

2008

The world's oldest church, which is believed to have once sheltered 70 disciples of Jesus Christ, is uncovered under St Georgeous Church in Rihab, near Amman.

2016

An enormous Nabataean platform measuring 56x49m and thought to be of ceremonial purpose is identified by satellite under the Petra sands.

Archaeology Museums in Jordan

If you want to see the finds from some of the key archaeological digs in Jordan, head for the following museums:

Jordan Museum (Amman; p51) Ain Ghazal fertility sculptures and examples of the Dead Sea Scrolls.

Salt Archaeological Museum (Salt; p107) Good coverage of domestic history.

Museum of Archaeology & Anthropology (Irbid; p97) Includes numismatic displays.

Petra Visitor Centre (Wadi Musa; p179) Some of the finds from Petra are temporarily housed in this excellent exhibition awaiting completion of a new Petra museum in 2018.

Biblical Sites of Jordan

From Abraham and Moses to John the Baptist and Jesus Christ, the founding fathers of the three great monotheistic traditions are intimately tied to the Jordanian landscape. Little wonder then that Jordan has been a destination of religious pilgrimage for centuries. The following are some of the most significant sites associated with the Good Book.

Locating Bible References

For hundreds of years pilgrims, historians and the culturally curious have been travelling to Jordan in search of the sites of biblical importance. The eastern banks of the Jordan River alone are home to no fewer than 100 such sites. The most famous are listed here, together with the biblical reference.

'Ain Musa or Ayoun Musa

Biblical reference *Then Moses raised his arm and struck the rock twice with his staff. Water gushed out, and the community and their livestock drank.* (Numbers 20:11)

Historical record The exact location of where Moses struck the rock is open to debate – it's thought to be either 'Ain Musa (Moses' Spring; p181), which is north of Wadi Musa near Petra, or Ayoun Musa (p138), near Mt Nebo.

For an illustrated and comprehensive listing of locations, Bible Places (www.bibleplaces.com) offers links to a pictorial library covering many biblical sites in Jordan.

Dead Sea

Biblical reference *...while the water flowing down to the Sea of Arabah was completely cut off...* (Joshua 3:16)

Historical record The Sea of Arabah (Dead Sea; p111), also known as the Salt Sea, is mentioned several times in the Bible.

Jebel Haroun

Biblical reference *Remove Aaron's garments and put them on his son Eleazar, for Aaron will be gathered to his people: he will die there. Moses did as the Lord commanded: they went up to Mount Hor in the sight of the whole community.* (Numbers 10:26–27)

Historical record Mt Hor is believed to be Jebel Haroun (p172) in the Ancient City at Petra. It is also revered by Muslims as a holy place.

Jebel Umm Al Biyara

Biblical reference *He* [the Judean King, Amaziah] *was the one who defeated ten thousand Edomites in the Valley of the Salt and captured Sela in battle...* (2 Kings 14:7)

Historical record The village on top of Umm Al Biyara (p172) mountain in Petra is believed to be the ancient settlement of Sela.

Biblical Sites of Jordan

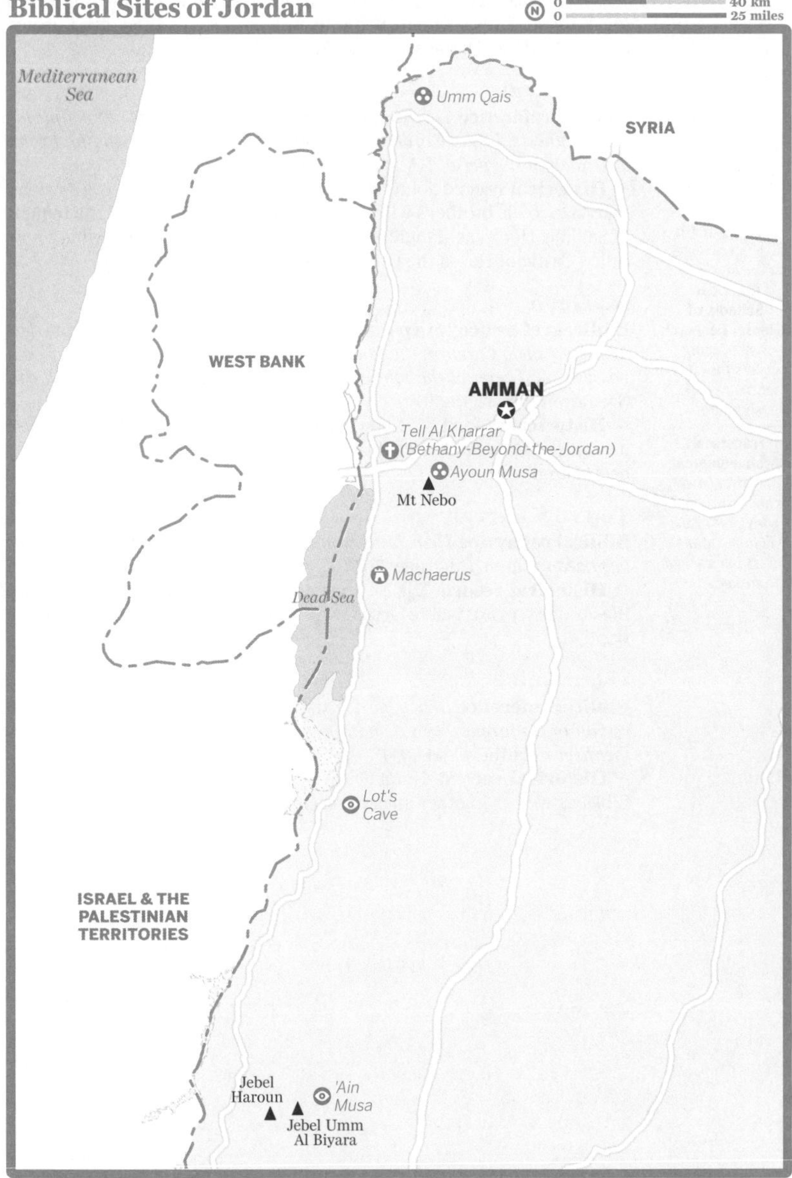

Lot's Cave

Biblical reference *Now Lot went up out of Zo'ar, and dwelt in the hills with his two daughters, for he was afraid to dwell in Zo'ar; so he dwelt in a cave with his two daughters.* (Genesis 19:30)

Historical record The cave (p123) where Lot and his daughters lived for years after Lot's wife turned into a pillar of salt is thought to be just off the Dead Sea Highway, not far from Safi.

Machaerus

Biblical reference *The King was sad, but because of his oaths and his dinner guests, he gave orders that her request be granted, and had John beheaded in the prison.* (Matthew 14:9–12)

Historical record John the Baptist had claimed that Herod Antipas' marriage to his brother's wife, Herodias, was unlawful. So, at the request of Salome, Herodias' daughter, John was supposedly killed at what's now called Castle of Herod the Great (p139).

Biblical Digs on the Web

American Schools of Oriental Research *(www.asor.org) Covers the sites of the Hebrew scriptures.*

Franciscan Archaeological Institute *(www.christusrex.org/www1/ofm/fai/FAImain.html) Covers biblical digs in Jordan.*

Mt Nebo

Biblical reference *Go up into...Mount Nebo in Moab, across from Jericho, and view Canaan, the land I am giving the Israelites as their own possession. There on the mountain that you have climbed you will die.* (Deuteronomy 32:49-50)

Historical record Mt Nebo (p136) is revered as a holy place because it is where Moses is reported to have died, although his tomb has never been found.

Tell Al Kharrar

Biblical reference *Then Jesus came from the Galilee to the Jordan to be baptised by John.* (Matthew 3:13)

Historical record Tell Al Kharrar is regarded as Bethany-Beyond-the-Jordan (p115) where Jesus was reputedly baptised by John the Baptist.

Umm Qais

Biblical reference *When he* [Jesus] *arrived at the other side in the region of Gadarenes, two demon-possessed men coming from the tombs met him.* (Matthew 8:28–34)

Historical record Umm Qais is known as Gadara (p101) in the Bible, as well as in other ancient scriptures.

People & Society

Many visitors enter Jordan with the sole priority of ticking off the antiquities. Some go in search of past heroes; others are led to Jordan in the spirit of pilgrimage and acquaintance with the 'soul posts' of their faith. Whatever their motivations to root out the past, however, invariably people return home impressed by the Jordan of today, of the way it has opened its doors to those in need and embraced a modern outlook towards the world at large.

Jordan's Bedouin Roots

Tradition of Hospitality

Ahlan wa sahlan! It's one of the most common greetings in Arabic and one that defines the way Jordanians relate to the people around them, especially guests. The root words mean 'people' or 'family' *(ahl)* and 'ease' *(sahl)*, so translated loosely the expression means 'be as one of the family and at your ease'. It's a gracious thought, and one that ends up in English simply as 'welcome' or (more commonly to tourists) 'welcome to Jordan'.

Bedouin traditions of hospitality and kindness are deeply ingrained in the Jordanian psyche. Rooted in the harsh realities of life in the desert, these traditions have been virtually codified into all social behaviour. Century-old notions of hospitality combine with a wonderful sense of humour to make Jordanians easy to connect with.

The Bedouin are known for their sense of humour, which they list – alongside courage, alertness and religious faith – as one of the four secrets of life, encouraging tolerance and humility.

Love of the Desert

More than 98% of Jordanians are Arab, descended from various tribes that migrated to the area from all directions of the Middle East over the

SOCIAL GRACES

Here are a few social graces that will help break the ice without breaking a friendship. If all else fails, there's not much harm that can't be undone with a smile, a box of baklava and a compliment about the lovable children.

Handshaking This is an important part of the ritual of greeting in Jordan but usually only between members of the same sex. If you witness an accident, for example, the first few moments will probably be taken up with copious handshaking, greeting and asking after each man's family...before a slanging match erupts about who is to blame.

Public Displays of Affection Don't think that seeing two men kissing gives you the right to do the same. All signs of affection, except between members of the same sex (and of the strictly platonic kind), is frowned upon in public. Not that you'd guess these days from the relaxed attitudes of trendsetters in the city who openly walk arm in arm with a loved one.

Hands and Arms Blundering with these limbs includes using your left hand to give something, forgetting to touch your heart when refusing something and, on that matter, forgetting to refuse something you intend eventually to accept.

Feet These appendages are both a host's and a guest's worst nightmare. For anyone contemplating a visit to a home or a mosque, the advice for feet is to wash them, unsock them and tuck them under when sitting on the floor.

centuries. Most tribes trace their lineage to the Bedouin, the original desert dwellers of Arabia, perceived by many as the representatives and guardians of the very essence of what it means to be Arab. Bedouins form the majority of the indigenous population, although today no more than 40,000 Bedouin can be considered truly nomadic. Living a traditional life of livestock rearing, the nomadic Bedouin who travel from oasis to oasis in quest of water are concentrated mainly in the Badia – the great desert plains of eastern Jordan.

The checked *keffiyah* (headdress) is an important national symbol – red and white for Bedouin; black and white for Palestinians. It's held in place by the black rope-like *agal*. There are no official dress restrictions for women and few wear a veil. Almost none wear full-body chador.

Despite the settlement of some Bedouin (recent examples include the Bdoul, who once roamed the hillsides of Petra but who now live for the most part in the modern settlement of Umm Sayoun), many Jordanians retain a deep sentimental attachment to the desert. This isn't always obvious given the littering and general despoliation of public access areas, such as at Wadi Rum, but it is evident in the way Jordanians claim kinship with the principal tenets of desert-dwelling – hospitality, loyalty, dignity, pride and courtesy.

Modern Caretakers of the Desert

Whether Zawaedha, Zalabia or Bdoul, whether from Wadi Rum, Wadi Musa or the great Badia beyond, the Bedouin are universally proud of 'their Jordan' and welcome guests who visit them in their ancient tribal lands. It's not surprising, then, that many of the country's Bedouin now make a living from tourism, and many feel it is their modern mission to reveal the wonders of their country to new generations of visitors. In some senses, the Bedouin have been doing the same, albeit for slightly different purposes, for centuries, offering bread and salt to those in need on the understanding that the same courtesy will be offered to them in return. The currency today is usually money, but the principle of easing the passage of strangers through traditional tribal territories remains unchanged. Unchanged, too, is the principle of 'word of mouth' in advertising friendly encampments, though today the internet has replaced the camel caravan as the *modus operandi*.

Not everything about the modern experience of the Bedouin has stayed the same, however. It is easy to romanticise the traditional approach – managing goats and sheep and looking for water – as simple and free, but the reality of life in the desert is uncompromisingly hard, entailing goat-hair beds and scorpions, insufferable heat and freezing nights, not enough to eat and being forever thirsty. Add to that the modern complexities of life (compulsory education, impinging urbanisation, and the tough and fickle demands of working with tourists) and it's easy to see that there's nothing simple or free in a modern Bedouin life.

While many aspects of Bedouin life have modernised, living arrangements under the *beit ash shaar* (goat-hair Bedouin tent) remain firmly divided between the private women's harem and the more public men's quarters.

It's little surprise then that while many regret the passing of the golden age of nomadic life, the majority of Jordan's indigenous population look towards settlement and the convenience that it brings. Today, therefore, as a visitor to Jordan, you are just as likely to run into the Bedouin on a mobile phone at the bus station or in public-assisted housing at the edge of Petra. They are wistful for the stories of their grandparents, but they are not nostalgic about the hardships. TV, internet and 4WD transport have changed their lives forever, but as they are not regretful of this, then neither should a visitor be!

Good Manners

There are many ways in which Jordan's Bedouin roots have influenced the national psyche. For the visitor, perhaps the most easily identifiable aspects of this inheritance is the value placed on good manners. Etiquette in Jordan has been refined over centuries of tribal interaction and is an important expression of national identity. Social mores cover all aspects of life from the length and depth of an introductory 'hello' to how many cups of coffee to be offered and accepted, and who offers what to whom – and in what order – at supper.

For a visitor, learning the subtleties of 'custom and manner' is challenging, but making the effort to fit in is invariably appreciated, particularly if visiting Jordanians at home.

Respect for the Royals

Another noticeable trait of the Bedouin inheritance is an ingrained tribal respect for local elders, or sheikhs. This character trait is extended to the ultimate leaders of the country. Claiming unbroken descent from Prophet Muhammad, Jordan's Hashemite royal family is a nationally beloved and regionally respected institution. All monarchies have their critics from time to time, not least for seeming arcane in their function, but Jordan's modern royal family has helped to redefine the royal image through benign and diplomatic governance (especially with regard to Middle East peace issues), as well as through a history of charitable works. It was evident that after the Arab Spring of 2011, despite protests against the government, there was limited enthusiasm for a republic. Jordanians look to their royalty for leadership and an example of how to live a modern life in the context of their largely Islamic and Arab heritage.

In a region where men are more commonly the public face of royal initiatives, Jordan has been unusual for the high profile of its royal women.

Crossing Cultures

Into the Wadi (Michele Drouart; 2000)

Married to a Bedouin (Marguerite van Geldermalsen; 2006)

THE ROYAL WOMEN OF JORDAN

Two influential women have helped shaped the modern face of Jordan. Both have used their marriage into royalty to make positive social changes and have set up nationally respected charities.

Queen Noor

Royal Connection Fourth wife of the former king, King Hussein (now deceased); married in 1978

Former Name Lisa Halaby; adopted the name Queen Noor upon conversion to Islam

Former Occupation Architect and urban planner

From Washington, DC; studied at Princeton

Background Born into a distinguished Arab-American family (her father served under the administration of John F Kennedy and was head of Pan-Am for a while)

Community Service Set up her own charity, the influential Noor Foundation

Public Relations Important role in explaining Jordan's stand against the 1990 Gulf War to American audiences, and active campaigner for women's rights, children's welfare and community improvement

Further Information See Queen Noor's website (www.nooralhusseinfoundation.org)

Queen Rania

Royal Connection Wife of the present king, King Abdullah; married in 1993

Former Name Rania Al Yassin

Former Occupation Business administration

From Kuwait; studied at the American University of Cairo

Background Born into a notable Jordanian family of Palestinian origin

Community Service Set up her own charity, the influential Jordan River Foundation

Public Relations Not afraid of a public profile; can be seen in activities as diverse as campaigning for the rights of women and advocating MOOCs (online education courses) to running the Dead Sea Marathon

Further Information See Queen Rania's website (www.queenrania.jo)

Visit many of the small women's cooperatives like Bani Hamida in Mukawir, and you are likely to find some mention of either Queen Noor or Queen Rania in the patronage or even funding of the project.

Daily Life

Importance of Family

Family ties are all-important to both modern and traditional Jordanians, and paying respect to parents is where the sense of obeisance to elders is engendered. Socialising generally entails some kind of get-together with the extended family, with lines drawn loosely between the genders. This is reflected in terms of physical divisions within the house, where separate seating areas are reserved for men and women.

Jordan has a regionally renowned education system; literacy levels are around 98% for Jordanian males and some report female literacy as 99%, the highest in the region. About 98% of children attend primary school, and school is compulsory from ages five to 14. More women than men attend university.

Meals are traditionally eaten on the floor, with everyone gathered around several trays of food shared by all. Old-school families are often quite hierarchical at meal times. The grandparents and male head of the house may eat in one circle, the latter's wife and the older children and other women in the family in another, and the small children in yet another. New-school families are too busy with gadgetry to be rigid about protocol.

The internet has brought about profound change and, in common with people the world over, youngsters in particular are obsessed with their phones. This hasn't dented the appetite for a family picnic or stroll around the streets, but it is signalling an individualisation within society that wasn't apparent in Jordan a decade ago. Elders look on in some dismay as the pastimes they inherited from previous generations – drinking tea, playing cards, smoking a *nargileh* (water pipe), watching European football on the TV, embroidering a marriage costume or preparing an elaborate family meal – begin to seem less and less relevant to the globally defined youth.

A DISHONOURABLE HOAX

In 2004 a book entitled *Forbidden Love,* written by Norma Khouri, arrived on the bookshelves. Within weeks the author (to the delight of her publisher, Random House) found she had a bestseller on her hands. Better and bigger than that, she had overnight become the convenient voice the West wanted to hear: an Arab woman speaking out against the supposed 'tyranny of Islam'. Soon she was fêted on chat shows and courted by newspaper journalists, and her tale assumed the quality of moral crusade taken up with indignation by worthy people around the world.

Her story was a harrowing one that described the death in Jordan of her childhood friend, the legendary Dalia: a killing carried out by the girl's Islamic knife-wielding father for a harmless flirtation with a Christian soldier. This event, together with the author's description of it, apparently led to Khouri's flight to the US from the benighted country of her birth and a fatwa being placed on her head. Comparisons with author Salman Rushdie begin to form...except that Rushdie never claimed his works of fiction were fact.

A 2008 documentary, *Forbidden Lies,* charts Khouri's exposure as a con artist and her book as a pack of lies. The very existence of Dalia is called into question and with it a pall of uncertainty covers the issue of 'honour killings', which is the book's central theme.

And this, of course, is the real tragedy behind one of the biggest literary hoaxes of the 21st century. Honour killings – where a woman is killed by members of the family to protect familial honour – do occur in Jordan, albeit in ever-reducing numbers. Sensationalist accounts that capitalise on the practice, however, undermine the work of various interest groups who try to work quietly and discreetly to change attitudes without compromising the sense of national pride.

The documentary *Crimes of Honour* by Shelley Saywell, filmed in Jordan and the West Bank, gives more information on this sensitive subject.

Marriage

Marriage is one area of Jordanian life that doesn't seem to have been much impacted by the pressures of modernity. Reflecting the sense of family allegiance, marriages are still mostly arranged for the benefit of the families involved, with matches commonly made between cousins. It is fair to say, however, that parents do not often enforce a wedding against their daughter's wish. In 2001 the legal age of marriage was lifted from 15 years old for women and 16 for men to 18 for both, although Islamic judges are still permitted to sanction underage marriages.

The marriage ceremony takes place either at the mosque, church or home of the bride or groom. After the marriage ceremony, the men of the family drive around the streets in a long convoy, sounding their horns, blasting out music and partying until sunrise.

Polygamy (by men) is rare, but it is legal. Men who marry more than once (Islam allows four wives if each wife is assured equal treatment) are obliged to inform both their first and their new wives. Amendments to the law in 2002 made it possible for women to file for divorce if they repay the dowry given by their husband. That said, the social stigma regarding divorce remains strong.

Jordan's Female Firsts

1979 *Government Minister*

1995 *Mayor (in Ajloun)*

1996 *Judge*

1997 *Taxi driver*

2010 *Attorney general*

2011 *Ambassador to Washington*

2013 *Carpenter*

2017 *Everest climbing team*

The Concept of Honour

In Jordan, a woman's 'honour' is still valued in traditional society, and sex before marriage or adultery is often dealt with harshly by other members of the woman's family. In rare cases it can lead to fatalities, with women in the family often complicit in the murder.

Jordan's legal code exempts a husband or close male relative for killing a wife caught in an act of adultery and offers leniency for murders committed in a 'fit of rage'. Most perpetrators are given short prison sentences, sending the message that the state in part condones these actions.

Internationally renowned journalist Rana Husseini is one among several high-profile Jordanians who are committed not just to bringing so-called 'honour killings' to the Jordanian public's attention but also to spreading intolerance towards the practice. Even King Abdullah has tried to impose tougher sanctions against honour killings, but little progress has thus far been made. Effecting radical change of deep-rooted cultural values is not something that can be accomplished overnight and only a change of attitude, rather than a change of law, is likely to be effective in driving the practice out.

On average (according to government statistics) 15 to 20 women are murdered each year for having sex out of wedlock, refusing an arranged marriage, leaving their husbands or simply being the victim of rape or sexual assault. Laws connected with rape, marriage and honour killing are at last being revised.

Confronting Modernity

A New Role for Women

Traditional concepts of honour *(ird)* run deep but sit uneasily with the freedoms many affluent Jordanian women have come to expect, largely thanks to universal access to one of the region's best education systems. Women are entitled to vote (Jordanian women got the vote in 1967 but didn't have a chance to use it for the first time until 1989) and a minimum of six women MPs is guaranteed by royal decree.

In 1991 only 14% of the labour force was made up of women; according to UN data, this figure rose to around one quarter in 2014, mainly in health and education but alarmingly slipped back to 14% in 2017 (reflecting a similar trend across the globe). In 2016 Jordan ranked a dispiriting 142nd out of 144 countries in terms of women in the workforce, and today only half of all women graduating from college gain employment. While some pioneering women have cut new ground in male-dominated industries, sports and cultural spheres, there remain few women in some key areas, such as media or the law profession (in 2015, for example, only 18% of judges were women). The low female employment data has triggered

PALESTINIAN REFUGEES

More than two million people in Jordan are registered Palestinian refugees, with around one half of Jordan's population estimated to be of Palestinian descent. The majority comprise Palestinians who fled, mostly from the West Bank, during the wars of 1948 and 1967, and from Kuwait after the Gulf War in 1990–91. Their numbers increased since 2012 as a result of the ongoing civil war in Syria.

Many Palestinians have exercised the right to Jordanian citizenship, and they now play an integral part in the political, cultural and economic life of Jordan. Others, however, continue to dream of a return to an independent Palestine. Some commentators suggest that this is partly why so many have resisted integration and continue to live in difficult conditions in refugee camps that dot the landscape.

Around 370,000 Palestinian refugees are housed in 10 official camps administered by the UN Relief & Works Agency (UNRWA), which is responsible for health, education and relief programs. The largest camps are centred around the north of Jordan where the original tent shelters have long since been replaced with more permanent structures and often resemble suburbs more than refugee camps. This is in contrast to the Za'atari camp on the Syrian border and Azraq camp to the east of Amman, set up to manage the crisis inflow of displaced refugees from Syria.

The following agencies give reliable statistics on all refugees in Jordan:

Department of Palestinian Affairs (www.unrwa.org)

UNHCR (UN Refugee Agency, www.unhcr.org)

a debate as to why women feature so insignificantly in the workforce, but it appears that this discussion has resulted in few tangible solutions to date.

Women Writers on Jordan

Nine Parts of Desire (Geraldine Brooks; 1995)

West of the Jordan (Laila Halaby; 2003)

At the beginning of the 21st century, women from more traditional communities in Jordan began to gain some financial independence and have a greater say in society. This was partially through the success of a number of Jordanian organisations that encouraged small-scale craft production and local tourism projects, many of which were sponsored by royalty. Sadly, many of these worthy initiatives have discontinued or proved too expensive to run. Some of the women who embraced their new entrepreneurial role blame regional political instability for the reversal of their fortunes and look forward to a revival in the kind of alternative tourism that flourished before the Arab Spring.

Urbanisation

Over the past decade, there has been an increasing polarisation in Jordanian society between town and country. In Amman, modern Western-leaning middle- and upper-class youths enjoy the fruits of a good education, shop in malls, drink lattes in mixed-sex Starbucks and obsess over the latest fashions or dreams of democracy. In rural areas, meanwhile, unemployment is high and many populations struggle with making ends meet.

Refugee Influxes

1948 *Palestinians (founding of Israel)*

1967 *Palestinians (Six Day War)*

1991 *Palestinians (Gulf War)*

2003 *Iraqis (Iraq War)*

Since 2011 *Syrians (Syrian Civil War)*

For this reason, economic migration is common in Jordan and many working-class families have at least one male who is temporarily working away from home, whether in Amman, the Gulf States or further abroad. The remittances sent home by these absent workers are increasingly important to family budgets, with each economically active person supporting, on average, four other people. The absence of a senior male role model, however, is changing the pattern of Jordanian family lives, and tensions inevitably rise between the expectations of those who are nostalgic for the traditions of home and those of the families left behind who are forced to steer their own course into a rapidly modernising environment.

Islam

Islam isn't the only religion in Jordan – around 2% of the population is Christian (mostly Greek Orthodox). The mixed inheritance, together with a long tradition of hosting visitors, has led Jordanians to be tolerant towards those of other beliefs and customs. Islam is, however, the predominant religion. For a visitor, understanding the country's Muslim roots will help make sense of certain customs and manners. In turn, it provides a guide to appropriate conduct and minimises the chance of giving offence.

Faith & Society in Jordan

It's probably fair to say that there is not the same overt dedication to faith as one sees in neighbouring countries, such as Saudi Arabia. However, this doesn't mean that Islam is any less central to Jordanian life. Islam governs what people wear, how they plan their lives, how they settle their disputes and how they spend their money. It gives a purpose for being and gives shape to the future. In other words, faith and culture seamlessly combine in Jordan, giving people a shared ethic upon which society is founded.

People of the Book

Founded seven centuries after the birth of Christ, Islam shares a common heritage with the two other great monotheistic faiths, Judaism and Christianity. For Muslims, Islam is the apogee of the monotheistic faiths but they traditionally attribute a place of great respect to Christians and Jews, whom they consider *ahl al kitab* (People of the Book).

The words *al hamdu lillah* (thanks be to God) frequently lace sentences in which good things are related and the words *in sha'allah* (God willing) mark sentences that anticipate the future. These expressions are not just linguistic decoration; they demonstrate a deep connection between society and faith.

Founding of Islam

Born into a trading family in Mecca (in present-day Saudi Arabia) in AD 570, the Prophet Muhammad began receiving revelations in 610, and after a time began imparting the content of Allah's message to the inhabitants of Mecca. Muhammad's call to submit to God's will was not universally well received, making more of an impact among the poor than among the wealthy families of Mecca, who feared his interference in the status quo.

By 622 Muhammad was forced to flee with his followers to Medina, an oasis town to the north of Mecca, where he continued to preach. This migration (the Hejira) marks the beginning of the Islamic calendar: year 1 AH. By 630 his followers returned to take Mecca, winning over many of the local tribes who swore allegiance to the new faith.

After Muhammad's death in 632, Arab tribes conquered the Middle East, Egypt and North Africa, Spain and eventually southern France, taking Islam with them. The Arabic language and Islamic faith remained long after the military conquests faded into history, uniting large parts of Europe, Africa and Asia in a shared cultural and religious ideology.

Sunnis & Shiites

Islam split into different sects soon after its foundation. When the Prophet died in 632, he left no instructions as to who should be his successor, nor the manner in which the future Islamic leaders (known as caliphs) should be chosen.

Mecca is Islam's holiest city. It's the home of the sacred Kaaba – a cube-shaped building allegedly built by Ibrahim (Abraham) and his son Ismail and housing a black stone of ancient spiritual focus. Muslims are enjoined to this day to face Mecca when praying. Medina is Islam's second holiest city.

In the ensuing power struggle, *shi'a* (partisans) supported the claim of Muhammad's cousin and son-in-law, while others supported the claim of the Umayyads. From that point the Muslim community split into two competing factions: the Shiites, who are loyal to the descendants of Muhammad, and the Sunnis, the orthodox bedrock of Islam.

Within Jordan most Muslims are Sunnis, belonging to the Hanafi school of thought. A minority of around 32,000 Druze in northeast Jordan (including the town of Azraq) follow a form of Shiite Islam.

Teachings

Despite modern connotations with fundamentalism and the violent beginnings of the faith, Islam is an inherently peaceful creed. The word 'Islam' means 'submission' or 'self-surrender'. It also means 'peace'. Taken as a whole, Islam is the attainment of peace – with self, society and the environment – through conscious submission to the will of God. To submit to the will of God does not just entail paying lip service to God through ceremony, but through all daily thoughts and deeds.

The principal teaching of Islam is that there is only one true God, creator of the universe. Muslims believe that the God of Islam is the same God of Christians and Jews, but that he has no son, and he needs no intermediary (such as priests). Muslims believe that the prophets – including Adam, Abraham and Jesus, and ending with the Prophet Muhammad – were sent to reveal God's word but that none of them were divine.

Islam, Judaism and Christianity share many of the same prophets: Abraham (Ibrahim), Jesus (Isa), John the Baptist (Yahya), Job (Ayyub), Joshua (Yosha), Lot (Lut), Moses (Musa) and Noah (Nuh). Muhammad is not considered divine, but rather the last of these prophets.

Historically, this creed obviously had great appeal to the nomadic peoples of the land we now call Jordan as they were given access to a rich spiritual life without having to submit to incomprehensible rituals administered by hierarchical intermediaries. Believers needed only to observe the transportable Five Pillars of Islam in order to fulfil their religious duty. This is true to this day and is perhaps one of the reasons why Islam is one of the world's fastest-growing religions.

The Five Pillars of Islam

A good Muslim is expected to carry out the following Five Pillars of Islam.

Hajj The pinnacle of a devout Muslim's life is the pilgrimage to the holy sites in and around Mecca. Hajj takes place in the last month of the Islamic calendar and Muslims from all over the world travel to Saudi Arabia for the pilgrimage and subsequent feast of Eid Al Adha. Returning pilgrims earn the right to be addressed as *haji*.

Salat This is the obligation of prayer, expressed five times a day when the muezzins call upon the faithful to pray before sunrise, at noon, midafternoon, at sunset and before midnight. Communal prayers are only obligatory on Friday, although the strong sense of community makes joining together in a masjid ('place of prostration', ie mosque) preferable at other times.

THE HOLY QURAN

Muslims believe that the Quran, the holy book of Islam, is the literal word of God, unlike the Bible or Torah, which they believe were inspired by God but were recorded subject to human interpretation. Communicated to the Prophet Muhammad directly in a series of revelations in the early 7th century, the Quran means 'recitation' and is not just the principal source of doctrine in Islam, but also a source of spiritual rapture in its own right. It is recited often with emotional elation, as a blessing to the reciter and the hearer. The use of the 'sacred' language of Arabic, with its unique rhythms, gives the recitation a sacramental quality that eludes translation, and many Muslims around the world still learn large portions of the Quran in its original form to feel closer to God's words.

HISTORICAL ORIGINS OF ISLAM

AD 570 Prophet Muhammad, founder of Islam, is born in Mecca.

610 Muhammad receives his first revelation, considered by Muslims as God's word and captured in the Quran.

622 Muhammad and his followers flee Mecca for Medina, marking the birth of the first Islamic state.

632 Muhammad dies and the Muslim capital moves to Damascus.

656 Ali bin Abi Taleb becomes caliph; his followers are known as Shiites.

661 Ali is assassinated by troops loyal to Muhammad's distant relative, separating the Muslim community into two factions.

680 Ali's son is murdered at Karbala, widening the gap between the two factions, Shiites and Sunnis.

Shahada This is the profession of the faith and the basic tenet of Islam: 'There is no God but Allah and Muhammad is his prophet' *(La il laha illa Allah Muhammad rasul Allah)*. This is part of the call to prayer, and is uttered at other events, such as births and deaths. People can often be heard muttering the first half of the sentence to themselves for moral support.

Sawm Ramadan, the ninth month of the Islamic calendar, commemorates the revelation of the Quran to Muhammad. As a renewal of faith, Muslims are required to abstain from sex and from letting anything (including cigarettes) pass their lips from dawn to dusk throughout the month.

Zakat Giving alms to the poor is an essential part of Islamic social teaching and, in some parts of the Muslim world, has been developed into various forms of tax as a way of redistributing funds to the needy. The moral obligation towards poorer neighbours continues to be emphasised at a personal and community level, and many Islamic groups run large charitable institutions, including, in Jordan, Amman's Islamic Hospital.

Islamic Customs

Muslims pray five times a day and follow certain rituals, washing their hands, mouth, ears, arms, feet, head and neck in running water. If no mosque is nearby and there is no water available, scouring with sand suffices; where there is no sand, the motions of washing must still be enacted.

Muslims must face Mecca (all mosques are oriented so that the *mihrab,* or prayer niche, faces this way – south-southeast in Jordan) and follow a set pattern of gestures and genuflections. Muslims do not require a mosque to pray, and you'll often see Jordanians praying by the side of the road or at the back of their shop; many keep a small prayer rug handy for such times.

In Jordan, which has a history of welcoming tourists to its world-class sites of largely pagan origin, people may be surprised if you take an interest in Islam, but they will also be delighted. Any sympathetic discussion of faith is treated as an olive branch in a region where religion has all too often led to conflict – as the great Crusader castles at Karak and Shobak and the heavily militarised border with Israel illustrates.

Websites on Islam

Al Bab *(www.al-bab.com) Comprehensive site with links to information and discussion on Islam.*

Islamicity *(www.islamicity.com) Good reference for non-Muslims interested in Islam.*

Traditional Crafts

For the visitor who chooses the right outlets, there is a special pleasure in buying something handmade, practical and aesthetically pleasing from Jordan, as the craftsperson very often earns money that directly benefits his or her community. Taking an interest in the crafts of Jordan, then, is not a remote aesthetic exercise. It represents sustainable tourism at its very best. Find out how to make your purchases count towards Jordan's regional cottage industries.

Made in Jordan

Walk the streets of Madaba, with bright coloured kilims flapping in the wind, hike to the soap-making villages of Ajloun or watch elderly Bedouin women threading beads at Petra, and the country's strong handicraft tradition is immediately apparent. The authorities have been quick to support this aspect of Jordan's heritage, and although the fortunes of craft cooperatives have suffered more than most in the economic downturn and resultant slump in tourism, they continue to be widespread. These enterprises result in benefits for local communities and ensure that Jordan's rich legacy of craft endures for future generations.

Fine examples of Bedouin jewellery, Jordanian crafts and traditional costumes are on display at the Folklore Museum (p55) and Museum of Popular Traditions (p55) at the Roman Theatre in Amman.

Weaving

Jordan has a long-established rug-making industry dating back to the country's pre-Islamic, Christian communities. *Mafrash* (rugs) are usually of the flat, woven kind, known as kilims, compared with carpets that have a pile. To this day, especially in Madaba and Mukawir, it's possible to watch kilims being made that are based on early Byzantine designs. Even if you hadn't intended to buy one of these woollen rugs, you'll find it impossible not to get carried away by the enthusiasm of the carpet vendors, who will good-naturedly unfurl all their rugs for you without much prospect of a sale.

Embroidery

Embroidery used to be an important skill among Jordanian women, who would traditionally embroider the clothes they would need as married women in their teenage years. Some still learn the craft as youngsters today, despite embroidery becoming something of a dying art. Embroidery among the elder generation continues to provide an occasion for women to socialise, often with a pot of tea spiced with a pinch of local gossip. Palestinian embroidery is famed throughout the region, and you'll see the characteristic red embroidery cross-stitch on traditional dresses, known as *roza,* in shops across Jordan. Purses featuring intricate flower designs in silk thread make delightful (and portable) mementos.

The cost of a kilim (anywhere between JD50 and JD500) depends on whether natural vegetable dyes are used, the length, thickness of thread, intricacy of pattern and age of the rug – the older the better.

Mosaics

The craft of mosaic-making has a noble and distinguished lineage in Jordan. Mosaics are made from tiny squares of naturally coloured rock called *tesserae.* The first part of the process is preparing the stone, which is hewn in blocks from the rock face and then cut into thin cuboid rods.

These are then snipped by pincers into the *tesserae*. The smallest *tesserae* make the most intricate designs but they are much harder to work with and the mosaics take longer to assemble. It's rather like the knots on a carpet – the more *tesserae* per centimetre, the finer and more valuable the mosaic. Many workshops in the Madaba area will ship items to a home country for visitors.

Copperware

Some of the oldest copper mines in the world are traceable in Jordan (especially near Feinan, now in the Dana Biosphere Reserve). Copper is used to make everyday utensils, as well as for heirlooms such as the family serving dish, copper tray or coffee pot. These pieces are mostly replicated for the tourist industry, but you can still find the genuine articles – with a bit of spit and polish, they'll light up the corner of a room back home. Quality pieces can be found in the antique shops in Amman, many of which are attached to top-end hotels. You won't find an antique older than about 50 years (and it's illegal to export anything older than 100 years), but the items are likely to have been much loved by the families who once used them.

Heather Colyer Ross looks into popular art forms in *The Art of Bedouin Jewellery* (1981), a useful asset for those contemplating purchasing some pieces.

Jewellery

A bride traditionally receives a gift of jewellery on her wedding day as her dowry, and this remains her personal property. The most common designs are protective silver amulets, such as the 'hand of Fatima' (daughter-in-law of the Prophet Muhammad). These are used as protection from evil spirits known as *djinn* ('genie' in English). Antique items such as silver headdresses decorated with Ottoman coins and ornately decorated Bedouin daggers (straight, rather than the famously curved Yemeni and Omani versions) are becoming harder to find. Many of the most beautiful

MAKING MOSAICS

Push the door open on a mosaic workshop and it's like entering the Hall of the Mountain King. Clouds of dust plume from the masonry saws and the workspace echoes with the screech of metal against rock and the persistent snapping of the workers' pincers as they cut stone rods into tiny, coloured squares. During our visit, all the workers engaged in this dedicated craft (from the stone-cutters to the assembly teams) were women. One of the ladies dusted her hands against her overcoat and, parking her mobile phone among the tweezers, the paste brush and the glue pot, gave us an ad hoc tour.

Artists, Mayzoon explained, sketch a design freehand or trace the image from books, in the same way as their ancient predecessors would have copied scenes from pattern books. Designs usually feature everyday life, with depictions of plants and animals (look for the chicken – almost every mosaic seems to feature one). Hunting and viniculture, personification of the seasons, and religious or mythological scenes are typical subjects. But it's the detail that captivates – the bell on a gazelle's neck, palm trees at an oasis, a wry human smile.

Once the design is in place, the *tesserae* are then painstakingly arranged – traditionally on a thick coating of wet lime and ash to form permanent flooring. Today they are more likely to be attached to wet plaster and affixed to wooden boards for use as table tops or wall decorations.

The tour concluded and Mayzoon returned to the assembly table. 'You took our photograph, no?' one of the ladies said. We were about to apologise when she added, 'Please, take it again. This time with all of us!' A shaft of brilliant sunshine cut through the dusty air, lighting up the eight faces gathered in intense concentration around the half-built mosaic. The team worked rhythmically together, tapping and snapping, inching and coaxing the stones into a tree of life. With a little definition in malachite and sandstone, the women could have found their own immortalisation in stone.

antique pieces were crafted by Circassian, Armenian and Yemeni silversmiths in the early 20th century. Much modern silver jewellery in Jordan, or the strings of beads made of regional stones, echo traditional designs.

Added-Value Craft

Traditional handicrafts in Jordan are not designed to be viewed in a museum, but to be bought and bartered over. Jordan's position at the crossroads of numerous caravan routes throughout the ages has made craft, the most practical and portable of all the arts, into a currency of practical benefit.

Several NGOs, such as the Noor Al Hussein Foundation and Jordan River Foundation, have spurred a revival of locally produced crafts as part of a national campaign to raise rural living standards, improve the status of rural women, provide income for marginalised families, nurture artists and protect the local environment. Nature shops figure prominently at the Wild Jordan Center in Amman and RSCN visitor centres in Ajloun, Azraq, Mujib, Dana and Wadi Rum.

If you want to spend your money where it counts, you may like to make contact with or buy from the outlets of community-based income-generating programs.

Beit Al Bawadi (p75) Quality ceramics bought here support local artisans, whom you can see working in the basement. Designs are both traditional and modern, some decorated with Arabic calligraphy, and pieces cost around JD50 to JD80.

Jordan River Foundation (p75) Supporting top-notch worthy causes by selling equally top-notch crafted items, this shop has become an institution in Amman. The showroom supports handloomed rugs from Bani Hamida and exquisite Palestinian-style embroidery. Cushions, camel bags, embroidery, baskets and Dead Sea products make it an excellent place to buy items of stylish decor. Only the highest-quality pieces make it into the showroom (reflected in the prices).

Madaba Tourism Development Association (www.visitmadaba.org) A voluntary community-based organisation, developing tourism products that use local skills and resources.

Made in Jordan (p188) This Wadi Musa shop sells quality crafts from local enterprises. Products include olive oil, soap, paper, ceramics, table runners, nature products from Wild Jordan in Amman, jewellery from Wadi Musa, embroidery from Safi, camel hair shawls, and bags from Aqaba as well as Jordan River Foundation goods. The fixed prices reflect the quality and uniqueness of each piece; credit cards are accepted.

Noor Al Hussein Foundation (p205) Maintains a showroom in Aqaba as well as links to now-independent projects selling NHF-labelled products in Iraq Al Amir, Salt and Wadi Musa (Nabataean Women's Cooperative).

Souk Jara (p75) A village initiative within the city of Amman, the Jebel Amman Residents Association spearheaded the now-famous Souk Jara street market. Expanded over the years to include food and drink stalls – and some regrettable plastic imports – the market retains its authentic craft roots.

Wild Jordan Center (p75) The nature store at the Wild Jordan Center sells products made in Jordan's nature reserves, including silver jewellery, organic herbs and jams from Dana, and candles made by Bedouin women as part of an income-generating project in Feynan. Decorated ostrich eggs are another speciality. All profits are returned to the craftspeople and to nature-reserve projects.

Good Buys

- *Silver jewellery (Wadi Musa, Petra)*
- *Handmade paper (Iraq Al Amir, Aqaba, Jerash)*
- *Ceramics (Salt)*
- *Painted ostrich eggs (Shaumari)*
- *Weavings (Mukawir)*
- *Traditional clothing (Madaba)*
- *Dead Sea soap (Dead Sea spas, Madaba)*
- *Handmade soap (RSCN shops, Ajloun, Amman)*

Shopping for Crafts

If you are after goods of a high quality, it pays to visit specialised craft centres as opposed to one-stop shopping in souvenir shops. Unfortunately, some shop owners have jumped on the cooperative bandwagon and claim to be part of charitable foundations when they are not. Check that a shop's sign exactly matches the outlet you are looking for!

GETTING A GOOD DEAL

Jordanians are committed shoppers and they make an art form out it, promenading the main street and popping into a shop to vex the owner without any intention of buying. Buying, meanwhile, is a whole separate entertainment, focused on the business of bartering.

Bartering implies that items do not have a value per se: their value is governed by what you are willing to pay balanced against the sum the vendor is happy to sell for. This subtle exchange, often viewed with suspicion by those from a fixed-price culture, is dependent on many factors, such as how many other sales the vendor has made that day, whether the buyer looks like a person who can afford an extra dinar or two, and even whether the vendor is in a good mood or not. Although bargaining when craft buying is essential, note that some cooperatives charge fixed prices.

As with all social interaction, there's an unwritten code of conduct that keeps negotiations sweet. Here are a few tips for making it an enjoyable experience.

- View bartering as your chance to decide what you are willing to pay for an item and then use your interpersonal skills to see if you can persuade the vendor to match it.
- Understand that haggling is a sociable activity, often conducted over piping-hot mint tea, so avoid causing offence by refusing hospitality too brusquely.
- Don't pay the first price quoted: this is often considered arrogant.
- Start below the price you wish to buy at so you have room to compromise – but don't quote too low or the vendor may be insulted.
- Never lose your temper: if negotiations aren't going to plan, simply smile and say *ma'a salaama* (goodbye) – you'll be surprised how often these words bring the price down.
- Resist comparing prices with other travellers; if they were happy with what they paid, they certainly won't be if you tell them you bought the same thing for less.
- Above all, remember that a 'good deal' in Jordan generally means a good deal more than just the exchange of money. It's a highlight of travelling in the country.

Duty Free

If you make a purchase at a shop with a Premier Tax Free sign, you pay the full purchase price but the sales tax will be refunded directly. Failing that, if you spend over JD350, keep your receipts, fill out a tax rebate form and leave the country within 90 days, you can get the 16% tax refunded to your credit card at a booth at the airport, just before check-in.

Export Restrictions

Exporting anything more than 100 years old is illegal, so don't buy any craft or artefact (including 'ancient' coins or oil lamps) described as 'antique' – if only because it probably isn't. If you're unsure about an item's provenance, contact the **Customs Department** (www.customs.gov.jo).

Flavours of Jordan

Eating in Jordan is primarily a social experience, whether conducted over a chat in Amman's cafes or sitting in cross-legged silence in a Bedouin tent. Anyone venturing beyond the bus-station kebab stands will quickly find that Jordanian food is not a tedious affair of falafel sandwiches but deliciously varied and culturally nuanced. Jordan is also beginning to be noted for its home-grown wines.

Cuisine

On the crossroads of Arab caravans, bringing spices from India and rice from Egypt, Jordan's hybrid cuisine has absorbed many traditions from its neighbours, particularly from Turkey and Lebanon. Jordan's home-grown fresh fruit and vegetables are a highlight. There are two distinct cuisines in Jordan, which for argument's sake we'll call pan-Arab and Bedouin.

Pan-Arab

The day starts for most Jordanians with a breakfast of eggs and locally produced olives, cheese, sour cream, *fuul madamas* (a fava bean dish with olive oil) and, of course, bread. Arab unleavened bread, *khobz*, is so ubiquitous at mealtimes it is sometimes called *a'aish* (life). A favourite breakfast staple is bread liberally sprinkled with *zaatar* (a blend of spices that includes hyssop, sumac and sesame) or sesame-encrusted rings of bread, which often come with a boiled egg. Either way, Jordanians are very sensitive about bread, and it is almost a crime to throw it away or wilfully waste it.

The word 'mezze' is derived from the Arabic *t'mazza*, meaning 'to savour in little bites'. Meat mezze usually comprise mutton, goat, chicken or lamb, but never pork – which is *haram* (forbidden) for Muslims. However, Jordan's Christian community is free to buy it – if they can find it.

Lunch is usually the main meal of the day, which could explain the habit of nap-taking in the afternoons. Invariably, lunch involves rice or potatoes and includes some form of seasonal vegetable, prepared as a slow-cooking stew with a meat bone or chicken. In a restaurant, or for a special occasion, *makloubeh* may be on the menu: a delicious dish of chicken, rice, vegetables and spices cooked together and turned 'upside down'. This popular dish is often garnished with cardamom and sultanas, and topped with slivers of onion, meat, cauliflower and fresh herbs, such as thyme or parsley.

The evening meal is a ragged affair of competing interests – children snacking over schoolwork, mothers preparing dishes for surprise visitors and fathers sneaking out for a kebab with friends. At the weekend, Jordanians go out as a family. In cities that could mean a Thai curry, while in small towns it will be the chef's special. In an Arab-style restaurant, the evening is whiled away over mezze – a variety of exquisite little delicacies, such as peppery rocket leaves, aromatic chopped livers, spicy aubergine dips or a dish of freshly peeled almonds.

Bedouin

Bedouin food consists of whatever is available at a particular time. Camel's milk and goat's cheese are staple parts of the diet, as are dried dates and water. Water takes on a particularly precious quality when it is rationed, and the Bedouin are renowned for consuming very little, particularly during the day when only small sips are taken, mostly to rinse the mouth.

The Bedouin speciality *mensaf* – consisting of lamb, rice and pine nuts, combined with yoghurt and the liquid fat from the cooked meat – was once reserved for special occasions. Now visitors can try such dishes in Wadi Rum and Wadi Musa. The dish is cooked in a *zerb* (ground oven), which consists of a hole in the sand and enough firewood to make glowing coals. The oven is sealed and the meat cooked for hours until succulent.

During Ramadan Muslims fast during daylight hours. They prepare a large predawn breakfast called *suhur* and eagerly await *iftar* (breaking the fast) at dusk. Always something of a celebration, this dish of the day is fun to share with hungry patrons at a busy restaurant.

Seasonal Specialities

Spring Lamb cooked in a *zerb* (ground oven) will ruin your palate for mutton. Fresh, frothy camel's milk is abundant and giant watermelons ripen in fields alongside the Desert Highway.

Summer The fruit harvest brings pomegranates, pistachios, peaches and limes. During Ramadan, fast with the locals (dawn to dusk) and see how hunger enhances the flavours of traditional evening sweetmeats.

Autumn Pluck dangling figs or grapes from the vine and sample corn drizzled with newly pressed olive oil from local groves. In the Jordan Valley bananas and mangoes ripen in subtropical warmth.

Winter Copper-coloured persimmons ripen for Christmas – a good time to try Bethany's 'Baptism Fish'. In winter it's not carnage on the roads – it's tomatoes. Crates of them fill the fields near Safi.

EATING ETIQUETTE

Travel in Jordan for any length of time and inevitably you'll be invited home for a meal, especially if you are travelling alone, and most especially if you are a woman. Jordanians are very accommodating of other people's habits but you will impress your hosts if you manage a few of the following courtesies.

Eating in Someone's House

- Bring a small gift of baklava or, better still, a memento from home.
- It's polite to be seen to wash your hands before a meal.
- Use only the right hand for eating or accepting food. The left is reserved for ablutions.
- Don't put food back on a communal plate: discard in a napkin.
- Your host will often pass the tastiest morsels to you; it's polite to accept them.
- The best part – such as the meat – is usually saved until last, so don't take it until offered.
- If you're sitting on the ground, don't stretch your legs out until after the meal.

Eating in a Restaurant

- Picking your teeth after a meal is acceptable and toothpicks are often provided.
- It's traditional to lavish food upon a guest. If you're full, try one more mouthful!
- Leave a little food on your plate. Traditionally, a clean plate is thought to invite famine.
- It's polite to accept a cup of coffee after a meal and impolite to leave before it's served.
- Avoid eating and drinking in public during daylight hours in Ramadan. Many rural restaurants close at this time.

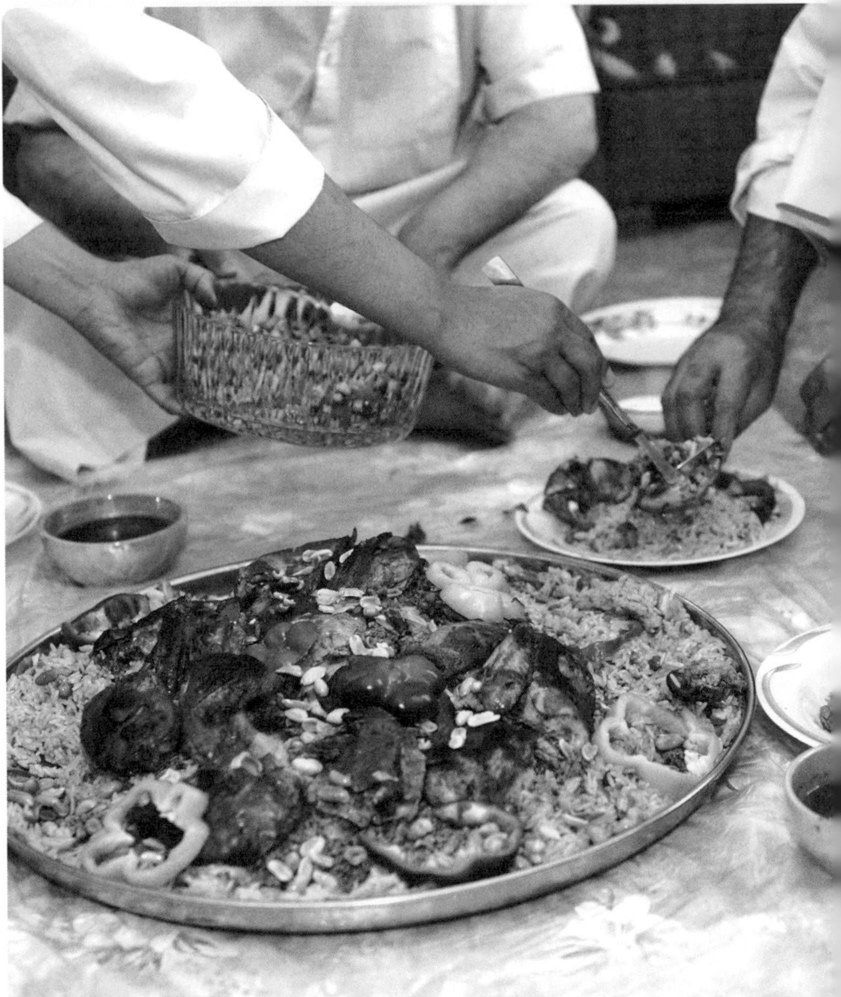

MOMEN KHAITI/LONELY PLANET ©

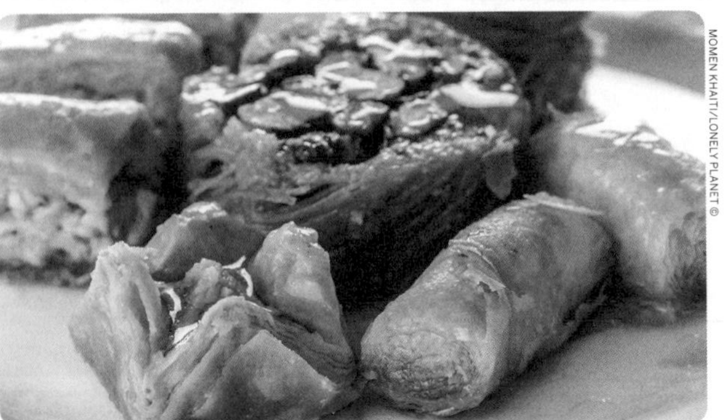

Top *Mensaf* (a Bedouin dish of lamb on a bed of rice)

Bottom Assorted Arabic sweets

Quick Eats

Local 'fast food' is safe, tasty and available in every town, usually from stands. The most popular dishes, none of which cost more than a couple of dinars, are as follows.

Shawarma Lamb or chicken sliced with great flourish from a revolving spit, mixed with onions and tomato and packed into flatbread.

Falafel Deep-fried balls of chickpea paste with spices, served in a piece of rolled-up *khobz* (bread) with varying combinations of pickled vegetables, tomato, salad and yoghurt.

Farooj Chicken roasted on spits in large grills in front of the restaurant, served with bread, raw onion and pickles.

Shish tawooq Spicy minced chicken kebabs, grilled over charcoal.

Cookbooks

Jordanian Cooking Step by Step (Lina Baydoun and Nada Halawani, 2009)

The New Book of Middle Eastern Food (Claudia Roden, 2000)

Vegetarian Options

Jordan, like many countries in the region, has a strongly carnivorous bias in the national diet – at least in restaurants. At home, people enjoy their vegetables and dairy products, and often consider meat as something to be enjoyed during special occasions.

Delicious vegetable and dairy dishes can be found in many restaurants in Jordan, especially mezze, but the concept of 'vegetarian' is still an alien one. As such, there may well be meat stock within a soup or animal fats used to prepare pastries. The following restaurants represent some of the best in terms of the variety of vegetarian options, but not for their non-meat pedigree.

Amman Wild Jordan Center (p69)
Azraq Azraq Lodge (p232)
Dana Biosphere Reserve Feynan Ecolodge (p151)
Jerash Lebanese House (p92)
Madaba Haret Jdoudna (p134)

COOKING YOUR OWN DINNER

It was an inauspicious start one cold day in winter: the knives were large, the onions eye-smartingly malevolent and the aubergines too big for their own good. But just as the Petra travellers were thinking this wasn't the activity for them, they caught sight of their fellow apprentices. With a smile of collusion across basins of parsley, they placed themselves in the hands of Mr Tariq, professional Petra chef and their teacher for the evening. Within moments, he had them shaving garlic with prodigious speed and chopping industrial quantities of tomatoes without them collapsing into sauce.

Petra Kitchen (p183) in downtown Wadi Musa is a novel idea. Instead of going out for supper, you pay a little extra to cook your own mezze, soup and a main course. The local experts who teach you how to cook Jordanian food give you valuable tips throughout the evening. If you get hooked on the flavours you learn to create, the dishes on the menu card change each night so within a week you could be returning home with a whole cookbook.

The experience of cooking in the company of strangers makes you realise that cooking in Jordan, just like dining, isn't about the locally grown vegetables or the handed-down recipes: it's about being sociable. One novice cook at Petra Kitchen commented that if they'd tasted the same meal at a restaurant, it would have tasted good but not as good as having prepared it themselves. This is probably because of the secret ingredients – namely the travellers' tales that spice up the flavours and the laughter that peppers each dish.

If the concept appeals, you can also put your culinary skills to the test at Beit Sitti (p65) in Amman.

Desserts

Jordanians have an incorrigibly sweet tooth, and there are pastry shops in every town dedicated to the sublime cuisine of baklava. The giant circular trays of filo pastry, trickled with honey, syrup and/or rose water and cut into lozenges, are almost works of art.

The sweetest highlight of travel in Jordan is *kunafeh,* a highly addictive dessert of shredded dough and cream cheese, smothered in syrup. Customers generally order desserts by weight: 250g is generally the smallest portion so have some friends (or a toothbrush) at the ready.

Jordan is locally famous for its dairy products, especially salty white cheese. A popular soft white cheese is *kashkawan* (or *kishkeh*), while haloumi and Lebanese-style *shinklish* have a firmer texture.

Drinks

Tea & Coffee

Tea and coffee are the major social lubricants in Jordan.

Tea *(shai)* is probably the more popular drink, taken without milk and in various degrees of sweetness: with sugar *(sukkar ziyada),* a little sugar *(sukkar qaleel)* or no sugar *(bidoon sukkar).* In most cafes you can ask for refreshing mint tea *(shai ma n'aana). Zaatar* (a blend of spices that includes hyssop, sumac and sesame) and *marrameeya* (sage) herbal teas are especially delicious in Dana.

Coffee *(qahwa)* is served strong, sweet and flavoured with cardamom, and usually contains thick sediment. You can specify a small espresso-sized cup *(finjan)* or large cup *(kassa kabira).* In traditional Bedouin areas, coffee is served in small porcelain bowls or small glasses and the host will always refill a guest's coffee cup. A good guest will accept a minimum of three cups but not more than five; gently 'dancing' the cup from side to side indicates you've had enough.

For men, Jordan's coffeehouses are great places to watch the world go by, write a letter, meet the locals and play a hand of cards, accompanied by the incessant clacking of domino and backgammon pieces and the gurgling of fruity *nargileh* (water pipes). Foreign women, with a bit of courage and modest attire, are usually tolerated. Traditional coffeehouses don't generally serve food.

Sahlab is a delicious traditional winter drink, served hot with milk, nuts and cinnamon. Look for it at hot-drink vendors, recognisable by their silver samovars.

Water is generally safe to drink in hotels and restaurants, and is available in earthenware ewers along rural roads; bottled water, however, minimises stomach upsets. Fresh pomegranate and rockmelon juices *(aseer)* are a regional highlight.

Alcoholic Drinks

In a predominantly Muslim country where alcohol is considered *haram* (forbidden) for most of the population, discreet imbibing of alcohol is acceptable for non-Muslims and the country supports a small wine industry and also a microbrewery. The latter was set up by a Christian Jordanian engineer who brought the concept of home-brewing from the US. The resulting Carakale brand (www.carakale.com/home) is a full-bodied beer much appreciated by aficionados.

Unlike the nascent brewing industry, viticulture has an ancient regional lineage. In contrast to neighbouring countries, however, Jordan's modern tradition of wine production was only revived a generation ago – almost single-handedly by Omar Zumot. A Christian from Amman who studied winemaking at a monastery in France, Zumot's organically produced St George wines give the lighter Mt Nebo wines a run for their money. If you're not convinced, it's easy to try both in top-end restaurants throughout Jordan.

In addition to beer and wine, arak (an aniseed-derived spirit) is drunk with enthusiasm by Christian Jordanians, in Amman and Madaba especially. Dilute with water to avoid the after-effects!

The Natural Environment

In Jordan you can breakfast in the desert, lunch under a pine tree and dine on bananas from the subtropical Jordan Valley. Not many countries exhibit such diversity within such a compact area. For the naturalist, this makes Jordan a dream. Thankfully, the authorities have been quick to recognise the country's wild appeal and have actively encouraged ecotourism. Whether you're a raptor enthusiast or casual fan of flowers, there's sure to be something to please you in Jordan's modest acreage.

The Land

At 91,860 sq km, Jordan is slightly smaller than Portugal or the US state of Virginia. Distances are short – it's only 430km from Ramtha, on the Syrian border in the north, to Aqaba in the south. TE Lawrence was pleased that he could cover Azraq to Amman in a hard, three-day camel ride. Today you can travel by car from tip to toe in around six hours. If you want to see anything, though, there's a lot to be said for the camel.

Geographically, Jordan can be divided into three major regions: the Jordan Valley, the East Bank Plateau and the desert.

Jordan's endemic plant species are represented in the Royal Botanic Garden, a 30-minute drive north of Amman. Featuring Jordan's national flower, the black iris, the gardens are the vision of conservation-minded Princess Basma and an impressive addition to Jordan's ecoprojects.

Jordan Valley Ecosystem

Jordan edges the Great Rift Valley, stretching from East Africa's lakes to southern Syria. The rift was created as the Arabian plate pulled away from the African plate, a geological event that gave rise to the Red Sea. Jordan's Wadi Araba, the Dead Sea and the Jordan Valley lie on this fault line. Sitting beside the effervescent springs at Hammamat Ma'in, it becomes obvious that this process of tectonic separation isn't yet complete.

Trickling through the northern part of the valley is the lowest-lying river on earth, the Jordan River, fed from the Sea of Galilee (Lake Tiberias), the Yarmouk River and hillside streams. This permanent fresh water has given rise to a humid, subtropical valley, highly fertile and intensively farmed.

Walking under the valley's flame and tamarisk trees you may see sunbirds and kingfishers or an endangered otter heading for the reeds. What you won't see is the lion, bear, elephant, rhino and herds of wild ass that Palaeolithic remains prove were once resident here.

Not everything in the region has changed, however. The fish in Madaba's famous mosaic, twisting back from certain death at the mouth of the Jordan River, show that the Dead Sea was as insupportable of life in Byzantine times as it is today. Change is all a matter of time scale, however. Go way back in history, between the two ice ages, and scientists speculate from recently discovered salt crystals under today's body of water that the Dead Sea area suffered an intense drought and perhaps evaporated, as it appears to be doing today.

Nature Guides

Field Guide to Jordan (Jarir Maani, 2008)

The Birds of the Hashemite Kingdom of Jordan (Ian J Andrews, 1995)

East Bank Plateau Ecosystem

High above the Jordan Valley – cut by a series of epic gorges carved out in slow motion by the wadis of Zarqa, Mujib and Hasa – is the hilly and temperate East Bank Plateau. It comprises the forested hills of northern Jordan (less than 1% of Jordan is wooded), rich in Aleppo pines, oak and red-barked strawberry trees, and home to ill-tempered wild boar, polecats, stone martens and porcupines.

Wildflowers, including pink hollyhocks, poppies and yellow daisies, bloom in magnificent abundance in spring. This is the time to spot the black iris (actually a deep purple), the national flower of Jordan.

'Jebel' is the Arabic word for arid mountain. Jebel Umm Adaani (1832m), the highest peak in Jordan, lives up to that description. 'Wadi' is the word for dry watercourse or flood channel. Wadi Mujib belies that description with its permanently flowing water.

The East Bank Plateau contains the main centres of population (Amman, Irbid, Zarqa and Karak) and has been crossed by caravans for centuries. The plateau landscape of fig and olive groves, occasional vineyards and closely cropped pastureland reflects this human interaction. If you hike near Madaba in the summer, you'll see Bedouin grazing their stock on the hillside; they descend to lower ground in winter to escape the bitter winds. Since the time of Moses, their husbandry has shaped the land, etching ancient paths around the closely cropped contours.

Pockets of pristine plateau wilderness remain towards the southern end of the plateau around Dana. This rocky wilderness of outstanding biodiversity is the habitat of elusive caracals (Persian lynx), felines with outrageous tufts of hair on the tips of their outsized ears. It is also home to ibex, endangered goats with enormous horns that cling to the craggy folds of limestone.

From a height of 600m to 900m above sea level, the plateau ends near the Red Sea port of Aqaba.

JORDAN'S BIODIVERSITY

Birds Jordan's location on the edge of the Great Rift Valley makes it an important migration route for birds. More than half a million birds transit between Russia, Central Europe and Africa, breaking their journey in Jordan's dwindling oases and wetlands. The Sinai Rosefinch, Jordan's national bird, can be spotted in and around Petra.

Animals A successful breeding program for the Nubian ibex by the Royal Society for the Conservation of Nature (RSCN; www.rscn.org.jo) began in Wadi Mujib Nature Reserve in 1989. Some have been reintroduced into the wild and the herds are increasing. An attempt to release oryx bred at Shaumari Wildlife Reserve into Wadi Rum initially met with less success, with some wandering over the border to Saudi Arabia, but the work to reintroduce Jordan's national animal continues.

Reptiles Jordan's brightly coloured reptiles are shy but considerably less elusive than the foxes and other fur- and feather-clad predators that feed on them. The bright turquoise Sinai agama and the changing coloration of the chameleon are two of many striking inhabitants of Jordan's jebel landscape. Around 35 snake species have been recorded in Jordan, some of which are venomous; they are seldom aggressive unless provoked.

Invertebrates In arid areas of Jordan, scorpions are common but shy nocturnal residents. It's worth knocking out boots in the morning to check for stowaways.

Fish The Gulf of Aqaba, part of the Red Sea, sustains 230 species of coral and 1000 types of fish.

Plants Jordan boasts more than 2500 species of wild plants, including 20 species of orchid. *Wildflowers of Jordan & Neighbouring Countries* by Dawud MH Al Eisawi has useful photographs that are helpful in identification. A trip to the Royal Botanic Garden outside Amman is a good way to become familiar with native species, including Jordan's famous black iris.

Desert Ecosystem

On its eastern flank, the East Bank Plateau glides gradually into the desert. More than 90% of Jordan is desert, but it's home to only 5% of the population. The forbidding volcanic basalt rock of the northeast gives way to soft-whittled sandstone and granite in the south and the famous escarpments of Wadi Rum. In between, the stony wasteland known as the Badia slides into 1000km of nothingness, interrupted only by the occasional succulent, a wandering camel or camouflaged lizard.

When you travel along empty Route 10, it's impossible to imagine that anything could survive such desolation. But then, miraculously, you reach Azraq Wetland Reserve, a desert oasis attracting great numbers of migrating birds. Herons and egrets fish patiently among the croaking toads, and predators such as the desert fox, wolf and jackal lurk beyond the fringes of the oasis waiting for a careless desert hare to run out of luck.

Top Goat, Dana Biosphere Reserve

Bottom Azraq Wetland Reserve

Some desert species ran out of luck a long time ago, hunted to extinction before conservation became part of the modern sensibility. In Shaumari Wildlife Reserve (newly reopened after a decade of redevelopment) there's a chance to see the animals that once roamed these plains before they are reintroduced to the wild.

The Dead Sea might be virtually barren, but the surrounding cliffs are not: small oases of date palm and hanging gardens of fern hide noisy Tristram's Grackle (a native starling), and the sandstone bluffs shelter the elusive and endangered Nubian ibex.

Protected Areas

Established in 1966, the **Royal Society for the Conservation of Nature** (RSCN; www.rscn.org.jo) is an unusual NGO in that it has a national mandate to run biodiversity projects on behalf of the nation. It is now Jordan's main environmental agency.

The RSCN has been successful in its founding remit: to help save animal and plant species from extinction and to reintroduce several locally extinct species, such as the Arabian oryx. Over the past two decades, however, the RSCN has developed a much wider focus, recognising that tourism has an important role to play. The result has been a modern and highly successful program of ecotourism projects, centred on RSCN reserves.

Jordan's Nature Reserves

The RSCN maintains nine reserves and helps manage the Wadi Rum protected area. It is also in the process of setting up a reserve at Burqu in eastern Jordan to protect the sand cat among other desert species. These reserves should not be confused with Jordan's 'national parks', which are unstructured, recreational areas, such as Zay National Park, near Salt.

Ajloun Forest Reserve (p94; 13 sq km, established 1988) This pretty reserve has easy trails, pistachio and oak forest, spring flowers and cottage industries.

Azraq Wetland Reserve (p229; 12 sq km, 1977) In spring and autumn, hundreds of migratory birds can be seen from a bird hide and boardwalk in this refuge amid the damaged and shrunken marshland.

Dana Biosphere Reserve (p148; 320 sq km, 1989) A spectacular wilderness area with various trails, Dana encompasses rugged mountains and desert with 600 species of plants, 200 species of bird and over 40 species of mammal.

Dibeen Forest Reserve (p93; 8 sq km, 2005) One of the last Aleppo pine forests left in Jordan, Dibeen protects endangered species such as the Persian squirrel.

Fifa Reserve (27 sq km, 2011) Rare subtropical vegetation, home to migratory waterbirds.

Mujib Biosphere Reserve (p121; 212 sq km, 1988) Used for the captive breeding of Nubian ibexes, Mujib has an impressive ecotourism program, with canyon walks and waterfall rappelling.

Qatar Nature Reserve An arid terrain on the edge of the Wadi Araba escarpment.

Shaumari Wildlife Reserve (p229; 22 sq km, 1975) This small reserve was established to reintroduce the locally extinct Arabian oryx, ostrich, gazelle and onager.

Wadi Rum Protected Area (p209; 540 sq km, 1998) This beautiful desert – a Unesco site since 2011 and controlled by the Aqaba government – is the Bedouin heartland, offering camping, camel treks and 4WD excursions.

Yarmouk Nature Reserve (30 sq km, 2011) Undeveloped home to waterbirds, endangered gazelles and otters.

The RSCN conducts public awareness programs among Jordanians, especially children; sponsors environmental clubs; trains guides; combats poaching and hunting; and lobbies against mining, helping the uphill struggle to preserve the country's natural treasures for future generations.

Green Jordan & Ecotourism

Despite 'green' being something of a nascent concept in the Middle East, Jordan has shown both ingenuity and commitment for nearly two decades in embracing an environmentally friendly approach. This approach extends both to an assortment of environmental challenges and to tourism, which is perhaps the biggest challenge of all. Find out how you can minimise the impact of your visit in a country that at times is too popular for its own good.

Environmental Issues

Water

Swim across one of the infinity pools in Aqaba surrounded by lush gardens and you may not realise that Jordan has a chronic shortage of water. The facts are alarming. Relying mainly on rainwater and subterranean aquifers that are already in many cases overexploited, Jordan has sunk to the fifth-most water-impoverished country in the world. With 90% of Jordan's rivers already being diverted, a population increasing by more than 2% annually and persistent droughts, this situation is likely to worsen rather than improve. Currently, about 60% more water is used than replenished from natural sources and, by some estimates, the country is due to run out of water within 20 years.

Jordan has just 77 cu metres of renewable water per capita per year, compared to the UK's 2244 or Lebanon's 856. Anything under 500 cu metres is considered to be a scarcity of water.

Jordan is not alone in this problem. Water is a hot political issue across the region, contributing to several skirmishes over the years and continuing to spike relations between Jordan and its neighbours. After the 1994 peace treaty, Israel and the Palestinian Territories permitted Jordan to extract 50 million cu metres per year from the Sea of Galilee, but disputes rumble on over whether Jordan is getting its fair share.

Hunting

Visit a nature reserve in Jordan and you'll see lots of information about elusive animals that reside there, but the fact remains that a staggering 20 species of mammal have become extinct in Jordan in the past 100 years. Some were hunted and poached (especially after WWII, when weapons flooded the region), spelling the end for Jordan's lion, cheetah, bear, gazelle and wild ass. The last leopard was killed near Dana in 1986, although there have been unsubstantiated sightings since.

The continuing threats to bird and animal species (24 out of Jordan's remaining 77 species of mammals are globally threatened) include poor land management, such as deforestation; the pumping of water from vital areas such as the Jordan River, Dead Sea and the Azraq Wetlands; urban sprawl; unremitting use of pesticides, especially near water sources in the Jordan Valley; and air and water pollution.

Green Info on Jordan

EcoPeace Middle East *(www.ecopeaceme.org)*

Ministry of Environment *(www.kinghussein.gov.jo/geo_env.html)*

Overgrazing & Desertification

Survey Moses' promised land from Mt Nebo and you'll find little left of promise in the semi-arid landscape – that's if you can see it through the haze of dust kicked up by livestock. This once fertile land has been devastated by centuries of overgrazing and this, together with erosion and drought, has led to widespread desertification (the seemingly unstoppable spread of the desert to previously fertile, inhabited and environmentally sensitive areas). According to the Royal Society for the Conservation of Nature (RSCN), millions of hectares of fertile land have become infertile and uninhabitable. This means there are now fewer pastures for livestock and crops, and reduced land for native animals and plants. Jordan is home to about three million sheep and goats, but there is no longer enough pasture to feed them, resulting in their encroachment on nature reserves and urban fringes.

A successful breeding program of the Nubian ibex by the RSCN began in the Mujib Biosphere Reserve in 1989. Some have now been reintroduced into the wild and the herds are increasing well. The killifish, unique to the Azraq Wetlands, has recently been saved from extinction, and numbers are increasing.

Overcoming the Challenges

Recognising the threat environmental problems posed to the country, the Jordanian Parliament passed the Protection of the Environment Law in 1995. This included measures banning hunting and restricting grazing.

Environmental strategies have focused on addressing the water issue. Jordan's farmers (comprising around 5% of the population) use 75% of the water (quite often inefficiently), so modernising farming practices and plugging leaks in city pipelines is a priority. More radical approaches include the extraction of nonrenewable fossil water from aquifers near Wadi Rum and controversial plans, finalised in 2013, to construct a series of desalination plants, hydroelectric power stations and canals linking the Red Sea with the Dead Sea, thereby raising the level of the Dead Sea and creating a fresh water supply. In 2016 companies began to bid for the first US$900-million phase of the project, which involves the moving of 300 million cu metres of water along a conveyance system from the Red Sea to the Dead Sea. While the scheme has attracted condemnation from environmental quarters anxious about the unique composition of the Red Sea, there is deeper political concern that if the looming water crisis is not resolved swiftly, the predicted 'water wars' will replace oil crises as the major source of conflict in the near future.

TEN TOP ECO-EXPERIENCES

- Hike to see soapmakers at work in Ajloun Forest Reserve (p94).
- Savour a wild-berry smoothie in Amman's Wild Jordan Center (p69).
- Learn about Azraq's Chechens over a home-cooked feast at Azraq Lodge (p232).
- Buy a hand-loomed rug from the Bani Hamida Weaving Centre (p140).
- Wake up to birdsong at beautiful Rummana Campground (p151).
- Enjoy a vegetarian supper in candlelit Feynan Ecolodge (p151).
- Give your sunglasses an embroidered treat from the craft shop at Dana Biosphere Reserve (p148).
- Splash through the permanent pools of Mujib Biosphere Reserve (p121).
- Take a camel trip in the company of a Bedouin guide in Wadi Rum (p217).
- Stay overnight with the Bedouin at the Ammarin Bedouin Camp (p192) near Wadi Rum.

Ecotourism

Effects of Tourism

Tourism has caused a rapid increase in pollution from cars and industries, and has exacerbated the demand for precious water. In addition, vandalism and unwitting damage to sites such as Jerash and Petra, the effects of flash photography on fragile rock art, and rubbish left at hot springs have made some people wonder whether tourism is worth the trouble.

Since the 1960s Israel and the Palestinian Territories have drawn one-third of their water from the Jordan River; reduced to a trickle, the river comprises raw sewage and effluent from fish farms.

But it is not all doom and gloom. In a region only recently concerned with conservation, Jordan is ahead of the game with the authorities proving keen to promote sustainable tourism while maintaining the country's cultural heritage. This is illustrated through the preservation of Islamic values, promotion for arts and craft initiatives, and support for traditional lifestyles (as with the employment of Bedouin drivers in Wadi Rum).

The RSCN has been at the forefront of attempts to promote a more sustainable form of tourism through its various ecotourism projects. Such projects provide a major means of funding environmental programs.

It's not easy balancing the need for increased tourism against the environmental cost of more visitors. For example, tourism revenue at Wadi Rum is needed for the upkeep of the protected area, but it's hard to minimise the impact of more feet and wheels upon a fragile desert ecosystem. A balance can be achieved, however, with the cooperation of visitors.

Impact-Neutral Checklist

If you'd like to know how to minimise the negative impact of your visit, think about using the following checklist to inform the choices you make on the road.

Save water Every drop helps, given Jordan's chronic water shortage.

Use local guides and services This is an opportunity to learn about a unique way of life and help preserve local traditions.

In 2013 King Abdullah II inaugurated a new pipeline to extract 120 million cu metres of water annually from the 30,000-year-old aquifer in Diseh near Wadi Rum. The near-billion-dollar project took four years to complete, and involved drilling 64 wells and building a 325km pipeline from Diseh to Amman.

Buy wisely Profits are returned to local communities from specialist craft centres.

Dress and behave respectfully The liberalisation of customs and manners is seen by many Jordanians as a bad habit caught from the West and an erosion of their cultural and Islamic heritage.

Pay your dues Entrance fees are the lifeline that helps to maintain Jordan's reserves.

Spend money... This will help make your visit count more positively than surviving on muesli you brought from home.

...but don't give it away Tips should only be given for services rendered (such as buying a souvenir from kids at Petra) to discourage the counter-productive activity of begging.

Leave as found For as long as outsiders have been searching for, and stumbling over, the ancient monuments of Jordan, they have also been chipping bits off, hauling items home or leaving their contributions engraved on the stones. Please don't be one of their number.

Bag it and bin it This is the one time when you shouldn't follow local example; be a trendsetter instead and take your litter home.

Follow the rules As tempting as it may be to reach out for a starfish in the Red Sea, light a fire at an ad hoc campground, take a photo without someone's permission or skinny dip in a waterhole, these are acts that erode the natural and cultural heritage of the country.

Making Your Stay Count

There are lots of ways in which you can turn your visit from a potential burden into a blessing. By supporting responsible enterprises, you will be contributing positively to local communities. Also don't forget that you can add value to your purchases by shopping at community-friendly outlets.

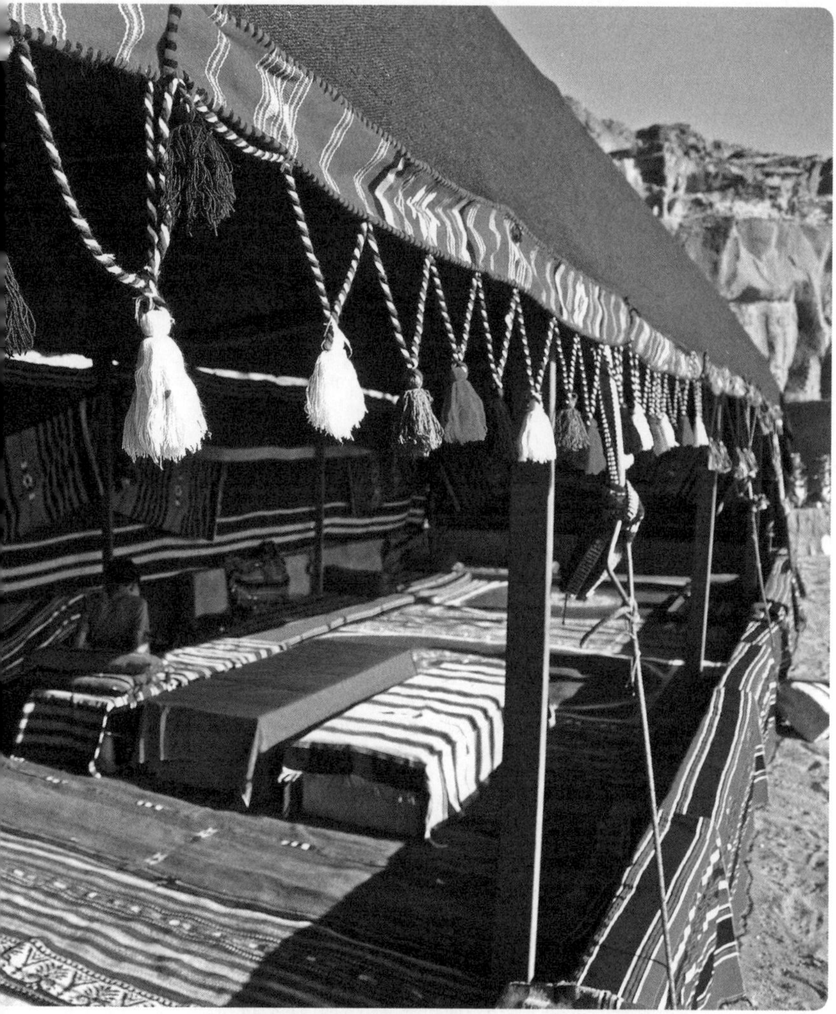

JOE WINDSOR-WILLIAMS/LONELY PLANET ©

Top Bedouin camp near Wadi Rum (p218)

Bottom A local guide on a camel, Wadi Rum (p209)

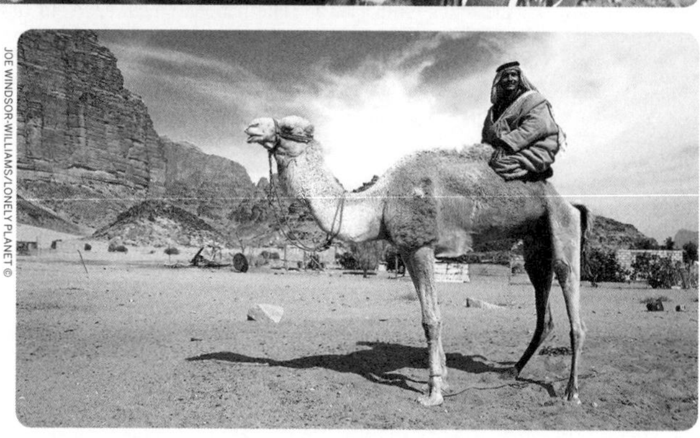

RSCN: A BYWORD FOR SUSTAINABLE TOURISM

Teamwork is a good way to describe the Royal Society for the Conservation of Nature's (RSCN) policy of environmental management. The RSCN directly employs hundreds of Jordanian people and has given employment opportunities to more than 16,000 Jordanians over the years. Its role includes getting corporate business involved to back eco-ventures (such as the chic cafe at the Wild Jordan Center within the RSCN headquarters building in Amman). Crucially, it also involves local communities, such as those of Ajloun or Dana, through income-generating projects that complement rather than threaten traditional lifestyles.

Thanks to the combined interests of all these 'stakeholders', the RSCN's work is high-profile in Jordan, with Jordanian nationals comprising a significant proportion of the tens of thousands of visitors who call in at one of the country's nature reserves each year.

With great accommodation serving wonderful food in beautiful places; walking, hiking and scrambling trails to suit all legs; and a series of shops that make you wish you'd packed a bigger suitcase, the RSCN's flagship reserves are a highlight of a 'sustainable visit' to Jordan.

Jordan's nature reserves represent about 1% of Jordan's total land area – a small percentage compared with land allocated in Saudi Arabia (9%) and the US (11%). When measured as a ratio of habitable land versus size of population, however, the figure is considerably more generous.

Things to Do

Abraham Path Initiative (www.abrahampath.org) Hike along a path from Ajloun to Pella in Jordan and connect to a cultural peace initiative that runs through Iraq, Israel and the Palestinian Territories, Egypt and Saudi Arabia. An excellent website aids planning and shows how to make the most of the journey by connecting with the local communities who stand to benefit from the passing trade of hikers.

Jordan Heritage Revival Company (www.jhrc.jo) Attend one of this company's accurate historical re-enactments, occasionally staged around the country, to keep alive Jordan's treasured continuity with the past. Donations for posing with Roman centurions at Petra go to support local community initiatives.

Jordan Trail (www.jordantrail.org) Follow Jordan's newest trail from north to south, supported by local in-country operators, and contribute therein to much needed local employment.

Sharhabil Bin Hassneh Ecopark (www.jordanecopark.com) Stay at an ecolodge or take the community-based tour along the Jordan River and learn more about cross-border issues, such as water conservation and peace-building – part of a larger ecological initiative to rehabilitate the Jordan Valley promoted by EcoPeace Middle East (www.ecopeaceme.org).

Wild Jordan (www.wildjordan.com) Book a tour along a trail established by Al Ayoun Society and support village projects near Ajloun. Similar community projects are run in Umm Qais and Dana.

Zikra Initiative (www.zikrainitiative.org) Get involved with a project that connects 'urbanites' (Jordanian and international city dwellers) to 'ruralists' – a modest participation fee helps fund microloans for village 'entrepreneurs'.

Places to Stay

RSCN (www.rscn.org.jo) Provides excellent ethical and sustainable accommodation within Jordan's reserves – reservations are necessary and can be made online.

Bedouin Cooperative Campgrounds Camps such as the Ammarin Bedouin (p192) near Little Petra, with an on-site museum showcasing the local tribe, and other camps at Wadi Rum and Diseh help preserve the Bedouin way of life.

Finding Fair Services

Jordan Inbound Tour Operators Association (www.jitoa.org) This voluntary umbrella organisation is a good place to research 'green' tour operators.

Survival Guide

Safe Travel

POST-ARAB SPRING

Jordan is safe to visit and, despite local dissatisfaction with issues such as Iraqi immigration, the Syrian refugee crisis, unemployment and high inflation, you are unlikely to feel any hint of the turmoil of neighbouring countries.

The democratic uprising during the Arab Spring of 2011 was only fleetingly experienced in Jordan. King Abdullah II is a respected leader and has wide public support for his efforts in introducing democratic reforms and curbing public corruption.

Terrorism

Jordan lives in a tough neighbourhood and has had to deal with the civil wars across the border in Syria and Iraq, as well as the aftermath of the Egyptian revolution and the ongoing Palestinian situation. For all this, the country is reassuringly calm and stable. That said, there are occasional demonstrations in support of the Palestinians in Karak, Tafila and Ma'an, and in the university areas of Irbid, Mu'tah and northern Amman, and occasional disturbances in the Zaatari camp for Syrian refugees.

The last major terrorist attack in Jordan was the 2005 suicide bombing of three hotels in Amman, which killed 60 people and injured 115, carried out by Iraqi Al Qaeda affiliates. A similar plot was foiled in 2012. Jordan strengthened its anti-terrorism laws in 2014 to clamp down on potential trouble from Syrian jihadists, and maintains close links to US and British security forces. One or two isolated incidents have occurred each year since 2014, none of which have dented Jordan's peaceful reputation.

Commitment to Safety

Over the past decade, the Jordanian government has invested significantly in tourism. Now, with so much at stake in terms of revenue, there is a collective desire among Jordanians to maintain Jordan's reputation as a safe destination. Some of the measures taken by the government for this purpose include the following:

- A high security presence in many tourist hotels throughout Jordan.
- Metal detectors at hotels and some public buildings.
- Tourist police are present at all major sites.
- Checkpoints monitor all border zones.

Some Dos

- Be vigilant in the cities, keeping clear of large public gatherings.
- Cooperate politely with security checks in hotel foyers and at road checkpoints.
- Keep abreast of the news in English-language newspapers published in Amman.
- Check the latest travel warnings online through your country's state department or ministry.
- Consult your embassy or consulate in Jordan for specific concerns.
- Register with your embassy or consulate on arrival if there have been recent public order issues.
- Trust the police, military and security services. They are overwhelmingly friendly, honest and hospitable, in common with their compatriots.

Some Don'ts

- Don't be paranoid – the chances of running into trouble are rare.
- Don't get involved if you witness political protests or civil unrest.

THE OTHER SIDE OF THE 'SCAM'

Taxi driver wouldn't use the meter? Paid more than a friend for the same item? These may sound like routine scams but there's often a legitimate reason. Jordanians take pride in their moral compass, and tourists on the whole are treated with respect and fairness. Here are some different perspectives given by service providers that may cast so-called scams in a different light.

Taxi fares? The fare is set by the government and hasn't been adjusted for inflation; taxi drivers usually agree on fair fares with locals, but it's harder to negotiate with tourists who don't speak Arabic.

Room rates? Small hotels have to respond to fluctuations in tourist numbers, or they go bust. For some, this means offering unrealistic rates in low season; for others, it means raising prices to cover investments made in anticipation of a good season.

Minibus overcharging? Foreigners don't like waiting until the bus is full – drivers are happy to leave early but it means making up the cost of a full load. As for luggage, that often takes up the place of a fee-paying passenger.

Double standards? When you're haggling, an item costs whatever a vendor is happy to sell for, balanced against whatever a buyer is happy to pay for during that one transaction. Comparison with other travellers' experiences can be a pointless exercise.

➡ Don't strike up conversations of a stridently political nature with casual acquaintances.

Government Travel Advice

The following government websites offer travel advisories and information on current hotspots.

Australian Department of Foreign Affairs & Trade (www.smarttraveller.gov.au)

British Foreign & Commonwealth Office (www.fco.gov.uk)

Canadian Department of Foreign Affairs & International Trade (www.dfait-maeci.gc.ca)

US State Department (http://travel.state.gov)

OTHER DANGERS

Minefields

Jordan is a signatory to the Ottawa International Mine Ban Treaty, and in 2012 became the first Arab country to declare itself free of landmines. Sections of the Jordan–Syria border previously contained large minefields. These have now been cleared, although there are unsubstantiated reports that more mines have been laid on the Syrian side recently because of that country's civil war.

Theft & Crime

Jordan has low levels of crime. Leaving your bag under the watchful eye of a member of staff at a bus station or hotel is generally safe, so avoid jumping to conclusions if something goes missing – locals have a lot to lose in a country where stealing from guests is particularly frowned upon.

Punishments are harsh and, in a country where unemployment is high, there is a serious chance of losing a job without much hope of recovering a livelihood in future. Inevitably, however, there are one or two scams to look out for.

Common Scams

Taken for a ride The taxi fare quoted on the meter is in fils, not in dinars, and visitors often misunderstand this when paying. Perhaps understandably, it is rare for a taxi driver to point out this mistake.

Crafty business Shop owners often claim something is locally crafted as part of a profit-share scheme, when in fact it is imported from abroad.

Money for old rope So-called antiques are often merely last year's stock that's gathered an authentic-looking layer of dust. Similarly, 'ancient' oil lamps and coins are seldom what they seem.

Full or five? At many petrol stations if you ask for 'full', the attendant fills up to the value of JD5, pleading misunderstanding, and then fills the tank and adds JD5 on top.

Your money or your lights! Some kids on the roads between Madaba and the Dead Sea have taken to holding up rental cars demanding sweets or 'One JD'. If the driver refuses, they stone the car, aiming in particular for the lights.

Cosy in a cave At Petra, a common scam is for men to befriend single women and offer them the moon, bedding down under the stars and promising them the world. The requests for money begin in the cold light of day and continue with different degrees of sophistication, often long after the love-struck visitor has returned home.

Women Travellers

ADOPTING THE RIGHT MINDSET

Plenty of women each year have travelled through Jordan alone (this writer included) and have enjoyed the experience thoroughly. That said, there are bound to be times when you will have male company in Jordan that you would rather do without. This may involve nothing more than irritating banter, proposals of marriage and declarations of love. On rarer occasions it will involve leering and physical contact – a grope in a bus, for example. Where possible, it's best to ignore such behaviour or pass it off as part of the experience, or a few sad individuals will spoil your whole trip. Needless to say, many women, such as the celebrated author Marguerite van Geldermalsen, have enjoyed male encounters enough to stay a lifetime, but it is important to gauge the sincerity of an admirer before being drawn into a relationship.

ATTITUDE TOWARDS WOMEN

Being highly gregarious as a nation, Jordanians will be surprised that you want to travel alone. Men, who have little or no contact with women, let alone sex, before marriage, may misinterpret this as an invitation to provide company. Stereotypes of foreign women based on Western films and TV convince some that all foreign women are promiscuous and will jump into bed at the drop of a hat.

AVOIDING TROUBLE

Dressing Appropriately

Nothing gives more offence in Jordan – a country with largely conservative and Islamic sensibilities – than baring too much flesh. To minimise harassment and to be respectful of local customs, it's imperative to dress appropriately, especially in small towns and rural areas.

In the trendy districts of Amman, such as Abdoun and Shmeisani, in large hotels and resorts, or even in the middle of Petra (where tour group parties generally wear whatever they feel like) you can dress as you would at home. Outside those areas, aim for

WATCH OUT FOR ROMEO

Some solo women travellers have reported being hoodwinked into relationships with local Bedouin men, particularly in Petra, that turn out to be nothing more than an opportunity for free sex and the chance of making money through hard luck stories. These come later, communicated through social media. While something of a common phenomenon in this part of the world, these scams have been perfected by some local men who have honed the art of deception to perfection, and women may need to be more alert to emotional blackmail than usual here.

The best advice is to treat offers of hospitality from attractive men, declarations of undying love and promises of platonic nights under the stars with scepticism if not caution. Dressing modestly is not only more culturally sensitive; it will also help keep unwanted attention to a minimum. Instances of physical harassment are rare and generally a good-natured but determined 'thanks but no thanks' is enough to ward off potential scammers. In the unusual circumstance where this is not the case, however, the incident should be reported to the police (or tourist police in Petra).

knee-length dresses or loose trousers, and cover your shoulders and upper arms.

On public beaches at the Dead Sea and in Aqaba, wear a swimsuit (and preferably a T-shirt and shorts) when swimming and save the bikinis for top-end resorts and dive centres. Never go topless – especially in the wadis where skinny dipping in freshwater pools is seldom as unseen as you might imagine.

Some foreign women go to the extent of covering their head, but this is inappropriate for non-Muslims in Jordan and can be misconstrued – particularly by the women of Jordan's Christian communities who do not wear headscarves.

Advice from Fellow Women Travellers

Some Dos

- Sit next to a woman if possible on public transport.
- Be cautious when venturing alone to remote parts of Petra, Jerash and Wadi Rum.
- Check for peepholes in rooms and bathrooms (particularly cigarette holes in curtains).
- Place a chair against your locked hotel room door in case of 'accidental' intrusions.
- Pay for a better hotel, generally associated with less hassle.
- Be suspicious of lovelorn guides, especially the handsome ones!
- Prepare a cover story – Jordanians will be mystified that you have no family or friends to travel with.
- Chat to men in the company of women – not all men are one-track minded.
- Wear a wedding ring – this will add to your respectability in Arab eyes. A photo of husband and kids will clinch it.
- Bring tampons and contraceptives – they're hard to find and embarrassing to purchase outside Amman.

Some Don'ts

- Don't go to a local bar unaccompanied.
- Don't make eye contact with strangers – dark glasses can help.
- Don't sit in the front seat of a chartered private or service taxi.
- Don't go outside with wet hair – this apparently implies you've had sex recently!

Public Spaces

It's not easy finding where to eat and drink, or even just sit, in public without becoming the centre of attention. Here are some guidelines.

Coffeehouses & Local Bars Often seen as a male domain; in some places the stares will evict you even if the landlord won't.

Midrange Bars & Cafes Almost always welcoming of women in Amman and Aqaba; less 'comprehending' (of your solo status) in smaller towns.

Public Beaches Magnet for unwanted attention; best to stick to resorts.

Restaurants Most have a 'family section' where women can eat alone and in peace.

Toilets Usually only one in small restaurants and bars; avoid where possible!

Tourist Sites Counter-intuitively, the best places to be 'alone' as a woman – though be on your guard for charmers with ulterior motives in Petra.

Responding to Persistent Harassment

Some behaviour may warrant a public scene: bystanders will quickly support you if someone has overstepped the mark. Say out loud *imshi* (clear off): this should deter most unwanted advances. Be firm but stay calm. Swearing or losing your temper will lose you public sympathy.

EMERGENCIES

Assault and rape are rare in Jordan, but if you do suffer a serious problem, follow this advice:

- Go to a police station or tourist police booth; the latter can be found at most tourist sites.
- Be clear about the facts: the tourist police in Jordan take reports seriously.
- Call ☎911, the nationwide emergency number; this central coordination point has English-speaking staff.

Directory A–Z

Accommodation

Jordan has accommodation to suit most budgets in the main cities but limited choice elsewhere. It's generally not necessary to book ahead except in the two peak seasons (September to October and March to mid-May). Holiday weekends are peak times in Aqaba and at the Dead Sea resorts.

RSCN Ecolodges Some of the best accommodation in Jordan is offered at sustainable lodges in the country's nature reserves.

Hotels Most hotels in Jordan are family-run enterprises with a long tradition of hospitality towards travellers.

Resorts Five-star luxury can be found at resorts in Amman, Aqaba, Wadi Musa and the Dead Sea.

Camping

For many people, spending a night under the stars – or at least under canvas – is a highlight of a trip to Jordan. One popular option is to sleep in a traditional 'house of hair' at a Bedouin camp in Wadi Rum. Facilities in these goat-wool tents are basic but it's a great experience.

Camping with your own tent is permitted in a few places in southern Jordan, especially in the desert surrounding Wadi Rum. Camping 'off piste' in the north is more problematic, not least because you'll have competition for the best spots from the Bedouin, and it's surprisingly hard to find a secluded place to pitch a tent.

Bringing a tent to save money on accommodation isn't cost effective as camping is rarely possible without your own transport. Besides, cheap rooms are plentiful in areas close to the major sites of interest.

Hotels

From homestays in Ajloun, family-run guesthouses in Madaba, ecolodges in nature reserves to the opulent pleasure palaces on the Dead Sea, Jordan offers some interesting hotel accommodation. Reservations are recommended during peak seasons, especially at the Dead Sea resorts, in Jerash, and for midrange and top-end hotels in Aqaba and Wadi Musa.

Breakfast varies from a humble round of bread with a triangle of processed cheese in budget hotels to a delicious assortment of locally made yoghurt, hummus, *fuul* (fava bean paste) and olives in midrange hotels. The buffet-style breakfasts at top-end hotels can fill up a hungry hiker for a week.

Wi-fi is available, usually for free, in most hotels but not necessarily in all the rooms.

BUDGET

Budget rooms are available in most towns and vary from stark and basic to simple and homely. Most are spotlessly clean.

Private rooms start from JD15/20 for singles/doubles, with less stark rooms with a private bathroom costing around JD25/35. Prices are negotiable, especially during quieter seasons. A few places in downtown Amman have dorm rooms, but these are otherwise not common; most budget places have 'triples' (rooms with three beds), which you can ask to share with other travellers, cutting the cost of accommodation considerably. In summer you can even sleep on the roof in some places for about JD8 per person with access to showers. There are no youth hostels in Jordan.

Some things to consider: many budget places are located above shops and cafes that can be noisy at night; avoid windowless rooms that are stifling hot in summer;

BOOK YOUR STAY ONLINE

For more accommodation reviews by Lonely Planet authors, check out http://lonelyplanet.com/hotels/. You'll find independent reviews, as well as recommendations on the best places to stay. Best of all, you can book online.

STAYING IN JORDAN'S NATURE RESERVES

A variety of accommodation, from camping and cabins to luxury rooms in ecofriendly lodges, is offered within most of Jordan's nature reserves. To see what is on offer in each reserve and to make an online booking, visit the website of the Royal Society for the Conservation of Nature (RSCN; www.rscn.org.jo). In some areas, such as the beautiful Dana Nature Reserve (open March to November), advance booking is required.

Camping in these reserves is not a cheap option. It is intended for those who are happy to pay extra to wake up in the wild and who want to contribute to the sustainable tourism ethic of the RSCN. Bookings can also be made through **Wild Jordan** (Map p52; ☎06 461 6523; www.wildjordan.com; Othman Bin Affan St, Downtown) in Amman.

winter in Jordan is bitterly cold so ensure the heater is working before checking in. Wi-fi may cost extra, and breakfast is not always included in the price.

Payment usually needs to be made in cash in Jordanian dinars.

MIDRANGE

Midrange hotels offer the best value for money in Jordan. They are often privately owned by families who take pride in welcoming their guests. The owners are a fount of local knowledge and provide assistance in catching transport or advising on sights of interest. Some even organise their own tours. Most family-run hotels offer some kind of home cooking for breakfast, and guests might even be asked to join the family if they have requested an evening meal.

There is at least one midrange hotel in towns you're likely to visit, with a good selection in Amman, Madaba, Wadi Musa (near Petra) and Aqaba. Rooms in midrange hotels usually have colour TV (sometimes featuring satellite stations such as CNN), fridge, heater (essential in winter), phone, reliable hot water and a private bathroom.

Prices are typically around JD50/65 for singles/doubles. Negotiation is sometimes possible, especially if you're staying for several days. Many midrange hotels accept credit cards, but it's best to ask before checking in.

TOP END

There are some excellent top-end hotels in Amman, Wadi Musa and Aqaba. Most have a travel agency within their shopping arcades from which you can hire a car and organise hotel bookings for the next part of your trip.

Most of the top-end hotels are owned by international chains, but they invariably reflect the local character of Jordan, with Arabian-style interior design, options for high-quality Middle Eastern dining, shops selling fine Jordanian handicrafts and bookshops with a selection of English-language titles on Jordan.

Independent travellers can often negotiate a walk-in rate. Outside peak seasons and holidays (when booking is essential), you may find a world-class room for a midrange price.

A tax and service charge of 26% is added to the bill in top-end hotels, although it's worth checking to see if this has already been included in a discounted rate. Major credit cards are accepted in all top-end hotels.

Rental Accommodation

Apartments for short-term rental can be a cost-effective way of making the most of a longer trip to Jordan. In Amman, the best places to check for apartments are the accommodation listings in the English-language newspapers, cultural-centre noticeboards, and signs displayed in the cafes around Rainbow Street (including the noticeboard at **Books@café** (Map p52; ☎06 465 0457; Omar Bin Al Khattab St; ⏰10am-midnight; 📶). Also see www.expatriates.com/classifieds/amm/housing available.

It generally costs about JD500 to JD1000 per month for a furnished apartment in a reasonable area of Amman (including bills). Short-term lets are also available in Aqaba, but in the rest of the country it's hard to find long-stay, self-catering accommodation for a period of less than six months.

Resorts

If you have only one night's luxury during your visit to Jordan, plan to stay in one of the Dead Sea resorts. Not only are these stylish hotels worth a visit in their own right, but they also offer the best access to the Dead Sea – an area where there is next to no alternative accommodation. Residents of one resort can use the facilities of the neighbouring hotels, which takes care of several nights' worth of entertainment in an area with no local nightlife.

Apart from the Dead Sea, there are also resorts in and around Aqaba – including the flagship resorts of the Mövenpick and Intercontinental chains. With access to the calm waters of the Red Sea, multiple pools, gyms and a selection of top-notch restaurants, they have brought a cosmopolitan experience to Jordan's second city.

Climate

Amman

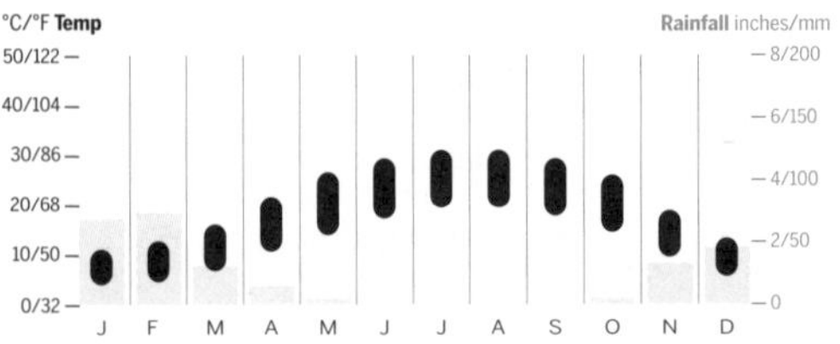

Aqaba

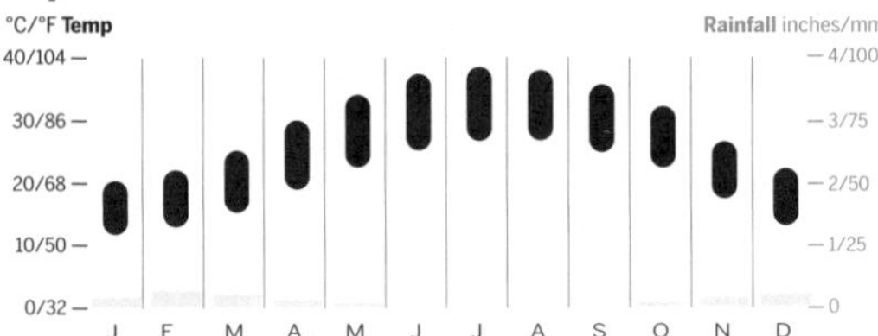

Customs Regulations

- 1L of alcoholic spirits or two bottles of wine
- 200 cigarettes or 25 cigars or 200g of tobacco
- A 'reasonable amount of perfume for personal use'
- Gifts up to the value of JD50 or the equivalent of US$150
- Prohibitions include drugs, weapons, and pornographic films and magazines
- Exporting anything more than 100 years old is illegal, so don't buy any souvenir (including 'ancient' coins or oil lamps) that is deemed to be 'antique'. If you're unsure about an item's provenance, contact the Customs Department (www.customs.gov.jo).

Electricity

Jordan takes a mix-and-match approach to electrical sockets. European round two- and three-pin plugs along with British square three-pin plugs are all used across the country, with frequency seemingly determined only by what the electrician had to hand during installation.

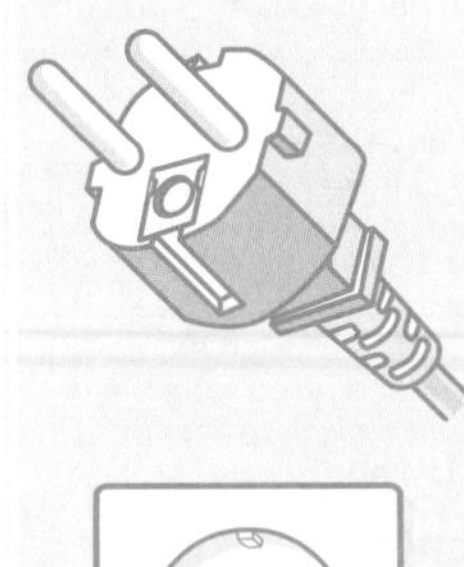

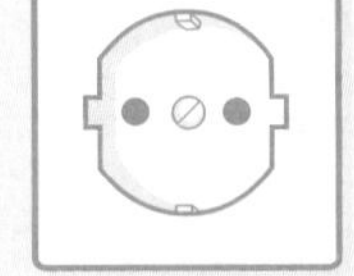

230V/50Hz

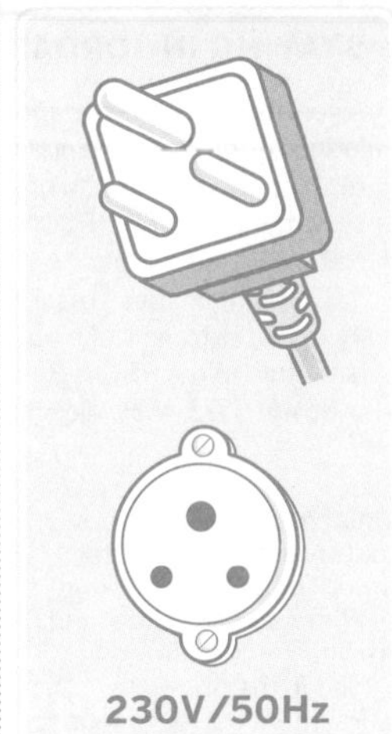

230V/50Hz

Embassies & Consulates

Most embassies and consulates are in Amman. In general, offices are open 9am to 11am Sunday to Thursday for visa applications and 1pm to 3pm for collecting visas.

Australian Embassy (☎06 580 7000; www.jordan.embassy.gov.au; 41 Kayed Al Armoti St, Abdoun)

Canadian Embassy (☎06 590 1500; www.canadainternational.gc.ca/jordan-jordanie; Zahran St)

Egyptian Embassy (☎06 560 5175; 22 Qortubah St, Jebel Amman; ⏰9am-noon Sun-Thu); there's also a **consulate** (☎03 201 6171; cnr Al Isteglal & Al Akhatal Sts; ⏰8am-3pm Sun-Thu) in Aqaba.

French Embassy (Map p56; ☎06 460 4630; www.ambafrance-jo.org; Al Mutanabbi St, Jebel Amman)

German Embassy (Map p56; ☎06 590 1170; www.amman.diplo.de; 31 Bin Ghazi St, Jebel Amman) Between 4th and 5th Circles.

Irish Consulate (Map p56; ☎06 553 3616; ireland_consulate@gmk.com.jo; Al Malek Al Hussein St, Jebel Amman)

Israeli Consulate (Map p58; ☎06 550 3500; http://embassies.gov.il/amman-en; Maysaloon St, Rabiyah)

Lebanese Embassy (Map p56; ☎06 592 9111; 17 Muhammad Ali Badir St) Near the UK embassy.

Netherlands Embassy (☎06 590 2200; www.nederlandwereldwijd.nl/landen/jordanie; 3 Abu Bakr Siraj Ad Din St) Near the 4th Circle.

UK Embassy (Map p56; ☎06 590 9200; www.gov.uk/government/world/organisations/british-embassy-amman; Dimashq St, Abdoun)

US Embassy (☎06 590 6000; https://jo.usembassy.gov; 20 Al Umawiyeen St, Abdoun)

Food

Eating in Jordan is primarily a social experience, whether conducted over a chat in Amman's cafes or sitting in cross-legged silence in a Bedouin tent. Anyone venturing beyond the bus-station kebab stands will quickly find that Jordanian food is not a tedious affair of falafel sandwiches but deliciously varied and culturally nuanced. Jordan is also beginning to be noted for its home-grown wines.

Gay & Lesbian Travellers

Homosexuality is illegal in most Islamic countries in the Middle East, but in Jordan gay sex is legal, and the age of consent is 16. Public displays of affection by heterosexuals are frowned upon, and the same rules apply to gays and lesbians, although same-sex hand-holding is a common sign of friendship in Jordan.

The legality of homosexuality shouldn't be confused with full societal acceptance, and discrimination and harassment are common. There is a subdued underground gay scene in Amman – if you're keen to explore it, keep your enquiries discreet. Gay-friendly venues that attract young, gay and straight crowds include the multipurpose **Books@café** (Map p52; ☎06 465 0457; Omar Bin Al Khattab St; ⏲10am-midnight; 📶) and the **Blue Fig Café** (☎06 592 8800; Al Emir Hashem Bin Al Hussein St; mains JD5-11; ⏲8.30am-1am) in Amman.

Check www.gayguide.net/middle_east and the gay and lesbian forum on Lonely Planet's Thorn Tree bulletin board (www.lonelyplanet.com/thorntree) for more information.

Insurance

Travel insurance that covers theft, loss and medical problems is essential. The policy should cover ambulance fees and emergency flights home.

Some policies specifically exclude 'dangerous activities', which can include motorcycling and even trekking. You must have insurance if you plan to dive in Aqaba – decompression-chamber treatment is an expensive business!

You may prefer a policy that pays doctors or hospitals directly. Alternatively, if you submit a claim after the event, ensure you keep all documentation. Some policies ask you to call back (reverse charges) to a centre in your home country where an immediate assessment of your problem is made.

Worldwide travel insurance is available at www.lonelyplanet.com/travel-insurance. You can buy, extend and claim online anytime – even if you're already on the road.

Internet Access

Wi-fi is standard (and mostly offered free) in hotels of most budgets, as well as many cafes and restaurants.

Legal Matters

The Jordanian legal system has evolved from distinct traditions. Civil and commercial law is largely based on British-style common law, while religious and family matters are generally covered by Islamic Sharia courts, or ecclesiastic equivalents for non-Muslims. In a nutshell:

- The legal age for driving and drinking is 18.
- The age of consent for men and women is 16.

SLEEPING PRICE RANGES

The following price ranges indicate the cost of a double room in high season. Rooms generally have private bathrooms unless stated otherwise.

$ Less than JD40

$$ JD40–90

$$$ More than JD90

EATING PRICE RANGES

The following price ranges refer to a main course. Especially at midrange and top-end restaurants, watch out for small print on menus adding the 16% sales tax and 10% service charge – increasing your bill by a quarter (where possible, all prices listed include taxes).

$ Less than JD5

$$ JD5–10

$$$ More than JD10

PRACTICALITIES

Discount Cards

- Buying a **Jordan Pass** (www.jordanpass.jo; with one/two/three days' entry to Petra JD70/75/80) represents a valuable way to save money – and time queuing for tickets.
- International Student Identity Card (ISIC) can be used for discounts at some tourist sites.
- University ID cards are not accepted.

Media

Radio Popular radio stations include Radio Jordan (96.3 FM), BBC World Service (1323 AM) and Popular Hits (99.6 FM).

Newspapers The key English-language newspaper is the *Jordan Times* (www.jordantimes.com).

TV Jordan's Channel 2 (French and English) and satellite channels (BBC, CNN, MTV, Al Jazeera) are available in most midrange and top-end hotels.

Smoking

- There are laws banning smoking in public places, but these are not always enforced, except in top-end hotels and restaurants in Amman, the Dead Sea and Aqaba.

Weights & Measures

- Jordan uses the metric system.

- You can be prosecuted under the law of your home country regarding age of consent, even when abroad.
- Travellers are expected to respect the law.
- Penalties for drug use of any kind are stiff.
- Criticising the king is illegal.
- Excessive speeding, drunk driving and seatbelt avoidance are not tolerated.
- If you break the law, your embassy can only contact your relatives and recommend local lawyers.

Maps

The Jordan Tourism Board's free *Map of Jordan* is a handy map, with a plan of Amman on the reverse. The Royal Geographic Centre of Jordan also publishes good maps, including a hiking map of Petra.

Several detailed maps are available outside Jordan: ITMB's 1:700,000 map *Jordan* is probably the easiest map to find, *Jordan* by Kümmerly and Frey is the best driving map, and the latest edition of GEO Project's *Jordan* (1:730,000) has an excellent map of Amman.

Money

Known as the 'jay-dee' among hip young locals, the currency in Jordan is the dinar (JD) and it is made up of 1000 fils. You'll often hear the terms piastre or *qirsh:* this refers to 10 fils (so 1 dinar equals 100 piastres). Often when a price is quoted the unit will be omitted, so if you're told that something is 25, it's a matter of working out whether it's 25 fils, 25 piastres or 25 dinars! Although it sounds confusing, it's usually obvious given the context, and most Jordanians wouldn't dream of ripping off a foreigner, with the possible exception of the occasional taxi driver.

Coins come in denominations of 1, 5, 10, 25 and 50 piastres (with the latter two marked as being quarter- and half-dinar respectively). Notes come in denominations of JD1, 5, 10, 20 and 50. Try to change larger notes as often as possible – when paying for petrol, for example, or for your hotel bill – as it can be hard to pay with large notes in small establishments.

ATMs

ATMs are available throughout the country and credit cards are widely used.

Bargaining

Bargaining is expected in Jordan but the margin of movement in terms of the starting and final price is not that great. In fact, haggling over small change is more about social exchange than getting a discount. There are helpful guidelines to get a good deal (p283), but in summary, fix on a maximum price the object is worth to you and if the seller matches it, that's a good price.

Changing Money

It's easy to change money in Jordan. Most major currencies are accepted in cash. US dollars, UK pounds and euros are easier to change than Australian or New Zealand dollars.

There are no restrictions on bringing dinars into Jordan. It's possible to change dinars back into some foreign currencies in Jordan.

Lebanese, Egyptian and Israeli currency can all be changed in Amman. Egyptian and Israeli currency are also easily changed in Aqaba. Banks and moneychangers charge about the same for exchanging cash, but large hotels charge more. There are small branches of major banks at the borders and airports.

Credit Cards

Most major credit cards are accepted at top-end hotels and restaurants, travel agencies, larger souvenir shops and bookshops. Commissions of up to 5% may be added to the bill, so it may be better to get a cash advance and pay with the paper stuff. Make a note of the emergency numbers on the back of your credit cards in case you lose them.

Duty Free

There are duty-free shops at Queen Alia International Airport and next to the Century Park Hotel in Amman, plus small outlets at the border crossings with Israel and the Palestinian Territories. Most upmarket shops offer tax rebates (p283).

Tax

Jordan has a sales tax of 16%, but it's generally only added to the bill in midrange and top-end restaurants. Midrange and top-end restaurants and hotels may add an additional 10% service charge. The Aqaba special economic zone has a sales tax of 5%, and many Jordanians head there on shopping sprees to take advantage of the lower consumer prices.

Tipping

Tipping is not routine in Jordan. To avoid counter-productive inflation, following local custom is recommended.

Top-end restaurants Around 10% is expected (often included in the bill).

Cafes and coffee shops Round up the bill to the nearest 500 fils.

Taxis In Amman, 10% is the norm. Elsewhere, return the loose change.

Petrol attendants Return loose change.

Hotels Around JD1 per bag. No obligation for cleaning staff.

Guides Around 10% per person.

Iraqi Money

If you are a collector of notes and coins, you may be interested in old Iraqi money, bearing the portrait of Saddam Hussein, for sale on street corners in downtown Amman. Even if they're fake, they're good as a conversational gambit with the Iraqi refugees who are selling them.

Opening Hours

Opening times vary widely across the country. Many sights, government departments and banks close earlier in winter and during Ramadan. The following opening hours are therefore a rough guide only. The official weekend in Jordan is Friday and Saturday, so expect curtailed hours on these days.

Banks 8am–3pm Sunday to Thursday

Restaurants noon–midnight daily

Cafes 9am–midnight daily

Bars and Clubs 9pm–1am daily

Shops 9am–8pm Saturday to Thursday; some close 2pm–4pm

Souqs 9am–8pm daily

PRACTICAL TIP: JORDAN PASS

The **Jordan Pass** (www.jordanpass.jo) is a highly recommended discount scheme offered by the Ministry of Tourism and Antiquities that is easily obtained and readily recognised throughout Jordan. If passes are purchased online before arrival, the cost of a tourist visa for three or more nights' stay in Jordan is waived, in addition to giving free entry to Petra, Jerash and more than 40 other attractions. There are three categories of pass that differ only in the number of days of entry covered at Petra – Jordan Wanderer (JD70; one day at Petra), Jordan Explorer (JD75; two days at Petra) and Jordan Expert (JD80; three days at Petra).

Photography

Some Jordanians, particularly women and the elderly, object to being photographed, so ask first. Persisting in taking a photograph against someone's wishes can lead to ugly scenes, so exercise courtesy and common sense. Children generally line up to be photographed.

Jordanians are very proud of their country and can be offended if you take pictures of anything 'negative' or suggestive of poverty and squalor; this may include the activity of a marketplace.

Photography in military zones and 'strategic areas' like bridges and public buildings is forbidden. Take particular care in the Eastern Desert as there are several sensitive military sites not far from the 'desert castles'. You also need to be careful along the Dead Sea Highway where there are numerous checkpoints protecting the sensitive border with Israel and the Palestinian Territories.

Post

Stamps are available from souvenir shops where postcards are sold, and there are postboxes around towns. Letters posted from Jordan take up to two weeks to reach Australia and the US, but often as little as three or four days to the UK and Europe. Every town has a post office, but parcels are best sent from Amman or Aqaba. For more detailed postal information, Jordan Post (www.jordanpost.com.jo) has an informative website.

Reliable courier companies include FedEx (www.fedex.com/jo), which has an office in Amman, and DHL (www.dhl.com), which has offices in Amman and Aqaba.

Public Holidays

During public holidays, government offices and banks close. Shops, moneychangers and restaurants generally remain open, and public transport functions normally. During Eid Al Fitr and Eid Al Adha many shops close as shop owners join their families on these important days of celebration.

Archaeological sites and nature reserves tend to be very crowded on Fridays and public holidays.

New Year's Day 1 January

Good Friday March/April

Labour Day 1 May

Independence Day 25 May

Army Day & Anniversary of the Great Arab Revolt 10 June

Christmas Day 25 December

The main Islamic holidays:

Islamic New Year First Day of Muharram.

Prophet's Birthday Celebrated on 12 Rabi' Al Awal.

Eid Al Isra Wal Mi'raj Celebrates the nocturnal visit of the Prophet Muhammad to heaven.

Ramadan Ninth month of the Islamic calendar.

Eid Al Fitr Starts at the beginning of Shawwal to mark the end of fasting in the preceding month of Ramadan.

Eid Al Adha Commemoration of Allah sparing Ibrahim (Abraham in the Bible) from sacrificing his son, Isaac. It also marks the end of the hajj.

Ramadan

During the holy month of Ramadan, Muslims refrain from eating, drinking, having sex and smoking during daylight hours in accordance with the fourth pillar of Islam. Even gum chewing is considered *haram* (forbidden).

Although many Muslims in Jordan do not follow the injunctions to the letter, most conform to some extent. Foreigners are not expected to follow suit, but it is bad form to eat, drink or smoke in public during this period.

Business hours during Ramadan are erratic and tempers tend to flare towards the end of the month. As the sun starts to dip, many villages turn into ghost towns as people go home to break their fast. Tourist attractions and hotel restaurants remain open and public transport generally functions normally, but the serving of alcohol may be restricted to room service or simply be unavailable.

Telephone

Mobile Phones

There is expansive coverage in Jordan for mobile phone networks. Local SIM cards can be used for international calls and can be topped up with readily available prepaid cards. 4G is increasingly available.

Two main service providers are Zain (www.zain.com) and Orange (www.orange.jo), both of which offer a full range of plans and prepaid SIM cards (ID required to purchase).

Phone Codes

Jordan's country code is ☎962.

To make a call to a landline, you must precede the six- or seven-digit number with a two-digit area code.

- ☎02 Northern Jordan
- ☎03 Southern Jordan
- ☎05 Jordan Valley, central and eastern districts
- ☎06 Amman district
- ☎07 Prefix for eight-digit mobile phone numbers
- ☎0800 Prefix for toll-free numbers
- ☎1212 Local directory assistance (Amman)
- ☎131 Local directory assistance (elsewhere)
- ☎132 or ☎133 International directory assistance

Emergency & Important Numbers

Jordan's country code	☎962
International access code	☎00
Ambulance, fire, police	☎911

Time

Jordan is two hours ahead of GMT/UTC in winter and three hours ahead from April through September, when daylight saving time is in effect. Note that Jordan's daylight saving time is slightly out of sync with summer clock changes in Europe.

ISLAMIC HOLIDAYS

HEJIRA YEAR	NEW YEAR	PROPHET'S BIRTHDAY	RAMADAN BEGINS	EID AL FITR	EID AL ADHA
1440	11 Sep 2018	20 Nov 2018	6 May 2019	4 Jun 2019	11 Aug 2019
1441	31 Aug 2019	9 Nov 2019	24 Apr 2020	24 May 2020	31 Jul 2020
1442	21 Aug 2020	29 Oct 2020	14 Apr 2021	14 May 2021	21 Jul 2021
1443	9 Aug 2021	18 Oct 2021	2 Apr 2022	2 May 2022	9 Jul 2022

INFLATION & TRAVEL COSTS

If there is one bone of contention between our readers and those involved with tourism in Jordan, it is the issue of prices. Many travellers expect to find prices unchanged and become suspicious of hotel owners and taxi drivers who charge more than expected. By the same token, many service providers in Jordan feel frustrated when travellers insist on prices that may be unrealistic or were quoted in a guidebook several years earlier.

In most instances, prices for accommodation, food and transport in Jordan have remained stable for the past three years, but that is largely the result of a deliberate policy to save the effects of inflation impinging on an already weakened tourism trade. This is unlikely to remain the case for the foreseeable future. Instability among neighbouring countries and continued immigration have all contributed to high inflation. For some, a slump in tourism because of regional tension means there is no option but to put prices up. For others, it means being forced to offer unrealistic discounts.

While every effort is made to ensure that our published prices for entrance fees, tours, accommodation, restaurants, food items and private transport is accurate at the time of writing, treat them only as a *guide* to pricing, not a definitive statement of costs.

There is one piece of good news for those trying to estimate the cost of their trip to Jordan. Public bus prices, which are heavily subsidised by the government, have only minimally increased over the past few years, and there is no suggestion of an imminent price hike in this sector.

There are no time differences within Jordan. Jordan is on the same time zone as Israel and the Palestinian Territories, Syria and Egypt.

Toilets

Almost all hotels and restaurants, even in the budget category, now have Western-style toilets. Where squat toilets are provided, the hose is used for ablutions and a water bucket is used for flushing.

Toilet paper (the use of which is considered an unsanitary practice in most Middle Eastern countries) is seldom available, except in the midrange and top-end hotels and restaurants. Local people prefer to use the hose and then deposit any toilet paper (used for drying purposes) in the basket by the side of the toilet bowl; these baskets should be used to avoid blockages as the sewer system is not designed for paper. For those who can't do without it, toilet paper can be bought in most grocery shops throughout Jordan.

If caught short in the desert or hillsides of Jordan, it is imperative you choose a spot well away from water courses and bury the outcome in as deep a pit as possible.

Tourist Information

Jordan has a good network of tourist offices and visitor centres. The main tourist office in Amman is located on the ground floor of the **Ministry of Tourism** (Map p56; ☎ext 254 06 460 3360; ground fl, Al Mutanabbi St, Jebel Amman; ⏰8am-9pm) in Jebel Amman.

The comprehensive website of the Jordan Tourism Board (JTB; www.visitjordan.com) has regularly updated information. JTB also publishes some excellent brochures in several languages.

Travellers with Disabilities

In 2000 Jordan celebrated its first-ever Olympic gold medal, won by the female athlete Maha Barghouthi in the Sydney Paralympics. It was a proud moment for Jordan, and it threw a spotlight on people with disabilities – albeit briefly. Almost two decades on, and Jordan is still not a great place for travellers with disabilities. Although Jordanians are happy to help, cities are crowded and the traffic is chaotic, roadside kerbs can be uncommonly high and visiting tourist attractions – such as the vast archaeological sites of Petra and Jerash – involves long traverses over uneven ground.

There is some good news, however:

- The Jordanian government has legislated that wheelchair access must be added to all new public buildings.
- Entry to some attractions, including Petra, is free for those with disabilities.
- Horse-drawn carriages are provided at Petra for visitors with disabilities to help with access to the Siq and Treasury.
- There is a useful website (www.accessiblejordan.com) providing some key information for those travelling with a mobility impairment in Jordan. This includes information for the elderly and for mums with strollers!

ETIQUETTE

While Jordanians are quite hard to offend in general, they do appreciate some common courtesies.

Greetings Men shake hands (or kiss cheeks) with other men but not always with women. If in doubt, touch your heart instead.

Controlled temper Getting angry in public is considered unacceptable. Find a calm way to settle a dispute (for example, in a car accident).

Hands The left hand is reserved for ablutions. Pass food and shake hands with the right hand.

Feet Shoes are considered unclean. Remove shoes in houses and mosques, and avoid pointing the soles of feet at others.

Taboo subjects Discussion about sensitive subjects like politics are best avoided.

Respect Jordan has a conservative culture. Avoid wearing tight or revealing clothing or taking photos without permission.

Religious norms Muslims fast during Ramadan. Avoid eating and drinking in public at that time and never offer a Muslim alcohol.

Accessible Travel Online Resources

Download Lonely Planet's free Accessible Travel guide from http://lptravel.to/AccessibleTravel.

Visas

Visas, required by all visitors, are available on arrival (JD40 for most nationalities) at the international airports and most of Jordan's land borders. It makes sense for most travellers to buy a Jordan Pass (www.jordanpass.jo) online before entering the country: this waives the cost of a visa in addition to giving free access to many sites in Jordan, including Petra.

At the Airport

Visas are issued on arrival at the immigration desks in the airport in Amman. There's no form filling involved. Payment must be made in Jordanian dinars.

At Land Borders

Visas for Jordan are issued at Sheikh Hussein Bridge from Israel, but not at King Hussein Bridge or Wadi Araba. The Jordan Pass is recognised at all land borders. Borders with Iraq and Syria are open but are considered unsafe.

Note that currently it's not possible to get a visa on arrival in Jordan at King Hussein Bridge or at Wadi Araba. Check the latest status of Jordan's border crossings on the Jordan Tourism Board website (http://international.visitjordan.com/GeneralInformation/GettingAround/Bordercrossings.aspx).

Via the Aqaba Economic Zone

If you arrive in Jordan's southern city of Aqaba by air on an international flight or by sea from Nuweiba in Egypt, you are entitled to a free visa as part of the free-trade agreement with the Aqaba Special Economic Zone Area (ASEZA).

Multiple-Entry Visas

Multiple-entry visas (from JD60) must be obtained in advance from Jordanian consulates or embassies outside the country. In the Middle East, you can find Jordanian embassies in all the neighbouring states, including Israel and the Palestinian Territories. You may want to avoid getting a Jordanian multiple-entry visa from the latter, however, if you intend to travel elsewhere in the region because many Arab countries refuse entry to those who have Israeli stamps or documentation in their passports.

Visa Extensions

In Amman and Aqaba visas can easily be extended, for a charge of JD40, for stays of up to three months. The process is simple but involves a little running around, although you're unlikely to spend more than 30 minutes in each office.

- Ask staff at your hotel to write a short letter confirming where you are staying.
- Ask them to fill out two copies of a small card (or photocopy) that states all the hotel details.
- Fill out the application form for an extension on the back of this card (it's in Arabic but staff at your hotel can help you read it and answers can be in English).
- Take the form, letter, photocopies of the front pages of your passport and the Jordanian visa page, and your passport to the relevant police station.
- Plan to arrive at the police station between 10am and

3pm Saturday to Thursday (best to go early).

➡ Wait for the extension (usually granted on the spot). After assembling the necessary paperwork, it takes about 30 minutes to complete the registration process at a police station. You may be required to have an HIV test, which usually takes 24 hours to process. The maximum stay allowed on an extended tourist visa is six months. Failure to register results in a fine of JD1.500 for every day you have overstayed. This is payable when you extend, or on departure from Jordan at a counter just before immigration at Queen Alia International Airport in Amman.

In Amman, you can start the process of lodging your visa extension paperwork at **Al Madeenah Police Station** (Map p52; ☎06 465 7788; 1st fl, Al Malek Faisal St, Downtown), opposite the Arab Bank.

Volunteering

RSCN (www.rscn.org.jo) If you are keen to learn more about Jordan's ecological projects, there are limited opportunities to work within some of the country's nature reserves on a three-month voluntary program. Board and lodging are generally offered in return for a variety of services, such as working in the visitor centres. These posts are best filled by local Jordanian people, but if you have a specialist skill in management or conservation, you may strike it lucky.

Royal Botanic Garden (RBG; www.royalbotanicgarden.org; Rumman) The Royal Botanic Garden near Rumman north of the capital welcomes volunteers, particularly those with a horticultural bent.

For further ideas, see www.volunteerabroad.com/jordan.cfm.

Work

There's not much in the way of casual work in Jordan as all such jobs are in hot demand from Palestinian and Iraqi refugees. If you are interested in staying longer in the country and have a specific skill or qualification, it's best to apply for work before leaving home. That way, your employer will be responsible for paying for your air ticket and will sponsor your work permit.

Diving

Qualified dive instructors or divemasters may be able to get work at one of the diving centres in Aqaba, particularly during peak season (September to March). Keep in mind, however, that positions are hotly contested by locals.

Language Teaching

English-teaching opportunities are open to those with TOEFL qualifications. The British Council (www.britishcouncil.org/jordan.htm) recruits teachers from the UK; you need the RSA Preparatory Certificate (the Diploma is preferred) or equivalent and at least two years' work experience. Contact them before arriving in Jordan. Casual vacancies within Jordan occasionally arise: address your CV to the Teaching Centre Manager.

AMIDEAST (www.amideast.org/jordan) runs the other top language school. Like the British Council, teachers are mostly recruited before arrival in Jordan.

Transport

GETTING THERE & AWAY

Ever since Swiss explorer Jean Louis Burckhardt rediscovered Petra for the Western world in the 19th century, tourists have been visiting Jordan, resulting in well-established and efficient inbound and onward travel routes. Most notable of these are the routes to Israel and the Palestinian Territories, and the ferry across the Red Sea from Aqaba to Nuweiba in Egypt, though check travel advisories before taking the latter route as the security situation in Nuweiba (part of South Sinai) is changeable. The once popular Amman–Damascus route is off limits because of the civil war in Syria.

As Amman is well connected with other Arab countries by air, it's possible to combine a trip with Dubai in the United Arab Emirates and other destinations in the Arabian Peninsula as well as to neighbouring capitals.

Flights, cars and tours can be booked online at lonelyplanet.com/bookings.

Entering the Country

Entering Jordan is straightforward whether by air, land or sea, with visas and money exchange facilities available at all borders.

Always carry your passport with you when travelling around sensitive areas, such as near the border of Israel and the Palestinian Territories, along the Dead Sea Highway and roads linking the Dead Sea Highway to interior towns. Checkpoints and passport checks are common in all these areas.

It is important to remember that you may have difficulty entering some Middle Eastern countries from Jordan if you have a visa stamp in your passport from Israel, although generally visitors are given a loose-leaf Israeli entry card not a stamp.

Main Entry Points

Queen Alia International Airport (south of Amman) The Airport Express Bus (JD3) runs to Amman every 30 minutes (from 6.30am to 5pm); the night bus runs hourly (5pm to midnight). Taxis cost JD20 to downtown Amman (around 45 minutes). Car hire is available in the arrivals hall.

Ferry Terminal (south of Aqaba) A taxi costs JD8 and takes 20 minutes from the ferry terminal and border to the centre of town.

Wadi Araba (Yitzhak Rabin) Border A taxi from the border costs JD11 and takes 15 minutes to central Aqaba (JD50, two hours to Petra).

Air

Queen Alia International Airport (☎06 401 0250; www.qaiairport.com), about 35km south of Amman, is the country's main gateway. Recently

CLIMATE CHANGE & TRAVEL

Every form of transport that relies on carbon-based fuel generates CO_2, the main cause of human-induced climate change. Modern travel is dependent on aeroplanes, which might use less fuel per kilometre per person than most cars but travel much greater distances. The altitude at which aircraft emit gases (including CO_2) and particles also contributes to their climate change impact. Many websites offer 'carbon calculators' that allow people to estimate the carbon emissions generated by their journey and, for those who wish to do so, to offset the impact of the greenhouse gases emitted with contributions to portfolios of climate-friendly initiatives throughout the world. Lonely Planet offsets the carbon footprint of all staff and author travel.

subject to an impressive refurbishment, it has ATMs, foreign exchange counters, a post office and left-luggage counter. The departure lounge has several cafes and a good range of duty-free gift items, including Arabic sweets and some souvenirs. Car-rental agencies are located in the arrivals building.

The only other international airport is at Aqaba, where some international carriers stop en route to Amman. Flights to Sharm El Sheikh in Egypt are handled from here. Charter flights from Europe tend to come and go depending on regional stability, but at the time of writing a new low-cost carrier was about to be announced, operating out of Aqaba.

The national airline, Royal Jordanian (www.rj.com), is well established with a good safety record. It has direct flights to most major cities in Europe and all Middle Eastern capitals, and runs short flights from Amman to Aqaba (twice daily). Royal Wings (www.royalwings.com.jo), a subsidiary of Royal Jordanian, has smaller planes and runs expensive charter flights.

A number of airlines fly to Jordan:

Air Arabia (www.airarabia.com)

Air France (www.airfrance.com)

British Airways (www.ba.com)

Emirates (www.emirates.com)

Fly Dubai (www.flydubai.com)

Gulf Air (www.gulfair.com)

Iraqi Airways (www.ia.com.iq)

KLM (www.klm.com)

Kuwait Airways (www.kuwaitairways.com)

Lufthansa Airlines (www.lufthansa.com)

Qatar Airways (www.qatarairways.com)

Saudi Arabian Airlines (www.saudia.com)

Turkish Airlines (www.turkishairlines.com)

Land

It's easy to reach Jordan by land from Israel and the Palestinian Territories. Foreign residents of Saudi Arabia (and transit passengers who can show they have no other way of reaching Jordan) are also able to cross Saudi Arabia and enter Jordan by land.

Most overland travellers arrive in Jordan by bus or service taxi, though it's also possible to bring your own vehicle.

Note that currently it's not possible to get a visa on arrival in Jordan at King Hussein Bridge or at Wadi Araba. Check the latest status of Jordan's border crossings on the Jordan Tourism Board website (http://international.visitjordan.com/GeneralInformation/GettingAround/Bordercrossings.aspx).

DEPARTURE TAX

Jordan's departure tax for travellers is JD8 by land and sea, and JD15 by air. If you are leaving by air, the departure tax is generally included in the ticket price.

Getting to/from Jordan's Borders

Egypt

Most people travel between Jordan and Egypt by boat. It's quicker and cheaper, however, to travel overland via Israel and the Palestinian Territories using the Wadi Araba border (but be aware of the Israeli border-stamp stigma before making a decision and the current need to apply for a Jordanian visa in advance of using this crossing). If you choose this route:

➡ Take a taxi to Wadi Araba border crossing and another taxi between Yitzhak Rabin and Taba border crossing on the Egyptian border.

➡ Taxis also run from either border to Eilat and there are buses from Eilat to either border.

➡ The whole trip takes about 1½ hours.

Israel & the Palestinian Territories

There are currently no direct services between Amman and Jerusalem or Tel Aviv. Of the three border crossings, Sheikh Hussein Bridge, King Hussein Bridge and Wadi Araba, King Hussein Bridge is the most commonly used and easiest to reach from Amman, but may require extra time and patience as there are often delays.

KING HUSSEIN BRIDGE (ALLENBY BRIDGE)

Take a service taxi from Amman's **Abdali Bus Station** (Map p56; Al Malek Al Hussein St, Jebel Amman) to King Hussein Bridge (JD10, 45 minutes) or there's a single daily **JETT bus** (Map p58; ☎06 566 4146; www.jett.com.jo; Al Malek Al Hussein St, Shmeisani) (JD10, one hour, 7am). A private taxi to the bridge costs around JD25. Public transport stops at the immigration terminal for locals; make sure you're dropped at the second terminal, for foreigners.

The two border posts are 5km apart. Buses (JD7 plus JD1.500 per piece of luggage, 10 minutes to one hour – depending on waiting time) shuttle between the two borders (expect long delays). It's not possible to walk or take a private vehicle across this border. Try to sit at the front of the bus so you can be near the front of the queue at Israeli immigration.

Jordanian immigration officials won't stamp your passport here – you're given an exit form instead. If you're coming back to Jordan, you can return at this crossing within two weeks without needing a new visa. Longer than this, you'll need to return via the Sheikh Hussein Bridge (or get a new visa at the Jordanian embassy in Tel Aviv). There's an exit fee of JD8.

At Israeli immigration, make sure you are given the immigration form with your photo on it, which is issued rather than a stamp in the passport.

Be prepared for slow progress at the border – plan for a couple of hours, and leave early to make the complete Amman–Jerusalem run in case of security delays. Sunday morning (ie after the weekend) and around holidays are the busiest – and therefore slowest – times to cross. If you're in a rush, a VIP service at the terminal is available to rush you through both immigration and security on both sides. This typically costs around JD80.

To get to Jerusalem from the border, take a sherut (Israeli shared taxi; around 42NIS plus 5NIS for luggage, 30 minutes) to Jerusalem's Damascus Gate.

Travelling in the other direction, there's an Israeli exit tax of 174NIS. If you intend to return to Israel, keep the Jordanian entrance form safe – you will have to present it on exiting the border.

The border is open 8am to 8pm Sunday to Thursday and 8am to 1pm Friday and Saturday. The border is closed for Yom Kippur and Eid Al Adha.

SHEIKH HUSSEIN BRIDGE (JORDAN BRIDGE)

Regular service taxis travel between the West bus station at Irbid and the border (JD15, 45 minutes). Private taxis cost JD50 from Irbid. You can ask Jordanian immigration not to stamp your passport here.

Buses cross the bridge (around JD2) roughly every 30 minutes.

Taxis go to the Beit She'an bus station (10 minutes) for onward connections. To get to Tel Aviv, it's quickest to get from Beit She'an to Afula and change there.

Travelling in the other direction, take a bus to Tiberias and change at Beit She'an (6km from the border). From there, take another bus to the Israeli border (arrive early because there are few buses).

Israeli exit tax is 100NIS at this border. The transfer bus across the bridge to the Jordanian side costs around 10NIS.

The border crossing here is considerably faster than at the King Hussein Bridge. It's also more convenient if you're travelling in a small group and can share transport costs.

The border is open 8am to 10pm Sunday to Thursday and 9am to 8pm Friday and Saturday. The border is closed for Yom Kippur and the Islamic New Year (but not for Eid Al Adha).

WADI ARABA (YITZHAK RABIN)

Taxis run between Aqaba and the border (JD10, 15 minutes). There's an exit fee of JD8.

You can walk the short distance across the border in a matter of minutes.

Buses run to central Eilat, 2km away (five minutes). Taxis cost around 50NIS.

Travelling in the other direction, buses from Jerusalem to Eilat will stop at the turn-off for the border (five minutes), a short walk away.

Israeli exit tax is 100NIS at this border. Currently you can't obtain a visa for Jordan at this border.

The border is open 6.30am to 8pm Sunday to Thursday and 8am to 8pm Friday and Saturday. The border is closed for Yom Kippur and the Islamic New Year.

Saudi Arabia

Getting a visa, even a transit visa, to Saudi Arabia is very difficult. If you are eligible for a visa, the main land route for public transport is at Al Umari, south of Azraq. The other two crossing points are Ad Durra, south of Aqaba, and further east at Al Mudawwara. Several companies run services to and from Jeddah and Riyadh from Amman's Abdali Bus Station.

The air-conditioned JETT bus travels to Jeddah, Riyadh and Dammam.

Elsewhere in the Middle East

For other destinations in the Middle East, travellers need time, patience and, most importantly, the necessary visas. Most trips involve long, hot journeys with frustrating delays so most people end up flying.

JETT has a coach service to Cairo (JD35), twice per week departing from the international bus office in Amman. Check with the JETT office ahead of your departure as schedules and prices change frequently.

Sea

Visiting Egypt is both a popular side trip from Aqaba or feasible as part of an onward journey. As Jordan has no land borders with Egypt, the journey involves a short boat ride to either Nuweiba or Taba (check travel advisories before taking these routes). At most times of the year this is a matter of turning up and buying your ticket. During hajj (pilgrimage to Mecca; late August or September for the next few years; dates move with the Islamic calendar), however, when Aqaba is abuzz with thousands of Egyptian pilgrims returning home from Mecca, you may find the journey becomes something more epic. Most nationalities can obtain Egyptian tourist visas on the boat or on arrival at Nuweiba (the Egyptian consulate in Aqaba also issues visas). Note that full visas are not issued in Taba, only the two-week Sinai Visitor Pass.

There are two main boat services to Egypt, which leave from the passenger terminal just south of Aqaba. Departure times are often subject to change so check with Arab Bridge Maritime (www.abmaritime.com.jo), which operates the services, before travelling.

The fast boat to Taba (US$60, one hour) leaves daily at 10pm. Fares for children aged between six and 12 are US$38 (under six US$32). The return ferry leaves Taba at 1.30pm.

There is also a slower regular service (US$45, three hours) departing twice daily at 11am and 2pm. It's notorious for being delayed (voyages can take up to 12 hours if the sea is rough) or even cancelled, although the night departure, which carries heavy commercial traffic, is regarded as being more consistent. Fares are reduced for children aged under eight (US$23). Services from Nuweiba leave at noon and 1pm.

Departure tax (JD8) is not included in the ticket prices. You need to show your passport to buy tickets. Note that fares from Nuweiba must be paid for in US dollars, but there are currency exchange facilities at the terminals at Aqaba and Nuweiba.

Passports are collected on the boat in both directions and handed back on arrival at immigration. Bear in mind, if you are travelling from Egypt, you will arrive in Aqaba too late for public transport to Petra or Wadi Rum, so you'll have to stay in Aqaba or pick up a taxi from the city centre.

GETTING AROUND

Public transport is limited to intercity buses and buses that serve the needs of local communities, making it hard for travellers to reach key destinations without time and patience.

Car Hiring a car is recommended, especially for visiting the Dead Sea, Eastern Desert and King's Highway. Driving is on the right.

Private Minibus Some hotels in Amman, Madaba, Petra and Aqaba organise minibus shuttle services and/or tours to key tourist destinations, including Eastern Desert sights.

Taxi Many locals get around by shared taxi. Negotiating a half- or whole-day rate with a taxi driver is a useful alternative to car hire.

Air

There is only one domestic air route, between Amman and Aqaba.

Royal Jordanian (www.rj.com) Flights twice daily (one way around JD52, one hour).

Royal Wings (www.royalwings.com.jo) A subsidiary of Royal Jordanian, offering expensive charter flights.

Bicycle

Cycling can be fun or sheer folly depending on the time of year. From March to May and September to November are the best times to get on your bike – you won't have to battle the stifling summer heat or the bitter winter winds. Spare parts aren't always common in Jordan, so carry a spare tyre, extra chain links, spokes, two inner tubes, repair kit and tool kit with spanner set. Also bring a

ISRAELI BORDER-STAMP STIGMA

Given historic tensions between Arab countries and Israel, any evidence of a visit to Israel in your passport (such as an entry or exit stamp from a Jordanian border crossing) can potentially bar you from entering a number of countries in the region in the future, so if you're combining your stay in Jordan with a trip to Israel, there are a few things to bear mind.

➡ When you enter or leave Israel, immigration officials issue you with a separate immigration form instead of stamping your passport. Keep this safe, as losing it can cause big problems.

➡ If you're crossing into Israel from Jordan via the King Hussein Bridge, you can ask the Jordanian officials to stamp a piece of paper instead of your passport. Alternatively, you can fly into and out of Ben Gurion airport in Tel Aviv (there are direct flights from Amman).

➡ Proof of having visited Israel isn't a problem for every Arab or Middle Eastern country. It's fine for Jordan, Egypt, Turkey, Tunisia and Morocco. Officially, Bahrain, Qatar, the UAE and Oman will refuse you entry if you have evidence of a visit to Israel in your passport, but in reality they don't always look for an offending stamp. Lebanon, Iran, Saudi Arabia, Libya, Yemen, Iraq and Syria will all automatically refuse you entry.

low-gear set for the hills and a couple of water containers; confine your panniers to a maximum of 15kg. If you don't want to bring your bike, the cycling outfit **Bike Rush** (Map p80; ☎07 9945 4586; www.facebook.com/bikerush; Al Jafn St, 8th Circle; ⏲noon-9pm Sat-Thu) offers bike hire from its Amman shop (with delivery to your address too), as well as weekly vehicle-supported bike trips around the country.

Bus

Local Bus

The two largest cities, Amman and Irbid, have efficient, cheap public bus networks. There are often no timetables available at chaotic local bus stations. Locals are always willing to help though.

Minibus

Public minibuses are the most common form of public transport. They normally only leave when full, so waiting times of an hour or more are inevitable, especially in rural areas. Tickets are normally bought on the bus. Standing is not usually allowed, and some seat shuffling often takes place to ensure that unaccompanied foreign men or women do not sit next to members of the opposite sex. Locals signify that they want to get off by rapping a coin on a side window.

Tourist Bus

The larger air-con buses offer a speedy and reliable service, departing according to a fixed schedule. They don't stop en route to pick up passengers. Tickets should ideally be bought a day in advance.

The national bus company **JETT** (Map p58; ☎06 566 4146; www.jett.com.jo; Al Malek Al Hussein St, Shmeisani) operates the most comfortable bus service from Amman to Aqaba. It also has services to King Hussein Bridge (7am daily) border crossing and Petra (6.30am daily).

Car & Motorcycle

Jordan is an easy country to drive in (with the exception of Amman), and there are some spectacular routes linking the high ground with the Jordan Valley below sea level. Indeed, there aren't many countries where you can claim to be driving uphill to the sea, but if you're on the Dead Sea Highway heading for the Red Sea, Jordan is one of them!

Strictly speaking, you don't need an International Driving Permit (IDP) to drive in Jordan unless you plan on crossing any borders, but it may help to have one if you are in an accident.

Bringing Your Own Vehicle

If you are travelling with your own vehicle, refer to the following checklist of items to bring with you (contact your local automobile association for details):

- The vehicle's registration papers and liability insurance
- *Carnet de passage en douane* (passport for the vehicle that acts as a temporary waiver of import duty)
- Specifications of any expensive spare parts, such as a gearbox, on board (designed to prevent car-import rackets)
- Spare parts and some mechanical knowledge for motorcycles

Royal Automobile Club of Jordan (www.racj.com) can arrange a carnet.

Checkpoints

There are a number of checkpoints in Jordan, and drivers are expected to stop at these. Foreigners are often waved through without any fuss, though you may have to show your passport. As such, always keep your passport, driving licence, hire agreement or proof of ownership and registration papers handy.

Fuel & Spare Parts

Petrol stations can mostly be found on the outskirts of major towns and at some junctions. Along the Desert Highway (the only fully dual carriageway), there are plenty of stations. There are fewer along the King's Highway and *very* few along the Dead Sea Highway. Unleaded petrol *(khal min ar rasas)* is only reliably available in Amman and even then at only a few petrol stations.

Garages with mechanics can be found in the outskirts of most towns. They can handle most repairs. Check with your car-hire company before letting them loose on a rental.

4WDs

Four-wheel drives are only necessary if you're going to remote parts of the desert, such as Burqu. You are highly advised to have prior experience of off-road driving before attempting soft sand: getting stuck in 45°C heat, for example, is a recipe for disaster if you don't know what you're doing. In Wadi Rum, it's easier (and more rewarding for both parties) to hire a 4WD with a Bedouin driver from the visitor centre rather than trying to go it alone in a hired vehicle.

If you're determined, 4WD vehicles can be hired from reputable agencies in Aqaba and Amman; they are far more expensive than normal sedans, costing at least JD150 per day.

Hire

Hiring a car is a great way of getting the most out of Jordan, especially if travelling the King's Highway or Dead Sea area. Drivers over 65 years of age should check whether they are eligible to hire a car with each particular agency as some have upper as well as lower age restrictions.

There are many car-hire agencies in Amman (King Abdullah Gardens in Shmeisani is lined with international and local hire offices), a few in Aqaba and one or two irregularly staffed offices at Queen Alia International Airport and the King Hussein border with Israel and the Palestinian Territories. Most car-hire agencies outside of these areas usually consist of an office with one guy, one desk, one telephone and one car for hire (usually his!). The best deals are in Amman, where competition among agencies is fierce.

Daily rates run at around JD50. This usually includes unlimited kilometres, although many agencies specify a minimum hire of 48 hours. You can normally drop off the hire car in another city (such as Aqaba) for an extra fee. All companies require a deposit of up to JD400 payable upon pick-up (usually by credit card) and refunded upon return of the car.

Road maps are not provided by car-hire agencies, but child-restraining seats are generally available for an extra fee.

Most agencies only hire to drivers over 21 years old; some stipulate that drivers must be at least 26 years. It's not possible to drive a hire car from Jordan into neighbouring countries.

Insurance

Most car-hire rates come with basic insurance that involves a deductible of up to JD400 (ie in case of an accident you pay a maximum of JD400). Most agencies offer additional Collision Damage Waiver (CDW) insurance for an extra JD7 to JD10 per day, which will absolve you of all accident costs (in some cases a maximum of JD100 excess).

Insurance offered by major companies often includes Personal Accident Insurance and Theft Protection, which may be covered by your travel insurance policy from home. Read the conditions of the contract carefully before signing – an English translation should always be provided.

WHAT TO DO IN AN ACCIDENT

- Don't move the vehicle.
- Find a policeman from the local station to attend the scene immediately.
- Get a police report (essential for insurance – Arabic is OK) and contact the car-hire company.
- If there's a serious injury, call ☎911 for emergency services; you'll be answered by English-speaking staff.
- Contact your travel insurance company at home and your embassy/consulate in Amman.
- If your own car is involved, your driving licence and passport will be held by the police until the case is reviewed in a local court – which may take weeks.
- Beware: drivers are always considered guilty if they hit a pedestrian, regardless of the circumstances.

If you're driving into Jordan in a private vehicle, compulsory third-party insurance must be purchased at the border from about JD40 (valid for one month). You also pay a nominal customs fee of JD5 for 'foreign car registration' (obtainable at the borders with Jordan and the ferry terminal in Nuweiba, Egypt).

Road Conditions

The condition of roads varies; unsigned speed humps are common, usually at the entrance to a town but also across main highways. It's important to note that the term 'highway' doesn't mean dual carriageway in Jordan – simply a main thoroughfare.

Despite the small population and relatively well-maintained roads, accidents are alarmingly frequent.

If you're driving around Jordan, read the following carefully:

- Signposting is erratic – generally enough to get you on your way but not enough to get you all the way to your destination.
- Most road signs are in English but are inconsistently transliterated (eg 'Om Qeis' or 'Umm Qais').
- Brown signs denote tourist attractions, blue signs are for road names and green signs are for anything Islamic, such as a mosque.
- Take care when it's raining: water and sand (and sometimes oil) make a lethal combination on the roads.
- The Jordanian road system makes more use of U-turns than flyovers.
- Beware herds of goats and camels crossing all roads, including highways.
- Petrol stations are not that common, so fill up when you see one.
- Straddling two lanes and overtaking using the slow lane are common practices and it's not unknown for someone to reverse along a dual carriageway or travel the wrong way along a hard shoulder to reach the nearest turning.

Road Rules

Visitors from any country where road rules are rigorously obeyed may be shocked by the traffic in Jordan, especially in Amman. Indicators are seldom used, the ubiquitous horn is preferred over slowing down and pedestrians must take their chances. But anyone who has driven elsewhere in the Middle East may find the traffic comparatively well behaved. Provided that you

OVERLAND TRANSPORT IN A HURRY

It is possible to get from Petra to Jerusalem (and vice versa) in a day, and also to a handful of other popular travel destinations across the Middle East.

Petra & Jerusalem via Amman & the West Bank

Taking this route means you may be able to avoid evidence of a visit to Israel in your passport. Beware of long delays at the border.

- From Petra, catch a bus to Amman's South bus station (three hours), a service taxi or bus to King Hussein Bridge (Allenby Bridge; one hour), a bus across the border (often a three-hour delay; border closed by noon Friday and Saturday) and a service taxi or bus to Jerusalem's Damascus Gate (30 minutes).
- This route also works in reverse, to get from Jerusalem to Petra.

Petra & Jerusalem via Aqaba & Eilat

If you're arriving in Jordan at Wadi Araba (Yitzhak Rabin), you must have a visa in advance.

- From Petra, catch a bus to the main bus station at Aqaba (2½ hours) and then a service taxi or bus to Wadi Araba (Yitzhak Rabin) border (15 minutes).
- Walk across the border (30 minutes; open every day) and then take a service taxi or bus to Eilat (15 minutes) and a bus to Jerusalem's Damascus Gate (five hours).
- This route also works in reverse.

Petra & Sharm El Sheikh via Aqaba & Nuweiba

Note that travelling by public transport from Sharm El Sheikh or Nuweiba to Wadi Rum or Petra requires an overnight stop in Aqaba. The security situation in South Sinai, where Nuweiba is located, is changeable; check travel advisories before attempting this route.

- From Petra, catch a bus to the main bus station at Aqaba (2½ hours) and then a service taxi or bus to the ferry terminal (30 minutes) and catch a boat at 11pm to Nuweiba (one hour). From here, take the bus to Sharm El Sheikh (2½ hours).
- Catch a bus from Sharm El Sheikh to Nuweiba ferry terminal (three hours) and then catch the 1pm boat to the ferry terminal south of Aqaba (three hours) followed by a service taxi or bus to Aqaba (30 minutes).
- Catch a private taxi to Petra or stay overnight in Aqaba and catch a bus to Petra the following day (2½ hours).
- Be aware that the Aqaba–Nuweiba ferry can be prone to long delays in both directions.

Petra & Mt Sinai via Aqaba

At the Wadi Araba crossing you can only get a visa for the Sinai Peninsula, so if you want to travel further than Sharm El Sheikh, this trip needs some careful planning: full visas can be obtained in advance from the Egyptian consulate in Aqaba or the Egyptian embassy in Amman. Note that the security situation is changeable in Taba and Mt Sinai; check travel advisories before attempting this route.

- From Petra, catch a bus to the main bus station in Aqaba (2½ hours) and then a service taxi to the Wadi Araba (Yitzhak Rabin) border crossing (15 minutes) and walk across the border (30 minutes).
- Catch a service taxi or bus to Taba (15 minutes) and a service taxi to Mt Sinai (three hours).
- While the reverse trip is not possible in a day on public transport, you can avoid a night's stay in Aqaba by taking a private taxi.

minimise driving in Amman and take reasonable care, you're unlikely to encounter too many difficulties.

Vehicles drive on the right-hand side of the road in Jordan. The general speed limit inside built-up areas is 50km/h or 70km/h on multilane highways in Amman, and 90km/h to 110km/h on the national highways.

Wearing a seatbelt is compulsory, though many Jordanians remain reluctant to use them. Traffic police are positioned at intervals along the highways.

Hitching

Hitching is never entirely safe, and we don't recommend it. Travellers who hitch should understand that they are taking a small but potentially serious risk. Hitching is sometimes used as a means of transport in Jordan in areas where public transport is limited or nonexistent, such as parts of the King's Highway and to the desert castles east of Amman.

Picking Up Hitchers

On remote routes like the Wadi Mujib stretch of the King's Highway, where public transport is limited or even nonexistent, it's common for Jordanians to pick up hitchhikers. If you're driving and choose to do the same, take the same safety precautions you would anywhere else. You shouldn't charge for the lift.

Taxis

Yellow private taxis work like ordinary taxis and can be chartered for the day. In Amman most drivers use the meter – note that fares are displayed in fils not dinars. Outside Amman, negotiate a reasonable fare before you set off. Taking a private taxi in Jordan is generally safe for women but those travelling alone may prefer the anonymity of sitting in the back seat.

White service taxis *(servees)* run along set routes within and between many towns, as well as between Jordan and neighbouring countries. They are shared by more than one passenger and usually have writing and numbers (in Arabic) indicating their route. They usually only leave when full. They cost up to twice as much as a minibus and about 50% more than a local bus, but are quicker because they stop less often along the way to pick up passengers. To avoid waiting for passengers, or to give yourself extra room, you can always pay for an extra seat. In contrast to private taxis, female travellers are likely to be ushered into the front seat if the back seats are occupied by men: this is an accepted practice for local women as well as visitors.

Tours

An alternative to a group tour organised from abroad is to arrange your own private mini-tour with a Jordanian travel agency. Many of these can arrange hiking or archaeological itineraries and provide a car and driver.

For hiking and activities in Jordan's nature reserves contact the tourism department of the Royal Society for the Conservation of Nature (www.rscn.org.jo), which can arrange short activity breaks or entire itineraries. For an extended trip to Wadi Rum it's best to contact a local Bedouin agency, such as the recommended Wadi Rum Mountain Guides (www.bedouinroads.com).

If you're travelling independently, and on a tight budget, jumping on a budget-priced organised tour from Amman (offered by many budget hotels) to a remote destination like the desert castles of eastern Jordan is far easier, and often cheaper, than doing it yourself.

Atlas Travel & Tourist Agency (www.atlastours.net) Also offers side trips to Israel and the Palestinian Territories and Lebanon.

Desert Guides Company (www.desertguides.net) Trekking, mountain-bike and adventure trips.

Engaging Cultures Travel (www.engagingcultures.com) Highly regarded small group and tailor-made tours from Amman, with strong emphasis on culturally immersive experiences.

Golden Crown Tours (www.goldencrowntours.com) Offers archaeological, religious and adventure tours.

Jordan Beauty Tours (www.jordanbeauty.com) Local tour operator offering archaeological and biblical tours, as well as hiking, camel trips, diving and cross-border tours to Israel.

La Beduina (www.labeduinatours.com) Specialist tours, including hiking, cooking, horse and camel riding, and yoga tours.

Petra Moon Tourism (Map p180; ☎07 9617 0666; www.petramoon.com; Tourism St; all-day horse rides to Jebel Haroun US$100, min 3 people) The most professional agency in Wadi Musa for arranging trips inside Petra and around Jordan (including Wadi Rum and Aqaba).

Tropical Desert Trips (www.td-adventures.com) Active tours, including hiking, climbing, canyoning and desert exploration.

Zaman Tours & Travel (www.zamantours.com) Adventure tours, camping, camel treks and hiking.

Health

Prevention and common sense is the key to staying healthy when travelling in Jordan. Infectious diseases occur, but these can be avoided with a few simple precautions. If you need vaccinations, remember to visit the doctor around eight weeks before travelling as some require multiple injections; this will also give time to ensure immunity on arrival as some vaccinations take time to come into effect.

The most common reason for travellers needing medical help is as a result of traffic accidents, which can partly be avoided if you wear a seatbelt, even though no one else in Jordan seems to bother, and stick to the speed limit on Jordan's less than perfect roads.

Medical facilities are generally very good, particularly in Amman where there are some excellent modern hospitals. In case of an emergency, contact your embassy or consulate where you will at least receive sound local advice. Don't forget to take out health insurance before you leave!

BEFORE YOU GO

Insurance

You are strongly advised to have insurance before travelling to Jordan. Check it covers the following:

- direct payments to health providers (or reimbursement later) for expenditure while in Jordan
- assistance in locating the nearest source of medical help
- emergency dental treatment
- repatriation home or air transport to better medical facilities elsewhere

Medical Checklist

Items you should consider packing:

- acetaminophen/paracetamol (Tylenol) or aspirin
- antibacterial ointment (eg Bactroban) for cuts and abrasions
- antidiarrhoeal drugs (eg loperamide)
- antihistamines (for hay fever and allergic reactions)
- insect repellent containing DEET (for the body)
- insect spray containing Permethrin (for clothing, tents and bed nets)
- iodine tablets or other water-purification tablets
- oral rehydration salts
- sunblock

Travelling with Medication

Bring medications in their original clearly labelled containers. A signed and dated letter from your physician describing your medical conditions and medications, including generic names, is also a good idea. If carrying syringes or needles, be sure to have a physician's letter documenting their medical necessity and keep these handy when entering or exiting any of Jordan's borders.

Websites

Consult your government's travel health website before departure:

Australia (www.dfat.gov.au/travel)

Canada (www.travelhealth.gc.ca)

UK (www.doh.gov.uk)

US (www.cdc.gov/travel)

In addition to government health websites, the following provide useful health information:

Centers for Disease Control (www.cdc.gov) Overview of the health issues facing travellers to Jordan and neighbouring countries.

MD Travel Health (www.mdtravelhealth.com) Complete travel-health recommendations for every country, updated daily, also at no cost.

World Health Organization (www.who.int/ith) Publishes a free, online book, *International Travel and Health,* revised annually.

Further Reading

International Travel Health Guide (Stuart R Rose, MD)

The Travellers' Good Health Guide (Ted Lankester) An especially useful health guide for volunteers and long-term expatriates working in the Middle East.

Traveller's Health (Dr Richard Dawood)

Travel with Children (Lonely Planet) Includes advice on travel health for younger children.

IN JORDAN

Availability & Cost of Health Care

Health-care provision is of a high standard in Jordan and any emergency treatment not requiring hospitalisation is free. The availability of health care can be summarised as follows:

- Modern, well-equipped public and private hospitals in Amman, Irbid, Aqaba and Karak.
- Good regional hospitals in Madaba, Ramtha and Zarqa.
- Basic health centres (all towns).
- Fairly modern and well-equipped dental surgeries in cities.
- Well-stocked pharmacies (most towns) dispensing advice as well as medicines.
- All doctors (and most pharmacists) speak English; many have studied abroad.
- Telephone numbers for pharmacies and hospitals in all cities are listed in the English-language newspapers.
- Ambulance number in Jordan: ☎911.

Food & Water

Water

Tap water in Jordan is generally safe to drink, but for a short trip it's better to stick to bottled water. This is readily available but check the seal has not been broken. Alternatively, you can boil tap water for 10 minutes, use water purification tablets or a filter.

The tap water in southern Jordan, particularly Wadi Rum, comes from natural springs at Diseh and so is extremely pure. Avoid drinking water from wadis in the wild as pools may have been used as waterholes for livestock. In the Jordan Valley, amoebic dysentery can be a problem.

If you get stuck in the desert without water, remember that you are more likely to be seriously ill (and even die) from dehydration than you are from an upset stomach, however unpleasant it may be. In summary, if water is offered and you need it, worry about its provenance later!

Avoiding Diarrhoea

The risk of becoming sick from unhygienic food preparation in Jordan is slim, especially if you follow this advice:

- Avoid tap water unless it has been boiled, filtered or chemically disinfected (iodine tablets).

TRAVEL PROBLEMS & PREVENTION

PROBLEM	SYMPTOMS	PREVENTION/TREATMENT
Deep Vein Thrombosis (DVT) – formation of blood clots in the legs during long plane flights; some clots may break off and travel through the blood vessels to the lungs, where they may cause life-threatening complications.	Swelling or pain of the foot, ankle or calf, usually but not always on just one side. Chest pain and difficulty in breathing – immediately seek medical attention.	Walk about the cabin. Perform isometric compressions of the leg muscles (ie contract the leg muscles while sitting). Drink plenty of fluids. Avoid alcohol and tobacco.
Jet Lag – common when crossing more than five time zones.	Insomnia, fatigue, malaise, nausea	Drink plenty of fluids (nonalcoholic). Eat light meals. Upon arrival, seek exposure to natural sunlight and readjust your schedule (for meals, sleep etc) as soon as possible.
Motion Sickness	Nausea	Antihistamines such as dimenhydrinate (Dramamine) and meclizine (Antivert, Bonine). A herbal alternative is ginger.

RECOMMENDED VACCINATIONS

The following vaccinations are recommended for most travellers to Jordan:

- diphtheria and tetanus – single booster recommended if you've not had one in the previous 10 years
- hepatitis A – a single dose at least two to four weeks before departure gives protection for up to a year; a booster 12 months later gives another 10 years or more of protection
- hepatitis B – now considered routine for most travellers
- measles, mumps and rubella – two doses of MMR recommended unless you have previously had the diseases; young adults may require a booster
- polio – generally given in childhood and should be boosted every 10 years
- typhoid – recommended if you're travelling for more than a couple of weeks
- yellow fever – vaccination is required for entry into Jordan for all travellers over one year of age if coming from infected areas such as sub-Saharan Africa and parts of South America

Note that some vaccinations should not be given during pregnancy, to people with allergies and to very young children – discuss this with your doctor.

- Beware of ice cream that may have melted and then been refrozen (eg a power cut in the last day or two).
- Be careful of shellfish, such as mussels, oysters and clams, particularly outside of Aqaba, as well as the raw-meat dishes available in Lebanese restaurants.
- Eat meals only at busy restaurants and be cautious of buffets that may have been standing for more than a day.

Infectious Diseases

Diphtheria & Tetanus

Diphtheria is spread through close respiratory contact. It causes a high temperature and severe sore throat. Sometimes a membrane forms across the throat requiring a tracheostomy to prevent suffocation. Vaccination is recommended for those likely to be in close contact with the local population in infected areas. The vaccine is given as an injection alone, or with tetanus (you may well have had this combined injection as a child), and lasts 10 years.

Hepatitis A

Hepatitis A is spread through contaminated food (particularly shellfish) and water. It causes jaundice and, although it is rarely fatal, can cause prolonged lethargy and delayed recovery. Symptoms include dark urine, a yellow colour to the whites of the eyes, fever and abdominal pain. Hepatitis A vaccine (Avaxim, VAQTA, Havrix) is given as an injection; hepatitis A and typhoid vaccines can also be given as a single-dose vaccine, hepatyrix or viatim.

Hepatitis B

Infected blood, contaminated needles and sexual intercourse can all transmit hepatitis B. It can cause jaundice and affects the liver, occasionally causing liver failure. All travellers should make this a routine vaccination. Many countries now give hepatitis B vaccination as part of routine childhood vaccination. The vaccine is given singly, or at the same time as the hepatitis A vaccine (hepatyrix). A course will give protection for at least five years. It can be given over four weeks, or six months.

HIV

This is spread via infected blood and blood products, sexual intercourse with an infected partner and from an infected mother to her newborn child. It can be spread through 'blood to blood' contacts, such as contaminated instruments during medical and dental procedures, acupuncture, body-piercing and sharing used intravenous needles.

Reliable figures aren't available about the number of people in Jordan with HIV or AIDS (even the lead UN agency, UNAIDS, lacks data) but given the strict taboos in Jordanian society about drugs, homosexuality and promiscuity, the disease is relatively rare. Contracting HIV through a blood transfusion is about as unlikely as in most Western countries, and anyone needing serious surgery will probably be sent home anyway.

You may need to supply a negative HIV test in order to get a second visa extension for a stay of longer than three months.

Polio

Generally spread through either contaminated food or water, polio is one of the

SYMPTOM SORTER

PROBLEM	SYMPTOMS	TREATMENT	PREVENTION
Diarrhoea – occurs usually after eating unhygienically prepared food.	Onset of loose stools.	Take oral-rehydration solution containing salt and sugar; sip weak black tea with sugar; drink soft drinks allowed to go flat and diluted 50% with clean water.	Drink plenty of fluids; eat in busy restaurants; wash your hands regularly.
	More than four or five loose stools.	Antibiotic (usually a quinolone drug); antidiarrhoeal agent (such as loperamide).	As above
	Bloody diarrhoea persistent for more than 72 hours; accompanied by fever, shaking chills or severe abdominal pain.	Seek medical attention; in an emergency you can make up a solution of six teaspoons of sugar and half a teaspoon of salt to 1L of boiled or bottled water.	As above
Heat exhaustion – occurs following heavy sweating and excessive fluid loss with inadequate replacement of fluids and salt.	Headache, dizziness and tiredness; dehydration; dark yellow urine.	Replace fluids with water or fruit juice or both; cool with cold water and fans; take salty fluids through soup or broth; add a little more table salt to foods than usual.	Get fit before planning a long hike; acclimatise to the heat before exercise; wear a hat and cover your neck in the sun; avoid the midday sun in summer; wear sunscreen.
Heat stroke – occurs when the body's heat-regulating mechanism breaks down.	Excessive rise in body temperature; cessation of sweating; irrational and hyperactive behaviour; eventually loss of consciousness and death.	Give rapid cooling by spraying the body with water and fanning; seek emergency fluid and electrolyte replacement by intravenous drip.	As above
Mosquito bite – can spread dengue fever but not malaria.	Irritation; infection.	Don't scratch the bites; apply antiseptic.	Use DEET-based insect repellents; sleep under mosquito netting.
Bed bugs	Very itchy, lumpy bites.	Apply lotion from pharmacy.	Spray mattress or move hotel!
Scabies	Itchy rash, often between fingers.	Apply lotion from pharmacy; treat those you are in contact with.	As above
Snake bite	Pain; swelling.	Seek medical attention.	Wear boots, socks and long trousers when hiking; avoid holes and crevices; be careful handling wood piles.
Scorpion bite	Intense pain.	Seek medical attention.	Check your shoes in the morning, particularly if you are camping near Little Petra.

IF BITTEN BY A SNAKE

- Don't panic: half of those bitten by venomous snakes are not actually injected with poison (envenomed).
- Immobilise the bitten limb with a splint (eg a stick).
- Apply a bandage over the site, with firm pressure, similar to bandaging a sprain.
- Do not apply a tourniquet, or cut or suck the bite.
- Get the victim to medical help as soon as possible so that antivenin can be given if necessary.

vaccines given in childhood and should be boosted every 10 years, either orally (a drop on the tongue), or as an injection. Polio may be carried asymptomatically, although it can cause a transient fever and, in rare cases, potentially permanent muscle weakness or paralysis. Polio is not currently present in Jordan but is prevalent in neighbouring countries.

Rabies

Spread through bites or licks on broken skin from an infected animal, rabies is fatal. Animal handlers should be vaccinated, as should those travelling to remote areas where a reliable source of post-bite vaccine is not available within 24 hours. Three injections are needed over a month. If you've come into physical contact with an infected animal and haven't been vaccinated, you'll need a course of five injections starting within 24 hours or as soon as possible after the injury. Vaccination does not provide you with immunity, it merely buys you more time to seek appropriate medical help.

Tuberculosis

Tuberculosis (TB) is spread through close respiratory contact and occasionally through infected milk or milk products. BCG vaccine is recommended for those likely to be mixing closely with the local population. It is more important for those visiting family or planning a long stay, and those employed as teachers and healthcare workers. TB can be asymptomatic, although symptoms can include cough, weight loss or fever, months or even years after exposure. An X-ray is the best way to confirm if you have TB. BCG gives a moderate degree of protection against TB. It causes a small permanent scar at the site of injection, and is usually only given in specialised chest clinics. As it's a live vaccine it should not be given to pregnant women or immunocompromised individuals. The BCG vaccine is not available in all countries.

Typhoid

This is spread through food or water that has been contaminated by infected human faeces. The first symptom is usually fever or a pink rash on the abdomen. Septicaemia (blood poisoning) may also occur. Typhoid vaccine (typhim Vi, typherix) will give protection for three years. In some countries, the oral vaccine Vivotif is also available.

Yellow Fever

Yellow-fever vaccination is not required for Jordan, but you *do* need a yellow-fever certificate, from a designated clinic, if arriving from an infected area, or if you've been in an infected area in the two weeks before arriving in Jordan.

Environmental Hazards

Jordan is not a dangerous place to visit, but it does have a few hazards unique to desert environments. Some visitors get themselves into trouble hiking through the desert in the heat of the day, especially around Wadi Rum. While heat-related problems are the most common, don't forget that the desert can be bitterly cold in winter: there is a real risk of hypothermia if camping between December and February without adequate bedding.

Language

Arabic is the official language of Jordan. Note that there are significant differences between MSA (Modern Standard Arabic) – the official lingua franca of the Arab world, used in schools, administration and the media – and the colloquial language, ie the everyday spoken version. The Arabic variety spoken in Jordan (and provided in this chapter) is known as Levantine Arabic.

Read our coloured pronunciation guides as if they were English and you'll be understood. Note that a is pronounced as in 'act', aa as the 'a' in 'father', ae as the 'ai' in 'air', aw as in 'law', ay as in 'say', e as in 'bet', ee as in 'see', i as in 'hit', oo as in 'zoo', u as in 'put', gh is a guttural sound (like the French 'r'), r is rolled, dh is pronounced as the 'th' in 'that', th as in 'thin' and kh as the 'ch' in the Scottish *loch*. The apostrophe (') indicates the glottal stop (like the pause in the middle of 'uh-oh'). The stressed syllables are indicated with italics.

BASICS

Hello.	.مرحبا	mer·*ha*·ba
Goodbye.	.خاطرَك .خاطرِك	*khae*·trak (m) *khae*·trik (f)
Yes.	.ايه	'eeh
No.	.لا	laa
Please.	.اذا بتريد .اذا بتريدي	*'i*·za bit·*reed* (m) *'i*·za bit·*ree*·dee (f)
Thank you.	.شكراً	*shuk*·ran
Excuse me.	.عفواً	*'af*·wan
Sorry.	.آسف./آسفة	*'aa*·sif/*'aas*·fe (m/f)

How are you?
كيفك؟/كيفـِك؟ *kay*·fak/*kay*·fik (m/f)

Fine, thanks. And you?
.منيح./منيحة mneeh/*mnee*·ha (m/f)
وأنت/أنتي؟ oo 'ent/*'en*·tee (m/f)

What's your name?
شو اسمَك؟ shoo 'es·mak (m)
شو اسمِك؟ shoo 'es·mik (f)

My name is ...
... اسمي 'es·mee ...

Do you speak English?
بتحكي انجليزي؟ *btah*·kee 'inj·*lee*·zee

I don't understand.
.ما فهمتْ maa fa·*he*·met

Can I take a photo?
بتسمحني اخذ صورة؟ btsa·*mah*·nee *'aa*·khud *soo*·re

ACCOMMODATION

Where's a ...?	وين ...؟	wayn ...
campsite	مخيّم	mu·*khay*·yam
guesthouse	بيت الضيوف	bayt id·du·*yoof*
hotel	فندق	*fun*·duk
youth hostel	فندق شباب	*fun*·du' sha·*baeb*

Do you have a ... room?	في عندكن غرفة ...؟	fee *'ind*·kun *ghur*·fe ...
single	بتخت منفرد	bi·*takht* mun·*fa*·rid
double	بتخت مزدوّج	bi·*takht* muz·*daw*·wej
twin	بتختين	bi·takh·*tayn*
How much is it per ...?	قديش لـ...؟	kad·*deesh* li·...
night	ليلة	*lay*·le
person	شخص	shakhs

Can I get another (blanket)?
اعطني/اعطيني (بطانية) تاني. *'a'*·ti·nee/*'a'*·*tee*·nee (ba·taa·*nee*·ye) *tae*·nee (m/f)

The (air conditioning) doesn't work.
(المكيف) مانه شغال. (il·mu·*kay*·yef) *mae*·nu sha·*ghael*

SIGNS

Entrance	مدخل
Exit	مخرج
Open	مفتوح
Closed	مغلق
Information	معلومات
Prohibited	ممنوع
Toilets	دوراتُ المياه
Men	الرجال
Women	النساء

DIRECTIONS

Where's the ...? وين الـ...؟ wayn il·...
- **bank** بنك bank
- **market** سوق sook
- **post office** مكتب البريد *mak*·tab il·ba·*reed*

Can you show me (on the map)?
بتورجني (عالخريطة)؟ btwar·*ji*·nee ('al·kha·*ree*·te)

What's the address?
شو العنوان؟ shoo il·'un·*waen*

Could you please write it down?
اذا بتريد/بتريدي 'i·za bit·*reed*/bit·*ree*·dee
اكتبه/اكتبيه؟ 'ik·*tu*·bu/'ik·tu·*beeh* (m/f)

How far is it?
قديش هو بعيد kad·*deesh hu*·wa ba·'*eed*
من هون؟ min hoon

How do I get there?
كيف بوصل لهناك؟ kayf *boo*·sal la·hu·*naek*

It's ... هو/هي ... *hu*·we/*hi*·ye ... (m/f)
- **behind ...** خلف ... khalf ...
- **in front of ...** قدام ... kad·*daem* ...
- **near to ...** قريب من ... ka·*reeb* min ...
- **next to ...** جنب ... jinb ...
- **on the corner** عند الزاوية 'ind az·*zae*·wi·ye
- **opposite ...** مواجه ... mu·*wae*·jeh ...
- **straight ahead** للقدام lil·kad·*daem*

Turn left/right.
اتجه 'it·*ta*·jih
ليسار/لشمال. li·ya·*saer*/li·shi·*mael* (m)
اتجهي 'it·*taj*·hee
ليسار/لشمال. li·ya·*saer*/li·shi·*mael* (f)

EATING & DRINKING

Can you recommend a ...? بتوصي بـ...؟ *btoo*·see bi·...
- **bar** بار baar
- **cafe** مقهى *mak*·ha
- **restaurant** مطعم *mat*·'em

I'd like a/the ..., please. بدي ... لو سمحت. *bid*·dee ... law sa·*maht*
- **nonsmoking section** قسم غير المدخنين kism ghayr il·mu·dakh·khi·*neen*
- **table for (four)** طاولة لـ(أربع اشخاص) *tae*·wi·le li·('*ar*·ba·'at 'esh·*khaes*)

What would you recommend?
بشو بتوصي؟ *bi*·shoo *btoo*·see

What's the local speciality?
شو الوجبة الخاصة؟ shoo il·*waj*·be il·*khae*·se

Do you have vegetarian food?
في عندكن fee '*ind*·kun
طعام نباتي؟ ta·'*aem* na·*bae*·tee

I'd like (the) ..., please. بدي ... لو سمحت. *bid*·dee ... law sa·*maht*
- **bill** الحساب il·hi·*saeb*
- **drink list** قائمة المشروبات *kae*·'i·met il·mash·roo·*baet*
- **menu** قائمة الطعام *kae*·'i·met it·ta·'*aem*
- **that dish** ذالك الوجبة *zae*·lik il·*waj*·be

Could you prepare a meal without ...? بتقدروا تحضروا وجبة بدون ...؟ btak·*de*·roo tu·had·*de*·roo *waj*·be bi·*doon* ...
- **butter** زبدة *zeb*·de
- **eggs** بيض bayd
- **meat stock** مرق لحم mirk lahm

I'm allergic to ... أنا عندي حساسية من ... '*a*·na '*in*·dee ha·sae·*see*·ye min ...
- **dairy produce** الألبان il·'al·*baen*
- **gluten** الغلوتين il·ghloo·*teen*
- **nuts** المكسرات il·mu·kas·si·*raet*
- **seafood** الطعام البحري it·ta·'*aem bah*·ree

Drinks

beer	بيرا	*bee*·ra
coffee	قهوى	*kah*·way
orange juice	عصير برتقال	'a·*seer* bur·te·*kael*
mineral water	مياه معدنية	mee·*yaah* ma'·da·*nee*·ye
red wine	نبيذ احمر	nbeez '*ah*·mer
tea	شاي	shaay
white wine	نبيذ ابيض	nbeez '*ib*·yad

EMERGENCIES

Help! ساعد! *sae*·'id (m)
ساعدي! sae·'*i*·dee (f)

Go away! روح!/روحي! rooh/*roo*·hee (m/f)

Call ...! اتصل بـ...! 'it·*ta*·sil bi·...
a doctor دكتور duk·*toor*
the police الشرطة ish·*shur*·ta

I'm lost.
أنا ضائع. 'a·na *dae*·'i' (m)
أنا ضائعة. 'a·na dae·'*i*·'e (f)

Where are the toilets?
وين الحمامات؟ wayn il·ham·mae·*maet*

I'm sick.
أنا مريض. 'a·na ma·*reed* (m)
أنا مريضة. 'a·na ma·*ree*·de (f)

I'm allergic to (antibiotics).
أنا حساسي/ 'a·na ha·*sae*·see/
حساسية من ha·sae·*see*·ye min
(مضاد حيوي). (mu·*daed* ha·*ya*·wee) (m/f)

SHOPPING & SERVICES

Where's a ...? وين ...؟ wayn ...
department store محل المنوعات *ma*·hal il·mu·naw·wa·*'aet*
grocery store بقالة ba·*kae*·le
newsagency وكالة الأنباء wi·*kae*·let il·'en·*baa'*
souvenir shop محل التذكارات *ma*·hal it·tiz·kae·*raet*
supermarket سبر مركت *su*·ber·markt

I'm looking for ...
بدور عن ... bi·*daw*·wer 'an ...

Can I look at it?
ورجني ياه؟ *war*·ji·nee yaah (m)
ورجيني ياه؟ war·*jee*·nee yaah (f)

Do you have any others?
في عندكن غيره؟ fee '*ind*·kun *ghay*·ru

It's faulty.
هو خربان. *hu*·we khar·*baen*

How much is it?
قديش هقه؟ kad·*deesh ha* ku

Can you write down the price?
اكتب الهق. '*ik*·tub il·*hak* (m)
اكتبي الهق. 'ik·*tu*·bee il·*hak* (f)

That's too expensive.
هيدا غالي اكتير. *hay*·dae *ghae*·lee 'ik·*teer*

What's your lowest price?
شو احسن سعر shoo '*ih*·sen si'r
طبعكن؟ ta·*ba'*·kun

There's a mistake in the bill.
في خطأ بالحساب. fee *kha*·ta' bil·hi·*saeb*

Where's an ATM?
وين جهاز الصرافة؟ wayn je·*haez* is·sa·*rae*·fe

Where's a foreign exchange office?
وين مكتب صرافة؟ wayn *mak*·teb sa·*rae*·fe

What's the exchange rate?
شو سعر التحويل؟ shoo si'r it·tah·*weel*

Where's the local internet cafe?
وين أقرب مقهى wayn '*ak*·reb *ma'*·ha
الانترنت؟ il·'in·*ter*·net

How much is it per hour?
قديش بتكلف kad·*deesh* bit·*kal*·lef
لساعة وحدة؟ la·*sae*·'a *wah*·de

Where's the nearest public phone?
وين أقرب تلفون wayn '*ak*·reb te·li·*foon*
عمومي؟ 'u·*moo*·mee

I'd like to buy a phonecard.
بدي اشتري *bid*·dee '*ish*·ta·ree
بطاقة تلفون. bi·*tae*·ke te·li·*foon*

TIME & DATES

What time is it?
كم الساعة؟ kam 'is·*sae*·'e

It's one o'clock.
الساعة وحدة. 'is·*sae*·'e *wah*·de

NUMBERS

1	١	واحد	*waa*·hed
2	٢	اثنين	'it·*nayn*
3	٣	ثلاثة	ta·*laa*·te
4	٤	اربع	*'ar*·ba'
5	٥	خمسة	*kham*·se
6	٦	ستة	*sit*·te
7	٧	سبعة	*sab*·'a
8	٨	ثمانية	ta·*maa*·ne
9	٩	تسعة	*tis*·'a
10	١٠	عشرة	*'ash*·re
20	٢٠	عشرين	'ish·*reen*
30	٣٠	ثلاثين	ta·laa·*teen*
40	٤٠	اربعين	'ar·be·*'een*
50	٥٠	خمسين	kham·*seen*
60	٦٠	ستين	sit·*teen*
70	٧٠	سبعين	sab·*'een*
80	٨٠	ثمانين	ta·ma·*neen*
90	٩٠	تسعين	tis·*'een*
100	١٠٠	مية	*mi*·'a
1000	١٠٠٠	الف	'elf

Note that Arabic numerals, unlike letters, are read from left to right.

ARABIC ALPHABET

Arabic is written from right to left. The form of each letter changes depending on whether it's at the start, in the middle or at the end of a word or whether it stands alone.

WORD-FINAL	WORD-MEDIAL	WORD-INITIAL	ALONE	LETTER
ـا	ـاـ	اـ	ا	alef'
ـب	ـبـ	بـ	ب	'ba
ـت	ـتـ	تـ	ت	'ta
ـث	ـثـ	ثـ	ث	'tha
ـج	ـجـ	جـ	ج	jeem
ـح	ـحـ	حـ	ح	'ha
ـخ	ـخـ	خـ	خ	'kha
ـد	ـدـ	دـ	د	daal
ـذ	ـذـ	ذـ	ذ	dhaal
ـر	ـرـ	رـ	ر	'ra
ـز	ـزـ	زـ	ز	'za
ـس	ـسـ	سـ	س	seen
ـش	ـشـ	شـ	ش	sheen
ـص	ـصـ	صـ	ص	saad
ـض	ـضـ	ضـ	ض	daad
ـط	ـطـ	طـ	ط	'ta
ـظ	ـظـ	ظـ	ظ	'dha
ـع	ـعـ	عـ	ع	ain'
ـغ	ـغـ	غـ	غ	ghain
ـف	ـفـ	فـ	ف	'fa
ـق	ـقـ	قـ	ق	kuf
ـك	ـكـ	كـ	ك	kaf
ـل	ـلـ	لـ	ل	lam
ـم	ـمـ	مـ	م	mim
ـن	ـنـ	نـ	ن	nun
ـه	ـهـ	هـ	ه	'ha
ـو	ـوـ	وـ	و	waw
ـي	ـيـ	يـ	ي	'ya
		ء		hamza
ـأ	ـئـَ ـؤَ	أَ	أَ	a
ـأُ	ـئُـ ـؤُ	أُ	أُ	u
ـإِ	ـئِـ ـؤِ	إِ	إِ	i
ـأْ	ـئْـ ـؤْ	أْ	أْ	' (glottal stop)
ـآ	ـآـ	آ	آ	aa
ـُو	ـُوْـ	أُو	أُو	oo
ـِيْ	ـِيْـ	إِيْ	إِيْ	ee
ـَوْ	ـَوْـ	أَوْ	أَوْ	aw
ـَيْ	ـَيْـ	أَيْ	أَيْ	ay

It's (two) o'clock.
هي (تنتين). *hi*·ye (tin·*tayn*)

Half past (two).
(تنتين) ونصّ. (tin·*tayn*) oo nus

At what time ...?
امتى ...؟ *'em*·ta ...

At ...?
في ... fee ...

yesterday ...	مبارح ...	*mbae*·reh ...
tomorrow ...	بكرة ...	*buk*·ra ...
morning	صبح	*su*·beh
afternoon	بعد ظهر	ba'd zuhr
evening	مسا	ma·*sae*
Monday	يوم الأتنين	yawm il·'it·*nayn*
Tuesday	يوم التلات	yawm il·ta·*laat*
Wednesday	يوم الاربعة	yawm il·*'ar*·ba·'a
Thursday	يوم الخميس	yawm il·kha·*mees*
Friday	يوم الجمع	yawm il·*jum*·'a
Saturday	يوم السبت	yawm is·*sabt*
Sunday	يوم الاحد	yawm il·*'a*·had

TRANSPORT

Please take me to (this address).
اوصلني عند (هيدا العنوان). *'oo*·*sal*·nee 'ind (*hay*·dae il·'un·*waen*)

Please ...	... اذا بتريد	*'i*·za bit·*reed* ...
stop here	قف هون	kif hoon
wait here	استنّا هون	*stan*·naa hoon

Public Transport

Is this the ... to (Petra)?	...هيدا الـ لـ(بيترا)؟	*hay*·dae il· ... la·(*bee*·tra)?
boat	سفينة	*sfee*·ne
bus	باص	baas
plane	طائرة	*tae*·'i·re
train	قطار	ki·*taar*

What time's the ... bus?	أمتى الباص...؟	*'em*·ta il·*baas*...
first	اول	*'aw*·wel
last	اخر	*'ae*·khir
next	قادم	*kae*·dim
One ... ticket (to Beirut), please.	تذكرة ... (لبيروت) اذا بتريد.	*taz*·ki·re ... (la·bay·*root*) *'i*·za bit·*reed*
one-way	ذهاب	za·*haeb*
return	ذهاب وایاب	za·*haeb* oo wee·*yaeb*

How long does the trip take?
الرحلة, كم ساعة بتاخذ؟ ar·*rih*·le kam *sae*·'a bi·*tae*·khud

Is it a direct route?
الطريق مباشر؟ it·ta·*reek* mu·*bae*·shir

What station/stop is this?
شو هيدا المحطة/الموقف؟ shoo *hay*·dae il·*mhat*·te/il·*maw*·kif

Please tell me when we get to ...
اولي/اوليلي لما منوصل عند ... *'oo*·lee/*'oo*·*lee*·lee *lam*·ma *mnoo*·sal 'ind ... (m/f)

How much is it to ...?
قديش الاجرة لـ ...؟ kad·*deesh* il·*'uj*·re la ...

Driving and Cycling

I'd like to hire a ...	... بدي استأجر	*bid*·dee 'is·*ta'*·jir ...
4WD	سيارة ذات الدفع الرباعي	say·*yae*·re zaat id·*daf'* er·ru·*bae*·'ee
car	سيارة	say·*yae*·re

with a driver
ومعها سائق oo *ma*·'aa *sae*·'i'

with air conditioning
بالمكيف bil·mu·*kay*·yef

How much for ... hire?	قديش الاجرة لـ...؟	*'ad*·*deesh* il·*'uj*·re la·...
daily	يوم	yawm
weekly	أسبوع	*'us*·*boo'*

Is this the road to (Tyre)?
هيدا الطريق لـ(صور)؟ *hay*·dae it·ta·*ree'* la·(soor)

I need a mechanic.
لازمني ميكانيكي. lae·*zim*·nee mee·kaa·*nee*·kee

I've run out of petrol.
خلص البنزين بسيارتي. *kha*·las il·bi·*trool* bi·say·*yae*·re·tee

I have a flat tyre.
اطار السيارة ما فيه هواء. *'i*·*taer* is·say·*yae*·re ma *fee*·hu ha·*wae*

QUESTION WORDS

When?	امتى؟	*'em*·ta
Where?	وين؟	wayn
Who?	مين؟	meen
Why?	ليش؟	leesh

GLOSSARY

This glossary lists terms used in this book that may be unfamiliar to those living outside Jordan. Most are Arabic words commonly used in Jordan but some abbreviations are also included. See p340 for architectural terminology, which may come in handy when visiting ancient sights such as Petra and Jerash.

abeyya – women's floor-length, black over-garment
abu – father of...
agal – black headrope used to hold a keffiyeh in place
ain (ayoun) – spring or well
amir – see *emir*
arak – alcoholic spirit
ASEZA – Aqaba Special Economic Zone Authority
Ayyubid dynasty – the dynasty founded by Saladin (Salah ad-Din) in Egypt in 1169
bab (abwab) – gate
Badia – stony desert
Bedouin (pl Bedu) – nomadic desert dweller
beit – house
beit ash-sha'ar – goat-hair Bedouin tent
bin – son of...; also *ibn*
caliph – Islamic ruler
caravanserai – large inn enclosing a courtyard, providing accommodation and a marketplace for caravans
Circassians – Muslims from the Caucasus who emigrated to Jordan in the 19th century
Decapolis (Latin) – literally '10 cities'; this term refers to a number of ancient cities in the Roman Empire, including Amman and Jerash
deir – monastery
eid – Islamic feast
Eid al-Adha – Feast of Sacrifice marking the pilgrimage to Mecca
Eid al-Fitr – Festival of Breaking the Fast, celebrated throughout the Islamic world at the end of Ramadan
emir – Islamic ruler, leader, military commander or governor; literally 'prince'
haj – the pilgrimage to Mecca
hammam(at) – natural hot springs; also a Turkish steam bath
haram – forbidden area
hejab – woman's headscarf
ibn – son of...; also *bin*
il-balad – downtown; the centre of town
imam – religious leader
jebel – hill or mountain
JETT – Jordan Express Travel & Tourism; the major private bus company in Jordan
JTB – Jordan Tourism Board
keffiyeh – checked scarf worn by Arab men
kilim – flat, woven mat
Koran – see *Quran*
Kufic – a type of highly stylised old Arabic script
mafrash – rugs
maidan – town or city square
malek – king
malekah – queen
Mamluk dynasty – Muslim dynasty named for a former slave and soldier class; mamluk is literally 'slaves'
medina – old walled centre of any Islamic city
mezze – starters, appetisers
mihrab – niche in the wall of a mosque that indicates the direction of Mecca
minaret – tower on top of a mosque
muezzin – mosque official who calls the faithful to prayer, often from the minaret
Nabataean – ancient trading civilisation based around Petra
nargileh – water pipe used to smoke tobacco (used mainly by men)
oud – Arabic lute
PLO – Palestine Liberation Organisation
qala'at – castle or fort
qasr – castle or palace
qibla – direction of Mecca
Quran – holy book of Islam
qusayr – small castle or palace
Ramadan – Muslim month of fasting
RSCN – Royal Society for the Conservation of Nature
Saladin – (Salah ad-Din in Arabic) Kurdish warlord who re-took Jerusalem from the Crusaders; founder of the Ayyubid dynasty
servees – service taxi
sheesha – see *nargileh*
sheikh – venerated religious scholar, dignitary or venerable old man
siq – gorge or canyon (usually created by tectonic forces rather than by wind or water)
souq – market
tell – ancient mound created by centuries of urban rebuilding
Trans-Jordan – Jordan's original name
Umayyad dynasty – first great dynasty of Arab Muslim rulers
umm – mother of...
UNRWA – UN Relief & Works Agency
wadi – valley or river bed formed by watercourse, dry except after heavy rainfall (plural: *widyan*)
zerb – Bedouin oven, buried in the sand

Dining & Drinking Glossary

Note that, because of the imprecise nature of transliterating Arabic into English, spellings will vary. For example, what we give as *kibbeh* may appear variously as *kubbeh, kibba, kibby* or even *gibeh.*

Mezze

baba ghanouj – (literally 'father's favourite'), dip of mashed eggplant (aubergine) and tahini
balilah – snack of boiled salty legumes
basterma – pastrami, popular from Armenia to Lebanon
buraik – meat or cheese pie

fatayer – triangles of pastry filled with white cheese or spinach; also known as *buraik*

fatteh – garlicky yoghurt and hummus, sometimes with chicken

fattoosh – salad with sumach (a red spice mix), tomatoes and shreds of crouton-like deep-fried bread

fuul medames – squashed fava beans with chillies, onions and olive oil

gallai – sautéed tomato, garlic, onion and peppers topped with cheese and pine nuts on Arabic bread

hummus – cooked chickpeas ground into a paste and mixed with tahini (a sesame-seed paste), garlic and lemon

kibbeh – Lebanese-style kofta made with minced lamb, bulgur/cracked wheat and onion; served raw or deep fried

labneh – cream-cheese dip

makdous – pickled eggplant, walnut and olive-oil dip

manaqeesh – Arabic bread with herbs

manoucha/manaqish – baked breads or pies with thyme (*zaatar*) and cheese

mosabaha – hummus with whole chickpeas in it

mouhamara – walnut, olive oil and cumin dip

muttabal – eggplant dip similar to *baba ghanouj* but creamier

sambousek – meat and pine-nut pastry

shanklish – tangy and salty dried white cheese, sometimes grilled, sometimes in a salad

tabbouleh – salad of cracked (bulgur) wheat, parsley and tomato

treedah – egg, yoghurt and meat

yalenjeh – stuffed vine leaves

Main Dishes

fareekeh – similar to *maqlubbeh* but with cracked wheat

fasoolyeh – bean stew

gallayah – traditional Bedouin meal of chicken with tomatoes, other vegetables, garlic and Arabic spices

kofta – meatballs, often in a stew

maqlubbeh – steamed rice topped with grilled slices of eggplant or meat, grilled tomato, cauliflower and pine nuts

mulukiyyeh – spinach stew with chicken or meat pieces

musakhan – baked chicken served on bread with onions, olive oil and pine nuts

sawani – meat or vegetables cooked on trays in a wood-burning oven

sawda dajaj – chicken livers with grenadine syrup and lemon

shish tawouq – grilled boneless chicken served with bread and onions

shwarma – chicken or lamb sliced off a spit and stuffed in a pocket of pita-type bread with chopped tomatoes and garnish

Dessert

ftir jibneh – large pastries

haliwat al-jibneh – a soft doughy pastry filled with cream cheese

halva – soft sesame paste, like nougat

kunafa – shredded dough on top of cream cheese smothered in syrup

ma'amoul – biscuits stuffed with dates and pistachio nuts and dipped in rose water

m'shekel – a form of baklava

muhalabiyya – rice pudding, made with rose water

wharbat – triangular pastries with custard inside

Staples

beid – egg

ejja – omelette

jibna – cheese

khobz – bread

labneh – yoghurt

makarone – all varieties of pasta

ruz – rice

shurba – soup

sukkar – sugar

Meat & Fish

farooj – chicken

hamour – a grouper-like fish from the Red Sea

kibda – liver

samak – fish

Vegetables

adas – lentils

banadura – tomato

batata – potato

khadrawat – vegetables

khiyar – cucumber

Fruit

battikh – watermelon

burtuqal – orange

inab – grape

mish-mish – apricot

moz – banana

rumman – pomegranate

tamr – date

tin – fig

tufah – apple

Other Dishes & Condiments

fil fil – chillies

sumach – red-spice mix

tahini – sesame-seed paste

torshi – pink pickled vegetables

tum – garlic

zaatar – thyme blend

zayt – olive oil

zaytun – olives

Drinks

asir – juice

karkade – sweetened hibiscus tea

maya at-ta'abiyya – mineral water

qahwa – coffee

sefeeha – lemon and mint drink

shai – tea

Architecture Glossary

Reading a guidebook to some of Jordan's most famous sights can seem like an exercise in linguistics encompassing Latin, Nabataean, Greek, Arabic and the languages of geography and classical architecture. Listen to any tour guide, especially at Petra and at Jerash, and you'll assume they're expert in all of them. But you don't have to be a polyglot to make the most of Jordan's wonders. Have a quick *shoofti* – Arabic word meaning 'you (female) looked' – at the glossary of architectural terms following and you'll soon know your pediments from your porticos.

agora – open meeting space for commerce

baetyls – divine stones

capitals – carved tops of columns

cardo maximus – Roman main street, running north–south

colonnade – row of columns

Corinthian – look for fluted columns with leafy capitals

decumanus – Roman main street, from east to west

Doric – look for unfluted columns with plain 'book-shaped' capitals

forum – open public space for meetings

high place – sacred site on mountaintop

hippodrome – stadium, usually for horseracing and chariot racing

Ionic – look for fluted columns with ram-horn (two curls in opposite directions) capitals

loculi – grave

macellum – indoor market building

necropolis – cemetery

nymphaeum – literally 'temple of the Nymphs'; public baths, fountains and pools

pediment – triangular crowning feature on front of building

portico – structure supported by columns

propylaeum – gateway or grand entrance

stele – commemorative stone or column with inscriptions

temenos – sacred courtyard

tetrapylon – an archway with four entrances

triclinium – Roman dining room

Behind the Scenes

SEND US YOUR FEEDBACK

We love to hear from travellers – your comments keep us on our toes and help make our books better. Our well-travelled team reads every word on what you loved or loathed about this book. Although we cannot reply individually to your submissions, we always guarantee that your feedback goes straight to the appropriate authors, in time for the next edition. Each person who sends us information is thanked in the next edition – the most useful submissions are rewarded with a selection of digital PDF chapters.

Visit **lonelyplanet.com/contact** to submit your updates and suggestions or to ask for help. Our award-winning website also features inspirational travel stories, news and discussions.

Note: We may edit, reproduce and incorporate your comments in Lonely Planet products such as guidebooks, websites and digital products, so let us know if you don't want your comments reproduced or your name acknowledged. For a copy of our privacy policy visit lonelyplanet.com/privacy.

OUR READERS

Many thanks to the travellers who used the last edition and wrote to us with helpful hints, useful advice and interesting anecdotes: Alan Tyers, Brooke Hart, Grace Park, Gudrun Broegger, Kendra Litke, Khaled Jarrah, Maria Gruber-Hatheier, Martijn Huijnen, Michael Henrickson, Natalie Holroyd, Owen Morton, Peter Hourigan, Phil Brownhill, Ralf Plechinger, Ray VarnBuhler, Remko Donga, Susan Lindsey, Tom Benhamou

WRITER THANKS

Jenny Walker

Returning to Jordan is always a pleasure, thanks to the strength of welcome unfailingly received. Over many years of writing and updating the Lonely Planet *Jordan* guide, I have inevitably become indebted to friends in Jordan who have helped shape the information in the general sections of this edition. Alas, there isn't space to do justice to individuals here, but I acknowledge their collective help with gratitude. My biggest thanks, however, are reserved, as ever, to my beloved Sam (Owen), husband, co-researcher and fellow traveller.

Paul Clammer

Thanks to Hakim al-Tamimi and Mahmoud Freihat at the Jordan Tourism Board. In Amman, thanks to Muna Haddad, Nabil Tarzi, Daniel Robards, Jon Killpack and Ayman Abd Alkareem. Thanks of course also to Susan Andrew and Soda. Thanks to Odeh Sawalhah and Ammar al-Damseh in Madaba, and to Atallah Dakhilallah in Wadi Rum. Hugs to the brilliant 'Team Feynan' – Kirsten Alana, Jill Robinson, Theresa Jackson, Daniella Van Haltren, Rajesh Oja, Bradley Moss and Tim Neville. Finally, thanks and love above all to Robyn, for everything as always.

ACKNOWLEDGEMENTS

Climate map data adapted from Peel MC, Finlayson BL & McMahon TA (2007) 'Updated World Map of the Köppen-Geiger Climate Classification', Hydrology and Earth System Sciences, 11, 163344.

Illustration pp168-9 by Michael Weldon

Cover photograph: Treasury, Petra; Neil Farrin/Getty©

THIS BOOK

This 10th edition of Lonely Planet's *Jordan* guidebook was curated by Jenny Walker, who also researched and wrote it, along with Paul Clammer. The previous edition was also written by Paul Clammer and Jenny Walker. This guidebook was produced by the following:

Destination Editor Lauren Keith

Product Editors Jenna Myers, Saralinda Turner

Senior Cartographer Julie Sheridan

Book Designer Jessica Rose

Assisting Editors Janet Austin, Sarah Bailey, Katie Connolly, Emma Gibbs, Victoria Harrison, Anne Mulvaney, Kristin Odijk, Fionn Twomey

Cover Researcher Naomi Parker

Thanks to Sunny Fitzgerald, Shona Gray, Anne Mason, Alison Ridgway

Index

Map Pages **000**
Photo Pages **000**

Map Pages **000**
Photo Pages **000**

Map Legend

Sights
- Beach
- Bird Sanctuary
- Buddhist
- Castle/Palace
- Christian
- Confucian
- Hindu
- Islamic
- Jain
- Jewish
- Monument
- Museum/Gallery/Historic Building
- Ruin
- Shinto
- Sikh
- Taoist
- Winery/Vineyard
- Zoo/Wildlife Sanctuary
- Other Sight

Activities, Courses & Tours
- Bodysurfing
- Diving
- Canoeing/Kayaking
- Course/Tour
- Sento Hot Baths/Onsen
- Skiing
- Snorkelling
- Surfing
- Swimming/Pool
- Walking
- Windsurfing
- Other Activity

Sleeping
- Sleeping
- Camping
- Hut/Shelter

Eating
- Eating

Drinking & Nightlife
- Drinking & Nightlife
- Cafe

Entertainment
- Entertainment

Shopping
- Shopping

Information
- Bank
- Embassy/Consulate
- Hospital/Medical
- Internet
- Police
- Post Office
- Telephone
- Toilet
- Tourist Information
- Other Information

Geographic
- Beach
- Gate
- Hut/Shelter
- Lighthouse
- Lookout
- Mountain/Volcano
- Oasis
- Park
- Pass
- Picnic Area
- Waterfall

Population
- Capital (National)
- Capital (State/Province)
- City/Large Town
- Town/Village

Transport
- Airport
- Border crossing
- Bus
- Cable car/Funicular
- Cycling
- Ferry
- Metro station
- Monorail
- Parking
- Petrol station
- Subway station
- Taxi
- Train station/Railway
- Tram
- Underground station
- Other Transport

Routes
- Tollway
- Freeway
- Primary
- Secondary
- Tertiary
- Lane
- Unsealed road
- Road under construction
- Plaza/Mall
- Steps
- Tunnel
- Pedestrian overpass
- Walking Tour
- Walking Tour detour
- Path/Walking Trail

Boundaries
- International
- State/Province
- Disputed
- Regional/Suburb
- Marine Park
- Cliff
- Wall

Hydrography
- River, Creek
- Intermittent River
- Canal
- Water
- Dry/Salt/Intermittent Lake
- Reef

Areas
- Airport/Runway
- Beach/Desert
- Cemetery (Christian)
- Cemetery (Other)
- Glacier
- Mudflat
- Park/Forest
- Sight (Building)
- Sportsground
- Swamp/Mangrove

Note: Not all symbols displayed above appear on the maps in this book

OUR STORY

A beat-up old car, a few dollars in the pocket and a sense of adventure. In 1972 that's all Tony and Maureen Wheeler needed for the trip of a lifetime – across Europe and Asia overland to Australia. It took several months, and at the end – broke but inspired – they sat at their kitchen table writing and stapling together their first travel guide, *Across Asia on the Cheap*. Within a week they'd sold 1500 copies. Lonely Planet was born.

Today, Lonely Planet has offices in Franklin, London, Melbourne, Oakland, Dublin, Beijing and Delhi, with more than 600 staff and writers. We share Tony's belief that 'a great guidebook should do three things: inform, educate and amuse'.

OUR WRITERS

Jenny Walker

Petra; Plan, Understand & Survival Guide chapters

Despite having travelled to over 120 countries from Mexico to Mongolia and Latvia to Lesotho, Jenny Walker's main interest is in the Middle East where she has been Associate Dean (PD) of Caledonian College of Engineering in Muscat for the past eight years. Her first involvement with the region was as a student, collecting bugs for her father's book on entomology in Saudi Arabia. She went on to write a dissertation on Doughty and Lawrence (Stirling University), an MPhil thesis on the Arabic Orient in British Literature (Oxford University), and she is currently writing a PhD on the Arabian desert as trope (Nottingham Trent University) in contemporary British literature. Jenny has written extensively on the Middle East for Lonely Planet for more than a decade.

Paul Clammer

Amman; Jerash, Irbid & the Jordan Valley; Dead Sea Highway; Madaba & the King's Highway; Aqaba, Wadi Rum & the Desert Highway; Azraq & the Eastern Desert Highway

Paul has worked as a molecular biologist, tour leader and travel writer. Since 2003 he has worked as a guidebook author for Lonely Planet, contributing to over 25 LP titles, covering destination swathes of South and Central Asia, West and North Africa and the Caribbean. In recent years, he has lived in Morocco, Jordan, Haiti and Fiji, as well as his native England. Find him online at paulclammer.com or on Twitter as @paulclammer.

Published by Lonely Planet Global Limited
CRN 554153
10th edition – Jul 2018
ISBN 978 1 78657 575 3

10 9 8 7 6 5 4 3 2 1
Printed in Malaysia